# Essential Math for GCSE Found

CW01468481

## Michael White

This book covers the material required for the GCSE Foundation Tier (grades C to G).

To allow for the range of abilities, each part of the book is written in 2 sections. The M exercises should be suitable for most students at this level. E exercises are generally more demanding. They may provide extension work following the M exercise or they may cover a related but more demanding topic.

Constant revisiting of topics is essential for exam success. Throughout this book, the author provides 'Can you still?' sections to encourage this continual reviewing process.

The author is most concerned about students' awareness of money matters. Each unit contains a 'Watch your money!' section. The purpose of this is to facilitate discussion and highlight each area.

Thanks are due to AQA, CCEA, Edexcel, OCR and WJEC for kindly allowing the use of questions from their past examination papers. The answers are solely the work of the author and are not rati ed by the examining groups.

The author is indebted to the contributions from Hilary White and Peter Gibson.

First published 2006 by
Elmwood Press
80 Attimore Road
Welwyn Garden City
Herts AL8 6LP
Tel. 01707 333232

ISBN 9781 902 214 702

© Michael White
Reprinted 2008, 2010

Typeset and illustrated by Domex e-Data Pvt. Ltd.

Printed by NPE Print Communications

# Contents

# NUMBER 1

**In this unit you will learn how to:**
- understand place value in numbers
- round off numbers
- add and subtract whole numbers
- multiply whole numbers
- divide whole numbers
- add and subtract negative numbers
- multiply and divide negative numbers
- do calculations in the correct order
- WATCH YOUR MONEY! – wages

## Place value

There are 1423 students in the Blue School.

14**2**3 The 3 digit represents 3 students

1**4**23 The 4 digit represents 400 students

14**2**3 The 2 digit represents 20 students

**1**423 The 1 digit represents 1000 students

### M1. 1

In Questions **1** to **5** , write down the value of each digit of the number.

**1** There are 2541 students in High Grass College.

**2** There are 1384 students in King Arthur's School.

**3** Forest Green School has 1279 pupils.

**4** There are 865 pupils in Cragg High School.

**5** Cleeve College has 3714 students.

**6**   What is the value of the underlined digit in each number below?

(a) 6<u>7</u>5   (b) 71<u>4</u>   (c) 137<u>8</u>   (d) <u>3</u>619   (e) 40<u>6</u>

(f) 5<u>7</u>14   (g) 37<u>8</u>1   (h) <u>5</u>369   (i) 5<u>1</u>8   (j) 3<u>6</u>72

(k) 372<u>6</u>   (l) <u>5</u>064   (m) 4<u>1</u>07   (n) 8<u>7</u>10   (o) 691<u>5</u>

**7**   | 6 |   | 8 |   | 3 |

(a) Using all the 3 cards above, what is the *largest* number you can make?

(b) Using all the 3 cards above, what is the *smallest* number you can make?

**8**   | 7 |   | 1 |   | 4 |

(a) Using all the 3 cards above, what is the *largest* number you can make?

(b) Using all the 3 cards above, what is the *smallest* number you can make?

## Tenths, hundredths, thousandths

### 🔑 Key Facts

The digit after the decimal point shows tenths

0.<u>1</u>   the 1 means $\dfrac{1}{10}$          0.<u>6</u>   the 6 means $\dfrac{6}{10}$          27.<u>8</u>   the 8 means $\dfrac{8}{10}$

The second digit after the decimal point shows hundredths

0.0<u>1</u>   the 1 means $\dfrac{1}{100}$          27.1<u>8</u>   the 8 means $\dfrac{8}{100}$

The third digit after the decimal point shows thousandths

0.00<u>1</u>   the 1 means $\dfrac{1}{1000}$          0.00<u>6</u>   the 6 means $\dfrac{6}{1000}$          27.34<u>8</u>   the 8 means $\dfrac{8}{1000}$

**1** The 3 in the number 12.731 means $\dfrac{3}{100}$.

What is the value of the underlined digit in each number below:

(a) 0.8$\underline{2}$      (b) 0.9$\underline{1}$3      (c) 0.$\underline{5}$86      (d) 0.30$\underline{7}$

(e) 0.$\underline{9}$      (f) 0.51$\underline{7}$      (g) 0.36$\underline{8}$      (h) 0.4$\underline{2}$8

(i) $\underline{7}$.89      (j) 5.$\underline{2}$38      (k) 2$\underline{8}$.6      (l) $\underline{1}$5.37

(m) 17.8$\underline{2}$6      (n) 26.10$\underline{8}$      (o) $\underline{3}$6.029      (p) 78.5$\underline{2}$6

(q) 106.9$\underline{7}$      (r) 2$\underline{7}$1.638      (s) 386.59$\underline{1}$      (t) 836.7$\underline{0}$4

**2** Which number is the larger: $\boxed{0.1}$ or $\boxed{0.01}$ ?

**3** Which number is the larger: $\boxed{0.08}$ or $\boxed{0.7}$ ?

**4** Which number is the largest: $\boxed{0.09}$ or $\boxed{0.5}$ or $\boxed{0.008}$ ?

**5** $\boxed{A}$ $\boxed{B}$ $\boxed{\bullet}$ $\boxed{C}$ $\boxed{D}$ $\boxed{E}$

(a) Tom has 5 cards: $\boxed{7}$ $\boxed{3}$ $\boxed{8}$ $\boxed{4}$ $\boxed{6}$

Tom must place the cards on spaces $\boxed{A}$ $\boxed{B}$ $\boxed{C}$ $\boxed{D}$ $\boxed{E}$ above to make the *largest* number possible. Write down the number he makes.

(b) Tom must now place the cards on spaces $\boxed{A}$ $\boxed{B}$ $\boxed{C}$ $\boxed{D}$ $\boxed{E}$ above to make the *smallest* number possible. Write down the number he makes.

(c) Sasha has 6 cards: $\boxed{4}$ $\boxed{9}$ $\boxed{1}$ $\boxed{6}$ $\boxed{5}$ $\boxed{8}$

Sasha must place 5 of her cards on spaces $\boxed{A}$ $\boxed{B}$ $\boxed{C}$ $\boxed{D}$ $\boxed{E}$ above to make the *largest* number possible. Write down the number she makes.

(d) Sasha must now place 5 of her cards on spaces $\boxed{A}$ $\boxed{B}$ $\boxed{C}$ $\boxed{D}$ $\boxed{E}$ above to make the *smallest* number possible. Write down the number she makes.

People often round off numbers when giving information

**THE PLANET**

Around 100,000 people attended the Concert ..
....................

*Daily Times*

Janet scoops just under £3 million on the Lottery....
....................

**Daily Herald**

About 120 people feared dead.......

## 🔑 Key Facts

| Rounding to the nearest 10 | Rounding to the nearest 100 |
|---|---|
| Look at the units column.<br>5 or more, round up.<br>Less than 5, round down.<br>49 rounds to 50<br>74 rounds to 70<br>65 rounds to 70 | Look at the tens and units columns.<br>50 or more, round up.<br>Less than 50, round down.<br>368 rounds to 400<br>327 rounds to 300<br>850 rounds to 900 |
| Rounding to the nearest 1000 | Rounding to the nearest whole number |
| Look at the hundreds, tens and units columns.<br>500 or more, round up.<br>Less than 500, round down.<br>1361 rounds to 1000<br>2724 rounds to 3000<br>8500 rounds to 9000 | Look at the tenths column (this is the first digit after the decimal point).<br>5 or more, round up.<br>Less than 5, round down.<br>2.5 rounds to 3<br>7.38 rounds to 7<br>£6.65 rounds to £7 |

### M1. 2

Round to the nearest 10

| 1 | 64 | 2 | 47 | 3 | 39 | 4 | 82 | 5 | 23 |
| 6 | 15 | 7 | 71 | 8 | 38 | 9 | 7 | 10 | 43 |
| 11 | 75 | 12 | 97 | 13 | 307 | 14 | 289 | 15 | 461 |
| 16 | 238 | 17 | 423 | 18 | 819 | 19 | 1324 | 20 | 6149 |

Round to the nearest 100

| | | | | |
|---|---|---|---|---|
| **21** 230 | **22** 360 | **23** 480 | **24** 610 | **25** 720 |
| **26** 750 | **27** 673 | **28** 308 | **29** 852 | **30** 695 |
| **31** 747 | **32** 896 | **33** 656 | **34** 718 | **35** 1350 |
| **36** 2715 | **37** 4582 | **38** 1639 | **39** 2193 | **40** 5417 |

Copy the sentences in Questions **41** to **46** , writing the number to the nearest 1000

**41** The van cost £ 16580.

**42** Jack flew 2813 miles to New York

**43** Hale Brewery sold 16293 bottles of beer last week.

**44** The 'Harry Potter' book has 678 pages.

**45** Ramesh won £ 38625 last month.

**46** 482,301 people live in Bristol.

Round to the nearest whole number.

**47** 7.8    **48** 3.2    **49** 2.5    **50** 12.3    **51** 8.34

Round to the nearest pound.

**52** £ 3.17    **53** £ 2.91    **54** £ 7.36    **55** £ 12.81    **56** £ 24.50

Round to the nearest kilogram.

**57** 7.2 kg    **58** 3.5 kg    **59** 14.3 kg    **60** 8.72 kg    **61** 23.26 kg

A headteacher says there are 800 students in Sand High School. This number is rounded off to the nearest 100.

Which of the numbers below could be the exact number of students in Sand High School?

820   701   791   752   861   850   831   750

Answer

820        791   752        831   750

are all possible answers.

Round off each number below to:

(a) the nearest 10    (b) the nearest 100    (c) to the nearest 1000

**1** 2317          **2** 4628          **3** 6278          **4** 4191

**5** 997           **6** 3283          **7** 8169          **8** 17451

**9** A golf club has 600 members. This number is rounded off to the nearest 100.

Which of the numbers below could be the exact number of members of the golf club?

550    610    650    619    583    529    665

**10** The table below shows the population (in millions) of some countries:

| Population (millions) | |
|---|---|
| China | 1131 |
| India | 871 |
| USA | 251 |
| Brazil | 153 |
| Pakistan | 126 |
| Japan | 124 |
| Mexico | 90 |

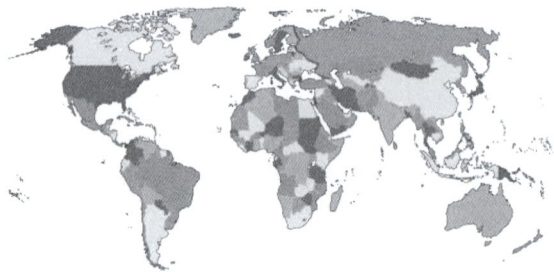

Write down each country and round off the number to the nearest 100.

**11** The home of Chelsea football club is Stamford Bridge. One Saturday around 50,000 people watch a game at Stamford Bridge. This number is rounded off to the nearest 1000.

Which of the numbers below could be the exact number of people at Stamford Bridge?

50,351   50,564   49,681   50,018   49,394   50,500   49,499   49,899

**12** Work out these answers with a calculator and then round off the answers to the *nearest whole number.*

(a) $5817 \div 57$      (b) $18.4 \times 2.17$      (c) $207 \div 0.7$      (d) $221 \div 19$

(e) $3.82 \times 4.05$      (f) $89.6 \div 5.3$      (g) $897 \div 17$      (h) $14.8 \times 0.87$

(i) $1.83 \div 0.07$      (j) $2725 \div 13$      (k) $63.3 \times 2.9$      (l) $83.4 \div 17$

$$4275 + 306 \qquad\qquad 867 - 248$$

Line up units with units
Line up tens with tens
Line up hundreds with hundreds
and so on

$$
\begin{array}{r}
4275 \\
+\ 306 \\
\hline
4581 \\
\hline
1
\end{array}
\qquad\qquad
\begin{array}{r}
8\ {}^{5}\!6\ {}^{1}7 \\
-2\ 4\ 8 \\
\hline
6\ 1\ 9
\end{array}
$$

## M1. 3

Copy and complete.

**1**
$$
\begin{array}{r}
98 \\
+\ 64 \\
\hline
\end{array}
$$

**2**
$$
\begin{array}{r}
216 \\
+\ 71 \\
\hline
\end{array}
$$

**3**
$$
\begin{array}{r}
378 \\
+\ 214 \\
\hline
\end{array}
$$

**4**
$$
\begin{array}{r}
2587 \\
+\ 3179 \\
\hline
\end{array}
$$

**5**
$$
\begin{array}{r}
6781 \\
+\ 2194 \\
\hline
\end{array}
$$

**6**
$$
\begin{array}{r}
87 \\
-\ 48 \\
\hline
\end{array}
$$

**7**
$$
\begin{array}{r}
73 \\
-\ 29 \\
\hline
\end{array}
$$

**8**
$$
\begin{array}{r}
126 \\
-\ 71 \\
\hline
\end{array}
$$

**9**
$$
\begin{array}{r}
563 \\
-\ 148 \\
\hline
\end{array}
$$

**10**
$$
\begin{array}{r}
2847 \\
-\ 386 \\
\hline
\end{array}
$$

**11**
$$
\begin{array}{r}
893 \\
+\ 284 \\
\hline
\end{array}
$$

**12**
$$
\begin{array}{r}
527 \\
+\ 292 \\
\hline
\end{array}
$$

**13**
$$
\begin{array}{r}
376 \\
-\ 128 \\
\hline
\end{array}
$$

**14**
$$
\begin{array}{r}
829 \\
-\ 463 \\
\hline
\end{array}
$$

**15**
$$
\begin{array}{r}
3718 \\
+\ 587 \\
\hline
\end{array}
$$

**16**
$$
\begin{array}{r}
581 \\
-\ 273 \\
\hline
\end{array}
$$

**17**
$$
\begin{array}{r}
8172 \\
+\ 3218 \\
\hline
\end{array}
$$

**18**
$$
\begin{array}{r}
2160 \\
-\ 1317 \\
\hline
\end{array}
$$

**19**
$$
\begin{array}{r}
5863 \\
-\ 2194 \\
\hline
\end{array}
$$

**20**
$$
\begin{array}{r}
86148 \\
+\ 31683 \\
\hline
\end{array}
$$

**21**

| 1 | | 2 | | 3 |
|---|---|---|---|---|
| | | 4 | | |
| 5 | 6 | | | |
| | | | 7 | |
| 8 | | | | |

Copy and complete the crossnumber using the clues.

Clues across
1 $737 + 187$
4 $471 - 228$
5 $1274 - 390$
7 $387 - 329$
8 $27383 + 36876$

Clues down
1 $382 + 576$
2 $561 - 137$
3 $13872 + 9417$
6 $417 + 417$
7 $826 - 771$

1. Find the sum of 318 and 187

2. Find the sum of the four numbers 49, 386, 172 and 563

> The *sum* of 51 and 38 means 51 + 38
>
> The *difference* of 51 and 38 means 51 – 38

3. Find the difference between 268 and 189

4. Find the difference between 637 and 476

5. What is the total of the three numbers 58, 124 and 186?

Copy and complete Questions 6 to 14 by writing the missing number in the box.

6. $220 + \square = 575$    7. $450 + \square = 610$    8. $785 - \square = 320$

9. $833 - \square = 525$    10. $864 + \square = 987$    11. $1238 - \square = 850$

12. $\square + 478 = 820$    13. $1650 - \square = 789$    14. $\square - 384 = 531$

Copy and complete the squares below:

15.

| +   | 38  | 87  |     | 66  |
|-----|-----|-----|-----|-----|
| 109 | 147 |     |     |     |
| 326 |     |     | 571 |     |
|     |     |     |     | 229 |
|     |     |     |     | 512 |

16.

| +   |     | 148 | 516 |     |
|-----|-----|-----|-----|-----|
| 384 | 827 |     |     |     |
|     |     |     | 400 |     |
| 87  |     |     |     | 331 |
| 226 |     |     |     |     |

17. Joe has £ 383. He needs to save £ 760 to buy a laptop. How much more money does he need?

18. Tina has collected the following money from a sponsored run: £ 22, £ 39, £ 21, £ 6, £ 18, £ 54, £ 31, £ 28, £ 42. How much money has she collected in total?

19. Sparrow Electrical Goods sell the following:

    (a) What is the total cost of all 5 items?

    (b) How much more does the Dishwasher cost than the Freezer?

    (c) What is the difference in the prices of the Fridge and the Microwave?

| Washing machine | £ 389 |
|-----------------|-------|
| Fridge          | £ 225 |
| Dishwasher      | £ 412 |
| Microwave       | £ 87  |
| Freezer         | £ 149 |

**20** The table below shows how many students were absent from school one week.

| Year | Monday | Tuesday | Wednesday | Thursday | Friday |
|------|--------|---------|-----------|----------|--------|
| 7 | 11 | 12 | 7 | 13 | 16 |
| 8 | 3 | 7 | 6 | 4 | 9 |
| 9 | 10 | 13 | 13 | 7 | 11 |
| 10 | 17 | 13 | 14 | 19 | 21 |
| 11 | 16 | 14 | 21 | 22 | 18 |

(a) How many students in total were absent on Monday?

(b) How many students in total were absent on Wednesday?

(c) What is the difference in the total number of students absent on Wednesday compared to Monday?

(d) What is the difference in the total number of students absent on Friday compared to Tuesday?

**21** A rock concert was supposed to be watched by 80,000 people maximum. One night the Police estimate that 112,350 people have managed to watch the concert. How many *extra* people were able to see the concert that night?

**22** Sid's car shows 52,487 miles on the milometer at the start of the year. At the end of the year it shows 68,279 miles. How many miles did Sid's car cover during that year?

## Multiplying and dividing by 10, 100 and 1000

$586 \times 10 = 5860$      $\times 10$      digits move 1 place to the left

$586 \times 100 = 58600$      $\times 100$      digits move 2 places to the left

$586 \times 1000 = 586000$      $\times 1000$      digits move 3 places to the left

$79000 \div 10 = 7900$      $\div 10$      digits move 1 place to the right

$79000 \div 100 = 790$      $\div 100$      digits move 2 places to the right

$79000 \div 1000 = 79$      $\div 1000$      digits move 3 places to the right

Write the answers only.

**1** $769 \times 10$

**2** $31 \times 1000$

**3** $268 \times 1000$

**4** $416 \times 100$

**5** $24 \times 100$

**6** $3861 \times 10$

**7** $6300 \div 10$

**8** $81700 \div 10$

**9** $397000 \div 10$

**10** $418000 \div 1000$

**11** $527000 \div 100$

**12** $4800 \div 100$

**13** $51600 \div 100$

**14** $31600 \times 10$

**15** $530 \times 100$

**16** $417000 \div 100$

**17** $684000 \div 1000$

**18** $5370 \times 1000$

**19** Ned earns £ 100 each week. How much money does he earn in one year (52 weeks)?

**20** Molly does a sponsored swim. Her total sponsorship money is £ 13 for each length of the swimming pool. How much money does Molly get if she swims 100 lengths?

**21** A factory makes 110,000 sweets during one week. The sweets are packed equally into 1000 boxes. How many sweets are there in each box?

Copy and complete.

**22** $\boxed{\phantom{000}} \times 10 = 8930$

**23** $\boxed{\phantom{000}} \times 100 = 46000$

**24** $\boxed{\phantom{000}} \div 100 = 218$

**25** $\boxed{\phantom{000}} \div 1000 = 49$

**26** $\boxed{\phantom{000}} \div 10 = 8410$

**27** $\boxed{\phantom{000}} \times 100 = 9300$

**28** $621 \times \boxed{\phantom{000}} = 62100$

**29** $480000 \div \boxed{\phantom{000}} = 480$

**30** $710 \times \boxed{\phantom{000}} = 71000$

**31** $\boxed{\phantom{000}} \div 100 = 3820$

**32** $\boxed{\phantom{000}} \div 10 = 9240$

**33** $87600 \div \boxed{\phantom{000}} = 8760$

**34** $\boxed{316} \rightarrow \boxed{\times 10} \rightarrow \boxed{\phantom{00}} \rightarrow \boxed{\times 100} \rightarrow \boxed{\phantom{00}} \rightarrow \boxed{\div 10} \rightarrow \boxed{\phantom{00}} \rightarrow \boxed{\div 100} \rightarrow \boxed{\phantom{00}}$

**35** $\boxed{\phantom{00}} \rightarrow \boxed{\times 100} \rightarrow \boxed{864000} \rightarrow \boxed{\div 100} \rightarrow \boxed{\phantom{00}} \rightarrow \boxed{\div 10} \rightarrow \boxed{\phantom{00}}$

(a) $3 \times 20$
$= 3 \times 2 \times 10$
$= 6 \times 10$
$= 60$

(b) $30 \times 20$
$= 3 \times 10 \times 2 \times 10$
$= 3 \times 2 \times 10 \times 10$
$= 6 \times 10 \times 10$
$= 60 \times 10$
$= 600$

(c) $50 \times 700$
$= 5 \times 10 \times 7 \times 100$
$= 5 \times 7 \times 10 \times 100$
$= 35 \times 10 \times 100$
$= 350 \times 100$
$= 35000$

(d) $80 \div 20$ is the same as $8 \div 2$ which equals 4

Before dividing 2 numbers you may divide *both* numbers by 10, 100 or 1000 which will make the division easier

(e) $280 \div 40$ is the same as $28 \div 4$ which equals 7

(f) $36000 \div 6000$ is the same as $36 \div 6$ which equals 6

## E1. 4

Work out

| | | | | | | | |
|---|---|---|---|---|---|---|---|
| **1** | $6 \times 30$ | **2** | $8 \times 50$ | **3** | $40 \times 7$ | **4** | $3 \times 90$ |
| **5** | $60 \times 6$ | **6** | $70 \times 30$ | **7** | $80 \times 50$ | **8** | $9 \times 400$ |
| **9** | $30 \times 400$ | **10** | $60 \times 800$ | **11** | $700 \times 20$ | **12** | $800 \times 200$ |
| **13** | $300 \times 90$ | **14** | $800 \times 700$ | **15** | $400 \times 600$ | | |

**16** 20 people each save £400. How much do they save in total?

**17** A school buys 30 boxes of drawing pins. Each box contains 200 drawing pins. How many drawing pins are there in total?

Work out

| | | | | | |
|---|---|---|---|---|---|
| **18** | $120 \div 30$ | **19** | $360 \div 40$ | **20** | $540 \div 60$ |
| **21** | $180 \div 90$ | **22** | $400 \div 50$ | **23** | $4800 \div 600$ |
| **24** | $7200 \div 900$ | **25** | $5600 \div 800$ | **26** | $32000 \div 4000$ |
| **27** | $27000 \div 9000$ | **28** | $48000 \div 8000$ | **29** | $4200 \div 70$ |
| **30** | $8100 \div 90$ | **31** | $21000 \div 700$ | **32** | $32000 \div 800$ |

**33** 60 people share a Lottery win of £300 000. How much does each person get?

**34** 720 000 packets of crisps are packed equally into 8000 boxes. How many packets of crisps are in each box?

Copy and complete

**35** ☐ × 30 = 150   **36** ☐ × 40 = 1200   **37** ☐ × 700 = 14000

**38** ☐ × 800 = 56000   **39** ☐ × 60 = 3000   **40** ☐ ÷ 30 = 50

**41** ☐ ÷ 500 = 70   **42** 25000 ÷ ☐ = 500   **43** 7000 × ☐ = 210000

**44** 20 → ×40 → ☐ → ×30 → ☐ → ÷600 → ☐ → ÷10 → ☐

**45** 300 → ÷10 → ☐ → ×50 → ☐ → ×30 → ☐ → ÷90 → ☐

*Can you still?*

**(1A)** **Round off numbers**

*Can you still?*

Round to the nearest 100.

**1.** 771          **2.** 850          **3.** 1723          **4.** 2198

Round to the nearest 10.

**5.** 18          **6.** 73          **7.** 449          **8.** 251

Round to the nearest whole number.

**9.** 8.9          **10.** 6.7          **11.** 3.16          **12.** 6.5

Round to the nearest 1000.

**13.** 8312          **14.** 7900          **15.** 28184          **16.** 53582

Work out these answers *WITH A CALCULATOR* and then round off the answers to the *nearest whole number*.

**17.** 4.9 × 3.61          **18.** 2142 ÷ 38          **19.** 1.97 ÷ 0.03          **20.** 17.6 × 31.8

# Short multiplication

**1** Copy and complete the grids below. Time yourself on the first grid. Try to improve your time on the second grid.

| × | 7 | 2 | 10 | 8 | 6 | 3 | 11 | 9 | 4 | 5 |
|---|---|---|----|---|---|---|----|---|---|---|
| 7 | 49 | | | | | | | | | |
| 2 | | | | | | | | | | |
| 10 | | | | | | | | | | |
| 8 | | | | | | | | | | |
| 6 | | | 48 | | | | | | | |
| 3 | | | | | | | 9 | | | |
| 11 | | | | | | | | | | |
| 9 | | | | | | | | | | |
| 4 | | | | | | | | | | |
| 5 | | | | | | | | | | |

| × | 2 | 9 | 6 | 3 | 5 | 11 | 0 | 8 | 7 | 4 |
|---|---|---|---|---|---|----|---|---|---|---|
| 2 | | | | | | | | | | |
| 9 | | | | | | | | | | |
| 6 | | | | | | | | | | |
| 3 | | | | | | | | | | |
| 5 | | | | | | | | | | |
| 11 | | | | | | | | | | |
| 0 | | | | | | | | | | |
| 8 | | | | | | | | | | |
| 7 | | | | | | | | | | |
| 4 | | | | | | | | | | |

Work out

**2** $\begin{array}{r} 31 \\ \times\, 3 \\ \hline \end{array}$
　　**3** $\begin{array}{r} 34 \\ \times\, 4 \\ \hline \end{array}$
　　**4** $\begin{array}{r} 61 \\ \times\, 4 \\ \hline \end{array}$
　　**5** $\begin{array}{r} 39 \\ \times\, 5 \\ \hline \end{array}$

**6** $\begin{array}{r} 89 \\ \times\, 7 \\ \hline \end{array}$
　　**7** $\begin{array}{r} 26 \\ \times\, 8 \\ \hline \end{array}$
　　**8** $\begin{array}{r} 416 \\ \times\, 4 \\ \hline \end{array}$
　　**9** $\begin{array}{r} 325 \\ \times\, 5 \\ \hline \end{array}$

**10** $\begin{array}{r} 513 \\ \times\, 3 \\ \hline \end{array}$
　　**11** $\begin{array}{r} 245 \\ \times\, 7 \\ \hline \end{array}$
　　**12** $\begin{array}{r} 216 \\ \times\, 6 \\ \hline \end{array}$
　　**13** $\begin{array}{r} 137 \\ \times\, 4 \\ \hline \end{array}$

**14** $\begin{array}{r} 436 \\ \times\, 8 \\ \hline \end{array}$
　　**15** $\begin{array}{r} 309 \\ \times\, 7 \\ \hline \end{array}$
　　**16** $\begin{array}{r} 154 \\ \times\, 6 \\ \hline \end{array}$
　　**17** $328 \times 6$

**18** $208 \times 5$
　　**19** $9 \times 246$
　　**20** $6 \times 3152$
　　**21** $6384 \times 7$

**22** One night 73 people watch a film at the cinema. They each pay £ 7. How much money do they all pay in total?

**23** Ralph likes collecting fossils. Each month he collects 8 new fossils. How many fossils will Ralph collect in 3 years (36 months)?

**24** Sandra and her 5 friends are going to Spain on holiday. They each have to pay £ 418. How much do Sandra and her friends have to pay in total?

**25** A fast-food restaurant sold 326 'special meals' at £ 4 each. How much money did they get for all 326 'special meals'?

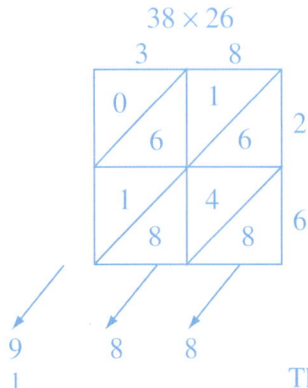

Using grids                    Traditional method

$38 \times 26$

|   | 3 | 8 |   |
|---|---|---|---|
|   | 0 / 6 | 1 / 6 | 2 |
|   | 1 / 8 | 4 / 8 | 6 |

add
along
the
diagonals

$38 \times 26$

```
      38
  ×   26
     228   (38 × 6)
     760   (38 × 20)
     988
```

9  8  8
1

The answer is 988

## E1. 5

Work out

**1**   $23 \times 16$    **2**   $16 \times 35$    **3**   $93 \times 27$    **4**   $68 \times 46$

**5**   $76 \times 52$    **6**   $59 \times 34$    **7**   $64 \times 28$    **8**   $417 \times 76$

**9**   $398 \times 59$    **10**   $68 \times 409$    **11**   $623 \times 67$    **12**   $518 \times 43$

**13**   $28 \times 338$    **14**   $81 \times 716$    **15**   $543 \times 728$

**16**   64 people each pay £ 724 to go on a holiday in the USA. How much do the 64 people pay in total?

**17**   On average, a person in the UK laughs 15 times each day. How many times will a person laugh in one year (52 weeks)?

**18**   A person sheds 18 kg of skin in his or her lifetime. How much skin would be shed by 500 people over their lifetimes?

**19**   In 2003, single men in the UK spent an average of £ 186 on a first date. How much in total would 73 single men have spent on their first dates?

**20**

| TV | £ 527 |
|---|---|
| CD player | £ 218 |

How much will 34 televisions and 19 CD players cost in total?

(a)   $625 \div 5$

$$\begin{array}{r} 1\ 2\ 5 \\ 5\overline{)6^1 2^2 5} \end{array}$$

(b)   $936 \div 4$

$$\begin{array}{r} 2\ 3\ 4 \\ 4\overline{)9^1 3^1 6} \end{array}$$

(c)   $3073 \div 7$

$$\begin{array}{r} 0\ 4\ 3\ 9 \\ 7\overline{)3^3 0^2 7^6 3} \end{array}$$

**M1. 6**

### Part One

Copy and complete the following division problems.

**1**   $6 \div 3 =$ ?      **2**   $8 \div 4 =$ ?      **3**   $48 \div 8 =$ ?      **4**   $88 \div 11 =$ ?

**5**   $16 \div 2 =$ ?      **6**   $10 \div 2 =$ ?      **7**   $49 \div 7 =$ ?      **8**   $90 \div 9 =$ ?

**9**   $20 \div 5 =$ ?      **10**   $99 \div 11 =$ ?      **11**   $50 \div 5 =$ ?      **12**   $96 \div 12 =$ ?

**13**   $24 \div 6 =$ ?      **14**   $14 \div 7 =$ ?      **15**   $54 \div 6 =$ ?      **16**   $100 \div 10 =$ ?

**17**   $28 \div 4 =$ ?      **18**   $15 \div 3 =$ ?      **19**   $0 \div 7 =$ ?      **20**   $5\frac{1}{2} \div 5\frac{1}{2} =$ ?

### Part Two      Work out

**1**   $3\overline{)99}$          **2**   $2\overline{)42}$          **3**   $4\overline{)48}$          **4**   $7\overline{)84}$

**5**   $5\overline{)65}$          **6**   $6\overline{)72}$          **7**   $7\overline{)847}$          **8**   $9\overline{)558}$

**9**   $8\overline{)128}$          **10**   $9\overline{)729}$          **11**   $2\overline{)678}$          **12**   $6\overline{)3372}$

**13**   $3\overline{)729}$          **14**   $5\overline{)725}$          **15**   $4\overline{)1028}$          **16**   $8\overline{)1856}$

**17**   $6\overline{)1296}$          **18**   $7\overline{)343}$          **19**   $9\overline{)6561}$          **20**   $6\overline{)2796}$

**21**   $8\overline{)2056}$          **22**   $5\overline{)1025}$          **23**   $6\overline{)7776}$          **24**   $7\overline{)5082}$

**25**   $3050 \div 10$          **26**   $1387 \div 1$          **27**   $38199 \div 7$          **28**   $14032 \div 8$

**29**   $31386 \div 6$          **30**   $3490 \div 5$          **31**   $28926 \div 9$          **32**   $15638 \div 7$

(a) How many teams of 5 can you make from 113 people?

Work out $113 \div 5$     $\dfrac{0\ 2\ 2}{5\overline{)1^1 1^1 3}}$ remainder 3

Here we round *down*. You can make 22 teams and there will be 3 people left over.

(b) An egg box holds 6 eggs. How many boxes do you need for 231 eggs?

Work out $231 \div 6$     $\dfrac{3\ 8}{6\overline{)23^5 1}}$ remainder 3

Here we round *up* because you must use complete boxes. You need 39 boxes altogether .

## E1. 6

Write the answers with a remainder.

| | | | |
|---|---|---|---|
| **1** $2\overline{)432}$ | **2** $4\overline{)716}$ | **3** $6\overline{)895}$ | **4** $3\overline{)164}$ |
| **5** $8\overline{)514}$ | **6** $9\overline{)375}$ | **7** $5\overline{)2642}$ | **8** $2\overline{)7141}$ |
| **9** $1079 \div 7$ | **10** $2132 \div 5$ | **11** $4014 \div 8$ | **12** $235 \div 6$ |
| **13** $657 \div 10$ | **14** $8327 \div 10$ | **15** $85714 \div 6$ | **16** $4826 \div 9$ |
| **17** $2007 \div 7$ | **18** $9998 \div 9$ | **19** $6732 \div 11$ | **20** $84563 \div 7$ |

In the Questions below, round the answer up or down, depending on which is more sensible.

**21** There are 27 children in a class. How many teams of 4 can be made?

**22** Tickets cost £ 7 each. I have £ 100. How many tickets can I buy?

**23** Tins of spaghetti are packed 8 to a box. How many boxes are needed for 943 tins?

**24** Five people can travel in one car. 83 people are to be transported. How many cars are needed?

**25** A tennis coach has 52 tennis balls. A box holds 4 tennis balls. How many boxes does the tennis coach have?

You can divide large numbers in the same way as you do short division.

$962 \div 26$

Write out the 26 times table by adding on 26 each time.

The most you will need are 9 numbers.

Write out the division leaving a space between each digit in 962.

26
52
78
104
130
156
182
208
234

$$\begin{array}{c} 0 \\ 26\overline{)9\,6\,2} \end{array} \implies \begin{array}{c} 0\ 3 \\ 26\overline{)9\,9\,6\,2} \end{array} \implies \begin{array}{c} 0\ 3\ 7 \\ 26\overline{)9\,9\,6\,18\,2} \end{array} \implies 962 \div 26 = 37$$

Look at the times table. 26 divides into 96 '3' times. $3 \times 26 = 78$ so the remainder is $96 - 78 = 18$. Write this in front of the 2.

## M1. 7

Work out

| | | | | | |
|---|---|---|---|---|---|
| **1** | $504 \div 14$ | **2** | $513 \div 19$ | **3** | $400 \div 16$ |
| **4** | $552 \div 24$ | **5** | $559 \div 13$ | **6** | $408 \div 17$ |
| **7** | $704 \div 22$ | **8** | $625 \div 25$ | **9** | $798 \div 21$ |
| **10** | $812 \div 28$ | **11** | $884 \div 34$ | **12** | $851 \div 37$ |
| **13** | $630 \div 35$ | **14** | $972 \div 27$ | **15** | $702 \div 39$ |

**16** To change months into years, we divide by 12. Find the age in years of each person below:

Charlie
348 months

Tessa
516 months

Ron
984 months

Teresa
180 months

**17** 840 packets of crisps are packed into 24 boxes. How many packets of crisps are there in each box?

**1** Copy and complete the crossnumber using the clues.

| 1 | | | 2 | | 3 |
|---|---|---|---|---|---|
| | | 4 | | | |
| 5 | 6 | | 7 | 8 | |
| | 9 | | | | |
| 10 | | | 11 | | |
| | | 13 | | | |
| 14 | | | | 15 | |

| | Clues across | | Clues down |
|---|---|---|---|
| 1 | $874 \div 23$ | 1 | $5372 \div 17$ |
| 2 | $9504 \div 18$ | 2 | $7436 \div 13$ |
| 4 | $1598 \div 34$ | 3 | $9493 \div 11$ |
| 5 | $3536 \div 52$ | 6 | $9828 \div 12$ |
| 7 | $3888 \div 16$ | 8 | $5978 \div 14$ |
| 9 | $1152 \div 64$ | 10 | $6540 \div 15$ |
| 10 | $2058 \div 42$ | 11 | $2871 \div 87$ |
| 11 | $4836 \div 13$ | 12 | $6318 \div 26$ |
| 13 | $2117 \div 29$ | 13 | $4788 \div 63$ |
| 14 | $8764 \div 14$ | | |
| 15 | $3818 \div 46$ | | |

**2** There are 380 children in a school. How many classes of 31 children can be made? How many children would be left over?

**3** Tom has to put 1000 bottles into crates. One crate will take 24 bottles. How many crates will Tom need?

**4** How many 27p stamps can I buy with a £20 note?

**5** A party of 17 people are going on holiday to Greece. The total holiday bill is £7191. How much does each person have to pay?

*Can you still?*

*Can you still?*

**1B  Add and subtract**

Work out

**1.** $573 + 64$          **2.** $937 + 418$          **3.** $561 - 38$

**4.** $572 - 419$          **5.** $4174 + 629$          **6.** $6834 - 458$

**7.** $3218 + 4627$          **8.** $6134 - 816$          **9.** $7428 - 2917$

Copy and complete Questions ⑩ to ⑮ by writing the missing number in the box.

**10.**  $371 + \boxed{\phantom{000}} = 518$     **11.**  $523 + \boxed{\phantom{000}} = 741$     **12.**  $681 - \boxed{\phantom{000}} = 251$

**13.**  $\boxed{\phantom{000}} + 334 = 620$     **14.**  $1369 - \boxed{\phantom{000}} = 817$     **15.**  $\boxed{\phantom{000}} - 265 = 306$

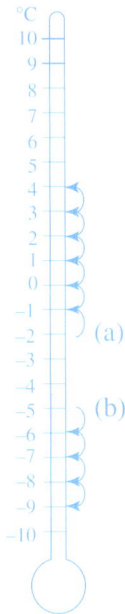

**Examples**

(a) The temperature is –2°C.    It *rises* by 6°C.
What is the new temperature?

Start at –2

Go *up* 6

Answer is 4

So new temperature is 4°C

(b) The temperature is –5°C. It *falls* by 4°C.
What is the new temperature?

Start at –5

Go *down* 4

Answer is –9

So the new temperature is –9°C

## M1. 8

**1** Copy and complete the table below by moving up or down the thermometer to find the new temperature.

| Temperature °C | Change °C | New temperature °C |
|---|---|---|
| 4 | falls by 5 | |
| 1 | falls by 6 | |
| –3 | rises by 2 | |
| –6 | falls by 3 | |
| –4 | rises by 7 | |
| –9 | rises by 6 | |
| 5 | rises by 3 | |
| 0 | falls by 7 | |
| –2 | falls by 3 | |
| 6 | falls by 10 | |

In questions **1** to **3** put the numbers in order, smallest first:

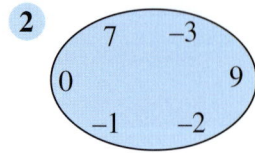

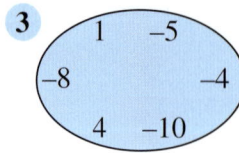

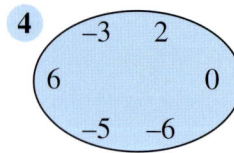

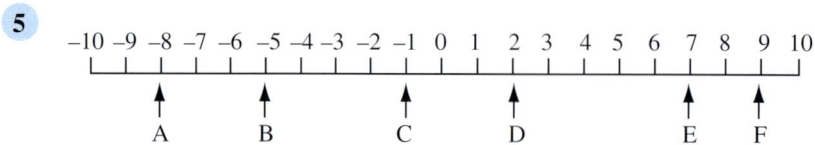

**2**
7   −3
0        9
−1   −2

**3**
1    −5
−8       −4
4   −10

**4**
−3   2
6        0
−5   −6

**5**

−10 −9 −8 −7 −6 −5 −4 −3 −2 −1 0 1 2 3 4 5 6 7 8 9 10

A     B        C    D        E   F

The *difference* in temperature between C and D is 3°C. Give the difference in temperature between:

(a)   E and F        (b)   B and C        (c)   D and E

(d)   A and B        (e)   A and C        (f)   B and E

**6**   The temperature in Birmingham at midday is 15°C. During the night it falls by 16°C. What is the new temperature?

**7**   One night the temperature in Plymouth is 1°C and the temperature in Newcastle is −3°C. How much colder is Newcastle than Plymouth?

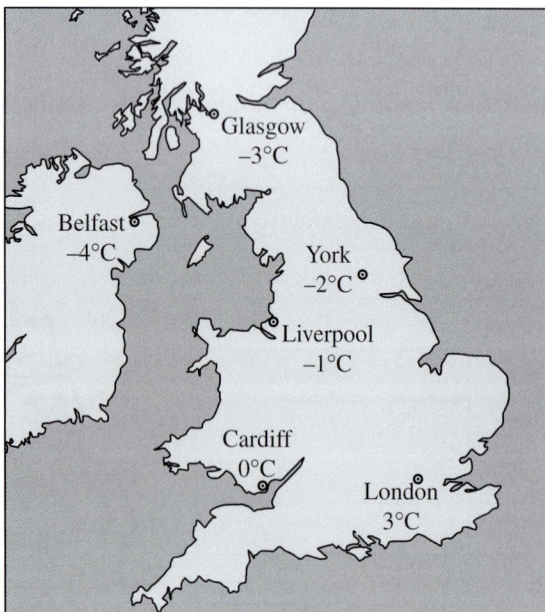

Glasgow
−3°C

Belfast
−4°C

York
−2°C

Liverpool
−1°C

Cardiff
0°C

London
3°C

**8**   Which city has the highest temperature?

**9**   Which city has the lowest temperature?

**10**   What is the difference in temperature between York and London?

**11**   What is the difference in temperature between Belfast and Liverpool?

**12**   During the day, the temperature in Glasgow rises by 10°C. What is the new temperature?

**13**   During the day, the temperature in Liverpool rises by 15°C and the temperature in Belfast rises by 17°C. Which city now has the higher temperature, Liverpool or Belfast?

**14** Work out

(a) $3 - 6$      (b) $-5 - 1$      (c) $-5 + 1$      (d) $-3 + 3$

(e) $-8 + 5$      (f) $3 - 9$      (g) $2 - 10$      (h) $-4 - 5$

(i) $-8 + 6$      (j) $-10 + 6$      (k) $-7 - 2$      (l) $-6 + 5$

**15** Copy and complete the table below:-

| Old temperature °C | Change °C | New temperature °C |
|---|---|---|
| -2 | rises by 7 | |
| | rises by 3 | 2 |
| | falls by 6 | -4 |
| -8 | falls by 2 | |
| | rises by 7 | 0 |
| -6 | | -2 |
| -12 | rises by 8 | |
| | rises by 3 | -1 |
| | falls by 5 | -7 |
| -10 | | -14 |

# 🔑 Key Facts

**Two signs together**

$8 - -5$ can be read as '8 take away negative 5'. This is sometimes written as $8 - (-5)$.

It is possible to replace two signs next to each other by one sign as follows:

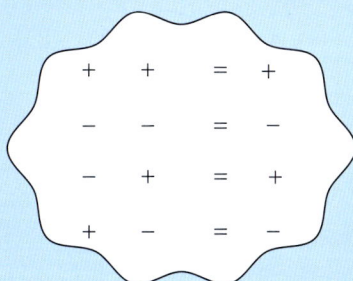

| | | | |
|---|---|---|---|
| + | + | = | + |
| − | − | = | − |
| − | + | = | + |
| + | − | = | − |

'same signs: +'

'different signs: −'

When two signs next to each other have been replaced by one sign in this way, the calculation is completed using the number line as before.

**Examples**

(a) $-6 + -2$          (b) $3 - -4$          (c) $-4 + -2$

$= -6 - 2$           $= 3 + 4$            $= -4 - 2$

$= -8$               $= 7$                $= -6$

**1** Work out

(a) $3 + -1$     (b) $8 + -5$     (c) $-4 - 2$     (d) $-2 + -3$

(e) $8 + -3$     (f) $4 - -2$     (g) $-3 + -4$     (h) $-2 - -1$

(i) $7 - 10$     (j) $4 + -6$     (k) $-6 - 3$     (l) $-8 - -4$

(m) $7 - -1$     (n) $5 - -4$     (o) $-1 + -6$     (p) $-12 + 5$

**2** John is overdrawn at the bank by £ 70 (This means he owes the bank £ 70). If John pays in £ 100, how much money will he have in the bank?

**3** Cassie is overdrawn at the bank by £ 60. How much money will she have in the bank if she:

(a)  pays in £ 100     (b)  pays in £ 70     (c)  pays in £ 140?

**4** Todd has £ 36 in his bank account. He buys some clothes for £ 150 with his bank card. How much money does he now owe the bank?

**5** Lola wants to buy a pair of shoes for £ 60. She has £ 12 in her bank account. The bank will allow her to go up to £ 50 overdrawn. Can she use her bank card to buy the shoes?

**6** Work out

(a) $-4 + 3$     (b) $-9 - 1$     (c) $4 - -7$     (d) $-8 - -2$

(e) $6 + -4$     (f) $-3 + -8$     (g) $7 - 13$     (h) $-9 + 5$

(i) $-9 - 5$     (j) $-9 - -5$     (k) $-4 - -10$     (l) $-5 - 6$

(m) $3 + -10$     (n) $-6 + -2$     (o) $-3 - -4$     (p) $-8 + 4 - 3$

(q) $-7 - 2 + 10$     (r) $-5 - -1 - 6$     (s) $4 - 7 + -2$     (t) $-8 + -5 - -5$

Copy and complete the boxes below:

**7**
$$-6 + 4 = -2$$
$$\square - 2 = -3$$
$$-8 - -7 = \square$$
$$-6 + 1 = \square$$
$$\square - -2 = 7$$

**8**
$$7 + -3 = \square$$
$$\square + -4 = -2$$
$$\square - 7 = -8$$
$$6 - \square = -1$$
$$-3 + \square = 1 - 10$$

**9**
$$-3 - -2 = \square$$
$$-9 + -3 = \square$$
$$\square - -7 = -2$$
$$-8 - \square = -2$$
$$\square + -6 = -12$$

**10** **Check** your answers to Questions **6** to **9** by *using a calculator*. Make sure your teacher shows you the correct button to use for negative numbers.

# 🔑 Key Facts

When a positive number is multiplied by a negative number the answer is negative.

When two negative numbers are multiplied together the answer is positive.

For division, the rules are the same as for multiplication.

**Examples**

$$-3 \times (-7) = 21 \qquad 5 \times (-3) = -15 \qquad -12 \div 3 = -4$$

$$20 \div (-2) = -10 \qquad -40 \div (-20) = 2 \qquad -1 \times (-2) \times (-3) = -6$$

## M1. 9

Work out

1  (a) $3 \times -5$      (b) $6 \times -3$      (c) $-4 \times -6$      (d) $-3 \times -7$

2  (a) $-8 \times -4$      (b) $-7 \times 6$      (c) $-2 \times -6$      (d) $4 \times -9$

3  (a) $5 \times -6$      (b) $3 \times -1$      (c) $-9 \times -5$      (d) $-4 \times -4$

4  (a) $-10 \div 5$      (b) $-28 \div 4$      (c) $-25 \div -5$      (d) $30 \div -6$

5  (a) $-60 \div -10$      (b) $-42 \div 7$      (c) $21 \div -7$      (d) $-18 \div -3$

6  (a) $48 \div -8$      (b) $-24 \div -4$      (c) $-35 \div -7$      (d) $-49 \div 7$

Copy and complete the squares below:

7

| × | −3 | −6 | 8 | −2 |
|---|---|---|---|---|
| 7 | −21 | | | |
| −5 | | | | |
| −4 | | | | |
| 9 | | | | |

8

| × | −7 | 4 | −3 | |
|---|---|---|---|---|
| 4 | −28 | | | −32 |
| | 42 | | | |
| | | | 15 | |
| | | | | −56 |

23

Work out

**9**   (a) $45 \div -9$    (b) $-120 \div -10$    (c) $-81 \div -9$    (d) $-63 \div 7$

**10**   (a) $12 \times -13$    (b) $-24 \times -16$    (c) $-17 \times 14$    (d) $-23 \times -34$

**11**   (a) $-2 \times -2$      (b) $-2 \times -2 \times -2$    (c) $-2 \times -2 \times -2 \times -2$

**12**   (a) $-3 \times -3 \times -3$    (b) $-4 \times 2 \times -4$    (c) $-10 \times -1 \times 3 \times -2$

**13**   **Check** your answers to Questions **7** and **8** by *using a calculator*. Make sure your teacher shows you the correct button to use for negative numbers.

## E1. 9

Each empty square contains either a number or an operation $(+, -, \times, \div)$. Copy each square and fill in the missing details. The arrows are equals signs.

**1**

| 20 | ÷ | -4 | → |  |
|---|---|---|---|---|
| ÷ |  | × |  |  |
|  |  | -3 | → | 30 |
| ↓ |  | ↓ |  |  |
| -2 | × |  | → |  |

**2**

| -30 | × | -2 | → |  |
|---|---|---|---|---|
| ÷ |  |  |  |  |
|  |  | × | → | -20 |
| ↓ |  | ↓ |  |  |
| 6 |  | -8 | → | -48 |

**3**

| -8 | ÷ |  | → | 4 |
|---|---|---|---|---|
|  |  |  |  |  |
| 3 | × | -6 | → |  |
| ↓ |  | ↓ |  |  |
| -24 |  | 12 | → | -2 |

**4**

| -8 | + | -4 | → |  |
|---|---|---|---|---|
| - |  | + |  |  |
| 2 |  | 12 | → | -10 |
| ↓ |  | ↓ |  |  |
|  | + |  | → |  |

**5**

| -11 | - | -1 | → |  |
|---|---|---|---|---|
| + |  |  |  |  |
| 6 |  | 8 | → | -2 |
| ↓ |  | ↓ |  |  |
|  | - | 7 | → |  |

**6**

| -10 | - |  | → | -8 |
|---|---|---|---|---|
| - |  | - |  |  |
| -4 |  | 7 | → | 3 |
| ↓ |  | ↓ |  |  |
|  |  | - | → |  |

**7**

| -10 | ÷ | 5 | → |  |
|---|---|---|---|---|
| × |  | - |  |  |
| -2 |  |  | → | -18 |
| ↓ |  | ↓ |  |  |
|  |  | -4 | → | -5 |

**8**

| 30 | ÷ |  | → | -6 |
|---|---|---|---|---|
| - |  |  |  |  |
| 40 |  | -8 | → | -5 |
| ↓ |  | ↓ |  |  |
|  | × | 3 | → |  |

**9**

| -16 | + |  | → | -12 |
|---|---|---|---|---|
|  |  | × |  |  |
| -8 | - |  | → |  |
| ↓ |  | ↓ |  |  |
| 2 |  | -24 | → | -48 |

24

## 🔑 Key Facts

Everyone has agreed to work out problems in the same order so that there is only one correct answer.

The table below shows the order.

| Brackets | ( ) | do first | 'B' |
|---|---|---|---|
| O | | | 'O' |
| Division | ÷ | do this pair next | 'D' |
| Multiplication | × | | 'M' |
| Addition | + | do this pair next | 'A' |
| Subtraction | − | | 'S' |

Remember the word 'BODMAS' (The 'O' is just used to make a word)

(a) $14 - 6 \div 2$

$= 14 - 3$

$= 11$

(b) $(14 - 6) \div 2$

$= 8 \div 2$

$= 4$

(c) $14 \times 2 + 3 \times 5$

$= 28 + 15$

$= 43$

## M1. 10

Work out the following: Show every step in your working.

1  $5 + 3 \times 2$

2  $7 + 4 \times 4$

3  $28 \div 7 + 6$

4  $20 \div 4 + 5$

5  $(5 + 3) \times 3$

6  $(6 + 2) \times 5$

7  $36 \div (5 + 1)$

8  $40 \div (4 + 4)$

9  $24 \div 4 + 8$

10  $42 \div 7 + 3$

11  $8 \times (3 + 4)$

12  $3 \times 10 + 4$

13  $40 \div (7 + 3)$

14  $3 \times 8 + 9$

15  $5 \times (8 + 3)$

16  $6 + 2 \times 4 + 3$

17  $(6 + 2) \times (4 + 3)$

18  $(6 + 2) \times 4 + 3$

19  $(7 + 13) \div 5 + 4$

20  $10 + 24 \div (6 + 2)$

21  $(8 + 7) \div (2 + 1)$

22  $35 - 3 \times 5$

23  $8 + 9 + 10 \div 2$

24  $(3 + 8 + 9) \div 4$

25  $5 + 3 \times 4 \div 2$

26  $5 + 21 \div 3 + 6$

27  $8 + 4 \times 7 + 2$

**28** $49 \div 7 + 3$   **29** $(6 + 4) \div 2 + 3 \times 3$   **30** $9 + 8 \div 2 + 4 \times 5$

**31** $12 + 12 \div 3 + 3$   **32** $(3 + 8 + 9) \div 10$   **33** $5 + 7 + 8 \div 2$

**34** $(5 + 7 + 8) \div 2$   **35** $3 \times 12 \div 3 + 1$   **36** $(11 + 24) \div (10 - 3)$

**37** $15 + 5 \div 5$   **38** $(15 + 5) \div 5$   **39** $(12 - 3) \div (2 + 3 + 4)$

## E1. 10

Work out the following, show every step in your working.

**1** $8 + 2 \times 4$   **2** $12 - 2 \times 3$   **3** $(8 - 3) \times 4$

**4** $15 \div 3 - 1$   **5** $17 + 9 \div 3$   **6** $4 + 39 \div 13$

**7** $15 + 4 \times 10$   **8** $50 - 11 \times 3$   **9** $48 \div (20 - 8)$

**10** $(14 + 3) \times 2$   **11** $7 + 7 \times 7$   **12** $32 - 5 - 11$

**13** $9 + 3 \times 3 - 4$   **14** $16 - (8 \times 1) + 3$   **15** $3 + 15 \div (9 - 6)$

**16** $(6 \times 5) - (12 \div 3)$   **17** $100 - (88 \div 4)$   **18** $(100 + 3) \div (104 - 101)$

**19** $8 + 32 \div 4 - 5$   **20** $40 \div 8 - 24 \div 8$   **21** $3 \times (4 \times 5 - 1)$

Copy each question and write brackets so that each calculation gives the correct answer.

**22** $3 + 2 \times 5 = 25$   **23** $7 + 4 \times 4 = 44$

**24** $5 \times 2 + 3 = 25$   **25** $8 + 3 \times 6 = 26$

**26** $5 \times 9 - 4 = 25$   **27** $6 \times 15 - 6 = 54$

**28** $40 - 25 \times 3 = 45$   **29** $63 - 7 \div 8 = 7$

**30** $42 \div 6 + 1 = 6$   **31** $18 - 12 \div 12 \div 4 = 2$

**32** $16 + 14 \div 2 = 15$   **33** $7 + 25 \div 4 = 8$

**34** $7 + 3 \times 8 - 5 = 30$   **35** $13 + 2 \times 4 = 60$

**36** $3 + 8 + 19 \div 3 = 10$   **37** $5 + 6 \times 10 - 4 = 66$

## WATCH YOUR MONEY! – Wages

**1** Do you have a job?

**2** How are you paid- per hour, per day, for each task?

**3** Discuss **1** and **2** with your class and teacher.

**4** Which jobs are well paid and which jobs are badly paid? Why?

> **Minimum wage**
>
> In 2004: minimum hourly wage for 16–17 year olds was £3
>
> for 18–21 year olds was £3.80
>
> for over 21 year olds was £4.85

### WYM1

Work out how much you earn if you work for:

**1** 10 hours at £4 per hour

**2** 7 hours at £5 per hour

**3** 9 hours at £6 per hour

**4** 12 hours at £4 per hour

**5** 8 hours at £5 per hour

**6** 8 hours at £4.10 per hour

**7** 10 hours at £3.90 per hour

**8** 15 hours at £4.20 per hour

**9** How much does Shelley earn if she works in a shop for 7 hours at £4.70 per hour?

**10** How much does Mark earn if he works for 14 hours at £4.50 per hour?

**11** Ron works for 16 hours at £3.85 per hour. How much does he earn?

**12** Margaret works for 20 hours at £4.25 per hour. How much does she earn?

**13** How much did Alan earn last week if he worked for 18 hours at £4.75 per hour?

**14** Pippa worked at 30 hours last week at £5.05 per hour. How much did she earn?

**15** Steven worked for 25 hours at £4.85 per hour. Natasha earned £4.65 per hour for 27 hours. Who earned more money and by how much?

## 1. Understanding place value

What is the value of the underlined digit in each number below?

(a) <u>4</u>19    (b) 46<u>2</u>1    (c) 0.7<u>9</u>    (d) 12.<u>6</u>8    (e) 31.82<u>7</u>

## 2. Rounding off numbers

Round the numbers below to    (i) the nearest 10

(ii) the nearest 100

(iii) the nearest 1000

(a) 3289    (b) 5614    (c) 12324    (d) 22831

(e) Round off 3.5 to the nearest whole number.

(f) Round off 7.82 to the nearest whole number.

## 3. Adding and subtracting whole numbers

Work out

(a) $39 + 53$    (b) $67 + 248$    (c) $3617 + 2394$

(d) $86 - 49$    (e) $263 - 146$    (f) $5126 - 3811$

## 4. Multiplying whole numbers

Work out

(a) $7 \times 8$    (b) $70 \times 80$    (c) $243 \times 4$    (d) $384 \times 6$

(e) $46 \times 27$    (f) $39 \times 78$    (g) $27 \times 419$    (h) $362 \times 53$

## 5. Dividing whole numbers

Work out

(a) $684 \div 4$    (b) $984 \div 3$    (c) $2282 \div 7$

(d) $864 \div 16$    (e) $1608 \div 24$    (f) $3286 \div 62$

(g) 289 children are going on an ice-skating trip. One coach holds 48 children. How many coaches are needed for this trip?

## 6. Adding and subtracting negative numbers

(a) The temperature in Sydney is $34°$ C. The temperature in Moscow is $-12°$ C. What is the difference in the temperatures?

(b) The temperature in Moscow in part (a) rises by $9°$ C. What is the new temperature in Moscow?

Work out

(c) $7 - 10$    (d) $-8 + 4$   (e) $-6 - -2$   (f) $7 + -3$

(g) $-3 - -4$   (h) $-8 - 4$   (i) $-7 - -5$   (j) $-4 + -3$

## 7. Multiplying and dividing negative numbers

Work out

(a) $8 \times -3$      (b) $-4 \times -6$     (c) $-7 \times 4$     (d) $-20 \div 10$

(e) $-40 \div -5$    (f) $-9 \times 8$      (g) $-48 \div 6$     (h) $-63 \div -9$

## 8. Doing calculations in the correct order

Work out

(a) $5 + 2 \times 4$           (b) $20 - (7 + 4)$    (c) $(9 + 7) \div 4$    **Remember:**

(d) $(6 + 10) \div (10 - 2)$    (e) $12 + 8 \div 2$    (f) $(7 - 2) \times 9$     'BODMAS'

Copy the Questions for parts (g) and (h) then write brackets so that each calculation gives the correct answer.

(g) $7 \times 4 + 5 = 63$      (h) $10 - 7 \times 8 + 2 = 30$

This machine multiplies all numbers by 7 then subtracts 2.

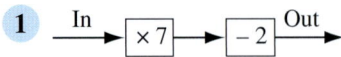

**1**    In → $\times 7$ → $-2$ → Out

(a) Complete this table

| In | Out |
|----|-----|
| 5  | 33  |
| 2  |     |
| 7  |     |

(b) 26 comes **out** of the machine. What was put **in**?    (AQA)

**2** The map shows the positions and heights of six mountains.

(a) Write the names of the six mountains in order of height. Put the highest mountain first.

(b) Helvellyn is added to the list of mountains in part (a). It is fourth in the list. What can be said about the height of Helvellyn?    (OCR)

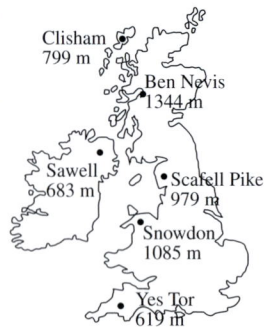

Clisham 799 m
Ben Nevis 1344 m
Sawell 683 m
Scafell Pike 979 m
Snowdon 1085 m
Yes Tor 619 m

**3** (a) Write the number forty six thousand six hundred and two in figures.

(b) Write your answer to part (a) to the nearest thousand.

**4** Work out    (a) $563 \times 78$    (b) $793 \div 26$    (EDEXCEL)

**5** As a gas cools it eventually turns to liquid. Radon gas turns to liquid at $-62°C$. Argon gas turns to liquid at $-186°C$.

(a) What is the difference between the two temperatures?

(b) In each of the statements below, write a possible temperature. (Temperatures below $-273°C$ are not possible.)

   (i) At ......°C radon is a gas.

   (ii) At ......°C argon is a liquid.    (OCR)

**6** Nick fills a van with large wooden crates.

The weight of each crate is 69 kg.

The greatest weight the van can hold is 990 kg.

Work out the greatest number of crates that the van can hold.    (EDEXCEL)

**7** (a) (i) Write down the number **fifty two thousand six hundred and two** in figures.

    (ii) Write down **fifty two thousand six hundred and two** to the nearest thousand.

  (b) (i) Write down 20 387 in words.

    (ii) Write down 20 387 to the nearest hundred.

**8** These maps show the temperatures at midday and at midnight on a certain day in five different places.

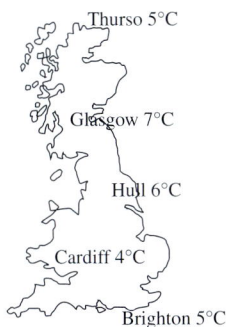
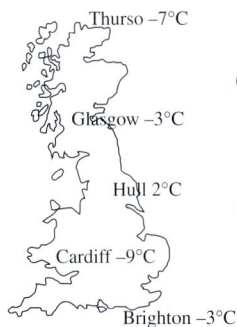

    **Midday**        **Midnight**

(a) Which place was the warmest at midday?

(b) How much colder was Cardiff than Glasgow at midnight?

(c) Which place had the greatest drop in temperature from midday to midnight?

(d) Which place had the least difference in temperature from midday to midnight?

(AQA)

**9** In this question you must **NOT** use a calculator.

You must show **ALL** your working.

Asif buys 37 ovens at £412 each.

Work out the total cost.

**10** A first class stamp costs 26p.

  (a) What is the greatest number of first class stamps you can buy for £2?

Jean buys 10 first class stamps.

She pays with a £5 note.

  (b) How much change should she get?        (EDEXCEL)

**11** A gardener buys 375 trays of plants. There are 54 plants in a tray.

How many plants is this altogether?        (CCEA)

# NUMBER 2

**2**

**In this unit you will learn how to:**

- square and square root numbers
- cube and cube root numbers
- use powers
- find factors and prime numbers
- find multiples and the Lowest Common Multiple (LCM)
- find the Highest Common Factor (HCF)
- break down numbers into prime factors
- find equivalent fractions
- cancel fractions
- put fractions in order of size
- convert between fractions and decimals
- order decimals
- WATCH YOUR MONEY! – wages – overtime

---

## Square numbers

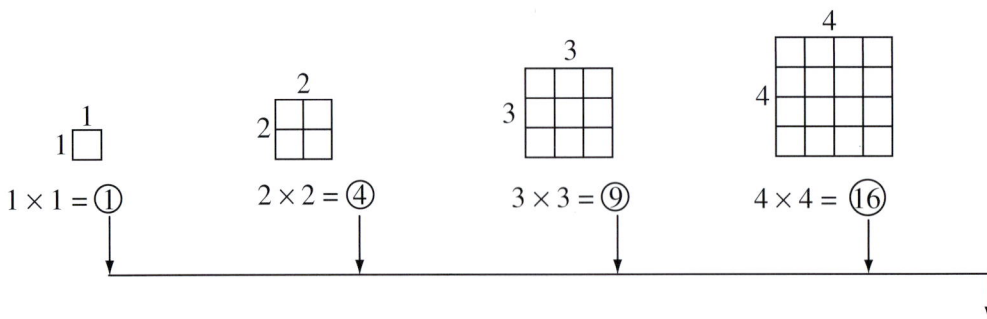

$1 \times 1 = ①$    $2 \times 2 = ④$    $3 \times 3 = ⑨$    $4 \times 4 = ⑯$

When a whole number is multiplied by itself, we get a *square number*

$3 \times 3 = 9$    We write this as $3^2$ (3 squared)

so $5^2 = 5 \times 5 = 25$

A *calculator* has a button for squaring $\boxed{x^2}$ Use this button with your teacher to make sure you know how to use it correctly.

## 🔑 Key Facts

The square root of a number $n$ is the number which is multiplied by itself to give that number $n$.

The square root of 36 is **6** because $\mathbf{6 \times 6} = 36$

The symbol for square root is $\sqrt{\phantom{x}}$ so $\sqrt{36} = 6$

$\sqrt{49} = 7$ because $7 \times 7 = 49$

A *calculator* has a button for finding square roots $\boxed{\sqrt{\phantom{x}}}$ or $\boxed{\sqrt{x}}$. Use this button with your teacher to make sure you know how to use it correctly.

### M2. 1

**1**  $1(1 \times 1)$ and $4(2 \times 2)$ are the first two square numbers. Write down the first 12 square numbers.

**2**  'In your head', find the value of

   (a) $4^2$   (b) $8^2$   (c) $9^2$   (d) $10^2$   (e) $20^2$

Work out

**3**  $10^2 + 7^2$      **4**  $8^2 - 5^2$      **5**  $8^2 - 6^2$

**6**  $7^2 + 4^2$      **7**  $3^2 + 5^2$      **8**  $(7 - 3)^2$

**9**  $10^2 - 4^2$      **10**  $(20 - 11)^2$      **11**  $1^2 + 2^2 + 3^2 + 4^2$

**12**   length / length

> If you multiply the length of one side of a square by itself, you will find the area of the square

   (a) What is the length of one side of a square if the area is 9?

   (b) What is the length of one side of a square if the area is 49?

   (c) What is the length of one side of a square if the area is 100?

**13**  Write down the square root of 64.

**14** Work out

(a) $\sqrt{1}$  (b) $\sqrt{25}$  (c) $\sqrt{81}$  (d) $\sqrt{4}$  (e) $\sqrt{16}$

**15** Work out

(a) $\sqrt{100} - \sqrt{64}$  (b) $\sqrt{81} + \sqrt{49}$  (c) $\sqrt{(47 - 11)}$  (d) $\sqrt{25} + \sqrt{9}$

You may **use a calculator** for the rest of the questions.

**16** Work out

(a) $17^2$  (b) $28^2$  (c) $114^2$  (d) $0.4^2$  (e) $3.8^2$  (f) $0.1^2$

**17** Work out

(a) $\sqrt{289}$  (b) $\sqrt{576}$  (c) $\sqrt{2500}$  (d) $\sqrt{1681}$  (e) $\sqrt{8.41}$  (f) $\sqrt{0.09}$

**18** Work out

(a) $\sqrt{0.16}$  (b) $\sqrt{0.25}$  (c) $\sqrt{0.36}$  (d) $\sqrt{0.49}$  (e) $\sqrt{0.64}$

(f) Can you write down the value of $\sqrt{0.81}$ without using a calculator?

**19** Find a pair of square numbers which give a total of:

(a) 65  (b) 10  (c) 29  (d) 73  (e) 61

**20** Work out  (a) $\sqrt{(10^2 - 6^2)}$  (b) $\sqrt{(13^2 - 12^2)}$  (c) $\sqrt{(100^2 - 80^2)}$

## Cube numbers

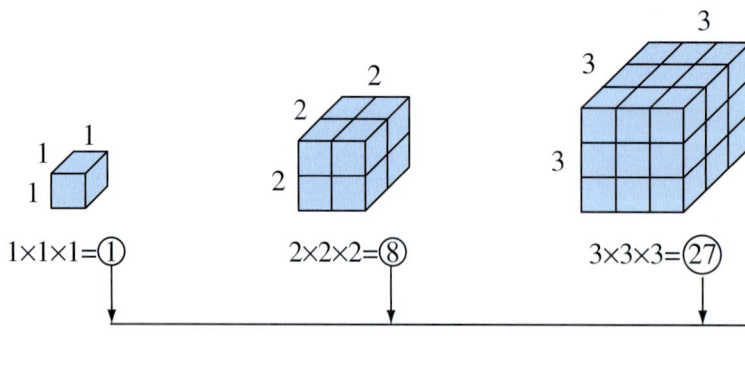

$1 \times 1 \times 1 = \textcircled{1}$    $2 \times 2 \times 2 = \textcircled{8}$    $3 \times 3 \times 3 = \textcircled{27}$

when a whole number is multiplied by itself 3 times, we get a *cube number*

$2 \times 2 \times 2 = 8$   we write this as $2^3$ (2 cubed)

so $1^3 = 1 \times 1 \times 1 = 1$     (this is 1 cubed. Sometimes we say 1 to the *power* 3)

34

## 🔑 Key Facts

The cube root of a number $n$ is the number which is multiplied by itself 3 times to give that number $n$.

The cube root of 8 is **2** because $\mathbf{2 \times 2 \times 2 = 8}$

The symbol for cube root is $\sqrt[3]{\phantom{x}}$

so $\sqrt[3]{8} = 2$

$\sqrt[3]{1} = 1$ because $1 \times 1 \times 1 = 1$ $(1^3 = 1)$

A *calculator* has a button for finding cube roots $\boxed{\sqrt[3]{\phantom{x}}}$ or $\boxed{\sqrt[3]{x}}$. The power button $\boxed{x^y}$ or root button $\boxed{\sqrt[y]{x}}$ can also be used. Use these buttons with your teacher to make sure you know how to use them correctly.

**E2. 1**

**1**
$1^3 = 1 \times 1 \times 1 = 1$
$2^3 = 2 \times 2 \times 2 = 8$
$3^3 = 3 \times 3 \times 3 = ..$
$4^3 = ...... = ..$

Copy and complete this list of cube numbers down to $10^3$.

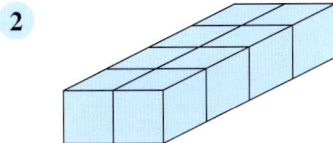

**2**

Can all these small cubes be used to make one large cube? If yes, draw the large cube made from the small cubes.

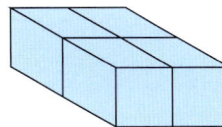

**3** Can all these small cubes be used to make one large cube? If yes, draw the large cube made from the small cubes.

**4** What number multiplied by itself 3 times will give an answer of 27?

**5** Work out

(a) $\sqrt[3]{27}$    (b) $\sqrt[3]{8}$    (c) $\sqrt[3]{125}$    (d) $\sqrt[3]{64}$    (e) $\sqrt[3]{216}$

(Use your answer to Question **1** to help you)

You may **use a calculator** for the rest of the questions

**6**   Work out

(a) $14^3$   (b) $21^3$   (c) $1.5^3$   (d) $0.1^3$   (e) $0.2^3$

**7**   Evaluate (this means 'work out the value of')

(a) $\sqrt[3]{3375}$   (b) $\sqrt[3]{13824}$   (c) $\sqrt[3]{64000}$   (d) $\sqrt[3]{0.027}$   (e) $\sqrt[3]{0.064}$

**8**   Work out

(a) $\sqrt[3]{(2 + 5^2)}$   (b) $\sqrt[3]{(3 + 5^2 + 6^2)}$   (c) $\sqrt[3]{(11^2 + 9^2 + 4^2 - 2)}$

**9**   Evaluate

(a) $\sqrt{(5^2 + 3^2 + 2)}$   (b) $(\sqrt{25} - \sqrt{9})^3$   (c) $(\sqrt[3]{343} - \sqrt{4})^3$

**10**   Work out

(a) $\sqrt{(2 \times 2 \times 3 \times 3)}$   (b) $\sqrt{(3 \times 3 \times 5 \times 5 \times 6 \times 6)}$

(c) $\sqrt[3]{(3 \times 3 \times 3 \times 5 \times 5 \times 5)}$

## Powers

# 🔑 Key Facts

$3 \times 3$ is written as $3^2$ ← power 2

$3 \times 3 \times 3$ is written as $3^3$ ← power 3

$3 \times 3 \times 3 \times 3$ is written as $3^4$

the power 4 means multiply 4 lots of 3 together

For $3^4$ we say '3 to the power 4'

'3 to the power 5' is $3^5$ which means $3 \times 3 \times 3 \times 3 \times 3$

Numbers written using powers are said to be in index form.

81 written in *index form* is $3^4$ (because $3 \times 3 \times 3 \times 3 = 81$)

20 written in *index form* is $2^2 \times 5$ (because $2 \times 2 \times 5 = 20$)

$2^4$ means $2 \times 2 \times 2 \times 2$

Copy and complete the following:

1   $8^4$ means _ _ _ _ _ _ _            2   $6^5$ means _ _ _ _ _ _ _

3   $10^4$ means _ _ _ _ _ _ _           4   $12^2$ means _ _ _ _ _ _ _

5   $7^5$ means _ _ _ _ _ _ _            6   $3^7$ means _ _ _ _ _ _ _

7   $8^6$ means _ _ _ _ _ _ _            8   $2^8$ means _ _ _ _ _ _ _

Write the following in index form

9   $4 \times 4 \times 4 \times 4 \times 4$            10   $2 \times 2 \times 2 \times 2 \times 2 \times 2$

11   $5 \times 5 \times 5$            12   $3 \times 3 \times 3 \times 3 \times 3 \times 3 \times 3 \times 3$

13   $10 \times 10 \times 10 \times 10 \times 10$            14   $6 \times 6 \times 6 \times 6$

15   Which is larger?   $2^4$   or   $3^3$

16   Which is larger?   $4^3$   or   $2^6$

Work out the value of the following:

17   $3^2 \times 5$       18   $2^3 \times 3$       19   $2^4 \times 3$       20   $6^2 \times 2$

21   $5^2 \times 2^2$       22   $3^3 \times 2$       23   $4^2 \times 2^2$       24   $4^2 \times 2^3$

25   Copy and complete this table, *using a calculator* when needed.

| We say | We write | We work out | Answer |
| --- | --- | --- | --- |
| 3 to the power 4 | $3^4$ | $3 \times 3 \times 3 \times 3$ | 81 |
| 2 to the power 5 | | $2 \times 2 \times 2 \times 2 \times 2$ | |
| 7 to the power 3 | $7^3$ | | |
| 8 to the power 4 | | | |
| | $4^7$ | | |
| 9 to the power 5 | | | |
| 10 to the power 6 | | | |

**(2A)** **Add and subtract negative numbers (see Unit 1)**

1  The temperature in Toronto is –1°C. It falls by 6°C. What is the new temperature?

2  The temperature in Oslo is –8°C. The temperature in Athens is 23°C. What is the difference in temperature?

3  Work out

(a)  –2 – 5  (b)  –3 + 5  (c)  –6 + 1  (d)  3 – 6

(e)  2 – –4  (f)  2 – 4  (g)  –4 – –2  (h)  –6 – –1

(i)  –6 – 1  (j)  5 – 6  (k)  –5 – –6  (l)  –4 – 3

4  Copy and complete the boxes below:

(a)  ☐ – 4 = –6  (b)  3 – ☐ = 5  (c)  –4 – ☐ = –9

## Factors and prime numbers

A *factor* is a number which divides exactly into another number (there will be no remainder).

If 2 divides into a number exactly, that number is an *even* number (2, 4, 6, 8, …).

If 2 does *not* divide into a number exactly, that number is an *odd* number (1, 3, 5, 7, …).

A *prime* number can only be divided by two different numbers (these are the numbers 1 and itself). The first four prime numbers are 2, 3, 5, 7, …

### M2. 3

Reminder: All the factors of 10 are $\boxed{1, 10}$ $\boxed{2, 5}$ so the factors of 10 are 1, 2, 5, 10.

Write down all the factors of the following numbers:

**1**  8 (4 factors)  **2**  16 (5 factors)  **3**  11 (2 factors)  **4**  15 (4 factors)

**5**  24 (8 factors)  **6**  19  **7**  35  **8**  28

| **9** | 40 | **10** | 23 | **11** | 30 | **12** | 42 |
|---|---|---|---|---|---|---|---|
| **13** | 17 | **14** | 26 | **15** | 50 | | |

**16** Write down the numbers given in Questions **1** to **15** which are *odd* numbers.

**17** Write down the numbers given in Questions **1** to **15** which are *even* numbers.

**18** Write down the numbers given in Questions **1** to **15** which are *prime* numbers (remember: this means they have *2 factors only*).

**19** 1, 2, 4, 5, 10 and 20 are all the factors of which number?

**20** 1, 2, 11 and 22 are all the factors of which number?

**21** Harry picks his National Lottery numbers by choosing the first six prime numbers. The winning numbers are drawn as below:

|  5  |  42  |  1  |  13  |  40  |  6  |

Does Harry win a small prize for picking 3 correct numbers?

**22** Which numbers between 20 and 30 have 7 as a factor?

**23** Write down the next 4 odd numbers after 49.

**24** Add together all the prime numbers less than 20.

## Multiples and the Lowest Common Multiple

## 🔑 Key Facts

*Multiples* are the numbers in a multiplication table.    6, 12, 18, 24, 30, ... are multiples of 6.

The *Lowest Common Multiple* (LCM) of two or more numbers is the smallest number which each of these numbers will divide into.

Here, for example, we find the LCM of 4 and 10.

The multiples of 4 are 4, 8, 12, 16, ⑳, 24, ....

The multiples of 10 are 10, ⑳, 30, ....

The *lowest* number in both lists is 20

The LCM of 4 and 10 is 20.

Copy and complete the first 10 multiples of the number in the first box:

**1** | 4 | 8 | 12 | 16 | □ | □ | □ | □ | □ | □ |

**2** | 7 | 14 | □ | □ | □ | □ | □ | □ | □ | □ |

**3** | 8 | □ | □ | □ | □ | □ | □ | □ | □ | □ |

**4** | 30 | □ | □ | □ | □ | □ | □ | □ | □ | □ |

**5** | 16 | □ | □ | □ | □ | □ | □ | □ | □ | □ |

Copy and draw a circle around the numbers which are *not* multiples of:

**6** | 5 | 11 25 35 54      **7** | 9 | 36 22 38 91      **8** | 6 | 23 18 54 42

**9** Here are the first six multiples of 6 and 10

6 :   6   12   18   24   30   36

10 :   10   20   30   40   50   60

Write down the Lowest Common Multiple (LCM) of 6 and 10 (ie the lowest number which is in both lists).

**10** Copy and complete the first five multiples of 4 and 6

4: 4   8   □ □ □

6: 6   □ □ □ □

Write down the LCM of 4 and 6.

**11** Find the Lowest Common Multiple of each of these pairs of numbers:

    (a) 3 and 10     (b) 3 and 7     (c) 5 and 9     (d) 10 and 7

    (e) 3 and 6     (f) 8 and 20     (g) 12 and 15     (h) 12 and 20

**12** In the game of 'Fizzbuzz', people take it in turns to count up one number at a time. When a multiple of 3 is reached, the person must say 'Fizz'. When a multiple of 5 is reached, the person must say 'Buzz'. If a multiple of both 3 and 5 is reached, the person says 'Fizzbuzz'.

Write down the first 2 numbers when the person would have to say 'Fizzbuzz'.

## Highest Common Factor

All the factors of 21 are 1, 3, ⑦, 21

All the factors of 28 are 1, 2, 4, ⑦, 14, 28

The highest factor in both lists is 7

This is called the Highest Common Factor (HCF)

**1** Copy and complete the sentences below:

(a) All the factors of 12 are 1, 2, 3, ☐, ☐, ☐

(b) All the factors of 18 are 1, 2, 3, ☐, ☐, ☐

(c) The Highest Common Factor of 12 and 18 is ☐

**2** Copy and complete the sentences below:

(a) All the factors of 20 are 1, 2, ☐, ☐, ☐, ☐

(b) All the factors of 30 are 1, 2, ☐, ☐, ☐, ☐, ☐, ☐

(c) The HCF of 20 and 30 is ☐

**3** (a) List all the factors of 32

(b) List all the factors of 40

(c) Write down the HCF of 32 and 40

**4** (a) List all the factors of 24

(b) List all the factors of 36

(c) Write down the HCF of 24 and 36

**5** Find the Highest Common Factor of

(a) 8 and 10    (b) 10 and 40    (c) 15 and 35    (d) 15 and 40

(e) 12 and 20    (f) 16 and 40    (g) 11 and 13    (h) 16 and 48

**6** Find the HCF of

(a) 4, 6 and 12    (b) 10, 20 and 45    (c) 24, 48 and 60

# 🔑 Key Facts

Factors of a number which are also prime numbers are called prime factors.

We can find these prime factors by using a 'factor tree' or by dividing by prime numbers again and again.

**Example**

Find the prime factors of 36.

**Method 1**

**Factor tree**

```
        36          Split into 4 and 9
       /  \         because 4 × 9 = 36
      4    9
     /\   /\        Split 4 into 2 × 2
    2  2 3  3       Split 9 into 3 × 3
```

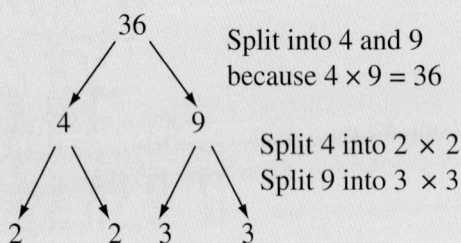

Stop splitting when
all numbers are prime
numbers

We can say 36 = $\underbrace{2 \times 2 \times 3 \times 3}_{\text{prime factors}}$

**Method 2**

**Dividing by prime numbers**

Divide by any
prime number ↓

```
2 | 36
2 | 18   ← 36 ÷ 2 = 18
3 |  9   ← 18 ÷ 2 = 9
3 |  3   ←  9 ÷ 3 = 3
     1   ←  3 ÷ 3 = 1
```

Stop when you get 1

These are the prime factors.

We can say 36 = 2 × 2 × 3 × 3

**The product of prime factors**

When we write 36 = 2 × 2 × 3 × 3, the prime factors 2, 2, 3 and 3 are multiplied together. This is called a *product*.

2 × 2 × 3 × 3 is the *product of its prime factors*.

**Index form**

2 × 2 = $2^2$          3 × 3 = $3^2$

so 36 = 2 × 2 × 3 × 3 can be written as $2^2 \times 3^2$

The answer written like
this using powers is said
to be in *index form*.

**1** Work out

(a) $2 \times 2 \times 5$     (b) $2 \times 3 \times 5$     (c) $3 \times 3 \times 5$

(d) $2 \times 3 \times 7$     (e) $3 \times 5 \times 11$     (f) $2 \times 2 \times 5 \times 5$

**2** Copy and complete these factors trees:

(a)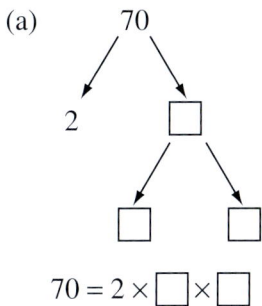

$70 = 2 \times \square \times \square$

(b)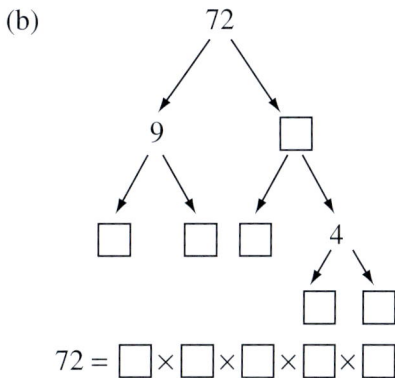

$72 = \square \times \square \times \square \times \square \times \square$

**3** Copy and complete the boxes below:

(a)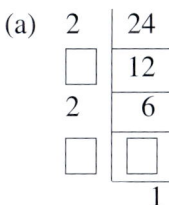

$24 = \square \times \square \times \square \times \square$

(b)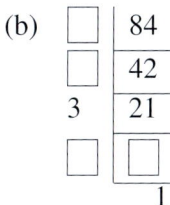

$84 = \square \times \square \times \square \times \square$

**4** Using any method, write the following numbers as products of prime factors:

(a) 18    (b) 28    (c) 22    (d) 32    (e) 48    (f) 50

(g) 81    (h) 96    (i) 200    (j) 120    (k) 196    (l) 392

**5** Copy the numbers below and put a circle round all the common factors for each pair of numbers.

(a) $180 = 2 \times 2 \times 3 \times 3 \times 5$

$120 = 2 \times 2 \times 2 \times 3 \times 5$     Write down the HCF of 180 and 120.

(b) $720 = 2 \times 2 \times 2 \times 2 \times 3 \times 3 \times 5$

$600 = 2 \times 2 \times 2 \times 3 \times 5 \times 5$    Write down the HCF of 720 and 600.

(c) $3850 = 2 \times 5 \times 5 \times 7 \times 11$

$140 = 2 \times 2 \times 5 \times 7$     Write down the HCF of 3850 and 140.

Can you still?

Can you still?

**2B** **Multiply and divide negative numbers (see Unit 1)**

1 Work out

    (a) $2 \times -3$     (b) $4 \times -5$     (c) $-6 \times -2$     (d) $-5 \times 6$

    (e) $-8 \div 2$     (f) $15 \div -3$     (g) $-24 \div -3$     (h) $-42 \div -7$

    (i) $-9 \div 3$     (j) $-10 \times 8$     (k) $-30 \div -6$     (l) $20 \div -5$

2 Copy and complete the boxes below:

    (a) $-3 \times \boxed{\phantom{00}} = 12$   (b) $5 \times \boxed{\phantom{00}} = -45$   (c) $\boxed{\phantom{00}} \times -4 = -20$

    (d) $10 \div \boxed{\phantom{00}} = -5$   (e) $\boxed{\phantom{00}} \div 4 = -9$   (f) $\boxed{\phantom{00}} \times -5 = 40$

3 Work out

    (a) $(-3)^2$   (b) $(-5)^2$   (c) $(-9)^2$   (d) $-1 \times -1 \times -1$   (e) $2 \times -4 \times 2$

## Equivalent fractions

### Cancelling Fractions

We often like to make the numerator (top number) and denominator (bottom number) as small as possible by dividing the numerator and denominator by the same number.

This is called 'cancelling down the fraction'.

$\frac{2}{8}$ is the same as $\frac{1}{4}$ $\frac{2}{8}$      $\frac{2}{8} \overset{\div 2}{\underset{\div 2}{=}} \frac{1}{4}$

**M2. 5**

Write the equivalent fractions shown by the shaded areas in each pair of diagrams.

**7**  =     **8**  =     **9**  = 

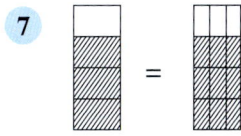

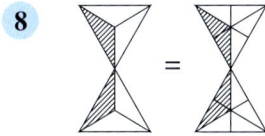

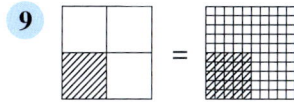

Copy and complete these equivalent fractions by filling in the box.

$\left(\text{Example: } \dfrac{7}{10} = \dfrac{\Box}{30} \implies \dfrac{7}{10} \overset{\times 3}{\underset{\times 3}{=}} \dfrac{21}{30}\right)$

**10** $\dfrac{1}{6} = \dfrac{\Box}{12}$    **11** $\dfrac{7}{8} = \dfrac{\Box}{16}$    **12** $\dfrac{1}{2} = \dfrac{\Box}{8}$    **13** $\dfrac{3}{5} = \dfrac{\Box}{20}$

**14** $\dfrac{4}{5} = \dfrac{\Box}{20}$    **15** $\dfrac{5}{6} = \dfrac{\Box}{12}$    **16** $\dfrac{5}{8} = \dfrac{\Box}{24}$    **17** $\dfrac{4}{7} = \dfrac{\Box}{21}$

**18** $\dfrac{3}{4} = \dfrac{\Box}{20}$    **19** $\dfrac{8}{9} = \dfrac{\Box}{45}$    **20** $\dfrac{3}{10} = \dfrac{\Box}{60}$    **21** $\dfrac{2}{5} = \dfrac{8}{\Box}$

**22** $\dfrac{4}{9} = \dfrac{12}{\Box}$    **23** $\dfrac{1}{2} = \dfrac{9}{\Box}$    **24** $\dfrac{3}{8} = \dfrac{15}{\Box}$    **25** $\dfrac{7}{10} = \dfrac{\Box}{80}$

**26** $\dfrac{3}{20} = \dfrac{24}{\Box}$    **27** $\dfrac{5}{7} = \dfrac{30}{\Box}$    **28** $\dfrac{7}{9} = \dfrac{\Box}{54}$    **29** $\dfrac{4}{11} = \dfrac{24}{\Box}$

**30** $\dfrac{2}{9} = \dfrac{20}{\Box}$    **31** $\dfrac{6}{7} = \dfrac{\Box}{42}$    **32** $\dfrac{9}{100} = \dfrac{\Box}{300}$    **33** $\dfrac{4}{25} = \dfrac{32}{\Box}$

---

## E2. 5

Copy the Questions below and fill in each box.

**1** $\dfrac{6}{8} = \dfrac{\Box}{4}$    **2** $\dfrac{2}{10} = \dfrac{\Box}{5}$    **3** $\dfrac{3}{9} = \dfrac{1}{\Box}$    **4** $\dfrac{9}{12} = \dfrac{3}{\Box}$

**5** $\dfrac{6}{10} = \dfrac{\Box}{5}$    **6** $\dfrac{9}{15} = \dfrac{\Box}{5}$    **7** $\dfrac{9}{24} = \dfrac{\Box}{8}$    **8** $\dfrac{4}{8} = \dfrac{\Box}{2}$

**9** $\dfrac{25}{30} = \dfrac{\Box}{6}$    **10** $\dfrac{3}{24} = \dfrac{\Box}{8}$    **11** $\dfrac{8}{10} = \dfrac{\Box}{5}$    **12** $\dfrac{8}{12} = \dfrac{\Box}{3}$

**13** $\dfrac{10}{30} = \dfrac{1}{\Box}$    **14** $\dfrac{6}{18} = \dfrac{1}{\Box}$    **15** $\dfrac{12}{24} = \dfrac{\Box}{2}$    **16** $\dfrac{30}{40} = \dfrac{3}{\Box}$

**17** Cancel each fraction below to its lowest terms.

(a) $\dfrac{8}{20}$  (b) $\dfrac{4}{10}$  (c) $\dfrac{7}{21}$  (d) $\dfrac{4}{18}$

(e) $\dfrac{4}{12}$  (f) $\dfrac{20}{30}$  (g) $\dfrac{12}{18}$  (h) $\dfrac{20}{24}$

(i) $\dfrac{32}{36}$  (j) $\dfrac{6}{15}$  (k) $\dfrac{14}{42}$  (l) $\dfrac{18}{30}$

(m) $\dfrac{27}{45}$  (n) $\dfrac{28}{36}$  (o) $\dfrac{45}{90}$  (p) $\dfrac{44}{66}$

(q) $\dfrac{24}{60}$  (r) $\dfrac{18}{72}$  (s) $\dfrac{75}{100}$  (t) $\dfrac{54}{81}$

**18** Which of the fractions below are the same as $\dfrac{5}{8}$?

(a) $\dfrac{15}{25}$  (b) $\dfrac{45}{80}$  (c) $\dfrac{10}{16}$  (d) $\dfrac{20}{40}$  (e) $\dfrac{30}{48}$  (f) $\dfrac{40}{64}$

**19** Which of the fractions below are the same as $\dfrac{4}{7}$?

(a) $\dfrac{12}{21}$  (b) $\dfrac{24}{48}$  (c) $\dfrac{40}{70}$  (d) $\dfrac{20}{35}$  (e) $\dfrac{12}{28}$  (f) $\dfrac{36}{65}$

**20** Find the fractions in the table which are equivalent to the given fraction. Rearrange the letters to make a word using the clue. The first Question is done for you.

(a) Find fractions $= \dfrac{1}{2}$

Clue: country

| | | | |
|---|---|---|---|
| $\frac{3}{4}$ | P | $\frac{2}{4}$ | G |
| $\frac{1}{3}$ | U | $\frac{4}{7}$ | H |
| $\frac{5}{10}$ | E | $\frac{6}{12}$ | E |
| $\frac{3}{5}$ | Y | $\frac{3}{6}$ | C |
| $\frac{8}{16}$ | E | $\frac{21}{42}$ | R |

The fractions equivalent to $\dfrac{1}{2}$ are:

$$\dfrac{5}{10} \quad \dfrac{8}{16} \quad \dfrac{2}{4} \quad \dfrac{6}{12} \quad \dfrac{3}{6} \quad \dfrac{21}{42}$$

E  E  G  E  C  R

Now rearrange the letters to make the name of a country:

GREECE

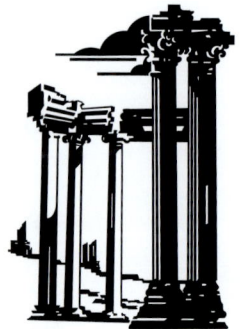

46

(b) Find fractions $= \frac{1}{10}$    (c) Find fractions $= \frac{3}{4}$    (d) Find fractions $= \frac{1}{4}$    (e) Find fractions $= \frac{2}{3}$

Clue: country | | Clue: fruit | | Clue: school subject | | Clue: sport | |
---|---|---|---|---|---|---|---
$\frac{8}{80}$ | N | $\frac{6}{8}$ | R | $\frac{8}{20}$ | T | $\frac{14}{22}$ | N
$\frac{6}{50}$ | P | $\frac{9}{12}$ | E | $\frac{2}{8}$ | G | $\frac{18}{21}$ | A
$\frac{5}{60}$ | U | $\frac{7}{14}$ | T | $\frac{5}{20}$ | E | $\frac{20}{30}$ | O
$\frac{4}{20}$ | Y | $\frac{8}{24}$ | I | $\frac{6}{25}$ | F | $\frac{4}{6}$ | Y
$\frac{2}{20}$ | A | $\frac{5}{7}$ | X | $\frac{3}{12}$ | H | $\frac{32}{49}$ | B
$\frac{9}{90}$ | I | $\frac{5}{12}$ | B | $\frac{4}{16}$ | N | $\frac{60}{90}$ | K
$\frac{8}{24}$ | M | $\frac{15}{20}$ | P | $\frac{4}{7}$ | A | $\frac{16}{24}$ | E
$\frac{3}{30}$ | C | $\frac{9}{15}$ | M | $\frac{25}{100}$ | L | $\frac{12}{18}$ | C
$\frac{5}{50}$ | H | $\frac{25}{50}$ | C | $\frac{20}{80}$ | I | $\frac{16}{25}$ | R
$\frac{9}{108}$ | U | $\frac{75}{100}$ | A | $\frac{12}{48}$ | S | $\frac{14}{21}$ | H

*Can you still?*    *Can you still?*

(2C)  **Do calculations in the correct order – BODMAS (see Unit 1)**

**Work out**

**1.** $3 + 8 \times 2$                **2.** $28 \div (3 + 4)$     **3.** $(6 + 2) \times 5$          **4.** $9 \times (6 - 4)$

**5.** $(8 + 1) \times (7 - 5)$    **6.** $30 \div 5 + 4$       **7.** $(5 - 1) \times 5 + 7$     **8.** $(8 + 4) \div (5 - 2)$

**9.** $25 - 3 \times 4$            **10.** $22 + 8 \div 2$     **11.** $36 \div 4 + 8$          **12.** $36 \div (4 + 8)$

**13.** $20 - 20 \div 4$          **14.** $(8 - 3) \times 3$     **15.** $(9 + 1) \div (7 - 2)$   **16.** $6 + 8 \div 2 + 4$

Copy each question below and write brackets so that each calculation gives the correct answer.

**17.** $7 + 4 \times 3 = 33$   **18.** $25 - 20 \times 4 = 20$   **19.** $9 + 21 \div 6 = 5$   **20.** $7 - 2 \times 5 + 1 = 30$

## 🔑 Key Facts

Get the denominator the same for each fraction so that you can easily compare the fractions.

---

Place $\dfrac{3}{4}, \dfrac{5}{8}$ and $\dfrac{4}{5}$ in order, smallest first.

Get the denominators the same for each fraction. 4, 8 and 5 all divide exactly into 40.

$$\overset{\times 10}{\underset{\times 10}{\dfrac{3}{4} = \dfrac{30}{40}}} \qquad \overset{\times 5}{\underset{\times 5}{\dfrac{5}{8} = \dfrac{25}{40}}} \qquad \overset{\times 8}{\underset{\times 8 \ \ 40}{\dfrac{4}{5}\ \dfrac{32}{\ \ }}}$$

Put the fractions in order, smallest first: $\quad \dfrac{25}{40} \quad \dfrac{30}{40} \quad \dfrac{32}{40}$

$$\downarrow \qquad \downarrow \qquad \downarrow$$

so the answer is $\quad \dfrac{5}{8} \qquad \dfrac{3}{4} \qquad \dfrac{4}{5}$

---

### M2. 6

**1** Write down the larger fraction:

(a)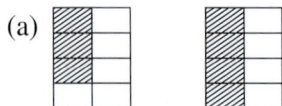

$\dfrac{3}{8}$    or    $\dfrac{1}{2}$

(b)

$\dfrac{2}{5}$    or    $\dfrac{3}{10}$

**2**    $\dfrac{1}{2} = \dfrac{\square}{6}$      $\dfrac{1}{3} = \dfrac{\square}{6}$

Which is larger, $\dfrac{1}{2}$ or $\dfrac{1}{3}$?

**3**   $\dfrac{3}{4} = \dfrac{\square}{8}$      Which is larger, $\dfrac{3}{4}$ or $\dfrac{7}{8}$?

**4**   Write down the *larger* fraction:

(a) $\dfrac{1}{4}$ or $\dfrac{1}{3}$    (b) $\dfrac{1}{10}$ or $\dfrac{1}{5}$    (c) $\dfrac{3}{8}$ or $\dfrac{3}{4}$

(d) $\dfrac{3}{4}$ or $\dfrac{2}{3}$    (e) $\dfrac{2}{5}$ or $\dfrac{7}{20}$    (f) $\dfrac{4}{7}$ or $\dfrac{3}{5}$

**5**   Place in order, *smallest first*:

(a) $\dfrac{1}{3}, \dfrac{1}{2}, \dfrac{1}{6}$    (b) $\dfrac{1}{2}, \dfrac{3}{8}, \dfrac{3}{4}$    (c) $\dfrac{1}{6}, \dfrac{2}{3}, \dfrac{7}{12}$

(d) $\dfrac{3}{10}, \dfrac{1}{2}, \dfrac{2}{5}$    (e) $\dfrac{7}{10}, \dfrac{4}{5}, \dfrac{13}{20}$    (f) $\dfrac{3}{4}, \dfrac{11}{16}, \dfrac{5}{8}$

**6**   Write down the *smaller* fraction:

(a) $\dfrac{3}{5}$ or $\dfrac{11}{20}$    (b) $\dfrac{7}{10}$ or $\dfrac{13}{20}$    (c) $\dfrac{3}{4}$ or $\dfrac{13}{16}$

(d) $\dfrac{8}{9}$ or $\dfrac{9}{10}$    (e) $\dfrac{5}{6}$ or $\dfrac{4}{7}$    (f) $\dfrac{7}{40}$ or $\dfrac{1}{5}$

*Can you still?*

**2D**   **Use squares, square roots, cubes and cube roots (see Unit 2)**

*Can you still?*

**Work out**

**1.** $3^2$    **2.** $8^2$    **3.** $\sqrt{36}$    **4.** $\sqrt{81}$    **5.** $10^2$    **6.** $\sqrt{400}$

**7.** Which is larger,    (a) $2^2$ or $\sqrt{100}$     (b) $\sqrt{81}$ or $4^2$

**8.** Write down the first 3 cube numbers.

**Work out**

**9.** $\sqrt[3]{8}$    **10.** $\sqrt[3]{1}$    **11.** $3^3$    **12.** $4^3$    **13.** $2^3$

**14.** $9^2 - 3^2$    **15.** $\sqrt{64} + \sqrt{16}$    **16.** $(4 + 2)^2$    **17.** $\sqrt{(61 - 52)}$

**18.** Find two square numbers which add up to 41.

# 🔑 Key Facts

## Changing decimals into fractions.

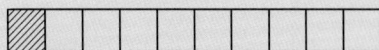 0.1 means $\frac{1}{10}$

 $0.7 = \frac{7}{10}$

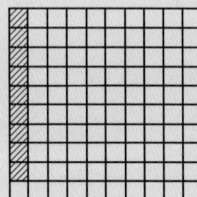 $0.09 = \frac{9}{100}$

If you change a decimal into a fraction, *cancel* the fraction if you can.

$$0.2 = \frac{2}{10} \overset{\div 2}{\underset{\div 2}{=}} \frac{1}{5}$$

$$0.34 = \frac{34}{100} \overset{\div 2}{\underset{\div 2}{=}} \frac{17}{50}$$

## Changing fractions into decimals.

If you can find an equivalent fraction with the denominator (bottom part) equal to 10, 100 or 1000, it will be easier to find the decimal value.

$$\frac{3}{5} \overset{\times 2}{\underset{\times 2}{=}} \frac{6}{10} = 0.6$$

$$\frac{7}{20} \overset{\times 5}{\underset{\times 5}{=}} \frac{35}{100} = 0.35$$

$$\frac{101}{200} \overset{\times 5}{\underset{\times 5}{=}} \frac{505}{1000} = 0.505$$

Change denominator to **10**    Change denominator to **100**    Change denominator to **1000**

## Note.

If you cannot easily change the denominator into 10, 100 or 1000, divide the numerator (top part) by the denominator (bottom part), as shown below.

(a) Change $\frac{1}{3}$ to a decimal

We work out $1 \div 3$
$$3\overline{)1.{}^1 0{}^1 0{}^1 0{}^1 0 \ldots} \quad \begin{array}{c} 0.3\,3\,3\,3\ldots \end{array}$$

We write $\frac{1}{3} = 0.\dot{3}$

We say 'nought point three recurring'

(the 3 carries on forever!)

Write True or False for each of the following statements.

**1**  $0.3 = \dfrac{3}{10}$      **2**  $0.07 = \dfrac{7}{100}$      **3**  $0.08 = \dfrac{1}{8}$

**4**  $0.5 = \dfrac{1}{2}$      **5**  $0.049 = \dfrac{49}{100}$      **6**  $0.079 = \dfrac{79}{1000}$

**7**  $0.4 = \dfrac{2}{5}$      **8**  $0.25 = \dfrac{1}{4}$      **9**  $0.217 = \dfrac{217}{1000}$

**10**  $0.7 = \dfrac{1}{7}$      **11**  $0.75 = \dfrac{3}{4}$      **12**  $0.81 = \dfrac{81}{100}$

Change the following decimals to fractions in their most simple form.

**13**  0.11      **14**  0.04      **15**  0.9      **16**  0.6

**17**  0.002      **18**  0.37      **19**  0.012      **20**  0.8

**21**  0.35      **22**  0.015      **23**  0.08      **24**  0.45

**25**  0.008      **26**  0.36      **27**  0.125      **28**  0.375

**29**  Which is larger 0.43 or $\dfrac{41}{100}$?

**30**  Which is larger 0.7 or $\dfrac{3}{5}$?

Copy Questions **31** to **36** below and fill in the boxes.

**31**  $\dfrac{4}{5} = \dfrac{\square}{10} = 0.\square$      **32**  $\dfrac{3}{20} = \dfrac{\square}{100} = 0.\square\square$

**33**  $\dfrac{7}{25} = \dfrac{\square}{100} = 0.\square\square$      **34**  $\dfrac{17}{50} = \dfrac{\square}{100} = 0.\square\square$

**35**  $\dfrac{9}{25} = \dfrac{\square}{100} = \square$      **36**  $\dfrac{11}{200} = \dfrac{\square}{1000} = \square$

Convert the fractions below to decimals.

**37** $\dfrac{1}{20}$     **38** $\dfrac{9}{20}$     **39** $\dfrac{2}{5}$     **40** $\dfrac{1}{25}$

**41** $\dfrac{3}{25}$     **42** $\dfrac{21}{25}$     **43** $\dfrac{29}{100}$     **44** $\dfrac{3}{200}$

**45** $\dfrac{1}{4}$     **46** $\dfrac{21}{200}$     **47** $\dfrac{1}{8}$     **48** $\dfrac{73}{200}$

**49** $\dfrac{7}{8}$     **50** $\dfrac{3}{4}$     **51** $\dfrac{119}{1000}$     **52** $\dfrac{17}{20}$

Change the following fractions to decimals by dividing the numerator by the denominator.

**53** $\dfrac{2}{3}$     **54** $\dfrac{5}{11}$     **55** $\dfrac{2}{9}$

**56** $\dfrac{7}{9}$     **57** $\dfrac{1}{6}$     **58** $\dfrac{5}{6}$

To change $\dfrac{3}{11}$ to a decimal we work out $3 \div 11$

$$11\overline{)3.{}^{3}0{}^{8}0{}^{3}0{}^{8}0{}^{3}0{}^{8}0\ldots} = 0.\,2\,7\,2\,7\,2\,7\ldots$$

$$\dfrac{3}{11} = 0.\dot{2}\dot{7}$$

## Ordering decimals

# 🔑 Key Facts

Write the set of decimals in a line with the decimal points in a column.

Fill in any empty spaces with zeros. This makes it easier to compare the decimals.

Arrange 0.29, 0.209, 0.09 and 0.2 in order, starting with the smallest.

| Write in column | Put in zeros | Arrange in order |
|---|---|---|
| 0.29 | 0.290 | 0.09 |
| 0.209 | 0.209 | 0.2 |
| 0.09 | 0.090 | 0.209 |
| 0.2 | 0.200 | 0.29 |

In Questions **1** to **10** , answer True or False.

**1** 7.2 is less than 7.02

**2** 0.03 is more than 0.003

**3** 0.8 is equal to 0.800

**4** 0.51 is more than 0.15

**5** 0.004 is more than 0.04

**6** 3 is equal to 3.00

**7** 0.83 is less than 0.847

**8** 0.08 is less than 0.083

**9** 0.2 is less than 0.028

**10** 0.71 is less than 0.089

> means 'more than'    < means 'less than'

Copy and complete questions **11** to **18** by writing >, < or = in the box.

**11** 0.7 ☐ 0.73

**12** 0.18 ☐ 0.2

**13** 0.81 ☐ 0.82

**14** 0.6 ☐ 0.60

**15** 0.09 ☐ 0.83

**16** 3.1 ☐ 3.06

**17** 5.17 ☐ 5.2

**18** 0.187 ☐ 0.3

**19** Here is a pattern of numbers based on 4.

Write a similar pattern based on 3 and extend it from 30000 down to 0.0003. Write the numbers in figures and in words.

| | |
|---|---|
| four thousand | 4000 |
| four hundred | 400 |
| forty | 40 |
| four | 4 |
| nought point four | 0.4 |
| nought point nought four | 0.04 |

In Questions **20** to **34** , arrange the numbers in order of size, smallest first.

**20** 0.08, 0.8, 0.008

**21** 0.4, 0.41, 0.042

**22** 0.72, 0.702, 0.73

**23** 0.832, 0.83, 0.85

**24** 0.06, 0.61, 0.063

**25** 0.52, 0.503, 0.053, 0.51

**26** 0.014, 0.017, 0.1, 0.107

**27** 0.03, 0.303, 0.31, 0.32, 0.034

**28** 0.81, 0.806, 0.812, 0.087, 0.82

**29** 0.061, 0.06, 0.064, 0.603, 0.61

**30** 0.107, 0.11, 0.121, 0.13, 0.015

**31** 3.6, 3.16, 3.04, 3.2, 3.18

**32** 8.1, 8.13, 8.021, 8.14, 8.019

**33** 0.51, 5.02, 0.53, 5.1, 5.17

**34** 1.72, 1.07, 1.16, 1.03, 0.19

**35** Here are numbers with letters.

Put the numbers in order, smallest first. Write down just the letters. Write out the sentence clearly.

| M | O | S | Y | S | T |
|---|---|---|---|---|---|
| 0.02 | 0.3 | 0.07 | 0.029 | 0.402 | 0.019 |

| H | E | T | A | R |
|---|---|---|---|---|
| 0.072 | 0.002 | 0.4 | 0.018 | 0.31 |

**36**

| O | D | G | U |
|---|---|---|---|
| 0.031 | 0.05 | 0.17 | 0.038 |

| O | Y | H | N |
|---|---|---|---|
| 0.061 | 0.03 | 0.006 | 0.108 |

| W | O | I |
|---|---|---|
| 0.01 | 0.007 | 0.1 |

Here are numbers with letters.

Put the numbers in order, smallest first. Write down just the letters. Write out the sentence clearly.

**37** Here we have fractions and decimals.

Write the numbers in order to find a word.

| P | S | N |
|---|---|---|
| $\frac{3}{4}$ | 0.01 | $\frac{5}{6}$ |

| H | E | A | R |
|---|---|---|---|
| $\frac{1}{50}$ | 0.81 | 0.035 | $\frac{3}{10}$ |

## WATCH YOUR MONEY! – Wages – overtime

Overtime is money paid for working more than the agreed number of hours each week.

Overtime is often paid at a different rate such as 'time and a half' or 'double time' (for example, evening work is often paid at 'time and a half' and weekend work is often 'double time').

**Note**

The average UK salary (in 2004) was £ 24, 600 = £ 12.81 per hour (based on a 48 week year and a 40 hour week).

Jess the mechanic is paid £8 per hour and overtime at 'time and a half'.

One week, Jess works for 40 hours plus 5 hours overtime. How much will Jess earn that week?

pay for 40 hours is 40 × £8 = £320

('time and a half' pay rate = £8 × 1.5 = £12)

pay for 5 hours overtime = 5 × £12 = £60

total pay = £320 + £60 = £380

## WYM2

1   Andy is paid £ 5 per hour for a 40 hour week.

Overtime is paid at time and a half.

How much will he be paid for a full week plus two hours overtime?

2   Jane is paid £ 6 per hour for a 40 hour week.

Overtime is paid at time and a half.

How much will she be paid for a full week plus 5 hours overtime?

3   Sid is paid £ 9 per hour for a 35 hour week.

Overtime is paid at double time.

How much will he be paid for a full week plus 6 hours overtime?

4   **Alf's Cheese Factory**

| Pay Rate: |
| --- |
| £ 6 per hour |
| Overtime paid at time and a half |

Work out how much the following people are paid for one week's work:

(a) Emma: 30 hours plus 4 hours overtime.

(b) Billy: 35 hours plus 6 hours overtime.

(c) Jack: 32 hours plus 7 hours overtime.

(d) Sarah: 40 hours plus 10 hours overtime.

(e) Ashley: 40 hours plus 8 hours overtime.

£ £ £ £ £ £ £ £ £ £

**5** Arnie is paid £ 4.50 per hour for 20 hours plus 5 hours overtime at time and a half. How much was he paid?

**6** Tamsin is paid £ 5.20 per hour for 30 hours plus 8 hours overtime at time and a half. How much was she paid?

**7** Sophie is paid £ 5.30 per hour for 40 hours plus 4 hours overtime at *double time*. How much was she paid?

**8** Max is paid £ 7.40 per hour for 35 hours plus 4 hours overtime at time and a half. How much was he paid?

**9** Work out the amount of pay for each part below:

(a) £ 6.80 per hour. 30 hours plus 6 hours overtime at time and a half.

(b) £ 4.70 per hour. 40 hours plus 5 hours overtime at double time.

(c) £ 5.60 per hour. 32 hours plus 6 hours overtime at time and a half.

(d) £ 6.90 per hour. 38 hours plus 4 hours overtime at time and a half.

**10**

## BRIDGE MOTORS

**Pay rate: £ 8.50 per hour**

**Saturday overtime: time and a half**

**Sunday overtime: double time**

Jake works at Bridge Motors. He works for 40 hours then does 4 hours on Saturday and 3 hours on Sunday. How much money does Jake earn?

**11** Tamsin works at Bridge Motors. She works for 36 hours then does 3 hours on Saturday and 6 hours on Sunday. How much money does Tamsin earn?

**12** Jenny earns £ 5.40 per hour.

Simon earns £ 5.20 per hour.

Jenny works for 35 hours plus 6 hours overtime at time and a half.

Simon works for 35 hours plus 7 hours overtime at time and a half.

Who earns the most money and by how much?

---

### 1. Square and square root numbers

Work out

(a) $7^2$    (b) $5^2$    (c) $\sqrt{16}$    (d) $\sqrt{9}$    (e) $4^2 - 3^2$

(f) Which of these are square numbers?

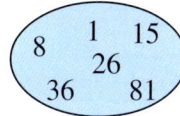

8  1  15
26
36  81

---

### 2. Cube and cube root numbers

Work out

(a) $2^3$    (b) $4^3$    (c) $\sqrt[3]{64}$    (d) $\sqrt[3]{8}$    (e) $5^3$

(f) Which of these are cube numbers?

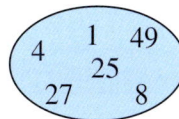

4  1  49
25
27  8

---

### 3. Using powers

Copy and complete the following:

(a) $3^4$ means · · · · · · · ·    (b) $2^5$ means · · · · · · · · ·

Write the following in index form:

(c) $6 \times 6 \times 6$    (d) $5 \times 5 \times 5 \times 5$    (e) $3 \times 3 \times 3 \times 3 \times 3 \times 3$

(f) Work out the value of $2^6$

---

### 4. Finding factors and prime numbers

Write down all the factors of    (a) 18    (b) 32

(c) Which of these are prime numbers?

6  3  10
12  5
17  7

(a) Write down the first five multiples of 6.

(b) Write down two multiples of 7 which lie between 40 and 50.

(c) Write down any multiple of 4 which lies between 22 and 30.

Find the Lowest Common Multiple of each of these groups of numbers:

(d) 5 and 3    (e) 8 and 12    (f) 3, 4 and 8.

### 6. Finding the Highest Common Factor (HCF)

(a) List all the factors of 15

(b) List all the factors of 20

(c) Write down the Highest Common Factor of 15 and 20

Find the Highest Common Factor of:

(d) 16 and 24    (e) 21 and 35    (f) 8, 12 and 20

### 7. Breaking down numbers into prime factors

Write the following numbers as products of prime factors:

(a) 12    (b) 36    (c) 54    (d) 100    (e) 144

### 8. Finding equivalent fractions

Copy and complete these equivalent fractions by filling in the box.

(a) $\dfrac{7}{8} = \dfrac{\square}{24}$    (b) $\dfrac{5}{9} = \dfrac{\square}{36}$    (c) $\dfrac{2}{7} = \dfrac{10}{\square}$

(d) $\dfrac{2}{3} = \dfrac{\square}{27}$    (e) $\dfrac{20}{25} = \dfrac{\square}{5}$    (f) $\dfrac{9}{30} = \dfrac{3}{\square}$

### 9. Cancelling fractions

Cancel each fraction below to its lowest terms.

(a) $\dfrac{6}{10}$    (b) $\dfrac{9}{24}$    (c) $\dfrac{15}{40}$    (d) $\dfrac{12}{28}$    (e) $\dfrac{42}{56}$    (f) $\dfrac{24}{72}$

## 10. Putting fractions in order of size

Write down the larger fraction:

(a) $\dfrac{1}{5}$ or $\dfrac{1}{4}$    (b) $\dfrac{2}{3}$ or $\dfrac{3}{5}$    (c) $\dfrac{5}{7}$ or $\dfrac{5}{9}$

Place in order, *smallest first*:

(d) $\dfrac{2}{5}, \dfrac{1}{4}, \dfrac{3}{8}$    (e) $\dfrac{5}{6}, \dfrac{3}{4}, \dfrac{2}{3}, \dfrac{7}{12}$

## 11. Converting between fractions and decimals

Change the following decimals to fractions in their most simple form:

(a) 0.37    (b) 0.08    (c) 0.8    (d) 0.028    (e) 0.42

Convert the fractions below to decimals:

(f) $\dfrac{7}{20}$    (g) $\dfrac{3}{5}$    (h) $\dfrac{2}{25}$    (i) $\dfrac{19}{25}$    (j) $\dfrac{5}{9}$    (k) $\dfrac{7}{11}$

## 12. Ordering decimals

(a) Which is larger, 0.04 or 0.3?

(b) Which is larger, 0.028 or 0.17?

In the Questions below, arrange the numbers in order of size, smallest first:

(c) 0.7, 0.071, 0.07

(d) 0.062, 0.064, 0.63, 0.6

(e) 0.32, 0.318, 0.034, 0.331

(f) 2.83, 2.183, 2.318, 2.14, 2.714, 2.049

**1** Here are two fractions $\frac{3}{5}$ and $\frac{2}{3}$.

Explain which is the larger fraction.

You may use the grids to help with your explanation.

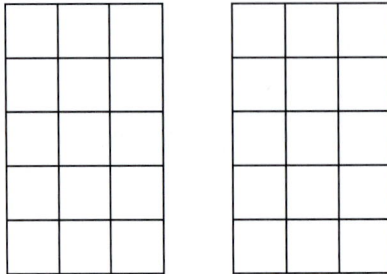

(EDEXCEL)

**2** Write the following fractions in order of size with the smallest first. Show your working.

$$\frac{3}{5} \qquad \frac{1}{2} \qquad \frac{5}{8}$$

(CCEA)

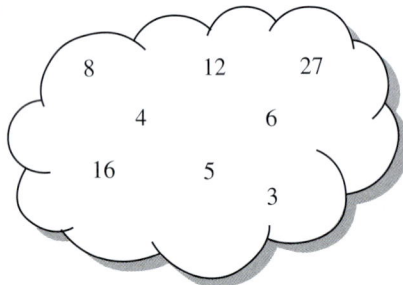

**3** Using only the numbers in the cloud, write down

8    12    27

4    6

16    5

3

(i) all the multiples of 6,

(ii) all the square numbers,

(iii) all the factors of 12,

(iv) all the cube numbers.    (EDEXCEL)

**4** (a) Work out

(i) $10^3$    (ii) $\frac{2^5}{4^2}$

(b) 21    22    23    24    25    26    27    28    29

From these numbers choose one which is

(i) a cube number,

(ii) a prime number.    (OCR)

**5** (a) Write 0.35 as a fraction. Give your answer in its simplest form.

(b) Write $\dfrac{3}{8}$ as a decimal. (EDEXCEL)

**6** (a) Write down all the factors of 10.

(b) Write down all the prime numbers between 20 and 30.

(c) Work out the cube of 6. (EDEXCEL)

**7** (i) Write 45 as a product of prime factors.

(ii) What is the lowest common multiple of 45 and 75? (AQA)

**8** Write these five fractions in order of size. Start with the smallest fracton.

$$\dfrac{3}{4} \quad \dfrac{1}{2} \quad \dfrac{3}{8} \quad \dfrac{2}{3} \quad \dfrac{1}{6}$$ (EDEXCEL)

**9** (i) $p$ and $q$ are prime numbers.

Find the values of $p$ and $q$ when $p^3 \times q = 24$.

(ii) Write 18 as a product of prime factors.

(iii) What is the lowest common multiple of 24 and 18? (AQA)

# SHAPE 1

**3**

**In this unit you will learn how to:**

- identify acute, obtuse, reflex and right angles
- label angles
- find angles on a straight line and angles at a point
- find vertically opposite angles and angles in a triangle
- use isosceles and equilateral triangles
- find alternate and corresponding angles
- use reflection symmetry and rotational symmetry
- recognise planes of symmetry
- find angles in polygons
- find angles in quadrilaterals
- recognise common quadrilaterals
- WATCH YOUR MONEY! – pricing your holiday

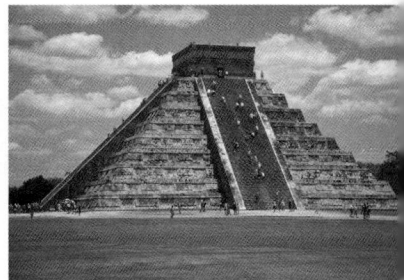

## Acute, obtuse, reflex and right angles

## 🔑 Key Facts

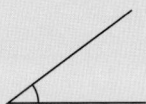 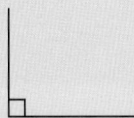 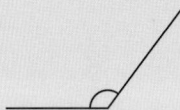 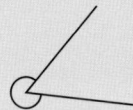

| An **acute** angle | A **right** angle | An **obtuse** angle | A **reflex** angle |
|---|---|---|---|
| is **less** than a $\frac{1}{4}$ turn (90°) | is a $\frac{1}{4}$ turn (90°) | is **more** than a $\frac{1}{4}$ turn (90°) and **less** than a $\frac{1}{2}$ turn (180°) | is **more** than a $\frac{1}{2}$ turn (180°) |

**1** Which of these angles are acute?

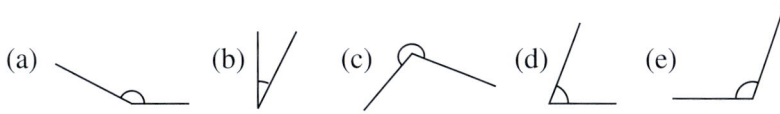

(a)  (b)  (c)  (d)  (e)

**2** Which of these angles are obtuse?

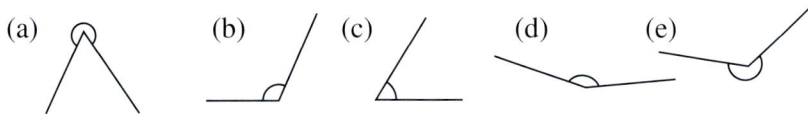

(a)  (b)  (c)  (d)  (e)

**3** Which of these angles are reflex?

(a)  (b)  (c)  (d)  (e)

**4** For each of these angles say whether they are acute, obtuse or reflex:

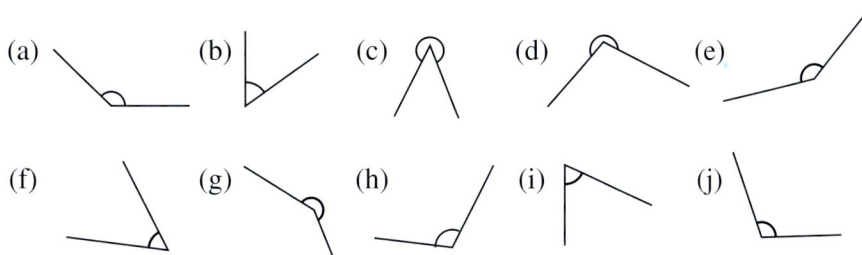

(a)  (b)  (c)  (d)  (e)

(f)  (g)  (h)  (i)  (j)

**5** For each shape, say whether the angles marked are acute, obtuse or reflex:

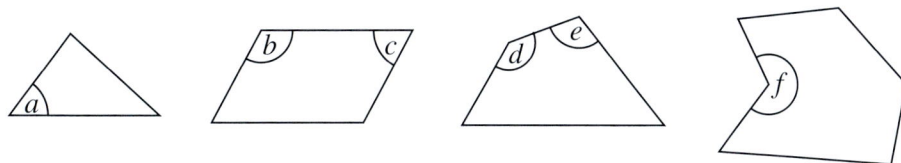

**6** (a) Draw a triangle with an obtuse angle:

(b) Draw a quadrilateral (a shape with 4 sides) with a reflex angle.

(c) Can you draw a triangle with a reflex angle inside it?

This is called angle *BCD* or angle *DCB*.

We write this as $B\hat{C}D$ or $D\hat{C}B$.

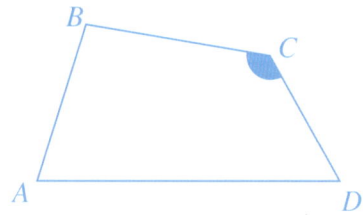

**E3. 1**

Name the shaded angles below:

**1**

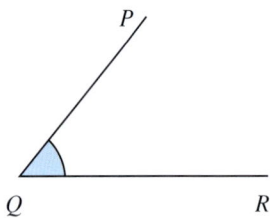

**2**

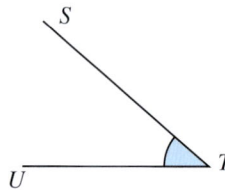

**3**

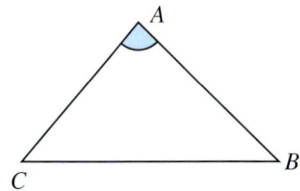

**4**

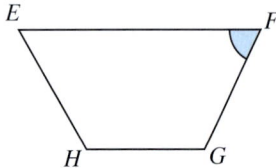

**5**

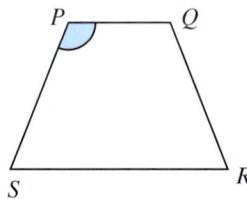

**6**

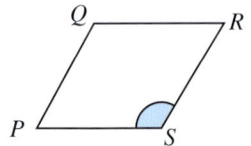

**7**

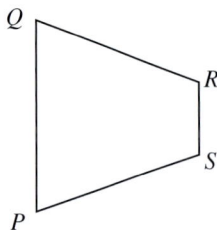

Is angle *PSR* acute or obtuse?

**8**

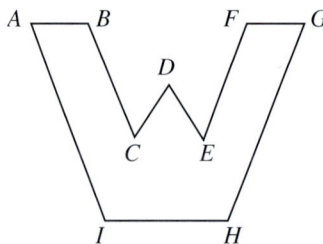

(a) Name 3 acute angles.

(b) Name 3 obtuse angles.

(c) Is $G\hat{H}I$ acute or obtuse?

(d) Is $B\hat{A}I$ acute or obtuse?

Write down the size of each angle stated below:

**9**

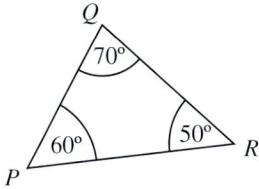

(a) $P\hat{R}Q$  (b) $Q\hat{P}R$

**10**

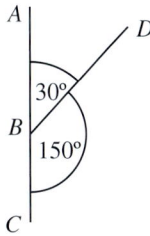

(a) $D\hat{B}C$  (b) $A\hat{B}D$

**11**

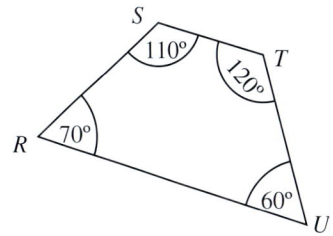

(a) $T\hat{S}R$  (b) $T\hat{U}R$

## Angles on a straight line and angles at a point

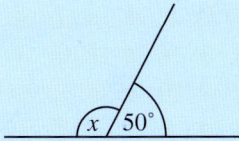
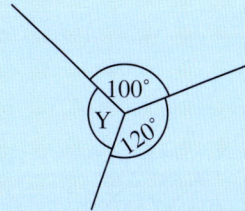
### M3. 2

Find the angles marked with the letters.

**1**

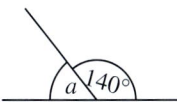

**2**

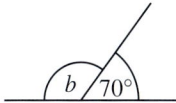

**3**

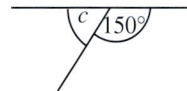

**4**

20°
d

**5**

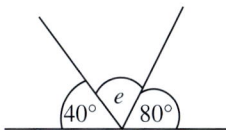

**6**

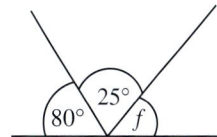

**7**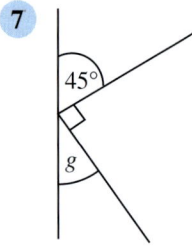
45°

g

**8**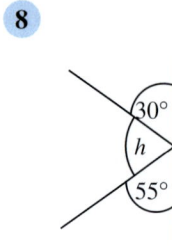
30°

h

55°

**9**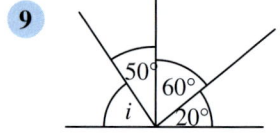
50° 60°

i 20°

**10**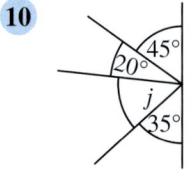
45°

20°

j

35°

**11**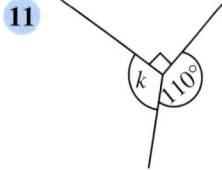
k 110°

**12**
120° ℓ

160°

**13**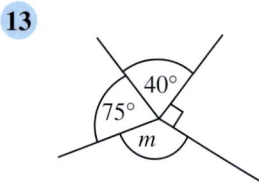
40°

75°

m

**14**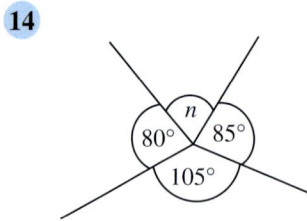
n

80° 85°

105°

**15**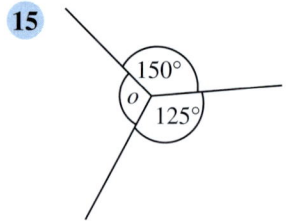
150°

o 125°

**16**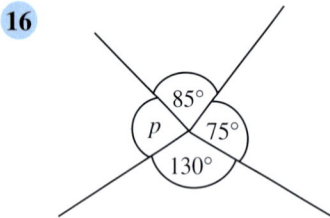
85°

p 75°

130°

**17**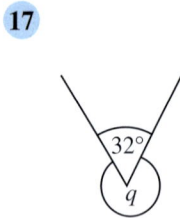
32°

q

**18**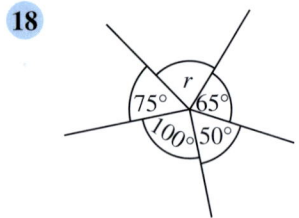
r

75° 65°

100° 50°

**19**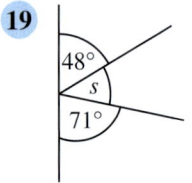
48°

s

71°

**20**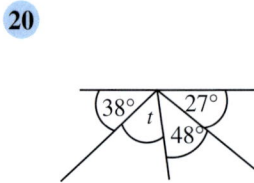
38° t 27°

48°

**21**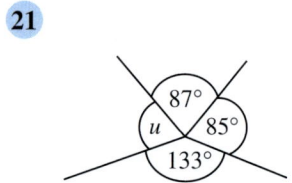
87°

u 85°

133°

**22**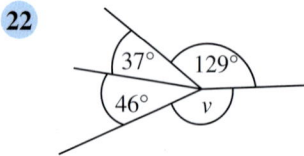
37° 129°

46° v

**23**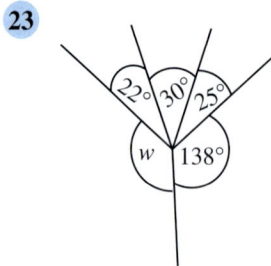
22° 30° 25°

w 138°

**24**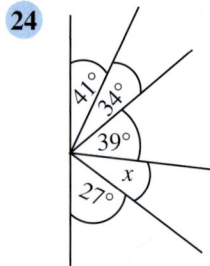
41° 34°

39°

x

27°

## Key Facts

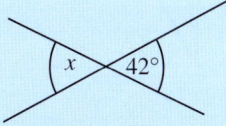

$x = 42°$
When 2 lines intersect the opposite angles are equal.
ie. vertically opposite angles are equal.

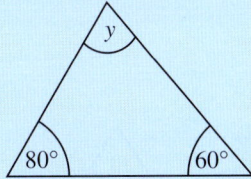

$y + 80° + 60° = 180°$
$y = 40°$
The angles in a triangle add up to 180°.

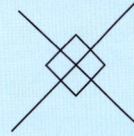

Lines which cross or meet at right angles are called **perpendicular** lines.

### E3. 2

Find the angles marked with the letters.

**1**

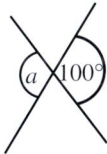

**2**

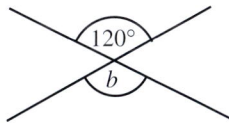

**3**

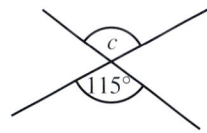

**4**

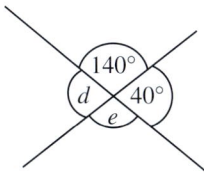

**5**

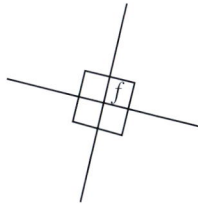

**6**

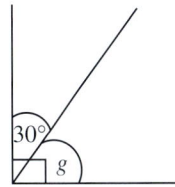

**7**

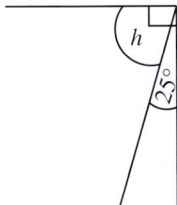

**8**

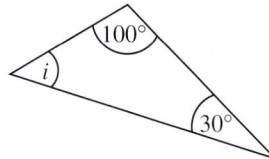

**9**

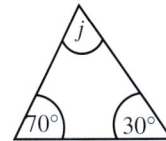

**10**

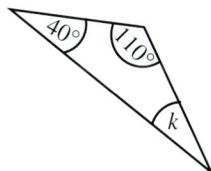

**11**

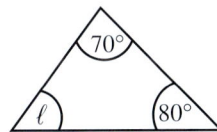

**12**

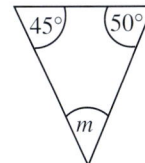

**13**
65°
$n$

**14**
58°
$o$
47°

**15**
26°
112°
$p$

**16**
$q$
$r$ 117°
63°

**17**
30°
70°
$s$ $t$

**18**
20°
85°
$u$ $v$

**19**
37°
$x$ $w$ 84°

**20**
$z$
80°
$y$
130°

**21**
40°
80°
$a$
$b$

**22**
65° 57°
$c$
$d$

**23**
$f$
134° $e$
72°

**24**
67°
$g$
$h$ 71°

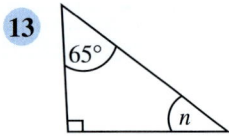

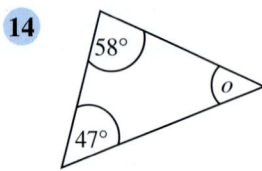

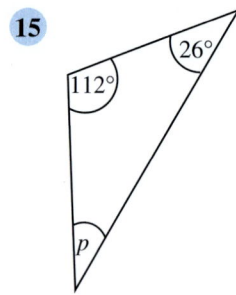

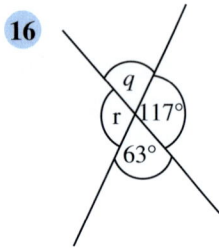

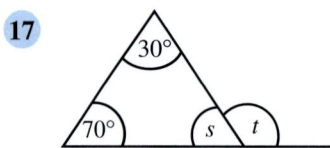

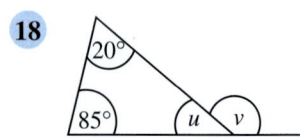

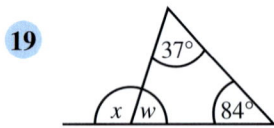

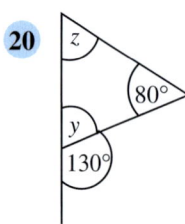

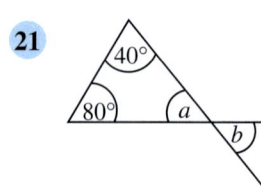

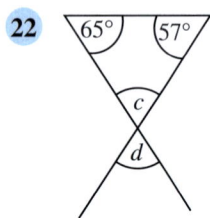

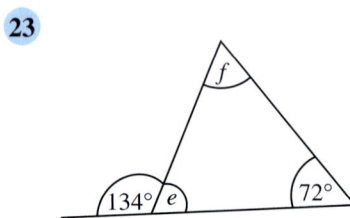

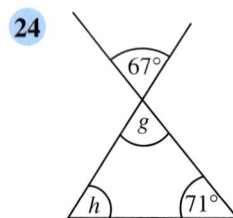

**25** Which two lines are perpendicular?

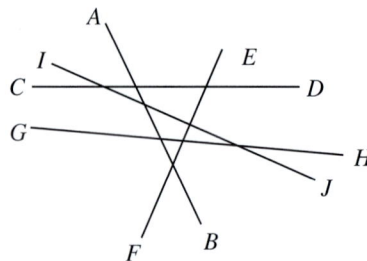

A
I
E
C —————— D
G
H
J
F B

68

(a)

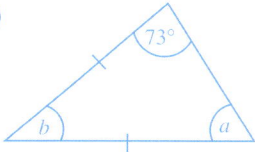

$a = 73°$ (isosceles triangle)
$b + 73° + 73° = 180°$ (angles in a triangle add up to 180°)

$b = 34°$

(b)

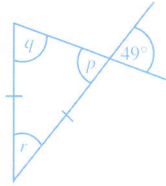

$p = 49°$ (vertically opposite)
$q = p = 49°$ (isosceles triangle)
$r + 49° + 49° = 180°$ (angles in a triangle add up to 180°)

$r = 82°$

**M3. 3**

Find the angles marked with letters.

**1**

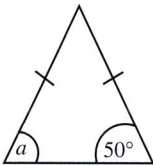

**2**

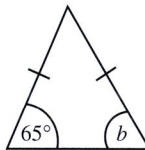

**3**

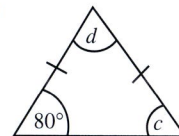

**4**

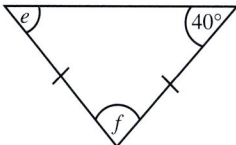

**5**

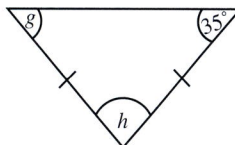

**6**

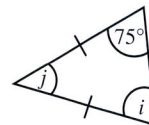

**7**

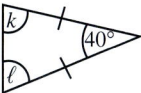

**8**

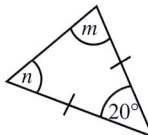

**9**

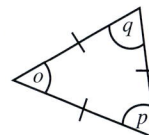

**10**

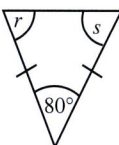

**11**

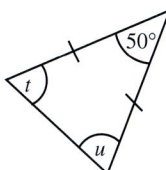

**12**

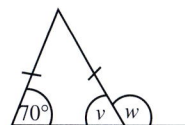

**13**

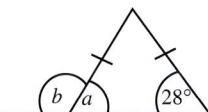

**14**

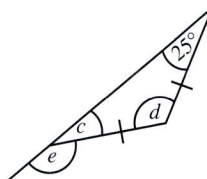

**15**

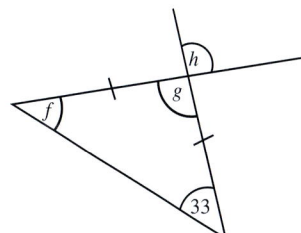

69

**16**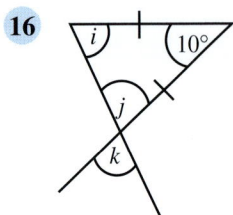

**17**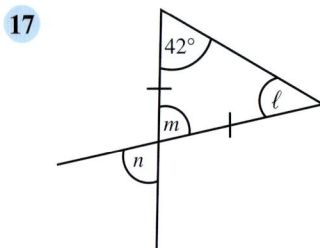

**18**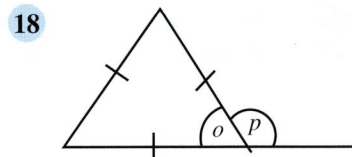

**19**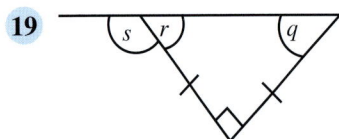

**20**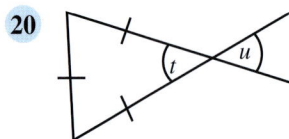

## Alternate and corresponding angles

# Key Facts

Many people think of alternate angles as 'Z' angles.

Many people think of corresponding angles as 'F' angles.

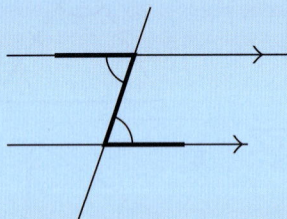

Alternate angles are equal

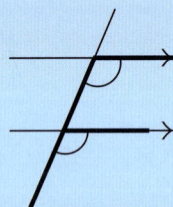

Corresponding angles are equal

(a)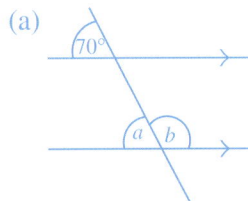

(b)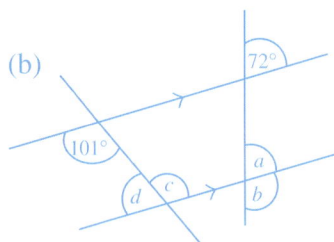

$a = 70°$ (corresponding angles)

$b = 110°$ ($a$ and $b$ are angles on a straight line which add upto 180°)

$a = 72°$ (corresponding)

$b = 108°$ (angles on a straight line add up to 180°)

$c = 101°$ (alternate)

$d = 79°$ (angles on a straight line add up to 180°)

Find the angles marked with letters.

**1**

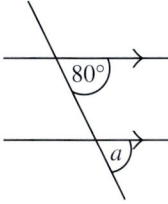

**2**

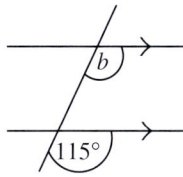

**3**

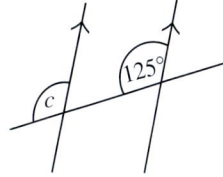

**4**

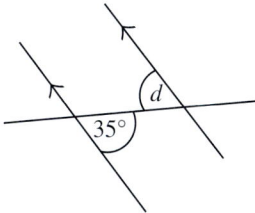

**5**

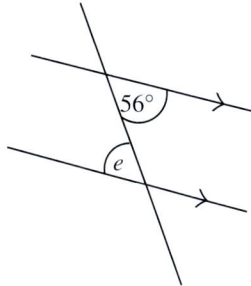

**6**

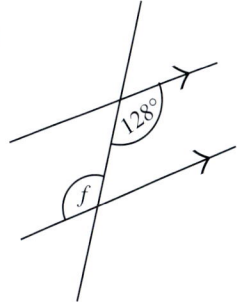

**7**

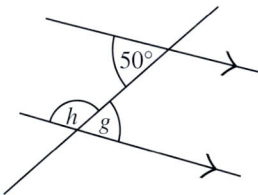

**8**

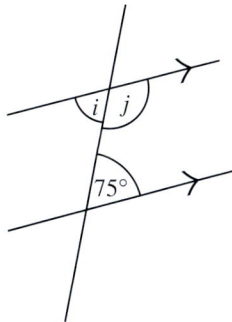

**9**

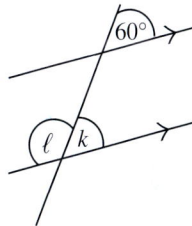

**10**

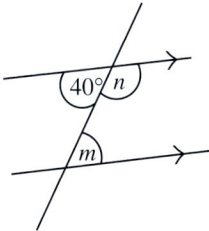

**11**

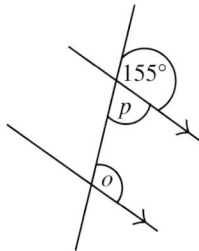

**12**

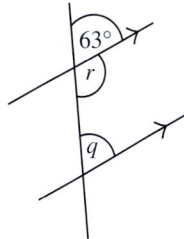

**13**

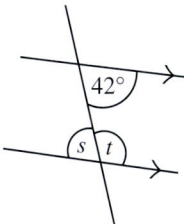

**14**

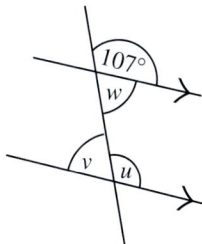

**15**

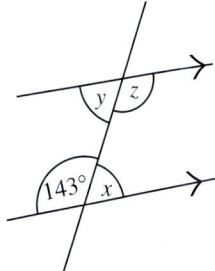

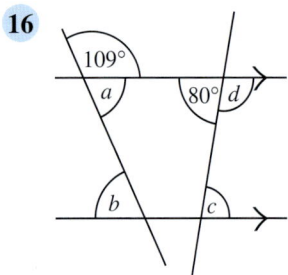

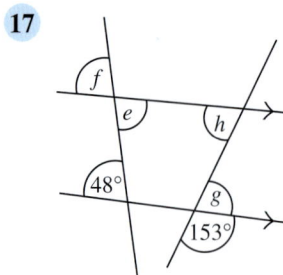

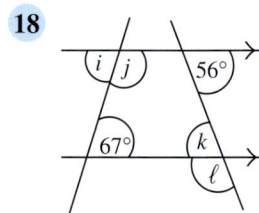

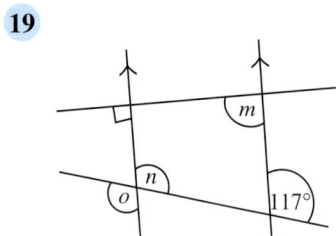

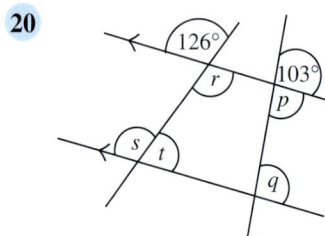

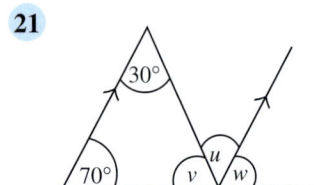

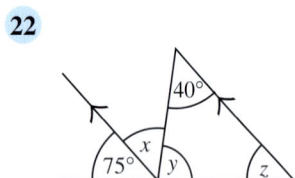

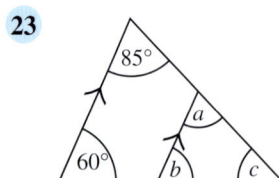

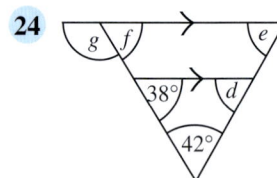

**16**

109°
a
80° d
b
c

**17**

f
e
h
48°
g
153°

**18**

i j
56°
67°
k
ℓ

**19**

m
n
o
117°

**20**

126°
r
103°
p
s
t
q

**21**

30°
70°
u
v w

**22**

40°
x
75° y
z

**23**

85°
a
60°
b
c

**24**

g f
e
38°
d
42°

Can you still?

**3A**  **Factors and Multiples (see Unit 2)**

Can you still?

1. Write down all the *factors* of:

   (a)  10      (b)  25      (c)  24

2. Which numbers below have 4 *factors* only?

   ⑮      ⑦      ⑯      ㉒

3. Which of the numbers below are *multiples* of 6?

   ⑰      ⑫      ㉒      ㉚      ⑲      ㊷

4.  (a) Write down the  first six *multiples* of 7

    (b) Write down the  first eight *multiples* of 5

    (c) Write down the Lowest Common Multiple of 5 and 7

5. Find the Lowest Common Multiple of each of these pairs of numbers:

   (a)  4 and 7      (b)  6 and 9      (c)  8 and 6

## Key Facts

A shape has a line of symmetry if one side is a reflection of the other along the line. One side folds exactly onto the other along the line.

Line of symmetry

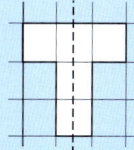

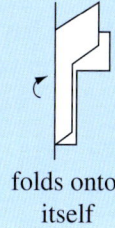

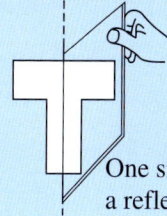

folds onto itself

One side is a reflection of the other

---

**M3. 4**

**1** Which of these road signs have one or more lines of symmetry?

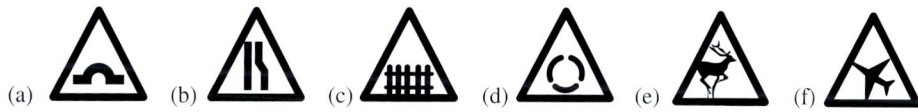

(a)   (b)   (c)   (d)   (e)   (f)

**2** Which of these signs have a line of symmetry?

(a)   (b)   (c)   (d)   (e)   (f)

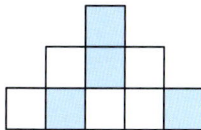

**3** Copy this shape into your book.

Shade one more square so that the shape has a line of symmetry.

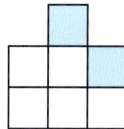

**4** Copy this shape into your book.

Shade two more squares so that it has a line of symmetry.

**5** Each of these shapes have a line of symmetry

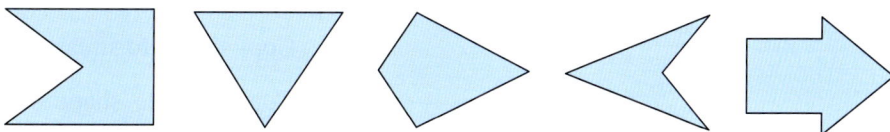

Copy them into your book and draw on a dotted line to show the line of symmetry.

**6** Sketch these shapes in your book.
Draw on their line of symmetry using a dotted line.

Hint: Turn them around to help see their line of symmetry

**7** These shapes have more than one line of symmetry.
Sketch them in your book and draw on all the lines of symmetry.

more than 3

more than 4

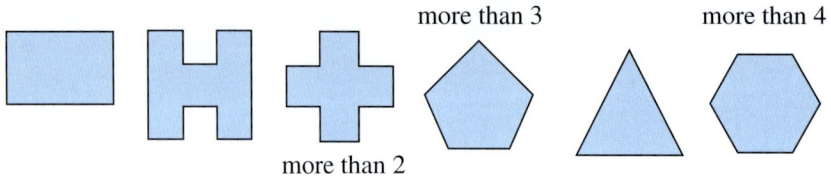

more than 2

**8** Copy these shapes. Mark on all their lines of symmetry.

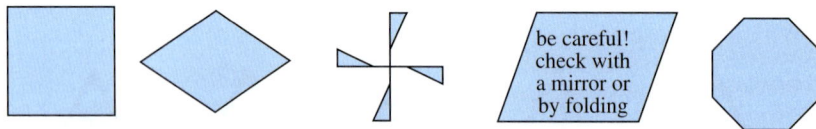

be careful!
check with
a mirror or
by folding

**9**

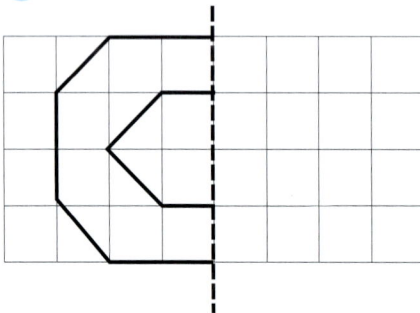

Copy this onto squared paper.

Complete the shape so that the dotted line is a *line of symmetry*.

**10**

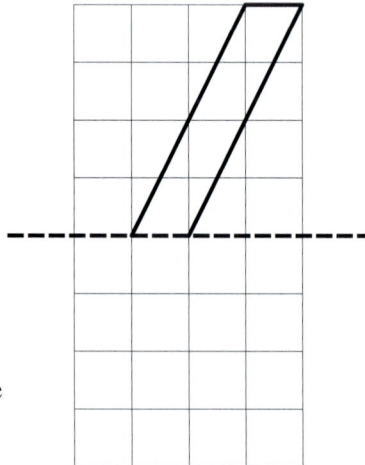

Copy this onto squared paper.

Complete the shape so that the dotted line is a *line of symmetry*.

74

## Key Facts

A shape has **rotational symmetry** if it fits onto itself when rotated (turned) before it gets back to its starting position.

The shape A fits onto itself three times when rotated through a complete turn. It has rotational symmetry of **order three**.

If a shape can only fit onto itself in its starting position, it has rotational symmetry of **order one**.

### E3. 4

For each shape write down the order of rotational symmetry (use tracing paper if you wish).

1 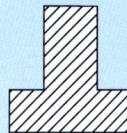  2 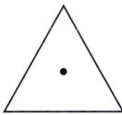  3   4

5 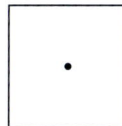  6 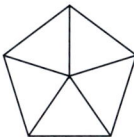  7   8

9   10   11 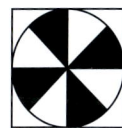  12

13  14  15  16

# 🔑 Key Facts

A plane of symmetry divides a 3-D shape into two identical halves. One half must be the mirror image of the other half.

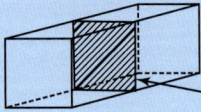

A plane of symmetry must be shown fully as a clear slice through the 3-D shape. Each half of the cuboid on each side of the plane of symmetry is symmetrical.

Note: a 3-D shape may have more than one plane of symmetry.

**M3. 5**

**1** Draw each shape below and show one plane of symmetry.

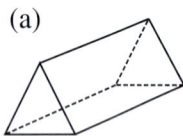

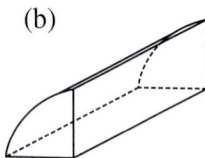

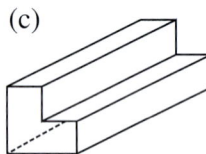

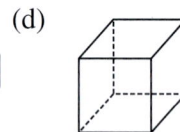

(a)    (b)    (c)    (d)

**2** Write down how many planes of symmetry each shape below has.

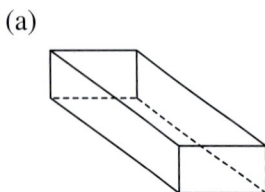

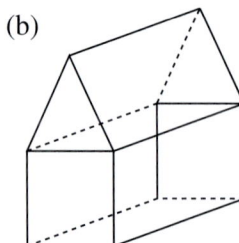

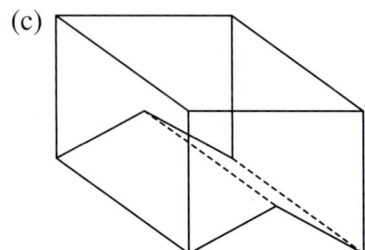

(a)    (b)    (c)

**(3B)** **Prime Factors and Highest Common Factors (see Unit 2)**

**1.** Copy and complete these factor trees:

(a)

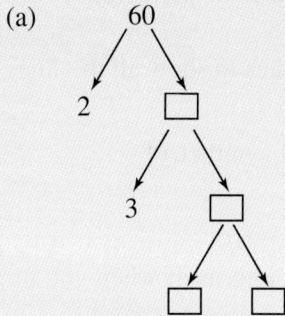

$60 = 2 \times \square \times 3 \times \square$

(b)

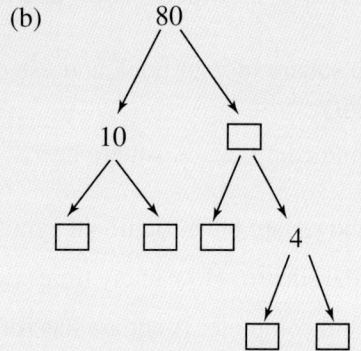

$80 = \square \times \square \times \square \times \square \times \square$

**2.** $20 = \underbrace{2 \times 2 \times 5}$

'a product of its prime factors'

Using any method, write the following numbers as products of prime factors:
(a) 30    (b) 36    (c) 50    (d) 144

**3.** (a) List all the factors of 28

(b) List all the factors of 21

(c) Write down the Highest Common Factor of 21 and 28

**4.** Using any method, find the Highest Common Factor of:

(a) 24 and 60     (b) 45 and 75     (c) 135 and 81

## Quadrilaterals – Four sided shapes

M3. 6

You will need some punched strips and tracing paper.

**1** Which of these shapes is a quadrilateral?

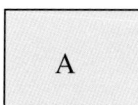

**2** The diagram shows a square.

(a) What is special about its angles?

(b) What is special about its sides?

**3** (a) Draw a square in your book.

(b) Use dashes to show equal sides and little squares to show right angles.

**4** (a) Draw a square in your book and use dotted lines to show all the lines of symmetry.

(b) Copy and complete: A square has .... lines of symmetry.

**5** (a) Does the square have rotational symmetry?

(b) Trace the square. How many times does it fit into itself when you turn it?

(c) Copy and complete: A square has rotational symmetry of order ...

**6**

make a square

2 cm

2 cm 2 cm

2 cm

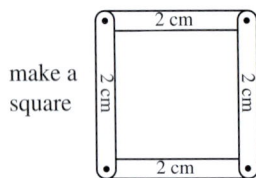

squash your square to make this shape it is called a rhombus

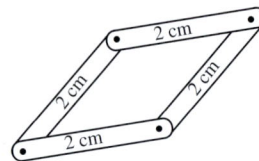

2 cm

2 cm 2 cm

2 cm

rhombus

(a) What is special about the sides of a rhombus?

(b) What is special about its opposite angles?

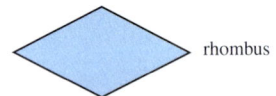

**7** (a) Draw a rhombus in your book.

(b) Use dashes to show equal sides and curves to show equal angles.

**8** (a) How many lines of symmetry does a rhombus have?

(b) Draw another rhombus in your book. Show its lines of symmetry using dotted lines.

**9** (a) Does the rhombus have rotational symmetry?

(b) Trace the rhombus. How many times does it fit into itself when you turn it?

(c) Copy and complete: A rhombus has rotational symmetry of order ....

**10** Which of these shapes are rhombuses?

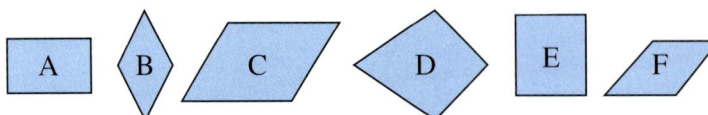

A    B    C    D    E    F

78

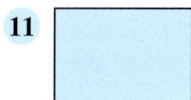

**11** 

(a) Draw a rectangle in your book.

(b) Mark any equal sides using dashes.

(c) Mark any parallel lines using arrows.

(d) Mark any right angles using little squares.

**12** (a) Draw a rectangle in your book. Show its lines of symmetry with dotted lines.

(b) Copy and complete: A rectangle has .... lines of symmetry.

**13** (a) Does a rectangle have rotational symmetry?

(b) Trace the rectangle. How many times does it fit into itself when you turn it?

(c) Copy and complete: A rectangle has rotational symmetry of order ....

**14**

 make a rectangle.

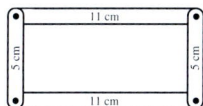

squash your rectangle to make this shape. It is called a parallelogram.

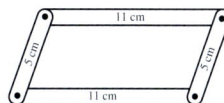

(a) Copy this parallelogram into your book.

(b) Why do you think it is called a parallelogram?

(c) Mark any parallel sides with arrows.

(d) Mark any equal angles with curves.

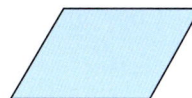

**15** (a) How many lines of symmetry does a parallelogram have?

(b) Trace the parallelogram. Cut it out. Try and fold it onto itself.

(c) Copy and complete: A parallelogram has ... lines of symmetry.

**16** (a) Does the parallelogram have rotational symmetry?

(b) Trace the parallelogram. How many times does it fit into itself when you turn it?

(c) Copy and complete: A parallelogram has rotational symmetry of order ...

**17** Which of these shapes are parallelograms?

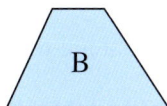

**18** Copy and complete each shape below to make a parallelogram

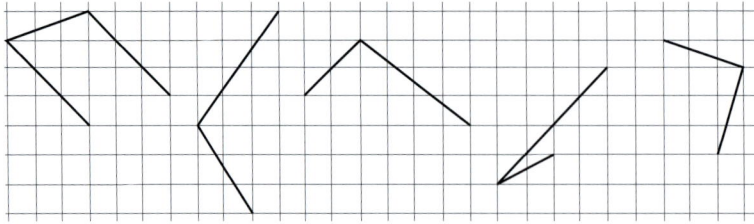

**19** Take the parallelogram from Question **14** apart.

Take the same four strips.

Make a quadrilateral which is not a parallelogram and not a rectangle.

This shape is called a kite.

**20** (a) Draw a kite in your book.

(b) Mark any equal sides with dashes.

(c) Mark any equal angles with curves. (check with a protractor!)

**21** (a) Draw another kite in your book using dotted lines to show any lines of symmetry.

(b) Copy and complete: A kite has ... line of symmetry.

**22** diagonal ←

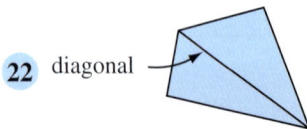

This line across from one corner to another is called a **diagonal**.

Copy this **square**.
Draw on both its diagonals. What angle do they meet at?

**23** Trace these special **quadrilaterals.**

Draw the diagonals on each shape.

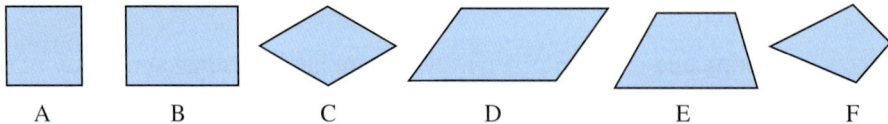

A      B      C      D      E      F

(a) Which of the quadrilaterals have diagonals that meet at right-angles:

(b) Which of the quadrilaterals have diagonals that are the same length?

(c) Which have diagonals which are also lines of symmetry?

## Angles in quadrilaterals

Find the angles marked with letters.

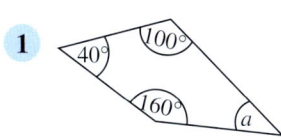

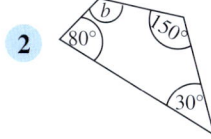

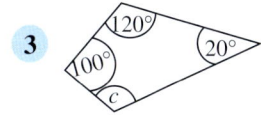

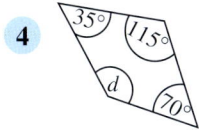

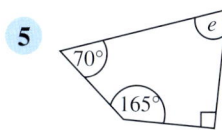

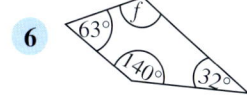

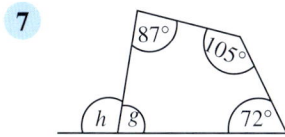

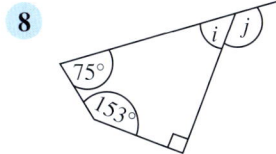

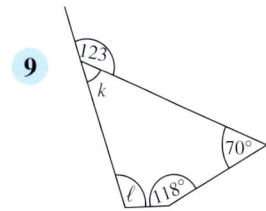

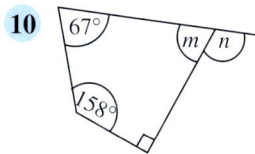

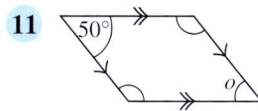

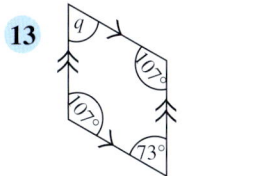

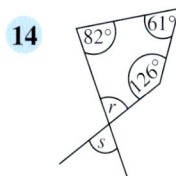

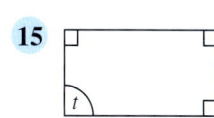

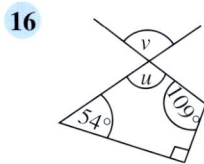

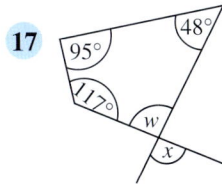

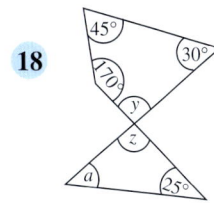

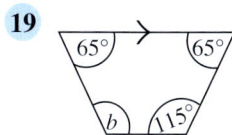

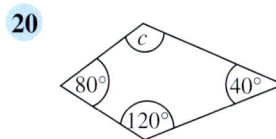

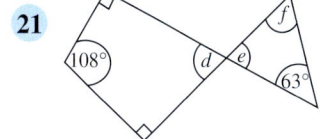

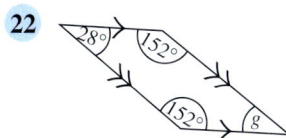

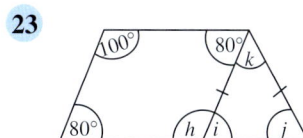

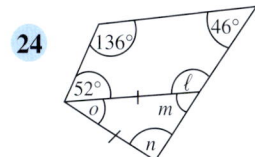

**1** 40° 100° 160° a

**2** b 80° 150° 30°

**3** 120° 100° 20° c

**4** 35° 115° d 70°

**5** 70° e 165°

**6** 63° f 140° 32°

**7** 87° 105° h g 72°

**8** 75° i j 153°

**9** 123° k 70° ℓ 118°

**10** 67° m n 158°

**11** 50° o

**12** 55° 125° 125° p

**13** q 107° 107° 73°

**14** 82° 61° 126° r s

**15** t

**16** v u 100° 54°

**17** 95° 48° 117° w x

**18** 45° 30° 170° y z a 25°

**19** 65° 65° b 115°

**20** c 80° 40° 120°

**21** 108° d e f 63°

**22** 28° 152° 152° g

**23** 100° 80° k 80° h i j

**24** 136° 46° 52° ℓ o m n

81

## 3C Fractions (see Unit 2)

In Questions **1** to **8**, copy and fill in the empty box:

**1.** $\dfrac{1}{3} = \dfrac{\Box}{12}$    **2.** $\dfrac{2}{5} = \dfrac{\Box}{30}$    **3.** $\dfrac{3}{10} = \dfrac{\Box}{40}$    **4.** $\dfrac{2}{3} = \dfrac{10}{\Box}$

**5.** $\dfrac{5}{9} = \dfrac{15}{\Box}$    **6.** $\dfrac{4}{7} = \dfrac{\Box}{35}$    **7.** $\dfrac{12}{15} = \dfrac{\Box}{5}$    **8.** $\dfrac{20}{28} = \dfrac{\Box}{7}$

Cancel each fraction below to its lowest terms:

**9.** $\dfrac{5}{20}$    **10.** $\dfrac{3}{9}$    **11.** $\dfrac{10}{40}$    **12.** $\dfrac{12}{20}$    **13.** $\dfrac{16}{24}$

**14.** $\dfrac{30}{50}$    **15.** $\dfrac{20}{45}$    **16.** $\dfrac{30}{42}$    **17.** $\dfrac{21}{56}$    **18.** $\dfrac{72}{88}$

**19.** Which of the fractions below are the same as $\dfrac{3}{4}$?

$$\dfrac{12}{50} \qquad \dfrac{15}{20} \qquad \dfrac{12}{16} \qquad \dfrac{30}{45} \qquad \dfrac{24}{32}$$

**20.** Which of the fractions below are the same as $\dfrac{2}{9}$?

$$\dfrac{6}{27} \qquad \dfrac{20}{90} \qquad \dfrac{25}{100} \qquad \dfrac{16}{72} \qquad \dfrac{18}{63}$$

## Mixed angle problems

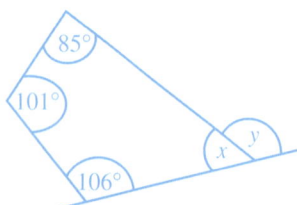

Find angles $x$ and $y$

$x = 68°$ (angles in a quadrilateral add up to 360°)

$y = 112°$ (angles on a straight line add up to 180°)

Find the angles marked with letters (Exam Questions often want reasons. Ask your teacher if you must write down all the reasons)

**1**
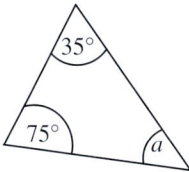

**2**
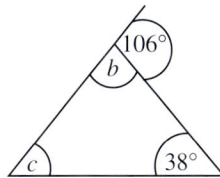

**3**
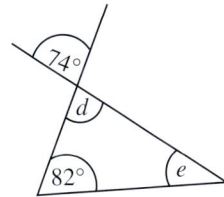

**4**
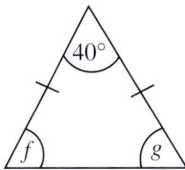

**5**
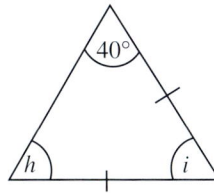

**6**
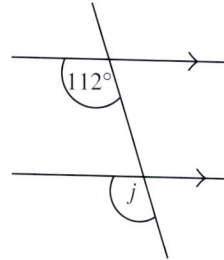

**7**
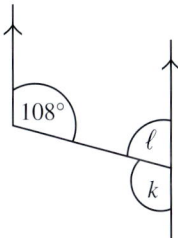

**8**
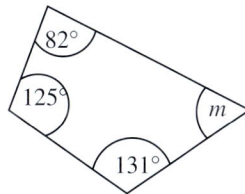

**9**
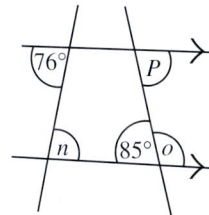

**10**
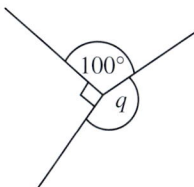

**11**
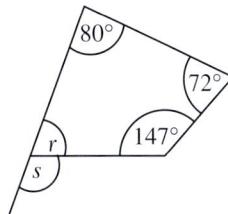

**12**
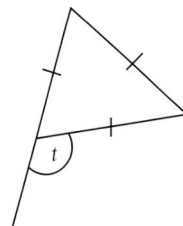

**13**
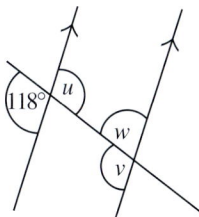

**14**
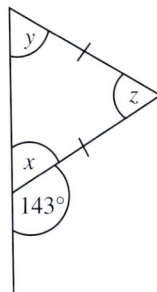

**15**
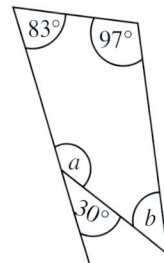

**16**

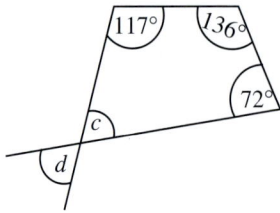

**17**

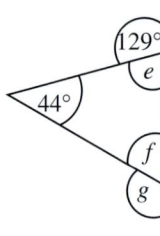

**18**

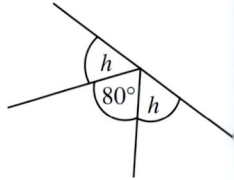

**19**

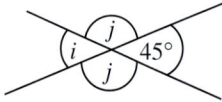

**20**

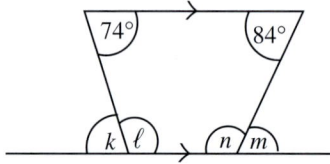

**21**

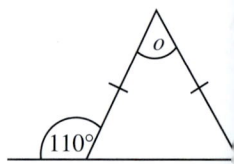

**22**

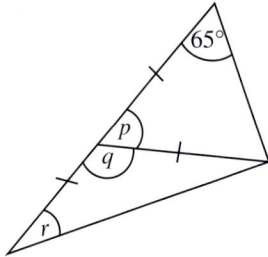

**23**

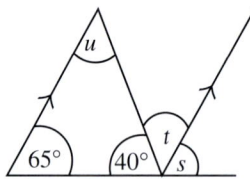

**24**

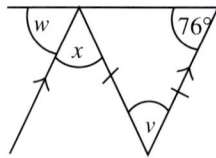

## Angle proof

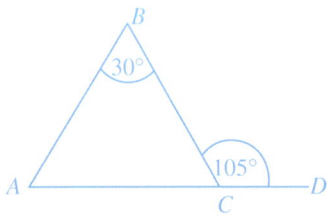

Prove that triangle $ABC$ is isosceles.

Give all your reasons clearly.

$A\hat{C}B = 180° - 105° = 75°$ (angles on a straight line)

$B\hat{A}C = 180° - 30° - 75° = 75°$ (angle in a triangle add up to 180°)

$A\hat{C}B = B\hat{A}C$ so triangle $ABC$ is isosceles.

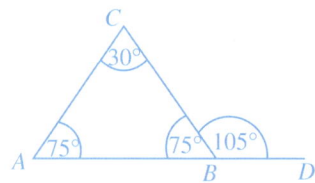

**1**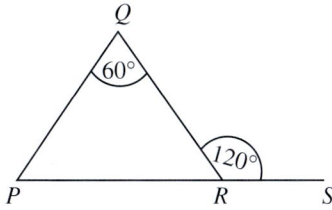

Prove that triangle *PQR* is equilateral.

**2**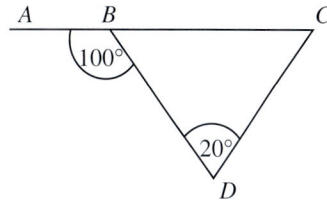

Prove that triangle *BCD* is isosceles.

**3** Copy and complete this proof for the sum of the angles in a triangle.

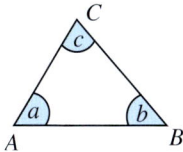 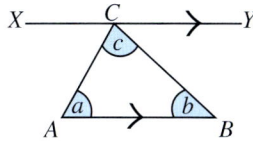 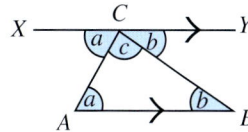

Here is triangle *ABC*.

Draw line *XCY* parallel to *AB*.

$A\hat{B}C = Y\hat{C}B$ (alternate angles)
$B\hat{A}C = \square$ (alternate angles)
$a + b + c = \square$ (angles on a straight line) angles in a triangle $a + b + c = 180°$

**4**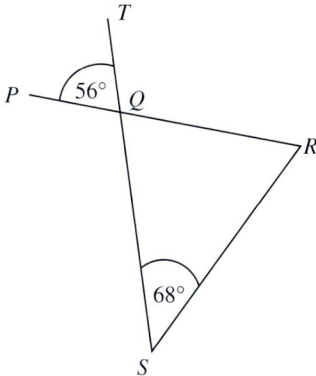

Prove that triangle *QRS* is isosceles.

Give all your reasons clearly.

**5** Copy and complete this proof for the sum of the angles in a quadrilateral.

Draw any quadrilateral *ABCD* with diagonal *BD*.

Now $a + b + c = \square$ (angles in a triangle add up to 180°)

and $d + e + f = \square$ (angles in a triangle add up to 180°)

so $a + b + c + d + e + f = \square$

This proves the result.

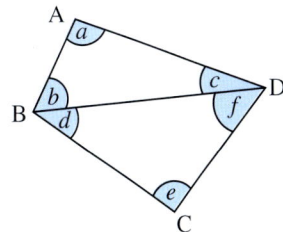

🔑 # Key Facts

A polygon is a shape with straight sides.

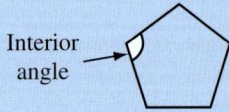

Interior angle →

A polygon with 5 sides is called a pentagon

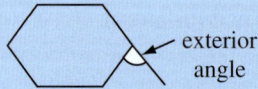

exterior angle ←

A polygon with 6 sides is called a hexagon

A **regular** polygon has equal sides and equal angles.

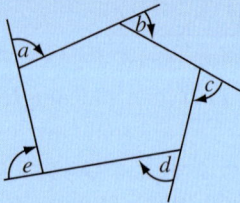

$a$  $b$  $c$  $e$  $d$

Put all the exterior angles together. We can see that the sum of the angles is 360°. This is true for any polygon.

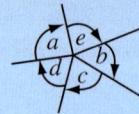

$a$ $e$ $b$ $d$ $c$

Exterior angles of a polygon add up to 360°

Note – in a regular polygon, all exterior angles are equal.

---

Find the value of angle $x$.

Sum of exterior angles = 360°

There are 8 sides so 8 equal exterior angles.

One exterior angle = 360° ÷ 8 = 45°

$x$  45°  ⇨  $x$  45°

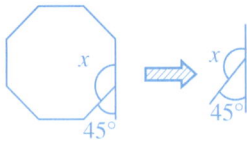

interior and exterior angles add up to 180°

so $x + 45° = 180°$

so $x = 135°$

**1** Each shape below is a *regular* polygon.

Find the angles marked with letters.

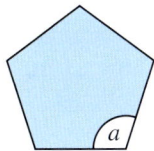

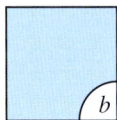

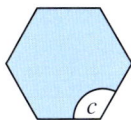

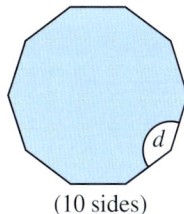

(10 sides)

**2** Find the angles marked with letters.

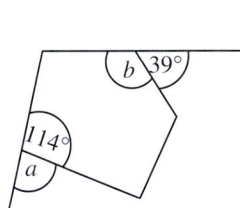

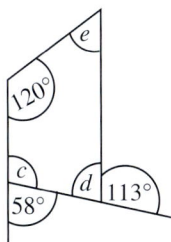

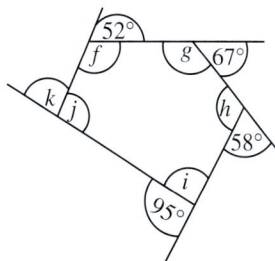

**3** A dodecagon has 12 sides.

(a) Find the size of each exterior angle of a *regular* dodecagon.

(b) Write down the size of the interior angle for the same shape.

**4** (a) Find the size of each exterior angle of a *regular* nonagon (9 sides)

(b) Write down the size of the interior angle for the same shape.

**5** Find the exterior angles of *regular* polygons with
   (a) 15 sides    (b) 20 sides    (c) 60 sides    (d) 90 sides

**6** Find the interior angle of each polygon in Question **5** .

**7** Each exterior angle of a *regular* polygon is 8°. How many sides has the polygon?

**8** Each exterior angle of a *regular* polygon is 20°. How many sides has the polygon?

**9** This diagram shows the interior and exterior angles of a *regular* polygon. How many sides has the polygon?

interior angle

exterior angle

168°  12°

**10** Find the size of the interior angle of a *regular* polygon with 24 sides.

The table below shows the prices in £'s per person for two adults to share a twin/double room in different hotels in a European city. The price includes travelling by air from the UK and includes breakfast in the hotel.

| Hotels | Hotel Rio | | Tulip Hotel | | Carling Hotel | | Hotel Eden | |
|---|---|---|---|---|---|---|---|---|
| departure date | 1 night | extra night | 1 night | extra night | 1 night | extra night | 1 night | extra night |
| 01 Apr – 27 Oct | 174 | 77 | 185 | 84 | 210 | 99 | 216 | 105 |
| 28 Oct – 10 Nov | 161 | 62 | 185 | 84 | 198 | 86 | 191 | 85 |
| 11 Nov – 5 Dec | 161 | 62 | 171 | 73 | 210 | 99 | 190 | 84 |
| 6 Dec – 21 Dec | 161 | 62 | 171 | 73 | 210 | 99 | 216 | 105 |
| 22 Dec – 5 Jan | 174 | 77 | 187 | 88 | 219 | 103 | 216 | 105 |
| 6 Jan – 10 Jan | 174 | 77 | 185 | 84 | 214 | 101 | 212 | 101 |
| 11 Jan – 20 Jan | 159 | 60 | 171 | 73 | 187 | 81 | 186 | 75 |
| 21 Jan – 2 Mar | 159 | 62 | 171 | 73 | 187 | 81 | 188 | 77 |
| 3 Mar – 10 Mar | 161 | 63 | 175 | 74 | 192 | 83 | 218 | 107 |
| 11 Mar – 18 Mar | 161 | 62 | 175 | 74 | 198 | 86 | 220 | 109 |
| 19 Mar – 31 Mar | 179 | 81 | 191 | 86 | 215 | 103 | 228 | 117 |

Weekend supplement: £12 per person for Friday and Saturday departures.

Seasonal supplement of £12 per person applies for departures between:
28 Apr–3 May, 28–31 May, 26–30 Aug, 24–27 Dec, 30 Dec–2 Jan.

'Weekend supplement' means each person pays £12 extra if they depart on a Friday or Saturday.

'Seasonal supplement' means each person pays £12 extra if they depart on the dates shown.

(a) 2 people want to spend 4 nights at the Carling Hotel, leaving on 15<sup>th</sup> November.
How much will this cost?
Look along the '11 Nov–5 Dec' row and stop at the Carling Hotel column. The cost per person is £210 plus £99 for each extra night.
Total cost per person for 4 nights = 210 + 297 = £507.
Total cost for 2 people = 507 × 2 = £1014.

(b) 4 people want to spend 3 nights at the Tulip hotel. They want to depart for their holiday on 7th August which is a Saturday. How much will the holiday cost for these 4 people?

Look along the '01 Apr–27 Oct' row and stop at the Tulip hotel column. The cost per person is £185 plus £84 for each extra night.

Total cost per person for 3 nights = $185 + 84 \times 2 = £353$

Depart on Saturday so weekend supplement = £12

Total cost per person = £365

Total cost for 4 people = $365 \times 4 = £1460$.

**Remember**

There is also the cost of getting to the airport, spending money, money for main meals, travel insurance and other items.

## WYM3

1  2 people want to spend 3 nights at the Hotel Eden leaving on 23rd January. How much will this cost?

2  Mr. and Mrs. Rowan want to spend 2 nights at the Carling Hotel, leaving on 10th May which is a Friday. How much will the holiday cost?

3  4 people want to spend 5 nights at the Hotel Rio, leaving on the 3rd March. What is the total cost of this holiday?

4  2 people want to spend 4 nights at the Hotel Rio, leaving on the 20th September, which is a Saturday. How much will the holiday cost for these 2 people?

5  A party of 10 people want to spend 2 nights at the Tulip hotel leaving on the 27th August (a seasonal supplement will be payable). What is the total cost of the holiday?

6  Jack and Susan are celebrating their Silver Wedding anniversary by spending 3 nights at the Carling Hotel. They plan to depart on 9th December, which is a Friday. How much will this holiday cost?

7  6 people want to spend 7 nights at the Hotel Eden, departing on the 20th March. What is the total cost of this holiday?

8  4 people want to spend 6 nights at the Hotel Rio, leaving on 28th May (a seasonal supplement will be payable). How much will this holiday cost?

1. Identifying acute, obtuse, reflex and right angles

For each of these angles say whether they are acute, obtuse, reflex or a right angle:

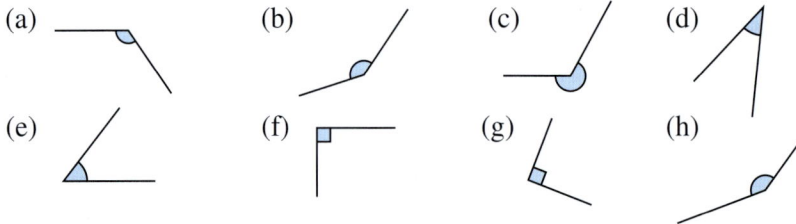

(a)    (b)    (c)    (d)

(e)    (f)    (g)    (h)

2. Labelling angles

Name each shaded angle below: (example: $B\hat{A}C$)

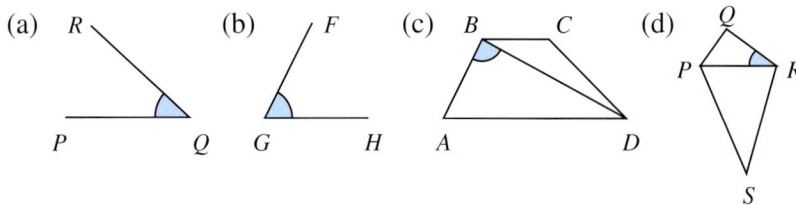

(a) R    (b) F    (c) B    C    (d) Q

P    Q    G    H    A    D    P    R

S

3. Finding angles on a straight line and angles at a point

Find the angles marked with the letters.

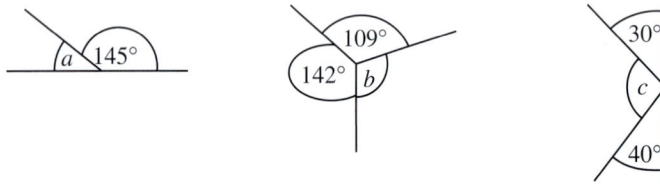

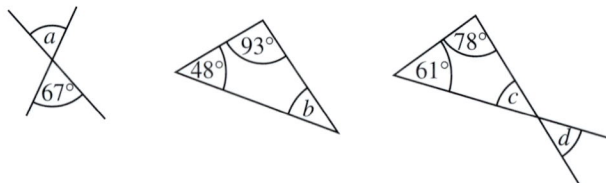

$a$ 145°

109°
142° $b$

30°
$c$
40°

4. Finding vertically opposite angles and angles in a triangle

Find the angles marked with the letters.

$a$
67°

93°
48°    $b$

78°
61°    $c$
$d$

## 5. Using isosceles and equilateral triangles

Find the angles marked with the letters

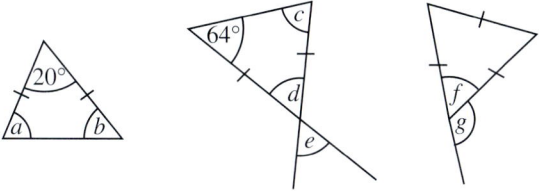

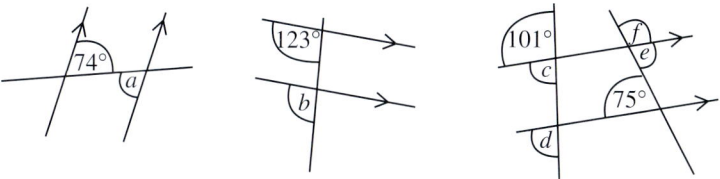

## 6. Finding alternate and corresponding angles

Find the angles marked with the letters

## 7. Using reflection symmetry and rotational symmetry

For each shape below, write down how many lines of symmetry it has and the order of rotational symmetry.

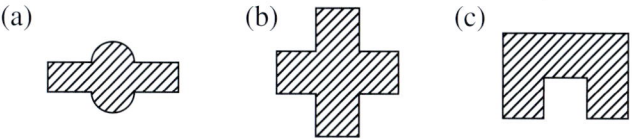

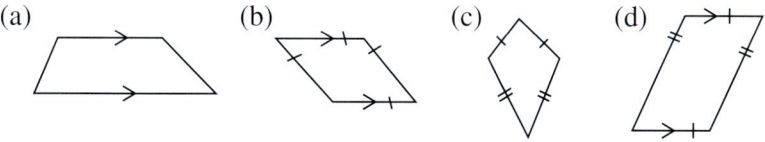

(a)        (b)        (c)

## 8. Recognising common quadrilaterals

Name the shapes below and for each shape, write down

  (i)  how many lines of symmetry it has and

  (ii)  its order of rotational symmetry.

(a)        (b)        (c)        (d)

91

## 9. Finding angles in quadrilaterals and polygons

Find the angles marked with the letters

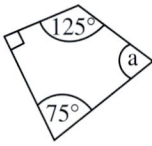
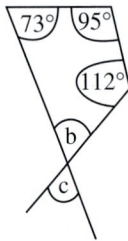
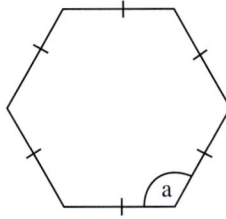
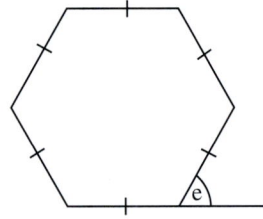

## Mixed examination questions

**1**

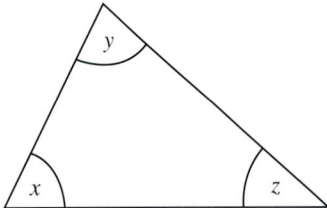

(i) The diagram shows a triangle

Which of the following correctly describes angle $x$?

acute angle,       obtuse angle,

reflex angle,      right-angle.

(ii) What is the value of $x + y + z$?

(AQA)

**2**

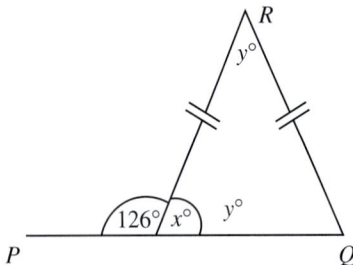

$PQ$ is a straight line.

(a) Work out the size of the angle marked $x°$.

(b)  (i) Work out the size of the angle marked $y°$.

     (ii) Give reasons for your answer.

(EDEXCEL)

**3**  State the order of rotational symmetry for each tile below.

(a)
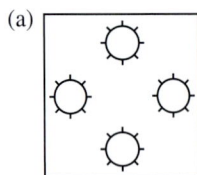

(b)
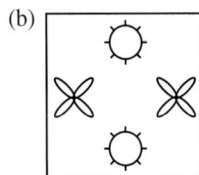

(c)
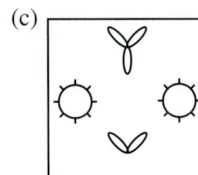

**4** The diagram shows a rectangle.

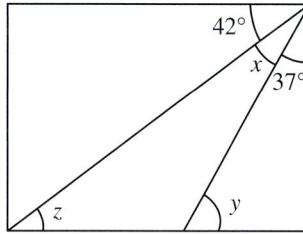

Work out the size of angles $x$, $y$ and $z$. (AQA)

**5**

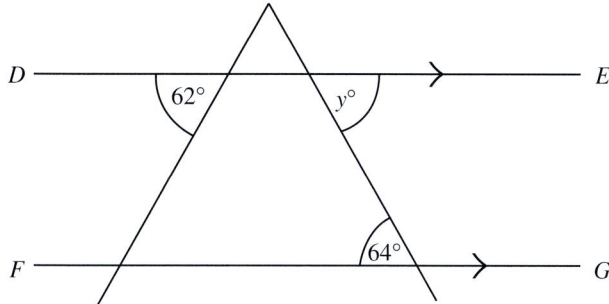

$DE$ is parallel to $FG$.

Find the size of the angle marked $y°$. (EDEXCEL)

**6** Shade two more squares on the diagram so that the final pattern has line symmetry AND rotational symmetry.

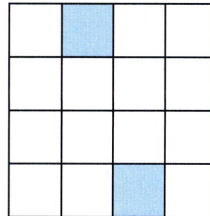

(AQA)

**7**

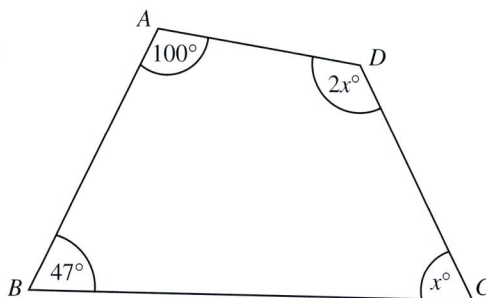

$ABCD$ is a quadrilateral.

Work out the size of the largest angle in the quadrilateral.

(EDEXCEL)

# ALGEBRA 1

# 4

**In this unit you will learn how to:**

– use letters and symbols in algebra

– substitute numbers for letters

– substitute numbers into formulas

– collect like terms

– simplify terms

– multiply out brackets

– take out common factors

– WATCH YOUR MONEY! – Money for your holiday

## Substitution

## 🔑 Key Facts

Letters can be used in place of numbers to solve problems:

Example – shoes cost £40

               shoes cost £$x$

$a + b$ is an algebraic *expression*

$3a$ means $3 \times a$           $ab$ means $a \times b$

$a^2$ means $a \times a$          $7a + 2$ means '$7 \times a$ then add 2'

$\dfrac{a}{b}$ means $a \div b$         $7(a + 2)$ means '$a + 2$ then multiply by 7'

$a^3$ means $a \times a \times a$     $4a^2$ means '$a \times a$ then multiply by 4'

$(4a)^2$ means '$4 \times a$ then square the answer'

94

Find the value of each expression when $a = 3$, $b = 2$ and $c = 5$

$ab = 3 \times 2 = 6$

$c^2 = 5 \times 5 = 25$

$5a - 1 = 5 \times 5 - 1 = 24$

$4(b + 3) = 4 \times (2 + 3) = 4 \times 5 = 20$

$\dfrac{c}{b} = 5 \div 2 = 2.5$

$(3b)^2 = (3 \times 2)^2 = 6^2 = 6 \times 6 = 36$

$3b^2 = 3 \times b \times b = 3 \times 2 \times 2 = 12$

# 🔑 Key Facts

**Remember:** BODMAS. The order of operations is Brackets then $\div$ $\times$ $+$ $-$

## M4. 1

In Questions **1** to **20** find the value of each expression when
$a = 6$
$b = 2$
$c = 4$

**1**  $4a$

**2**  $a + b + c$

**3**  $2a - b$

**4**  $a + b - c$

**5**  $bc$

**6**  $3c - 5$

**7**  $ab$

**8**  $7b + 2c$

**9**  $c^2$

**10**  $a^2$

**11**  $a^2 + b^2$

**12**  $4(b + c)$

**13**  $3(a - c)$

**14**  $b(a + c)$

**15**  $\dfrac{a - c}{b}$

**16**  $a(c - b)$

**17**  $a(b + c)$

**18**  $b(2a - c)$

**19**  $\dfrac{3b + a}{c}$

**20**  $\dfrac{6c}{a}$

In Questions **21** to **40** find the value of each expression when $x = 3$
$y = 0$
$z = 8$

**21** $6x$

**22** $2z$

**23** $3x - z$

**24** $4z + x$

**25** $3z + 7$

**26** $x + z$

**27** $x + z - y$

**28** $z - 2x$

**29** $14 + 2z$

**30** $3x - 2y$

**31** $x^2$

**32** $y^2 + x^2$

**33** $xy$

**34** $yz$

**35** $xyz$

**36** $x^2 + y^2 + z^2$

**37** $3(2x + z)$

**38** $x(z - y)$

**39** $4(x^2 + z^2)$

**40** $\dfrac{10x}{5x}$

In Questions **41** to **49** find the value of each expression

**41** $3x + 2$ if $x = 4$

**42** $5x - 7$ if $x = 6$

**43** $2a + 9$ if $a = 5$

**44** $b^2 + 4$ if $b = 6$

**45** $6(a - 3)$ if $a = 5$

**46** $x^2 - 6$ if $x = 5$

**47** $8 + 2b$ if $b = 4$

**48** $9(x^2 - 3)$ if $x = 2$

**49** $a(5a - 9)$ if $a = 3$

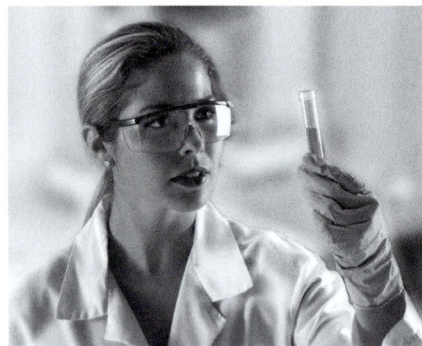

## E4. 1

In Questions **1** to **20** find the value of each expression when $x = 5$
$y = 4$
$z = 7$

**1** $y^2 + z^2$

**2** $x^2$

**3** $4x^2$

**4** $(4x)^2$

**5** $(2y)^2$

**6** $2z^2$

**7** $3y^2$

**8** $xyz$

**9** $2(x^2 + y^2)$

**10** $2y + 3x$

**11** $x^2 + y^2 + z^2$

**12** $2x^2 - y^2$

**13** $y(3z - 2x)$

**14** $z(4x + 2y)$

**15** $\dfrac{21(x - y)}{z}$

**16** $6(x^2 - y^2)$

**17** $y(2z + 3y)$

**18** $(2x)^2 - 2x^2$

**19** $6(3x + y^2)$

**20** $\dfrac{5z + x}{y}$

In Questions **21** to **29** find the value of each expression

**21** $x^2 - 3$, if $x = 7$      **22** $2b^2$, if $b = 3$      **23** $3a^2$, if $a = 1$

**24** $7(p - 2)$, if $p = 2$      **25** $(4a)^2$, if $a = 1$      **26** $3x$, if $x = -2$

**27** $20 + b$, if $b = -6$      **28** $3 - 6x$, if $x = 2$      **29** $5(a - 6)$, if $a = 2$

In Questions **30** to **45** find the value of each expression when    $a = 4$
$$b = -2$$
$$c = -3$$

**30** $bc$      **31** $5a + 3b$      **32** $3c - 2$      **33** $2b + 4c$

**34** $b^2$      **35** $a^2 + b^2$      **36** $2c^2$      **37** $3(4b - 2)$

**38** $b(a + c)$      **39** $abc$      **40** $9c$      **41** $(3b)^2$

**42** $8(a - b)$      **43** $24 - c$      **44** $5c + 10$      **45** $3a + 2b - c$

## Using formulas

If base = 9 cm and height = 6 cm

then $b = 9$ and $h = 6$

Area A $= \dfrac{bh}{2}$

so   A $= \dfrac{9 \times 6}{2} = 27$

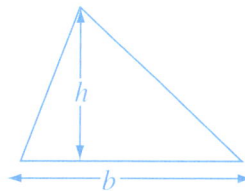

**M4. 2**

In Questions **1** to **12** you are given a formula. Find the value of the letter required in each case.

**1**   $a = 5b + 2$        **2**   $x = 7y - 6$

     Find $a$ when $b = 3$        Find $x$ when $y = 3$

**3**   $a = \dfrac{b}{4} + 5$        **4**   $c = \dfrac{d}{3} - 2$

     Find $a$ when $b = 20$        Find $c$ when $d = 15$

**5** $g = 4h + 9$

Find $g$ when $h = 6$

**6** $p = 2(q + 8)$

Find $p$ when $q = 3$

**7** $m = n + 3p$

Find $m$ when $n = 8$ and $p = 6$

**8** $p = 6q + 2r$

Find $p$ when $q = 4$ and $r = 5$

**9** $v = 2(3w + 2y)$

Find $v$ when $w = 4$ and $y = 5$

**10** $a = \dfrac{4b + 7c}{5}$

Find $a$ when $b = 4$ and $c = 2$

**11** $x = 3y + 6z - 8$

Find $x$ when $y = 4$ and $z = 2$

**12** $e = \dfrac{f}{3} + \dfrac{d}{4}$

Find $e$ when $f = 15$ and $d = 28$

In Questions **13** to **16** use the formula $s = ut$ to find the value of $s$ ($s$ means distance, $u$ means speed and $t$ means time taken).

**13** $u = 7, t = 8$

**14** $u = 47, t = 16$

**15** $u = 23, t = 41$

**16** $u = 4.1, t = 3.6$

In Questions **17** to **20** use the formula $v = at + u$ to find the value of $v$.

**17** $a = 7, t = 6$ and $u = 43$

**18** $a = 17, t = 32$ and $u = 217$

**19** $a = 3.6, t = 7$ and $u = 8.9$

**20** $a = 5.2, t = 3.6$ and $u = 7.17$

**21**

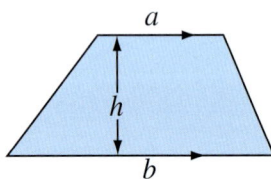

The area $A$ of a trapezium can be found using the formula $A = \dfrac{1}{2}h(a + b)$

$\left(\dfrac{1}{2}h \text{ means } \dfrac{1}{2} \text{ of } h\right)$

Find the area of a trapezium when $h = 8$, $a = 8.9$ and $b = 6.1$

**22**

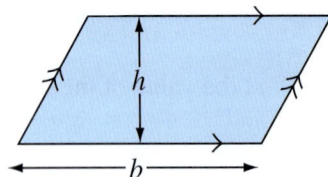

The area $A$ of a parallelogram can be found using the formula

$$A = bh$$

Find the area of a parallelogram when $b = 6.2$ and $h = 4.9$

**23** $a = \dfrac{v - u}{t}$ Use the formula to find the value of $a$ when $v = 11$, $u = 4$ and $t = 0.5$

**24** $x$ and $y$ are connected by the formula $x = 5(2y - 3)$. Find $x$ when $y = 5.6$

**25** $c$, $d$ and $e$ are connected by the formula

$$c = \sqrt{(d^2 + e^2)}$$

Find $c$ when $d = 3$ and $e = 4$

**1** Below are several different formulas for $z$ in terms of $x$. Find the value of $z$ in each case.

    (a) $z = 10x - 6$ when $x = 3.5$

    (b) $z = \dfrac{5x + 3}{2}$ when $x = 3$

    (c) $z = 4(3x + 7)$ when $x = 2$

**2** Using the formula $a = 100 + 2b$, find the value of $a$ when

    (a) $b = 6$      (b) $b = 100$      (c) $b = \dfrac{1}{2}$

**3** In the formulas below $v$ is given in terms of $a$ and $t$. Find the value of $v$ in each case.

    (a) $v = 7t + 3a$ when $t = 4$ and $a = 5$

    (b) $v = 8t + 5a - 12$ when $t = 3$ and $a = 4$

    (c) $v = at + 6$ when $a = 4$ and $t = 8$

**4** Here are some polygons.

| Number of sides : | 3 | 4 | 5 |
|---|---|---|---|
| Sum of angles : | 180° | 360° | 540° |

The sum of the angles in a polygon with n sides is given by the formula

sum of angles $= (n - 2) \times 180°$

    (a) Find the sum of the angles in a hexagon (6 sides)

    (b) Find the sum of the angles in a polygon with 102 sides

    (c) Show that the formula gives the correct answer for the sum of the angles in a pentagon (5 sides)

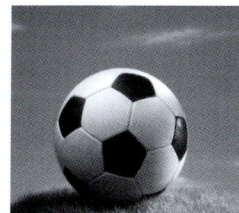

**5** Here is a formula $h = t^2 - 7$. Find the value of $h$ when

    (a) $t = 6$    (b) $t = 1$    (c) $t = -3$

**6** Using the formula $C = N^2 - P^2$

    find the value of $C$ when

    (a) $N = 8$ and $P = 5$    (b) $N = 4$ and $P = 7$

    (c) $N = -3$ and $P = -6$

**7** Using the formula $V = 3B^2$ find the value of $V$ when

    (a) $B = 5$    (b) $B = 10$    (c) $B = -2$    (d) $B = -8$

**8** An estimate for the volume of a cylinder of radius $r$ and height $h$ is given by the formula $V = 3r^2h$

    (a) Find the value of $V$ when $r = 10$ and $h = 2$

    (b) Find the value of $V$ when $r = 5$ and $h = 4$

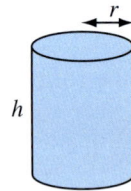

**9** Find the value of $c$ using formulas and values given.

    (a) $c = mx + 7$;   $m = 5$   $x = -1$

    (b) $c = 2t + t^2$;   $t = 3$

    (c) $c = 2pq + p^2$;   $p = 3$   $q = 2$

    (d) $c = (a + b^2)$;   $a = 5$   $b = -2$

**10** If $T = a^2 + 3a - 5$, find the values of $T$ when

    (a) $a = 3$    (b) $a = 10$    (c) $a = 1$

**11** The total surface area $A$ of the solid cuboid shown is given by the formula

$$A = 2bc + 2ab + 2ac$$

    Find the value of $A$ when $a = 2, b = 3, c = 4$

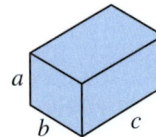

**12** Using the formula $P = QR + S$, find the value of $P$ when

    (a) $Q = -2, R = -4, S = -5$    (b) $Q = -3, R = 5, S = 10$

In the Questions below round off the answers to the **nearest whole number**.

**13** Using the formula $x = \dfrac{y + z}{z - y}$ find the value of $x$ when

(a) $y = 6, z = 11$     (b) $y = 0.3, z = -2.8$

**14** Using the formula $A = \dfrac{2B + C}{B + 3C}$ find the value of $A$ when

(a) $B = -7, C = 4$     (b) $B = -24, C = -2$

**15** Here is a formula $M = \sqrt{(4N - 1)}$. Find the value of $M$ when

(a) $N = 6$     (b) $N = 20$     (c) $N = 5.8$

**16**

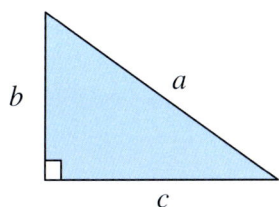

For any right-angled triangle:

$$a = \sqrt{(b^2 + c^2)}$$

Find the value of $a$ when

(a) $b = 7, c = 2$     (b) $b = 12, c = 5$     (c) $b = 8, c = 15$

**17** Using the formula $R = 8 - \sqrt{S}$, find the value of $R$ when

(a) $S = 3$     (b) $S = 38$     (c) $S = 300$

**18**

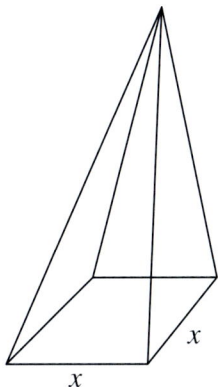

The volume $V$ of this pyramid is given by the formula

$$V = \frac{x^2 h}{3}$$

where $h$ is the height of the pyramid.

Find the value of $V$ when

(a) $x = 4, h = 10$     (b) $x = 5, h = 7$     (c) $x = 20, h = 15$

**19** Using the formula $f = \dfrac{uv}{u + v}$, find the value of $f$ when

(a) $u = 6, v = 4$     (b) $u = 8, v = 20$     (c) $u = 5, v = 32$

## Key Facts

$a + b$ cannot be added together because the *term a* is not like the term b
$a + 3a = 4a$ because the term *a* is like the term $3a$
$a$ and $3a$ are *like terms*

**Examples**

(a) $6a + 4b + 2a + 3b = 8a + 7b$   (b) $5p + p + 3p = 9p$

(c) $ab + 3b + 2b = ab + 5b$   (d) $4x^2 + 3x + 2x^2 + 6x = 6x^2 + 9x$
    (*ab* is *not* like 3*b*)

(e) $7a + 3 + 2a = 9a + 3$

### M4. 3

Collect like terms

**1** $3a + 4b + 2a$    **2** $5a + 6a + a$    **3** $3a + 4a + 4b$

**4** $4p + 8q + 3p$    **5** $9p + 2p + 5q$    **6** $3p + 4q + 5q + 4p$

**7** $8p + 5p + 6q + 2q$    **8** $7x + 5y - 3x$    **9** $7x + 3y - 7x$

**10** $5x + 7y - 4y$    **11** $5a + 6a - 2a$    **12** $6x + 9x + 4y$

**13** $8x - 3x + 4x$    **14** $9x - 5x + 2y$    **15** $6a + 3 + 5a - 2$

**16** $9x - 3 + 3x - 5x$    **17** $8p + 4q + 4q - 3p$    **18** $6c + 3c - 2 + 5c$

**19** $8a + 3a + 7a + 4$    **20** $6x + 4y + 5y - 2x$    **21** $6c + 3 + 6 - 3c$

Find the perimeter of each shape in Questions **22** to **25**. Simplify each answer.

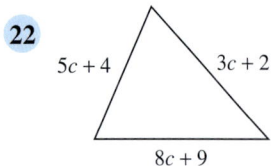

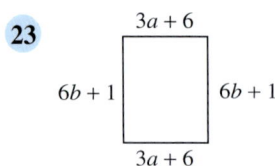

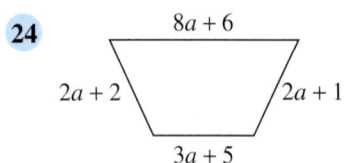

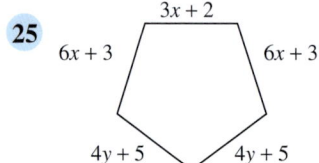

**22** Triangle with sides $5c + 4$, $3c + 2$, $8c + 9$

**23** Rectangle with sides $3a + 6$, $6b + 1$, $6b + 1$, $3a + 6$

**24** Trapezium with sides $8a + 6$, $2a + 2$, $2a + 1$, $3a + 5$

**25** Pentagon with sides $3x + 2$, $6x + 3$, $6x + 3$, $4y + 5$, $4y + 5$

102

Simplify Questions **26** to **35**.

**26** $8m - 3m + 2n$      **27** $8a - 3a + 6b + 2b$

**28** $a + 6b - a - 3b$      **29** $8x + 7y + 3x + 6x$

**30** $9a + 3a + 10 - 4a$      **31** $5x - 2x + 8x + 6 - 2$

**32** $4p + 6q + 3q - 8q - 2p$      **33** $5a + 8 - 3 + 2 + 3a$

**34** $6a + 9a - 10a + 3b - 2$      **35** $8x - 6x + 2y + 3x - y$

## E4. 3

Simplify

**1** $8a + a$      **2** $-5c + 7c$      **3** $-7a + a$

**4** $-b + 6b$      **5** $-a + a$      **6** $8a - 3b + 2a + 6b$

**7** $8p + 3q - p + 4q$      **8** $4m - 2n + 6m$      **9** $3a + 2b - 5a - b$

**10** $a + 4b - a - 3b$      **11** $4a + b - 3b - 2a$      **12** $6x + 2x - 8x - 3x$

**13** $6p - 2 + 8 - 2p$      **14** $5p - 3p - 6p - 2$      **15** $5a - 1 - 1 - a$

**16** $6x - 3y + 2y - x$      **17** $3a + 6a + 8 - 10$      **18** $5c - 2c - c - 7$

**19** $8p - 3p + 2q - 8p$      **20** $9a - 3 - 6 - 4a$      **21** $6x - 3x - 8 + 3$

**22**

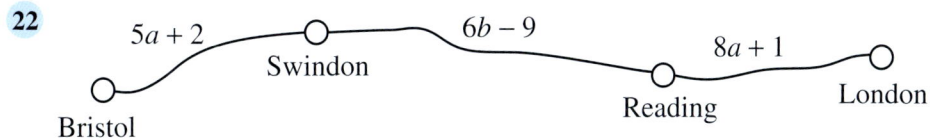

Bristol — $5a + 2$ — Swindon — $6b - 9$ — Reading — $8a + 1$ — London

Use algebra to show how far it is between:

  (a) Bristol and London

  (b) Bristol and Reading

  (c) Swindon and London

**23**

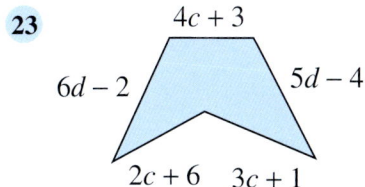

Find the perimeter of this shape.

Simplify your answer.

Simplify Questions **24** to **41**.

**24** $3x + x^2 + 5x$

**25** $4x^2 + 3x^2 + 5x^2$

**26** $3x^2 + 6x + 2x + 4x^2$

**27** $8a^2 + 3a + 4a^2 + 6a$

**28** $3ab + a + 2ab$

**29** $6ab + 3a + 2a + 2ab$

**30** $4xy + 2xy - 3xy$

**31** $5xy - 2 - 3 - 2xy$

**32** $9ab + 3ab + 6 + 5ab$

**33** $6xy - 3xy + 5xy - 2xy$

**34** $7ab + 3ab - 2a + 4b$

**35** $5xy - 2xy + 3x - 6x$

**36** $4a^2 + a^2 + 9 - 2$

**37** $7a^2 - 3a + 5a^2 - 2a$

**38** $3ab + 2a^2 + 4ab + 5a^2$

**39** $6x^2 + 3x + 3x^2 - x + y^2 - y$

**40** $8a + 3a^2 - 2a + 4ab - a^2$

**41** $5pq + 3pq - p + 6p - 10pq$

Can you still?

## (4A) Fractions–Decimals (see Unit 2)

Can you still?

Change the fractions below into decimals:

**1.** $\dfrac{7}{100}$  **2.** $\dfrac{19}{100}$  **3.** $\dfrac{3}{4}$  **4.** $\dfrac{1}{5}$  **5.** $\dfrac{3}{20}$  **6.** $\dfrac{9}{25}$

Change the decimals below into fractions:

**7.** 0.3   **8.** 0.67   **9.** 0.25   **10.** 0.4   **11.** 0.08   **12.** 0.32

In Questions **13** to **15** below, write down which number is the larger:

**13.** $\boxed{0.7}$ or $\dfrac{4}{5}$   **14.** $\boxed{0.28}$ or $\dfrac{6}{25}$   **15.** $\dfrac{7}{20}$ or $\boxed{0.34}$

## Simplifying terms

(a) $4a \times 2 = 8a$    $c \times c = c^2$

(b) $3a \times 2a = 6a^2$   {multiply numbers first then the letters}

(c) $3m \times 2n = 6mn$     $5y \times y = 5y^2$

(d) $6a \div 2 = 3a$     $28n \div 7 = 4n$

### M4. 4

Do the following multiplications and divisions.

**1** $4x \times 2$    **2** $3x \times 5$    **3** $8x \times 2$    **4** $4y \times 2$

**5** $5y \times 4$    **6** $7a \times 6$    **7** $8x \times 10$    **8** $4a \times 9$

**9** $3d \times 6$    **10** $6 \times 4c$    **11** $9 \times 4p$    **12** $5 \times 9x$

**13** $7 \times 2c$    **14** $9 \times 3d$    **15** $6 \times 8x$    **16** $8x \div 4$

**17** $24x \div 4$    **18** $4p \div 2$    **19** $20x \div 4$    **20** $21A \div 3$

**21** $27Q \div 9$    **22** $42n \div 6$    **23** $9A \div 3$    **24** $36N \div 4$

**25** $16r \div 4$    **26** $90t \div 9$    **27** $48T \div 4$    **28** $35a \div 5$

**29** $80R \div 10$    **30** $12b \div 3$    **31** $a \times a$    **32** $c \times c$

**33** $Q \times Q$    **34** $3c \times c$    **35** $4p \times p$    **36** $5d \times d$

**37** $r \times 2r$    **38** $B \times B$    **39** $c \times 5c$    **40** $a \times 6a$

**41** $2a \times 4b$    **42** $3y \times 6y$    **43** $7a \times 2a$    **44** $5t \times 5t$

### E4. 4

Do the following multiplications and divisions.

**1** $3a \times 2b$    **2** $6x \times 3y$    **3** $5p \times 2q$    **4** $7e \times 3e$

**5** $8m \times 3n$    **6** $6c \times 9c$    **7** $3x \times 8x$    **8** $2B \times 8B$

**9** $5P \times 9Q$    **10** $3v \times 12u$     **11** $8c \div 2$    **12** $15A \div 3$

**13** $64p \div 8$    **14** $72x \div 9$     **15** $a \times b \times c$    **16** $3a \times 2b \times 2c$

**17** $4x \times 3y \times 5z$    **18** $2a \times 6b \times 3c \times 2d$

In Questions **19** to **33** answer 'true' or 'false'.

**19** $c \times d = cd$     **20** $n \times n = n^2$

**21** $2n \times 3n = 5n^2$     **22** $a \times 3a = 3a^2$

**23** $p + p = p^2$     **24** $3 \times a = a \times 3$

**25** $8n \times 4n = 32n^2$     **26** $10a \div 2 = 5a$

**27** $3c \times 12d = 36cd$     **28** $12p \div 3 = 9p$

**29** $3a - a = 3$     **30** $4n + 4n = 8n^2$

**31** $n \times n \times n = n^3$     **32** $a + a^2 = a^3$

**33** $m \times 3 \times n = 3mn$

Simplify

**34** $m \times -m$    **35** $2a \times -3b$    **36** $-4c \times 5d$    **37** $-2x \times -4y$

**38** $-9y \div 3$    **39** $-6a \div -2$    **40** $-8P \div 4$    **41** $-6c \times -3d$

**42** $8x \times -5y$    **43** $28q \div -4$    **44** $-9y \times 6$    **45** $3a \times -7a$

**46** $-14x \div -2$    **47** $18a \times -3b$    **48** $-9P \times -6P$

*Can you still?*

**4B** **Negative numbers (see Unit 1)**

*Can you still?*

Work out

**1.** $-3 + 1$    **2.** $-8 - 2$    **3.** $-6 + 7$    **4.** $-9 + 3$    **5.** $2 - 10$

**6.** $-5 - -1$    **7.** $-10 - 3$    **8.** $-9 - -4$    **9.** $-9 - 4$    **10.** $-5 - -5$

**11.** $-6 \times 4$    **12.** $-8 \times -3$    **13.** $-6 \times -5$    **14.** $-6 \times 3$    **15.** $8 \times -2$

**16.** $-8 \div 2$    **17.** $-24 \div -3$    **18.** $-36 \div 9$    **19.** $42 \div -7$    **20.** $-56 \div -8$

## Multiplying out brackets

(a) Multiply out $2(3 + 5)$ means $2 \times 3$ add $2 \times 5 = 6 + 10 = 16$

(b) Multiply out $2(a + b)$ means $2 \times a$ add $2 \times b = 2a + 2b$

(c) Expand $3(5a - 4)$ means $3 \times 5a$ subtract $3 \times 4 = 15a - 12$

(d) Expand $a(b + c)$ means $a \times b$ add $a \times c = ab + ac$

(e) Multiply out $p(2q - 3)$ means $p \times 2q$ subtract $p \times 3 = 2pq - 3p$

(f) Expand $n(n + 2)$ means $n \times n$ add $n \times 2 = n^2 + 2n$

(g) Expand $5n(2n + 3)$ means $5n \times 2n$ add $5n \times 3 = 10n^2 + 15n$

### M4. 5

Multiply out

**1** $2(a + 3)$     **2** $8(2y - 1)$     **3** $6(4x - 2)$     **4** $5(3x + 4)$

**5** $7(3x - 5)$     **6** $4(7y + 2)$     **7** $5(a - b)$     **8** $2(2a + b)$

**9** $7(3x + y)$     **10** $3(x + 2y)$     **11** $6(3x + 2)$     **12** $4(p + q)$

**13** $4(p + 2q)$     **14** $6(3a - 5b)$     **15** $9(4c + 8d)$     **16** $x(x + y)$

**17** $x(2x + y)$     **18** $a(b - c)$     **19** $a(b + a)$     **20** $p(p - q)$

**21** $c(2c + d)$     **22** $p(p + 3)$     **23** $a(a - 7)$     **24** $3a(a + 1)$

**25** $5x(y + 2)$     **26** $3b(c + 2d)$     **27** $4a(a + 2b)$     **28** $3m(2m - 5n)$

**29** $6a(4b - 8c)$     **30** $3x(2x + 3y)$

(a) Multiply out $-4(x - 2)$ means $-4 \times x$ and $-4 \times -2 = -4x + 8$

(b) Expand $-3(2a + 4)$ means $-3 \times 2a$ and $-3 \times 4 = -6a - 12$

(c) Expand $-a(a + b)$ means $-a \times a$ and $-a \times b = -a^2 - ab$

(d) Multiply out $-b(b - c)$ means $-b \times b$ and $-b \times -c = -b^2 + bc$

Expand

**1** $-2(x + 6)$    **2** $-5(y - 3)$    **3** $-3(a - 2)$    **4** $-2(x + 4)$

**5** $-5(c + 10)$    **6** $-2(3x - y)$    **7** $-4(3p - 5)$    **8** $-5(2a + 1)$

**9** $-4(8b - 2)$    **10** $-3(2c + 4)$    **11** $-3(5a + 2)$    **12** $-6(3x - 3)$

**13** $-4(5a - 6)$    **14** $3(3b - 7)$    **15** $7(1 - 2x)$    **16** $-a(b + c)$

**17** $-e(f - g)$    **18** $-x(x - y)$    **19** $-p(2p + q)$    **20** $-y(3y + z)$

**21** $-x(2x - y)$    **22** $-a(a + b)$    **23** $-m(m - n)$    **24** $-(3x - y)$

**25** $-(2p + 5q)$    **26** $-3a(a + b)$    **27** $2b(3a - 2b)$    **28** $5x(3x - 2y)$

---

(a) Simplify    $2(3n + 1) + 3n$    { multiply out brackets first }

         $= 6n + 2 + 3n$    { now collect like terms }

   Answer $= 9n + 2$

(b) Simplify    $3(2a + 2) + 4(a + 1)$

         $= 6a + 6 + 4a + 4$

   Answer $= 10a + 10$

---

Simplify

**1** $2(x + 3) + 5$        **2** $5(2x + 1) + 3$

**3** $4(3x + 2) + 2x$        **4** $5(3x + 4) + 7x$

**5** $9(2x + 3) - 14$        **6** $3(2a + 4) - 2a$

**7** $6(4a + 3) - 8a$        **8** $9(3y + 2) - 6$

**9** $5(a + 2) + 2(2a + 1)$        **10** $3(x + 4) + 6(x + 2)$

**11** $6(x + 1) + 3(2x + 4)$

**12** $5(2a + 3) + 4(a - 2)$

**13** $3(4a + 8) + 2(a - 3)$

**14** $7(2x + 3) + 4(3x + 1)$

**15** $4(2d + 2) + 6(3d + 4)$

**16** $6x + 9 + 3(4x + 2)$

**17** $3a + 2(4a + 7) - 10$

**18** $8(2x + 1) + 3(4x - 1)$

**19** $6a + 3(2a + 4) + 2(5a + 4)$

**20** $3x + 2(3x + 4) + 5(2x - 1)$

---

(a) Simplify $\underbrace{5(2a + 1)}\underbrace{- 3(a - 2)}$

$= 10a + 5 - 3a + 6$

⬆ Note

$= 7a + 11$

(b) Simplify $\underbrace{8(x + 3)}\underbrace{- 2(2x + 4)}$

$= 8x + 24 - 4x - 8$

⬆ Note

$= 4x + 16$

---

**E4. 6**

Expand and simplify

**1** $3(4a + 2) - 2(a - 2)$

**2** $5(3x + 1) - 3(3x - 2)$

**3** $6(2x + 3) - 4(2x + 2)$

**4** $5(3a + 2) - 3(2a + 1)$

**5** $3(4d + 1) - 2(6d - 5)$

**6** $9y - 5(y + 2) - 3$

**7** $11x + 2 - 3(2x - 5)$

**8** $6a + 2(3a + 1) - 7 + 2a$

**9** $9(x + 2) - 4 + 2(2 - 3x)$

**10** $6(c + 3) - 2(2c - 4)$

**11** $7(3a + 2) - 2(5a - 4)$

**12** $8(c + 9) - 3(2c + 6)$

**13** $5(2c + 6) - 4(c + 5)$

**14** $8x - 4(x - 9) - 10$

**15** $3a + 11 - 2(a + 3)$

**16** $9(3a + 4) + 2a - 4(2a - 3)$

**17** $15(n + m) - 6(2n - m)$

**18** $8(2a + b) - 3(3a + 2b)$

**19** $5(3x + 6) - 4(2x - 3)$

**20** $8x + 6(2 - x) + 2(3x + 5)$

## Key Facts

**Multiplying out 2 brackets**

Each term in one bracket must be multiplied by each term in the other bracket.

Consider $(a+b)(c+d)$

| | |
|---|---|
| F | $(a+b)(c+d)$ multiply the First terms in each bracket $\Rightarrow$ $ac$ |
| O | $(a+b)(c+d)$ multiply the Outer terms in each bracket $\Rightarrow$ $+ad$ |
| I | $(a+b)(c+d)$ multiply the Inner terms in each bracket $\Rightarrow$ $+bc$ |
| L | $(a+b)(c+d)$ multiply the Last terms in each bracket $\Rightarrow$ $+bd$ |

First ⎫
Outer ⎬ follow this order each time to make sure you do not miss any terms
Inner ⎪
Last ⎭

$\Rightarrow$ $(a+b)(c+d) = ac + ad + bc + b$

---

(a) Multiply out $(x + 3)(x + 5)$

$(x + 3)(x + 5)$

$\phantom{=}$ F $\phantom{x}$ O $\phantom{x}$ I $\phantom{x}$ L
$= x^2 + 5x + 3x + 15$

these middle 2 terms can be collected together

$= x^2 + 8x + 15$

(b) Expand $(x + 4)(x + 2)$

$(x + 4)(x + 2)$

$= x^2 + 2x + 4x + 8$

$= x^2 + 6x + 8$

---

**M4. 7**

**1** Copy and complete the following

(a) $(x + 3)(x + 4)$

$= x^2 + 4x + \square + 12$

$= x^2 + \square + 12$

(b) $(x + 1)(x + 6)$

$= \square + 6x + x + \square$

$= \square + 7x + \square$

(c) $(x + 9)(x + 4)$

$= x^2 + \square + \square + 36$

$= x^2 + \square + 36$

110

Expand the following

**2** $(x + 2)(x + 6)$  **3** $(p + 1)(p + 5)$  **4** $(a + 3)(a + 7)$

**5** $(m + 2)(m + 8)$  **6** $(y + 3)(y + 6)$  **7** $(n + 1)(n + 1)$

Multiply out the following:

**8** $(x + 7)(x + 3)$  **9** $(y + 4)(y + 5)$  **10** $(p + 3)(p + 10)$

**11** $(a + 9)(a + 7)$  **12** $(f + 4)(f + 8)$  **13** $(y + 6)(y + 8)$

Find the area of each rectangle below

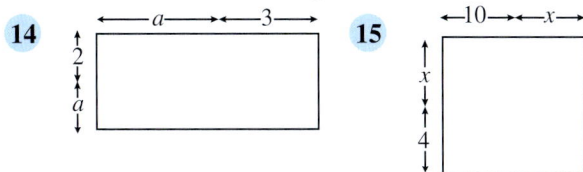  **15**

Expand  **16** $(x + 3)(x + 3)$  **17** $(x + 3)^2$  **18** $(x + 5)^2$

**19** $(x + 8)^2$  **20** $(x + 2)^2$  **21** $(x + 9)^2$

---

(a)  Expand $(x - 4)(x + 2)$

$(x - 4)(x + 2)$

$= x^2 + 2x - 4x - 8 = x^2 - 2x - 8$

(b)  Expand $(x - 5)^2$

$(x - 5)(x - 5)$

$= x^2 - 5x - 5x + 25 = x^2 - 10x + 25$

---

**E4. 7**

(1)  Copy and complete the following

(a) $(x + 2)(x - 6)$

$= x^2 - \square + 2x - 12$

$= x^2 - \square - 12$

(b) $(a - 5)(a + 3)$

$= \square + 3a - 5a - \square$

$= \square - 2a - \square$

(c) $(m - 7)^2 = (m - 7)(m - 7)$

$= m^2 - \square - \square + \square$

$= m^2 - \square + \square$

Expand  **2** $(m + 3)(m - 1)$  **3** $(n - 5)(n + 2)$  **4** $(b - 8)(b + 3)$

**5** $(x - 6)(x + 8)$  **6** $(c - 8)(c - 3)$  **7** $(q - 2)(q - 7)$

**8** $(f - 2)(f - 10)$  **9** $(a + 9)(a - 4)$  **10** $(y - 4)(y - 9)$

**11** $(x - 4)(x - 4)$  **12** $(x - 4)^2$  **13** $(x - 6)^2$

**14** $(m - 1)^2$  **15** $(y - 10)^2$  **16** $(a - 8)^2$

**17** $(2 + n)(n + 3)$  **18** $(x + 5)(6 + x)$  **19** $(y + 4)(3 - y)$

**20** $(x + 1)^2 + (x + 3)^2$  **21** $(n + 4)^2 + (n - 2)^2$

**(4C) Ordering decimals (see Unit 2)**

For each Question below write out the decimals in order of size, starting with the smallest.

**1.** 0.04, 0.4, 0.35

**2.** 0.1, 0.09, 0.089

**3.** 0.04, 0.14, 0.2, 0.53

**4.** 1.2, 0.12, 0.21, 1.12

**5.** 2.4, 2.04, 0.85, 0.09

**6.** 0.73, 0.37, 0.703, 0.4, 0.137

**7.** 0.091, 0.19, 0.109, 0.901, 0.91

**8.** 0.86, 0.816, 0.608, 0.68, 0.628, 0.806

## Common factors

# 🔑 Key Facts

We know that $3(a + b)$ is the same as $3a + 3b$ so $3a + 3b = 3(a + b)$

Consider

$3a$  $+ 3b$

$3 \times a$    $3 \times b$

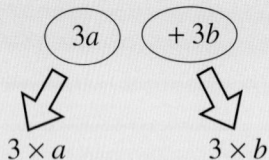

3 is *a factor* of both $3a$ and $3b$

so 3 is the *common factor* of $3a$ and $3b$

Common factors can be extracted from algebraic expressions.

Take out common factor 3.

$3a + 3b$ ⟹ Write remaining terms in a bracket ⟹ $3(a + b)$

Multiply out bracket to check you have the same expression you started with

This is called '*factorising*' $3a + 3b$

**Examples**

Factorise $7x - 7y$

$7x$ and $7y$ have common factor 7

so $7x - 7y = 7(x - y)$

Factorise $5a + 10b$

5 divides into $5a$ and $10b$

so $5a$ and $10b$ have common factor 5

so $5a + 10b = 5(a + 2b)$

112

Copy and complete

**1** $6a + 15 = 3(2a + \square)$

**2** $9c + 6 = 3(3c + \square)$

**3** $5x - 15 = 5(x - \square)$

**4** $12a + 18 = 6(\square + 3)$

**5** $15m + 20 = 5(\square + \square)$

**6** $7n - 35 = 7(\square - \square)$

**7** $8x + 32 = \square(x + \square)$

**8** $9x + 36 = 9(\square + \square)$

**9** $14a - 35 = 7(2a - \square)$

**10** $16n - 24 = 8(2n - \square)$

**11** $45x + 36 = \square(\square + \square)$

**12** $48a - 40 = \square(\square - \square)$

Factorise the expressions below:

**13** $8a + 10$

**14** $6x + 27$

**15** $5x - 20$

**16** $6m + 42$

**17** $25a - 35$

**18** $16x - 4$

**19** $27p - 18$

**20** $18a + 24b$

**21** $16x + 40y$

**22** $14a - 21b$

**23** $24m - 20n$

**24** $21x + 28y$

**25** $56a + 32b$

**26** $20x - 10y$

**27** $36x - 27y$

**28** $72c + 40d$

**29** $10a + 15b + 25c$

**30** $6p + 9q + 3r$

**31** $7x + 14y - 7z$

**32** $9a - 9b - 21c$

**33** $24m + 12n + 16p$

**34** $42a + 35b - 14$

**35** $18a - 27b + 36c$

**36** $28x - 36y + 16$

Letters as well as numbers can be the common factors.

(a) Factorise $ab + ac$

$ab$ and $ac$ have common factor $a$

So $ab + ac = a(b + c)$   **multiply out to check the answer is correct**

(b) Factorise $5ac + 15bc$

$5ac$ and $15bc$ have common factor $5c$

so $5ac + 15bc = 5c(a + 3b)$

Factorise $4x^2 - 6x$

$4x^2$ and $6x$ have common factor $2x$

so $4x^2 - 6x = 2x(2x - 3)$

Copy and complete

**1** $xy + xz = x(y + \square)$

**2** $ab - ac = a(\square - \square)$

**3** $x^2 + 6x = x(x + \square)$

**4** $5a + a^2 = a(5 + \square)$

**5** $3b^2 - 12b = 3b(\square - \square)$

**6** $cd + c^2 = c(\square + \square)$

**7** $3xy + 15xz = 3x(y + \square)$

**8** $8ab - 24bc = 8b(\square - \square)$

**9** $12x^2 - 8x = \square(3x - \square)$

**10** $6m^2 - m = \square(6m - \square)$

Factorise the expressions below:

**11** $ef + fg$

**12** $p^2 + 3p$

**13** $7a - a^2$

**14** $x^2 - 8x$

**15** $a^2 + 5a$

**16** $2pq + 4pr$

**17** $8ab - 12bc$

**18** $6xy - 9yz$

**19** $5x^2 - 15x$

**20** $5st + 35s$

**21** $8pr - 40pq$

**22** $6ab + 4b$

**23** $3a^2 + 8a$

**24** $12x - 16x^2$

**25** $x^2 + xy$

**26** $3x^2 + 21xy$

**27** $20ab - 50b$

**28** $a^2b - a^2c$

**29** $a^2 + abc$

**30** $5x^2 - 6xy$

**31** $20p^2 - 30pq$

**32** $36abc - 16b^2$

**33** $49x^2 + 42xy$

**34** $63a^2 - 35ab$

## WATCH YOUR MONEY! – Money for your holilday

**Exchange rate**

This is the amount of foreign money you will get in exchange for £1.

At the time of writing:

| | |
|---|---|
| £1 = 1.45 euros (Europe) | £1 = 51.18 rubles (Russia) |
| £1 = 1.82 dollars (USA) | £1 = 19.84 pesos (Mexico) |
| £1 = 196 yen (Japan) | £1 = 6.84 riyals (Saudi Arabia) |
| £1 = 11.98 rand (South Africa) | £1 = 2.39 dollars (Australia) |

## Converting pounds into foreign money

> Multiply the number of pounds by the chosen exchange rate

### Examples

£1 = 1.82 dollars (USA)

so £10 = 10 × 1.82 = 18.2 dollars

£1 = 51.18 rubles (Russia)

so £300 = 300 × 51.18 = 15354 rubles.

## Converting foreign money into pounds

> Divide the foreign money by the chosen exchange rate

### Examples

£1 = 196 yen (Japan)

4508 yen = 4508 ÷ 196 = £23

£1 = 1.45 euros

150 euros = 150 ÷ 1.45 = £103.448276

= £103.45 (to the nearest penny)

> Beware!

When converting your money, the bank (or whatever organization you use) will charge you a fee. This is called the 'commission'.

Different organizations charge different amounts of commission. Always look around for the best deal.

### WYM4

Using the exchange rate at the start of this section, convert the following amount of money.

1  £200 into euros

2  £350 into pesos

3  £150 into Australian dollars

4  £900 into rand

5  300.3 american dollars into pounds

6  11904 pesos into pounds

7  13328 yen into pounds

8  £454 into riyals

9  1015 euros into pounds

10  17970 rand into pounds

11 A digital radio cost £164 in the UK. Sarah sees a similar digital radio for 31360 yen in Japan. In which country is the digital radio cheaper?

12 Jonathan was lucky enough to have two holidays last year, one in France and one in Australia. A can of cola was 1.16 euros in France and 1.68 dollars in Australia. In which country was the can of cola cheaper?

13 Candice comes back from holiday in Mexico with 992 pesos. Shabina returns from holiday in the USA with 98.28 dollars. Who has more money left?

14 Stephen takes 547.2 riyals to a Bureau de change to convert them into pounds. The Bureau de Change charges 4% commission. How much money does Stephen get back?

15 Maggie takes 2047.2 rubles to a bank to change them into pounds. The bank charges 3% commission. How much money does Maggie get back?

## TEST YOURSELF ON UNIT 4

### 1. Substituting numbers for letters

Find the value of each expression below:

(a) $5a$ if $a = 3$

(b) $3x - 4$ if $x = 7$

(c) $p^2$ if $p = 9$

(d) $2(c + d)$ if $c = 3, d = 8$

(e) $a(3b + 4)$ if $a = 5, b = 3$

(f) $5 + 7a$ if $a = -2$

(g) $3b^2$ if $b = 2$

### 2. Using formulas

(a) $y = 6x - 1$    Find the value of $y$ when $x = 3$

(b) $a = \dfrac{b}{4} + 6$    Find the value of $a$ when $b = 20$

(c) $V = IR$    Find the value of $V$ when $I = 6.2, R = 20.1$

(d) $v = u + at$    Find the value of $v$ when $u = 10, a = 5, t = 7$

(e) $f = \dfrac{u + v}{u}$    Find the value of $f$ when $u = 0.6, v = 3.6$

Simplify

(a) $3x + 7y + 3x$  (b) $9a + 6b - 4a$  (c) $4p + 2 + 3p$

(d) $8m - 2m + 3n + n$  (e) $5 + 2x - 2 + 3x$  (f) $6x - 5x$

(g) $3p + 2q - q$  (h) $x^2 + x^2 + x^2$  (i) $4a + 2ab + 3ab$

## 4. Multiplying and dividing terms

Simplify

(a) $5a \times 3$  (b) $7 \times 2c$  (c) $A \times A$  (d) $3b \times 2b$

(e) $6p \div 2$  (f) $45b \div 5$  (g) $6m \times 4n$  (h) $12F \div 3$

## 5. Multiplying out brackets

Expand (this means 'multiply out')

(a) $3(x + 7)$  (b) $6(2a - b)$  (c) $5(x + 5y)$  (d) $p(q + 6)$

(e) $a(2a - 5)$  (f) $b(2b + 3c)$  (g) $3x(y - 2x)$  (h) $-4(2a - b)$

(i) $(x + 3)(x + 7)$  (j) $(y + 2)(y - 6)$  (k) $(p - 2)^2$

## 6. Multiplying out brackets and collecting like terms

(a) $5(a + 2) + 3$  (b) $5(2x + 4) - 3x$

(c) $3(x + 2) + 5(x + 6)$  (d) $4(2m + 3) + 5(3m + 1)$

(e) $3(6a + 3) - 2(2a - 5)$  (f) $4x - 3(x - 2)$

## 7. Extracting common factors

(a) $5x + 15$  (b) $8a - 24$  (c) $35p - 21$  (d) $4a + 10b - 8c$

(e) $cd + ce$  (f) $x^2 - 4xy$  (g) $6pq - 10qr$  (h) $5a^2 + 30ab$

**1** Use the formula $v = u + at$

to calculate $v$ when $u = 5$, $a = 3$ and $t = 10$.

**2** (a) Simplify    (i) $5c + 2c - 3c$     (ii) $5p - 8r + 12r - 6p$

(b) Find the value of

    (i) $5x + 2y$ when $x = 3$ and $y = 6$.

    (ii) $4g - 2h$ when $g = 2$ and $h = -4$.        (EDEXCEL)

**3** (a) Simplify $3a - 2a + a$.

(b) What is the value of $x^2 + 5$ when $x$ is $-3$?        (AQA)

**4** Tom spilt some coffee on his Maths work.

It had already been marked correct.

Part of the work could no longer be seen.

$$3x + 2y - 4z + \boxed{\phantom{xxxxxxxxx}} = 5x + y$$

Work out the expression that has been covered by the spill.        (OCR)

**5** (a) Simplify $2x - x + 1$.

(b) Find the value of $3x + y^2$ when $x = -2$ and $y = 3$.        (AQA)

**6** (a) In this question $a = 5$, $b = -4$ and $c = 3$.

    Work out    (i) $a^2 + b$     (ii) $\dfrac{ab}{2c - b}$

(b) Multiply out the brackets $7(2x + 3y)$.        (OCR)

**7** Simplify

(a) $x + x + x$

(b) $2a + 4b + a - 2b$

(c) Expand $3(a + 2)$

(d) Expand and simplify $2(x - 1) + 3(2x + 1)$        (EDEXCEL)

**8** (a) Simplify      (i) $5p + 3q - 4q$      (ii) $3x \times 4y$

(b) Multiply out  (i) $5(3h - 2)$          (ii) $-(3r - 4)$                    (EDEXCEL)

**9** This is an approximate rule to change a temperature in degree Celsius ($C$), into one in degrees Fahrenheit ($F$):

**Double the Celsius temperature then add 30**

(a) Write this approximate rule as a formula for $F$ in terms of $C$.

(b) Use your formula, or otherwise, to find

(i) $F$ when $C = 54$        (ii) $C$ when $F = 54$                        (CCEA)

**10** Multiply out the brackets and simplify this expression.

$3(2x + 3) + 2(4x - 1)$                                    (OCR)

**11** Factorise      (i) $10x + 15$      (ii) $x^2 - 3x$                    (OCR)

**12** Factorise      $a^2 + 3a$.                                    (AQA)

**13**

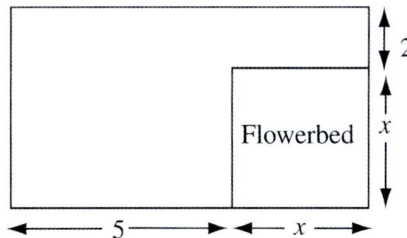

The diagram represents a garden in the shape of a rectangle.

All measurements are given in metres.

The garden has a flowerbed in one corner.

The flowerbed is a square of side $x$.

(a) Write down an expression, in terms of $x$, for the shortest side of the garden.

(b) Find an expression, in terms of $x$, for the perimeter of the garden. Give your answer in its simplest form.                    (EDEXCEL)

# NUMBER 3

**5**

In this unit you will learn how to:

In this unit you will learn how to:

– write one number as a fraction of another number

– find a fraction of a number

– convert improper fractions and mixed numbers

– add and subtract fractions

– multiply fractions

– divide fractions

– WATCH YOUR MONEY! – Mobile phones

## One number as a fraction of another number

### M5. 1

**1** Which of these squares are split into quarters?

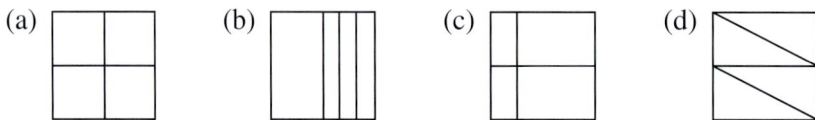

(a)  (b)  (c)  (d) 

**2** What fraction of each of these shapes is shaded?

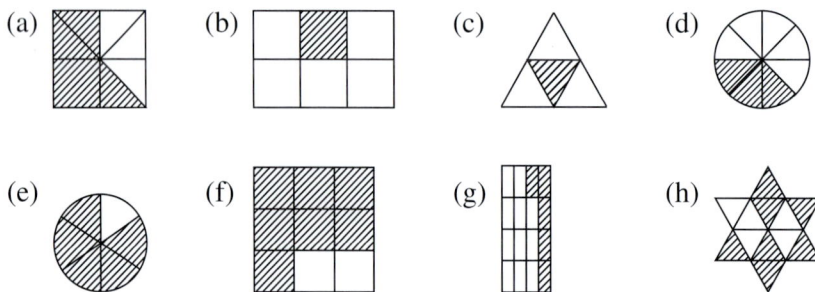

(a)  (b)  (c)  (d) 

(e)  (f)  (g)  (h)

**3** In a class of 33 students, 18 are girls.

   (a) What fraction of the class are girls?

   (b) What fraction of the class are boys?

**4** What fraction of these people have spiky hair?

**5** In a class of 30 students, 25 are right-handed. What fraction are left-handed? (Try and cancel your answer)

**6** What fraction of these shapes are squares?

**7** 2, 3 and 5 are prime numbers.

What fraction of these numbers are prime?

| 8 | 2 | 5 | 6 | 4 | 5 | 2 |
|---|---|---|---|---|---|---|
| 6 | 8 | 4 | 4 | 2 | 9 | 3 |
| 9 | 8 | 9 | 3 | 6 | 4 | 8 |

**8** What fraction of £1 is:

   (a) 10p   (b) 25p   (c) 40p   (d) 3p   (e) 65p   (f) 48p

> Try to cancel your answers

**9** What fraction of the numbers from zero to ninety-nine contain the number 8?

**10** Find $\dfrac{1}{4}$ of:   (a) 12   (b) 28   (c) 52   (d) 100

**11** Find $\dfrac{1}{3}$ of:   (a) 15   (b) 27   (c) 24   (d) 60

**12** Find $\dfrac{1}{5}$ of:   (a) 15   (b) 40   (c) 60   (d) 100

Work out

**13** $\dfrac{1}{10}$ of £70   **14** $\dfrac{1}{7}$ of £49   **15** $\dfrac{1}{8}$ of 48 g   **16** $\dfrac{2}{3}$ of 12

**17** $\dfrac{3}{4}$ of 16   **18** $\dfrac{3}{5}$ of 40   **19** $\dfrac{4}{7}$ of 21   **20** $\dfrac{7}{10}$ of 50

**21** $\dfrac{2}{3}$ of these sheep are sold.

How many sheep are sold?

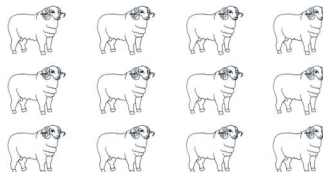

**22** The petrol tank of a car holds 60 litres. How much petrol is in the tank when it is $\frac{3}{5}$ full?

**23** $\frac{9}{10}$ of your body is made up of water.

Terri weighs 70 kg. How much of her body is water?

Work these out. You may **use a calculator** if you need to:

**24** $\frac{3}{4}$ of 24    **25** $\frac{3}{4}$ of £64    **26** $\frac{2}{9}$ of £378    **27** $\frac{2}{3}$ of 1275 m

**28** $\frac{3}{5}$ of 270    **29** $\frac{2}{3}$ of £144    **30** $\frac{3}{8}$ of £4976    **31** $\frac{1}{8}$ of 12 litres

**32** $\frac{2}{5}$ of 40    **33** $\frac{5}{8}$ of 112 cm    **34** $\frac{5}{7}$ of 175 kg    **35** $\frac{1}{10}$ of £75

---

A TV costs £440. In a sale $\frac{3}{8}$ of the price is knocked off.

How much does the TV cost now?

$\frac{3}{8}$ of 440 = (440 ÷ 8) × 3 = 55 × 3 = £165. 'Knockoff' £165.

TV costs 440 − 165 = £275

---

**E5. 1**

Work out

**1** $\frac{3}{4}$ of 44    **2** $\frac{3}{7}$ of 63    **3** $\frac{5}{6}$ of 18    **4** $\frac{4}{5}$ of 125

**5** Jenny earns £36 for her Saturday job. Jenny got $\frac{1}{3}$ extra as a Christmas bonus.

How much money does Jenny get in total?

**6** A packet of jelly tots has $\frac{3}{5}$ extra.

If a packet normally has 45 g in it, how much does it weigh now?

122

**7** | Sofa normal price £320
Sale
$\frac{3}{8}$ off!

How much does the sofa cost in the sale?

**8** Jesse's new jeans are 96 cm long when she buys them. After washing they shrink to $\frac{7}{8}$ of their previous length. What is the new length of the jeans?

**9** Dom has £28. He spends $\frac{3}{4}$ of his money on a Christmas present. How much money does he have left?

**10** Here are calculations with letters. Put the answers in order of size, smallest first. Write down the letters to make a word.

| C $\frac{4}{5}$ of 45 | F $\frac{5}{9}$ of 45 | R $\frac{3}{10}$ of 60 |
|---|---|---|

| E $\frac{3}{4}$ of 36 | P $\frac{2}{7}$ of 21 | T $\frac{7}{8}$ of 48 | E $\frac{5}{6}$ of 18 |
|---|---|---|---|

**11** Ollie gets £96 for Christmas. He spends $\frac{1}{2}$ of it on clothes and $\frac{3}{8}$ of it on music.

How much money does Ollie have left?

*Can you still?*

**5A** **Calculate angles (see Unit 3)**

*Can you still?*

Find the angles marked with the letters.

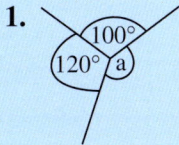

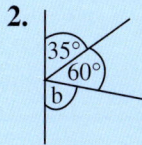

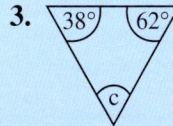

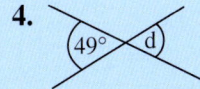

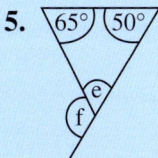

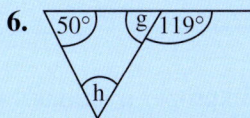

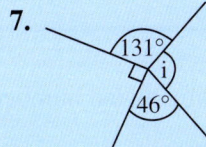

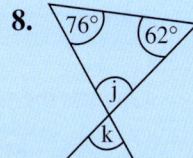

**1.** 100° 120° a

**2.** 35° 60° b

**3.** 38° 62° c

**4.** 49° d

**5.** 65° 50° e f

**6.** 50° g 119° h

**7.** 131° i 46°

**8.** 76° 62° j k

123

# Improper fractions and mixed numbers

Change the following improper fractions to mixed numbers.

**1** ⊘ ⊘ ⊘ ⊘ $\dfrac{7}{2}$  **2** ⊗ ⊗ ⊗ $\dfrac{13}{6}$

**3** ⊕ ⊕ ⊕ $\dfrac{11}{4}$  **4** ⊘ ⊘ ⊘ ⊘ $\dfrac{11}{3}$

**5** $\dfrac{9}{4} = 2\dfrac{\square}{4}$  **6** $\dfrac{15}{7} = \square\dfrac{\square}{7}$  **7** $\dfrac{25}{8} = \square\dfrac{\square}{8}$  **8** $\dfrac{7}{4} = \square\dfrac{\square}{4}$

**9** $\dfrac{20}{7}$  **10** $\dfrac{19}{9}$  **11** $\dfrac{5}{2}$  **12** $\dfrac{35}{6}$  **13** $\dfrac{23}{3}$  **14** $\dfrac{17}{2}$

**15** $\dfrac{41}{8}$  **16** $\dfrac{29}{5}$  **17** $\dfrac{17}{6}$  **18** $\dfrac{29}{9}$  **19** $\dfrac{44}{5}$  **20** $\dfrac{27}{4}$

---

Change $2\dfrac{3}{8}$ to an improper fraction.

Multiply whole number by denominator   $2 \times 8 = 16$

Add the numerator.        $16 + 3 = 19$

Put sum over denominator.        $\dfrac{19}{8}$

$2\left(=\dfrac{16}{8}\right) + \dfrac{3}{8}$  ⇨  $2\dfrac{3}{8} = \dfrac{19}{8}$

---

Change the following mixed numbers to improper fractions.

**1** ⊗ ⊗ ⊘ $2\dfrac{1}{3}$  **2** ⊘ ⊘ ⊘ ⊘ $3\dfrac{1}{2}$

**3** $4\dfrac{3}{4} = \dfrac{19}{\square}$  **4** $5\dfrac{2}{3} = \dfrac{17}{\square}$  **5** $4\dfrac{1}{2} = \dfrac{\square}{2}$  **6** $5\dfrac{3}{4} = \dfrac{\square}{4}$

**7** $6\frac{1}{3}$  **8** $3\frac{7}{8}$  **9** $4\frac{2}{3}$  **10** $5\frac{3}{5}$  **11** $3\frac{2}{9}$  **12** $4\frac{3}{7}$

**13** $8\frac{3}{4}$  **14** $7\frac{4}{9}$  **15** $9\frac{5}{7}$  **16** $6\frac{2}{5}$  **17** $8\frac{6}{7}$  **18** $5\frac{3}{8}$

Can you still?

Can you still?

(5B)  **Find angles in isosceles and equilateral triangles (see Unit 3)**

Find the angles marked with the letters.

**1.**

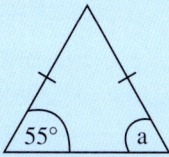

**2.**

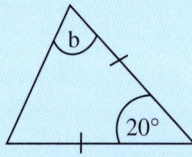

**3.**

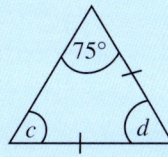

**4.**

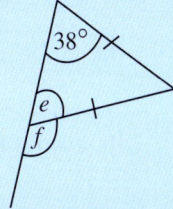

**5.**

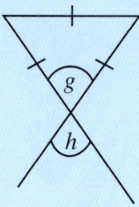

**6.**

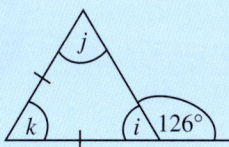

**7.**

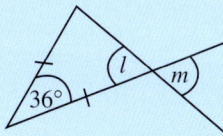

**8.**

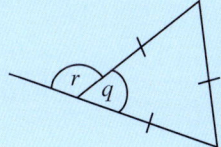

## Adding and subtracting fractions

(a) $\frac{1}{7} + \frac{2}{7} = \frac{3}{7}$ ⟶ add the numerators (top numbers)
⟶ denominator (bottom number) stays same.

(b) $\frac{3}{5} - \frac{2}{5} = \frac{1}{5}$ ⟶ subtract the numerators
⟶ denominator says same

(c) $\frac{1}{5} + \frac{1}{10} = \frac{2}{10} + \frac{1}{10} = \frac{3}{10}$   The denominators must be the same before adding.

(d) $\frac{3}{4} - \frac{1}{6} = \frac{9}{12} - \frac{2}{12} = \frac{7}{12}$   $\frac{3}{4} \overset{\times 3}{\underset{\times 3}{=}} \frac{9}{12}$ and $\frac{1}{6} \overset{\times 2}{\underset{\times 2}{=}} \frac{2}{12}$

Work out

**1** $\dfrac{2}{5} + \dfrac{1}{5}$    **2** $\dfrac{2}{7} + \dfrac{3}{7}$    **3** $\dfrac{5}{7} + \dfrac{1}{7}$    **4** $\dfrac{2}{9} + \dfrac{5}{9}$

**5** $\dfrac{3}{8} + \dfrac{3}{8}$    **6** $\dfrac{3}{10} + \dfrac{2}{10}$    **7** $\dfrac{5}{7} - \dfrac{3}{7}$    **8** $\dfrac{10}{11} - \dfrac{7}{11}$

**9** $\dfrac{11}{20} - \dfrac{3}{20}$    **10** $\dfrac{9}{10} - \dfrac{2}{10}$    **11** $\dfrac{8}{9} - \dfrac{5}{9}$    **12** $\dfrac{5}{8} - \dfrac{3}{8}$

**13** Add $\dfrac{2}{11}$ onto:    (a) $\dfrac{1}{11}$    (b) $\dfrac{3}{11}$    (c) $\dfrac{6}{11}$    (d) $\dfrac{7}{11}$    (e) $\dfrac{8}{11}$

**14** Subtract $\dfrac{2}{9}$ from :    (a) $\dfrac{7}{9}$    (b) $\dfrac{4}{9}$    (c) $\dfrac{8}{9}$    (d) $\dfrac{3}{9}$    (e) $\dfrac{5}{9}$

In Questions **15** to **17** , which answer is the odd one out?

**15** (a) $\dfrac{3}{7} + \dfrac{1}{7}$    (b) $\dfrac{6}{7} - \dfrac{2}{7}$    (c) $\dfrac{2}{7} + \dfrac{1}{7}$

**16** (a) $\dfrac{9}{10} - \dfrac{2}{10}$    (b) $\dfrac{3}{10} + \dfrac{6}{10}$    (c) $\dfrac{3}{10} + \dfrac{4}{10}$

**17** (a) $\dfrac{3}{5} + \dfrac{1}{5}$    (b) $\dfrac{4}{5} - \dfrac{1}{5}$    (c) $\dfrac{2}{5} + \dfrac{2}{5}$

Copy and complete Questions **18** to **20**

**18** $\dfrac{1}{5} + \dfrac{2}{3}$

$= \dfrac{3}{15} + \dfrac{\square}{15}$

$= \dfrac{\square}{15}$

**19** $\dfrac{3}{4} - \dfrac{2}{7}$

$= \dfrac{\square}{28} - \dfrac{\square}{28}$

$= \dfrac{\square}{28}$

**20** $\dfrac{3}{8} + \dfrac{3}{10}$

$= \dfrac{\square}{40} + \dfrac{\square}{40}$

$= \dfrac{\square}{\square}$

Work out

**21** $\dfrac{1}{3} + \dfrac{2}{15}$    **22** $\dfrac{5}{8} - \dfrac{1}{4}$    **23** $\dfrac{4}{5} + \dfrac{1}{10}$    **24** $\dfrac{1}{6} + \dfrac{2}{3}$

**25** $\dfrac{2}{5} + \dfrac{3}{10}$    **26** $\dfrac{5}{8} - \dfrac{1}{2}$    **27** $\dfrac{1}{10} - \dfrac{1}{20}$    **28** $\dfrac{7}{8} - \dfrac{1}{2}$

**29** $\dfrac{1}{3} - \dfrac{1}{4}$    **30** $\dfrac{1}{2} + \dfrac{1}{3}$    **31** $\dfrac{2}{3} + \dfrac{1}{4}$    **32** $\dfrac{3}{4} - \dfrac{1}{3}$

Copy and complete Questions **33** to **35** by changing to improper fractions

**33** $1\dfrac{1}{2}+\dfrac{1}{4}$  $\qquad$ **34** $2\dfrac{1}{4}+\dfrac{2}{3}$  $\qquad$ **35** $2\dfrac{1}{5}+1\dfrac{3}{4}$

$=\dfrac{\square}{2}+\dfrac{1}{4}$  $\qquad\qquad$ $=\dfrac{\square}{4}+\dfrac{2}{3}$  $\qquad\qquad$ $=\dfrac{\square}{5}+\dfrac{\square}{4}$

$=\dfrac{\square}{4}+\dfrac{1}{4}$  $\qquad\qquad$ $=\dfrac{\square}{12}+\dfrac{\square}{12}$  $\qquad\quad$ $=\dfrac{\square}{20}+\dfrac{\square}{20}$

$=\dfrac{\square}{4}=\square\dfrac{\square}{4}$  $\qquad\quad$ $=\dfrac{\square}{12}=\square\dfrac{\square}{12}$  $\qquad$ $=\dfrac{\square}{20}=\square\dfrac{\square}{20}$

Work out

**36** $2\dfrac{1}{3}+\dfrac{5}{8}$  $\quad$ **37** $1\dfrac{7}{8}+\dfrac{5}{6}$  $\quad$ **38** $5\dfrac{1}{2}+\dfrac{3}{5}$  $\quad$ **39** $2\dfrac{1}{3}+1\dfrac{1}{2}$

**40** Match each Question to the correct answer:

A $\boxed{\dfrac{3}{5}\ +\ 1\dfrac{1}{10}}$  $\qquad$ P $\boxed{2\dfrac{5}{8}}$

B $\boxed{1\dfrac{7}{8}\ +\ \dfrac{3}{4}}$  $\qquad$ Q $\boxed{1\dfrac{19}{20}}$  $\qquad$ S $\boxed{1\dfrac{4}{15}}$

C $\boxed{1\dfrac{7}{10}\ +\ \dfrac{1}{4}}$  $\qquad$ R $\boxed{1\dfrac{7}{10}}$

**41** Work out

(a) $1\dfrac{1}{2}-\dfrac{3}{8}$  (b) $1\dfrac{9}{10}-\dfrac{2}{5}$  (c) $2\dfrac{1}{10}-\dfrac{2}{3}$  (d) $3\dfrac{1}{4}-1\dfrac{1}{2}$

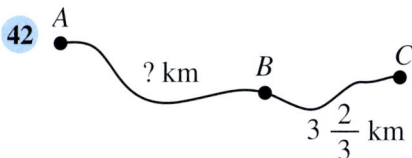

**42**

$A$

$B$  $\qquad$ $C$

? km

$3\dfrac{2}{3}$ km

The total distance along the road from $A$ to $C$ is $8\dfrac{1}{4}$ km.

What is the distance between $A$ and $B$ along the road?

**43** Work out

(a) $2\dfrac{3}{4}-\dfrac{2}{5}$  (b) $3\dfrac{1}{4}-1\dfrac{1}{10}$  (c) $3\dfrac{3}{5}-1\dfrac{1}{2}$

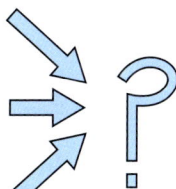

**A** The diagram shows that $\frac{1}{2}$ of $\frac{1}{3} = \frac{1}{6}$.

We say $\frac{1}{2} \times \frac{1}{3} = \frac{1}{6}$

To multiply fractions, multiply the numerators and multiply the denominators

(a) $\frac{1}{3} \times \frac{2}{5} = \frac{2}{15}$     (b) $\frac{1}{2} \times \frac{1}{5} = \frac{1}{10}$     (c) $\frac{1}{2} \times \frac{2}{3} = \frac{2}{6} = \frac{1}{3}$ by cancelling

(d) $1\frac{1}{5} \times \frac{2}{3}$                          (e) $\frac{2}{15} \times 20$                          (f) $2\frac{1}{2} \times 3\frac{2}{5}$

$= \frac{2\cancel{6}}{5} \times \frac{2}{\cancel{3}_1}$ (cancel)        $= \frac{2}{\cancel{15}_3} \times \frac{\cancel{20}^4}{1}$        $= \frac{1\cancel{5}}{2} \times \frac{17}{\cancel{5}_1}$

$= \frac{4}{5}$                          $= \frac{8}{3} = 2\frac{2}{3}$                          $= \frac{17}{2} = 8\frac{1}{2}$

**B** How many halves are there in 3?

Answer: 6

So: $3 \div \frac{1}{2} = 6$

Notice that $3 \times \frac{2}{1} = \frac{6}{1} = 6$

To divide two fractions, turn the second fraction upside-down and then multiply

(a) $\frac{1}{2} \div \frac{3}{4} = \frac{1}{2} \times \frac{4}{3} = \frac{4}{6} = \frac{2}{3}$

(b) $\frac{2}{9} \div \frac{3}{5} = \frac{2}{9} \times \frac{5}{3} = \frac{10}{27}$

(c) $2\frac{1}{2} \div \frac{2}{3} = \frac{5}{\cancel{2}_1} \times \frac{\cancel{2}^1}{3} = \frac{5}{3} = 1\frac{2}{3}$

Work out

**1** (a) $\dfrac{1}{2}$ of $\dfrac{1}{4}$    (b) $\dfrac{1}{3}$ of $\dfrac{1}{3}$    (c) $\dfrac{1}{4}$ of $\dfrac{1}{3}$    (d) $\dfrac{1}{2}$ of $\dfrac{1}{6}$

**2** Draw this rectangle and put in more lines to show that $\dfrac{1}{4}$ of $\dfrac{1}{3} = \dfrac{1}{12}$

**3** (a) $\dfrac{1}{5}$ of $\dfrac{1}{6}$    (b) $\dfrac{1}{3}$ of $\dfrac{1}{5}$    (c) $\dfrac{1}{6}$ of $\dfrac{1}{4}$    (d) $\dfrac{1}{4}$ of $\dfrac{1}{5}$

**4** (a) $\dfrac{1}{2}$ of $\dfrac{3}{4}$    (b) $\dfrac{2}{3}$ of $\dfrac{3}{4}$    (c) $\dfrac{1}{4}$ of $\dfrac{2}{3}$    (d) $\dfrac{1}{2}$ of $\dfrac{2}{5}$

(cancel your answers where possible)

**5** (a) $\dfrac{4}{5}$ of $\dfrac{2}{7}$    (b) $\dfrac{1}{5}$ of $\dfrac{5}{6}$    (c) $\dfrac{1}{3}$ of $\dfrac{3}{4}$    (d) $\dfrac{2}{3}$ of $\dfrac{3}{5}$

Work out the following Questions (you must cancel your answers where possible):

**6** $\dfrac{2}{3} \times \dfrac{1}{7}$    **7** $\dfrac{1}{9} \times \dfrac{1}{10}$    **8** $\dfrac{3}{4} \times \dfrac{1}{5}$    **9** $\dfrac{5}{7} \times \dfrac{14}{15}$

**10** $\dfrac{1}{3} \times \dfrac{1}{8}$    **11** $\dfrac{2}{3} \times \dfrac{1}{8}$    **12** $\dfrac{3}{4} \times \dfrac{2}{3}$    **13** $\dfrac{2}{9} \times \dfrac{3}{8}$

**14** $\dfrac{1}{9} \times \dfrac{1}{4}$    **15** $\dfrac{3}{4} \times \dfrac{1}{9}$    **16** $\dfrac{3}{5} \times \dfrac{5}{9}$    **17** $\dfrac{7}{9} \times \dfrac{3}{14}$

**18** A house contains 40 pieces of furniture. A family take $\dfrac{7}{10}$ of the furniture to their new house.

Work out $\dfrac{7}{10}$ of 40.

**19** Copy and complete the Questions below:

(a) $\dfrac{3}{8} \times 16 = \dfrac{3}{\cancel{8}_{1}} \times \dfrac{\cancel{16}^{2}}{1} = \dfrac{\square}{\square} = \square$

(b) $\dfrac{2}{3} \times 6 = \dfrac{2}{3} \times \dfrac{6}{\square} = \dfrac{\square}{\square} = \square$

Work out

**20** $\dfrac{2}{5} \times 20$    **21** $\dfrac{3}{4} \times 20$    **22** $\dfrac{1}{8} \times 6$

Copy and complete Questions **23** to **25** .

**23** $\dfrac{3}{4} \times 1\dfrac{2}{5}$

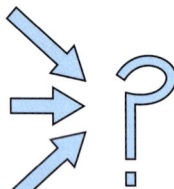

$= \dfrac{3}{4} \times \dfrac{\square}{5}$

$= \dfrac{\square}{20}$

$= \square\dfrac{\square}{20}$

**24** $3\dfrac{1}{3} \times 2\dfrac{1}{2}$

$= \dfrac{\square}{3} \times \dfrac{\square}{2}$

$= \dfrac{\square}{3} \times \dfrac{5}{1}$ (cancel)

$= \dfrac{\square}{3} = \square\dfrac{\square}{3}$

**25** $\dfrac{1}{20} \times 15$

$= \dfrac{1}{20} \times \dfrac{15}{1}$

$= \dfrac{1}{4} \times \dfrac{\square}{1}$ (cancel)

$= \dfrac{\square}{4}$

Work out

**26** $3\dfrac{1}{2} \times \dfrac{8}{21}$

**27** $1\dfrac{1}{4} \times \dfrac{3}{5}$

**28** $1\dfrac{2}{3} \times 1\dfrac{1}{5}$

**29** $3\dfrac{1}{2} \times 1\dfrac{1}{21}$

**30** $2\dfrac{1}{4} \times 3\dfrac{1}{5}$

**31** $4\dfrac{1}{2} \times 2\dfrac{2}{3}$

**32** $\dfrac{2}{5} \times 1\dfrac{1}{3}$

**33** $1\dfrac{1}{9} \times 5\dfrac{2}{5}$

**34** Match each Question to the correct answer:

A $\boxed{2\dfrac{1}{2} \quad \times \quad \dfrac{2}{5}}$

B $\boxed{1\dfrac{1}{2} \quad \times \quad 1\dfrac{1}{3}}$

C $\boxed{1\dfrac{3}{4} \quad \times \quad 1\dfrac{1}{2}}$

P $\boxed{2}$

Q $\boxed{2\dfrac{5}{8}}$

R $\boxed{1}$

Copy and complete Questions **35** to **37** :

**35** $\dfrac{1}{4} \div \dfrac{1}{3}$

$= \dfrac{1}{4} \times \dfrac{\square}{1}$

$= \dfrac{\square}{4}$

**36** $\dfrac{2}{7} \div \dfrac{5}{9}$

$= \dfrac{2}{7} \times \dfrac{\square}{5}$

$= \dfrac{\square}{\square}$

**37** $\dfrac{1}{8} \div \dfrac{5}{7}$

$= \dfrac{1}{8} \times \dfrac{\square}{5}$

$= \dfrac{\square}{\square}$

Work out

**38** $9 \div \dfrac{1}{3}$

**39** $2 \div \dfrac{1}{2}$

**40** $8 \div \dfrac{1}{4}$

**41** $6 \div \dfrac{1}{5}$

**42** $1 \div \dfrac{1}{10}$

**43** $12 \div \dfrac{1}{3}$

**44** $3 \div \dfrac{1}{2}$

**45** $7 \div \dfrac{1}{9}$

**46** Match each Question to the correct answer:

A $\dfrac{1}{6} \div \dfrac{3}{4}$    B $\dfrac{3}{8} \div \dfrac{5}{7}$    C $\dfrac{1}{6} \div \dfrac{3}{8}$

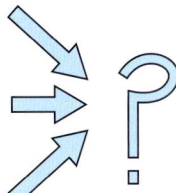

P $\dfrac{21}{40}$    S $\dfrac{21}{13}$    Q $\dfrac{4}{9}$    R $\dfrac{2}{9}$

Work out

**47** $1\dfrac{1}{5} \div \dfrac{3}{10}$  **48** $4\dfrac{1}{2} \div \dfrac{7}{10}$  **49** $2\dfrac{1}{10} \div 3\dfrac{1}{5}$  **50** $5\dfrac{3}{8} \div 2\dfrac{1}{2}$

**51** $2\dfrac{5}{8} \div \dfrac{1}{2}$  **52** $1\dfrac{2}{5} \div 1\dfrac{3}{20}$  **53** $1\dfrac{1}{5} \div 2\dfrac{1}{10}$  **54** $2\dfrac{9}{20} \div 5\dfrac{3}{10}$

**55** $3\dfrac{1}{2} \div \dfrac{5}{16}$  **56** $3\dfrac{3}{5} \div 1\dfrac{7}{10}$  **57** $1\dfrac{1}{3} \div \dfrac{5}{6}$  **58** $6\dfrac{5}{6} \div 2\dfrac{1}{3}$

**59** A recipe for a cake uses $\dfrac{2}{3}$ of a pound of sugar. How many cakes can be made from 6 pounds of sugar?

**60** A farmer has $37\dfrac{1}{2}$ kg of potatoes. He packs them into $2\dfrac{1}{2}$ kg bags. How many bags of potatoes will the farmer have?

## WATCH YOUR MONEY! – Mobile phones

**1** Do you have a mobile phone?

**2** If yes, which one?

**3** Why did you choose this phone?

**4** When do you use your phone most often?

| Monday to Friday (during the day) | or | Monday to Friday (during the evening) | or | At the weekend |

**5** How many minutes do you spend on the phone per day?

| 0 | or | 1–5 | or | 6–15 | or | 16–30 | or | 31–60 | or | more than 60 |

**6** How many texts do you send per day?

[0] or [1–5] or [6–10] or [11–15] or [more than 15]

**7** What are the advantages and disadvantages of having a mobile phone?

**8** Collect the above class data together with your teacher. Discuss the main findings.

### Mobile phone bills

### Contracts

You often pay a fixed monthly amount which allows you a certain number of minutes of phone calls and a certain number of text messages. You may have to pay extra if you exceed your limit.

### Pay As You Go

You pay money in advance (sometimes by buying cards which allow you a certain amount of money on your phone). As soon as you have used up all your money, you have to buy more phone credit in advance.

### Remember

Text messages are usually cheaper to send than making phone calls.

### The best deal?

A tariff is a way of paying to use a mobile phone. The best tariff depends on how many minutes you use your phone for and what time of the day you use the phone.

### WYM5

Compare these two tariffs.

| TARIFF P |
|---|
| 4p per minute anytime |

| TARIFF Q |
|---|
| £ 9 per month plus 1p per minute anytime |

The best choice depends on how many minutes are used.

**1** 20 minutes on tariff P would cost 20 × 4p = 80p. Copy and complete this table for tariff P.

| minutes | 0 | 20 | 40 | 100 | 200 | 300 | 400 |
|---|---|---|---|---|---|---|---|
| cost (£) | 0 | 0.80 | 1.60 | | | | |

132

**2** (a) Copy the axes opposite onto squared paper.

(b) Plot points from the tariff P table and join them up to make a straight line.

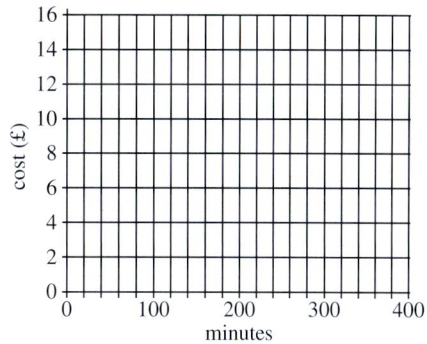

**3** 20 minutes on tariff Q would cost £9, then add on (20 × 1p) which is £0.20. 20 minutes cost £9.20.

Copy and complete this table for tariff Q.

| minutes | 0 | 50 | 100 | 200 | 300 | 400 |
|---------|---|----|-----|-----|-----|-----|
| cost (£) | 9 | | | | | |

**4** Plot points from the tariff Q table using the *same axes* as before. Join them up to make a straight line.

Your graph should look like this.

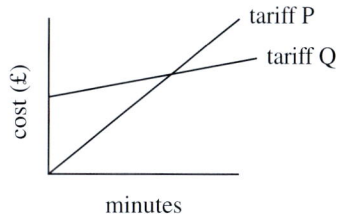

**5** After how many minutes do the 2 lines cross?

**6** What is the cost on both tariffs when the 2 lines cross?

**7** If the number of minutes you use your mobile phone is less than your answer to Question **5**, which tariff is cheaper for you?

**8** If the number of minutes you use your mobile phone is more than your answer to Question **5**, which tariff is cheaper for you?

**9** Compare these two tariffs.

| TARIFF Y £5 per month plus 2p per minute | TARIFF Z 4.5p per minute anytime |
|---|---|

(a) Repeat Questions **1** to **4** for these new tariffs.

(b) After how many minutes is the cost the same for both tariffs?

(c) Which tariff would you advise if you use your mobile phone for 150 minutes?

(d) Which tariff would you advise if you use your mobile phone for 320 minutes?

## TEST YOURSELF ON UNIT 5

### 1. Writing one number as a fraction of another number

(a) There are 29 people on a bus. 17 are women. What fraction of people on the bus are women?

(b) There are 11 animals waiting to be seen by a vet. 5 of the animals are dogs, the rest are cats. What fraction of the animals are cats?

(c)
What fraction of these noughts and crosses are the crosses?

(d) What fraction of the days of the week begin with the letter T?

### 2. Finding a fraction of a number

Find

(a) $\frac{1}{3}$ of £18     (b) $\frac{1}{8}$ of £24     (c) $\frac{2}{3}$ of £21     (d) $\frac{5}{6}$ of 42 kg

(e)
Table £350
SALE
$\frac{1}{7}$ off
What is the price of the table in the sale?

(f) Geena earns £300 each week. One week she gets paid $\frac{3}{10}$ extra for overtime. How much money does she get paid that week?

### 3. Converting improper fractions and mixed numbers

Change the following improper fractions to mixed numbers.

(a) $\frac{23}{4}$     (b) $\frac{9}{2}$     (c) $\frac{17}{5}$     (d) $\frac{32}{5}$

Change the following mixed numbers to improper fractions.

(e) $2\frac{1}{4}$     (f) $5\frac{2}{3}$     (g) $3\frac{2}{7}$     (h) $4\frac{3}{8}$

134

## 4. Adding and subtracting fractions

Work out

(a) $\dfrac{3}{7} + \dfrac{2}{7}$     (b) $\dfrac{4}{7} - \dfrac{1}{5}$     (c) $\dfrac{1}{4} + \dfrac{1}{3}$     (d) $\dfrac{3}{7} + \dfrac{2}{5}$

(e) $2\dfrac{1}{2} + \dfrac{3}{5}$     (f) $1\dfrac{7}{8} - \dfrac{3}{4}$     (g) $\dfrac{5}{6} + 2\dfrac{1}{4}$     (h) $2\dfrac{1}{3} + 1\dfrac{3}{4}$

## 5. Multiplying fractions

Work out

(a) $\dfrac{1}{3}$ of $\dfrac{1}{8}$     (b) $\dfrac{2}{5} \times \dfrac{1}{3}$     (c) $\dfrac{2}{7} \times \dfrac{3}{4}$     (d) $\dfrac{3}{8} \times \dfrac{4}{5}$

(e) $\dfrac{10}{11} \times \dfrac{22}{30}$     (f) $3\dfrac{2}{3} \times 1\dfrac{4}{5}$     (g) $\dfrac{8}{9} \times 12$     (h) $4\dfrac{3}{4} \times 3\dfrac{1}{5}$

## 6. Dividing fractions

Work out

(a) $\dfrac{1}{9} \div \dfrac{1}{8}$     (b) $\dfrac{2}{7} \div \dfrac{5}{9}$     (c) $\dfrac{3}{8} \div 6$     (d) $5\dfrac{1}{2} \div 3$

(e) $1\dfrac{1}{6} \div \dfrac{4}{9}$     (f) $3\dfrac{2}{5} \div 2\dfrac{1}{2}$     (g) $8\dfrac{1}{2} \div 5\dfrac{1}{4}$     (h) $4\dfrac{5}{6} \div 4\dfrac{2}{3}$

**1** (a) Shade $\frac{2}{3}$ of the shape below.

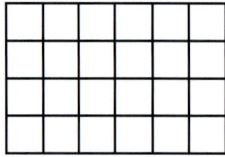

(b) (i) What fraction of the shape below is shaded?

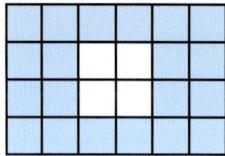

(ii) What fraction of this shape is not shaded? (WJEC)

**2** Work out, giving your answer as a fraction in its simplest form.

(a) $\frac{2}{5} \times \frac{1}{4}$    (b) $\frac{2}{5} - \frac{1}{4}$ (OCR)

**3** Work out    (i) $\frac{3}{4} - \frac{1}{3}$    (ii) $\frac{3}{8} \div 6$

**4** This is a drawing of a bolt. It is not drawn to scale.

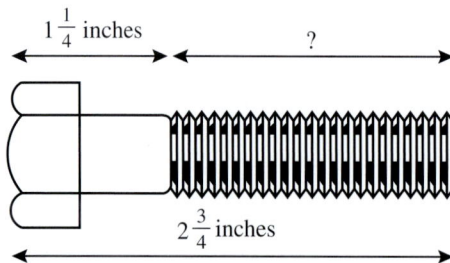

Calculate the length marked '?'. (OCR)

**5** I planted $\frac{1}{4}$ of my garden with vegetables, $\frac{3}{8}$ of my garden with roses and the rest as lawn. What fraction of the garden have I left for lawn? (AQA)

**6** Calculate $2\frac{3}{8} + 1\frac{1}{2}$. (CCEA)

**In this unit you will learn how to:**
- convert between fractions and percentages
- express one number as a percentage of another number
- find a percentage of a number
- find percentage increases and decreases
- convert between percentages and decimals
- find percentage changes
- do compound interest-type problems
- use percentage multipliers
- find ratios
- deal with direct proportion
- share in a given ratio
- WATCH YOUR MONEY! – Bank accounts 1

## Fractions and percentages

## 🔑 Key Facts

Per cent means 'out of 100'.

Percentages are fractions with denominator (bottom number) equal to 100.

63% means $\dfrac{63}{100}$     7% means $\dfrac{7}{100}$

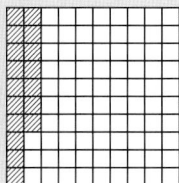

17 out of 100 small squares are shaded.

Fraction shaded $= \dfrac{17}{100}$

Percentage shaded $= 17\%$

**Example**

In a survey about favourite drinks, 37 out of 100 people said they preferred wine. Write this as a percentage.

$\dfrac{37}{100} = 37\%$ so 37% of the people said they preferred wine.

**1**

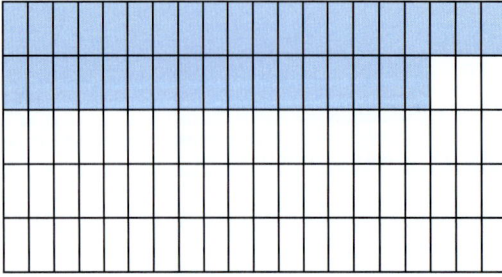

(a) What fraction of the large rectangle is shaded?

(b) What percentage of the large rectangle is shaded?

**2** 5 out of every 100 Britons donate blood at least once a year. Write down the percentage of Britons who donate blood at least once a year.

**3** 70% of people in Great Britain drive to work. What percentage of people do *not* drive to work?

**4** If 35% of a rectangle is shaded, what percentage of the rectangle is *not* shaded?

**5** 57 out of every 100 workers in the UK would choose a different job if they could have their time again. Write this as a percentage.

**6** Approximately 67% of the earth's surface is covered with water. What percentage of the earth's surface is land?

**7** 75% of women make their bed every day but only 45% of men do.

(a) What percentage of women do *not* make their bed every day?
(b) What percentage of men do *not* make their bed every day?

**8** 12 out of every 100 British people are left-handed. Write down the percentage of British people who are left-handed.

**9** Cleator Moor, near Whitehaven in Cumbria, has the highest percentage of Christians in the country (89%). What percentage of the people in Cleator Moor are *not* Christians?

**10** In 2001, 40% of 16 to 74-year-olds in Fairlight, near Hastings, were retired, the highest percentage of retired people in England and Wales. What percentage of 16 to 74-year-olds in Fairlight were *not* retired?

**Changing percentages into fractions**

$41\% = \dfrac{41}{100}$

$18\% = \dfrac{18}{100} \overset{\div 2}{\underset{\div 2}{=}} \dfrac{9}{50}$

cancel when you can

$35\% = \dfrac{35}{100} \overset{\div 5}{\underset{\div 5}{=}} \dfrac{7}{20}$

cancel when you can

**Changing fractions into percentages**

(a)

$50\% = \dfrac{50}{100} \overset{\div 50}{\underset{\div 50}{=}} \dfrac{1}{2}$    so $\dfrac{1}{2}$ means 50%

To change a fraction into a percentage, multiply the fraction by 100

(b) Change $\dfrac{7}{24}$ into a percentage

$\dfrac{7}{24} \times 100$    Use calculator

$\dfrac{7}{24} \times 100 = 29.16666...$

= 29% (to the nearest whole number)

---

### E6. 1

**1** Change these percentages into fractions. Cancel the answers when possible.

(a) 10%    (b) 3%    (c) 11%    (d) 40%    (e) 75%    (f) 15%

(g) 80%    (h) 22%    (i) 32%    (j) 95%    (k) 48%    (l) 5%

**2** Carl gave Michelle 30% of his CD's. What *fraction* of his CD's did Carl give to Michelle?

**3** Nina used 55% of the petrol in her car when travelling from Manchester to Newcastle. What *fraction* of her petrol did she use?

**4** Zak spent 64% of his money in town on Saturday. What *fraction* of his money did he spend?

**5** Change these fractions into percentages (remember: multiply by 100 unless you can see a quicker way).

(a) $\dfrac{1}{4}$   (b) $\dfrac{7}{100}$   (c) $\dfrac{4}{5}$   (d) $\dfrac{7}{20}$   (e) $\dfrac{3}{4}$   (f) $\dfrac{3}{25}$   (g) $\dfrac{9}{25}$

(h) $\dfrac{9}{100}$   (i) $\dfrac{2}{5}$   (j) $\dfrac{7}{10}$   (k) $\dfrac{14}{25}$   (l) $\dfrac{9}{10}$   (m) $\dfrac{17}{20}$   (n) $\dfrac{21}{50}$

**6** Ivan ran $\frac{39}{50}$ of a marathon race before he had to drop out. What percentage of the race did he manage to run?

**7** Silvio scored 13 out of 25 in a test. What percentage was this?

**8** Jane has to use $\frac{11}{20}$ of her money to pay her rent. What percentage of her money does she use to pay her rent?

**9** Use a calculator to change these fractions into percentages (give your answers to the nearest whole number).

(a) $\frac{12}{17}$    (b) $\frac{8}{29}$    (c) $\frac{5}{16}$    (d) $\frac{11}{40}$    (e) $\frac{13}{16}$    (f) $\frac{12}{41}$

(g) $\frac{6}{37}$    (h) $\frac{29}{39}$    (i) $\frac{58}{73}$    (j) $\frac{9}{32}$    (k) $\frac{26}{27}$    (l) $\frac{88}{143}$

**10** In a cricket match, Michael Vaughan scored $\frac{29}{49}$ of his team's runs. What percentage of his team's runs did he score? (Give your answer to the nearest whole number)

---

## Expressing one number as a percentage of another number

### 🔑 Key Facts

Write the two numbers as a fraction of each other then multiply by 100 to change into a percentage.

Suppose there are 25 cars in the staff car park. 9 of the cars were made in Japan. What percentage of the cars were made in Japan?

$$\frac{9}{25} \times 100 = \frac{9}{\overset{}{\underset{1}{25}}} \times \frac{\overset{4}{\cancel{100}}}{1} = \frac{36}{1} = 36\%$$

140

**1** (a) Write down 6 as a percentage of 25 (b) Write down 9 as a percentage of 50

(c) Write down 8 as a percentage of 20 (d) Write down 40 as a percentage of 200

**2**

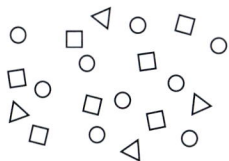

What percentage of these shapes are:

(a) squares

(b) circles

(c) triangles

**3** 13 people in a class of 25 have blonde hair. What percentage of the class have blonde hair?

**4** Mehur scored 13 out of 20 in his maths exam and 18 out of 50 in his science exam.

(a) What percentage did Mehur score in his maths exam?

(b) What percentage did Mehur score in his science exam?

(c) Which exam did Mehur do better in?

**5** In a box of 20 chocolates, 14 of them are milk chocolates. What percentage are milk chocolates?

**6** In a school of 800 students, there are 472 girls.

(a) What is the percentage of *girls* in the school?
(b) What is the percentage of *boys* in the school?

**7** 250 people go to a rock concert. 145 of the people are male.

(a) What is the percentage of *males* at the rock concert?
(b) What is the percentage of *females* at the rock concert?

**8** This table shows the number of cars of each colour in a car park.

What percentage of the total number of cars were:

(a) red (b) blue (c) white

(d) gold (e) yellow (f) green

| colour | number of cars |
|--------|----------------|
| red | 18 |
| blue | 12 |
| white | 6 |
| gold | 3 |
| yellow | 15 |
| green | 6 |
| total | 60 |

**9** In a survey, 150 people were asked about smoking. 45 people said they smoke. The rest of the people said they do *not* smoke. What percentage of the people said they do *not* smoke?

**10** 2 twins, Meg and Charlie, sat 5 exams. The results are opposite.

Find the percentage that Meg scored in *each* subject.

Write down who got the higher marks in most subjects.

| subject | Meg | Charlie |
|---------|-----|---------|
| english | $\dfrac{17}{20}$ | 79% |
| maths | $\dfrac{14}{25}$ | 50% |
| science | $\dfrac{23}{50}$ | 52% |
| art | $\dfrac{26}{40}$ | 62% |
| geography | $\dfrac{42}{60}$ | 75% |

## E6. 2

Use a calculator for the Questions in this exercise. Give your answers to the nearest whole number.

**1** Change these test scores into percentages:

(a) $\dfrac{13}{40}$  (b) $\dfrac{36}{42}$  (c) $\dfrac{5}{16}$  (d) $\dfrac{54}{72}$  (e) $\dfrac{45}{63}$  (f) $\dfrac{23}{30}$

**2** Brenda saves £5 each week out of her Saturday job. If she gets paid £17.50, work out the percentage of her wage that she saves.

**3** A chocolate bar weighs 68 g. If 47 g of the bar is nougat, work out what percentage of the bar is nougat.

**4** A house costs £115, 000. Sam must pay a deposit of £10, 000. What is the deposit as a percentage of the total cost of the house?

**5**

$$1^2 = 1 \times 1 = 1$$
$$2^2 = 2 \times 2 = 4$$
$$3^3 = 3 \times 3 = 9$$
$$4^4 = 4 \times 4 = 16$$

These are the first 4 square numbers.

Look at the picture opposite. What percentage of the numbers are square numbers?

**6** Orange squash is to be made with 24 ml of juice and 126 ml water. What is the percentage of juice in the *whole* drink?

**7**

| S | M | O | K | I |
|---|---|---|---|---|
| N | G | I | S | B |
| A | D | F | O | R |
| Y | O | U | R | H |
| E | A | L | T | H |

What percentage of the letters in the square are

(a) the letter H

(b) vowels (A, E, I, O, U)

**8** In the 'horror' of the First World War, the numbers of people killed from the main countries are shown.

Work out the percentage of people killed who came from (a) Britain (b) France (c) Germany. What a tragic waste of life!

| | |
|---|---|
| Germany | 1,800,000 |
| Russia | 1,700,000 |
| France | 1,384,000 |
| Austria–Hungary | 1,290,000 |
| Britain | 743,000 |
| Italy | 615,000 |
| Roumania | 335,000 |
| Turkey | 325,000 |
| Others | 454,000 |
| Total | 8,646,000 |

**9** Peter asks people what their favourite drink was. The results are shown in this table.

Write down the percentage of people who like *each* type of *drink*.

| drink | number of people |
|---|---|
| juice | 21 |
| wine | 18 |
| cola | 32 |
| lemonade | 21 |
| beer | 34 |
| cider | 12 |
| total | 138 |

**10**

BARCLAYS PREMIERSHIP

| | | HOME | | | | | AWAY | | | | | |
|---|---|---|---|---|---|---|---|---|---|---|---|---|
| | P | W | D | L | F | A | W | D | L | F | A | GD | Pts |

| | P | W | D | L | F | A | W | D | L | F | A | GD | Pts |
|---|---|---|---|---|---|---|---|---|---|---|---|---|---|
| 1 CHELSEA | 16 | 6 | 2 | 0 | 15 | 3 | 6 | 1 | 1 | 16 | 3 | +25 | 39 |
| 2 EVERTON | 17 | 6 | 1 | 2 | 11 | 9 | 5 | 2 | 1 | 10 | 5 | +7 | 36 |
| 3 ARSENAL | 16 | 5 | 3 | 0 | 23 | 9 | 5 | 1 | 2 | 19 | 11 | +22 | 34 |
| 4 MAN UTD | 16 | 6 | 3 | 0 | 12 | 3 | 3 | 3 | 2 | 10 | 7 | +12 | 30 |
| 5 MIDDLESBRO | 17 | 4 | 3 | 1 | 13 | 9 | 4 | 2 | 3 | 16 | 13 | +7 | 29 |
| 6 ASTON VILLA | 16 | 5 | 3 | 0 | 14 | 4 | 1 | 4 | 3 | 7 | 13 | +4 | 25 |
| 7 LIVERPOOL | 16 | 6 | 0 | 1 | 15 | 5 | 1 | 3 | 5 | 9 | 13 | +6 | 24 |
| 8 CHARLTON | 17 | 4 | 2 | 2 | 12 | 8 | 3 | 1 | 5 | 7 | 19 | -8 | 24 |
| 9 BOLTON | 17 | 4 | 2 | 2 | 12 | 8 | 2 | 3 | 4 | 14 | 17 | +1 | 23 |
| 10 PORTSMOUTH | 16 | 5 | 1 | 2 | 15 | 11 | 1 | 3 | 4 | 7 | 12 | -1 | 22 |
| 11 TOTTENHAM | 17 | 2 | 2 | 4 | 11 | 12 | 4 | 2 | 3 | 5 | 5 | -1 | 22 |
| 12 NEWCASTLE | 17 | 3 | 3 | 3 | 16 | 16 | 2 | 3 | 3 | 12 | 16 | -4 | 21 |
| 13 MAN CITY | 17 | 3 | 3 | 3 | 10 | 6 | 2 | 2 | 4 | 11 | 12 | +3 | 20 |
| 14 FULHAM | 16 | 3 | 0 | 5 | 8 | 15 | 2 | 2 | 4 | 10 | 12 | -9 | 17 |
| 15 NORWICH | 17 | 2 | 4 | 3 | 12 | 15 | 0 | 5 | 3 | 5 | 13 | -11 | 15 |
| 16 BIRMINGHAM | 16 | 1 | 4 | 3 | 5 | 7 | 1 | 4 | 3 | 7 | 11 | -6 | 14 |
| 17 C PALACE | 17 | 2 | 2 | 5 | 8 | 11 | 1 | 3 | 4 | 9 | 13 | -7 | 14 |
| 18 BLACKBURN | 17 | 1 | 5 | 2 | 10 | 14 | 1 | 3 | 5 | 6 | 16 | -14 | 14 |
| 19 SOUTHAMPTON | 17 | 2 | 5 | 2 | 13 | 13 | 0 | 2 | 6 | 4 | 13 | -9 | 13 |
| 20 WEST BROM | 17 | 1 | 4 | 4 | 7 | 14 | 0 | 3 | 5 | 8 | 18 | -17 | 10 |

This table shows the Barclays Premiership in December 2004.

(a) What percentage of the teams begin with the letter 'B'?

(b) What percentage of the teams have played 17 games (look down the 'P' column)?

(c) What percentage of the teams have *more than* 25 points (look down the 'Pts' column)?

143

**(6A)** **Convert between fractions and decimals (see Unit 2)**

1  Change these decimals into fractions. (cancel answers where possible)

   (a) 0.3   (b) 0.2   (c) 0.29   (d) 0.36   (e) 0.72

2  Change these fractions into decimals.

   (a) $\dfrac{31}{100}$   (b) $\dfrac{9}{10}$   (c) $\dfrac{7}{20}$   (d) $\dfrac{1}{4}$   (e) $\dfrac{16}{25}$

3  Match up each decimal with its equivalent fraction (Warning: one of the fractions is not needed).

A 0.84

B 0.6

C 0.21

D 0.55

E 0.75

F 0.28

P $\dfrac{7}{25}$

Q $\dfrac{3}{5}$

R $\dfrac{28}{50}$

S $\dfrac{3}{4}$

T $\dfrac{21}{100}$

U $\dfrac{21}{25}$

V $\dfrac{11}{20}$

## Percentage of a number

**Common percentages**

$50\% = \dfrac{1}{2}$      $25\% = \dfrac{1}{4}$      $75\% = \dfrac{3}{4}$      $33\tfrac{1}{3}\% = \dfrac{1}{3}$      $66\tfrac{2}{3}\% = \dfrac{2}{3}$

(a)  25% of 60

$= \dfrac{1}{4} \times 60$

$= 60 \div 4 = 15$

(b)  75% of 36

$= \dfrac{3}{4} \times 36$

$= (36 \div 4) \times 3 = 27$

(c)  $66\tfrac{2}{3}\%$ of 24

$= \dfrac{2}{3} \times 24$

$= (24 \div 3) \times 2 = 16$

**Multiples of 10%**      $10\% = \dfrac{1}{10}$

To work out 20%, find 10% then multiply by 2

To work out 30%, find 10% then multiply by 3 and so on

**1** Find 50% of:

    (a) 80    (b) 42    (c) 28    (d) 120    (e) 9    (f) 25

**2** Find 25% of:

    (a) 80    (b) 28    (c) 48    (d) 100    (e) 200    (f) 30

**3** Find 75% of:

    (a) 20    (b) 32    (c) 80    (d) 12    (e) 400    (f) 52

**4** There are 280 children in a school. 75% of the children play sport for a school team. How many children play for a school team?

**5** Find $33\frac{1}{3}\%$ of:

    (a) 12    (b) 30    (c) 60    (d) 18

**6** Find $66\frac{2}{3}\%$ of:

    (a) 15    (b) 21    (c) 45    (d) 60    (e) 300    (f) 72

**7** Find 10% of:

    (a) 80    (b) 90    (c) 20    (d) 200    (e) 50    (f) 600

**8** Find 30% of:

    (a) 80    (b) 90    (c) 20    (d) 200    (e) 50    (f) 600

**9** Find 70% of:

    (a) 40    (b) 10    (c) 80    (d) 40    (e) 300    (f) 140

**10** Find 5% of:

    (a) 80    (b) 20    (c) 60    (d) 140    (e) 30    (f) 90

**11** Find 15% of: (hint: work out 10% and 5% then add together)

    (a) 80    (b) 60    (c) 120    (d) 200    (e) 50    (f) 30

**12** 25% of a chocolate bar is caramel. If the chocolate bar weighs 60 g, how much is caramel?

145

**13** An egg is made up of 60% egg white, 30% yolk and the rest is shell.

    (a) What percentage of the egg is shell?

    (b) If the egg weighs 50 g, what is the weight of the yolk?

**14** Find the odd one out
    (a) 50% of £30    (b) 20% of £80    (c) 25% of £60

**15** Find the odd one out

    (a) 5% of £160    (b) 25% of £36    (c) 10% of £80

**16** $66\frac{2}{3}$% of adults like a cup of tea first thing in the morning. If 150 adults were asked, how many said they liked a cup of tea first thing in the morning?

**17** 160 people walked through a shop. 5% of these people had their noses pierced. How many of these people had their noses pierced?

**18** 360 people were asked if they had flown at any point in their life. 70% said they had flown. How many people was that?

**19** Copy the 2 grids below:

| 60 | 38 | 3 |  | 63 | 90 | 38 | 11 |  | 66 | 15 |
|----|----|---|--|----|----|----|----|--|----|----|
|    |    |   |  |    |    |    |    |  |    |    |

| 40 | 12 | 63 | 50 | 9 |  | 9 | 50 | 90 | 9 | 50 |
|----|----|----|----|---|--|---|----|----|---|----|
|    |    |    |    |   |  |   |    |    |   |    |

There is a hidden message.

Answer the Questions listed below then write the letter under the answer number in your grids.

Example. Letter U is 15% of 20    Answer: 3 Write the letter 'U' under all the 3's in the grid.

| letter A is 40% of 30 | letter O is 10% of 380 |
|---|---|
| letter E is 20% of 250 | letter S is $33\frac{1}{3}$% of 27 |
| letter I is 75% of 88 | letter T is 30% of 50 |
| letter K is 90% of 70 | letter U is 15% of 20 |
| letter M is 80% of 50 | letter W is 5% of 220 |
| letter N is 25% of 360 | letter Y is $66\frac{2}{3}$% of 90 |

## Key Facts

**Harder percentages**

$1\% = \dfrac{1}{100}$    To find 1% of a number, divide the number by 100

Find 23% of a number.
Divide the number by 100 to find 1% then multiply by 23 to find 23% of the number.

---

(a) Find 12% of 2300

1% of 2300 = 2300 ÷ 100

12% of 2300 = (2300 ÷ 100) × 12

= 276

(b) Work out, to the nearest penny:

6% of £12.99

$$\overset{1\%}{\overbrace{(12.99 \div 100)}} \times 6$$

= 0.7794

= £0.78, to the nearest penny.

**Note** $\boxed{4.5}$ on a calculator display means £4.50 if the number is showing £'s.

---

## E6. 3

*Use a calculator when needed.*

**1** Find 1% of:

    (a) 600    (b) 400    (c) 350    (d) 850    (e) 65    (f) 9

**2** Find 3% of:

    (a) 600    (b) 400    (c) 350    (d) 850    (e) 65    (f) 9

**3** Find 9% of:

    (a) 200    (b) 700    (c) 300    (d) 650    (e) 320    (f) 8

**4** Find 24% of:

    (a) 500    (b) 800    (c) 450    (d) 240    (e) 68    (f) 3

**5** Find 81% of:

    (a) 300    (b) 400    (c) 150    (d) 750    (e) 49    (f) 7

**6** Find 17.5% of:

(a) 200    (b) 120    (c) 380    (d) 685    (e) 72    (f) 4

Work out

**7** 9% of £450    **8** 4% of £770    **9** 47% of £185

**10** 7% of £550    **11** 85% of £600    **12** 8% of £350

**13** 48000 people watch Liverpool play Everton. 62% of the people are Liverpool supporters. How many Liverpool supporters watch the match?

**14** 53% of the students in a school are girls. If there are 1300 students in the school, how many are girls?

**15** Find the odd one out

(a) 3% of 68    (b) 8% of £32    (c) 12% of £17

**16** Match each Question to the correct answer:
(the answers have been rounded off to the nearest penny)

A  37% of £8.65          P  £1.48

B  9% of £16.40          Q  £1.87

C  12% of £15.62         R  £3.20

**17** Work out, correct to the nearest penny:

(a) 12% of £17.60    (b) 26% of £91    (c) 14% of £8.50

(d) 29% of £6.87    (e) 67% of £11.27    (f) 18% of £28.53

(g) 6.5% of £174    (h) 9.2% of £9.25    (i) 12.5% of £38.17

**18** 9% of a cereal is sugar. How much sugar is there in a 750 g box of cereal?

**19** Sean has £850. He uses 37.2% of his money to buy a new music centre. How much did he spend on the music centre?

**20** Which is larger?

(a) 7.3% of £8.99    or    (b) 9.4% of £6.81

**(6B)** **Substitute numbers for letters (see Unit 4)**

In Questions **1** to **8** find the value of each expression when

$$a = 3$$
$$b = 1$$
$$c = 5$$

**1.** $2a$      **2.** $c - a$      **3.** $bc$      **4.** $3a + 2c$

**5.** $c^2$      **6.** $a^2 + b^2$      **7.** $a(b + c)$      **8.** $6c - 4b$

In Questions **9** to **16** find the value of each expression when

$$x = 6$$
$$y = 2$$
$$z = 4$$

**9.** $7y$      **10.** $x^2$      **11.** $yz$      **12.** $3x + 2z$

**13.** $5(x - z)$      **14.** $\dfrac{x}{y}$      **15.** $y(x + z)$      **16.** $xyz$

**17.** $a = b + 9c$      Find $a$ when $b = 4$ and $c = 3$

**18.** $f = \dfrac{m}{4} - 6$      Find $f$ when $m = 32$

## Percentage increase and decrease

Find the given percentage then '*add on*' for '*increase*' or '*subtract*' for '*decrease*'.

(a) Increase £70 by 10%

     10% of 70 = 70 ÷ 10 = 7

     70 + 7 = £77
     ↑
     increase

(b) Decrease £90 by 20%

                10%
     20% of 90 = (90 ÷ 10) × 2 = 18

     90 − 18 = £72
     ↑
     decrease

Do *not* use a calculator.

1. (a) Increase £60 by 10%  (b) Increase £90 by 30%
   (c) Increase £30 by 60%  (d) Decrease £50 by 40%
   (e) Decrease £300 by 25%  (f) Increase £800 by 7%
   (g) Reduce (decrease) £30 by $33\frac{1}{3}$%  (h) Reduce £200 by 4%
   (i) Decrease £60 by 5%  (j) Increase £20 by 30%

2. A music store is having a sale, with 25% *off* all prices. A guitar normally costs £360. What will it cost in the sale?

3. After one year, a car *loses* 20% of its value. If the car cost £7000 when it was bought, how much will it cost after one year?

4. A shop increases all its prices by 5%. If the price of a computer was £840, what is the new price?

5. A 750 g Cornflake packet has 10% extra free. How much does it weigh now?

In Questions 6 to 14 below:

(a) How much is the price reduced by?   (b) What is the sale price?

6.
Computer £600
SALE
20% off

7.
Jacket £90
SALE
10% off

8.
Bike £90
SALE
25% off

9.
Dress £80
SALE
75% off

10.
Watch £92
SALE
50% off

11.
Table £420
SALE
30% off

12.
Digital radio £90
SALE
$33\frac{1}{3}$% off

13.
Bed £350
SALE
40% off

14.
Bracelet £64
SALE
75% off

15. A restaurant adds a 10% service charge to its bills. If a meal costs £50, how much will it cost with the service added?

16. The price of a house was £160 000. During one year, the price increases by 3%. What is the new price of the house?

17. Hilary weighs 70 kg. She goes on a diet and loses 10% of her weight. How much does she now weigh?

**18** Rosie earns £22 000 each year. She gets a pay rise of 4%. How much does she now earn each year?

**19** Increase £400 by 17.5% (hint: find 10% then 5% then 2.5% and add them all together)

**20** Increase £560 by 17.5%

---

VAT is Value Added Tax. It is extra money that must be paid when buying many goods. The money is used by the Government to help run the country. It is usually 17.5%.

A printer costs £250 + VAT.

If VAT is 17.5%, work out how much the printer costs altogether.

$$17.5\% \text{ of } 250 = \overbrace{(250 \div 100)}^{1\%} \times 17.5 = 43.75$$

*add* the tax

printer costs 250 + 43.75 = £293.75

---

## E6. 4

*Use a calculator* when needed. Give answers to the nearest penny when needed.

**1**  (a) Increase a price of £90 by 5%  (b) Increase a price of £270 by 3%
  (c) Decrease a price of £75 by 7%  (d) Increase a price of £48 by 26%
  (e) Decrease a price of £320 by 8.5%  (f) Reduce a price of £ 39 by 83%
  (g) Increase a price of £7.40 by 11%  (h) Reduce a price of £463 by 62%
  (i) Decrease a price of £21 by 6.3%  (j) Decrease a price of £9.85 by 3.2%

**2** A restaurant gives a 10% discount for take-away meals ('discount' means money is 'knocked off'). A meal costs £ 47.50. How much will the meal cost with the discount?

**3** A railcard gives a 20% discount. How much would a £9.65 train journey cost if the railcard was used?

**4** The population of Hatton is 11500. If the population decreases by 2%, what is the new population?

**5** A computer costs £1099. Tom gets a 14% discount. How much will Tom pay for the computer?

**6** A bike costs £412 + VAT.

If VAT is 17.5%, work out how much the bike costs altogether.

**7** Copy and complete the table below:

| item | price (£) | VAT (17.5%) | price + VAT |
|---|---|---|---|
| TV | 325 | 56.88 | 381.88 |
| fridge | 217 | | |
| mobile phone | 185 | | |
| cd player | 133 | | |
| sofa | 899 | | |
| camera | 326 | | |
| car | 12121 | | |
| bed | 582 | | |
| computer game | 47 | | |
| guitar | 332 | | |

**8** A car is worth £4650. After an accident its value falls by 38%. How much is it worth now?

**9** A holiday is priced at £2118. World oil prices rise which means that the price of the holiday increases by 7.5%. What is the new price of the holiday?

**10** A bank pays 4% interest each year (this means if you put money in the bank for one year, you will get 4% of the money extra from the bank). If you put in £70, how much would you have after 1 year?

**11** A bank pays 5.2% interest each year.

If you put in £390, how much would you have after 1 year?

**12** Copy and complete the table below:

| money put into the bank (£) | interest each year | extra money (£) | total money after 1 year (£) |
|---|---|---|---|
| 80 | 3% | 2.40 | 82.40 |
| 500 | 5.5% | | |
| 360 | 2.9% | | |
| 25 | 5% | | |
| 2100 | 4.7% | | |
| 5350 | 3.85% | | |
| 473 | 5.05% | | |
| 204 | 4.79% | | |
| 8 | 5.8% | | |
| 791 | 6.7% | | |

**13** A new car costs £2320 + VAT (17.5%).

(a) What is the total price of the new car?

Its value decreases by 27% after one year.

(b) How much does the car cost after 1 year?

**14** A new watch costs £275 + VAT (17.5%).

(a) What is the total price of the new watch?

After a year-and-a-half the shop puts the watch in a sale when the price is reduced by 15%.

(b) How much does the watch cost in the sale?

**15** A new TV costs £550 + VAT (17.5%).

(a) What is the total price of the new TV?

In the New Year sales, the price of the TV is reduced by 18%.

(b) How much does the TV cost in the New Year sales?

*Can you still?*

**6C** **Collect like terms (see Unit 4)**

*Can you still?*

Simplify

**1.** $3a + 2a$　　　　　　**2.** $5a - a$　　　　　**3.** $2a + 3b + 5a$

**4.** $9x + 2y + 5x + 2y$　**5.** $3x + 7y - 3y$　**6.** $6p + 3q + 2q - p$

**7.** $9m - 2m + 3n - 2n$　**8.** $8a + 4 + a$　　**9.** $3m + 2n + 6m + 3$

Find the perimeter of each shape in Questions **10** and **11**. Simplify each answer.

**10.**

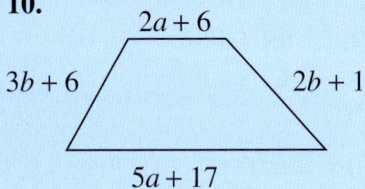

$2a + 6$

$3b + 6$　　　　$2b + 1$

$5a + 17$

**11.**

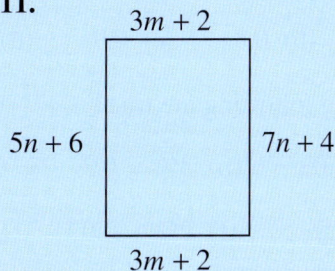

$3m + 2$

$5n + 6$　　　$7n + 4$

$3m + 2$

# Percentages and decimals

$$71\% = \frac{71}{100} = 0.71 \qquad\qquad 23\% = \frac{23}{100} = 0.23$$

**Note**

$$80\% = \frac{80}{100} = 0.80 = 0.8 \qquad \text{but} \qquad 8\% = \frac{8}{100} = 0.08$$

To change decimals into percentages, the first two numbers after the point give the percent:

$$0.73 = \frac{73}{100} = 73\% \qquad\qquad 0.59 = \frac{59}{100} = 59\%$$

**Note**

$$0.07 = \frac{7}{100} = 7\% \qquad \text{but} \qquad 0.7 = 0.70 = \frac{70}{100} = 70\%$$

## M6. 5

**1** Change these percentages into decimals:

   (a) 69%      (b) 31%      (c) 93%      (d) 21%      (e) 15%      (f) 60%

**2** Change these decimals into percentages:

   (a) 0.29     (b) 0.84     (c) 0.14     (d) 0.67     (e) 0.90     (f) 0.02

**3** Change these percentages into decimals:

   (a) 53%      (b) 28%      (c) 18%      (d) 40%      (e) 3%       (f) 92%

**4** Change these decimals into percentages:

   (a) 0.08     (b) 0.8      (c) 0.9      (d) 0.09     (e) 0.05     (f) 0.5

**5** Which of the following are true?

   (a) $3\% = 0.03$      (b) $3\% = 0.3$      (c) $70\% = 0.07$      (d) $70\% = 0.7$

   (e) $2\% = 0.2$      (f) $2\% = 0.02$      (g) $4\% = 0.4$      (h) $40\% = 0.4$

**6** Match up each percentage with its equivalent decimal (warning: one of the decimals is not needed).

A [ 60% ]    P [ 0.1 ]

B [ 1% ]    Q [ 0.06 ]

C [ 31% ]    R [ 0.01 ]

D [ 6% ]    S [ 3.1 ]

E [ 10% ]    T [ 0.6 ]

U [ 0.31 ]

**7** Change these percentage into decimals:

(a) 3.5%  (b) 6.7%  (c) 100%  (d) 120%  (e) 248%  (f) 192%

**8** In exercise E6.1, we changed fractions and percentages. Look back to remind yourself if you need to.

Copy and complete:

| Percentage | Decimal | Fraction |
|---|---|---|
| 21% | | |
| | 0.07 | |
| | | $\frac{19}{100}$ |
| 25% | | |
| | 0.3 | |
| | | $\frac{7}{10}$ |

**9** Copy and complete:

| Decimal | Percentage | Fraction |
|---|---|---|
| 0.32 | | |
| | 43% | |
| 0.06 | | |
| | | $\frac{7}{50}$ |
| | 80% | |
| | | $\frac{3}{20}$ |

(a) A holiday firm reduces its prices of a holiday from £1740 to £1479.

Find the percentage decrease.

actual decrease = 1740 − 1479

$$= 261$$

percentage decrease = $\left(\dfrac{261}{1740}\right) \times 100$

$$= 15\%$$

(b) Roger buys a box of shirts for £180 and sells them for £232.20.

Find the percentage profit.

actual profit = 232.20 − 180

$$= 52.20$$

percentage profit = $\left(\dfrac{52.20}{180}\right) \times 100$

$$= 29\%$$

Notice that in both calculations we divide by the *original value*.

## E6. 5

*Use a calculator* when needed. Give answers to the nearest whole number when needed.

1   Eddie's wages were increased from £120 to £129.60 per week. What was the percentage increase?

2   A CD player is bought for £60 and sold for £69. What is the percentage profit?

3   Sandra's weekly wage goes up from £240 to £252. What is the percentage increase?

4   Copy and complete the table below:

| original price (£) | final price (£) | actual increase or decrease(£) | percentage increase or decrease |
|---|---|---|---|
| 280 | 336 | | |
| 300 | 324 | | |
| 524 | 550.20 | | |
| 780 | 897 | | |
| 310 | 170.50 | | |
| 96 | 62.40 | | |

5   The value of a bike drops from £240 to £160 in one year. What is the percentage decrease in that year?

6   The population of a country increases from 2,374,000 to 2,445,220. What is the percentage increase?

**7** 'Dobbs Autos' has to reduce its workforce from 120 people to 93 people. What is the percentage decrease?

**8** Kevin bought a car for £7350 and sold it quickly for £8100. Calculate the percentage profit.

**9** Copy and complete the table below:

| old price (£) | new price (£) | actual profit or loss (£) | percentage profit or loss |
|---|---|---|---|
| 80 | 100 | | |
| 130 | 91 | | |
| 520 | 400 | | |
| 63 | 50 | | |
| 119 | 200 | | |
| 48 | 75 | | |

**10** Carla buys a house for £221,000. She sells it 3 years later for £247,520. What percentage profit does Carla make?

**11** Simon buys 300 cans of drink at 30p for each can. The cans are sold at a school disco for 36p a can. What is the percentage profit if all the cans are sold?

**12** The cost of a first-class stamp is increased from 28p to 29p. What is the percentage increase?

**13** The 'King's Arms' pub buys some of its items at the costs shown below and sells them at the prices shown below. Find the percentage profit on each item.

| Item | cost price | selling price |
|---|---|---|
| pint of lager | £1.20 | £2.70 |
| packet of crisps | 25p | 60p |
| pint of bitter | £1.15 | £2.50 |
| packet of nuts | 27p | 75p |

**14** Arnie the grocer bought 100 cabbages at 30p each. He sold 80 of the cabbages at 65p each. The other 20 cabbages went rotten and had to be thrown away. Find the percentage profit Arnie made on the 100 cabbages.

(a) Suppose £2000 is invested at 10% per annum (year) compound interest. How much money will there be after 2 years?

'**compound**' interest here means that the interest must be worked out separately for each year.

After 1 year: interest = 10% of 2000 = 200

total money = 2000 + 200 = £2200

money at start    interest
of year

Do a new calculation for the interest in the second year.

After 2 years: interest = 10% of 2200 = 220

money at
start of year

total money = 2200 + 220 = £2420

money at start of 2nd year    interest

(b) A car is bought for £12000. Each year, its value depreciates (goes down) by 5% of its value at the start of the year.

How much is the car worth after 2 years?

After 1 year: loss = 5% of 12000 = 600

value of car = 12000 − 600 = 11400

After 2 years: loss = 5% of 11400 = 570

value of car = 11400 − 570 = £10830

## Simple interest

This means work out the interest for one year then multiply by the number of years.

£2000 is invested at 10% per annum (year) simple interest. How much money will there be after 2 years?

interest = 10% of 2000 = 200
total interest for 2 years = 200 × 2 = 400
total money after 2 years = 2000 + 400 = £2400

money at start    total interest

*Use a calculator* when needed. Give answers to the nearest penny when needed.

**1** £5000 is invested at 10% per annum (year) compound interest. How much money will there be after 2 years?

**2** Ben invests £6000 in a bank at 5% per annum compound interest. How much money will be have in the bank after 2 years?

**3** A bank pays 6% per annum compound interest. How much will the following people have in the bank after the number of years stated?

(a) Kim: £9000 after 2 years.    (b) Freddie: £4000 after 3 years.

(c) Les: £2500 after 2 years.    (d) Olive: £600 after 2 years.

**4** A stereo loses 30% of its value every year. Tim bought it for £800. How much would it be worth after:

(a) 2 years?    (b) 3 years?

**5** The number of fish in a lake is decreasing by 5% each year. There are 10000 fish in the lake at the start of 2005. How many fish are there in the lake

(a) at the end of 2005?    (b) at the end of 2006?

**6** Inflation is how much more expensive things in the shop get each year. Inflation is about 3%.

If a pair of shoes costs £50, how much will the pair of shoes cost after:

(a) 2 years?    (b) 3 years?

**7** A new car is bought for £23000. Each year, its value depreciates (goes down) by 15% of its value at the start of the year. How much is the car worth after 3 years?

**8** The population of a country decreases by 4% of its value at the start of every year. If the population is 8 million, what will it be after 3 years?

**9** A bacteria culture starts with 4000 bacteria. Each hour the number of bacteria increases by 20%. How many bacteria will there be after 3 hours?

**10** Mohammed puts £200 in a bank at 6% p.a. (per annum) compound interest. Geena puts £210 in a bank at 4% p.a. compound interest.

(a) Who will have more money in the bank after 2 years?

(b) How much more?

£500 is invested in a bank at 14% per annum compound interest. How much money is in the bank after 5 years?

Use a *percentage multiplier* 1.14 (100% + 14% = 114%)

Now multiply by 1.14 every year to get the new amount.

Start with £500:

after 1 year:    $500 \times 1.14 = 570$

after 2 years:    $\times 1.14 = 649.80$ and so on

after 5 years: total money $= 500 \times \underbrace{1.14 \times 1.14 \times 1.14 \times 1.14 \times 1.14}_{\text{5 years}}$

$$= 962.70|729\ldots$$
$$= £962.71 \text{ (to the nearest penny)}$$

## E6. 6

*Use a calculator.* Give answers to the nearest penny when needed.

**1**  £800 is put in a bank with 10% p.a. (per annum) compound interest.

(a) Work out the total money in the bank after 3 years (use *percentage multiplier* 1.1).

(b) How much money is in the bank after 5 years?

(c) How much money is in the bank after 10 years? (just multiply £800 by 1.1 ten times)

**2**  Another bank pays 7% p.a. compound interest. If you put in £400, how much money would be in the bank after:

(a) 2 years?    (b) 3 years?    (c) 5 years?

**3**  A building society offers 4.7% p.a. compound interest. If you put £1200 into the building society, how much would you have 3 years later?

**4**  (a) What is the percentage multiplier to find a 15% decrease? (Hint: what percentage would you have left after you have taken off 15%?)

(b) The value of a car depreciates (goes down) by 15% of its value each year. Sally buys the new car for £16000.
How much will the car be worth after 7 years?

**5** The value of a washing machine depreciates by 25% of its value each year.

If a new washing machine costs £480, how much will it be worth after 6 years?

**6** A bank account gives 5% compound interest each year. Jack puts £600 into the bank. Copy and complete the table below:

| after | money in bank |
|---|---|
| 1 year | |
| 3 years | |
| 5 years | |
| 10 years | |

**7** A car loses 22% of its value each year. A car costs £19500 brand new. Copy and complete the table below:

| after | value of car |
|---|---|
| 2 years | |
| 4 years | |
| 5 years | |
| 10 years | |

**8** The mould on some bread has an area of $20 \, cm^2$. It grows by 8% each week. Copy and complete the table below, giving your answers to the nearest whole number.

| after | area of mould |
|---|---|
| 1 week | |
| 2 weeks | |
| 3 weeks | |
| 4 weeks | |

**9** A population decreases by 11% each year. At the end of year 2000, the population was 3,000,000. Copy and complete the table below, giving your answers to the nearest whole number.

| end of year | population |
|---|---|
| 2001 | |
| 2002 | |
| 2003 | |
| 2004 | |

**10** If a 15-year old person put £500 in a bank at 9% p.a. compound interest and left it in the bank for 50 years until retirement, how much money would be in the bank?

**Can you still?**

**6D** **Multiply out brackets (see Unit 4)**

**Can you still?**

**Expand (multiply out)**

**1.** $3(a + 3)$

**2.** $5(x - 3)$

**3.** $4(2x + 6)$

**4.** $5(7m - 2)$

**5.** $7(4a + 2b)$

**6.** $3(6y - 3z)$

**7.** $7(2x - 9y)$

**8.** $a(b + c)$

**9.** $m(m - 6)$

**10.** $-3(a + 4)$

**11.** $-5(x - 5)$

**12.** $-2(2b - 6)$

## Key Facts

We use ratio to compare parts of a whole.

In this diagram, there are 6 black squares and 2 white squares.

We say the *ratio* of black squares to white squares is 6 to 2.

This is written as 6:2

Both numbers in the ratio 6:2 can be divided by 2 so we can reduce the ratio 6:2 to its simplest from of 3:1

(a) In a class of 24 children, 14 are girls. Find the ratio of boys to girls. Give the answer in its simplest form.

There are 10 boys.
Ratio of boys to girls = 10:14
(10 and 14 can both be divided by 2)
Ratio of boys to girls = 5:7

(b) Are the ratios 15:25:30 the same as 3:5:6?
15, 25 and 30 can all be divided by 5

$15 \div 5 = 3$
$25 \div 5 = 5$
$30 \div 5 = 6$

so 15:25:30 = 3:5:6

---

**M6. 7**

Copy and fill in the boxes below:

1   The ratio of black to white is ☐ : ☐

2   The ratio of black to white is ☐ : ☐

3   The ratio of black to white is ☐ : ☐

In Questions **4** to **7** , copy the circles and colour them in to match the given ratio.

4   ○○○○○   The ratio of black to white is 3:2.

5   The ratio of black to white is 1:4.   ○○○○○

6   ○○○○○○   The ratio of *white* to *black* is 3:3.

**7** The ratio of *white* to *black* is 2:4.

**8** For the human body, write down the following ratios. Write the answers in their simplest form (example: thumbs to fingers is 2:8 = 1:4)

(a) feet to toes     (b) ears to nose     (c) eyes to fingers

**9** On a bus, there are 35 people. 25 of the people are female. Find the ratio of males to females. Give the ratio in its simplest form.

**10** One evening, a vet sees 16 dogs and 10 cats. Find the ratio of dogs to cats. Give the ratio in its simplest form.

**11** For each diagram below, write down the ratio of black to white in its simplest form.

(a) ● ● ● ○ ● ● ● ○     (b)

(c)          (d)

**12** Maaike makes some models using cubes of different colours.

(a) Model 1 must have red to blue in the ratio 1:2. She uses 4 red cubes. How many blue does she use?

(b) Model 2 must have yellow to green in the ratio 2:3. She uses 6 yellow cubes. How many green does she use?

(c) Model 3 must have green to blue in the ratio 3:5. She uses 10 blue cubes. How many green does she use?

(d) Model 4 must have white to yellow in the ratio 3:2. She uses 8 yellow cubes. How many white does she use?

(e) Model 5 must have white to black to red in the ratio 2:1:3. She uses 3 black cubes. How many white does she use?
How many red does she use?

**13** In a hall there are 45 chairs and 9 tables. Find the ratio of chairs to tables in its simplest form.

**14** In a class of 30 children, 18 are boys. Find the ratio of boys to girls in its simplest form.

**15** Change the following ratios to their simplest form.

(a) 15:10     (b) 8:12     (c) 9:15     (d) 10:22

(e) 30:20     (f) 42:49     (g) 12:16     (h) 35:20

(i) 18:24      (j) 18:30      (k) 40:25      (l) 24:60

(m) 8:4:2      (n) 6:9:12      (o) 40:15:25      (p) 8:18:14

**16** Frank spends £3 on Monday and 50p on Tuesday. Find the ratio of the money spent on Monday to the money spent on Tuesday (remember to change all the money to pence then give the answer in its simplest form)

**17** Tanya is 1.6 m tall and Sid is 2 m tall. Find the ratio of Tanya's height to Sid's height (remember: 1 m = 100 cm so 2 m = 200 cm and 1.6 m = 160 cm). Give the answer in its simplest form.

**18** Write the ratios below in their simplest form. Remember to get the units the same first.

(a) 50 cm:1 m      (b) 1 m:20 cm      (c) 2 m:20 cm      (d) 3 m:50 cm

(e) 25 cm:2 m      (f) 75 cm:3 m      (g) 5 m:40 cm      (h) 5 cm:2 m

(i) 50p:£2      (j) 50p:£5      (k) 5p:£2      (l) 80p:£8

## Direct proportion

5 doughnuts cost 80p.

How much will 12 doughnuts cost?

*Find the cost of 1 doughnut and then find the cost of 12.*

5 doughnuts cost 80p

1 doughnut costs 80 ÷ 5 = 16p

12 doughnuts cost 16p × 12 = 192p = £1.92

### E6. 7

*Do not use a calculator.*

**1** 6 pencils cost 54p. What do 5 pencils cost?

**2** 5 rulers cost £1.50. What do 2 rulers cost?

**3** 5 oranges cost 75p. What do 6 oranges cost?

**4** 8 bananas cost 64p. What do 5 bananas cost?

**5** Magazines cost £21 for 7. Find the cost of 3 magazines.

**6** 9 pizzas cost £45. How much will 7 pizzas cost?

**7** 8 rubbers cost 88p. How much will 5 rubbers cost?

**8** 7 shirts cost £84. Find the cost of 4 shirts.

**9** The total weight of 6 CDs is 72 grams. How much do 9 CDs weigh?

**10** 2 televisions cost £900. How much will 3 televisions cost?

**11** A car takes 20 minutes to travel 32 km. How far will the car travel in 40 minutes?

**12** 4 cups cost £2.80. How much will 5 cups cost?

*For the rest of the exercise you may use a calculator if needed.*

**13** Find the cost of 3 cakes if 9 cakes cost £15.30.

**14** 3 boxes weigh 14.1 kg. Find the weight of 13 boxes.

In Questions **15** to **18** , copy and complete the tables.

**15**

| number of grapefruit | cost |
|---|---|
| 8 | £2.80 |
| 1 | |
| 7 | |
| 10 | |
| 50 | |

**16**

| weight of potatoes | cost |
|---|---|
| 2.5 kg | £2.40 |
| 1 kg | |
| 5 kg | |
| 15 kg | |
| 17.5 kg | |

**17**

| pounds | dollars |
|---|---|
| 42 | 79.80 |
| 1 | |
| 8 | |
| 32.50 | |
| 75 | |

**18**

| pounds | euros |
|---|---|
| 9.20 | 15.18 |
| 1 | |
| 5 | |
| 15 | |
| 125 | |
| 63.40 | |

**19** Toni used 450 g of mince to make chilli con carne for 4 people. How much mince would have to be used to make chilli con carne for 10 people?

**20** 5 bottles of beer cost £13.30. Find the cost of 7 bottles of beer.

**21** 17 adults can go to the cinema for £116.45. How much would 12 adults pay?

**22** This recipe for macaroni cheese serves 6 people.

| 150 g | cheese |
|---|---|
| 300 g | plain flour |
| 250 g | margarine |
| 1 | onion |
| 3 | eggs |
| 30 g | butter |
| 3 | tablespoons of cold water |

How much of each ingredient is needed to serve 18 people?

**23** This recipe for chocolate sponge serves 8 people.

| 220 g | butter |
|---|---|
| 220 g | sugar |
| 2 | tablespoons of boiling water |
| 4 | eggs |
| 220 g | self-raising flour |
| 2 | tablespoons of cocoa |

How much of each ingredient is needed for 12 people?

**24** This recipe for pancakes serves 4 people.

| 120 g | plain flour |
|---|---|
| 280 ml | milk |
| 2 | eggs |

How much of each ingredient is needed for 6 people?

**25** This recipe for pizza serves 5 people.

| 250 g | cheese |
|---|---|
| 180 g | dough |
| 150 ml | tomato sauce |
| 25 g | pepperoni |

How much of each ingredient is needed for 9 people?

## Sharing in a given ratio

Share 40 oranges between Al and Jordan in the ratio 5:3.

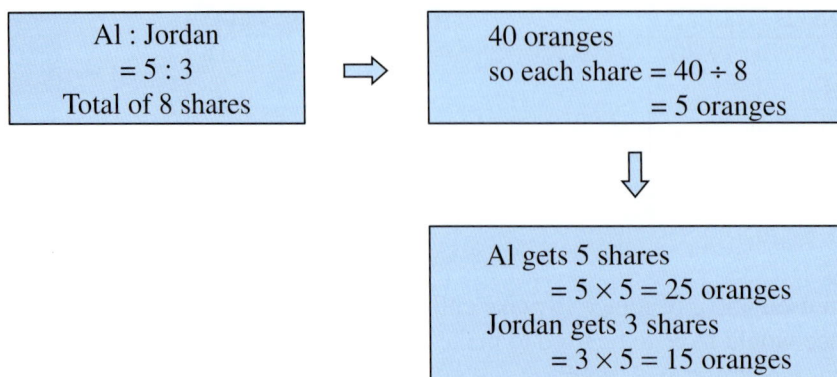

| Al : Jordan |
|---|
| = 5 : 3 |
| Total of 8 shares |

⟹

| 40 oranges |
|---|
| so each share = 40 ÷ 8 |
| = 5 oranges |

⟱

| Al gets 5 shares |
|---|
| = 5 × 5 = 25 oranges |
| Jordan gets 3 shares |
| = 3 × 5 = 15 oranges |

**1** (a) Divide £160 in the ratio 1:3      (b) Divide £90 in the ratio 5:4

   (c) Divide £240 in the ratio 7:5      (d) Divide 80 g in the ratio 2:3

   (e) Divide 300 g in the ratio 3:7      (f) Divide 450 g in the ratio 7:2

   (g) Divide 60 minutes in the ratio 3:1      (h) Divide £800 in the ratio 5:1:2

   (i) Divide £360 in the ratio 2:3:4      (j) Divide 5000 g in the ratio 8:5:7

**2** In a class the ratio of boys to girls is 4:3. If there are 28 children in a class, how many boys are there and how many girls?

**3** A woman divides £800 between Cath and Ben in the ratio 5:3. How much money do Cath and Ben each get?

**4** Colin and Lily share a bag of 35 sweets in the ratio 2:3. How many sweets does each person get?

**5** A metal bar is 27 cm long. If it is cut into 2 parts in the ratio 2:7 how long is each part?

**6** The ratio of men to women to children visiting the Eiffel Tower one day was 4:5:6. If 975 people visited the Eiffel Tower, find out how many were:

   (a) men      (b) women      (c) children

**7** £320 is shared between Omar, Molly and Sachin in the ratio 3:1:4. How much will each person get?

**8** Mr Hope has a BMW and a Mini. He puts 75 litres of petrol into the 2 cars so that the ratio of the petrol in the BMW to the Mini is 16:9. How much petrol is put into each car?

**9** A green paint is mixed from blue and yellow in the ratio 2:5. How much of each colour is needed to make 56 litres of paint?

**10** 900 g of alloy is made up of copper, tin and nickel in the ratio 7:3:5. How many grams of each metal are there?

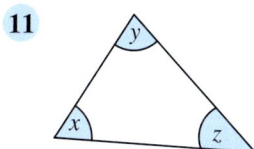

**11**

The angles $x$, $y$ and $z$ in a triangle are in the ratio 5:1:3.

Find the sizes of angles $x$, $y$ and $z$.

**12** The angles $p$, $q$, $r$ and $s$ in a quadrilateral are in the ratio 3:1:2:4

Find the sizes of angles $p$, $q$, $r$ and $s$

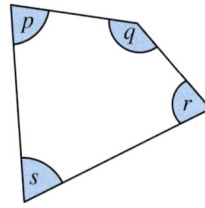

### Further questions on ratio

Lola and Dan are given some money in the ratio 6:5. If Lola gets £42, how much does Dan get?

| Lola gets 6 shares |
| Lola gets £42 |
| each share = 42 ÷ 6 |
| = £7 |

⟹

| Dan gets 5 shares |
| = 5 × 7 |
| = £35 |

## E6. 8

**1** Ribena is diluted with water in the ratio 1:6.

   (a) If 9 ml of ribena is used, how much water should be added?

   (b) If 60 ml of water is used, how much ribena should be added?

**2** Some money is shared between Hamish and Rory in the ratio 11:4. If Rory gets £60, how much will Hamish get?

**3** Gravel and cement are mixed in the ratio 5:3 to make mortar.

   (a) If 30 shovels of gravel are used, how many shovels of cement are needed?

   (b) If 12 shovels of cement are used, how many shovels of gravel are needed?

**4** For a school trip there needs to be a ratio of adults to young people of 2:17. How many adults are needed for a trip with 85 young people?

**5** A father's and son's ages are in the ratio 9:4. If the father is 45 years old, how old is the son?

**6** An orange paint is made by mixing red and yellow in the ratio 2:3.

   (a) How much yellow must be used if 16 litres of red are used?

   (b) How much red must be used if 36 litres of yellow are used?

   (c) How much red and how much yellow must be used to make 80 litres of orange?

**7** Bread is made from flour and yeast in the ratio 30:1

    (a) How much yeast is mixed with 870 g of flour?

    (b) How much flour is needed to mix with 350 g of yeast?

**8** A 'Pink Lady' cocktail is made in the ratio 1 measure gin to 2 dashes Grenadine.

    (a) If 6 measures of gin are used, how many dashes of Grenadine should be added?

    (b) How many measures of gin should be used for 28 dashes of Grenadine?

**9** At a college, the ratio of boys to girls is 5:8

    (a) If there are 10 boys in a class, how many girls would there be?

    (b) If there are 264 girls in the college, how many boys are there in the college?

**10** Sheila, Gill and Ron are given some money in the ratio 7:3:4. If Gill was given £72, what was the *total* amount of money given to all 3 people?

**11** In a factory the ratio of men to women is 5:2. If there are 235 men, how many women are there?

**12** A recipe is made from flour, butter and sugar in the ratio 6:3:2 How much flour and sugar is needed if 270 g of butter is used?

**13** Purple paint is made from red and blue paint in the ratio 2:5. If 35 litres of blue are used, how much purple paint would be mixed *in total*?

**14** Gunpowder is made up of potassium nitrate, sulphur and charcoal in the ratio 17:3:4.

    (a) If 9 kg of sulphur is used, how much potassium nitrate should be added?

    (b) If 20 kg of charcoal is used, how much sulphur should be added?

    (c) How much sulphur should be used to make 216 kg of gunpowder?

**15** The seven dwarves are given some money. It is shared between Dopey, Doc, Happy, Bashful, Grumpy, Sneezy and Sleepy in the ratio 8:9:4:3:10:7:12. If Grumpy gets £150, how much money do each of the seven dwarves get? What is the total amount of money?

Most people have an account with a bank or a building society. Money is kept safely in the bank. Bills can be paid directly from the bank or with a debit card. Cash can be withdrawn or cheques can be used.

**Writing a cheque**

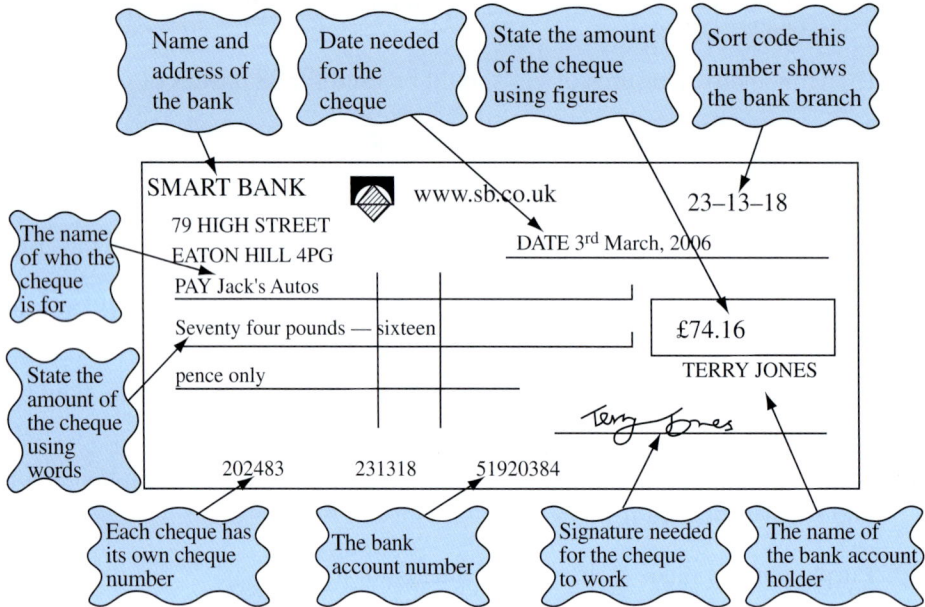

Name and address of the bank

Date needed for the cheque

State the amount of the cheque using figures

Sort code–this number shows the bank branch

The name of who the cheque is for

State the amount of the cheque using words

SMART BANK
79 HIGH STREET
EATON HILL 4PG
www.sb.co.uk
23–13–18
DATE 3rd March, 2006
PAY Jack's Autos
Seventy four pounds — sixteen
pence only
£74.16
TERRY JONES
Terry Jones
202483        231318        51920384

Each cheque has its own cheque number

The bank account number

Signature needed for the cheque to work

The name of the bank account holder

**Note**

- the amount in words must match the amount in figures.
- the cheque must be used within six months of the date.
- if you make a mistake when filling out a cheque, you may correct it so long as you write your signature by the mistake.
- the bank will not pay the money for your cheque if you do not have enough money in your bank account.

SMART BANK
1234 5678 9101 1121
JERRY JONES
VALID 07/04 THRU 07/09

**Cheque guarantee card**

Once you are over 18, your bank may allow you a cheque guarantee card. If the cheque guarantee card number is written on the back of the cheque, the bank will definitely pay the money (the maximum amount is usually £100).

**Being overdrawn**

If you spend more money than is in your bank account without arranging with the bank beforehand, you will go overdrawn. The bank will charge you extra money and you will *owe* them *even more money*. You will then have to sort it out quickly or you could run into even greater difficulties.

## WYM6

**1** Pat has £56 in her account. Her bank will charge her £30 if she goes overdrawn. She pays out two cheques, one of £39.19 and another of £27. How much will she now owe the bank?

**2** Zak's bank has agreed that he may go up to £50 overdrawn without paying a penalty. If he breaks the agreement, he will have to pay a £35 charge.

Zak has £32 in his account. He makes payments of £28, £16.29 and £34.96. How much will Zak now owe the bank?

**3** Chloe has the same agreement with her bank as Zak in Question **2**. Chloe has £93 in her account. She makes payments of £61.14, £73.06 and £25.32. How much will Chloe now owe the bank?

**4** Colin sends the following cheque to his phone company.

| | |
|---|---|
| SMART BANK ◈ www.sb.co.uk | 17–26–19 |
| 79 BRIDGE ROAD POLDEN P019 6XG | DATE 9th April, 2006 |

PAY Phone Easy

Eighty two pounds — twenty four pence only

£72.24

COLIN MAYS

*Colin Mays*

417327      172619      32718425

By looking at the cheque earlier in this section, write down:

(a) the sort code               (b) the bank account number

(c) the website address for the bank     (d) the cheque number

(e) The bank will not cash this cheque. Explain why.

**5** Lara has £128.16 in her bank account. She makes payments of £17.11, £32.68 and £41.23. What is the biggest cheque she could now pay out without going overdrawn?

**6** Investigate different banks. Find out if they pay interest on bank accounts. How much can you go overdrawn before you are charged? How much would the bank charge you if you went too much overdrawn? Discuss as a class.

### 1. Converting between fractions and percentages

Change these percentages into fractions. Cancel the answers when possible.

(a) 29%   (b) 20%   (c) 4%   (d) 71%   (e) 85%   (f) 12%

Change these fractions into percentages

(g) $\dfrac{3}{100}$   (h) $\dfrac{1}{2}$   (i) $\dfrac{51}{100}$   (j) $\dfrac{3}{10}$   (k) $\dfrac{7}{25}$   (l) $\dfrac{11}{20}$

### 2. Expressing one number as a percentage of another

(a) What percentage of these shapes are stars?

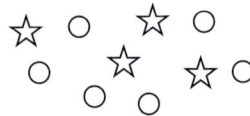

(b) Ned scored 9 out of 25 in his English test. Faye scored 8 out of 29 in her English test. Who got the higher percentage and by how much was it higher? (*You may use a calculator*)

(c) Mr. Seymour wants to buy a car for £12000. He pays a deposit of £1000. What is the deposit as a percentage of the total cost of the car? (*You may use a calculator*. Give your answer to the nearest whole number)

(d) What percentage of letters in the alphabet are vowels (a, e, i, o, u)? (*You may use a calculator*. Give your answer to the nearest whole number)

### 3. Finding a percentage of a number

(a) Find 25% of £36     (b) Find $33\frac{1}{3}$% of £36     (c) Find 10% of £90
(d) Find 30% of £90     (e) Find 5% of £40     (f) Find 15% of £40

*You may use a calculator* for the Questions below:

(g) Find 3% of £650     (h) Find 23% of £92     (i) Find 17% of £312

### 4. Finding percentage increases and decreases

(a) Increase £40 by 10%     (b) Decrease £70 by 20%
(c) Reduce £600 by 5%     (d) Decrease £120 by $66\frac{2}{3}$%

(e)

TV £560
SALE
30% off

What is the sale price of this TV?

(f) A music system costs £628 + VAT.

   If VAT is 17.5%, work out how much the music system costs in total?

(g) Increase £610 by 4%    (h) Decrease £385 by 12%

---

### 5. Converting between percentages and decimals

Change these percentages into decimals.

   (a) 29%   (b) 79%   (c) 34%   (d) 25%   (e) 70%   (f) 22%

Change these decimals into percentages:

   (g) 0.61   (h) 0.8   (i) 0.08   (j) 0.64   (k) 0.3   (l) 1.27

---

### 6. Finding percentage changes

*You may use a calculator.*

(a) A bike is bought for £310 and sold one year later for £250.

   What was the percentage loss? (Give your answer to the nearest whole number)

(b) A necklace is brought for £60 and sold for £75. What is the percentage profit?

(c) Callum earns £260 each week.

   His wage is increased to £275.60 each week. What is the percentage increase?

(d) A fairground drops its standard price of £2.50 a ride to £2 a ride. What is the percentage decrease?

---

### 7. Doing compound interest-type problems

(a) £4000 is invested at 5% per annum (year) compound interest. How much money will there be after 2 years?

(b) £32000 is invested at 10% per annum (year) compound interest. How much money will there be after 3 years?

(c) A car is bought for £16000. Each year, its value depreciates (goes down) by 4% of its value of the start of the year. How much is the car worth after 2 years?

## 8. Using percentage multipliers

*You may use a calculator.*

(a) What is the *percentage multiplier* to find a 12% increase? (Hint: what percentage would you have when you add on 12%)

(b) £700 is put in a bank at 12% p.a. (per annum) compound interest. How much money will be in the bank after 5 years? (Give your answer to the nearest penny)

(c) What is the *percentage multiplier* to find a 21% decrease?

(d) The value of a fridge depreciates by 21% of its value each year.

If a new fridge costs £270, how much will it be worth after 7 years? (Give your answer to the nearest penny)

## 9. Finding ratios

(a)  What is the ratio of black to white?

(b) There are 29 children in a class. 17 are boys. Find the ratio of boys to girls.

(c) Write down the ratio of black to white in its simplest form.

Change the following ratios to their simplest form:

(d) 9:24     (e) 60:15     (f) 50 cm:2 m     (g) 25p:£3

## 10. Dealing with direct proportion

(a) 9 apples cost 54p. What do 7 apples cost?

(b) 3 calculators cost £15. How much will 5 calculators cost?

(c) 7 bags of sugar weigh 5495 g. How much do 3 bags of sugar weigh?

## 11. Sharing in a given ratio

(a) The ratio of boys to girls in a class is 5:4. If there are 36 children in a class, how many boys are there and how many girls?

(b) £3000 is shared between Ally, Jane and Rob in the ratio 11:4:5.

How much money does each person get?

(c) Lemon squash is diluted using squash and water in the ratio 1:8. If 72 ml of water is used, how much squash must be added?

(d) Green paint is made from blue and yellow paint in the ratio 3:7. If 42 litres of yellow are used, how much blue paint must be used?

**1** (a) A dealer bought a mobile phone for £75 and sold it to make a 30% profit. For how much did he sell the phone?

    (b) Bushra has a mobile phone. She pays a charge of £12.50 per month and the phone calls cost 3 pence per minute. VAT of 17.5% is added to the total of charge and the calls. How much is Bushra's phone bill in a month when she has made calls for 170 minutes? (OCR)

**2** David's salary in 1998 was £17550. He was promoted in January 1999 and given an 18% increase in his salary. What is his new salary? (WJEC)

**3** (a) (i) Write 25% as a fraction.

       (ii) Write 0.2 as a fraction.

      (iii) Write $\dfrac{3}{10}$ as a percentage.

    (b) Write 25%, 0.2 and $\dfrac{3}{10}$ in order of size, smallest first.

    (c) Write 9% as (i) a fraction (ii) a decimal (OCR)

**4** Kelly bought 4 identical computer disks for £3.60.

Work out the cost of 9 of these computer disks.

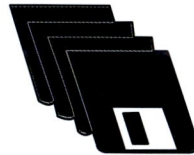

(EDEXCEL)

**5** A bar of Fruit & Nut chocolate normally weighs 200 g. The ratio by weight of a special offer bar to a normal bar is 5:4. What is the weight of a special offer bar? (AQA)

**6** This is a list of ingredients for making a pear & almond crumble for 4 people.

| Ingredients for 4 people. |
| --- |
| 80 g plain flour |
| 60 g ground almonds |
| 90 g soft brown sugar |
| 60 g butter |
| 4 ripe pears |

Work out the amount of each ingredient needed to make a pear & almond crumble for 10 people. (EDEXCEL)

**7** Alan, Brendan and Chloe shared £768 in the ratio 5:4:3. How much did each receive? (OCR)

**8** There are 800 students at Prestfield School.

144 of these students were absent from school on Wednesday.

(a) Work out how many students were **not** absent on Wednesday.

Trudy says that more than 25% of the 800 students were absent on Wednesday.

(b) Is Trudy correct? Explain your answer.

45% of these 800 students are girls.

(c) Work out 45% of 800.

There are 176 students in year 10.

(d) Write 176 out of 800 as a percentage.                    (EDEXCEL)

**9** (a) This year Jo's class has 160 maths lessons.

Next year they will have 20% fewer lessons.

How many maths lessons will they have next year?

(b) This year each lesson lasts 50 minutes.

Next year each lesson will be 20% longer.

How long will each lesson be next year?

(c) Jo thinks this means they will have exactly the same total amount of maths lesson time. She is wrong. By what percentage will it change?     (OCR)

**10** At the end of any year the value of a car is 20% lower than at the beginning of that year.

At the beginning of the year I bought a car for £5000.

Work out how much my car is worth 2 years later.                    (OCR)

**11** Josie invests £800 in an account that pays her 3% **simple** interest every year.

How much interest will she have been paid in total after 6 years?     (OCR)

**12** Each year the value of a cooker falls by 8% of its value at the beginning of that year. Sally bought a new cooker on 1st January 2001.

By 1st January 2002 its value fallen by 8% to £598.

(a) Work out the value of the new cooker on 1st January 2001.

(b) Work out the value of the cooker by 1st January 2005.
Give your answer to the nearest penny.                    (EDEXCEL)

# Coursework 1 – problem solving task  7

In this unit we will explore the problem solving task which accounts for 10% of your final GCSE grade.

### Advice

- Check carefully with your teacher if you do not understand the problem at the start.

- Make a plan (eg. the order of doing things, any data to collect, equipment needed, any questions to be asked).

- Use tables, charts and graphs.

- Check answers as you go along.

- Leave yourself enough time.

- Write down everything you do even if it goes wrong.

- Spend your time working on the problem, not on drawing a beautiful front cover which scores no marks.

- Make the problem as simple as you can at the start.

- Use calculators and computers if you need to.

- Use algebra to explain rules if you can.

- Explain why a rule works if you can.

### How is your work marked?

Three different 'strands' are being looked at:

Strand 1 –  deciding what to do at each stage then doing it!

Strand 2 –  showing what you have done, using tables, diagrams and graphs. Eventually using algebra clearly.

Strand 3 –  finding patterns and testing your ideas. Using algebra to make formulas and explaining why they work by looking closely at how the problem is made up.

We will highlight key points by exploring two possible coursework tasks.

**Task 1 – 'a feast'**

10 people can sit around a table at a feast.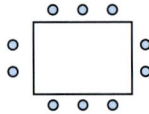

When 2 tables are put together, 16 people can sit around them.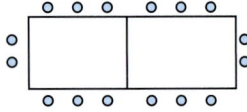

When 3 tables are put together, 22 people can sit around them.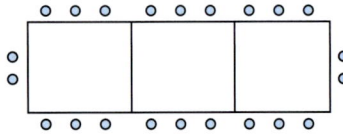

(a) How many people can sit around 20 tables?

(b) How many people can sit around any given number of tables? Investigate.

**Start simple**

Draw 4 tables.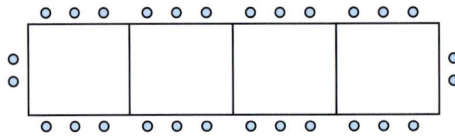

28 people

**Put results in a table**

| Number of tables | Number of people |
|---|---|
| 1 | 10 |
| 2 | 16 |
| 3 | 22 |
| 4 | 28 |

**Search for a pattern**

From my table I can see that the number of people goes up by 6 every time I add one table.

**Test the rule**

There should be $28 + 6 = 34$ people around 5 tables.

Check by drawing.

34 people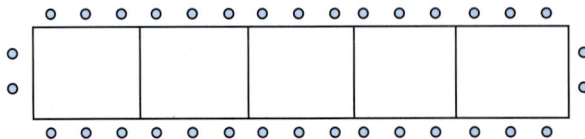

178

let $t$ = number of tables

let $p$ = number of people

look at the differences

| $t$ | $p$ |
|---|---|
| 1 | 10 |
| 2 | 16 |
| 3 | 22 |
| 4 | 28 |
| 5 | 34 |

+6
+6
+6
+6

The 1$^{st}$ difference is 6 so a formula will contain $6 \times t$

| $t$ | $p$ | $6t$ |
|---|---|---|
| 1 | 10 | 6 |
| 2 | 16 | 12 |
| 3 | 22 | 18 |
| 4 | 28 | 24 |
| 5 | 34 | 30 |

We need to add 4 onto each '$6t$' value to get the number of people $p$

$$p = 6t + 4$$

**Test the formula**

$t = 3 \Rightarrow p = (6 \times 3) + 4 = 22$

$t = 5 \Rightarrow p = (6 \times 5) + 4 = 34$

We have a formula that seems to work but we have not explained where it comes from by looking at the pattern of people around the tables. We cannot 'hit' a C grade without doing this.

**Justify the formula**

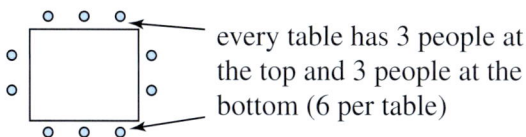

every table has 3 people at the top and 3 people at the bottom (6 per table)

2 tables have $6 \times 2 = 12$ people at the top and bottom

3 tables have $6 \times 3 = 18$ people at the top and bottom

so $t$ tables have $6 \times t = 6t$ people at the top and bottom

↑

our formula is $p = 6t + 4$

↑

There are the 2 people sitting on the left of the tables and the 2 people on the right no matter how may tables there are.

(a) How many people can sit around 20 tables?

$$p = 6t + 4 = (6 \times 20) + 4 = 124$$

124 people can sit around 20 tables.

(b) $p = 6t + 4$, where $p$ = number of people and $t$ = number of tables

The arrangement of tables could be changed.

eg.

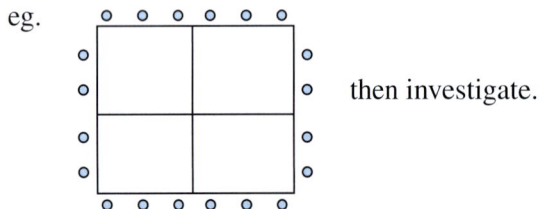

then investigate.

The shape of the tables could be changed.

eg.

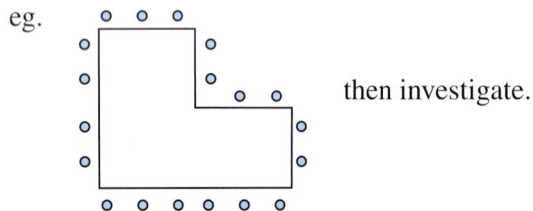

then investigate.

Key points have been highlighted. You must write down all the ideas you have at any stage. Always explain what you are doing and write a conclusion at the end. You can sum up your main formulas and state what else you might have looked at if you had been given the time.

Key points are now shown for another possible coursework task.

## Task 2 – 'the painted cube'

### Part A

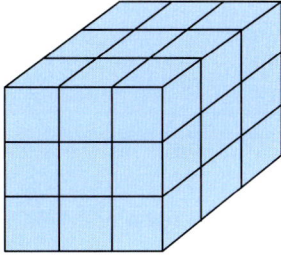

The outside faces of a 3 × 3 × 3 cube are painted blue.

Find out how many small cubes have:

(a) 3 blue faces      (b) 2 blue faces

(c) 1 blue face      (d) 0 blue faces

### Part B

Answer the same questions for a 20 × 20 × 20 cube.

### Part C

Investigate further.

{ Be practical }   Get some multilink cubes and explore simple models.

{ Put results in a table }

**Part A**

| 3 × 3 × 3 cube | |
|---|---|
| | number of cubes |
| 3 blue faces | 8 |
| 2 blue faces | 12 |
| 1 blue face | 6 |
| 0 blue faces | 1 |
| total | 27 |

{ Keep simple }

Look at a 2 × 2 × 2 cube

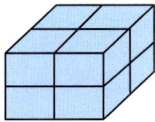

| 2 × 2 × 2 cube | |
|---|---|
| | number of cubes |
| 3 blue faces | 8 |
| 2 blue faces | 0 |
| 1 blue face | 0 |
| 0 blue faces | 0 |
| total | 8 |

Look at a 4 × 4 × 4 cube

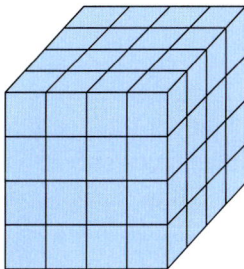

| 4 × 4 × 4 cube | |
|---|---|
| | number of cubes |
| 3 blue faces | 8 |
| 2 blue faces | 24 |
| 1 blue face | 24 |
| 0 blue faces | 8 |
| total | 64 |

181

3 red faces – always 8

| 2 blue faces | 2 × 2 × 2 cube | 3 × 3 × 3 cube | 4 × 4 × 4 cube |
|---|---|---|---|
| number of cubes | 0 | 12 | 24 |

The number is increasing by 12 each time. We would expect 36 for a $5 \times 5 \times 5$ cube. We need to test this or find a formula.

| 1 blue face | 2 × 2 × 2 cube | 3 × 3 × 3 cube | 4 × 4 × 4 cube |
|---|---|---|---|
| number of cubes | 0 | 6 | 24 |

We do not have enough numbers yet to be sure of a pattern.

| 0 blue faces | 2 × 2 × 2 cube | 3 × 3 × 3 cube | 4 × 4 × 4 cube |
|---|---|---|---|
| number of cubes | 0 | 1 | 8 |

These are cube numbers, $0^3$, $1^3$, $2^3$. We would expect $3^3 = 27$ for a $5 \times 5 \times 5$ cube.

Use algebra to find formulas

It is not practical to make a $5 \times 5 \times 5$ cube from multilink cubes. We could use differences to find a formula for 2 blue faces because this seems to go up by 12 each time.

It is better to look at exactly where each set of cubes is found on the larger cube.

**2 blue faces**

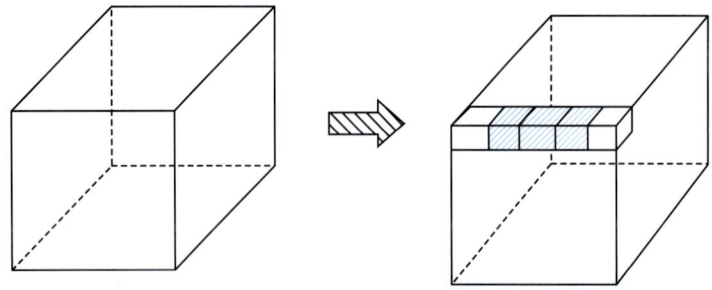

a cube has 12 edges        If each edge has $n$ cubes then subtract the 2 end cubes to leave the cubes with 2 blue faces only. Each edge has $(n - 2)$ cubes with 2 blue faces.

There are 12 edges so there are $12(n - 2)$ cubes with 2 blue faces.

Number of cubes with 2 blue faces $= 12(n-2)$

$3 \times 3 \times 3$ cube ($n = 3$), $12(n-2) = 12 \times (3-2) = 12$ cubes ✓

$4 \times 4 \times 4 \times$ cube ($n = 4$), $12(n-2) = 12 \times (4-2) = 24$ cubes ✓

This seems to work.

For a $5 \times 5 \times 5$ cube ($n = 5$), we would expect $12(n-2) = 12 \times (5-2) = 36$ cubes.

Justify the formula

We have already explained how this formula is made up because of how we used the diagrams to find the formula.

Find more formulas

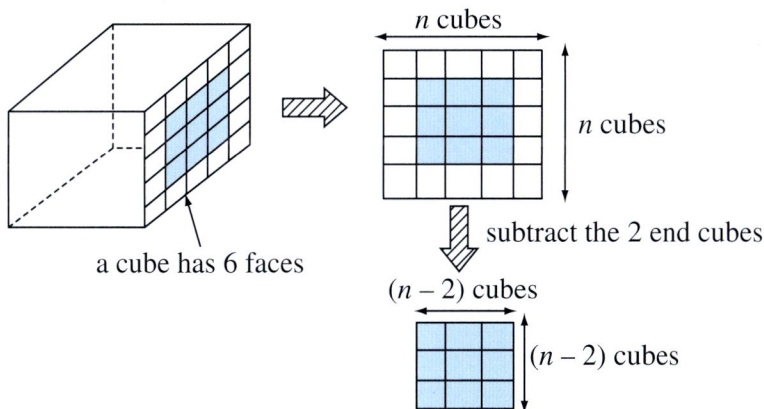

a cube has 6 faces

$n$ cubes

$n$ cubes

subtract the 2 end cubes

$(n-2)$ cubes

$(n-2)$ cubes

Number of cubes with 1 blue face $= (n-2) \times (n-2) = (n-2)^2$

There are 6 faces so there are $6(n-2)^2$ cubes with 1 blue face.

Test the formula

Number of cubes with 1 blue face $= 6(n-2)^2$

$3 \times 3 \times 3$ cube ($n = 3$), $6(n-2)^2 = 6 \times (3-2)^2 = 6 \times 1^2 = 6$ cubes ✓

$4 \times 4 \times 4$ cube ($n = 4$), $6(n-2)^2 = 6 \times (4-2)^2 = 6 \times 2^2 = 24$ cubes ✓

This seems to work.

For a $5 \times 5 \times 5$ cube ($n = 5$), we would expect $6(n-2)^2 = 6 \times (5-2)^2$

$$= 6 \times 3^2 = 54 \text{ cubes.}$$

There are always 8 cubes with 3 blue faces at each corner of the large cube.

For an $n \times n \times n$ cube, the total number of cubes $= n^3$

If the outer layer of the large cube is stripped off, it would reveal all the cubes with 0 blue faces. We would have an $(n-2) \times (n-2) \times (n-2)$ cube instead of an $n \times n \times n$ cube (2 cubes removed from each line of cubes when the outer layer is removed).

number of cubes with 0 blue faces $= (n-2)^3$

Test formulas    Test using numbers as with the earlier formulas.

Answer the problem

**Part B** For a $20 \times 20 \times 20$ cube ($n = 20$).

(a) number of cubes with 3 blue faces $= 8$

(b) number of cubes with 2 blue faces $= 12(n-2) = 12 \times (20 - 2) = 216$

(c) number of cubes with 1 blue face $= 6(n-2)^2 = 6 \times (20-2)^2$
$$= 6 \times 18^2 = 1944$$

(d) number of cubes with 0 blue faces $= (n-2)^3 = (20-2)^3$
$$= 18^3 = 5832$$

Check

Total number of cubes from above $= 8 + 216 + 1944 + 5832 = 8000$

Total number of cubes should be $n^3 = 20^3 = 8000$ ✓

Extend the problem

**Part C** – investigate further.

Cuboids could now be looked at.

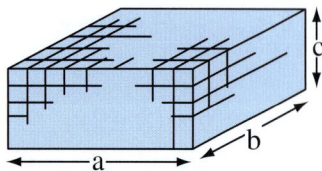

You could approach this in a similar way until your time runs out!

# SHAPE 2

**8**

### In this unit you will learn how to:

– recognise congruent shapes

– use co-ordinates

– translate shapes

– reflect shapes in mirror lines

– rotate shapes

– enlarge shapes

WATCH YOUR MONEY! –
Bank accounts 2

## Congruent shapes

---

### 🔑 Key Facts

   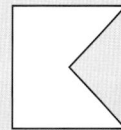

    *A*             *B*             *C*             *D*

Shapes *A*, *B*, *C* and *D* are exactly the same (even though *C* is upside down and *D* is on its side).

We say shapes *A*, *B*, *C* and *D* are congruent.

'**congruent**' means 'exactly the same size and shape'.

**Note**

If you are not sure if 2 shapes are congruent, use tracing paper. The shapes must fit on top of each other exactly (you may 'flip' the tracing paper upside down if you need to).

185

Use tracing paper if needed.

**1** Which shapes are *congruent* to shape *A*?

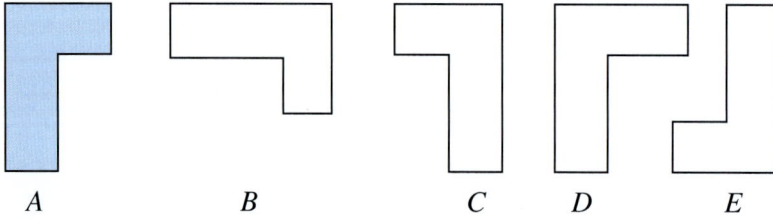

A     B     C     D     E

**2** Which shapes are congruent to shape *P*?

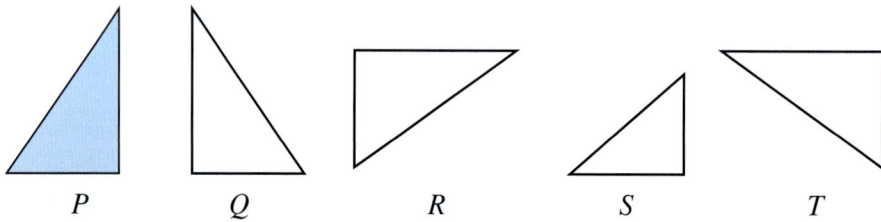

P     Q     R     S     T

**3** Which shapes are congruent to shape *P*?

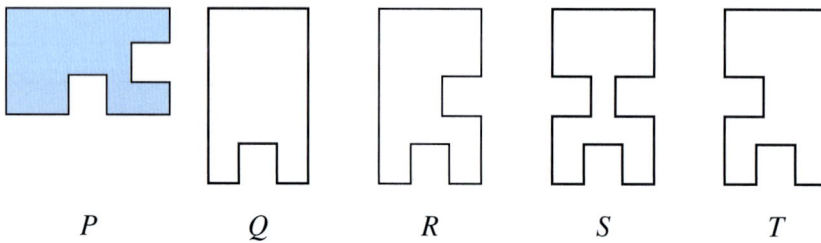

P     Q     R     S     T

**4** Which 2 shapes are congruent?

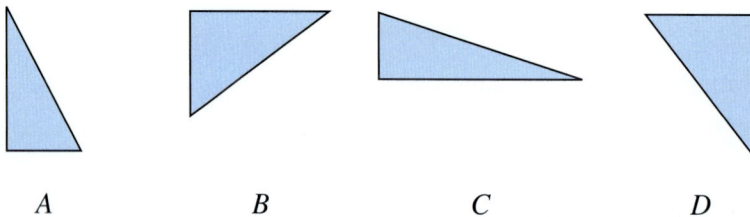

A     B     C     D

186

**5** Each shape below is congruent to 2 other shapes. Write down the letters of each group of congruent shapes.

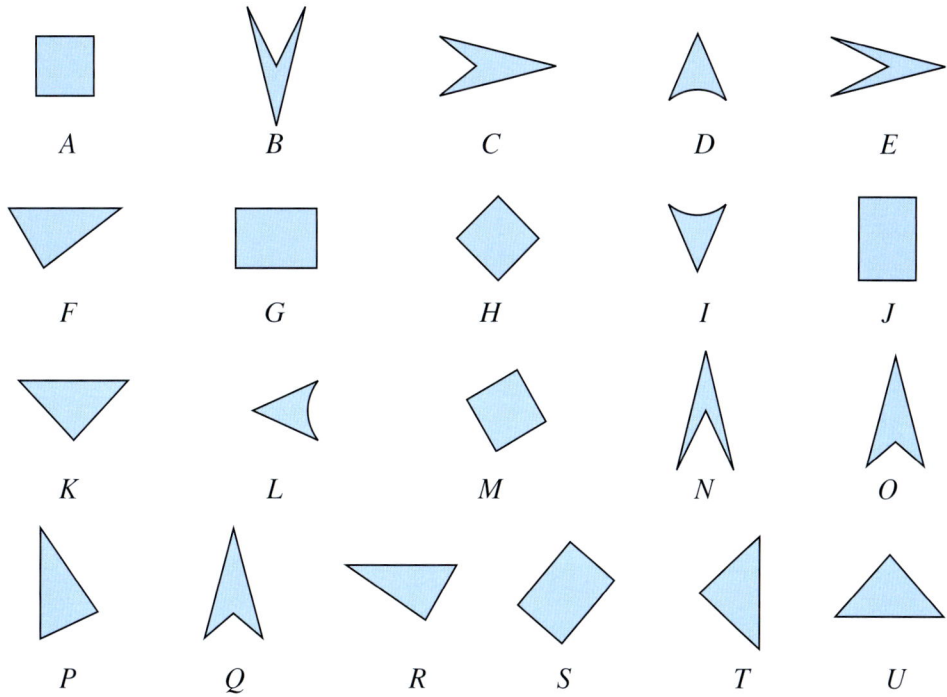

A  B  C  D  E

F  G  H  I  J

K  L  M  N  O

P  Q  R  S  T  U

Show how each of these shapes can be split into two congruent shapes.

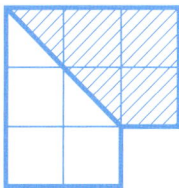

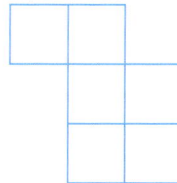

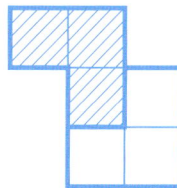

Copy each shape below.

Show how each shape can be split into two congruent shapes.

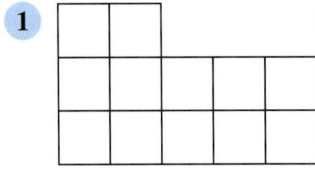

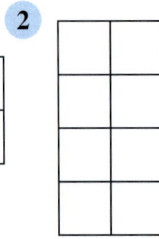

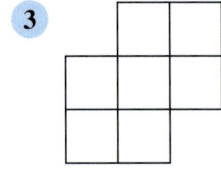

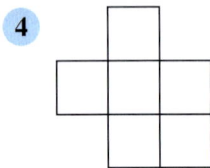

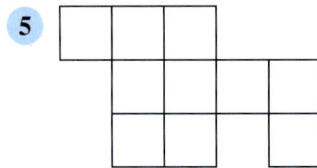

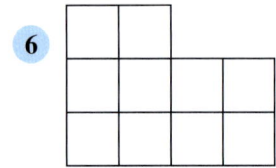

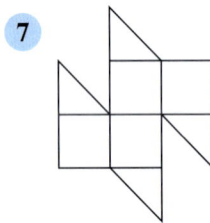

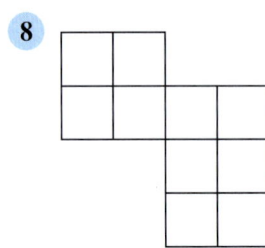

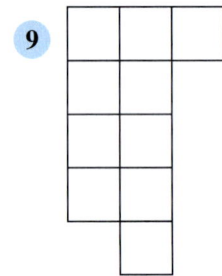

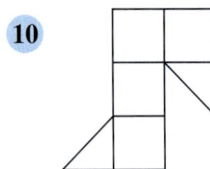

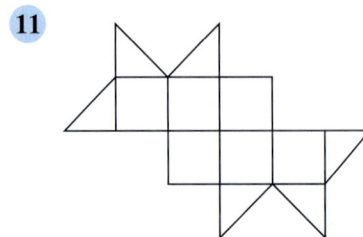

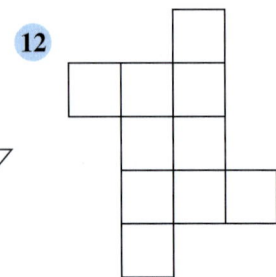

1

2

3

4

5

6

7

8

9

10

11

12

188

## Key Facts

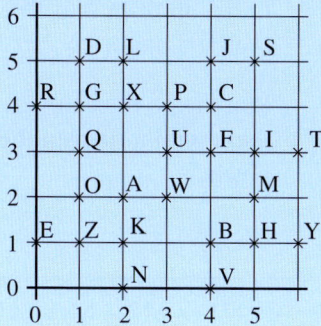

The position of a point on a grid is given by its co-ordinates. The *across* co-ordinate always comes first.

Point W is (3, 2)     Point N is (2, 0)

Point H is (5, 1)     Point R is (0, 4)

### M8. 2

**1** Use the grid above to spell out this message.

(5, 3)        (2, 5) (1, 2) (4, 0) (0, 1)        (4, 1) (2, 5) (5, 3) (2, 0) (1, 4)

**2** Use co-ordinates to write the word MATHEMATICS.

**3** Use the grid above to spell out this joke.  Read across.

(3, 2) (5, 1) (2, 2) (6, 3)     (2, 5) (5, 3) (0, 1) (5, 5)     (2, 2) (6, 3)

(6, 3) (5, 1) (0, 1)  (4, 1) (1, 2) (6, 3) (6, 3) (1, 2) (5, 2)  (1, 2) (4, 3)  (6, 3) (5, 1) (0)

(5, 5) (0, 1) (2, 2)  (2, 2) (2, 0) (1, 5)  (5, 5) (5, 1) (5, 3) (4, 0) (0, 1) (0, 4) (5, 5)

(2, 2)  (2, 0) (0, 1) (0, 4) (4, 0) (1, 2) (3, 3) (5, 5)  (3, 2) (0, 4) (0, 1) (4, 4) (2, 1).

**4** Write a message or joke of your own using co-ordinates.  Ask a friend to work out your message.

**5**

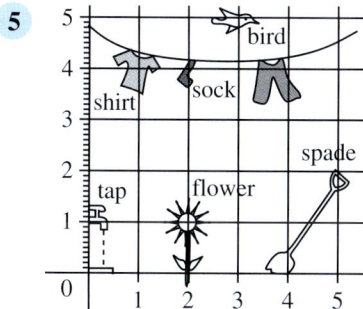

What are the co-ordinates of:

(a) the sock     (b)  the top of the spade

(c) The flower

What is at:

(d) (3, 5)    (e) (1, 4)    (f) (0, 1)

**6**

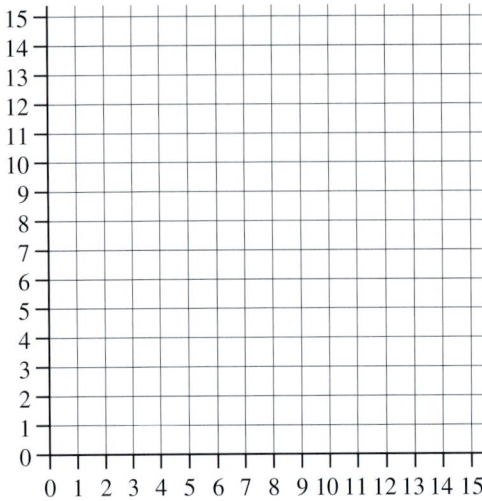

Draw a grid on squared paper as shown.

Label across from 0 to 15 (horizontal axis).

Label up from 0 to 15 (vertical axis).

Plot the points below and join them with a ruler in the order given.

| | | | | | |
|---|---|---|---|---|---|
| $(5, 5\frac{1}{2})$ | $(4, 5\frac{1}{2})$ | $(3, 6)$ | $(2\frac{1}{2}, 7)$ | $(2\frac{1}{2}, 8)$ | $(3, 9\frac{1}{2})$ |
| $(4, 10)$ | $(5, 10)$ | $(7\frac{1}{2}, 9\frac{1}{2})$ | $(8, 10)$ | $(9, 10)$ | $(9\frac{1}{2}, 9\frac{1}{2})$ |
| $(13\frac{1}{2}, 10)$ | $(14\frac{1}{2}, 9\frac{1}{2})$ | | | | |

On the same picture plot the points below and join them up with a ruler in the order given. Do not join the last point in the box above with the first point in the new box.

| | | | | |
|---|---|---|---|---|
| $(5, 10)$ | $(5, 10\frac{1}{2})$ | $(4\frac{1}{2}, 11)$ | $(4, 11)$ | $(4\frac{1}{2}, 12)$ |
| $(7, 12\frac{1}{2})$ | $(11\frac{1}{2}, 12)$ | $(11, 11)$ | $(10, 10)$ | $(10, 8)$ |
| $(12, 7\frac{1}{2})$ | $(12, 8)$ | $(13\frac{1}{2}, 9)$ | | |

| | | | | | |
|---|---|---|---|---|---|
| $(11, 0)$ | $(10, 2)$ | $(6, 2)$ | $(4, 0)$ | $(6, 2)$ | $(6, 3)$ | $(4, 4)$ |

$(13, 7)$  $(13, 8)$          $(8, 4\frac{1}{2})$  $(8, 5\frac{1}{2})$

$(4, 11)$  $(3\frac{1}{2}, 11)$  $(3, 10\frac{1}{2})$  $(3, 9\frac{1}{2})$          $(8, 5)$  $(7, 4)$  $(4, 4)$  $(3, 4\frac{1}{2})$  $(4, 5\frac{1}{2})$

| | | | | | |
|---|---|---|---|---|---|
| $(10, 2)$ | $(12, 6)$ | $(13, 6)$ | $(14, 7)$ | $(14, 8)$ | $(13\frac{1}{2}, 9)$ |
| $(13\frac{1}{2}, 13)$ | $(11, 14\frac{1}{2})$ | $(7, 14\frac{1}{2})$ | $(3, 13)$ | $(1, 11)$ | $(4\frac{1}{2}, 12)$ |

$(7\frac{1}{2}, 9\frac{1}{2})$  $(7\frac{1}{2}, 8\frac{1}{2})$  $(8, 8)$  $(9, 8)$  $(9\frac{1}{2}, 8\frac{1}{2})$  $(9\frac{1}{2}, 9\frac{1}{2})$

Draw a • at $(9, 9)$ and a • at $(4, 10)$    Colour me in?

**1**

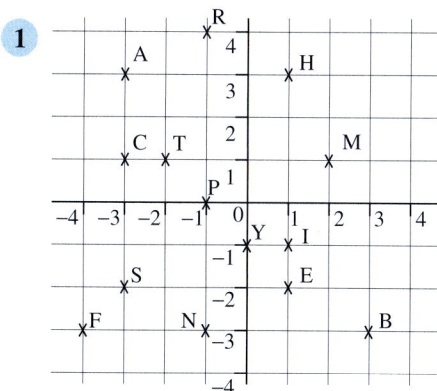

**Remember:** the 'across' co-ordinate always comes first.

Use the grid to spell out this message.

$(-2, 1)(1, 3)(1, -1)(-3, -2)$

$(1, -1)(-3, -2)$

$(1, -2)(-3, 3)(-3, -2)(0, -1)$

**2**

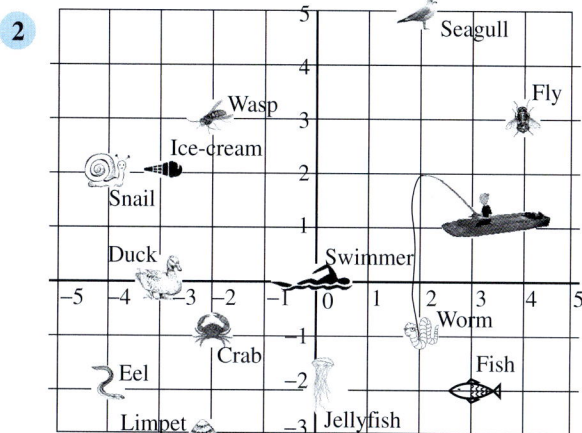

What are the co-ordinates of

(a) the fish          (b) the ice-cream

(c) the seagull  (d) the limpet

(e) the eel          (f) the jellyfish

What is at:

(g) $(2, -1)$  (h) $(-2, -1)$

(i) $(0, 0)$      (j) $(4, 3)$

(k) $(-3, 0)$  (l) $(-2, 3)$

**3**

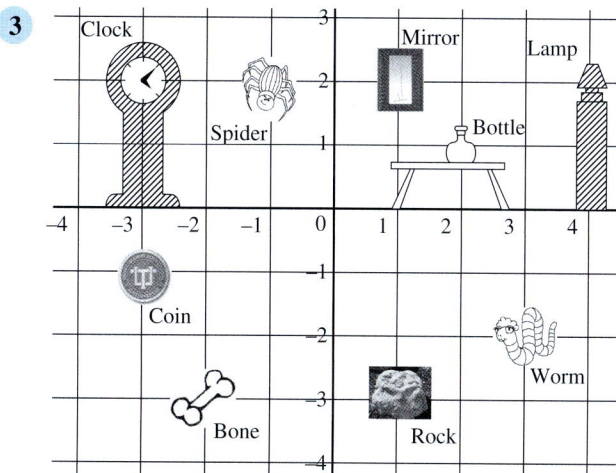

What are the co-ordinates of:

(a) the coin     (b) the spider

(c) the bottle  (d) the rock

What is at:

(e) $(2, 1)$      (f) $(-2, -3)$

(g) $(-3, 2)$  (h) $(1, 2)$

(i) $(3, -2)$

**4** Draw a horizontal axis from $-4$ to 8 and a vertical axis from $-8$ to 11.

Plot the points below and join them up with a ruler in the order given.

$(0, 1)$   $(-2, 1)$   $\left(-2\frac{1}{2}, \frac{1}{2}\right)$   $\left(-2\frac{1}{2}, -\frac{1}{2}\right)$   $\left(2, -\frac{1}{2}\right)$   $\left(4, -1\frac{1}{2}\right)$   $(5, -1)$   $\left(4, -1\frac{1}{2}\right)$

$(4, -3)$   $\left(3, -2\frac{1}{2}\right)$   $\left(-1\frac{1}{2}, -2\frac{1}{2}\right)$   $(0, -5)$   $\left(\frac{1}{2}, -5\frac{1}{2}\right)$   $(1, -7)$   $(6, -5)$   $\left(5\frac{1}{2}, -4\right)$

$\left(4, -4\frac{1}{2}\right)$   $(2, -5)$   $\left(\frac{1}{2}, -5\frac{1}{2}\right)$   $(-1, -7)$   $(0, -5)$

On the same picture plot the points below and join them up with a ruler in the order given. Do not join the last point in the box above with the first point in the new box.

$(6, -1)$   $(6, 1)$   $\left(6\frac{1}{2}, 3\right)$   $\left(6, 3\frac{1}{2}\right)$   $\left(5\frac{1}{2}, 3\right)$   $\left(5\frac{1}{2}, 2\right)$   $(5, 2)$

$(5, 7)$   $(4, 8)$   $(0, 8)$   $\left(-2, 6\frac{1}{2}\right)$   $(-2, 4)$   $\left(-2\frac{1}{2}, 3\right)$

$(6, 2)$ $(6, 3)$

$(4, 3)$   $(4, 2)$   $(3, 1)$   $(2, 1)$   $(1, 2)$   $(1, 3)$   $(2, 4)$   $(3, 4)$   $(4, 3)$   $\left(5\frac{1}{2}, 3\right)$

$\left(-2, 6\frac{1}{2}\right)$   $(-3, 7)$   $(-3, 8)$   $(-1, 10)$   $\left(1, 10\frac{1}{2}\right)$   $\left(5, 10\frac{1}{2}\right)$   $(7, 9)$

$(7, 0)$   $\left(6\frac{1}{2}, -1\right)$   $(6, -1)$   $\left(5\frac{1}{2}, -4\right)$

$\left(-2\frac{1}{2}, -\frac{1}{2}\right)$   $(-3, -1)$   $\left(-3, -2\frac{1}{2}\right)$   $\left(-1\frac{1}{2}, -2\frac{1}{2}\right)$

$(1, 3)$   $\left(\frac{1}{2}, 3\right)$   $\left(\frac{1}{2}, 2\right)$   $\left(-\frac{1}{2}, 1\right)$   $\left(-1\frac{1}{2}, 1\right)$   $\left(-2\frac{1}{2}, 2\right)$   $\left(-2\frac{1}{2}, 3\right)$

$\left(-1\frac{1}{2}, 4\right)$   $\left(-\frac{1}{2}, 4\right)$   $\left(\frac{1}{2}, 3\right)$

$(-2, -1)$ $\left(-2\frac{1}{2}, -2\right)$   |   $(-1, -1)$ $\left(-1\frac{1}{2}, -2\right)$   |   $(0, -1)$   $\left(-\frac{1}{2}, -2\right)$

$(1, -1)$ $\left(\frac{1}{2}, -2\right)$   |   $(2, -1)$ $\left(1\frac{1}{2}, -2\right)$   |   $(3, -1)$ $\left(2\frac{1}{2}, -2\right)$

Draw a • at $(2, 2)$ and a • at $(-2, 2)$

Colour me in?

## Key Facts

A **translation** means movement in a straight line (no turning).

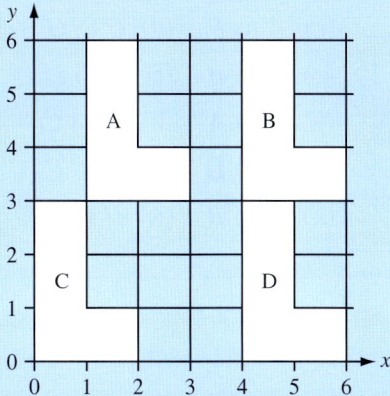

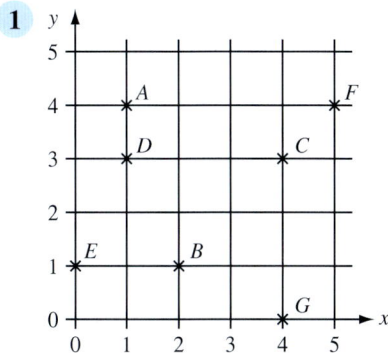

Describe the following *translations*. In each case, write down how many units left or right and how many units up or down.

(a) *A* to *B*

(b) *A* to *D*

(c) *B* to *C*

(d) *C* to *A*

Pick one corner (vertex) of the shape and follow where it moves to.

(a) 3 right, 0 up         (3R OU)

(b) 3 right, 3 down       (3R 3D)

(c) 4 left, 3 down        (4L 3D)

(d) 1 right, 3 up         (1R 3U)

---

**M8. 3**

**1**

Describe the following *translations*. In each case, write down how many units left or right and how many units up or down:

(a) *A* to *B*    (b) *A* to *C*

(c) *A* to *E*    (d) *A* to *G*

(e) *A* to *F*    (f) *B* to *C*

(g) *B* to *D*    (h) *B* to *G*

(i) *G* to *C*    (j) *C* to *F*

193

**2**

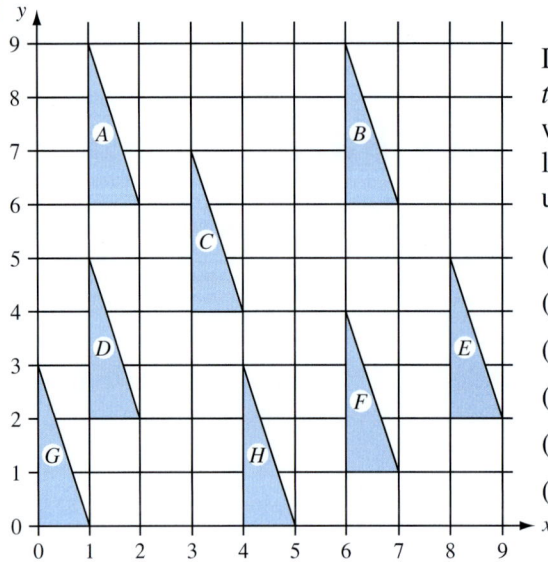

Describe the following *translations*. In each case, write down how many units left or right and how many units up or down:

(a) *A* to *C*    (b) *A* to *D*
(c) *A* to *F*    (d) *C* to *G*
(e) *E* to *B*    (f) *C* to *D*
(g) *B* to *A*    (h) *H* to *C*
(i) *F* to *D*    (j) *E* to *F*
(k) *G* to *B*    (l) *H* to *A*

**3**

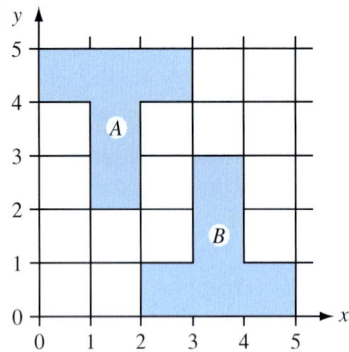

Shape *A* has moved to shape *B*.
*Explain* why this is *not* a translation.

**4**

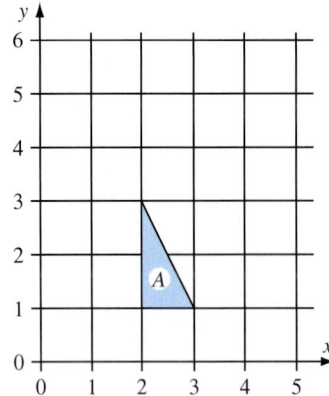

Copy the grid opposite and draw the triangle *A* as shown.

(a) Translate triangle *A* 1 unit to the right and 3 units up. Label the new triangle *B*.

(b) Translate triangle *A* 2 units to the left and 1 unit down. Label the new triangle *C*.

(c) Translate triangle *A* 1 unit to the left and 1 unit up. Label the new triangle *D*.

(d) Translate triangle *A* 0 units to the right and 2 units up. Label the new triangle *E*.

194

**Translation vector**

To describe a translation, we do not have to use the words 'left', 'right', 'up' and 'down'. We use a vertical bracket like this:

$$\begin{pmatrix} 2 \\ 3 \end{pmatrix}$$

The number at the *top* shows 2 units to the *right*.
(If the number at the top was $-2$ it would be 2 units to the *left*)

The number at the *bottom* shows 3 units *up*.
(If the number at the bottom was $-3$ it would be 3 units *down*)

**Note**

The vertical axis is often called the $y$-axis.
The horizontal axis is often called the $x$-axis.

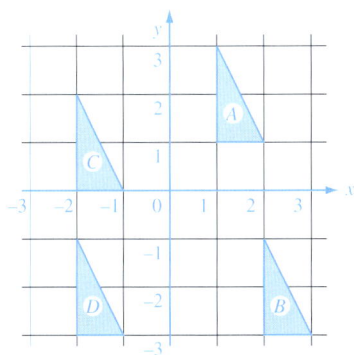

Use translation vectors to describe the following translations.

(a) $A$ to $B$     (b) $A$ to $C$

(c) $A$ to $D$     (d) $B$ to $C$

(a) $\begin{pmatrix} 1 \\ -4 \end{pmatrix}$    (b) $\begin{pmatrix} -3 \\ -1 \end{pmatrix}$    (c) $\begin{pmatrix} -3 \\ -4 \end{pmatrix}$    (d) $\begin{pmatrix} -4 \\ 3 \end{pmatrix}$

**E8. 3**

**1**

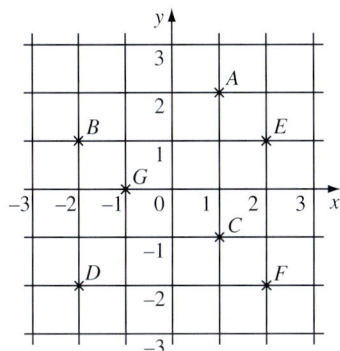

Use translation vectors to describe the following translations.

(a) $A$ to $B$     (b) $A$ to $F$

(c) $A$ to $G$     (d) $B$ to $C$

(e) $F$ to $G$     (f) $D$ to $G$

(g) $E$ to $B$     (h) $B$ to $F$

**2**

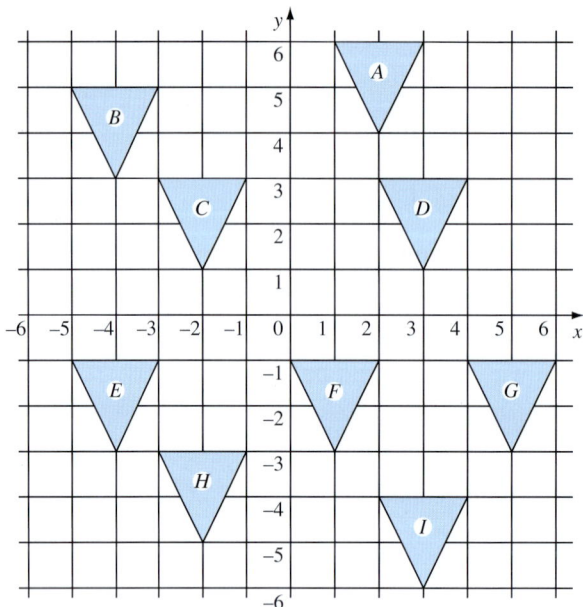

Use translation vectors to describe the following translations.

(a) *A* to *D*    (b) *A* to *G*

(c) *A* to *H*    (d) *A* to *I*

(e) *B* to *E*    (f) *B* to *H*

(g) *C* to *D*    (h) *C* to *A*

(i) *C* to *E*    (j) *D* to *B*

(k) *D* to *H*    (l) *E* to *G*

(m) *E* to *D*    (n) *F* to *C*

(o) *G* to *I*    (p) *G* to *B*

(q) *H* to *D*    (r) *I* to *C*

**3**

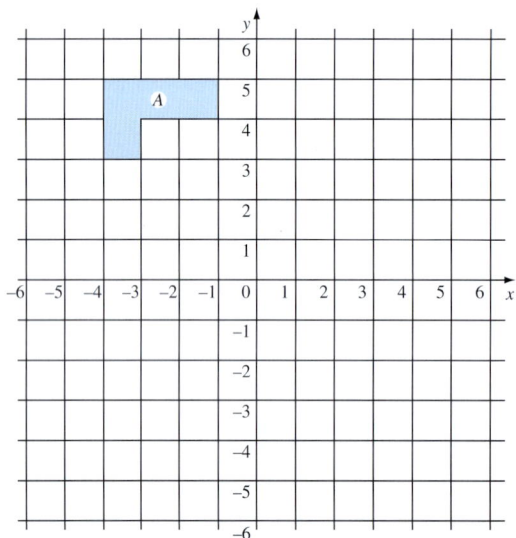

Copy the grid opposite and draw shape *A* as shown.

(a) Translate shape *A* through $\begin{pmatrix} 5 \\ 1 \end{pmatrix}$ Label the new shape *B*

(b) Translate shape *B* through $\begin{pmatrix} 2 \\ -3 \end{pmatrix}$ Label the new shape *C*

(c) Translate shape *C* through $\begin{pmatrix} -2 \\ -5 \end{pmatrix}$ Label the new shape *D*

(d) Translate shape *D* through $\begin{pmatrix} -4 \\ 4 \end{pmatrix}$ Label the new shape *E*

(e) Translate shape *E* through $\begin{pmatrix} -3 \\ -5 \end{pmatrix}$ Label the new shape *F*

(f) Use a translation vector to describe the translation that moves shape *E* to shape *B*

(g) Use a translation vector to describe the translation that moves shape *A* to shape *F*

(h) Use a translation vector to describe the translation that moves shape *D* to shape *B*

Reflect this shape in the mirror line.

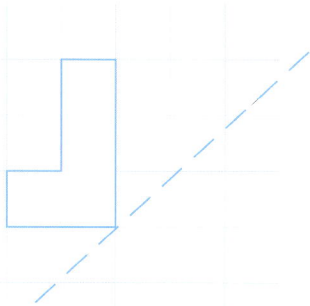

**Advice**
Turn the paper to
make the mirror line
vertical then draw the
reflection.

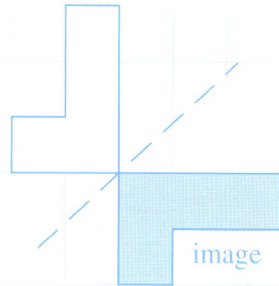

image

**M8. 4**

Draw each shape below and reflect in the mirror line.

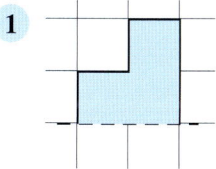

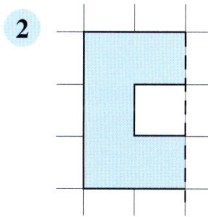

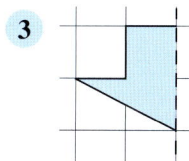

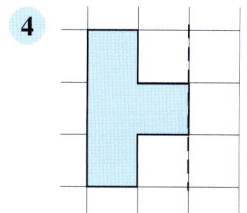

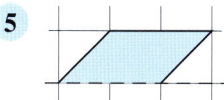

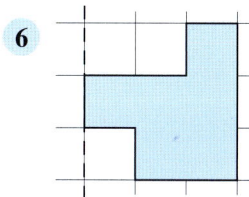

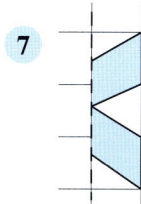

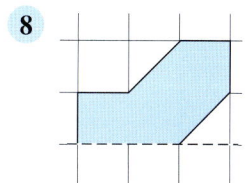

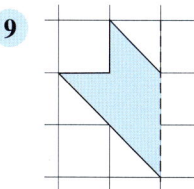

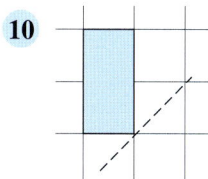

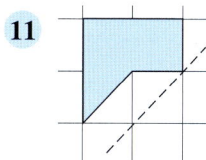

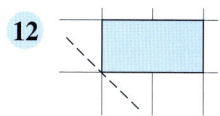

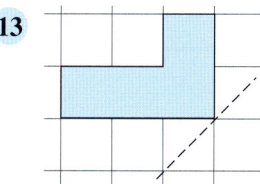

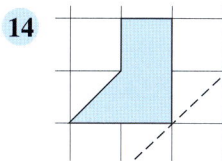

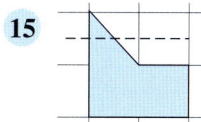

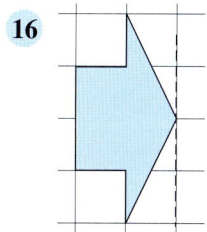

1

2

3

4

5

6

7

8

9

10

11

12

13

14

15

16

## Mirror line

The mirror line is sometimes called the *line of reflection*. We can sometimes give special names to these lines.

### Horizontal lines

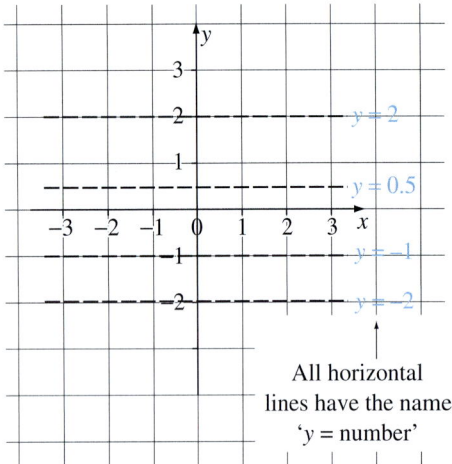

All horizontal lines have the name '$y$ = number'

### Vertical lines

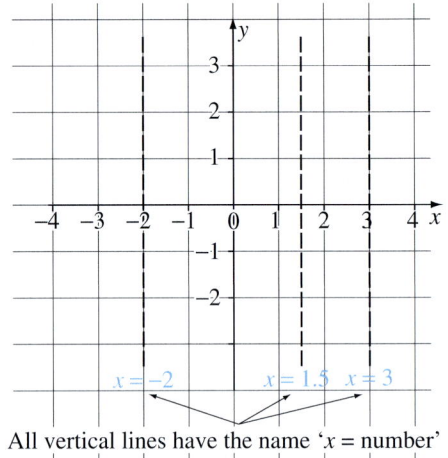

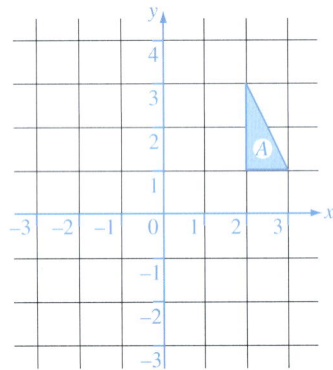

All vertical lines have the name '$x$ = number'

(a) Reflect triangle $A$ in the $x$-axis.
Label the image (new triangle) $B$.

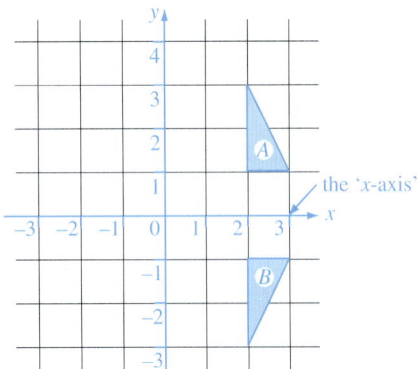

(b) Reflect triangle $A$ in the line $x = 1$.
Label the image (new triangle) $C$.

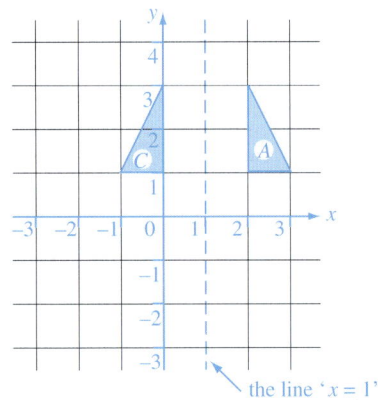

the '$x$-axis'

the line '$x = 1$'

**1**

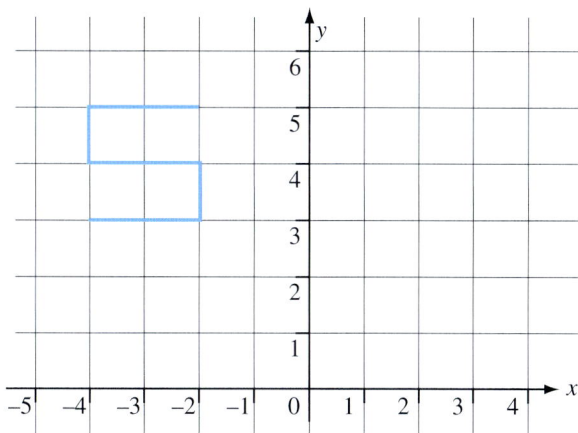

Copy this grid.
Copy the letter then
reflect it in the
$y$-axis.

**2** Copy this grid.
Copy the shape then
reflect it in the
$x$-axis.

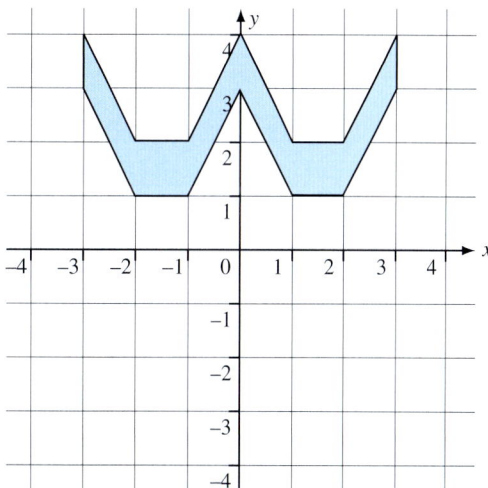

**3**

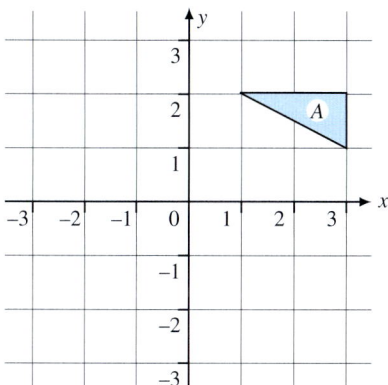

Copy the grid and shape opposite.

(a) Reflect triangle $A$ in the $y$-axis.
Label the image (new triangle) $B$.

(b) Reflect triangle $A$ in the $x$-axis.
Label the image $C$.

(c) Reflect triangle $C$ in the $y$-axis.
Label the image $D$.

(d) Describe how you could *transform*
(change) triangle $D$ into triangle $B$.

199

**4**

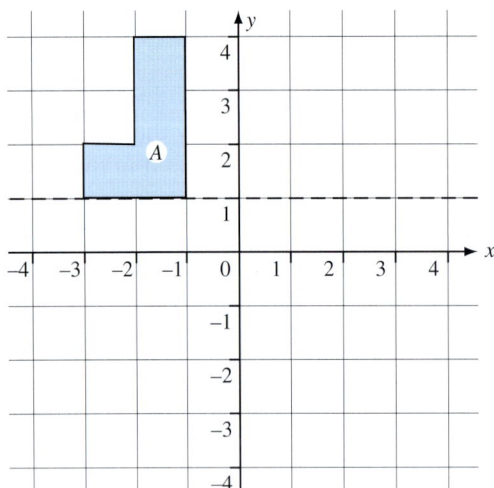

Copy the grid and shape opposite.

(a) Reflect shape $A$ in the $y$-axis. Label the image $B$.

(b) Reflect shape $A$ in the line $y = 1$ (the dotted line). Label the image $C$.

(c) Reflect shape $B$ in the line $y = 1$. Label the image $D$.

(d) Describe how you could *transform* (change) shape $C$ into shape $D$.

**5**

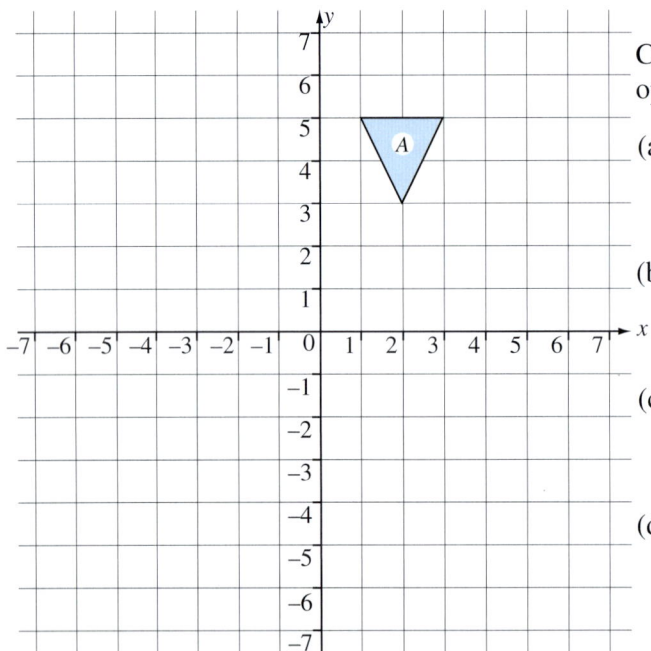

Copy this grid and shape opposite.

(a) Reflect shape $A$ in the $x$-axis. Label the image $B$.

(b) Reflect shape $B$ in the line $y = -2$. Label the image $C$.

(c) Reflect shape $C$ in the line $x = -1$. Label the image $D$.

(d) Reflect shape $D$ in the line $y = 1$. Label the image $E$.

(e) Reflect shape $E$ in the $y$-axis. Label the image $F$.

(f) Reflect shape $F$ in the line $y = 3$. Label the image $G$.

**6**

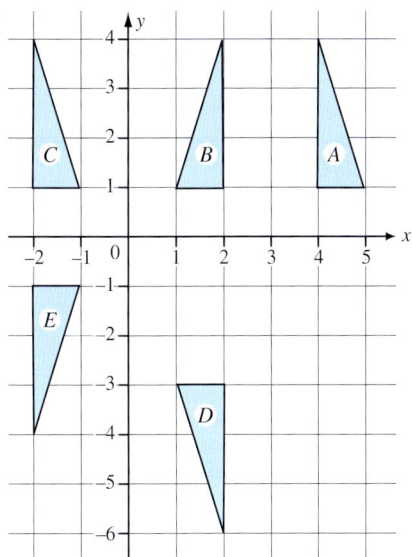

For each pair of triangles below, write down the name (equation) of the *line of reflection*.

(a)  *A* to *B*

(b)  *B* to *C*

(c)  *B* to *D*

(d)  *C* to *E*

Can you still?

**8A**  **Find a fraction of a number (see Unit 5)**

Can you still?

Work out

1.  $\frac{1}{4}$ of 24     2.  $\frac{3}{4}$ of 24     3.  $\frac{1}{6}$ of 30     4.  $\frac{5}{6}$ of 30

5.  $\frac{3}{8}$ of 56     6.  $\frac{2}{7}$ of 21     7.  $\frac{5}{9}$ of 36     8.  $\frac{7}{8}$ of 72

9.  | Computer £720 |
    | SALE |
    | $\frac{1}{5}$ off |

How much does the computer cost?

10.  Hal has £42. He spends $\frac{5}{7}$ of his money on a pair of trousers. How much money does he have left?

11.  A tin of beans contains 360 g. If the tin of beans contains $\frac{2}{9}$ extra in a special offer, how much does the tin now contain?

12.  Ginny scores 64% in an English exam. There is a mistake in the marking so that Ginny should have $\frac{3}{8}$ extra. What is her total mark now?

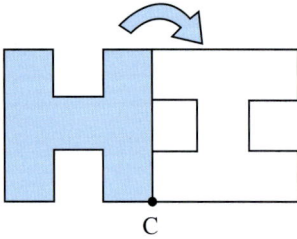

This shape has turned clockwise through a right angle (90° turn).

**Remember:** clockwise

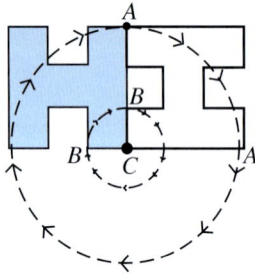

Each point in the shape rotates around a circle with its centre at the dot (C).

The dot (C) is called the **centre of rotation**.

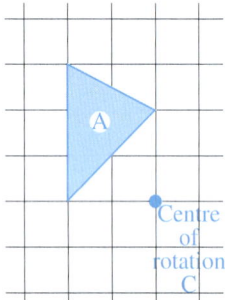

Rotate triangle *A* 90° anticlockwise about *C*.

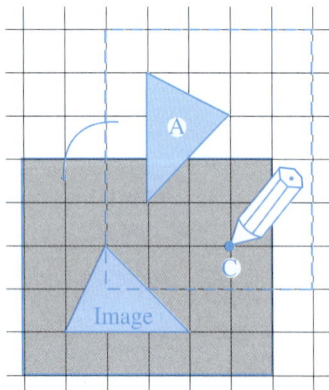

Trace the triangle. Hold your pencil on point *C*. Turn the tracing paper 90° anticlockwise to see the new position of the triangle.

**Note**

For 90° rotations, horizontal lines become vertical and vice versa.

Use tracing paper.

For each Question, draw the shape and the centre of rotation (C). Rotate the shape as indicated and draw the image.

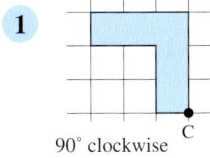

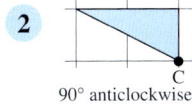

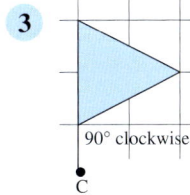

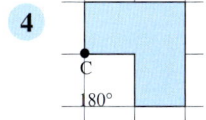

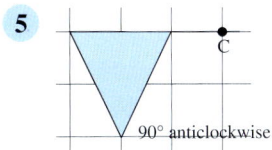

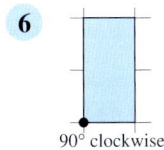

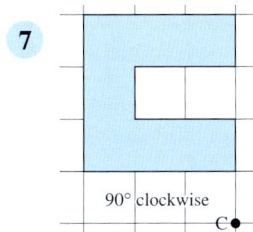

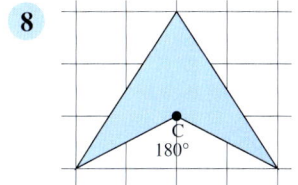

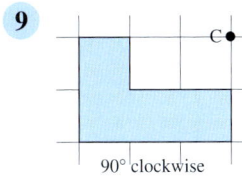

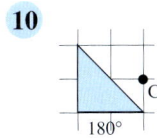

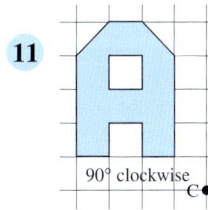

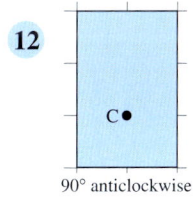

**1**
90° clockwise

**2**
90° anticlockwise

**3**
90° clockwise

**4**
180°

**5**
90° anticlockwise

**6**
90° clockwise

**7**
90° clockwise

**8**
180°

**9**
90° clockwise

**10**
180°

**11**
90° clockwise

**12**
90° anticlockwise

In Questions **13** to **16** copy each diagram. Draw the shaded shape on tracing paper. Place the tip of a pencil on different points until the shape can be rotated onto the other shape. Mark the centre of rotation with a dot.

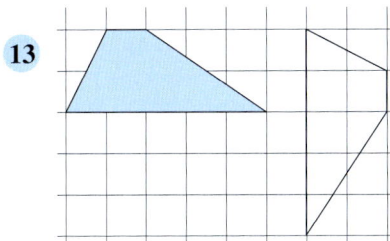

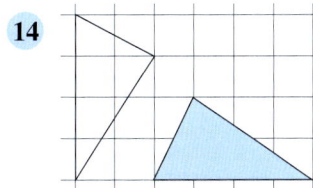

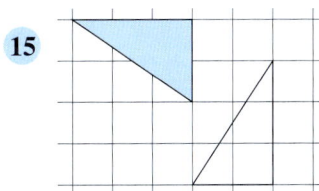

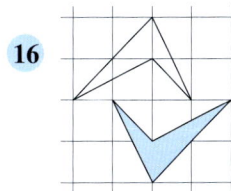

**13**

**14**

**15**

**16**

**17**

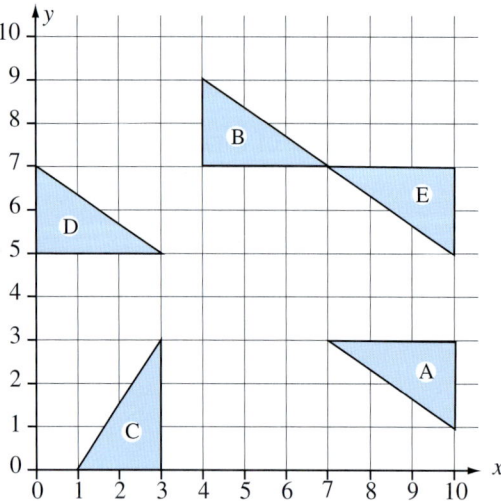

Find the co-ordinates of the centres of the following rotations:

(a) triangle *A* onto triangle *B*

(b) triangle *A* onto triangle *C*

(c) triangle *A* onto triangle *D*

(d) triangle *C* onto triangle *E*

# 🔑 Key Facts

**Note**    The point (0, 0) is called the '**origin**.'

We need 3 things to *describe fully* a rotation:

**1.** the angle

**2.** the direction (clockwise or anticlockwise)

**3.** the centre of rotation

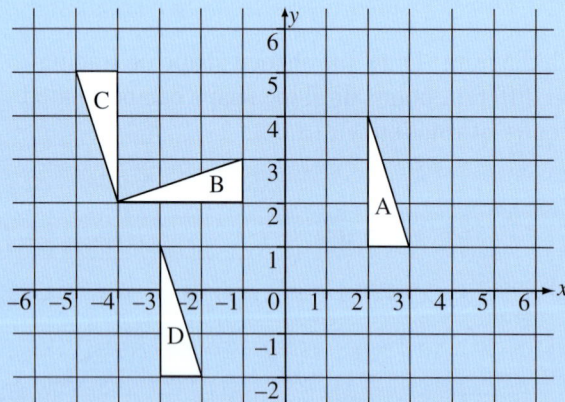

Describe fully the rotation which transforms:

(a) triangle *A* onto triangle *B*

(b) triangle *B* onto triangle *C*

(c) triangle *B* onto triangle *D*

For each answer, we must write down the angle, direction and centre of rotation.

(a) rotates 90° anticlockwise about (0, 0)

(b) rotates 90° anticlockwise about (− 4, 2)

(c) rotates 90° clockwise about (− 4, 1)

Use tracing paper

**1**

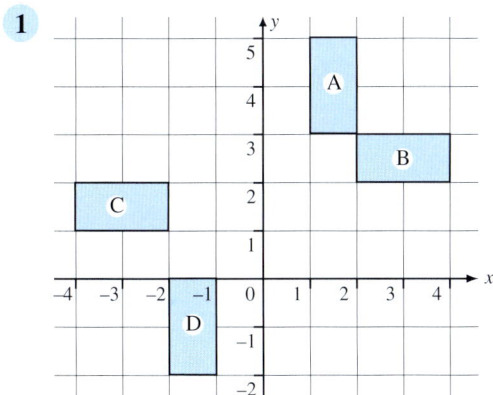

Describe *fully* the rotation which transforms:

(a) shape $A$ onto shape $B$

(b) $B$ onto $C$

(c) $C$ onto $D$

**2**

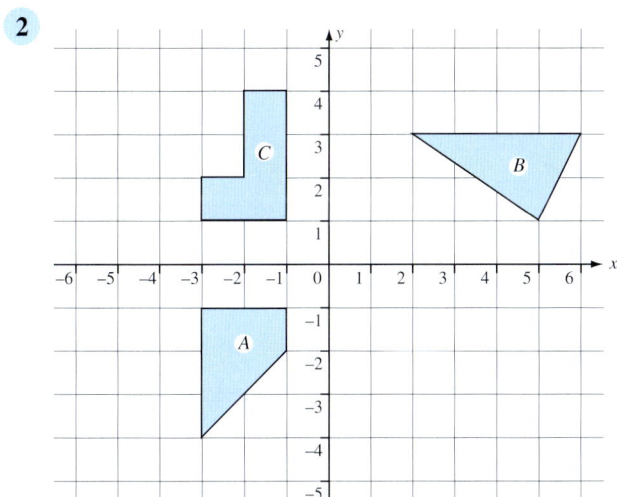

Copy the grid and shapes opposite.

(a) Rotate shape $A$ 90° anticlockwise about $(-3, -4)$. Label the image $P$.

(b) Rotate shape $B$ 90° clockwise about $(1, 0)$. Label the image $Q$.

(c) Rotate shape $C$ 90° clockwise about $(2, 1)$. Label the image $R$.

**3** (a) Draw $x$ and $y$ axes with values from $-5$ to $5$.

Draw rectangle $A$ with vertices (corners) at $(0, 2)$, $(0, 5)$, $(-2, 5)$, $(-2, 2)$.

(b) Rotate rectangle $A$ 180° about $(-2, 2)$. Label the image $B$.

(c) Rotate rectangle $B$ 90° clockwise about $(0, -1)$. Label the image $C$.

(d) Rotate rectangle $C$ 180° about $(2, 0)$. Label the image $D$.

(e) Rotate rectangle $D$ 90° clockwise about $(3, -2)$. Label the image $E$.

**4**

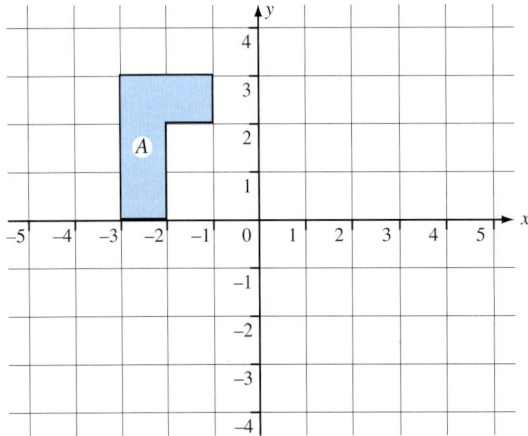

Copy the grid opposite. The x-axis goes from −5 to 5. The y-axis goes from −4 to 4. Shape A has vertices (corners) at (−1, 2), (−1, 3), (−3, 3), (−3, 0), (−2, 0) and (−2, 2).

(a) Rotate shape A 180° about (0, 2). Label the image B.

(b) Rotate shape B 90° clockwise about (1, 0). Label the image C.

(c) Rotate shape C 90° anticlockwise about (2, −2). Label the image D.

(d) Rotate shape D 90° anticlockwise about (0, −3). Label the image E.

(e) Rotate shape E 90° anticlockwise about (−5, 0). Label the image F.

**5** (a) Draw x and y axes with values from −6 to 6. Draw triangle A with vertices (corners) at (−5, 2), (−5, 6) and (−3, 5).

(b) Rotate triangle A 90° clockwise about (−4, −2). Label the image B.

(c) Rotate triangle B 90° clockwise about (6, 0). Label the image C.

(d) Rotate triangle C 180° about (1, 1). Label the image D.

(e) Rotate triangle D 90° anticlockwise about (−5, 1). Label the image E.

(f) Describe *fully* the rotation which transforms triangle E onto triangle A.

**6** (a) Draw the x axis from −4 to 4.

Draw the y axis from −3 to 3.

Draw triangle A with vertices at (−1, −2), (−2, −2), (−2, 0).

(b) Rotate triangle A 90° clockwise about (0, −1). Label the image B.

(c) Rotate triangle B 180° about (1, 1). Label the image C.

(d) Reflect triangle C in the x axis. Label the image D.

(e) Reflect triangle D in the line y = −2. Label the image E.

(f) Translate triangle E through $\begin{pmatrix} -5 \\ 1 \end{pmatrix}$. Label the image F.

(g) Describe *fully* the rotation which transforms triangle F onto triangle A.

An **enlargement** makes the shape larger (or smaller). The original and the enlargement must be exactly the same shape. All angles in both shapes stay the same.

**Note**

Enlarge this shape by a scale factor $\frac{1}{2}$

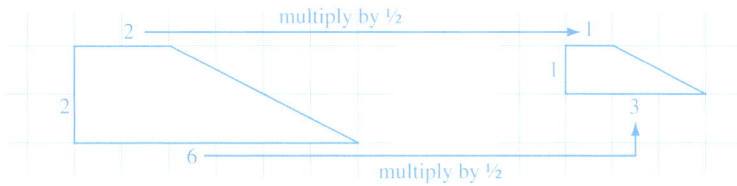

multiply by ½

multiply by ½

The shape gets smaller when the scale factor is a fraction between 0 and 1.

## M8. 6

Enlarge these shapes by the scale factor given. Make sure you leave room on your page for the enlargement!

1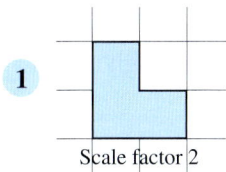
Scale factor 2

2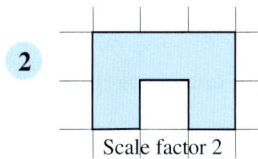
Scale factor 2

3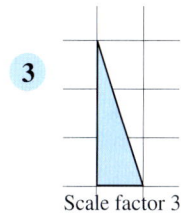
Scale factor 3

4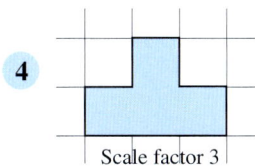
Scale factor 3

5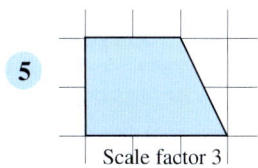
Scale factor 3

6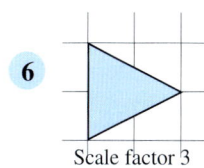
Scale factor 3

7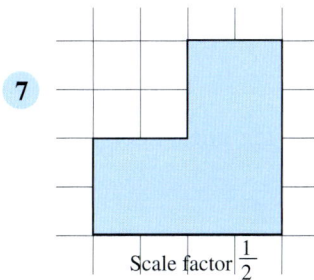
Scale factor $\frac{1}{2}$

8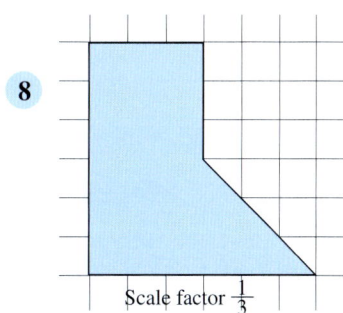
Scale factor $\frac{1}{3}$

9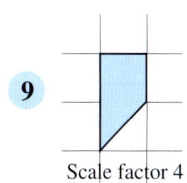
Scale factor 4

Look at each of the following pairs of diagrams and decide whether or not one diagram is an enlargement of the other. For each Question write the scale factor of the enlargement or write 'not an enlargement'.

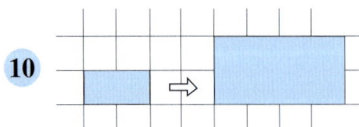

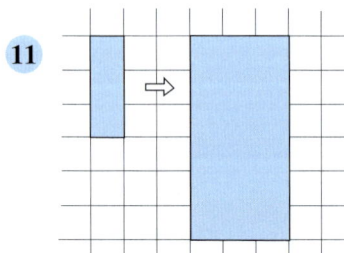

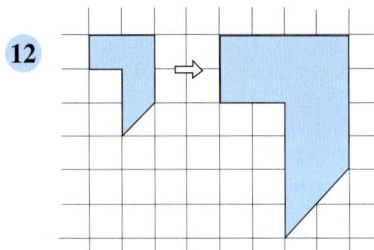

**10**

**11**

**12**

---

## Centre of enlargement

A *mathematical enlargement* always has a centre of enlargement as well as a scale factor.

The centre of enlargement is formed by drawing a broken line through a corner of the new shape and the same corner of the old shape.

Do this for each pair of points as shown in the diagram.

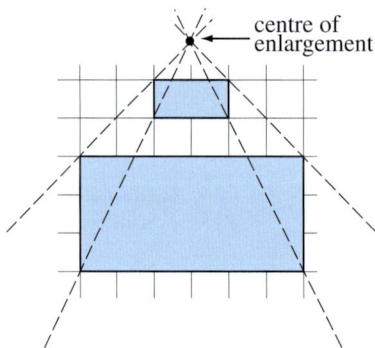

centre of enlargement

The centre of enlargement is the point where all the broken lines meet (intersect).

We need 2 things to describe fully an enlargement:
1. the **scale factor**
2. the **centre of enlargement**

## Drawing an enlargement

Draw an enlargement of triangle $A$ with scale factor 3 about the centre of enlargement $C$.

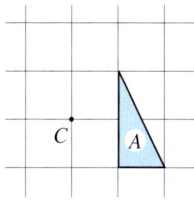

Join the centre $C$ to one vertex (corner) with a dotted line

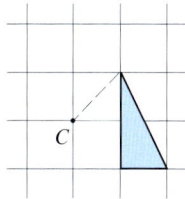

Multiply the length of the dotted line by the scale factor (do this by measuring or by counting squares) then draw the longer dotted line from $C$

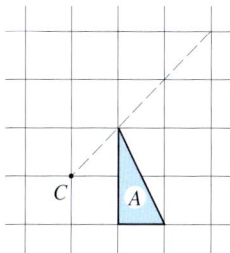

This shows where the top vertex will move to

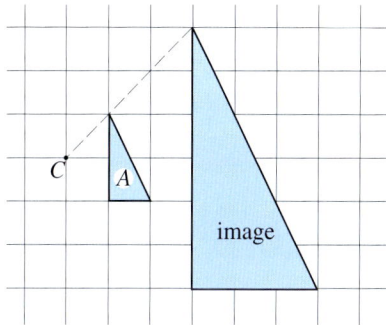

The rest of the enlarged shape can be drawn from this new vertex.

Describe fully the enlargement which transforms shape $A$ onto shape $B$.

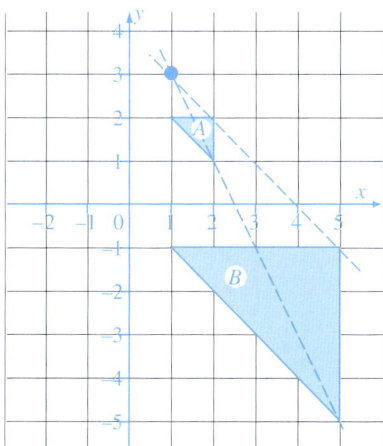

Draw broken lines through each corner of the new shape and the same corner of the old shape.

The centre of enlargement is where the broken lines meet (intersect).

Answer: enlargement by scale factor 4 about (1,3).

For Questions **1** to **5** , draw the grid and the 2 shapes then draw broken lines through pairs of points in the new shape and the old shape. Describe *fully* the enlargement which transforms shape *A* onto shape *B*.

**1**

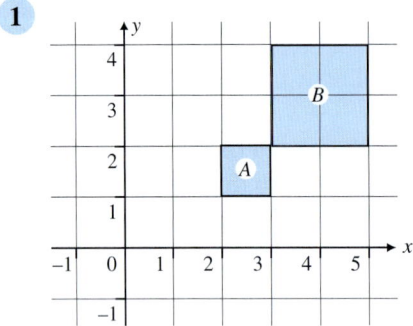

**2**

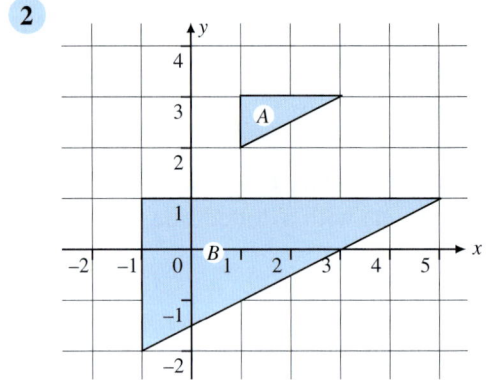

**3**

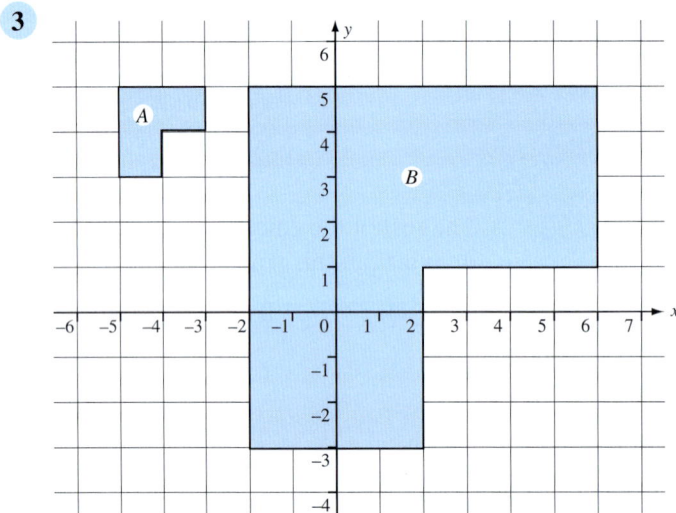

**4**

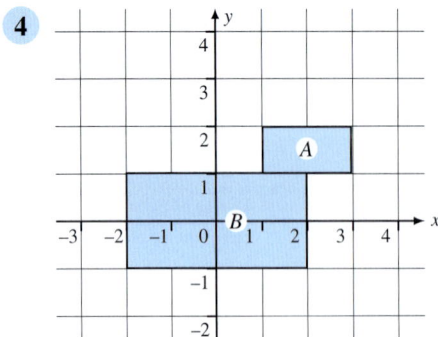

**5**

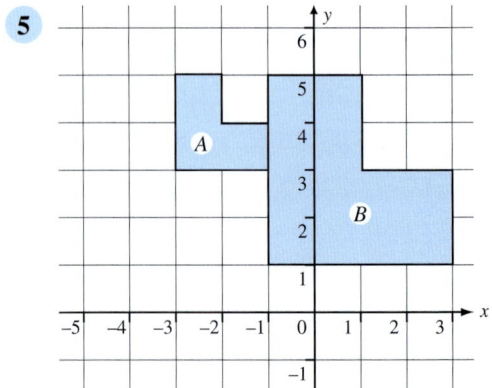

For Questions **6** to **11**, copy the diagram and then draw an enlargement using the scale factor and centre of enlargement (C) given.
Leave room for the enlargement!

**6**

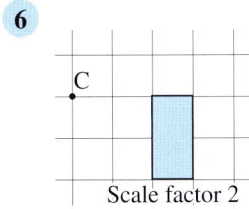

Scale factor 2

**7**

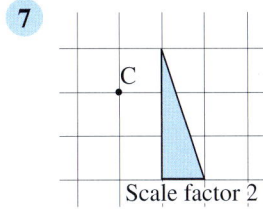

Scale factor 2

**8**

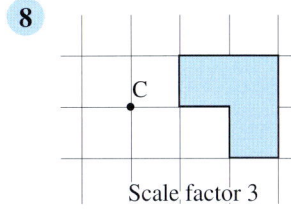

Scale factor 3

**9**

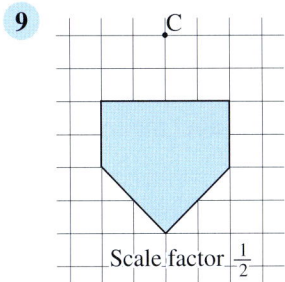

Scale factor $\frac{1}{2}$

**10**

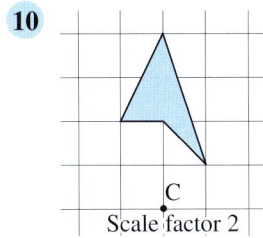

Scale factor 2

**11**

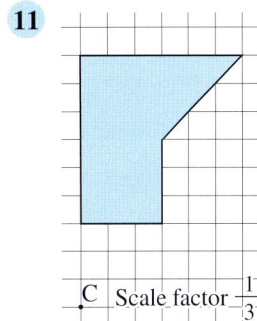

Scale factor $\frac{1}{3}$

**12** Look at your diagram for Question **8**

(a) Write down the area of the original shape.

(b) Write down the area of the enlarged shape.

(c) How many times bigger is the area of the enlarged shape? Compare this to the scale factor.

**13**

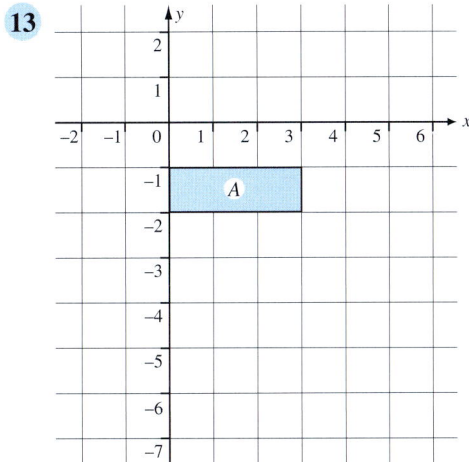

(a) Copy the grid and rectangle *A*. Enlarge rectangle *A* by scale factor 2 about $(0, 0)$. Label the image *B*.

(b) Write down the area of *A*.

(c) Write down the area of *B*.

(d) How many times bigger is the area of *B*? Compare this to the scale factor.

**14**

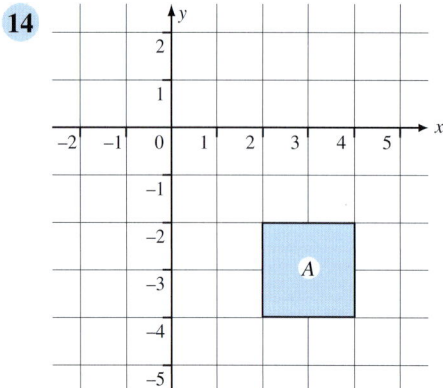

Copy the grid and square $A$

Enlarge square $A$ by scale factor $\frac{1}{2}$ about $(0, 0)$

Label the image $B$

**15** (a) Draw the $x$-axis from $-4$ to 8. Draw the $y$-axis from $-4$ to 6.
Draw the triangle $A$ with vertices (corners) at $(1, 3)$, $(1, 4)$, $(3, 4)$.
(b) Enlarge triangle $A$ by scale factor 2 about $(1, 5)$. Label the image $B$.
(c) Enlarge triangle $B$ by scale factor $\frac{1}{2}$ about $(-3, 1)$. Label the image $C$.
(d) Enlarge triangle $C$ by scale factor 3 about $(-2, 3)$. Label the image $D$.

**16** (a) Draw the $x$-axis from $-6$ to 6. Draw the $y$-axis from $-7$ to 7.
Draw the triangle $A$ with vertices at $(2, 2)$, $(2, 6)$, $(4, 6)$.
(b) Enlarge triangle $A$ by scale factor $\frac{1}{2}$ about $(0, 0)$. Label the image $B$.
(c) Reflect triangle $B$ in the $y$-axis. Label the image $C$.
(d) Enlarge triangle $C$ by scale factor 3 about $(-1, 4)$. Label the image $D$.
(e) Rotate triangle $D$ $90°$ clockwise about $(-1, -5)$. Label the image $E$.
(f) Enlarge triangle $E$ by scale factor $\frac{1}{3}$ about $(5, 1)$. Label the image $F$.

*Can you still?*

**(8B) Multiply and divide fractions (see Unit 5)**

*Can you still?*

Work out (cancel the answers if possible):

1. $\frac{1}{5}$ of $\frac{1}{4}$    2. $\frac{2}{3}$ of $\frac{6}{7}$    3. $\frac{2}{5} \times \frac{1}{8}$    4. $\frac{3}{4} \times \frac{5}{9}$

5. $\frac{1}{4} \times \frac{8}{9}$    6. $\frac{4}{5} \times \frac{10}{11}$    7. $\frac{3}{4} \times 28$    8. $\frac{2}{7} \times 21$

9. $\frac{1}{9} \div \frac{1}{5}$    10. $\frac{1}{3} \div \frac{4}{5}$    11. $\frac{3}{8} \div \frac{3}{10}$    12. $\frac{7}{9} \div \frac{5}{6}$

13. $\frac{3}{4} \div \frac{7}{8}$    14. $\frac{5}{9} \div 3$    15. $\frac{3}{5} \div 2$    16. $\frac{2}{11} \div \frac{4}{5}$

# Transformations

You may use tracing paper.

**1**

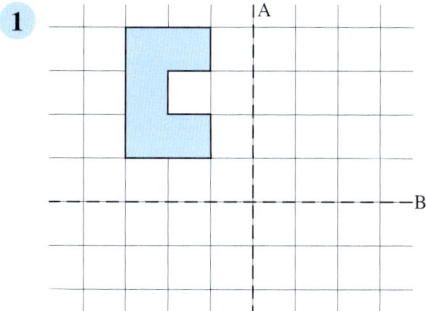

Copy the shape and the mirror lines.

(a) Reflect the shape in mirror line $A$.

(b) Reflect the image (new shape) in mirror line $B$.

**2**

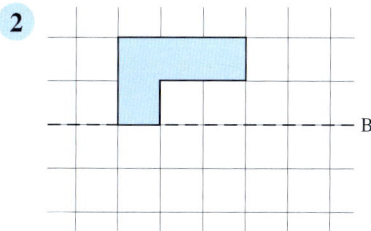

Copy the shape and the mirror line.

(a) Reflect the shape in the mirror line.

(b) Translate the image (new shape) 3 units to the right and 1 unit up.

**3**

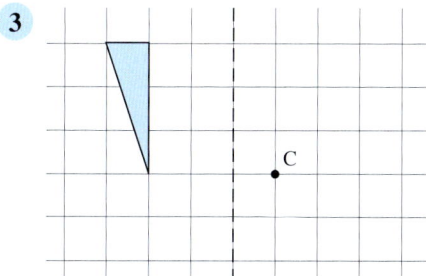

Copy the shape and the mirror line.

(a) Reflect the shape in the mirror line.

(b) Rotate the image 90° clockwise about the point $C$.

**4**

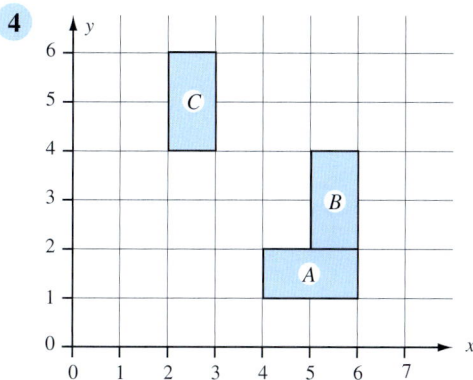

(a) Describe *fully* the rotation which moves shape $A$ onto shape $B$.

(b) Describe *fully* the translation which moves shape $B$ onto shape $C$.

213

**5**

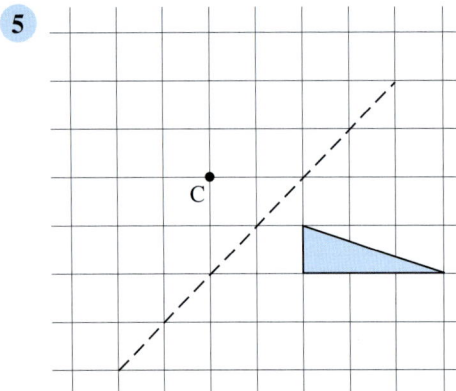

Copy the shape and the mirror line.

(a) Reflect the shape in the mirror line.

(b) Rotate the image 90° anticlockwise about the point $C$.

**6** Copy the shape.

(a) Rotate the shape 180° about the point $C$.

(b) Translate the image 4 units to the left and 2 units down.

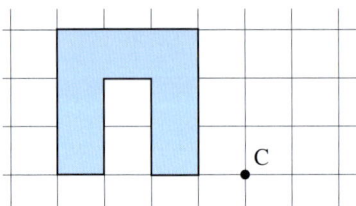

**7**

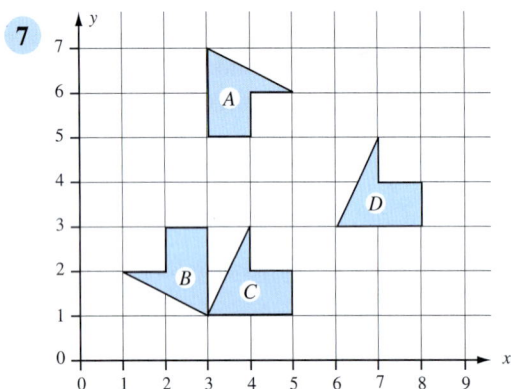

(a) Describe *fully* the rotation which moves shape $A$ onto shape $B$.

(b) Describe *fully* the rotation which moves shape $B$ onto shape $C$.

(c) Describe *fully* the translation which moves shape $C$ onto shape $D$.

*Can you still?*

**8C** **Multiply out brackets and collect like terms (see Unit 4)**

*Can you still?*

Simplify

**1.** $3(x + 4)$

**2.** $5(2x - 3)$

**3.** $4(3x + 6) + 2$

**4.** $4(2x + 1) + 7$

**5.** $3(x + 2) + 2(x + 3)$

**6.** $4(3x + 4) + 3(2x + 3)$

**7.** $8x + 5 + 4(3x - 1)$

**8.** $2(5x + 2) - 3(2x - 4)$

**9.** $5(x + 4) + 2(3x - 5)$

You may use tracing paper.

**1**

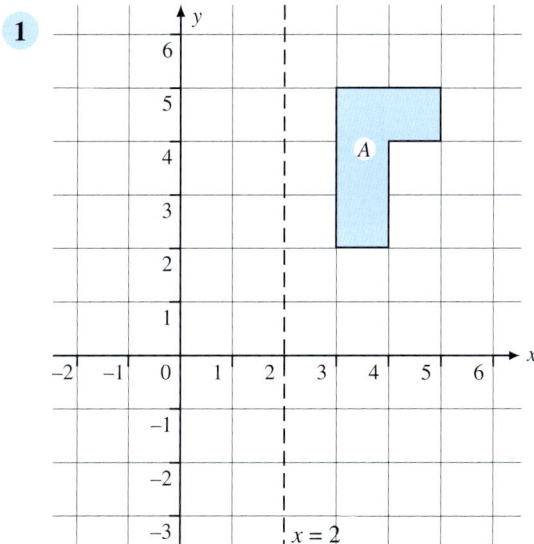

Copy the grid and shape opposite.

(a) Reflect shape $A$ in the line $x = 2$. Label the image $B$.

(b) Reflect shape $B$ in the line $y = 1$. Label the image $C$.

(c) Rotate shape $C$ 90° clockwise about $(1, -3)$. Label the image $D$.

**2**

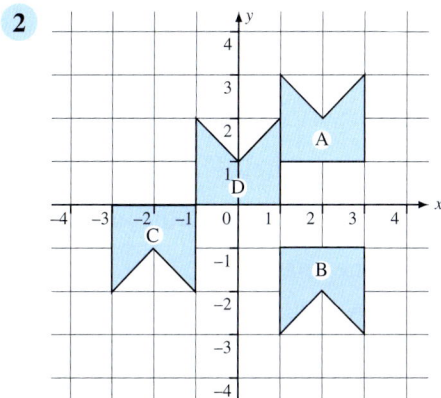

(a) Describe *fully* the transformation which transforms shape $A$ onto shape $B$.

(b) Describe *fully* the transformation which transforms shape $B$ onto shape $C$.

(c) Describe *fully* the transformation which transforms shape $C$ onto shape $D$.

(d) Describe *fully* the transformation which transforms shape $D$ onto shape $A$.

**3** (a) Draw the $x$-axis from $-4$ to 8.

Draw the $y$-axis from $-5$ to 5.

Draw triangle $A$ with vertices of $(1, 1)$, $(1, 2)$, $(3, 2)$.

(b) Enlarge triangle $A$ by scale factor 2 about $(0, 0)$. Label the image $B$.

(c) Rotate triangle $B$ 90° anticlockwise abut $(6, 4)$. Label the image $C$.

(d) Translate triangle $C$ through $\begin{pmatrix} -1 \\ -4 \end{pmatrix}$ Label the image $D$

(e) Reflect triangle $D$ in the line $x = 3$. Label the image $E$.

(f) Rotate triangle $E$ 90° clockwise about $(1, 0)$. Label the image $F$.

215

**4**

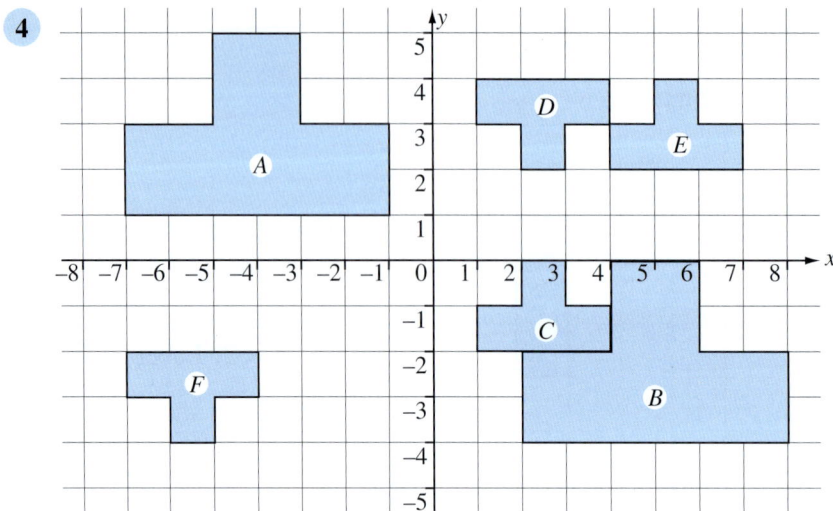

Describe *fully* the transformation which moves:

(a) shape $A$ onto shape $B$     (b) shape $B$ onto shape $C$

(c) shape $C$ onto shape $D$     (d) shape $D$ onto shape $E$

(e) shape $E$ onto shape $F$

**5** (a) Draw the $x$-axis from $-5$ to $10$.

     Draw the $y$-axis from $-8$ to $5$.

     Draw shape $A$ with vertices at $(2, 2)$, $(2, 4)$, $(3, 3)$, $(5, 3)$, $(5, 2)$.

   (b) Rotate shape $A$ $180°$ about $(3, 1)$. Label the image $B$.

   (c) Enlarge shape $B$ by scale factor 3 about $(1, 1)$. Label the image $C$.

   (d) Reflect shape $B$ in the $y$-axis. Label the image $D$.

   (e) Reflect shape $D$ in the line $y = 1$. Label the image $E$.

   (f) Describe *fully* the translation which moves shape $E$ onto shape $A$.

**6** (a) Draw the $x$-axis from $-8$ to $4$.

     Draw the $y$-axis from $-5$ to $5$.

     Draw shape $A$ with vertices $(-1, 2)$, $(-1, 5)$, $(-2, 5)$, $(-2, 3)$, $(-3, 3)$, $(-3, 5)$, $(-4, 5)$, $(-4, 2)$.

   (b) Rotate shape $A$ $90°$ anticlockwise about $(-4, 1)$. Label the image $B$.

   (c) Reflect shape $B$ in the line $x = -2$. Label the image $C$.

   (d) Reflect shape $C$ in the $x$-axis. Label the image $D$.

   (e) Rotate shape $D$ $90°$ clockwise about $(0, 0)$. Label the image $E$.

   (f) Describe *fully* the transformation that would move shape $E$ onto shape $A$.

To keep track of your money, the bank or building society will send you a regular **'statement'**.

ATM (Automated Teller Machine) – this shows cash taken out of a cash machine with a cash card

Balance brought forward – the amount of money in the account at the start of this period

D (overdrawn) – this shows the account is overdrawn and money is owed to the bank

CHQ – this shows any cheques paid out (202485 is the cheque number)

DD (Direct Debit) – this is money taken out of the account by an organisation to pay bills when permission has been given

CR (Credit) – this is any money paid into the account

MAE (Maestro card) – this is money paid out with a debit card

SO (standing order) – a regular payment of a fixed amount

Balance carried forward – the amount of money in the account at the end of this period

SMART BANK

Account Name
TERRY JONES

28 March to 27 April 2006

Sort code  Account Number
23-13-18     54920384

| Date | Payment type and details | Paid out | Paid in | Balance |
|---|---|---|---|---|
| 27 Mar | Balance brought forward | | | 278.10 |
| 28 Mar | ATM Cash | 50.00 | | 228.10 |
| 30 Mar | CHQ 202485 | 79.85 | | 148.25 |
| 5 Apr | DD BRITISH GAS | 63.10 | | 85.15 |
| 8 Apr | DD HENTON DISTRICT COUNCIL | 72.00 | | 13.15 |
| 9 Apr | CHQ 202486 | 25.51 | | 12.36 D |
| 12 Apr | CR My EMPLOYER | | 824.00 | 811.64 |
| 13 Apr | MAE PIZZA STALL | 42.83 | | 768.81 |
| 17 Apr | CR PAID IN AT SMART BANK | | 56.00 | 824.81 |
| 23 Apr | SO CRUK | 20.00 | | 804.81 |
| 24 Apr | MAE HENTON TANDOORI | 64.72 | | 740.09 |
| 27 Apr | Balance carried forward | | | 740.09 |

```
SMART BANK    ◈

Account Name
COLIN MAYS

3 April to 2 May 2006            Sort code    Account Number
                                 172619        32718425
```

| Date | Payment type and details | | Paid out | Paid in | Balance |
|------|------|------|------|------|------|
| 2 Apr | | Balance brought forward | | | 416.25 |
| 3 Apr | CHQ | 419330 | 63.10 | | ① |
| 5 Apr | DD | POLDEN WATER | 58.17 | | 294.98 |
| 9 Apr | CR | MY EMPLOYER | | 750.00 | ② |
| 14 Apr | MAE | PETROLGO | 28.64 | | ③ |
| 16 Apr | DD | MID ELECTRICITY | 67.00 | | 949.34 |
| 18 Apr | CHQ | 419331 | ④ | | 823.74 |
| 19 Apr | SO | MR. S. JONES | 38.45 | | ⑤ |
| 22 Apr | CR | PAID IN AT SMART BANK | | ⑥ | 850.29 |
| 23 Apr | MAE | HORTON STORE | 43.26 | | ⑦ |
| 28 Apr | MAE | AQUAPLAY | 21.95 | | ⑧ |
| 2 May | | Balance carried forward | | | ⑨ |

For Questions **1** to **9**, write down the correct amount of money for each box above.

**10** Explain what 'DD' shows on a bank statement.

**11** Explain what 'ATM' shows on a bank statement.

**12** Explain what 'D' shows on a bank statement.

## TEST YOURSELF ON UNIT 8

> 1. Recognising congruent shapes

Which shapes are congruent to shape *A*?

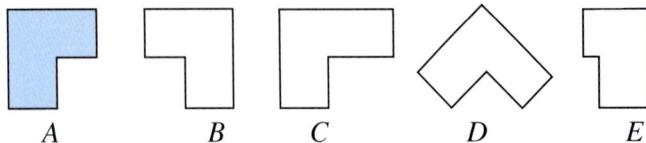

*A*      *B*      *C*      *D*      *E*

## 2. Using co-ordinates

(a)

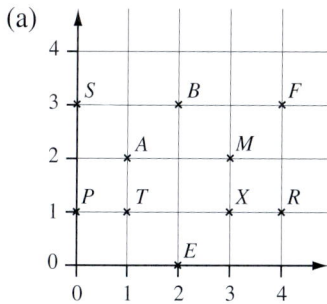

Write down the co-ordinates of each letter that spells the word A X E S

## 3. Translating shapes

(a)

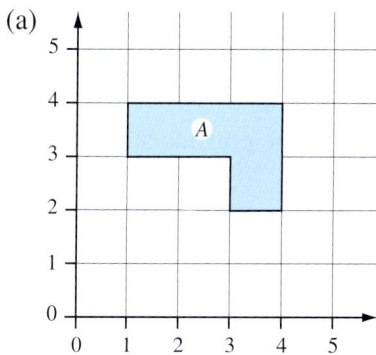

Copy the grid opposite and draw the shape shown.

(i) Translate shape *A* 1 unit to the left and 2 units down. Label the new shape *B*.

(ii) Translate shape *B* 2 units to the right and 3 units up. Label the new shape *C*.

(b)

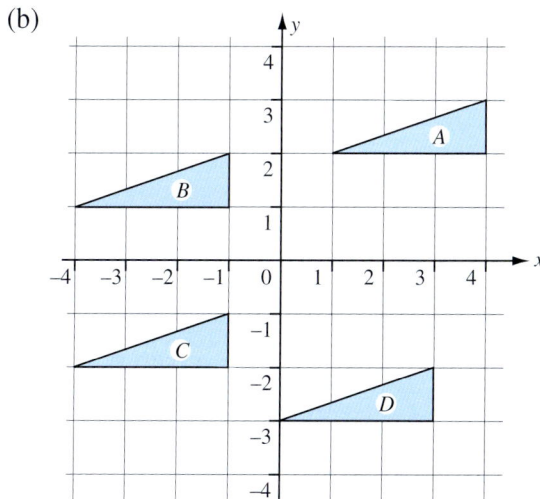

Describe the following translations.

(i) *A* to *C*

(ii) *A* to *D*

(iii) *D* to *B*

(iv) *B* to *A*

## 4. Reflecting shapes in mirror lines

Draw each shape below and reflect in the broken mirror line.

(a)

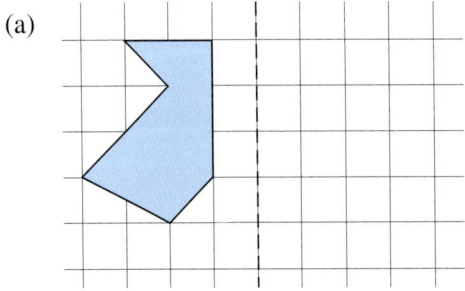

(b)

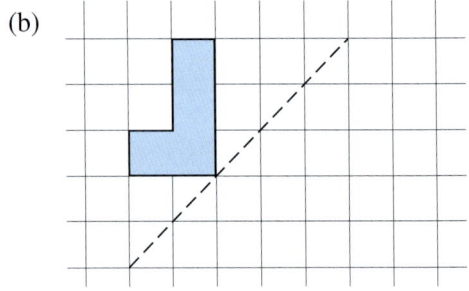

## 5. Rotating shapes

(a)

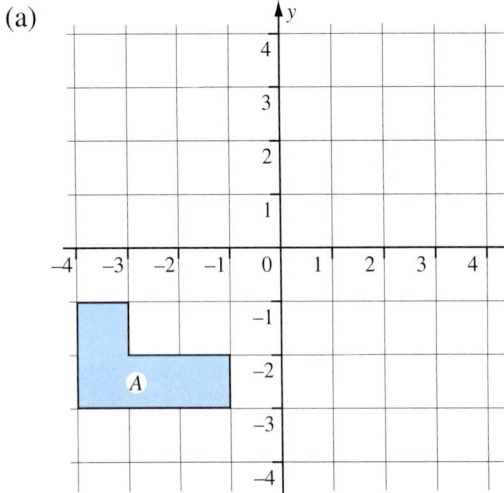

Copy the grid and shape *A* opposite.

(i) Rotate shape *A* 90° anticlockwise about (0, 0). Label the image *B*.

(ii) Rotate shape *A* 180° about (−1, −2). Label the image *C*.

(b)

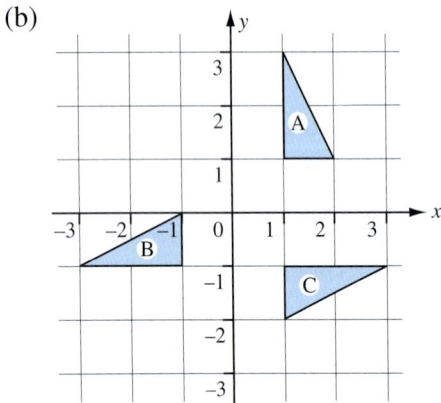

Describe *fully* the rotation which transforms:

(i) shape *A* onto *B*

(ii) shape *A* onto *C*

220

## 6. Enlarging shapes

Copy the diagrams below and then draw an enlargement using the scale factor and centre of enlargement (C) given.

(a)

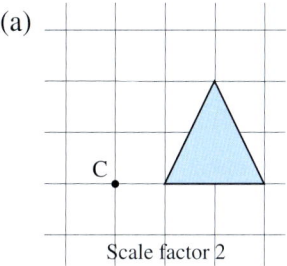

Scale factor 2

(b)

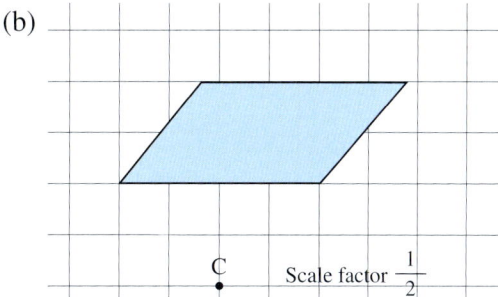

C • Scale factor $\frac{1}{2}$

(c)

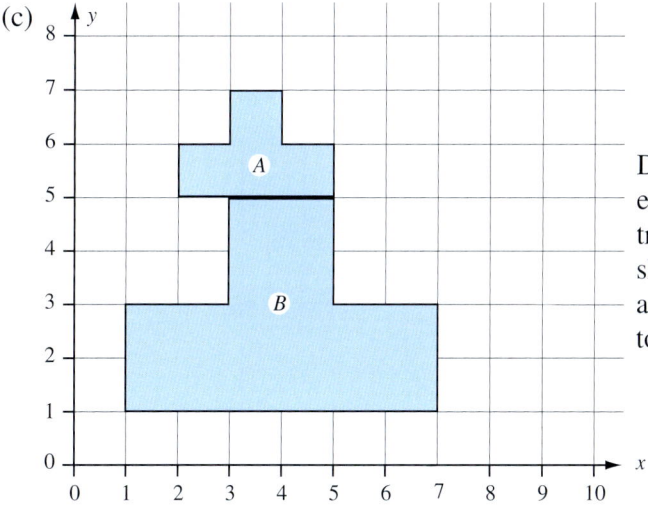

Describe *fully* the enlargement which transforms shape *A* onto shape *B* (draw the grid and 2 shapes if you need to)

## Mixed examination questions

**1** Which **two** of the following shapes are congruent to each other?

(a) (b) (c) (d)

(e) (f) (g)

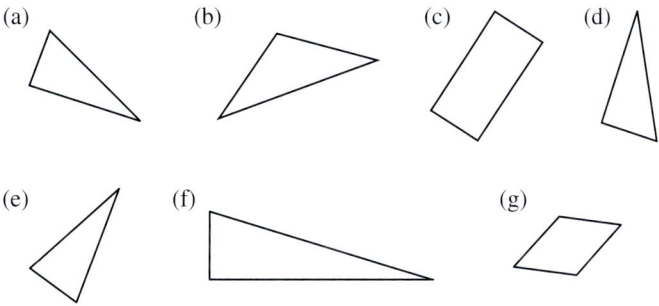

(WJEC)

221

**2**

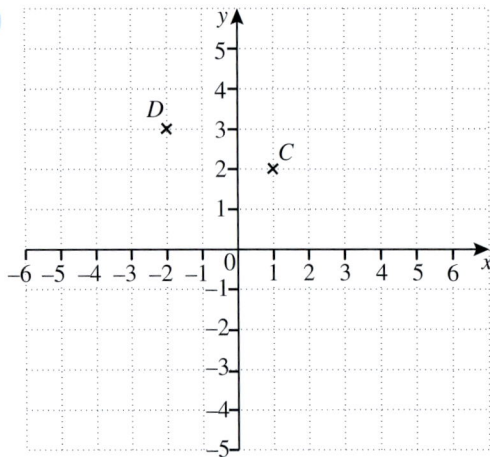

(a) Write down the co-ordinates of the points $C$ and $D$.

(b) Copy the grid and plot the points $E(-5, -1)$ and $F(2, -4)$.

Label each point clearly.

(OCR)

**3**　(a) Describe fully the single transformation which takes $A$ onto $B$.

(b) Describe fully the single transformation which takes $B$ onto $A$.

(c) $A$ is mapped onto $D$ by transformation $\begin{pmatrix} -2 \\ 3 \end{pmatrix}$.

Copy the grid and draw the position of $D$ on the diagram.

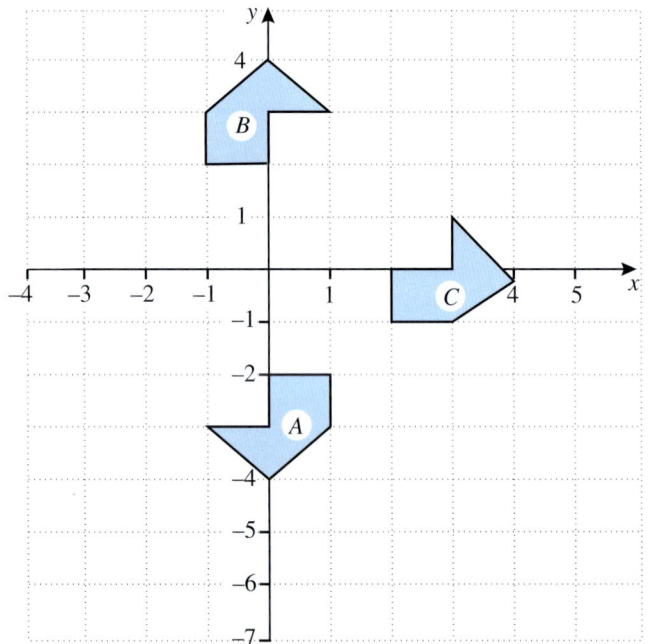

(AQA)

**4**

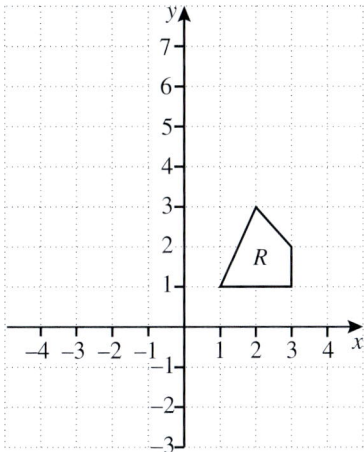

(a) Copy the grid opposite. *R* is mapped onto *S* by a reflection in the *y*-axis. Draw and label *S*.

(b) *S* is mapped onto *T* by reflection in the line $y = 4$. Draw and Label *T*.

(c) Describe fully the single transformation which maps *T* onto *R*.

(AQA)

**5** (a) Copy the grid opposite. Reflect the triangle *A* in the line $x = 4$. Label the image *P*.

(b) Translate triangle *A* by 4 squares to the left and 3 squares down.

Label the image *Q*.

(c) Triangle *B* is an enlargement of triangle *A*. Write down the scale factor of the enlargement.

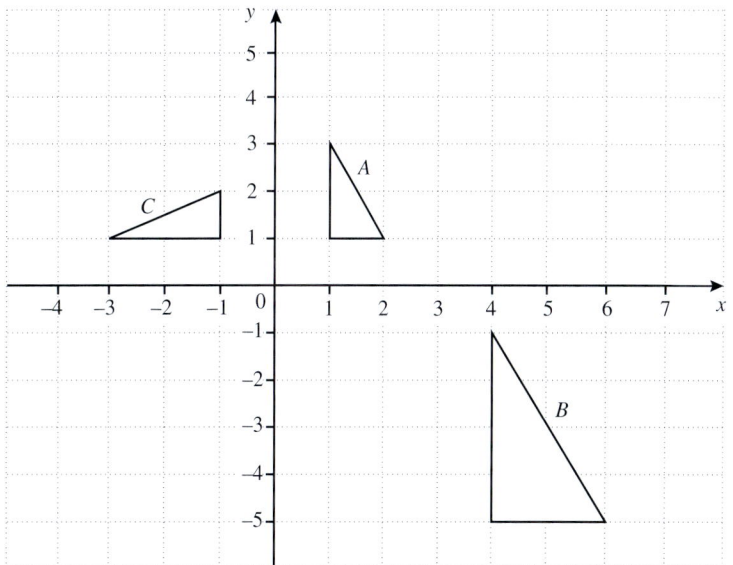

(d) Describe fully the single transformation that maps triangle *A* onto triangle *C*.

(OCR)

# NUMBER 5

**9**

**In this unit you will learn how to:**

– add and subtract decimals

– multiply decimals

– divide decimals by whole numbers

– divide by decimals

– round off numbers to the nearest
  10, 100, 1000 or whole number

– round off to decimal places

– estimate answers

– use a calculator

– round off to significant figures

– check answers

– WATCH YOUR MONEY! – VAT

---

## Adding and subtracting decimals

(a)  $3.2 + 4.31$      (b)  $0.27 + 5 + 14.2$      (c)  $8 - 3.7$

put a zero

```
    3.20
  + 4.31
    7.51
     ↑
```
(line up the points)

```
     0.27
     5.00
  + 14.20
   19.47
```
(write 5 as 5.00)

```
   7 ⁸̸ ¹0
  − 3.7
    4.3
```
(write 8 as 8.0)

---

### M 9.1

**1** Work out

(a)    13.6
    + 22.3

(b)    361.8
    + 32.7

(c)    7.34
    + 8.4

(d)  18.6
  +  13.4

(e)  30.75
  +  7.8

(f)  13.0
  +  0.39

(g)  17.5
  −  6.2

(h)  8.36
  −  2.8

(i)  14.0
  −  2.6

**2**

| 0.71 | 0.54 | 0.96 | 0.37 |
|------|------|------|------|
| 0.22 | 0.8  | 0.63 | 0.41 |
| 0.46 | 0.29 | 0.04 | 0.61 |
| 0.39 | 0.2  | 0.78 | 0.59 |

This grid is full of pairs of numbers which add up to 1. Write down every pair (there are 8 pairs of numbers).

**3** Copy and complete the following:

(a)  73.16
  +  0.52

(b)  3816.3
  +  507.2

(c)  2628.32
  −  316.21

(d)  68.17
  −  26.32

(e)  213.72
  −  61.36

(f)  362.7
  +  257.8

**4** Work out the following (Remember to line up the decimal point):

(a)  $1.7 + 3.27$

(b)  $5.16 + 4.99$

(c)  $0.082 + 3.07$

(d)  $6 + 0.31$

(e)  $8.28 + 4.19$

(f)  $38.64 + 13.8$

(g)  $47.3 - 21.8$

(h)  $63.7 - 28.8$

(i)  $38.4 - 16$

(j)  $7 - 4.4$

(k)  $12 - 6.3$

(l)  $7.7 - 5.39$

**E 9.1**

**1**

| 0.281 | 0.049 | 0.213 | 0.12  |
|-------|-------|-------|-------|
| 0.251 | 0.18  | 0.17  | 0.28  |
| 0.13  | 0.06  | 0.087 | 0.019 |
| 0.202 | 0.02  | 0.098 | 0.24  |

This grid is full of pairs of numbers which add up to 0.3. Write down every pair (there are 8 pairs of numbers).

**2** Work out

(a) $712.6 + 32.8 + 163.9$
(b) $807.3 + 216.8 + 36.7$
(c) $68.3 + 121.62 + 31.94$
(d) $61.87 - 13.9$
(e) $107.2 - 68.14$
(f) $2.174 - 1.38$

**3**

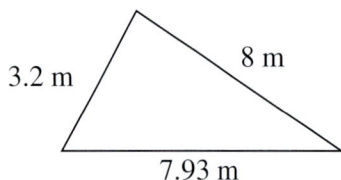

Find the perimeter of this triangle.

**4** How much change from a £20 note do you get if you spend:

(a) £3.72   (b) £14.53   (c) £11.06   (d) £6.85

(e) £4.48   (f) £3.99   (g) £8.63   (h) £17.57

**5** David has £50. He buys a book for £6.95 and a CD for £14.95. How much money does he have left?

**6** Geri has £40. She spends £13.87 on food and £15.50 on travel. How much money does she have left?

**7**

| | |
|---|---|
| TV | £487.50 |
| computer | £874.99 |
| CD player | £88.45 |
| printer | £124.75 |

Dan has £1600 to spend. Can he afford to buy all the items opposite? If so, how much money will he have left?

In Questions **8** to **10**, find the odd answer out.

**8** (a) $12.63 + 11.85 + 1.28$   (b) $20.3 + 4.19 + 1.37$   (c) $18.38 + 4.9 + 2.58$

**9** (a) $11.6 - 5.18$   (b) $14.4 - 7.88$   (c) $16 - 9.58$

**10** (a) $5.66 - 2.3$   (b) $16.96 - 13.7$   (c) $11.16 - 7.9$

**11** Which is larger?

A ( sum of 7.22 and 8 )   or   B ( difference between 23 and 7.68 )

**12** Find the missing digits

(a)
$$\begin{array}{r} \square \cdot 5\square \\ -4 \cdot \square 3 \\ \hline 3 \cdot 73 \end{array}$$

(b)
$$\begin{array}{r} 4 \cdot \square 7 \\ +\square \cdot 9\square \\ \hline 9 \cdot 03 \end{array}$$

(c)
$$\begin{array}{r} 3 \cdot 17\square \\ -\square \cdot 4\square 8 \\ \hline 0 \cdot \square 48 \end{array}$$

226

**9A** **Convert improper fractions and mixed numbers (see Unit 5)**

Change the following improper fractions to mixed numbers.

**1.** $\dfrac{9}{4}$     **2.** $\dfrac{13}{5}$     **3.** $\dfrac{27}{10}$     **4.** $\dfrac{17}{6}$     **5.** $\dfrac{38}{7}$

Change the following mixed numbers to improper fractions.

**6.** $3\dfrac{2}{3}$     **7.** $5\dfrac{1}{2}$     **8.** $7\dfrac{2}{5}$     **9.** $3\dfrac{6}{7}$     **10.** $8\dfrac{3}{4}$

## Multiplying decimals

(a) $4.23 \times 10 = 42.3$     (b) $0.0063 \times 100 = 0.63$     (c) $10.9 \times 1000 = 10900$

(d) $6 \times 0.1$

$= 6 \times \dfrac{1}{10}$

$= 6 \div 10$

$= 0.6$

(e) $0.7 \times 0.1$

$= 0.7 \times \dfrac{1}{10}$

$= 0.7 \div 10$

$= 0.07$

(f) $20.3 \times 0.01$

$= 20.3 \times \dfrac{1}{100}$

$= 20.3 \div 100$

$= 0.203$

### M 9.2

Work out

1   $6.12 \times 10$     2   $3.97 \times 10$     3   $0.618 \times 100$     4   $5.81 \times 100$

5   $0.093 \times 10$     6   $0.0081 \times 100$     7   $3.226 \times 1000$     8   $13.6 \times 1000$

9   $7.36 \times 100$     10  $0.0612 \times 1000$   11  $5.73 \times 100$     12  $3.298 \times 10$

13  $0.38 \times 1000$   14  $6.1 \times 1000$     15  $0.3 \times 100$     16  $0.5 \times 1000$

17  $0.1 \times 10$     18  $0.79 \times 1000$   19  $2.14 \times 10$     20  $0.824 \times 100$

Work out

21  $4 \times 0.1$     22  $0.2 \times 0.1$     23  $18 \times 0.01$     24  $7.4 \times 0.01$

25  $9 \times 0.1$     26  $0.8 \times 0.1$     27  $2 \times 0.01$     28  $15 \times 0.1$

**29** $19 \times 0.1$      **30** $0.36 \times 0.1$      **31** $64 \times 0.01$      **32** $5 \times 0.1$

**33** $25 \times 0.1$      **34** $1 \times 0.01$      **35** $87 \times 0.01$      **36** $0.4 \times 0.1$

**37** Here are 4 rules:

$$\boxed{\times 10} \quad \boxed{\times 0.1} \quad \boxed{\times 100} \quad \boxed{\times 0.01}$$

Copy each chain of numbers below and fill in the empty boxes with the correct rule (Remember: $\times 0.1$ means $\div 10$ and $\times 0.01$ means $\div 100$).

(a) $3.9 \rightarrow \square \rightarrow 39 \rightarrow \square \rightarrow 390 \rightarrow \square \rightarrow 3.9 \rightarrow \square \rightarrow 0.39$

(b) $670 \rightarrow \square \rightarrow 67 \rightarrow \square \rightarrow 6.7 \rightarrow \square \rightarrow 670 \rightarrow \square \rightarrow 6.7$

(c) $83.2 \rightarrow \square \rightarrow 8320 \rightarrow \square \rightarrow 832 \rightarrow \square \rightarrow 8.32 \rightarrow \square \rightarrow 0.832$

(d) $0.24 \rightarrow \square \rightarrow 24 \rightarrow \square \rightarrow 2.4 \rightarrow \square \rightarrow 240 \rightarrow \square \rightarrow 0.24$

---

When we multiply two decimal numbers together, the answer has the same number of figures after the decimal point as the total number of figures after the decimal point in the Question.

(a) $0.7 \times 0.4$

    $(7 \times 4 = 28)$

    so $0.\underline{7} \times 0.\underline{4} = 0.2\,8$

(b) $0.8 \times 0.009$

    $(8 \times 9 = 72)$

    so $0.8 \times 0.\underline{0}\,\underline{0}\,\underline{9} = 0.\underline{0}\,\underline{0}\,7\,2$

**Note:**

**When a number is multiplied by a decimal between 0 and 1, the answer will be smaller than the starting number.**

---

**E 9.2**

**1** Copy the Questions below and put the decimal point in the correct place in each answer.

(a) $3.8 \times 0.7 = 266$      (b) $0.3 \times 0.78 = 234$

(c) $8.6 \times 6 = 516$      (d) $0.17 \times 0.29 = 493$

(e) $3.1 \times 0.94 = 2914$      (f) $3.28 \times 2.8 = 9184$

(g) $0.619 \times 3.6 = 22284$      (h) $27 \times 0.19 = 513$

(i) $0.05 \times 1.67 = 835$      (j) $8 \times 1.084 = 8672$

**2** Work out

(a) $0.9 \times 0.4$      (b) $0.2 \times 0.8$      (c) $0.03 \times 0.7$

(d) $0.4 \times 0.04$      (e) $0.03 \times 0.6$      (f) $0.5 \times 0.007$

(g) $0.03 \times 0.4$      (h) $0.8 \times 0.7$      (i) $0.04 \times 0.003$

(j) $0.8^2$      (k) $0.3^2$      (l) $0.9^2$

**3** Work out

(a) $3 \times 0.72$      (b) $6.9 \times 4$      (c) $12.3 \times 5$

(d) $14.6 \times 6$      (e) $7 \times 13.2$      (f) $0.027 \times 8$

**4** Find the total cost of 3 kg of meat at £4.74 per kg.

**5** Find the total cost of 5 cereal packets at £1.89 for each packet.

**6** Find the total cost of 7 bottles of tomato ketchup at £1.63 for each bottle *and* 4 large packets of crisps at £1.28 for each packet.

**7** If 1 kg of cheese costs £5.29, find the cost of 4 kg.

**8** A new car tyre costs £41.49.

What is the total cost of 4 new tyres?

**9** Find the total cost of 6 batteries at £1.47 each.

**10** £1 = \$1.52. Change the money below to dollars by multiplying by 1.52.

(a) £3      (b) £7      (c) £8      (d) £20

**11** Work out

(a) $27 \times 0.02$    (b) $14 \times 0.05$    (c) $18 \times 0.03$    (d) $0.5 \times 0.05$

(e) $44 \times 0.02$    (f) $1.6 \times 0.4$    (g) $4.1 \times 0.5$    (h) $2.63 \times 0.3$

(i) $3.4 \times 0.6$    (j) $0.49 \times 0.7$    (k) $0.38 \times 0.02$    (l) $0.22 \times 0.03$

(m) $6.22 \times 0.07$    (n) $18.4 \times 0.8$    (o) $40.9 \times 0.3$

**12** Copy below and fill in the empty boxes.

(a) $0.4 \times 3 = \boxed{\phantom{x}}$      (b) $0.7 \times \boxed{\phantom{x}} = 4.2$

(c) $\boxed{\phantom{x}} \times 0.6 = 0.18$      (d) $0.02 \times \boxed{\phantom{x}} = 0.014$

(e) $0.8 \times \boxed{\phantom{x}} = 0.048$      (f) $\boxed{\phantom{x}} \times 0.06 = 0.0054$

## Dividing decimals by whole numbers

(a) $11 \div 8$

$$
\begin{array}{r}
1.\ 3\ 7\ 5 \\
8)\overline{11.^30\,^60\,^40}
\end{array}
$$

↑ ↑ ↑

Note the extra zeros

(b) $7.3 \div 4$

$$
\begin{array}{r}
1.\ 8\ 2\ 5 \\
4)\overline{7.^33\,^10\,^20}
\end{array}
$$

↑ ↑

Note the extra zeros

### M 9.3

Work out

**1** $3)\overline{18.6}$     **2** $4)\overline{36.48}$     **3** $6)\overline{20.46}$

**4** $6)\overline{15.36}$     **5** $7)\overline{34.3}$     **6** $9)\overline{39.15}$

**7** Divide the numbers below by 4.

    (a) 13.2     (b) 18.94     (c) 13     (d) 27

**8** Divide the numbers below by 8.

    (a) 21.12     (b) 3.6     (c) 17     (d) 31

Work out

**9** $18.52 \div 4$    **10** $14.82 \div 6$    **11** $205.2 \div 6$    **12** $18.93 \div 6$

**13** $1.085 \div 5$    **14** $26.67 \div 7$    **15** $1.96 \div 4$    **16** $70.28 \div 7$

**17** $8.7 \div 5$    **18** $0.58 \div 8$    **19** $0.02352 \div 6$    **20** $0.3724 \div 7$

**21** A prize of £259.50 is shared by six winners. How much should each person receive?

**22** Hannah and three of her friends go to the cinema. The tickets cost £23 in total. What is the cost of 1 ticket?

**23** Five people share the fuel cost of a car journey. The total fuel cost is £32.35. How much does each person pay?

**24** Tom, Sally and Cherie club together to buy some flowers for their dear old Gran. The flowers cost £37.35. How much does each person pay?

**25** Christmas crackers cost £11.94 for six. How much does each cracker cost?

**26** Four identical boxes weigh 193 kg in total. How much does each box weigh?

**27** A multipack containing 4 soap bars costs £2.52. Single soap bars can be bought for 67p each. How much do you save on each bar by buying the multi-pack?

**28** A piece of wood is 4.23 m long. It is cut into 9 equal parts. How long is each part?

## Dividing by decimals

To divide by a decimal, multiply both numbers by 10, 100, 1000, … so that the decimal you are dividing by becomes a whole number. Now divide the 2 numbers to get the answer.

(a) $3.2 \div 0.\underline{4}$

multiply both
numbers by 10

$= 32 \div 4$

$= 8$

(b) $5.517 \div 0.\underline{9}$

multiply both
numbers by 10

$= 55.17 \div 9$

$$\begin{array}{r} 6.\ 1\ 3 \\ 9\overline{)55.^117} \end{array}$$

(c) $3.5882 \div 0.\underline{0}\,\underline{0}\,\underline{7}$

multiply both
numbers by 1000

$= 3588.2 \div 7$

$$\begin{array}{r} 51\ 2.\ 6 \\ 7\overline{)358^18.^42} \end{array}$$

**Note:**

**When a number is divided by a decimal between 0 and 1, the answer will be larger than the starting number.**

### E 9.3

**1** Copy the Questions below and fill in the empty boxes

    (a) $4.6 \div 0.2 = \boxed{\phantom{x}} \div 2 = \boxed{\phantom{x}}$      (b) $3.2 \div 0.04 = \boxed{\phantom{x}} \div 4 = \boxed{\phantom{x}}$

    (c) $1.65 \div 0.5 = \boxed{\phantom{x}} \div 5 = \boxed{\phantom{x}}$      (d) $2.64 \div 0.002 = \boxed{\phantom{x}} \div 2 = \boxed{\phantom{x}}$

**2** Divide the numbers below by 0.5.

    (a) 3.5     (b) 4     (c) 6.5     (d) 8

**3** Divide the numbers below by 0.3.

    (a) 6     (b) 2.4     (c) 3.6     (d) 0.18

**4** Divide the numbers below by 0.7.

    (a) 2.8     (b) 6.3     (c) 21     (d) 0.42

Work out

**5** $7.2 \div 0.4$  **6** $3.8 \div 0.2$  **7** $1.84 \div 0.8$

**8** $14.98 \div 0.7$  **9** $0.084 \div 0.03$  **10** $0.496 \div 0.08$

**11** $0.444 \div 0.06$  **12** $3.25 \div 0.05$  **13** $26.6 \div 0.7$

**14** $0.075 \div 0.003$  **15** $0.144 \div 0.04$  **16** $0.065 \div 0.002$

**17** A bottle of lemonade holds 1 litre. How many glasses can be filled from this bottle if each glass holds 0.2 litres?

**18** A box of sweets contains 2.4 kg. How many packets can be filled from this box if each packet holds 0.15 kg?

In Questions **19** to **21**, find the odd answer out.

**19** (a) $0.63 \div 0.7$  (b) $0.57 \div 0.6$  (c) $0.72 \div 0.8$

**20** (a) $7.02 \div 0.09$  (b) $5.18 \div 0.07$  (c) $2.96 \div 0.04$

**21** (a) $8.82 \div 0.6$  (b) $7.4 \div 0.5$  (c) $11.84 \div 0.8$

**22** Each empty square below contains either a number or an operation $(+, -, \times, \div)$. Copy each square and fill in the missing details. The arrows are equal signs.

(a)

| 22.4 | ÷ | 7 | → |  |
|------|---|---|---|---|
| × |  | + |  |  |
| 0.1 | × |  | → | 0.01 |
| ↓ |  | ↓ |  |  |
|  | + |  | → |  |

(b)

| 6.52 | ÷ | 0.2 | → |  |
|------|---|-----|---|---|
| × |  | × |  |  |
| 10 | × |  | → | 1 |
| ↓ |  | ↓ |  |  |
|  | + |  | → |  |

**23** $147 \times 382 = 56154$

use this to work out:

(a) $1470 \times 382$

(b) $147 \times 38200$

(c) $14.7 \times 38.2$

(d) $1.47 \times 3820$

**24** $64.848 \div 28 = 2.316$

use this to work out:

(a) $64848 \div 28$

(b) $6484.8 \div 280$

(c) $0.64848 \div 0.028$

(d) $2316 \times 28$

**9B Calculate angles (see Unit 3)**

Find the angles marked with letters.

1.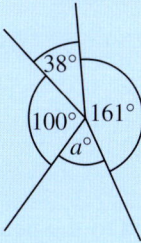

2.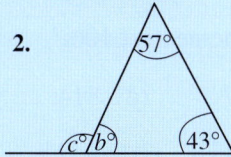

3.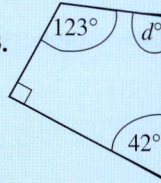

4.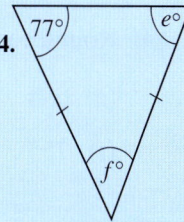

5.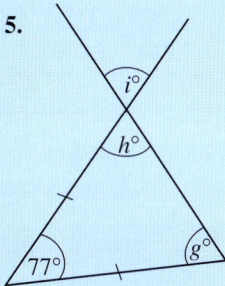

6.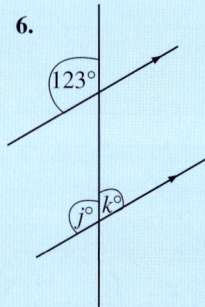

7.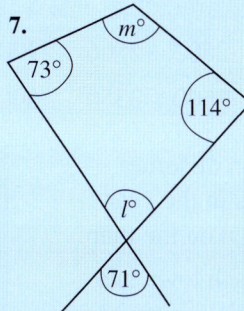

8.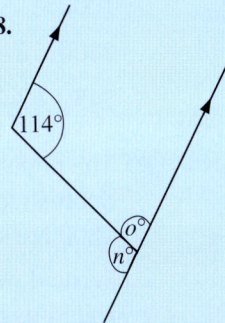

---

## Rounding off numbers

**1.** *Rounding to the nearest whole number.*

If the first digit after the decimal point is *5 or more* round *up*. Otherwise round down.

$68.3 \xrightarrow{\text{rounds to}} 68$

$49.8 \longrightarrow 50$

$3.5 \longrightarrow 4$

**2.** *Rounding to the nearest 100.*

If the digit in the tens column is 5 or more round up. Otherwise round down.

$387 \longrightarrow 400$

$138 \longrightarrow 100$

$3712 \longrightarrow 3700$

**M 9.4**

**1** Which of the numbers below will round to 70 when rounded to the nearest 10?

63   64   65   66   67   68   69   70   71   72   73   74   75   76   77

**2** Which of the numbers below will round to 140 when rounded to the nearest 10?

133   134   135   136   137   138   139   140   141   142   143   144   145   146   147   148

233

**3** Which of the numbers below will round to 400 when rounded to the nearest 100?

330  340  349  350  351  375  399  400  401  408

420  437  440  445  449  450  451  460

**4** Round each of these numbers to the nearest 100.

(a) 684  (b) 393  (c) 807  (d) 814  (e) 485

(f) 755  (g) 1586  (h) 2111  (i) 6394  (j) 3423

**5** Which of the numbers below will round to 3000 when rounded to the nearest 1000?

2400  2499  2500  2506  2700  2900  3000  3100  3300  3400

3450  3499  3500  3550  3600

**6** The population of some Scottish towns in the year 1800 are shown on the map.

Write down each town and round its population to the nearest 1000.

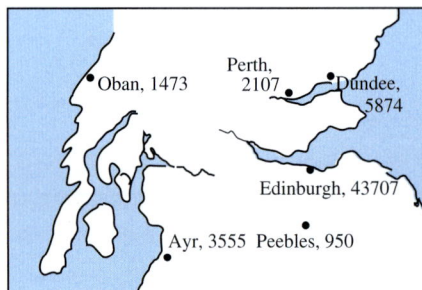

Oban, 1473  Perth, 2107  Dundee, 5874

Edinburgh, 43707

Ayr, 3555  Peebles, 950

**7** Round each of these numbers to the nearest whole number:

(a) 5.2  (b) 8.7  (c) 2.5  (d) 3.4  (e) 8.5

(f) 0.7  (g) 12.2  (h) 25.8  (i) 41.1  (j) 69.2

(k) 249.9  (l) 174.6  (m) 3.17  (n) 8.32  (o) 7.64

**8** Which of the numbers below are correctly rounded off?

(a) 67 $\longrightarrow$ 70  (to nearest 10)  (b) 4729 $\longrightarrow$ 4700  (to nearest 100)

(c) 3186 $\longrightarrow$ 3100 (to nearest 100)  (d) 38194 $\longrightarrow$ 38000 (to nearest 1000)

(e) 2743 $\longrightarrow$ 2750 (to nearest 10)  (f) 791 $\longrightarrow$ 800  (to nearest 10)

(g) 2.38 $\longrightarrow$ 3  (to nearest whole number)

(h) 5.16 $\longrightarrow$ 5  (to nearest whole number)

(i) 35 $\longrightarrow$ 30 (to nearest 10)

(j) 13.82 $\longrightarrow$ 13 (to nearest whole number)

**9** What is the smallest number that will round to 820 when rounded to the nearest 10?

**10** What is the largest whole number that will round to 2700 when rounded to the nearest 100?

**11** A newspaper reports that 42000 people went to a football match. If this number had been rounded to the nearest 1000, write down the lowest number of people that could have been at the football match.

**12** 12400 people live in the town of Tadcaster (to the nearest 100). Write down the greatest number of people that might live in Tadcaster.

## E 9.4

**1** Round each of these numbers to the nearest £1:
(a) £3.87  (b) £7.63  (c) £1.26  (d) £4.50  (e) £8.53

**2** Round each of these numbers to the nearest 1m:
(a) 6.7 m  (b) 3.12 m  (c) 11.4 m  (d) 7.89 m  (e) 0.84 m

**3** 3.$\underline{5}$178924 is 4 to the nearest whole number because the first digit after the decimal point is 5 or more so round up.

Round each of these numbers to the nearest whole number:
(a) 7.14862      (b) 3.471894      (c) 8.721893      (d) 5.07213

(e) 3.631089      (f) 12.941628      (g) 17.718253      (h) 11.31874

(i) 34.278914      (j) 0.825164

**4** Work out these answers on a calculator and then round off the answer to the nearest whole number.
(a) $321 \div 19$      (b) $898 \div 19$      (c) $78.1 \times 4.7$      (d) $302 \div 0.13$

(e) $7.16 \times 3.28$      (f) $28.2 \times 3.47$      (g) $83.7 \times 5.9$      (h) $13.2 \times 0.39$

(i) $382.7 \div 9.4$      (j) $507 \div 0.23$      (k) $85.6 \div 13$      (l) $2.33 \div 0.13$

**5** Work out a rough answer to each Question below by rounding each number to the nearest 10:
(a) $38 \times 11$      (b) $63 \times 29$      (c) $72 \times 41$

(d) $372 - 159$      (e) $249 - 82$      (f) $61 \times 49$

(g) $418 + 213$      (h) $1337 + 2181$      (i) $59 \times 89$

# Decimal places

## Rounding off to 1 decimal place

If the figure in the 2nd decimal place is 5 or more, round up. Otherwise do not.

$3.8\underline{7}2 = 3.9$      $14.4\underline{5} = 14.5$      $2.4\underline{3}7 = 2.4$

↑            ↑            ↑

5 or more     5 or more     less than 5
round up      round up      round down

## Rounding off to 2 decimal places

If the figure in the 3rd decimal place is 5 or more, round up. Otherwise do not.

$3.87\underline{2} = 3.87$      $15.52\underline{5} = 15.53$      $2.43\underline{7} = 2.44$

↑            ↑            ↑

less than 5     5 or more     5 or more
round down    round up      round up

### Note

5.96 rounded to the nearest whole number is 6

5.96 rounded to 1 decimal place is 6.0 (the zero is needed)

---

**M 9.5**

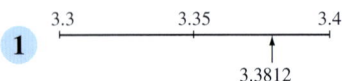

**1** Round 3.3812 to 1 decimal place.

(number line showing 3.3, 3.35, 3.4 with 3.3812 marked)

**2** Round these numbers to 1 decimal place.

(a) 6.31     (b) 5.83     (c) 8.37     (d) 6.75

(e) 0.352    (f) 9.841    (g) 12.618    (h) 15.747

**3** Which numbers below round to 7.3 (to 1 decimal place)?

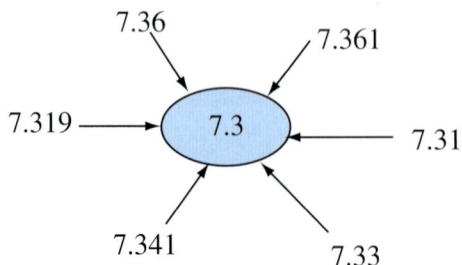

7.36     7.361

7.319 → **7.3** ← 7.31

7.341     7.33

**4** Round these numbers to 2 decimal places.

(a) 2.346     (b) 7.053     (c) 13.333     (d) 2.074

(e) 0.2365     (f) 23.676     (g) 0.9393     (h) 7.086

**5** Which numbers below round to 8.16 (to 2 decimal places)?

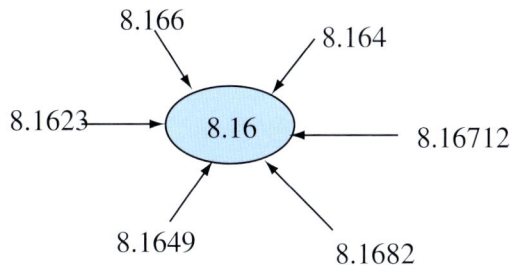

**6** Round these numbers to 3 decimal places.

(a) 2.1683     (b) 5.6414     (c) 8.3257     (d) 4.2318

(e) 7.2515     (f) 13.7109     (g) 17.3298     (h) 41.61352

**7** Work out these answers on a calculator and then round the answers correct to 2 decimal places.

(a) $9.76 \div 7$     (b) $0.38 \times 0.81$     (c) $2.57^2$     (d) $3186 \div 416$

(e) $0.89 \times 0.37$     (f) $19.32 \div 17$     (g) $3.9 \times 0.518$     (h) $0.87^2$

(i) $0.38 \div 51$     (j) $\sqrt{7.6}$     (k) $\sqrt{17}$     (l) $5.9 \div 37$

**8** (a) Measure the sides of each triangle below. Write down each length, in cm, correct to 1 decimal place.

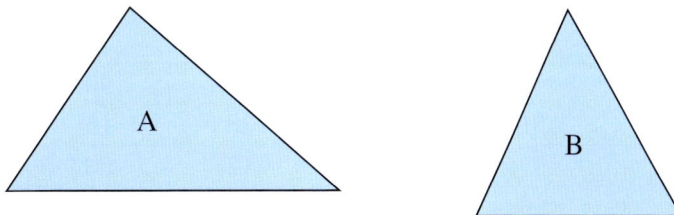

(b) For each triangle, add together the lengths of the 3 sides to find the perimeter.

## Key Facts

Jack worked out 7.02 × 8.9 equals 624.78. He can check his answer by rounding off numbers in the question.

7.02 is roughly 7     8.9 is roughly 9

so     7.02 × 8.9 is roughly 7 × 9 = 63

Clearly Jack's answer is wrong. He put the decimal point in the wrong place. His answer should have been 62.478.

**Examples**

Find rough answers to the questions below:

(a) 29.7 × 3.1          (b) 38.8 ÷ 1.981          (c) 12% of £68.99

is roughly 30 × 3          is roughly 40 ÷ 2          is roughly 10% of £70

= 90                              = 20                              $= \frac{1}{10}$ of £70 = £7

### E 9.5

Do *not* use a calculator.

From the table below, choose the most sensible **rough** answer from A, B or C.

|    | Calculation | A | B | C |
|----|-------------|------|------|--------|
| 1  | 7.78 × 8.95 | 32 | 72 | 720 |
| 2  | 3.1 × 97 | 300 | 90 | 30 |
| 3  | 4.16 × 6.99 | 28 | 15 | 280 |
| 4  | 603 ÷ 4.93 | 12 | 60 | 120 |
| 5  | 88.7 ÷ 0.97 | 90 | 300 | 900 |
| 6  | 604 × 10.46 | 4000 | 6000 | 600 |
| 7  | 68.6 × 39 + 271 | 400 | 100 | 4000 |
| 8  | 2.12 × 70.4 | 700 | 140 | 7 |
| 9  | $7.13^2$ | 14 | 50 | 200 |
| 10 | 728 ÷ 9.88 | 70 | 700 | 350 |
| 11 | 48% of £28300 | £28 | £280 | £14000 |
| 12 | 9% of £394.60 | £20 | £40 | £200 |

**13** A quick way of adding lots of figures on a shopping bill is to round every number to the nearest pound (eg. £2.37 becomes £2, £0.94 becomes £1, £0.36 becomes £0 and so on).

Use this method to estimate the total for each bill below:

(a)

| | |
|---|---|
| APPLE GRNNY SMTH | |
| 0.540 kg @£1.08/kg | £0.58 |
| CLEMENTINES | £1.69 |
| GRAPEFRUIT RED | £0.38 |
| CONFERENCE PEARS | £1.49 |
| CHICORY 160G | £1.08 |
| ORGANIC CARROTS | £0.84 |
| ORGNC/WATERCRESS | £1.39 |
| BANANAS | |
| 0.710 kg @£0.74/kg | £0.53 |
| MANGE TOUT 200G | £1.39 |
| ORGNC/WATERCRESS | £1.39 |
| CELERY | £0.53 |
| ORGANIC CARROTS | £0.84 |
| SALAD CRESS | £0.23 |
| SALAD CRESS | £0.23 |
| TTD CHC GNG BISC | £1.09 |
| GRAPES RD SEEDLS | |
| 0.425 kg @£2.99/kg | £1.27 |

(b)

| | |
|---|---|
| RTB BAGUETTE | £0.95 |
| RTB BAGUETTE | £0.95 |
| APPLES COX | |
| 1.495 kg @£1.49/kg | £2.23 |
| SATSUMAS | |
| 0.985 kg @£1.49/kg | £1.47 |
| JS CEYLON TEA | £0.82 |
| JS CEYLON TEA | £0.82 |
| JS SLC HVST FHSE | £0.69 |
| JS SLC HVST FHSE | £0.69 |
| ONIONS LARGE | |
| 0.225 kg @£0.64/kg | £0.14 |
| *2 40W BULBS | £0.45 |
| * LDT CORNET BOX | £3.29 |
| * COMP C/TKY/VEG | £1.46 |
| JS U/S BRT BUTTR | £1.09 |
| * 2 100W BULBS | £0.49 |
| GOUDA WHEEL | £3.66 |
| JS CHICKEN BURGR | £1.09 |

(c) Use a calculator to work out the exact total bill above.
Was the estimate larger or smaller than the exact total bill?

**14** Do not use a calculator.

Use sensible **rough** answers to match each Question below to the correct answer:

A  $7.1 \times 4.9$        P  101.7375

B  $41 \times 4.95$        Q  34.79

C  $8139 \div 80$        R  70.9

D  $0.99 \times 61$        S  202.95

E  $29.6 + 41.3$        T  60.39

**15** Keira earns £97 each week. *Estimate* how much Keira earns in one year (52 weeks) by rounding off to sensible rough numbers.

**16** Josh burns off 590 kcals each time he visits the Gym. *Estimate* how many kcals he burns off during 21 trips to the Gym?

**17**

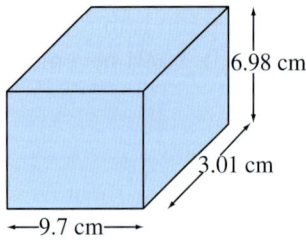

The volume of this box is $6.98 \times 3.01 \times 9.7$

*Estimate* the volume of this box.

**18** Do not use a calculator.

Use sensible **rough** answers to match each Question below to the correct answer:

| A | $203.1 \div 5$ | | P | $54.994$ |
|---|---|---|---|---|
| B | $6.2 \times 8.87$ | | Q | $9.4$ |
| C | $9.08^2$ | | R | $82.4464$ |
| D | $202.1 \div 21.5$ | | S | $200.6467$ |
| E | $39.89 \times 5.03$ | | T | $40.62$ |

*Can you still?*

*Can you still?*

**9C Convert between fractions, decimals and percentages**
**(see Unit 6)**

Put all the numbers below into groups of 3 so that the numbers in each group are equal to each other. $\left( \text{Example: } 6\% = 0.06 = \dfrac{3}{50} \right)$

$7\%$ $\qquad \dfrac{3}{50} \qquad\qquad \dfrac{7}{10}$

$0.6 \qquad\qquad 0.35 \qquad\qquad 0.06$

$\qquad\qquad 0.04 \qquad \dfrac{7}{100} \qquad \dfrac{1}{4}$

$\dfrac{7}{20} \qquad\qquad\qquad 6\% \qquad 60\%$

$\qquad\qquad 70\% \qquad\qquad 4\%$

$0.07 \qquad \dfrac{1}{25} \qquad\qquad 25\%$

$0.25 \qquad\qquad 0.7 \quad 35\% \qquad \dfrac{3}{5}$

## Using a calculator

**Money**

To work out £16.80 ÷ 6, key in $\boxed{16.8}$ $\boxed{÷}$ $\boxed{6}$ $\boxed{=}$

The answer is $\boxed{2.8}$   Remember this means £2.80

**Order of operations**   Make sure you always follow the rule BODMAS
*B*rackets first then *D*ivide, *M*ultiply, *A*dd and *S*ubtract
in that order.

(a) Work out $3.9 + \dfrac{2.4}{12}$

$\dfrac{2.4}{12}$ means $2.4 ÷ 12$ and Division must be done before Adding.

Key in $\boxed{2.4}$ $\boxed{÷}$ $\boxed{12}$ $\boxed{=}$ then $\boxed{+}$ $\boxed{3.9}$ $\boxed{=}$

Answer is 4.1

(b) Does $\dfrac{3.6}{1.8 + 5.4}$ equal 7.4 or 0.5?

$1.8 + 5.4 = 7.2$ so the denominator (bottom number) is larger than the
numerator (top number) which means the answer must be smaller than 1.

$\boxed{3.6}$ $\boxed{÷}$ $\boxed{1.8}$ $\boxed{+}$ $\boxed{5.4}$ $\boxed{=}$ gives 7.4.

This is wrong. All the denominator must be divided, not just 1.8.

## M 9.6

**1**  Work out the following. Give answers to the *nearest whole number*.

(a) $3.6 + 6.3 \times 1.8$

(b) $17 - 3.6 \times 2.1$

(c) $31 + 16 ÷ 0.8$

(d) $6.1 + \dfrac{3.8}{1.65}$

(e) $9.7 - \dfrac{6.1}{4.82}$

(f) $\dfrac{1.8 + 4.81}{3.7}$

(g) $(8.1 - 3.06) \times (4.7 + 2.93)$

(h) $\dfrac{11.3 - 6.28}{4.6}$

(i) $\dfrac{(8.91 + 3.6)}{0.69}$

(j) $\dfrac{(5.3 - 1.21)}{0.07}$

(k) $\dfrac{19.2 + 13.71}{1.08}$

(l) $\dfrac{(28.01 + 17.6)}{(32 - 29.7)}$

(m) $\dfrac{82.1 - 13.7}{31 + 1.6}$

(n) $\dfrac{47.28}{3.8 - 0.19}$

**2** Match each Question below to the correct answer:

A $(4.1 \times 2.6) - 1.9$

B $4.1 \times (2.6 - 1.9)$

C $2.6 \times (4.1 + 1.9)$

D $(2.6 \times 4.1) + 1.9$

E $1.9 \times (4.1 - 2.6)$

P $\boxed{15.6}$

Q $\boxed{8.76}$

R $\boxed{2.85}$

S $\boxed{2.87}$

T $\boxed{12.56}$

**3** Copy the grid below.

Use a calculator to fill in the grid using the clues (*ignore any decimal points*).

**Clues across**

**1.** $3.8 + 1.7 + 1.42$

**3.** $7 \times (3.6 - 1.9)$

**5.** $\dfrac{17.6}{0.4} - 3.88$

**7.** $4.9 \times 150$

**9.** $(0.62 + 0.08) \times 70$

**10.** $-24.1 - 2.3 + 61.2$

**11.** $-900 \times (-0.09)$

**12.** $4.9 \times \left(\dfrac{40}{0.8}\right)$

**Clues down**

**1.** $\dfrac{5.1 - 1.7}{0.5}$

**2.** $3.9 \times 4.8 \times 13.4$

**3.** $(3.1 + 1.8) \times (6.1 - 3.8)$

**4.** $121 - (31.2 - 4.85)$

**6.** $\dfrac{13.8 + 9.12}{0.25}$

**8.** $(15.1 - 7.6) \times 3.5 + 5.2$

**10.** $\dfrac{18.1 - 1.1}{0.38 + 0.12}$

**Squaring numbers**

$4^2 = 4 \times 4 = 16$      Calculator button $\boxed{x^2}$

$\boxed{4}$ $\boxed{x^2}$ gives 16

**Fractions**

Key in $\boxed{3}$ $\boxed{a\dfrac{b}{c}}$ $\boxed{4}$. This is $\dfrac{3}{4}$

$\boxed{3 \lrcorner 4}$
M+   M−   +   ×

Use the fraction button to work out $\dfrac{5}{6} - \dfrac{3}{4}$

The display should show $\boxed{1 \lrcorner 12}$ because the answer is $\dfrac{1}{12}$.

---

**E 9.6**

**1** Use a calculator to work out the following:

    (a) $14^2$      (b) $7.3^2$      (c) $4.2^2$      (d) $8.9^2$

    (e) $23^2$      (f) $\sqrt{225}$      (g) $\sqrt{361}$      (h) $\sqrt{10.24}$

    (i) $\sqrt{28.09}$      (j) $\sqrt{0.49}$      (k) $(3+12)^2$      (l) $(38-16)^2$

    (m) $\sqrt{(169-25)}$      (n) $\sqrt{(625-49)}$      (o) $3.4^2 + 6.7^2$      (p) $(5.9^2 - 2.1) \times 8$

**2** Use a calculator to match each Question below to the correct answer:

| | |
|---|---|
| A $\boxed{3^5}$ | P $\boxed{256}$ |
| B $\boxed{2^8}$ | Q $\boxed{4096}$ |
| C $\boxed{5^5}$ | R $\boxed{243}$ |
| D $\boxed{7^4}$ | S $\boxed{3125}$ |
| E $\boxed{4^6}$ | T $\boxed{7776}$ |
| F $\boxed{6^5}$ | U $\boxed{2401}$ |

**3** Write down the fractions shown on the calculator displays below:

(a) $\boxed{2\lrcorner 7}$    (b) $\boxed{5\lrcorner 9}$    (c) $\boxed{3\lrcorner 2\lrcorner 5}$

(d) $\boxed{6\lrcorner 4\lrcorner 9}$    (e) $\boxed{8\lrcorner 11}$    (f) $\boxed{7\lrcorner 2\lrcorner 7}$

**4** Use a calculator to work out

(a) $\dfrac{3}{7} + \dfrac{2}{5}$    (b) $\dfrac{5}{8} + \dfrac{3}{4}$    (c) $\dfrac{4}{9} - \dfrac{2}{11}$    (d) $1\dfrac{3}{4} \times 2\dfrac{1}{2}$

(e) $3\dfrac{1}{5} \times 4\dfrac{1}{2}$    (f) $8\dfrac{1}{4} \div \dfrac{3}{5}$    (g) $32 \div \dfrac{4}{7}$    (h) $\left(4\dfrac{1}{5}\right)^2$

**5** Copy and complete.

| + | $\dfrac{3}{8}$ | | $2\dfrac{1}{2}$ | $1\dfrac{2}{3}$ |
|---|---|---|---|---|
| $\dfrac{1}{4}$ | | | | |
| $\dfrac{3}{5}$ | | $\dfrac{19}{20}$ | | |
| | | | $4\dfrac{5}{6}$ | |
| | | $2\dfrac{13}{20}$ | | |

**6** Work out and give the answer correct to 2 decimal places.

(a) $3.1^3 \times (5.9 - 1.312)$    (b) $\dfrac{5.12}{(7.8 + 0.314)}$

(c) $3.8^2 - 2.17$    (d) $18.8 \div (2.8^2 - 2.95)$

(e) $\dfrac{(17.2 + 11.25)}{(3.89 + 1.63)}$    (f) $\dfrac{17.2 + 11.25}{3.89 + 1.63}$

(g) $\dfrac{16.18 - 3.892}{12.62 + 19.31}$    (h) $\dfrac{8.312}{(5.6^2 - 4.218)}$

(i) $\dfrac{5.1^2 + 6.34}{17.162 - 2.8^2}$    (j) $\dfrac{3.81^2 + 2.6^3}{1.41^2 - 1.317}$

**7** Copy this crossword puzzle and complete it using the clues below.
[The answers are calculator words]

### Across

2: $(3.08 + 0.701637) \times 10^6$      readable

5: $2 \times 71 \times 5$      greasy

6: $3 \div 500$      sticky

7: $555 - 44 + 3$      belongs to him

9: $0.6 - 0.22$      good when you're tired

11: $8 \times 4 \times (27 - 8)$      get out your wellies

13: $3^3 \div 30$      green light

14: $2000^2 - 68462$      surround

### Down

1: $60 \text{ million} + 436000 + 34$      hibernates in winter

3: $8 \times 9 \times 10 + 4^2 + 3$      for hair

4: $21 \times (40^2 + 67)$      not tight

6: $2^4 \times 5^3 \times 0.41 - 1$      part of a boat

8: $33333 - 1325$      not a good idea

10: $24 \times 25 + (1 + 2 + 3 + 4)$      you might need a spade

12: $10^3 - 65.5 \times 10$      female

## (9D) Percentage increase and decrease (see Unit 6)

Do *not* use a calculator.

1. Increase £80 by 5%
2. Decrease £70 by 30%

3. Jamie gets a 4% pay rise. If he now earns £15000 each year, how much will he earn after the pay rise?

4.
> Shoes £60
> SALE
> 15% off

What is the sale price of these shoes?

You may *use a calculator* for the Questions below.

5. Decrease £75 by 6%.
6. Increase £58 by 37%.

7. A computer costs £899 + VAT.
   If VAT is 17.5%, work out how much the computer costs altogether.

## Significant figures

For significant figures we approach from the left and start counting as soon as we come to the first figure which is not zero. Once we have started counting, we count any figure, zeros included.

(a) Round 63.8251 to 3 significant figures (3 s.f.)

63.8251

(Count 3 figures. The 'next' figure is 2 which is less than 5 so do not round up.)

63.8251 = 63.8 (to 3 s.f.)

(b) Round 8.0374 to 3 s.f.                    8.0374

(Count 3 figures. The 'next' figure is 7 which is more than 5 so round up.)

8.0374 = 8.04 (to 3 s.f.)

(c) 0.0654516 = 0.0655 (to 3 s.f.)

(d) 6382.7 = 6400 (to 2 s.f.)

Notice that we need the two noughts after the '4' as the original number 6382.7 is approximately 6400 not just 64.

**1** Write true or false for each statement below:

(a) $3.174 = 3.17$ (to 3 s.f.)   (b) $5.082 = 5.08$ (to 3 s.f.)

(c) $92.29 = 92.2$ (to 3 s.f.)   (d) $83.79 = 83.8$ (to 3 s.f.)

(e) $0.0818 = 0.082$ (to 2 s.f.)   (f) $0.0734 = 0.074$ (to 2 s.f.)

(g) $0.0605 = 0.061$ (to 2 s.f.)   (h) $32751 = 32000$ (to 2 s.f.)

(i) $81768 = 80000$ (to 1 s.f.)   (j) $472.23 = 480$ (to 2 s.f.)

**2** Which numbers below round to 3.96 (to 3 s.f.)?

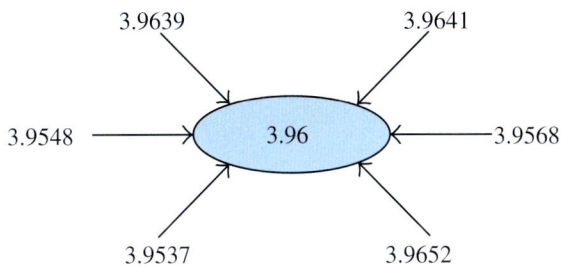

**3** Write the numbers below correct to 3 significant figures.

(a) 2.1875   (b) 32.896   (c) 0.8547   (d) 183.21

(e) 18.394   (f) 0.08756   (g) 48873   (h) 0.6555

(i) 3284.3   (j) 6278   (k) 0.02138   (l) 375899

**4** Write the following to the number of significant figures shown.

(a) 13.82 (2 s.f.)   (b) 7.891 (1 s.f.)   (c) 6.412 (2 s.f.)

(d) 0.83554 (3 s.f.)   (e) 1736.8 (3 s.f.)   (f) 51.382 (3 s.f.)

(g) 31777 (2 s.f.)   (h) 0.05483 (2 s.f.)   (i) 28639 (1 s.f.)

**5** Copy the grid below.

Use a calculator to fill in the grid using the clues (**ignore any decimal points**).
You **must** round answers to the number of significant figures shown.

| 1 | | 2 | | | 3 | 4 |
|---|---|---|---|---|---|---|
| | | | | 5 | | |
| 6 | 7 | | | | | |
| | | | 8 | | | |
| 9 | | 10 | | | | |
| | | 11 | | | 12 | |
| 13 | | | | 14 | | |

**Clues across**

**1** $1.9 \times 9.46$ (4 s.f.)

**3** $3 \div 0.27$ (2 s.f.)

**6** $2754.4 \times 0.3$ (2 s.f.)

**8** $3.81^2$ (4 s.f.)

**9** $\dfrac{38 + 69.4}{0.48}$ (3 s.f.)

**11** $2.2^3$ (2 s.f.)

**12** $(3.6 + 5.12) \times 1.01$ (2 s.f.)

**13** $5.6^2 + 0.417$ (3 s.f.)

**14** $\dfrac{3.1}{(2.83 - 1.9)}$ (2 s.f.)

**Clues down**

**1** $18 \div 9.1$ (3 s.f.)

**2** $30.8^2$ (1 s.f.)

**4** $1797.4853 \div 13$ (6 s.f.)

**5** $0.24 \times 0.17$ (2 s.f.)

**7** $0.36^2 + 1.7^2$ (3 s.f.)

**9** $29 \div 13$ (3 s.f.)

**10** $\dfrac{33}{0.12} + 142.9$ (3 s.f.)

**12** $99 - 16.182$ (2 s.f.)

## Checking answers

- Here are five calculations followed by sensible checks. Some checks involve 'undoing' the calculation.

  (a) $22.2 \boxed{\div} 6 = 3.7$      check    $3.7 \boxed{\times} 6 = 22.2$

  (b) $31.7 \boxed{-} 4.83 = 26.87$      check    $26.87 \boxed{+} 4.83 = 31.7$

  (c) $42.8 \boxed{\times} 30 = 1284$      check    $1284 \boxed{\div} 30 = 42.8$

  (d) $\sqrt{17} = 4.1231$      check    $4.1231^2$

  (e) $3.7 + 17.6 + 13.9 + 6.2$      check    $6.2 + 13.9 + 17.6 + 3.7$
  
                                                      (add in reverse order)

- Calculations can also be checked by rounding numbers to a given number of significant figures. This gives an estimate which helps to check if the answer is correct.

  (f) $\dfrac{6.1 \times 32.6}{19.3} = 10.3$ (to 3 s.f.)

  Check this answer by rounding each number to 1 significant figure and estimating.

  $$\frac{6.1 \times 32.6}{19.3} \approx \frac{6 \times 30}{20} \approx \frac{180}{20} \approx 9$$

  '$\approx$' means 'approximately equal to'.    This is close to 10.3 so the actual answer probably is 10.3

## E9.7

**1** Use a calculator to work out the following then check the answers as indicated.

(a) $92.5 \times 20 = \square$      check $\square \div 20 = \square$

(b) $14 \times 328 = \square$      check $\square \div 328 = \square$

(c) $63 - 12.6 = \square$      check $\square + 12.6 = \square$

(d) $221.2 \div 7 = \square$      check $\square \times 7 = \square$

(e) $384.93 \div 9.1 = \square$      check $\square \times 9.1 = \square$

(f) $13.71 + 25.8 = \square$      check $\square - 25.8 = \square$

(g) $95.4 \div 4.5 = \square$      check $\square \times 4.5 = \square$

(h) $8.2 + 3.1 + 19.6 + 11.5$      check $11.5 + 19.6 + 3.1 + 8.2$

(i) $\sqrt{39} = \square$      check $\square^2$

(j) $3.17 + 2.06 + 8.4 + 16$      check $16 + 8.4 + 2.06 + 3.17$

**2** The numbers below are rounded to 1 significant figure to *estimate* the answer to each calculation. Match each Question below to the correct answer.

A $\boxed{21.9 \times 1.01}$

B $\boxed{\dfrac{19.8^2}{(18.61 + 22.3)}}$

C $\boxed{7.8 \times 1.01}$

D $\boxed{\dfrac{\sqrt{98.7}}{8.78 + 11.43}}$

E $\boxed{\dfrac{21.42 + 28.6}{18.84 - 8.99}}$

P $\boxed{10}$

Q $\boxed{5}$

R $\boxed{0.5}$

S $\boxed{8}$

T $\boxed{20}$

**3** Do *not* use a calculator.

$281 \times 36 = 10116$

Work out

(a) $10116 \div 36$     (b) $10116 \div 281$     (c) $28.1 \times 3.6$

**4** Mavis is paid a salary of £49620 per year. Work out a rough estimate for her weekly pay. (Give your answer correct to one significant figure)

**5** In 1996, the population of France was 61 278 514 and the population of Greece was 9 815 972. Roughly how many times bigger is the population of France compared to the population of Greece?
(Hint: round the numbers to 1 significant figure).

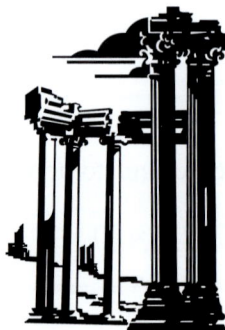

**6** *Estimate*, correct to 1 significant figure:

(a) $41.56 \div 7.88$

(b) $\dfrac{5.13 \times 18.777}{0.952}$

(c) $\dfrac{1}{5}$ of £14892

(d) $\dfrac{0.0974 \times \sqrt{104}}{1.03}$

(e) 52% of 0.394 kg

(f) $\dfrac{6.84^2 + 0.983}{5.07^2}$

(g) $\dfrac{2848.7 + 1024.8}{51.2 - 9.98}$

(h) $\dfrac{2}{3}$ of £3124

(i) $18.13 \times (3.96^2 + 2.07^2)$

This is money added to the prices of goods and services. This money is collected by the government.

The usual rate of VAT is 17.5%. Fuel for homes is charged at a lower rate of 5%. Some things like books are zero-rated. This means there is no VAT on books.

A TV costs £500 + VAT at 17.5%. How much does the TV cost?

VAT *without* a calculator

10% of 500 $= \dfrac{1}{10}$ of 500 $= 50$

5% of 500 $= 25$

2.5% of 500 $= 12.50$

Total: 17.5% of 500 $= 87.50$

VAT *with* a calculator,

17.5% means $\dfrac{17.5}{100}$

so 17.5% of 500 $= \dfrac{17.5}{100} \times 500$

$(17.5 \div 100 \times 500)$

so 17.5% of 500 $= 87.50$

TV costs £500 + £87.50 = £587.50
VAT

## WYM9

VAT is 17.5% in this Exercise.

**1** How much will each of the following cost?

(a) a computer costing £820 + VAT.

(b) a washing machine costing £450 + VAT.

(c) a cooker costing £630 + VAT.

**2**

'ELECTRICS'
Digital radio
£160
including VAT

Which digital radio is cheaper?

'SPARKS'
Digital radio
£140
plus VAT

**3** Lionel has a checkup and a filling at the dentist. He is charged £182 + VAT. How much does Lionel have to pay?

**4** Raneer has some new windows fitted. The windows cost £2750 + VAT. How much does Raneer pay?

**5** Copy and complete the garage bill below.

| brake pads | 43 |
|------------|----|
| brake fluid | 4 |
| labour | 45 |
| total | |
| VAT | |
| total bill | |

**6** Callie has a £400 limit. Can she afford to buy a dishwasher which costs £360 + VAT?

**7** Mary's grandparents offer her £300 towards a new music system. Mary has saved £200. She wants a music system which costs £420 + VAT. Has she enough money to buy this?

**8** Copy and complete the bill for certain bathroom items.

| bath | 199.50 |
|------|--------|
| sink | 89.70 |
| toilet | 112 |
| mirror | 26.80 |
| total | |
| VAT | |
| total bill | |

## TEST YOURSELF ON UNIT 9

### 1. Adding and subtracting decimals

Work out

(a) $\begin{array}{r} 14.9 \\ + 12.3 \\ \hline \end{array}$  (b) $\begin{array}{r} 6.71 \\ - 3.4 \\ \hline \end{array}$  (c) $\begin{array}{r} 17.0 \\ - 6.4 \\ \hline \end{array}$  (d) $\begin{array}{r} 19 \\ - 12.3 \\ \hline \end{array}$

(e) $4.6 + 9.17$    (f) $6.12 + 3 + 8.7$    (g) $28.4 - 16.8$

(h) How much change from a £20 note do you get if you spend £6.27?

## 2. Multiplying decimals

Work out

(a) $4.98 \times 10$     (b) $0.0342 \times 1000$     (c) $67 \times 0.1$     (d) $0.3 \times 0.1$

(e) $0.6 \times 0.03$     (f) $0.08 \times 6$          (g) $0.7^2$          (h) $21.2 \times 0.3$

## 3. Dividing decimals by whole numbers

Work out

(a) $4\overline{)13.28}$          (b) $8\overline{)18.00}$          (c) $7.035 \div 5$

(d) $15 \div 4$          (e) $0.768 \div 6$          (f) $3.6 \div 5$

(g) 4 friends split the cost of a meal equally. If the meal costs £63, how much does each friend have to pay?

## 4. Dividing by decimals

Copy the Questions below and fill in the empty boxes.

(a) $7.8 \div 0.2 = \square \div 2 = \square$

(b) $1.71 \div 0.3 = \square \div 3 = \square$

Work out

(c) $6.9 \div 0.3$     (d) $5.2 \div 0.05$     (e) $0.288 \div 0.8$     (f) $0.156 \div 0.01$

## 5. Rounding off numbers to the nearest 10, 100, 1000 or whole number

(a) Round each of these numbers to the nearest 10.
   (i) 23     (ii) 48     (iii) 75     (iv) 135     (v) 464

(b) Round each of these numbers to the nearest 100.
   (i) 382     (ii) 750     (iii) 1210     (iv) 8390     (v) 1650

(c) Round each of these numbers to the nearest 1000.
   (i) 3217     (ii) 8510     (iii) 17232     (iv) 21500     (v) 24320

(d) Round each of these numbers to the nearest whole number.
   (i) 6.7     (ii) 8.6     (iii) 3.12     (iv) 18.5     (v) 27.38

(a) Round these numbers to 1 decimal place.

   (i) 8.23      (ii) 6.35      (iii) 4.16      (iv) 14.34      (v) 8.162

(b) Round these numbers to 2 decimal places.

   (i) 3.387      (ii) 2.186      (iii) 15.384      (iv) 0.895      (v) 28.183

(c) Round these numbers to 3 decimal places.

   (i) 8.1932      (ii) 0.7235      (iii) 7.4864      (iv) 27.2087      (v) 14.81327

Do *not* use a calculator.

From the table below, choose the most sensible ROUGH answer from A, B or C.

|     | Calculation | A | B | C |
|-----|-------------|-----|-----|-----|
| (a) | $5.8 \times 2.03$ | 50 | 120 | 1200 |
| (b) | $8.12 \times 3.02$ | 240 | 24 | 60 |
| (c) | $805 \div 9.96$ | 800 | 80 | 8 |
| (d) | $41.2 \div 8.14$ | 320 | 50 | 5 |
| (e) | $68.6 - 19.14$ | 50 | 30 | 90 |
| (f) | $789 \times 10.33$ | 800 | 8000 | 80 |
| (g) | $8.95^2$ | 80 | 150 | 20 |
| (h) | $41.2 + 163 + 0.92$ | 300 | 200 | 50 |

Work out

(a) $8.3^2$

(b) $\dfrac{7}{12} \times \dfrac{3}{5}$

(c) $-12 \times (-0.3)$

(d) $(-7)^2$

(e) $2\dfrac{1}{5} + 3\dfrac{5}{7}$

(f) $\sqrt{14.44}$

(g) $2.7^3$

(h) $\dfrac{4+8}{0.5}$

(i) $4 + \left(\dfrac{8}{0.5}\right)$

(j) $\dfrac{13.6 - 5.9}{0.12 + 0.08}$

(k) $\dfrac{6.8^2}{15.8 - 15.79}$

(l) $\dfrac{\sqrt{28} - 12}{0.5^2}$

Write the following to the number of significant figures (s.f.) shown.

(a) 17.81 (3 s.f.)       (b) 23.69 (2 s.f.)       (c) 31.685 (3 s.f.)

(d) 213182 (3 s.f.)       (e) 384.67 (2 s.f.)       (f) 0.61087 (3 s.f.)

(g) 0.020714 (2 s.f.)       (h) 379418 (1 s.f.)       (i) 2374.23 (2 s.f.)

## 10. Checking answers

Do *not* use a calculator.

(a) If $38 \times 27 = 1026$,    does $1026 \div 27 = 38$?

(b) If $310 \times 23 = 7130$,    does $7130 \div 310 = 23$?

(c) If $2646 \div 42 = 63$,    does $2646 \div 63 = 42$?

(d) If $2646 \div 42 = 63$,    does $63 \times 42 = 2646$?

(e) If $14.61 + 13.093 = 27.703$,    does $27.703 - 13.093 = 14.61$?

(f) If $4.08^2 = 16.6464$,    does $\sqrt{16.6464} = 4.08$?

Estimate, correct to 1 significant figure:

(g) $59.89 \div 20.2$       (h) 24% of 792 kg

(i) $\dfrac{19.6 - 1.987}{\sqrt{4.01}}$       (j) $\dfrac{7.16^2}{3.912 + 0.99}$

## Mixed examination questions

**1** In a shop, Alan spends
£ 1.33 on milk
£ 3.14 on coffee
£ 0.74 on sugar

  **i** Calculate the total amount that Alan spends.

  **ii** Alan pays with a £10 note. How much change should be given?

  **iii** Barbara is organising a coach trip for 260 people. Each coach will hold 48 people. How many coaches will be needed?   (OCR)

**2** The prices of a bottle of red wine and a kilogram of cheddar cheese are shown.

What is the total cost of twelve bottles of red wine and a quarter of kilogram of cheddar cheese? (AQA)

**3** Nick takes 26 boxes out of his van.

The weight of each box is 32.9 kg.

Work out the **total** weight of the 26 boxes. (EDEXCEL)

**4** Three friends, Ali, Brenda and Chris, go to the cinema together. The total cost of their three tickets is £11.55. Each ticket costs the same. Work out the cost of one ticket. (AQA)

**5** Joe can do, on average, 4 calculations on his calculator every minute.

(a) How many calculations, on average, can he do in $7\frac{1}{2}$ minutes?

(b) Use your calculator to work out the value of $\sqrt{(15 + 27.25)}$ (EDEXCEL)

**6** The answers to the following calculations have been rounded to the nearest whole number. In each case the first digit of the answer is missing.
**Use estimation** to work out the missing first digit in each calculation.
Make clear the estimates you use.

$8.98^2 \times 2.43 = \square 96$ $\qquad$ $\dfrac{402 \times 87}{47} = \square 44$ (OCR)

**7** Use approximations to estimate the value of $\dfrac{9.67^2}{0.398}$.
You **must** show all your working. (AQA)

**In this unit you will learn how to:**
- draw straight line graphs
- draw curves from equations
- solve simultaneous equations graphically
- find gradients of straight lines
- read graphs
- use travel graphs
- WATCH YOUR MONEY! Electricity, gas and water

## Drawing straight line graphs

### M10. 1

**1** Write down the equations of the lines marked A, B and C.

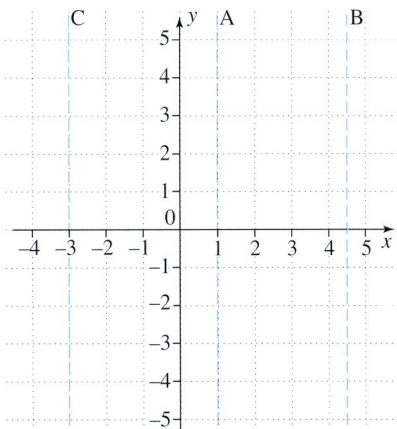

**2** Write down the equations of the lines marked P, Q, R and S.

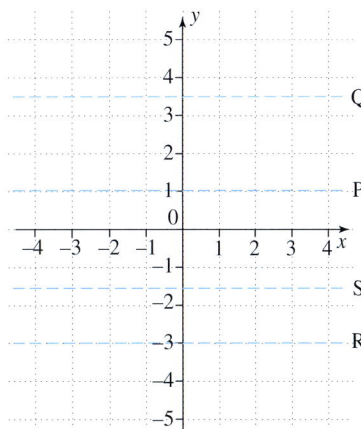

**3** (a) Draw axes like those above.

(b) Plot the points $A(4, 3)$, $B(-3, -2)$, $C(4, -1)$, $D(-3, 3)$

(c) Write down the equation of the line passing through

(i) $A$ and $C$    (ii) $B$ and $D$    (iii) $A$ and $D$

**4**

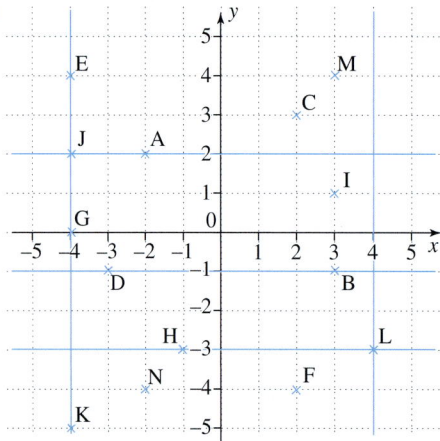

(a) J lies on the line $y = 2$. Which other letter lies on $y = 2$?

(b) Which letter lies on $x = 4$?

(c) Which letters lie on $y = -1$?

(d) Which letters lie on $x = -4$?

(e) How many letters lie on $y = -3$?

(f) Which letter lies on $y = 2$ *and* $x = -4$?

(g) Which letter lies on $x = 4$ *and* $y = -3$?

**5** The outside edge of Frank's face is made by straight lines.

Write down the equation of each line (2 of the lines will have the same equation).

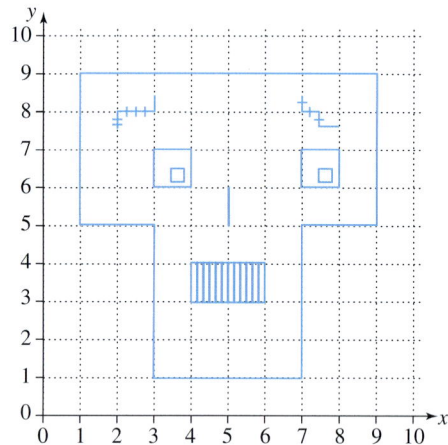

*Can you still?*    *Can you still?*

**10A** **Percentage Change (see Unit 6)**

1. Freddie's salary was increased from £5000 to £5500. What was the percentage increase?

2. In one year, Sandra's height increases from 160 cm to 164 cm. What is the percentage increase?

3. Tom bought a car for £12000. He sold the car for £9000. What was the percentage loss?

4. Carol buys 20 books for £120. She sells each book for £7.50. What percentage profit did Carol make?

5. A box of 50 CDs cost £400. All were sold in a sale for £7.50 each. What was the percentage loss on each CD?

## Sloping lines

Draw the straight line $y = x + 3$.

When $x = 1$, $y = x + 3 = 1 + 3 = 4 \rightarrow (1, 4)$

When $x = 2$, $y = x + 3 = 2 + 3 = 5 \rightarrow (2, 5)$

When $x = 3$, $y = x + 3 = 3 + 3 = 6 \rightarrow (3, 6)$

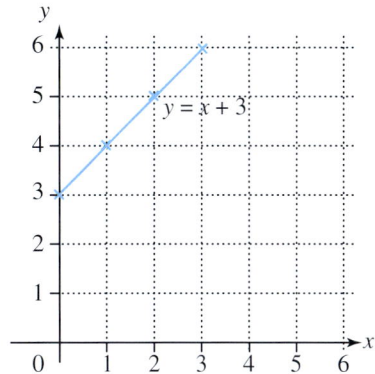

### Note

When working out the $y$-values, we usually write them in a table

| $x$ | 0 | 1 | 2 | 3 |
|-----|---|---|---|---|
| $y$ | 3 | 4 | 5 | 6 |

---

### E10. 1

(Check all your graphs with a computer or graphical calculator if your teacher wants you to!)

For Questions **1** to **5**, you will need to draw axes like these:

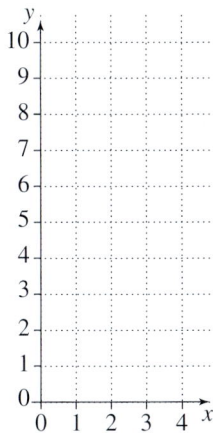

**1** Complete the table below then draw the straight line $y = x + 4$

| $x$ | 0 | 1 | 2 | 3 |
|-----|---|---|---|---|
| $y$ |   |   |   |   |

**2** Complete the table below then draw the straight line $y = x + 6$

| $x$ | 0 | 1 | 2 | 3 |
|-----|---|---|---|---|
| $y$ |   |   |   |   |

**3** Complete the table below then draw $y = 2x$

| $x$ | 0 | 1 | 2 | 3 |
|-----|---|---|---|---|
| $y$ |   |   |   |   |

**4** Complete the table below then draw $y = 2x + 2$.

| $x$ | 0 | 1 | 2 | 3 |
|---|---|---|---|---|
| $y$ | | | | |

**5** Complete the table below then draw $y = 3x + 1$.

| $x$ | 0 | 1 | 2 | 3 |
|---|---|---|---|---|
| $y$ | | | | |

**6** Using $x$-values from 0 to 4, complete a table then draw the straight line $y = 3x$ (make sure you draw the axes big enough).

**7** Using $x$-values from 0 to 5, complete a table then draw the straight line $y = 6 - x$.

**8** Using $x$-values from 0 to 5, complete a table then draw $y = 8 - x$.

**9** Draw $y = 2x + 3$ using $x$-values from 0 to 4.

**10** (a) Using $x$-values from 0 to 3, draw $y = x$ *and* $y = 6 - 2x$ on the *same graph*.

(b) Write down the co-ordinates where the two lines meet.

**11** Find the value of these when $x = -2$:

(a) $x + 3$   (b) $3x$   (c) $x - 2$   (d) $2x$   (e) $2x + 3$

**12** Find the value of $y$ when $x = -3$:

(a) $y = x + 1$   (b) $y = 2x$   (c) $y = x - 3$   (d) $y = 3x$   (e) $y = 3x - 2$

Check your answers to questions **11** and **12** before doing question **13**. Discuss any wrong answers with your teacher.

For Questions **13** to **17**, you will need to draw axes like these:

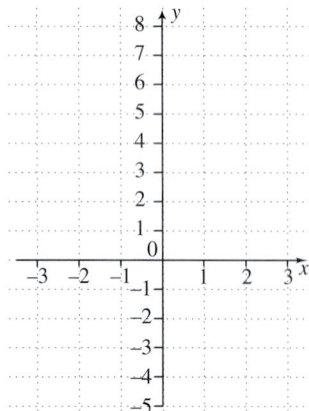

**13** Complete the table below then draw the straight line $y = x - 2$.

| $x$ | -2 | -1 | 0 | 1 | 2 |
|---|---|---|---|---|---|
| $y$ | | | | | |

**14** Complete the table below then draw the straight line $y = 2x + 4$.

| $x$ | -2 | -1 | 0 | 1 | 2 |
|---|---|---|---|---|---|
| $y$ | | | | | |

**15** Complete the table below then draw $y = x - 3$.

| $x$ | −2 | −1 | 0 | 1 | 2 |
|-----|----|----|---|---|---|
| $y$ |    |    |   |   |   |

**16** Complete the table below then draw $y = 2x - 1$.

| $x$ | −2 | −1 | 0 | 1 | 2 |
|-----|----|----|---|---|---|
| $y$ |    |    |   |   |   |

**17** Complete the table below then draw $y = -2x$.

| $x$ | −2 | −1 | 0 | 1 | 2 |
|-----|----|----|---|---|---|
| $y$ |    |    |   |   |   |

**18** Complete this table for $y = 3x - 1$.

| $x$ | −3 | −2 | −1 | 0 | 1 | 2 | 3 |
|-----|----|----|----|---|---|---|---|
| $y$ |    |    |    |   |   |   |   |

Draw an $x$-axis from −3 to 3 and a $y$-axis from −10 to 8.

Plot the points and draw the straight line $y = 3x - 1$.

**19** Using $x$-values from −2 to 2, complete a table then draw the straight line $y = 3x - 2$ (make sure you draw the axes big enough).

**20** Using $x$-values from −2 to 2, complete a table then draw $y = -3x$.

**21** Draw $y = 3 - 2x$ using $x$-values from −3 to 3.

**22** Draw $y = \dfrac{1}{2}x$ using $x$-values from −4 to 4.

**23** Draw an $x$-axis from −3 to 3 and a $y$-axis from −10 to 8. Using the *same* set of axes, draw

$$y = 4x \qquad\qquad y = 2x - 3$$

$$y = 1 - 2x \qquad\qquad y = 3x - 4$$

Label each line clearly.

**(10B)** **Compound Interest (see Unit 6)**

1. £4000 is invested at 5% per annum (year) compound interest. How much money will there be after 2 years?

2. £10,000 is invested at 10% per annum compound interest. How much money will there be after 3 years?

3. £6000 is invested at 4% per annum compound interest. How much money will there be after 2 years?

4. A new car is bought for £14000. Each year, its value depreciates (goes down) by 20% of its value at the start of the year. How much is the car worth after 2 years?

## Drawing curves

Draw $y = x^2 + 3$, using $x$-values from $-3$ to $3$.

| $x$ | $-3$ | $-2$ | $-1$ | 0 | 1 | 2 | 3 |
|-----|------|------|------|---|---|---|---|
| $y$ |      |      |      |   |   |   |   |

draw a table

$\Downarrow$

Start with $x = 0$ and positive $x$-values first

$y = 0^2 + 3 = 0 + 3 = 3$

$y = 1^2 + 3 = 1 + 3 = 4$

$y = 2^2 + 3 = 4 + 3 = 7$

$y = 3^2 + 3 = 9 + 3 = 12$

Now be careful with the negative $x$-values

$y = (-3)^2 + 3 = 9 + 3 = 12$

$-3 \times -3 = 9$

$y = (-2)^2 + 3 = 4 + 3 = 7$

$-2 \times -2 = 4$

$y = (-1)^2 + 3 = 1 + 3 = 4$

$-1 \times -1 = 1$

| $x$ | $-3$ | $-2$ | $-1$ | 0 | 1 | 2 | 3 |
|-----|------|------|------|---|---|---|---|
| $y$ | 12 | 7 | 4 | 3 | 4 | 7 | 12 |

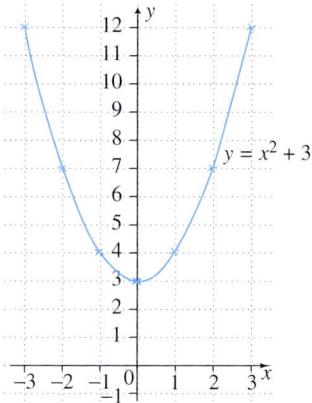

- draw axes so that *all* the points can be plotted

- plot each point

- join up all the points with a smooth curve

- label the curve with its equation

## M10. 2

(Check all your graphs with a computer or graphical calculator if your teacher wants you to!)

**1** Find the value of these when $x = 3$:

(a) $x^2$    (b) $x^2 + 1$    (c) $x^2 - 3$    (d) $x^2 + x$    (e) $x^2 + 2x$

**2** Find the value of these when $x = -4$:

(a) $x^2$    (b) $3x$    (c) $x^2 + 2$    (d) $x^2 - 6$    (e) $x^2 + x$

**3** Find the value of these when $x = -1$:

(a) $2x$    (b) $x^2$    (c) $x^2 + 3$    (d) $x^2 - x$    (e) $x^2 + 2x$

Check your answers to Questions **1** to **3**. Discuss with your teacher if the answers are not clear.

For Questions **4** to **8**, you will need to draw axes like these:

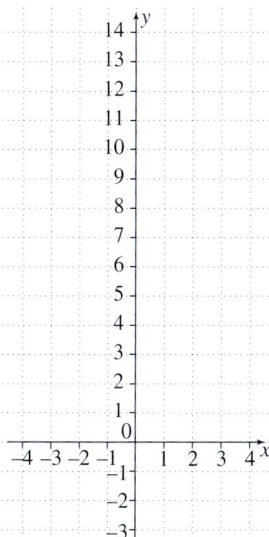

**4** Complete the table below then draw the curve $y = x^2$

| $x$ | −3 | −2 | −1 | 0 | 1 | 2 | 3 |
|---|---|---|---|---|---|---|---|
| $y$ | | | | | | | |

**5** Complete the table below then draw the curve $y = x^2 + 1$

| $x$ | −3 | −2 | −1 | 0 | 1 | 2 | 3 |
|---|---|---|---|---|---|---|---|
| $y$ | | | | | | | |

**6** Complete the table then draw $y = x^2 - 3$

| $x$ | −3 | −2 | −1 | 0 | 1 | 2 | 3 |
|---|---|---|---|---|---|---|---|
| $y$ | | | | | | | |

**7** Complete the table then draw $y = x^2 - 2$.

| $x$ | −3 | −2 | −1 | 0 | 1 | 2 | 3 |
|---|---|---|---|---|---|---|---|
| $y$ | | | | | | | |

**8** Complete the table then draw $y = x^2 + 5$.

| $x$ | −3 | −2 | −1 | 0 | 1 | 2 | 3 |
|---|---|---|---|---|---|---|---|
| $y$ | | | | | | | |

Discuss with your teacher the shape of each curve you have drawn in questions
**4** to **8**.

**9** (a) Complete the table below for $y = 2x^2$ ($2x^2$ means '$x^2$ then multiply by 2').

| $x$ | −3 | −2 | −1 | 0 | 1 | 2 | 3 |
|---|---|---|---|---|---|---|---|
| $y$ | 18 | | | | 2 | | |

$$x = 1 \text{ so } y = 2x^2 = x^2 \times 2 = (1)^2 \times 2 = 1 \times 2 = 2$$

(b) Draw an $x$-axis −3 to 3 (use 2 cm for 1 unit) and a $y$-axis from 0 to 18 (use 1 cm for 2 units).

Plot the points from the table and draw the curve $y = 2x^2$.

**10** (a) Complete the table below for $y = 3x^2$ ($3x^2$ means $x^2$ then 'multiply by 3').

| $x$ | −3 | −2 | −1 | 0 | 1 | 2 | 3 |
|---|---|---|---|---|---|---|---|
| $y$ | | 12 | | | | | |

(b) Draw an $x$-axis from −3 to 3 (use 2 cm for 1 unit) and a $y$-axis from 0 to 28 (use 1 cm for 2 units). Draw the curve $y = 3x^2$.

**11** Using $x$-values from −3 to 3, complete a table then draw $y = 2x^2 + 1$ (make sure you draw the axes big enough).

**12** (a) Using $x$-values from 1 to 6, complete a table for $y = \frac{6}{x}$ (you may use a calculator).

$\frac{6}{x}$ means $6 \div x$

| $x$ | 1 | 2 | 3 | 4 | 5 | 6 |
|---|---|---|---|---|---|---|
| $y$ | | | | | | |

(b) Draw an $x$-axis from 0 to 6 and a $y$-axis from 0 to 6. Draw the curve $y = \frac{6}{x}$.

**13** Using $x$-values from 1 to 6, complete a table then draw $y = \frac{12}{x}$ (make sure you draw the axes big enough).

**Curves with several terms**

Using $x$-values from $-3$ to 3 draw $y = x^2 + 4x - 1$.

Do each part separately in the table then add together at the end to find $y$.

| $x$ | $-3$ | $-2$ | $-1$ | 0 | 1 | 2 | 3 |
|---|---|---|---|---|---|---|---|
| $x^2$ | 9 | 4 | 1 | 0 | 1 | 4 | 9 |
| $+4x$ | $-12$ | $-8$ | $-4$ | 0 | 4 | 8 | 12 |
| $-1$ | $-1$ | $-1$ | $-1$ | $-1$ | $-1$ | $-1$ | $-1$ |
| $y$ | $-4$ | $-5$ | $-4$ | $-1$ | 4 | 11 | 20 |

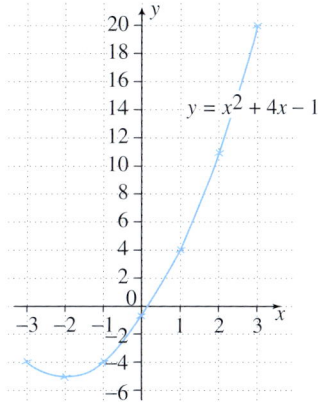

$y = x^2 + 4x - 1$

**Note**

A curve is called a 'quadratic' graph if the highest power of $x$ is $x^2$.

---

**E10. 2**

**1**

(a) Complete the table for $y = x^2 + x + 2$.

(b) Draw an $x$-axis from $-4$ to 2 and a $y$-axis from 0 to 14. Draw the curve $y = x^2 + x + 2$ (the bottom of the curve should be curved $\smile$ *not* flat $\diagdown\!\diagup$)

| $x$ | $-4$ | $-3$ | $-2$ | $-1$ | 0 | 1 | 2 |
|---|---|---|---|---|---|---|---|
| $x^2$ | | 9 | | | | | |
| $+x$ | | $-3$ | | | | | |
| $+2$ | 2 | 2 | 2 | 2 | 2 | 2 | 2 |
| $y$ | | 8 | | | | | |

For Questions **2** to **5**, you will need to draw axes like these:

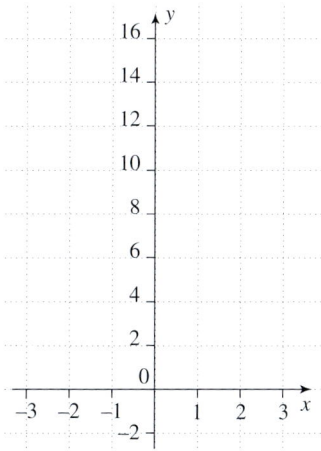

**2** Complete the table below then draw the curve $y = x^2 + x$.

| $x$ | $-3$ | $-2$ | $-1$ | 0 | 1 | 2 | 3 |
|---|---|---|---|---|---|---|---|
| $x^2$ | | | 1 | | | | 9 |
| $+x$ | | | $-1$ | | | | 3 |
| $y$ | | | 0 | | | | 12 |

**3** Complete the table below then draw the curve $y = x^2 + 2x$.

| $x$ | $-3$ | $-2$ | $-1$ | 0 | 1 | 2 | 3 |
|---|---|---|---|---|---|---|---|
| $x^2$ | | 4 | | | 1 | | |
| $-2x$ | | $-4$ | | | 2 | | |
| $y$ | | 0 | | | 3 | | |

4. (a) Complete the table then draw the curve $y = x^2 - 2x$.

   (b) Read off the value of $y$ from your curve when $x = 1.5$.

| $x$ | $-3$ | $-2$ | $-1$ | $0$ | $1$ | $2$ | $3$ |
|---|---|---|---|---|---|---|---|
| $x^2$ | | 4 | | | | | |
| $-2x$ | | 4 | | | | | |
| $y$ | | 8 | | | | | |

5. (a) Complete the table then draw the curve $y = x^2 - x + 2$.

   (b) Read off the value of $y$ from your curve when $x = 0.5$.

| $x$ | $-3$ | $-2$ | $-1$ | $0$ | $1$ | $2$ | $3$ |
|---|---|---|---|---|---|---|---|
| $x^2$ | 9 | | | | | | |
| $-x$ | 3 | | | | | | |
| $+2$ | 2 | | | | | | |
| $y$ | 14 | | | | | | |

6. Using $x$-values from $-4$ to $2$, complete a table then draw $y = x^2 + 3x - 2$ (make sure you draw the axes big enough).

7. $x^3$ means $x \times x \times x$ so $2^3 = 2 \times 2 \times 2 = 4 \times 2 = 8$

   Complete the table below then draw $y = x^3$.

| $x$ | $-3$ | $-2$ | $-1$ | $0$ | $1$ | $2$ | $3$ |
|---|---|---|---|---|---|---|---|
| $y$ | $-27$ | | | | | | |

8. Using $x$-values from $-3$ to $3$ draw:

   (a) $y = x^3 + 1$          (b) $y = x^3 + x$

   (c) $y = x^3 + 3x - 4$     (d) $y = x^3 + x^2 + 1$

   [All these curves are called 'cubic' graphs because the highest power of $x$ is $x^3$]

9. Using $x$-values from $1$ to $6$ draw:

   (a) $y = \dfrac{24}{x}$      (b) $y = \dfrac{1}{x}$

   [These curves are called 'reciprocal' graphs because $x$ is in the denominator.]

10. Using $x$-values from $-5$ to $5$, draw $y = \dfrac{10}{x^2}$ (be very careful when $x = 0$)

    Discuss this graph with your teacher.

In this unit we have drawn equations of straight lines where $y$ is on its own (examples: $y = 2x + 1$, $y = 3x - 2$)

If $x$ and $y$ are on the same side of the '=' sign (examples: $x + y = 2$, $2x - 3y = 6$), we can find the points to join up on a graph by using the cover-up method.

## 🔑 Key Facts

Draw $2x + 3y = 6$.

Use $\boxed{x = 0}$ so $2x = 0$    *Cover up* $2x$ in the equation.

$2x + 3y = 6$ becomes $\boxed{0} + 3y = 6$ so $\boxed{y = 2}$

Use $\boxed{y = 0}$ so $3y = 0$    *Cover up* $3y$ in the equation.

$2x + 3y = 0$ becomes $2x + \boxed{0} = 6$ so $\boxed{x = 3}$

*Always use $x = 0$ then $y = 0$.*

Plot the points $x = 0$, $y = 2$ and $x = 3$, $y = 0$ on the graph and join them up to get your straight line.

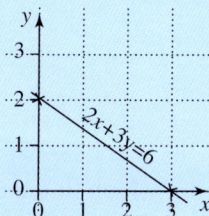

## M10. 3

**1**  (a) Draw these axes.

(b) If $x + 2y = 4$, find the value of $y$ when $x = 0$.

(c) If $x + 2y = 4$, find the value of $x$ when $y = 0$.

(d) Plot 2 points from (b) and (c) and join them up to make the straight line $x + 2y = 4$.

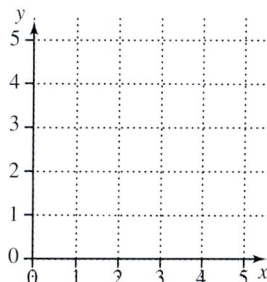

**2**   (a) Draw the same axes as in Question **1** .

     (b) Use $x = 0$ then $y = 0$ to find 2 points for $3x + y = 3$.

     (c) Draw the straight line $3x + y = 3$.

**3**   (a) Draw an $x$-axis from $x = 0$ to 10 and a $y$-axis from $y = 0$ to 10.

     (b) Use the cover-up method with $x = 0$ and $y = 0$ to draw $x + 5y = 10$.

**4**   (a) Draw the same axes as in Question **3** .

     (b) Use the cover-up method to draw $3x + 2y = 18$.

**5**   Draw each line below with the cover-up method. You need to find the 2 points first then draw the axes big enough.

     (a) $5x + 3y = 15$      (b) $2x + 5y = 10$      (c) $9x + y = 18$

     (d) $3x + 4y = 12$      (e) $6x + 5y = 30$      (f) $2x + 7y = 28$

## Simultaneous equations on a graph

If $x = 2$ and $y = 8$ then $4x + y = 16$

If $x = 3$ and $y = 4$ then $4x + y = 16$

There are many pairs of values of $x$ and $y$ which fit the equation $4x + y = 16$

There are also many pairs of values of $x$ and $y$ which fit the equation $15x - y = 3$

There is only *one pair* of values of $x$ and $y$ which satisfy both equations at the same time (*simultaneously*).

If $x = 1, y = 12$ then $4x + y = 16$ $\left.\right\}$   the 2 equations are called
If $x = 1, y = 12$ then $15x - y = 3$    *simultaneous equations.*

$x = 1$ and $y = 12$ are called the *solutions* of the *simultaneous equations.*

The solutions of simultaneous equations can be found by drawing a graph.

Solve the simultaneous equations

$3x + y = 6$ $\qquad$ $x + y = 4$

(a) Draw the line $3x + y = 6$

$\qquad$ when $x = 0$, $y = 6$

$\qquad$ when $y = 0$, $3x = 6$ so $x = 2$

(b) Draw the line $x + y = 4$

$\qquad$ when $x = 0$, $y = 4$

$\qquad$ when $y = 0$, $x = 4$

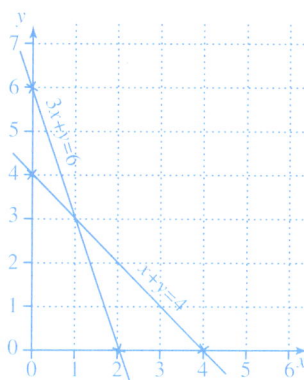

(c) The lines intersect at (1, 3).

$\qquad$ The solutions of these simultaneous equations are $x = 1$, $y = 3$.

## E10. 3

**1** Use the graph to solve the simultaneous equations

$$x + y = 7$$
$$2x - y = -1$$

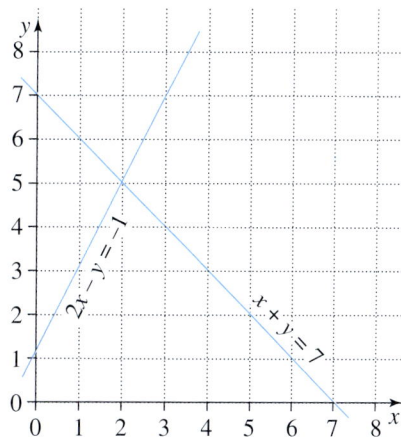

**2** Use the graph to solve the simultaneous equations.

(a) $2x + y = 8$

$\qquad$ $x + y = 5$

(b) $x - y = -5$

$\qquad$ $x + y = 5$

(c) $2x + y = 8$

$\qquad$ $x - y = -5$

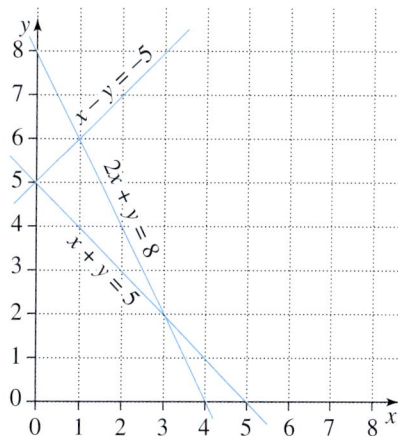

269

**3** (a) Draw $x$ and $y$ axes from 0 to 9.

(b) Use the cover-up method to draw the line $3x + 4y = 24$.

(c) Use the cover-up method to draw the line $3x + 2y = 18$.

(d) Write down the solutions of the simultaneous equations $3x + 4y = 24$
$$3x + 2y = 18$$

**4** (a) Draw $x$ and $y$ axes from 0 to 6.

(b) Draw the lines $x + y = 6$ and $y = x + 3$.

(c) Solve the simultaneous equations $x + y = 6$
$$y = x + 3$$

**5** (a) Draw $x$ and $y$ axes from 0 to 5.

(b) Solve graphically the simultaneous equations $x + y = 5$
$$y = x + 2$$

**6** (a) Draw $x$ and $y$ axes from 0 to 13.

(b) Solve graphically the simultaneous equations $x + 2y = 11$
$$2x + y = 13$$

**7** Use the graph to solve the simultaneous equations.

(a) $x + y = 11$

$x + 3y = 13$

(b) $2x - y = -2$

$x + y = 11$

(c) $x + 3y = 13$

$2x - y = -2$

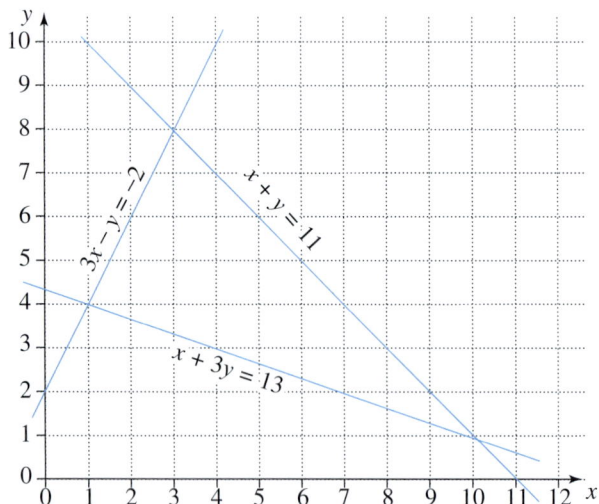

# Gradient

Have you ever seen signs like this?

This is the gradient – how steep the hill is.

The '**1 in 10**' means that the hill goes up 1 m for every 10 m across.

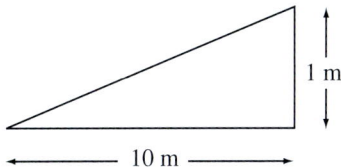

Gradient = 1 in 10 = $\dfrac{1}{10}$

The steeper the hill, the bigger the gradient.

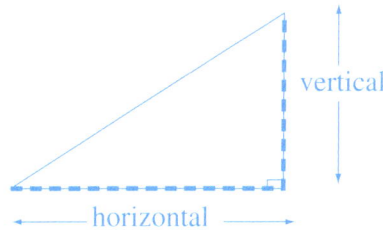

$$\text{Gradient} = \frac{\text{vertical distance}}{\text{horizontal distance}}$$

(a) Find the gradient of this line.

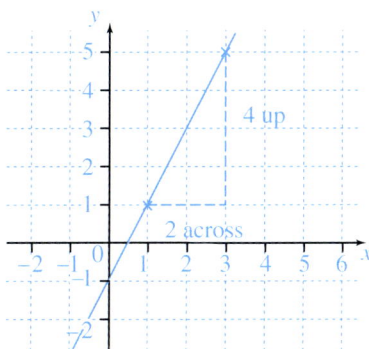

$$\text{Gradient} = \frac{4 \text{ up}}{2 \text{ across}} = \frac{4}{2} = 2$$

(b) Find the gradient of this line.

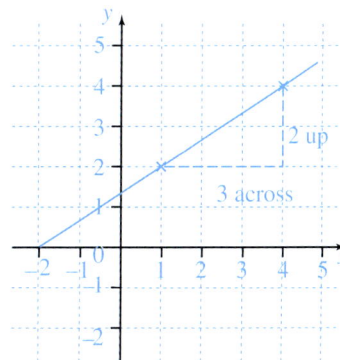

$$\text{Gradient} = \frac{2 \text{ up}}{3 \text{ across}} = \frac{2}{3}$$

Find the gradient of each line.

**1**

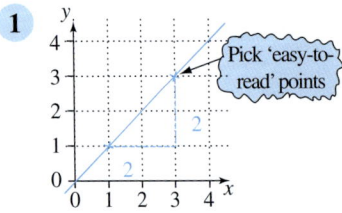

Pick 'easy-to-read' points

**2**

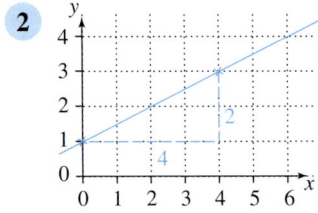

**3**

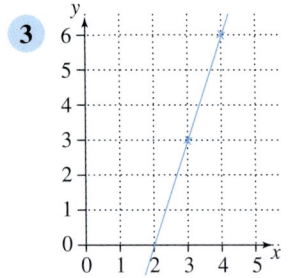

**4**

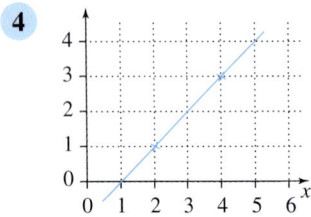

**5**

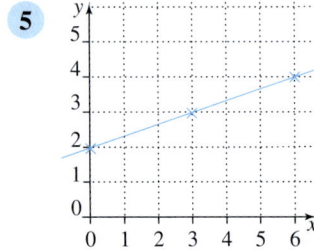

**6**

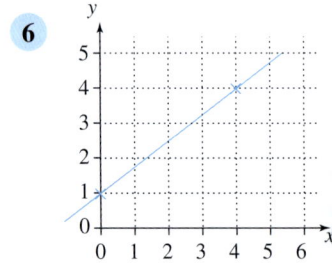

**7** Find the gradient of each line below:

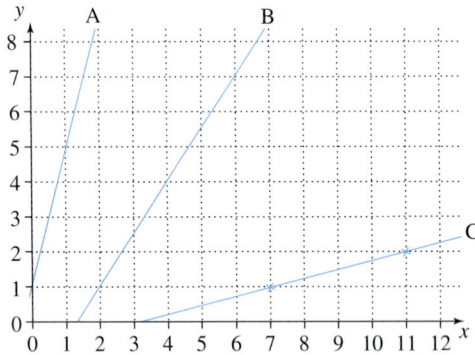

**8** Find the gradient of the line joining:

(a) *A* and *B*

(b) *A* and *D*

(c) *C* and *D*

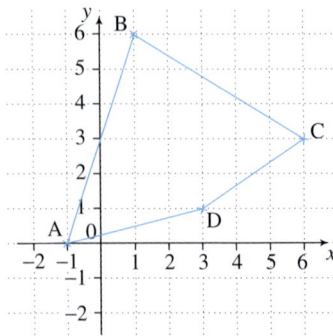

## Negative gradient

If a line slopes downwards to
the right, it has a
*negative gradient*.

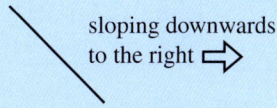

sloping downwards
to the right ⟹

Find the gradient of this line.

$$\text{Gradient} = \frac{4 \text{ down}}{2 \text{ across}}$$

$$= \frac{-4}{2}$$

$$= -2$$
↑

4 down

2 across

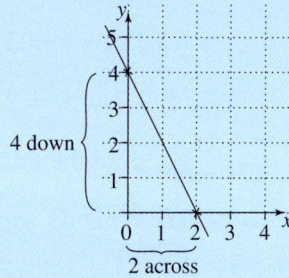

negative because line sloping downwards to the right

---

## E10. 4

Find the gradient of each line.

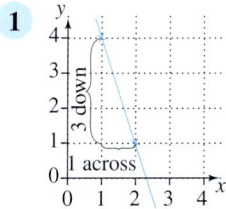

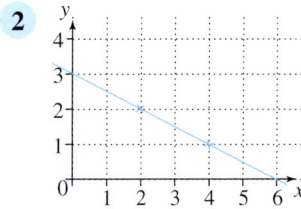

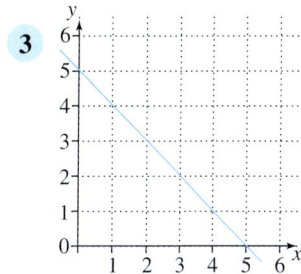

**1**

3 down

1 across

**2**

**3**

**4** Find the gradient of each line below:

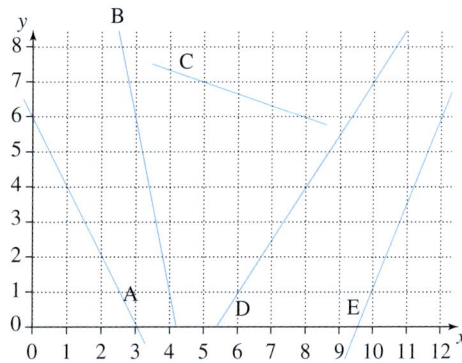

B

C

A

D

E

**5** You will need to draw axes like these:

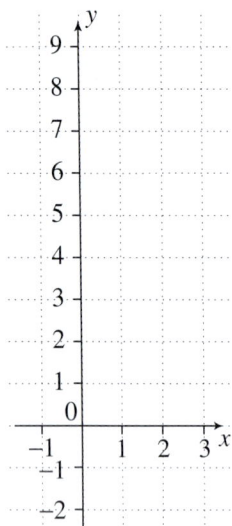

(a) Complete the table below then draw the straight line $y = 2x + 3$.

| $x$ | 1 | 2 | 3 |
|---|---|---|---|
| $y$ | | | |

(b) Use another table to draw $y = 2x$ on the same grid.

(c) Draw $y = 2x + 1$ on the same grid.

(d) Draw $y = 2x - 1$ on the same grid.

(e) Find the gradient of each line.

(f) What do you notice about the gradient of each line and its equation? *Discuss* with your teacher.

**6** The equation of any straight line can be written in the form $y = mx + c$ where $m$ is the gradient and $c$ is where the line crosses the $y$-axis.

(a) Which lines below have the same gradient?

$$y = 3x + 1 \quad y = 3x - 2 \quad y = 2x + 3 \quad y = 3 + 4x \quad y = 7 + 3x$$

(b) Which lines below are parallel?

$$y = x + 2 \quad y = 3 + 4x \quad y = 5 - x \quad y = 4x - 2 \quad y = 2x + 4$$

**7** Write down the gradient of each line below.

(a) $y = 7x - 1$    (b) $y = 9x + 4$    (c) $y = 6 + 2x$    (d) $y = \frac{1}{2}x + 3$

(e) $y = 4 - 2x$

*Can you still?*

**(10C)** **Sharing in a given ratio (see Unit 6)**

*Can you still?*

**1.** Divide £300 in the ratio 1:5

**2.** Divide 420 g in the ratio 3:7

**3.** £2500 is shared between Millie, Ken and Simon in the ratio 2:5:3  How much will each person get?

**4.** Lemon squash is diluted using squash and water in the ratio 2:9  If 40 ml of squash is used, how much water must be added?

**5.** The angles in a triangle are in the ratio 7:4:9  If the smallest angle is 36°, find the size of each of the other angles.

**M10. 5**

**1** A scientist records the height of a growing plant every day for 20 days.

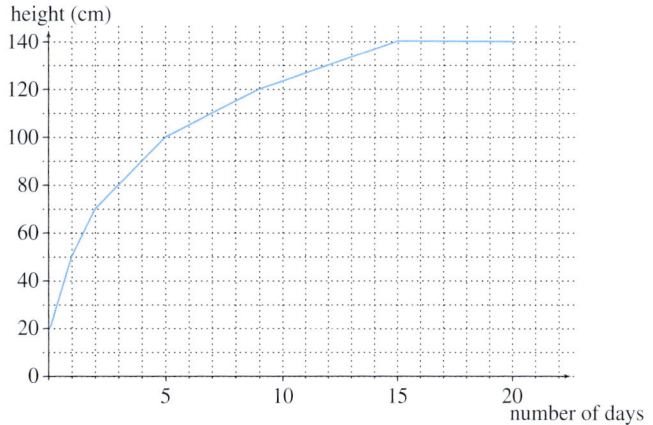

(a) What was the height of the plant after 5 days?

(b) After how many days was the height

    (i) 70 cm     (ii) 105 cm?

(c) What was the greatest increase in height in one day?

(d) What was the full-grown height of the plant?

**2** The graph below shows how many cars pass through a car wash during one day.

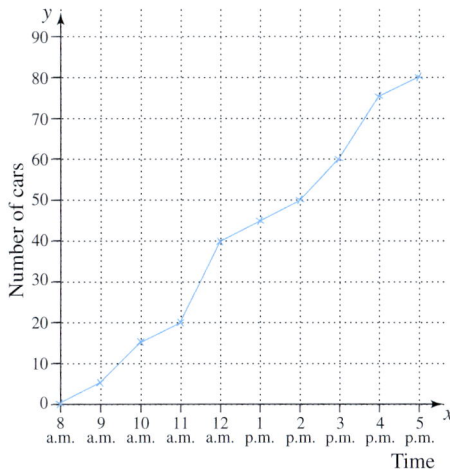

How many cars had passed through the car wash by the following times?

(a) 12 am     (b) 11:30 am

(c) 9:30 am     (d) 2:30 pm

(e) During which one hour period did *most* cars pass through the car wash. How many cars was this?

**3** The graph below shows how to convert miles into kilometres.

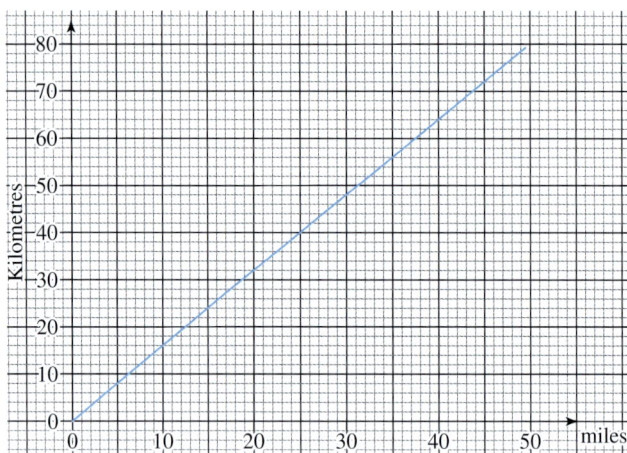

(a) How many kilometres is one small square worth on the vertical axis?

Use the graph to find how many kilometres are the same as:

(b) 25 miles    (c) 15 miles    (d) 45 miles    (e) 5 miles

Use the graph to find how many miles are the same as:

(f) 64 km    (g) 56 km    (h) 16 km    (i) 32 km

**4** The graph below shows how to convert pounds into euros.

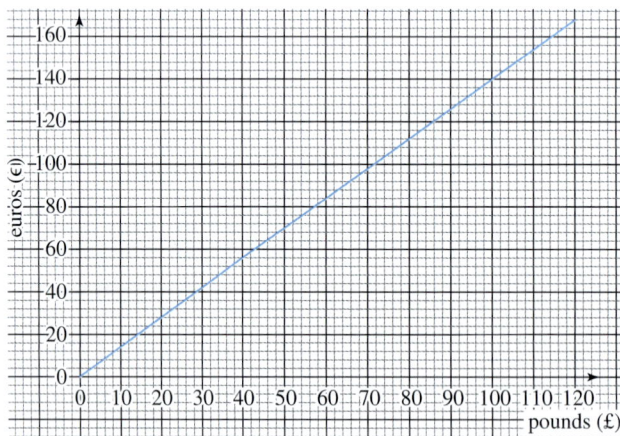

Use the graph to find how many euros are the same as:

(a) £ 20    (b) £ 80    (c) £ 50

Use the graph to find how many pounds are the same as:

(d) € 56    (e) € 84    (f) € 140

(g) Tim spends €154 on clothes in Paris. How many pounds has he spent?

**5** The number of people sitting down in a cinema was recorded every quarter of an hour. The results are shown below.

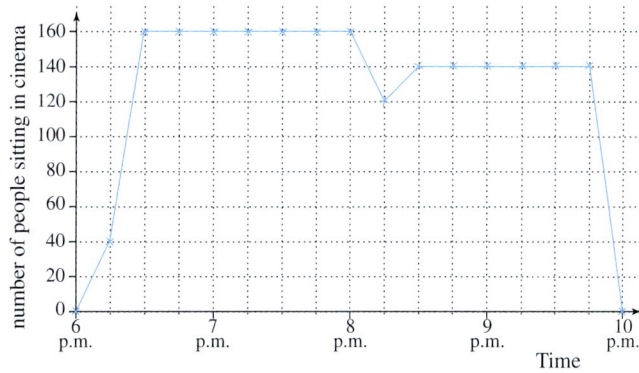

(a) How many people were sitting down at 7 p.m.?

(b) How many people were sitting down at 8:15 p.m.?

(c) When do you think the first film started?

(d) When do you think the second film started?

(e) How long did the first film last for?

(f) Which film was more popular?

## Travel graphs

### E10. 5

**1** Jennifer walked 18 km between 9 a.m. and 2 p.m. The graph below shows how far she had walked at various times.

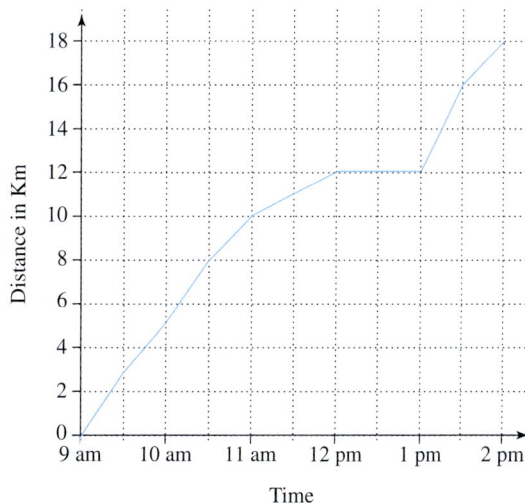

What distance had Jennifer walked by the following times?

(a) 9:30 a.m.      (b) 11:30 a.m.      (c) 1:30 p.m.

(d) 9:45 a.m.      (e) 1:15 p.m.      (f) 1:45 p.m.

(g) Between what times did Jennifer stop for a rest?

(h) During which half-hour interval did Jennifer walk the furthest?

     What distance was this?

**2** Colin and Kris run a 400-metre race. The graph below shows how far they had run at different times.

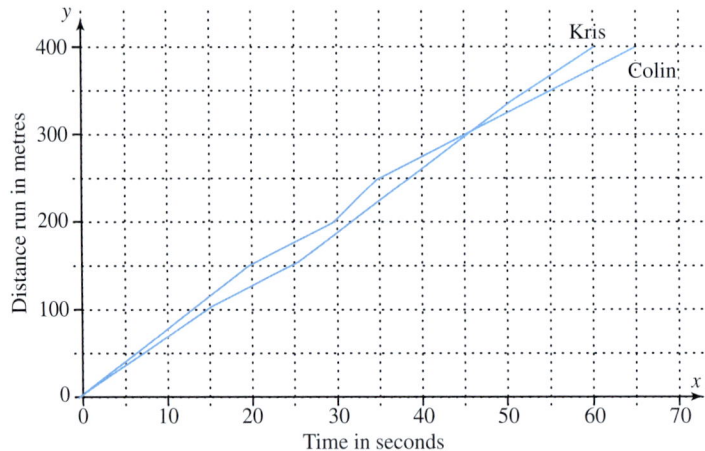

How far has Kris run after:

(a) 15 seconds?      (b) 25 seconds?      (c) 60 seconds?

(d) How long does it take Colin to run the first 150 metres?

(e) How long does it take Colin to run the first 250 metres?

(f) After how many seconds have Colin and Kris run the *same* distance?

(g) Who won the race?

**3** (a) Jack travels 40 km in 30 minutes. How far will he travel in 1 hour?

  (b) Sonia travels 9 km in 10 minutes. How far will she travel in 1 hour?

  (c) Kim travels 150 km in 2 hours. How far did she travel in 1 hour?

  (d) Sid travels 25 km in 15 minutes. How far will he travel in 1 hour?

**4** For each graph below find the speed of the journey from $A$ to $B$
(give the answer in km/h).

(a)

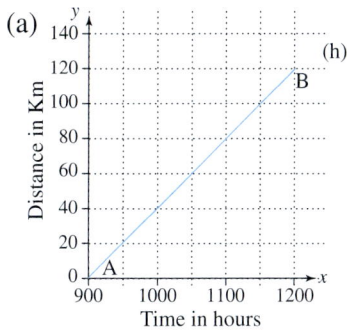

(b)

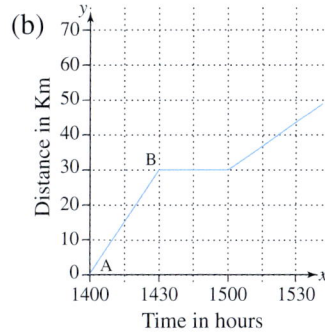

(c)

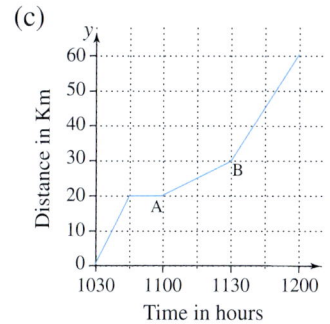

**5**

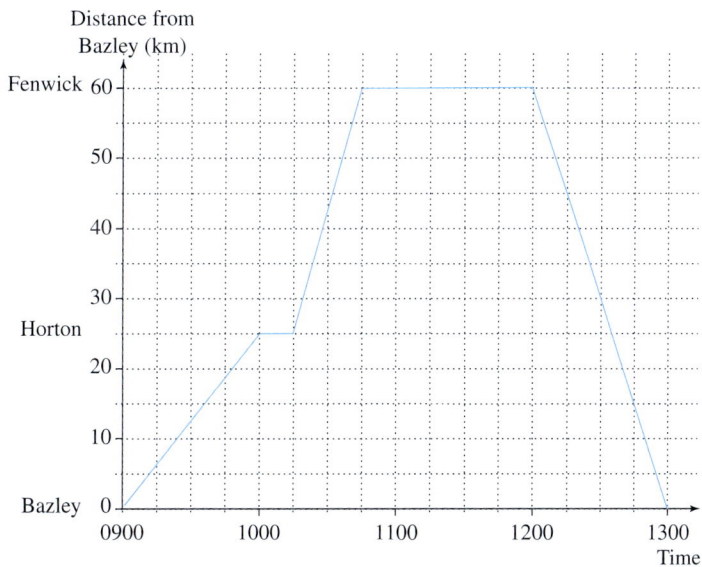

The graph above shows a car journey from Bazley.

(a) When did the car arrive back in Bazley?

(b) How long did the car stop in Horton?

(c) When did the car leave Horton after stopping?

(d) How long did the car stop in Fenwick?

(e) Find the speed (in km/h) of the car between Bazley and Horton.

(f) Find the speed (in km/h) of the car between Horton and Fenwick.

(g) Find the speed (in km/h) of the car from Fenwick back to Bazley.

279

In Questions **6** and **7** below, copy the axes then draw a travel graph to show each journey.

**6** Distance from home (km)

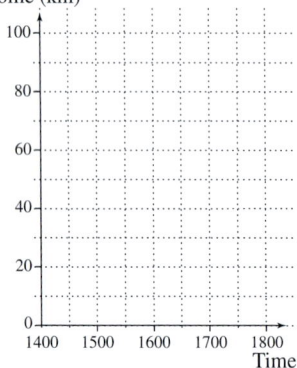

At 1400 Jason leaves home and drives 60 km in 1 hour at a steady speed. He stops at a café for $\frac{1}{2}$ hour. He travels another 40 km in $\frac{1}{2}$ hour. He then stops for 1 hour before returning home in 1 hour at a steady speed.

**7** Distance from hostel (km)

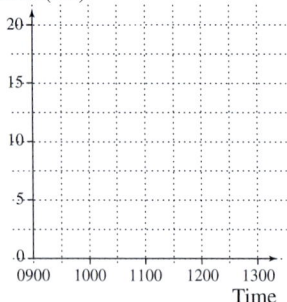

Some friends go for a long walk. They leave their hostel at 0900 and walk 4 km in $\frac{1}{2}$ hour at a steady speed. They walk 7 km during the next hour. They then rest for $\frac{1}{2}$ hour. They walk another 4 km in the next $\frac{1}{2}$ hour then return to the hostel in $1\frac{1}{2}$ hours at a steady speed.

**8** Distance

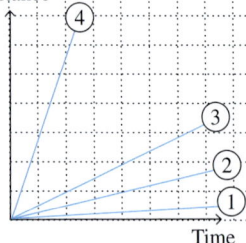

These four lines are the graphs for travel:

(A) in a car      (B) on foot

(C) on a bike      (D) in a rocket

Which graph is which?

**9** Which of the graphs below shows:

(A) steady speed    (B) car that speeds up    (C) car that slows down

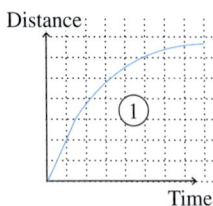

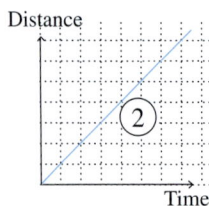

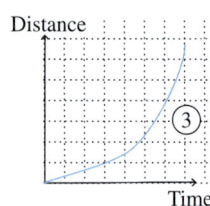

**10** Water is poured at a constant rate into each of the containers $A$, $B$ and $C$. Which of the graphs below fits each container?

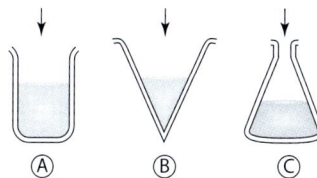

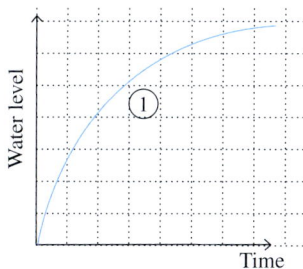

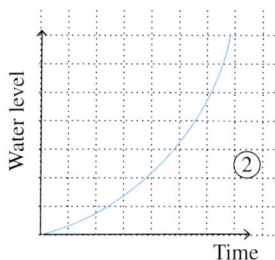

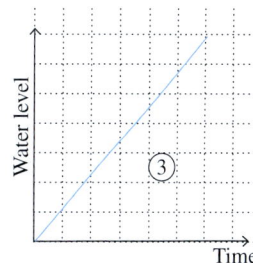

**11** Which of the graphs below best fits each of the following statements:

(A) After a poor start, car sales have increased massively this year.

(B) The price of milk has remained the same over the past year.

(C) The world's population continues to rise rapidly.

(D) The price of computers has fallen steadily over the last year.

(E) The number of visitors to a seaside resort rose in the Summer then dropped off towards Winter.

(F) The number of people going to the cinema in the UK has increased steadily this year.

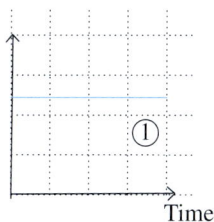

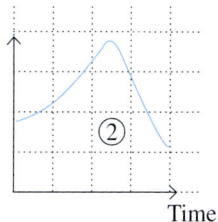

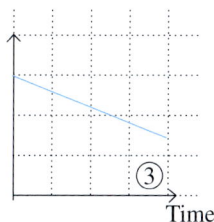

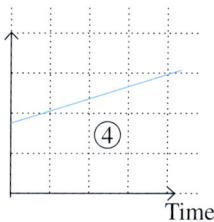

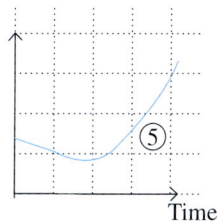

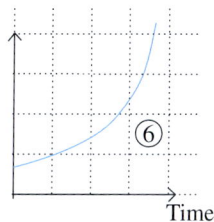

Some people say 'you don't get 'owt for nowt in this life'. Most things have to be paid for and that includes the electricity, gas and water you use in your home.

The amount of electricity, gas (and water in some homes) used is recorded on a *meter*. The meter is read every 3 months and a bill is sent. An electricity bill could look like the one below:

| Reading | Present | Previous | Units | Amount |
|---------|---------|----------|-------|--------|
| Units | 83757 | 81777 | 1980 at 7.600p | £150.48 |
| VAT | at 5% on £150.48 | | | £7.52 |
| Total bill | | | | £158.00 |

reading on meter this time

reading on meter last time

units of electricity used = present reading – previous reading

Value Added Tax for the government is 5% of the electricity bill

cost of one unit of electricity

number of units multiplied by the cost of one unit

**Payment**

Some people simply pay their bill when it arrives. Other people arrange to pay part of their bill each month. They are often given a small discount if they arrange to pay the bill each month.

Ally has received his electricity bill:

present reading = 61982 previous reading = 60732

cost of one unit of electricity = 7.6 p.

VAT is 5%.

How much does Ally have to pay?

units used = present – previous = 61982 – 60732 = 1250

cost of units = 1250 × 7.6 p = 9500 p = £95.00

$$\text{VAT} = 5\% \text{ of } £95.00 = \frac{5}{100} \times 95.00 = £4.75$$

Total bill = £99.75

**1** Nerys has received her electricity bill:

present reading = 53164          previous reading = 51083

cost of one unit of electricity = 9.3 p.

Copy and complete the bill below:

units used = present – previous = 53164 – ☐ = ☐

cost of units = ☐ × 9.3 p = ☐ p = £ ☐

$$\text{VAT} = 5\% \text{ of } \pounds\,\square = \frac{5}{100} \times \square = \pounds\,\square$$

Total bill = £ ____

**2** Work out the cost of each electricity bill below.

VAT is payable at 5% each time.

| Bill | present reading | previous reading | cost of one unit of electricity |
|------|-----------------|------------------|----------------------------------|
| a | 81659 | 80292 | 8.3 p |
| b | 23748 | 22095 | 7.6 p |
| c | 5186 | 4417 | 7.6 p |
| d | 63746 | 62640 | 9.4 p |
| e | 9187 | 8089 | 8.2 p |
| f | 5613 | 4688 | 11.4 p |
| g | 71248 | 69325 | 7.9 p |

### 1. Drawing straight line graphs

(a)

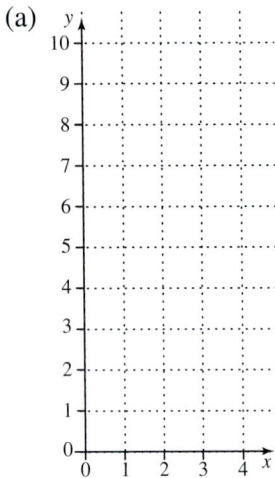

Draw these axes.

Complete the table below then draw $y = 4x + 1$.

| $x$ | 0 | 1 | 2 |
|-----|---|---|---|
| $y$ |   |   |   |

(b) Using $x$-values from 0 to 4, complete a table then draw $y = 7 - x$.

(c) Look at points on the straight line. Copy and complete the table below:

| $x$-coordinate | $y$-coordinate |
|----------------|----------------|
| 2 | 0 |
| 3 |   |
| 4 |   |
| 5 |   |

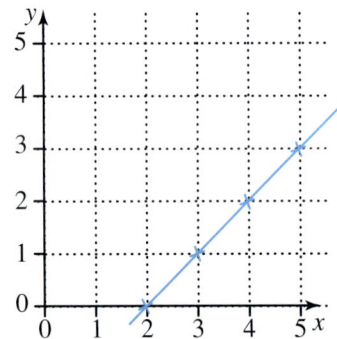

(d) Find a rule connecting the $x$-coordinate and the $y$-coordinate.  $y = \ldots\ldots$

### 2. Drawing curves from equations

(a) Complete the table below then draw the curve $y = x^2 + 2$.

| $x$ | −3 | −2 | −1 | 0 | 1 | 2 | 3 |
|-----|----|----|----|---|---|---|---|
| $y$ |    |    |    |   |   |   |   |

(b) Complete the table below then draw the curve $y = x^2 - 4$.

| $x$ | −3 | −2 | −1 | 0 | 1 | 2 | 3 |
|-----|----|----|----|---|---|---|---|
| $y$ |    |    |    |   |   |   |   |

284

## 3. Using the cover-up method for drawing straight lines

(a)

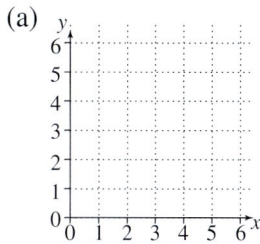

    (i) Draw these axes.

    (ii) Use $x = 0$ then $y = 0$ to find 2 points for $x + 3y = 6$.

    (iii) Draw the straight line $x + 3y = 6$.

(b) Draw $x$ and $y$ axes from 0 to 6.

    Draw the straight line $4x + 5y = 20$.

## 4. Solving simultaneous equations on a graph

(a) Use the graph to solve the simultaneous equations

$$2y - x = 4$$

$$x + y = 5$$

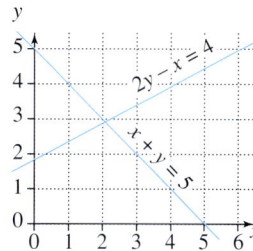

(b) Draw $x$ and $y$ axes from 0 to 6.

    Solve graphically the simultaneous equations $3x + y = 6$

$$x + y = 4.$$

(c) Draw $x$ and $y$ axes from 0 to 8.

    Solve graphically the simultaneous equations $2x + y = 8$

$$2x + 3y = 12.$$

## 5. Finding gradients of straight lines

Find the gradient of each line below:

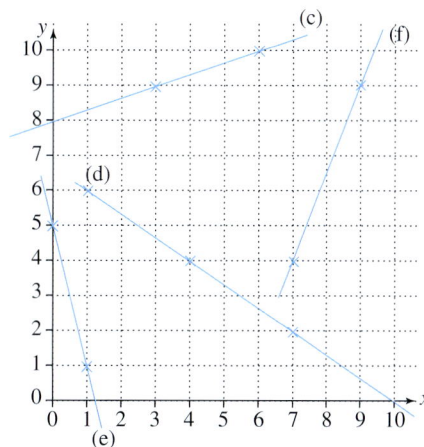

285

The graph below shows the weights of Ed and Serena during one year.

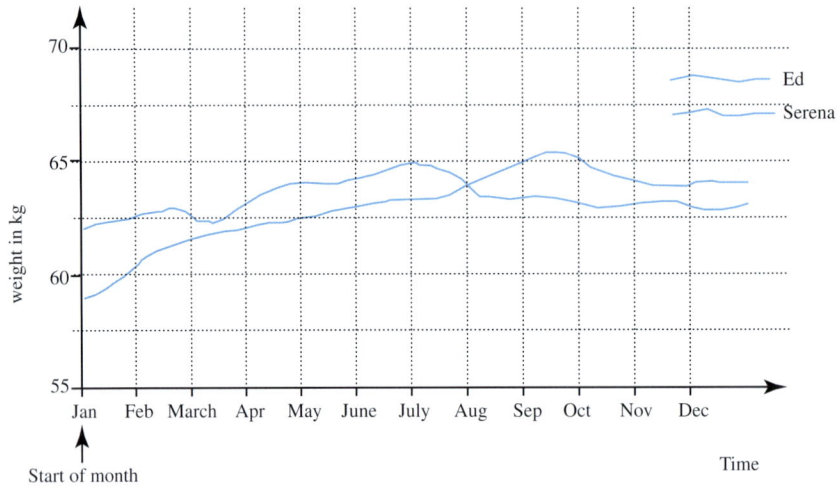

How much did Ed weigh at the start of:

(a) March?        (b) September?        (c) December?

(d) At the start of which month did Serena weigh 65 kg?

(e) How much did Serena weigh at the start of January?

(f) When did Ed and Serena weigh the *same* amount? How much did they weigh then?

(g) How much *more* did Serena weigh than Ed at the start of February?

(h) How much *more* did Ed weigh than Serena at the start of November?

## Mixed examination questions

**1.** (a) Copy and complete the table of values for $y = 2x + 3$

| $x$ | $-2$ | $-1$ | 0 | 1 | 2 | 3 |
|---|---|---|---|---|---|---|
| $y$ | | 1 | 3 | | | |

(b) Draw the graph of $y = 2x + 3$        (EDEXCEL)

**2.** The distance, by boat, from Poole Quay to Wareham is 12 miles. The diagram shows the distance-time graph of a boat trip from Poole Quay to Wareham and back.

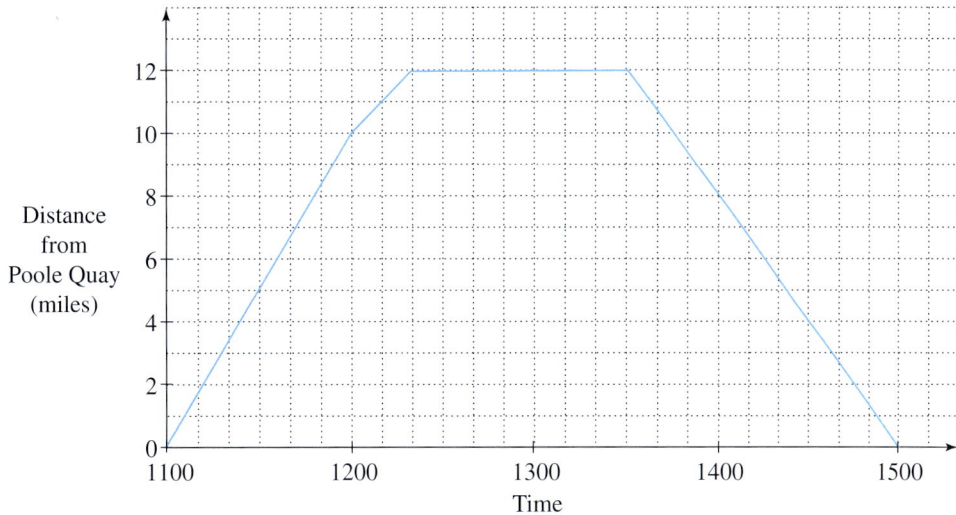

(a) Describe what happened to the speed of the boat at 1200 hours.

(b) How long did the boat stay in Wareham?

(c) What was the average speed of the boat on the return journey from Wareham to Poole Quay? (AQA)

**3.** (a) Complete the table of values for $y = 5 - x^2$.

| $x$ | $-3$ | $-2$ | $-1$ | 0 | 1 | 2 | 3 |
|-----|------|------|------|---|---|---|---|
| $y$ |      | 1    | 4    | 5 |   |   | $-4$ |

(b) Draw the graph of $y = 5 - x^2$ for values of $x$ from $-3$ to 3. (AQA)

**4.** The line $y + 4x = 14$ is shown on the right.

(a) On a copy of the diagram draw the line $y = 2x - 1$.

(b) Use your graph to solve the simultaneous equations

$$y + 4x = 14$$
$$y = 2x - 1$$

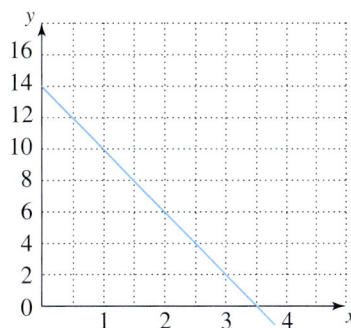

(CCEA)

# DATA 1

**In this unit you will learn how to:**

– use the probability scale

– use relative frequency

– find probabilities

– list possible outcomes

– deal with mutually exclusive events

– WATCH YOUR MONEY! – credit 1 – hire purchase.

## The probability scale

The probability of something happening is the likelihood or chance that it might happen.

If the probability of something happening is 'impossible', we say the probability is 0 (0% or 'no chance').

If the probability of something happening is 'dead certain', we say the probability is 1 (100% certain).

All the probabilities lie between 0 and 1.

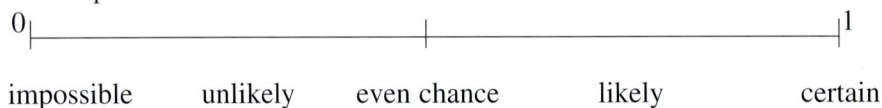

impossible     unlikely     even chance     likely     certain

This is the 'probability scale'.

Think about the probability of these events. Place them on a probability scale.

**A**  You will eat during the next week.

**B**  You will get 'heads' if you toss a coin.

**C**  It will rain on the 10th February.

**D**  You could swim to Australia without stopping.

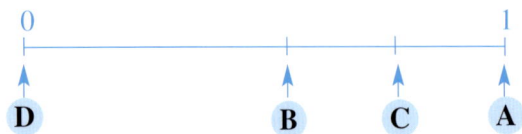

288

For each of these statements write one of these probabilities:

impossible   unlikely   even chance   likely   certain

**1**   Your teacher was born on a Monday.

**2**   You roll a dice and get a 3.

**3**   A baby will be born somewhere in the UK in the next hour.

**4**   It will rain on the 4ᵗʰ July.

**5**   You will brush your teeth sometime tomorrow.

**6**   You will drive a bus home tomorrow evening.

**7**   You will have a birthday in the next year.

**8**   You will choose a king if you pick one card from a pack of playing cards (there are 4 kings in a pack of 52 playing cards).

**9**   You will fly to the moon during the next year.

**10**   You will do *all* your maths homework for the rest of the year.

**11**   Think about the probability of the events below. Place them on a probability scale.

(a) Someone in your family will win the National Lottery Jackpot next week.

(b) You will wash your hair during the next week.

(c) There will be a school holiday during the next year.

(d) You will get 'tails' if you toss a coin.

(e) All pupils in your class will wear correct school uniform every day next term.

**12**   Think about the probability of the events below. Place them on a probability scale.

(a) It will snow on Christmas Day.

(b) The first person to walk into your next maths lesson will be a girl.

(c) You will go to the toilet during the next 24 hours.

(d) You roll a dice and get an 'odd' number.

(e) You will get married one day.

Can you still?

**11A**   **Use co-ordinates (see Unit 8)**

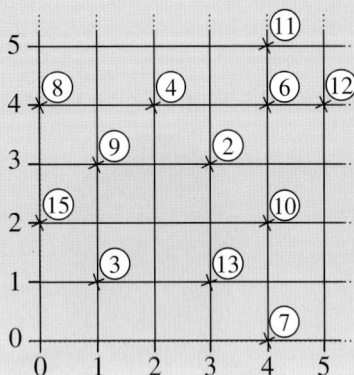

Write down the numbers at each of the co-ordinates given below:

(4, 5)     (1, 1)     (3, 1)     (3, 3)     (4, 0)

These numbers are a special type of number. Write down their name.

2.  Draw *x* and *y* axes with values from –5 to 5. Plot the points below and join them up in order.

   a) (–2, –3)     (–1, –3)     (0, –2)     (–2, 0)     (–2, 1)     (–3, 2)

      (–4, 1)     (–4, 3)     (–3, 4)     (–2, 4)     (0, 2)     (–1, 1)

      (–1, 0)     (1, –1)     (3, –1)     (3, 0)     (1, 2)     (0, 2)

   On the same grid, plot the points below and join them up in order.

   b) (2, –1)     (4, –3)     (3, –4)     (2, –2)     (0, –2)

   On the same grid, plot the points below and join them up in order.

   c) (–4, 1)     (–3, 3)     (–3, 4)     (–3, 2)

   d) Draw a dot at (–2, 3).

## Relative frequency

Sometimes it is useful to *estimate* the probability of something happening.

We collect data (maybe by doing an experiment). Each time the experiment is done is called a 'trial' (e.g. throwing a dice).

We use these results to estimate the chance of something happening. This estimate is called the *relative frequency*.

$$\text{Relative frequency of 'X' happening} = \frac{\text{number of times 'X' happens}}{\text{total number of trials}}$$

Maggie thinks her dice is biased (not fair). She throws the dice 600 times. The table below shows her results.

| Score | 1 | 2 | 3 | 4 | 5 | 6 |
|---|---|---|---|---|---|---|
| Frequency | 96 | 84 | 186 | 72 | 78 | 84 |

(a) How many times should each number come up if the dice is fair?

(b) From Maggie's results, estimate the probability of getting a '3' (this is called the relative frequency).

(c) Do you think the dice is fair?

**Answer:**

(a) 6 numbers so each number should come up 100 times.

(b) Relative frequency of getting a '3' = $\dfrac{186}{600}$ = 0.31        (using a calculator)

(c) The dice is not fair (it landed on '3' nearly twice as often as it should).

**1** Joe spins a coin 100 times. The coin lands on 'heads' 71 times and 'tails' 29 times.

(a) How many times should 'heads' come up if the coin is fair?

(b) From Joe's results, find the 'relative frequency' of getting 'heads'.

(c) Do you think the coin is fair? Explain the answer you give.

**2** Will thinks his dice is biased (not fair). He throws the dice 300 times. The table below shows his results.

| Score | 1 | 2 | 3 | 4 | 5 | 6 |
|---|---|---|---|---|---|---|
| Frequency | 51 | 46 | 47 | 54 | 53 | 49 |

(a) How many times should each number come up if the dice is fair.

(b) From Will's results, use a calculator to estimate the 'probability' of getting a '4'.

(c) Do you think the dice is fair? Discuss your answer with your teacher.

**3** Mary throws a drawing pin 200 times. It lands 'point down' 78 times.

(a) Use a calculator to find the relative frequency that the drawing pin will land 'point down'.

(b) How many times does the drawing pin land 'point up'?

(c) Find the relative frequency that the drawing pin will land 'point up'.

**4** Lola is throwing a 10-sided dice. She throws the dice 500 times. The table below shows her results.

| Score | 1 | 2 | 3 | 4 | 5 | 6 | 7 | 8 | 9 | 10 |
|---|---|---|---|---|---|---|---|---|---|---|
| Frequency | 44 | 48 | 51 | 50 | 47 | 52 | 40 | 82 | 45 | 41 |

(a) How many times should each number come up if the dice is fair?

(b) From Lola's results, use a calculator to estimate the probability of getting each score (1 up to 10).

(c) Do you think the dice is fair? Explain the answer you give.

**5** Gavin has to feed 900 people. He asks 60 people to choose their favourite meal from a menu of 3 dishes. The results are shown opposite.

(a) Estimate the probability that the first person to arrive for a meal would choose chicken kurma.

(b) Based on Gavin's survey, how many servings of *each* meal should he prepare to feed all 900 people?

| | |
|---|---|
| Cottage pie | 18 |
| Chicken kurma | 12 |
| Spaghetti bolognese | 30 |

*Can you still?*

(11B) **Translate and reflect shapes (see Unit 8)**

*Can you still?*

**1.**

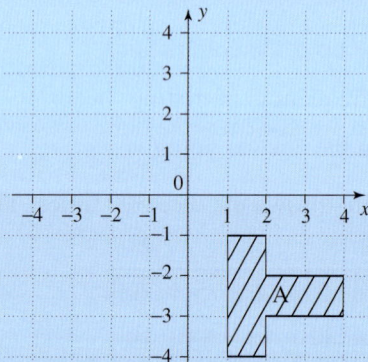

Copy this grid. Copy shape A.

(a) Reflect shape A in the x–axis. Label the image (new shape) B.

(b) Translate shape B through $\begin{pmatrix} -3 \\ -1 \end{pmatrix}$. Label the new shape C.

(c) Describe *fully* the translation which moves shape C onto shape A.

(d) Which shapes are *congruent* to shape A?

**2.**

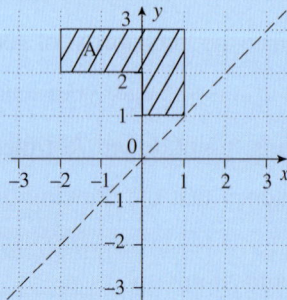

Copy this grid. Copy shape B.

(a) Reflect shape A in the broken mirror line. Label the image (new shape) B.

(b) Translate shape B through $\begin{pmatrix} -4 \\ 1 \end{pmatrix}$. Label the new shape C.

$$\text{Probability} = \frac{\text{the number of ways the event can happen}}{\text{the total number of possible outcomes}}$$

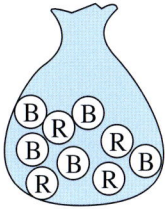

A bag contains 5 black beads and 4 red beads.
I take out one bead.

(a) The probability of taking out a black bead is $\frac{5}{9}$

We may write $p$ (black) $= \frac{5}{9}$

(b) The probability of taking out a red bead $= \frac{4}{9}$

(c) The probability of taking out a red or black bead $= \frac{9}{9} = 1$    (This is 'dead certain')

(d) The probability of taking out a yellow bead $= 0$     (This is impossible)

## M11.2

**1**  Mo has a bag of sweets.
She has 3 chews and 2 mints left.
She picks out a sweet.
What is the probability that she picks a mint?

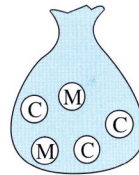

**2**  Tina rolls a dice.

What is the probability that she rolls a:

(a) 1?               (b) 3?               (c) 4?               (d) 3 or 4?

**3**  Billy has 9 cards as shown below:

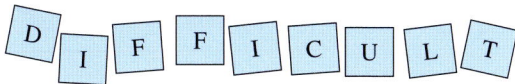

D I F F I C U L T

Billy picks a card at random.

What is the probability that he picks the letter:

(a) C?               (b) F?               (c) a vowel?

**4** Rowan has a box of chocolates.

These are 5 truffles, 4 toffees and 2 nuts.

Rowan picks a chocolate.

Find the probability that he chooses a:

(a) toffee           (b) truffle         (c) toffee or nut

**5**  Thelma spins this spinner.

Find the probability that she gets

(a) a 5     (b) an even number     (c) an odd number

**6** Ten discs numbered 1, 2, 2, 2, 3, 6, 8, 9, 9, 9, are placed in a bag. One disc is selected at random.

Find the probability that it is:

(a) an even number           b) 2           c) less than 6

**7** Phil has 15 pencils in his pencil case. 7 pencils are red, 5 are blue and the rest are green.

Phil takes out a pencil at random.

What is the probability that he takes out:

(a) blue?        (b) green?     (c) red or green?     (d) yellow?

**8** Sarah is taking part in a TV Quiz show. She must choose one box from a choice of 10 to win a prize. 4 boxes are empty, 5 boxes contain prizes for the home and 1 box has the 'star' prize.

What is the probability that Sarah will win:

(a) the 'star' prize? (b) nothing? (c) a prize for the home?

**9** One card is picked at random from a pack of 52.

Find the probability that it is:

(a) the Queen of clubs

(b) a red card

(c) a spade

**10**  A bag contains 12 balls. There are 5 red, 4 white and 3 yellow.

(a) Find the probability of selecting a red ball.

(b) The 4 white balls are replaced by 4 yellow balls. Find the probability of selecting a yellow ball.

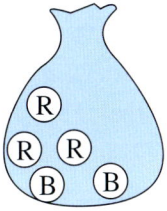

There are 3 red beads and 2 black beads in a bag. A bead is picked from this bag 75 times and replaced each time. How many red beads would you expect to get?

Probability of picking 'red' = $\dfrac{3}{5}$

Expect to get $\dfrac{3}{5}$ of 75

$= (75 \div 5) \times 3$

$= 15 \times 3$

$= 45$ reds.

## E11.2

**1**  A bag contains one white bead and 3 yellow beads. A bead is picked from the bag 80 times and replaced each time.

How many yellow beads would you expect to get?

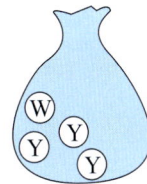

**2**  A dice is thrown 180 times.

How many times would you expect to get

(a) a 4      (b) a 3      (c) an even number      (d) a 2 or 3

**3**  A coin is spun 60 times. How many tails would you expect to get?

**4**  A box has 30 pencils in it. The probability of picking a red pencil is $\frac{1}{6}$. How many red pencils are in the box?

**5**  A bag has 25 beads in it. The probability of picking a white bead is $\frac{3}{5}$. How many white beads are in the bag?

**6**  In a game this spinner is spun 60 times. How many wins would you expect?

**7**  The chance of Jim playing football in a games lesson is $\frac{1}{4}$. There are 16 lessons in a term. How many times will Jim expect to play football?

**8**  A bag contains 7 red discs, 8 black discs and 5 white discs. Sandra pulls out one at random and then puts it back. If she does this 80 times, how many times would she pick:

(a) a red disc?      (b) a white disc?    (c) a black disc?

**9**  The probability that a train will arrive *on time* the next day at Swindon is 0.8. If 60 trains arrive at Swindon the next day, how many will be *on time*?

**10** The probability of getting a grade C or better in an English GCSE is 0.6. If 300 young people take their English GCSE, how many would you expect to get a grade C or better?

**11** Ann keeps trying her luck in the National Lottery. The probability that the first ball chosen will be hers is $\frac{6}{49}$. During one year, she plays 98 times.

How many times would she expect the first ball chosen to be hers?

**12** There are 15 balls in a bag. Sandeep takes a ball from the bag, notes its colour and then returns the ball to the bag. Sandeep does this 20 times.

| red | 6 |
|--------|----|
| yellow | 1 |
| black | 11 |
| green | 2 |

Here are the results.

(a) What is the smallest number of green balls there could be in the bag?

(b) Sandeep says 'There cannot be any white balls in the bag because there are no whites in my table'.

Explain why Sandeep is wrong.

(c) Sandeep takes one more ball from the bag. What is the most likely colour of the ball?

**13** The probability of it raining in November in Aberdeen is $\frac{5}{6}$. How many days would you expect it to rain in November?

**14** A bag has only blue and white balls in it. The probability of picking blue is $\frac{3}{4}$.

(a) What is the probability of picking a white ball?

(b) Ken picks a ball at random. He picks a white ball. What is the smallest number of white balls there could be in the bag?

(c) Ken then picks out another white ball. What is the smallest number of blue balls there could be in the bag?

**15** I have a two bags of beads.

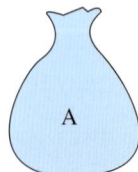

| A | B |
|---|---|
| 12 red beads | 11 red beads |
| 16 blue beads | 14 blue beads |

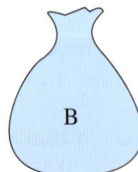

Which bag has the greater probability of getting a red counter? (you may *use a calculator* to help explain your answer)

(11C) **Rotate and enlarge shapes (see Unit 8)**

(You may use tracing paper)

1.

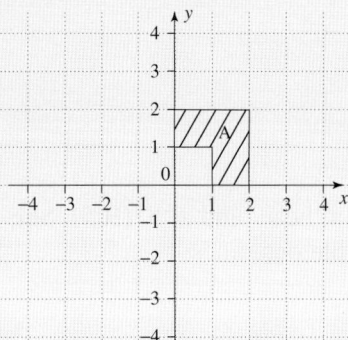

(a) Copy the grid. Copy shape A.

(b) Rotate shape A 180° clockwise about (0, 0). Label the image (new shape) B.

(c) Enlarge shape B by scale factor 2 about (0, 0). Label the image C.

2.

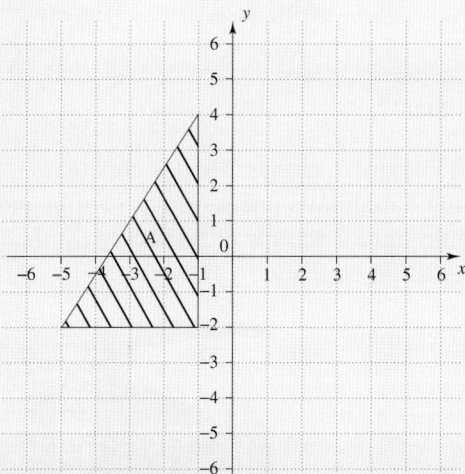

(a) Copy the grid. Copy shape A.

(b) Enlarge shape A by scale factor $\frac{1}{2}$ about (–3, –4). Label the image B.

(c) Rotate shape B 90° clockwise about (–1, –4). Label the image C.

## Listing possible outcomes

When more than one event occurs, it is usually helpful to make a list of all the possible outcomes. Use a system when making the list.

If you throw 2 coins, they could land as:

| 1st coin | 2nd coin |
|---|---|
| head | head |
| head | tail |
| tail | head |
| tail | tail |

there are 4 possible outcomes

1. For breakfast, Ellie eats cereal or toast. She drinks juice or tea.
Copy and complete the table below to show all the different breakfasts she might have.

| food | drink |
|------|-------|
| cereal | juice |
| | tea |
| | |
| toast | |

2. Ivy throws a coin and a dice. She could get a 'head' and a '5' (H 5). She could get a 'tail' and a '5'. List the 12 possible outcomes.

3. Here are 2 spinners. If I spin both spinners, I could get a 3 and a 9 (3, 9).

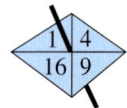

    a) List *all* the possible outcomes.

    b) How many possible outcomes are there?

4. Alfonso sells ice-cream in tubs which contain 2 scoops. He has chocolate chip, vanilla and raspberry ripple. A tub could have one scoop of vanilla and one scoop of raspberry ripple or it could have 2 scoops of raspberry ripple. List all the different kinds of tubs which can be made.

5. At a restaurant, each person has a starter, main course and desert.

    One evening the menu is:

    starter: melon or soup

    main course: lamb, turkey or pork

    dessert: apple pie, chocolate mousse or rhubarb crumble

    List all the different meals that could be ordered.

6. Four people, Tom, Sasha, Becky and Ronnie, work at a garage. Two people work at any one time. List all the possible pairs of people that could be working together at any one time.

7. Three coins are thrown together. List all the possible outcomes for the three coins.

**8** You can choose from 4 possible drinks in a drinks machine.

coke    fanta    sprite    diet coke

Zak buys one drink for himself and one for his friend. Write down all the possible pairs of drink Zak and his friend could have.

**9** Jack has 2 spinners. He spins both spinners and adds up the numbers to get a total. For example a '4' and a '3' give a total of 7.

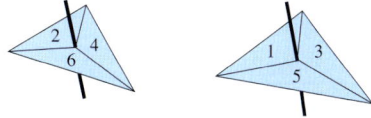

(a) Copy and complete this grid to show all the possible outcomes and totals.

(b) Find the probability of getting a total of 7.

| + | 1 | 3 | 5 |
|---|---|---|---|
| 2 | 3 |   |   |
| 4 |   | 7 |   |
| 6 |   |   |   |

**10**

| + | 1 | 2 | 3 | 4 | 5 | 6 |
|---|---|---|---|---|---|---|
| 1 |   |   |   |   |   |   |
| 2 |   |   |   |   |   |   |
| 3 |   | 5 |   |   |   |   |
| 4 |   |   |   |   |   |   |
| 5 |   | 7 |   |   |   |   |
| 6 |   |   |   |   |   |   |

2 dice are thrown. The numbers are then added together to get a total.

(a) Copy and complete this grid to show all the possible outcomes and totals.

(b) Find the probability of getting a total of 6.

(c) Find the probability of getting a total which is an even number.

(d) Find the probability of getting a score which is *more* than 9.

## Mutually exclusive events

Events are mutually exclusive if they cannot occur at the same time.

For example:

- selecting a queen
  selecting a '3' } from the same pack of cards

- tossing a 'head'
  tossing a 'tail'

- selecting a red ball from a bag
  selecting a white ball from the same bag

> The sum of the probabilities of mutually exclusive events is 1.

A bag contains balls which are either red, blue or yellow.

The probability of selecting a red is 0.3.

The probability of selecting a blue is 0.4.

What is the probability of selecting a yellow?

The probability of selecting a red *or* blue = 0.3 + 0.4 = 0.7 ('or' often suggests you *add* the probabilities)

Sum of probabilities = 1

Probability of selecting a yellow = 1– p (red or blue)

$$= 1 - 0.7$$

$$= 0.3$$

## E11.3

**1** Which of the following pairs of events are mutually exclusive?

(a) choose a club or an ace from a pack of cards.

(b) win or lose a football match.

(c) get a red light or green light on traffic lights.

(d) the sun shines or it rains.

(e) wear a blue tie or brown shoes.

(f) get a '3' or a '4' on a dice.

**2** Kerry has a drawer full of blue, black or red socks. The probability of choosing blue socks is 0.5. The probability of choosing black socks is 0.3.

(a) What is the probability of selecting blue *or* black socks?

(b) What is the probability of selecting red socks?

**3** In a Games lesson, students play football, basketball or hockey.

The probability of playing football is 0.4.

The probability of playing basketball is 0.5.

(a) What is the probability of playing football or basketball?

(b) What is the probability of playing hockey?

**4** In a football match the probability of Everton winning is 0.5. The probability of losing is 0.3. What is the probability of Everton drawing?

**5** A bag contains balls which are either yellow, blue or green.

The probability of selecting a yellow ball is 0.15.

The probability of selecting a blue ball is 0.55.

(a) Find the probability of selecting a green ball.

(b) Find the probability of selecting a ball which is *not* yellow.

**6** Emma has one drink for her breakfast. The table shows the probability of her choosing each drink.

| tea | coffee | orange juice | grape fruit juice |
|-----|--------|--------------|-------------------|
| 0.4 | $x$ | 0.3 | 0.1 |

(a) What is the probability of Emma choosing orange juice or grapefruit juice?

(b) What is the probability of Emma choosing coffee?

(c) During the month of April, how many days would you expect Emma to choose tea?

**7** Terry has a selection of shirts. The table shows the probability of Terry choosing a particular shirt colour.

| blue | white | yellow | red | green |
|------|-------|--------|-----|-------|
| 0.3 | 0.3 | 0.15 | $x$ | 0.05 |

(a) What is the probability of Terry choosing a yellow or green shirt?

(b) What is the probability of Terry choosing a red shirt?

(c) For every 50 times that Terry chooses a shirt, how many times would you expect him to choose a white shirt?

**8** The probability of pulling out a Queen from a pack of cards is $\frac{1}{13}$. What is the probability of *not* pulling out a Queen?

**9** 4 people play a game of poker. The probability of each person winning the game is shown below in the table.

| Darryl | Simon | Dan | Mark |
|--------|-------|-----|------|
| 0.35 | 0.25 | 0.25 | $x$ |

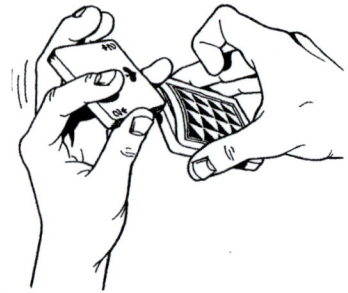

(a) What is the probability of Darryl or Simon winning?

(b) What is the probability of Mark winning.

(c) If they play 60 times, how many times would you expect Dan to win?

**10** Each time Cassie visits her grandfather he gives her some money. The table shows the probability of her getting a particular amount of money.

| £2 | £5 | £10 | £20 |
|----|----|-----|-----|
| $x$ | $\frac{1}{4}$ | $\frac{1}{8}$ | $\frac{1}{16}$ |

(a) Find the probability of getting £5 or £10.

(b) Find the probability of not getting £20.

(c) Find the probability of getting £2.

(d) For every 16 visits to her grandfather, how many times would Cassie expect to get £10?

**11** The probability of getting a square number when you throw a dice is $\frac{1}{3}$. What is the probability of *not* getting a square number?

**12** Every Friday night Jodie goes to a cinema, pub or restaurant. The probability of going to the cinema is $\frac{1}{2}$. The probability of going to the pub is $\frac{1}{4}$. What is the probability that Jodie goes to a restaurant?

If you do not have enough money to buy an item, you might buy *on credit*. There are different ways of doing this such as hire purchase, credit cards, store cards, bank overdrafts and personal loans.

**Make sure you know the true cost of buying on credit.**

This section deals with hire purchase.

> Hire purchase allows you to buy items straight away but you pay for them in instalments (usually monthly).
>
> You probably will not own the items until all the instalments have been paid. If you stop paying the instalments, the items could be taken back.

Music Centre £650
(or a 20% deposit plus 24 monthly payments of £27.50 each month)

If you buy the music centre on credit:

$$\text{deposit} = 20\% \text{ of } £650 = £130$$

$$24 \text{ monthly payments} = 24 \times £27.50 = £660$$

$$\text{total credit price} = £130 + £660 = £790$$

**How much extra does the hire purchase cost you?**

$$\text{extra cost} = £790 - £650 = £140$$

$\qquad\qquad\quad\uparrow\qquad\uparrow$

$\qquad\qquad$ Credit $\quad$ Cash

$\qquad\qquad$ price $\quad\ $ price

You would have to decide if you do not mind paying this *extra money* to be able to get this music centre.

GET WISE

If shops and other places offer interest-free periods, find out exactly what you have to pay in the end. It may *cost* you a lot of *extra money*.

1  A washing machine costs £420. You can buy it for a 10% deposit plus 36 equal monthly payments at £14.

(a) How much is the deposit?

(b) How much are the 36 monthly payments?

(c) What is the total credit price?

(d) How much extra does the hire purchase cost?

2  A TV costs £560. You can buy it for a 15% deposit plus 36 equal monthly payments of £15.50.

(a) How much is the deposit?

(b) How much are the 36 monthly payments?

(c) What is the total credit price?

(d) How much extra does the hire purchase cost?

3  Copy and complete the table below:

|  | item | cash price (£) | deposit (£) | number of monthly instalments (£) | each monthly instalment (£) | total credit price (£) | extra cost of hire purchase (£) |
|---|---|---|---|---|---|---|---|
| (a) | cooker | 735 | 100 | 24 | 30 | | |
| (b) | bike | 390 | 80 | 24 | 15 | | |
| (c) | car | 12400 | 3000 | 48 | 224 | | |
| (d) | phone | 230 | 40 | 12 | 17.50 | | |
| (e) | dishwasher | 465 | 55 | 36 | 14.99 | | |

4
| New windows £3250 | Pay a 20% deposit then *nothing for 2 years.* Followed by 12 equal monthly payments of £299. |
|---|---|

How much extra does the hire purchase cost?

5

Boiler    £ 4100
Pay a £1000 deposit then *nothing for 1 year.*
Finally 48 equal monthly payments of £85.

How much is saved by paying the cash price?

**1.** Using the probability scale

Think about the probability of the events below. Place them on a probability scale.

0 ⊢————————————————————⊣ 1

(a) You will have a drink in the next 24 hours.

(b) You will get a '2' when you throw a dice.

(c) A car will drive on a motorway today in the UK.

(d) If I put a stone in one of my hands, you will guess correctly which hand has the stone.

(e) Your school will be 'transported' to the planet Mars today.

**2.** Using relative frequency

Sabrina throws a shoe into the air. The shoe lands on its left side, right side or on its bottom.

She does this 50 times. The table below shows her results.

| left side | right side | bottom |
|-----------|------------|--------|
| 16        | 21         | 13     |

Use a calculator to find the relative frequency that the shoe lands on its:

(a) left side

(b) right side

(c) bottom

(d) If Sabrina threw the shoe 200 times, how many times would she expect it to land on its right side?

**3.** Finding probabilities

(a) Fiona has 8 cards as shown below?

R  E  M  E  M  B  E  R

Fiona picks a card at random.

What is the probability that she picks the letter:

(i) B?          (ii) E?          (iii) R?          (iv) a vowel?

(b) 12 discs numbered 1, 2, 3, 3, 5, 6, 6, 8, 9, 9, 10, 15 are placed in a bag.
One disc is selected at random. Find the probability that it is:

   (i) a prime number     (ii) a 6       (iii) a multiple of 3

(c) This pointer is spun 60 times. How many
times would you expect it to point to:

   (i) 2?

   (ii) an even number?

   (iii) a square number?

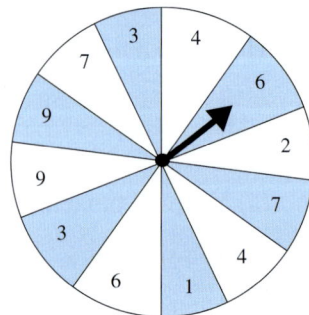

**4.** Listing possible outcomes

(a) Kyron throws a dice and spins the
spinner shown opposite.

He could get a '4' and a '3' (4, 3).
List *all* the possible outcomes. How
many possible outcomes are there?

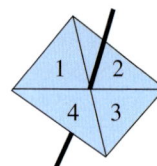

(b) Cath has to choose some of her school subjects from the option blocks
below:

| A | B | C |
|---|---|---|
| french | history | art |
| german | geography | dt |
| spanish | | |

She must choose one subject from column A, one from column B and one
from column C. List *all* the different groups of choices she could make
(combinations).

(c) How many combinations are there?

**5.** Dealing with mutually exclusive events

(a) The probability that Ivan is late in the morning is 0.01. What is the
probability that Ivan is *not* late in the morning?

(b) A bag contains balls which are either white, green or blue.
The probability of selecting a white ball is 1/3.
The probability of selecting a green ball is 1/2.

   (i) What is the probability of selecting a white *or* green ball?

   (ii) What is the probability of selecting a blue ball?

(c) Gwen likes a wide range of music. The table below shows the probability of Gwen listening to a particular type of music.

| rock | opera | jazz | classical |
|------|-------|------|-----------|
| 0.5 | 0.15 | $x$ | 0.05 |

   (i) What is the probability of Gwen listening to opera or classical music?

  (ii) What is the probability of Gwen listening to jazz?

 (iii) For the next 50 times that Gwen listens to music, how many times would you expect her to listen to rock music?

## Mixed examination questions

**1** (a) Marco is recycling his glass bottles.
He has one green (G), one brown (B) and one clear (C) bottle.

List the different orders he could recycle the three bottles. The first one is done for you.

| G | B | C |
|---|---|---|

(b) (i) Jane has 11 green, 7 brown and 2 clear bottles to recycle. She picks the first bottle at random.

What is the probability that it is brown?

  (ii) The probability that the first bottle she picks is a juice bottle is 0.4.

What is the probability that the first bottle she picks is not a juice bottle? (OCR)

**2** A sack contains a number of gold and silver discs.
An experiment consists of taking a disc from the sack at random, recording its colour and then replacing it.
The experiment is repeated 10, 50, 100, 150 and 200 times.
The table shows the results.

| Number of experiments | 10 | 50 | 100 | 150 | 200 |
|-----------------------|----|----|-----|-----|-----|
| Number of gold discs | 3 | 8 | 23 | 30 | 38 |

(a) Draw a graph to show how the relative frequency of a gold disc changes as the number of experiments increases.

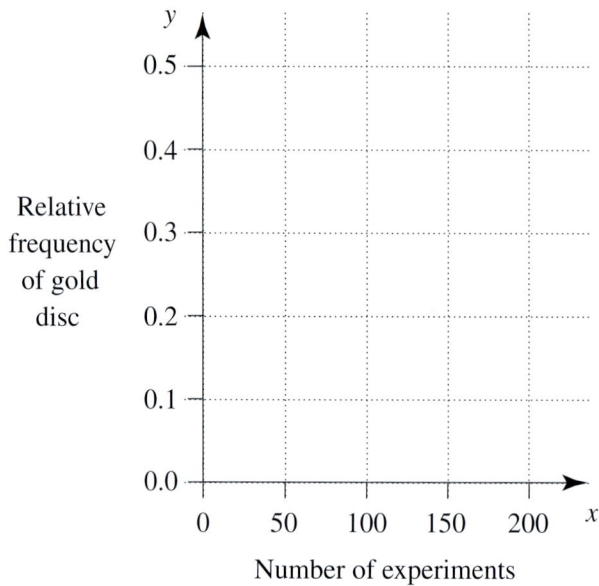

(b) The sack contains 1000 discs.
Estimate the number of gold discs in the sack.

(AQA)

3  The table shows information about a group of adults.

|  | Can drive | Cannot drive |
|---|---|---|
| Male | 32 | 8 |
| Female | 38 | 12 |

(a) One of these adults is chosen at random.
What is the probability that the adult can drive?

(b) A man in the group is chosen at random.
What is the probability that he can drive?

(c) A woman in the group is chosen at random.
The probability that she can drive is 0.76.
What is the probability that she cannot drive?

(d) Does the information given support the statement

"More women can drive than men"?

Explain your answer.

(AQA)

**4** (a) A bag contains 3 orange sweets and 2 yellow sweets.
   One sweet is chosen from the bag at random.
   Find the probability that it will be orange.

   (b) There are only red, green and blue counters in a box.
   The probability of a red or a green counter being chosen is given in the table below.

   | Colour | Red | Green | Blue |
   |---|---|---|---|
   | Probability | 0.4 | 0.2 | |

   (i) Work out the probability of choosing a blue counter.          (OCR)

**5** Rovers play Wanderers at football.
   The probability that Rovers win the match is 0.55.
   The probability that Wanderers win the match is 0.2.

   Find the probability that the result is a draw.          (OCR)

**6** The table shows the probability for the delivery time of letters posted first class.

   | Delivery time (days) | 1 | 2 | 3 or more |
   |---|---|---|---|
   | Probability | 0.7 | 0.2 | 0.1 |

   100 letters are posted first class.

   How many will be delivered in 1 or 2 days?          (AQA)

**In this unit you will learn how to:**

– find numbers in sequences

– find rules for sequences

– solve equations

– solve equations with brackets

– solve equations with the unknown on both sides

– set up equations and solve them

– solve equations by trial and improvement

– WATCH YOUR MONEY! – credit 2 – credit cards and store cards

## Sequences

- A number sequence is a list of numbers in special order.

- Each number in a sequence is called a *term*.

- The terms are connected by a rule.

  3, 8, 13, 18, 23... the rule is +5 each time.

- To find the rule that links the numbers, study the gaps.

2   3   5   8 ...

  +1  +2  +3

You can now see the pattern so the next number will be 8 + 4 = 12

**1** The numbers in boxes make a sequence. Find the next term.

(a) 2   5   8   11   ☐

(b) 15   13   11   9   ☐

(c) 4   9   14   19   ☐

(d) 3   4   6   9   ☐

In Questions **2** to **15** copy the sequences and write the *next 2 numbers*. What is the rule for each sequence?

**2** 2, 6, 10, 14…

**3** 7, 9, 11, 13…

**4** 7, 15, 23, 31…

**5** 16, 13, 10, 7…

**6** 23, 19, 15, 11…

**7** 5, 14, 23, 32…

**8** 4, 10, 16, 22...

**9** 10, 19, 28, 37...

**10** 5, 7, 10, 14...

**11** 1, 2, 4, 7...

**12** 18, 17, 15, 12...

**13** 80, 75, 65, 50...

**14** 5, 3, 1, -1...

**15** 2, 0, -2, -4...

In Questions **16** to **25** write down the missing numbers.

**16** 7, 11, ☐, 19, ☐

**17** 8, 11, ☐, 17, ☐

**18** 21, 16, ☐, 6, ☐

**19** 32, 26, 20, ☐, ☐

**20** 5, 12, ☐, 26, ☐

**21** –10, –8, ☐, –4, ☐

**22** 3, 0, ☐, –6, ☐

**23** 61, 57, 53, ☐, ☐

**24** ☐, 2, 0, –2, ☐

**25** 4, 5, 7, 10, ☐, ☐

**26** Do you remember the triangular numbers below?

1     3     6     10

Write down the next 3 triangular numbers?

**27** shape 1    shape 2    shape 3

How many lines are needed for

(a) shape 4,

(b) shape 5?

**28**  shape 1     shape 2     shape 3

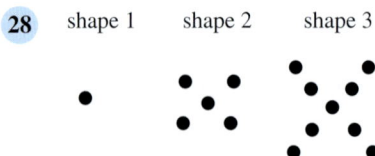

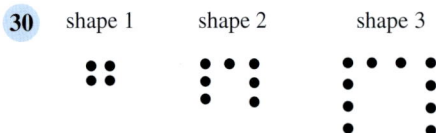

How many dots are needed for

(a) shape 4,

(b) shape 5?

**29**  shape 1     shape 2     shape 3

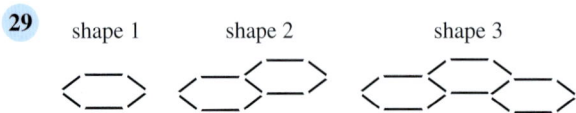

How many lines are needed for

(a) shape 4,

(b) shape 5?

**30**  shape 1     shape 2     shape 3

How many dots are needed for

(a) shape 4,

(b) shape 5?

## Key Facts

- If the sequence is not a clear adding or subtracting pattern, try multiplying or dividing.

  64, 16, 4, 1… the rule is $\div 4$ each time. The next number will be $1 \div 4$ which is $\frac{1}{4}$.

- If you study the gaps between numbers (we call these *differences*), the *differences* can make a sequence.

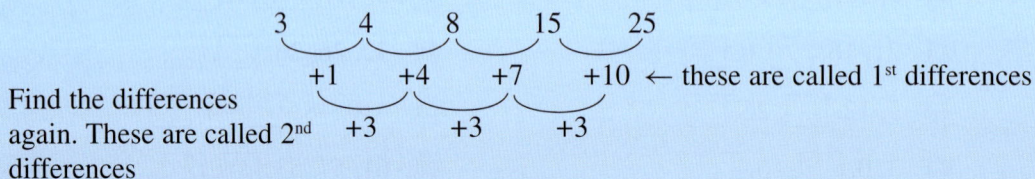

$$3 \quad\quad 4 \quad\quad 8 \quad\quad 15 \quad\quad 25$$

+1    +4    +7    +10  ← these are called 1st differences

Find the differences again. These are called 2nd differences    +3    +3    +3

So add 3 onto the 1st differences to give +13. Now +13 onto the term 25 to get 38 which is the next term in the sequence.

### E12.1

In Questions **1** to **12** copy the sequences and write the next *2 numbers*. What is the rule for each sequence?

**1**  1, 2, 4, 8...

**2**  1, 3, 9, 27...

**3**  5, 10, 20, 40...

**4**  800, 400, 200, 100...

**5**  $\frac{1}{2}$, 1, $1\frac{1}{2}$, 2...

**6**  2, 6, 18, 54...

**7** 1, 5, 25, 125...    **8** 243, 81, 27, 9...    **9** 2, 20, 200, 2000...

**10** 150, 140, 120, 90...    **11** 1.3, 1.7, 2.1, 2.5...    **12** 300, 30, 3, 0.3...

**13**  shape 1    shape 2    shape 3    shape 4    How many small squares are needed for (a) shape 5?

(b) shape 6?

In Questions **14** to **23** find the next 2 numbers in each sequence (it may help you to work out the 2nd differences).

**14** 1, 4, 9, 16, 25...    **15** 6, 7, 10, 15, 22...    **16** 4, 5, 7, 10, 14...

**17** 3, 5, 12, 24, 41...    **18** 1, 4, 10, 19, 31...    **19** 5, 6, 11, 20, 33...

**20** 2, 3, 7, 14, 24...    **21** 1, 9, 25, 49, 81...    **22** 4, 9, 19, 34, 54...

**23** 7, 8, 11, 16, 23...

**24** Find the next 2 numbers in the sequence below. Try to explain the pattern.

1, 1, 2, 3, 5, 8, 13...

**25** Find the next 2 numbers in the sequence 0, 0, 1, 1, 2, 4, 7, 13...

**26** This is Pascal's triangle.

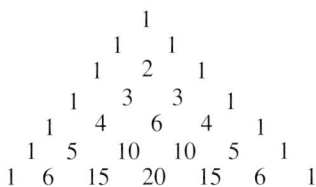

```
              1
           1     1
        1     2     1
      1    3     3    1
    1   4     6     4   1
  1   5   10    10    5   1
1   6   15   20   15   6   1
```

(a) Look carefully at how the triangle is made. Write down the next row. It starts: 1 7...

(b) Work out the *sum* of the numbers in each row of Pascal's triangle. What do you notice?

# Sequence rules

The *term-to-term* rule explains how one term in a sequence is connected to the next term.

28, 23, 18, 13... the term-to-term rule is 'subtract 5'.

3, 5, 9, 17... the term-to-term rule is 'double then subtract 1'.

The *position-to-term* rule explains how a term in a sequence is connected to its position in the sequence.

Find the position-to-term rule for the sequence below:

| Position $n$ | 1 | 2 | 3 | 4 |
|---|---|---|---|---|
| ↓ | ↓ | ↓ | ↓ | ↓ |
| term | 5 | 8 | 11 | 14 |

find the 1st difference        +3      +3      +3

If the 1st difference is the same, the rule will involve the '1st difference' *multiplied* by the 'position $n$'

i.e. $3 \times n$        (we write $3n$)

Work out the '$3n$' numbers and write them beneath the terms.

| Position $n$ | 1 | 2 | 3 | 4 |
|---|---|---|---|---|
| term | 5 | 8 | 11 | 14 |
| $3n$ | 3 | 6 | 9 | 12 |

We can see that we need to add 2 onto each '$3n$' value to get the term

so each term $= 3n + 2$

we call this the formula for the '$n^{th}$ *term*'

$$n^{th} \text{ term} = 3n + 2$$

We can check this formula by choosing a value of $n$, for example $n = 2$.
$n^{th}$ term $= 3n + 2 = 3 \times 2 + 2 = 8$ so the 2nd term $= 8$ which we can see is correct.

---

Find the $n^{th}$ term for the sequence 2, 6, 10, 14.

Draw a table showing positions and terms.

| Position $n$ | 1 | 2 | 3 | 4 |
|---|---|---|---|---|
| Rerm | 2 | 6 | 10 | 14 |
| $4n$ | 4 | 8 | 12 | 16 |

1st difference $= 4$
so work out '$4n$' values.

We need to subtract 2 from each '$4n$' value to get each term.

So the $n^{th}$ term $= 4n - 2$ (check with $n$ values of your choice)

---

**M12.2**

1  The first term of a sequence is 6 and the term-to-term rule is 'add 5'. Write down the first 5 terms of the sequence.

**2** Write down the term-to-term rule for the sequence 28, 21, 14, 7…

**3** You are given the first term and the rule of several sequences. Write down the first 5 terms of each sequence.

|      | First term | Rule        |
|------|------------|-------------|
| (a)  | 4          | add 7       |
| (b)  | 26         | subtract 3  |
| (c)  | 3          | double      |
| (d)  | 8000       | divide by 10 |

**4** Write down the term-to-term rule for each sequence below:

(a) 70, 64, 58, 52...          (b) 144, 72, 36, 18...

(c) 3.5, 5, 6.5, 8...          (d) 2, 6, 18, 54...

**5** The rule for the number sequences below is 'multiply by 3 then add 1'

Find the missing numbers.

(a) $3 \rightarrow 10 \rightarrow 31 \rightarrow 94 \rightarrow \boxed{\phantom{00}}$

(b) $\boxed{\phantom{00}} \rightarrow 7 \rightarrow 22 \rightarrow 67 \rightarrow 202$

**6** The rule for the number sequences below is 'multiply by 2 and take away 1'

Find the missing numbers.

(a) $2 \rightarrow 3 \rightarrow 5 \rightarrow 9 \rightarrow \boxed{\phantom{00}}$

(b) $\boxed{\phantom{00}} \rightarrow 7 \rightarrow 13 \rightarrow 25 \rightarrow 49$

**7** Here is a sequence:

3, 8, 13, 18...

The 1st difference is +5.

| Position $n$ | 1 | 2 | 3 | 4 |
|--------------|---|---|----|----|
| term         | 3 | 8 | 13 | 18 |
| $5n$         | 5 | 10 | 15 | 20 |

Copy the table which has a row for '$5n$'.

Copy and complete: 'The $n^{th}$ term of the sequence is $5n - \boxed{\phantom{0}}$'

**8** Use the tables below to help you find the $n^{th}$ term of each sequence.

(a) Sequence 8, 10, 12, 14...          (b) Sequence 3, 7, 11, 15...

| Position $n$ | 1 | 2 | 3 | 4 |
|--------------|---|----|----|----|
| term         | 8 | 10 | 12 | 14 |
| $2n$         | 2 | 4  | 6  | 8  |

| Position $n$ | 1 | 2 | 3 | 4 |
|--------------|---|---|----|----|
| term         | 3 | 7 | 11 | 15 |
| $4n$         | 4 | 8 | 12 | 16 |

$n^{th}$ term = $\boxed{\phantom{000000}}$          $n^{th}$ term = $\boxed{\phantom{000000}}$

(c) Sequence 5, 9, 13, 17

| Position $n$ | 1 | 2 | 3 | 4 |
|---|---|---|---|---|
| term | 5 | 9 | 13 | 17 |
| $4n$ | | | | |

$n^{th}$ term = [            ]

(d) Sequence 2, 5, 8, 11

| Position $n$ | 1 | 2 | 3 | 4 |
|---|---|---|---|---|
| term | 2 | 5 | 8 | 11 |
| $3n$ | | | | |

$n^{th}$ term = [            ]

**9** For each sequence below find the first difference to help you to make a table like the one in question **7** and use it to find the $n^{th}$ term.

(a) 3, 9, 15, 21...   (b) 4, 11, 18, 25...   (c) 13, 23, 33, 43...

(d) 8, 13, 18, 23...   (e) 1, 9, 17, 25...   (f) 7, 16, 25, 34...

**10** Make a table for each sequence below and write the $n^{th}$ term.

(a) 12, 10, 8, 6...   (b) 17, 13, 9, 5...

(c) 2.5, 3, 3.5, 4...   (d) 40, 31, 22, 13...

---

Here is a sequence of shapes made from sticks.

Let $n$ = shape number and $s$ = number of sticks

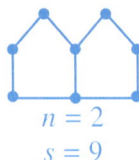

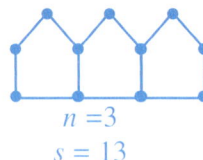

$n = 1$
$s = 5$

$n = 2$
$s = 9$

$n = 3$
$s = 13$

The next shape in the sequence is

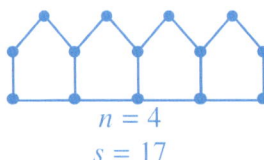

$n = 4$
$s = 17$

Make a table of values.

| $n$ | 1 | 2 | 3 | 4 |
|---|---|---|---|---|
| $s$ | 5 | 9 | 13 | 17 |
| $4n$ | 4 | 8 | 12 | 16 |

The 1st difference is +4.

Write the '$4n$' values under the table.

So the $n^{th}$ term = $4n + 1 \Rightarrow$ this means s = $4n + 1$

If we want to know how many sticks are needed for shape number 50 ($n = 50$), we can use the formula:

s = $4n + 1$ = $4 \times 50 + 1$ = 201 sticks   (much quicker than drawing pictures!)

**1** Here is a sequence of shapes made from squares. Let $n$ = shape number and $w$ = number of white squares.

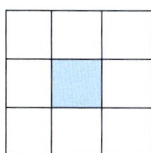  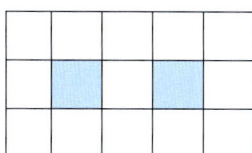  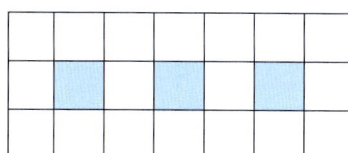

$n = 1$ $\quad\quad\quad\quad\quad\quad$ $n = 2$ $\quad\quad\quad\quad\quad\quad$ $n = 3$
$w = 8$ $\quad\quad\quad\quad\quad\quad$ $w = 13$ $\quad\quad\quad\quad\quad$ $w = 18$

(a) Draw the next shape in the sequence.

(b) How many white squares are in shape number 4?

(c) Complete the table of values. The 1st difference is +5. Write out the '5n' values. Use these to find a formula for the number of white squares ($w$) for the shape number $n$. Use values of $n$ to *check* if your formula is correct.

| $n$ | 1 | 2 | 3 | 4 |
|-----|---|----|----|---|
| $w$ | 8 | 13 | 18 | |

(d) Use your formula to find out how many white squares are in shape number 20.

**2** Here is a sequence of shapes made from hexagons.

Let $n$ = shape number and $w$ = number of white hexagons.

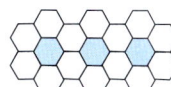

$n = 1$ $\quad\quad\quad\quad\quad$ $n = 2$ $\quad\quad\quad\quad\quad$ $n = 3$

(a) How many white hexagons are in each shape?

(b) How many white hexagons would be in the next shape in the sequence?

(c) Complete a table of values.

Find the 1st difference.
Find a formula for the number of white hexagons (w) for the shape number $n$.
Use values of $n$ to *check* if your formula is correct.

| $n$ | 1 | 2 | 3 | 4 |
|-----|---|---|---|---|
| $w$ | 6 | | | |

(d) Use your formula to find out how many white hexagons are in shape number 20.

For each of the sequences in Questions **3** and **7**,

(a) Draw the next shape in the sequence.

(b) Let $n$ = shape number and $s$ = number of sticks.
Complete a table of values for $n$ and $s$.

(c) Use the table and 1st difference to find a formula for the number of sticks ($s$) for the shape number $n$.
Use values of $n$ to *check* if each formula is correct.

(d) Use the formula to find out how many sticks are in shape number 50.

**3**

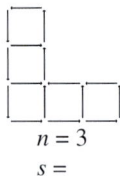

$n = 1$        $n = 2$        $n = 3$
$s = 4$        $s = 10$       $s =$

**4**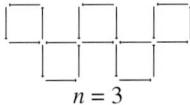

$n = 1$        $n = 2$        $n = 3$

**5**

 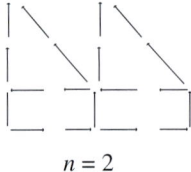 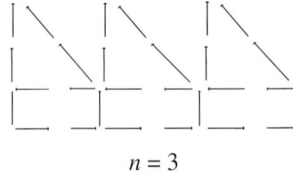

$n = 1$        $n = 2$           $n = 3$

**6**

$n = 1$        $n = 2$           $n = 3$

**7**

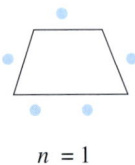 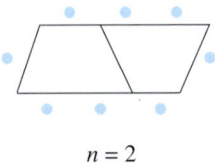 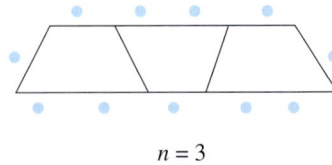

$n = 1$            $n = 2$            $n = 3$

**8**  This table can seat 5 people

The diagrams below show how many people can be
seated when tables are joined together.

$n = 1$            $n = 2$            $n = 3$

(a) Draw the diagram for 4 tables.

(b) Let $p$ = number of people and $n$ = number of tables. Make a table of values and use it to find a formula for the number of people according to how many tables.

(c) How many people could be seated with 20 tables?

**9** Ponds are surrounded by paving slabs as shown below:

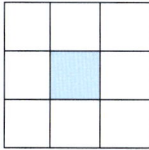 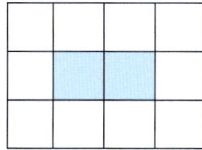 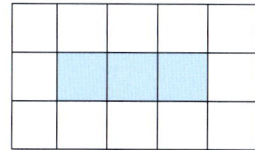

$n = 1$        $n = 2$        $n = 3$

(a) Draw the next shape in the sequence.

(b) How many white paving slabs surround each pond?

(c) Find a formula for the number of white slabs ($w$) surrounding each pond $n$ (use a table of values to help you).

(d) How many white slabs surround pond number 50?

*Can you still?*

**12A**   **Collect like terms (see Unit 4)**

*Can you still?*

Simplify

1. $6a + 3a$       **2.** $8a - 2a$       **3.** $3a + a$

**4.** $7x + 2y + 2x$       **5.** $2a + 5b - 3b$       **6.** $4x + 9y - 2y + 2x$

**7.** $3p + 5q + 2p - q$       **8.** $7x + 2 - 3x$       **9.** $4a + 3b + 2b + 5$

**10.** Eddie has £ $(5a + 2)$. He spends £ $(3a)$. How much money does he have left?

**11.** Linda is $(2m + 5n)$ cm tall. During the next year she grows $(3m + 2)$ cm. How tall is she now?

**12.** Milly is building a table. She will cut one piece of wood into 4 pieces each $(2x + 1)$ cm long. How long is the piece of wood she starts with?

## Key Facts

An '*equation*' contains an ' = ' sign.

$n + 3 = 7$ is an equation.

'Solve' $n + 3 = 7$ means 'Find the value of $n$ which fits the *equation*'.

$n = 4$ because $\boxed{4} + 3 = 7$

(a) Solve $n - 4 = 2$
$n = 6$ because $\boxed{6} - 4 = 2$

(b) Solve $3n = 18$
$3n$ means '$3 \times n$'
$n = 6$ because $3 \times \boxed{6} = 18$

(c) Solve $\dfrac{n}{3} = 2$

$\dfrac{n}{3}$ means '$n \div 3$'

$n = 6$ because $\dfrac{\boxed{6}}{3} = 2$

### M12.3

**1** Work out the missing numbers:

(a) $n + 6 = 10$ (b) $n + 2 = 5$ (c) $n + 6 = 9$ (d) $n - 4 = 1$ (e) $n - 8 = 3$

(f) $n - 20 = 7$ (g) $n - 5 = 12$ (h) $n + 10 = 32$ (i) $n - 1 = 9$ (j) $n + 7 = 14$

(k) $n + 9 = 12$ (l) $n - 7 = 9$

**2** Solve these equations:

(a) $x - 15 = 8$ (b) $x - 17 = 12$ (c) $x + 28 = 40$ (d) $x + 16 = 30$

(e) $x + 31 = 52$ (f) $x + 43 = 75$ (g) $x - 24 = 20$ (h) $x - 30 = 27$

**3** Solve these equations:

(a) $3 \times n = 21$ (b) $5 \times n = 30$ (c) $3 \times n = 12$ (d) $2 \times n = 32$ (e) $4n = 24$

(f) $10n = 70$ (g) $8n = 48$ (h) $3n = 27$ (i) $6n = 42$ (j) $7n = 56$

(k) $6n = 24$ (l) $8n = 40$

**4** Solve:

(a) $n \div 2 = 3$ (b) $n \div 4 = 3$ (c) $n \div 5 = 4$ (d) $n \div 2 = 5$

(e) $\dfrac{n}{5} = 6$ (f) $\dfrac{n}{4} = 8$ (g) $\dfrac{n}{10} = 7$ (h) $\dfrac{n}{6} = 6$

**5** Jim thinks of a number and then adds 7. If the answer is 15, what number did Jim think of?

**6** Teresa thinks of a number and then subtracts 8. If the answer is 9, what number did Teresa think of?

**7** Ed thinks of a number and then subtracts 14. If the answer is 13, what number did Ed think of?

**8** Candice thinks of a number and then multiplies it by 6. If the answer is 54, what number did Candice think of?

**9** Gemma thinks of a number and then multiplies it by 8. If the answer is 32, what number did Gemma think of?

**10** Solve:

(a) $x+8 = 20$  (b) $x+17 = 31$  (c) $3x = 15$  (d) $9x = 63$

(e) $x+43 = 61$  (f) $x-16 = 23$  (g) $\dfrac{x}{4} = 7$  (h) $x-32 = 21$

(i) $\dfrac{x}{7} = 5$  (j) $6x = 30$  (k) $x+88 = 110$  (l) $\dfrac{x}{3} = 12$

---

Sometimes the missing number may be a *negative number*.

(a) Solve $n + 6 = 2$  (b) Solve $n-3 = -8$  (c) $3n = -12$

$\quad n = -4$ because $\boxed{-4} + 6 = 2$  $\quad n = -5$ because  $\quad n = -4$ because

$\qquad\qquad\qquad$ $\boxed{-5} -3 = -8$  $\qquad$ $3 \times \boxed{-4} = -12$

---

**E12.3**

**1** Solve these equations:

(a) $n + 4 = 3$  (b) $n + 6 = 1$  (c) $n + 9 = 4$  (d) $n + 7 = 2$

(e) $n - 2 = -1$  (f) $n - 8 = -13$  (g) $n - 4 = -8$  (h) $n - 4 = -9$

(i) $n - 6 = -3$  (j) $n + 7 = 0$  (k) $n + 12 = 4$  (l) $n - 12 = -20$

**2** Solve:

(a) $4n = -20$  (b) $7n = -21$  (c) $5n = -35$  (d) $9n = -18$

(e) $6n = -36$  (f) $-5n = 30$  (g) $-9n = 27$  (h) $-3n = 24$

(i) $-7n = -28$  (j) $-6n = -42$  (k) $-3n = 18$  (l) $-10n = -60$

**3** Solve:

(a) $n \div 3 = -6$        (b) $n \div 2 = -8$        (c) $n \div 3 = -2$        (d) $\dfrac{n}{5} = -3$

(e) $\dfrac{n}{2} = -4$        (f) $\dfrac{n}{-3} = 7$        (g) $\dfrac{n}{-2} = 3$        (h) $\dfrac{n}{-1} = -6$

(i) $\dfrac{n}{-5} = 4$        (j) $\dfrac{n}{2} = -9$        (k) $\dfrac{n}{-2} = -2$        (l) $\dfrac{n}{7} = -2$

**4** If $2n = 1$ then $n = \frac{1}{2}$ because $2 \times \boxed{\frac{1}{2}} = 1$

This answer could also be written as $n = 0.5$
Solve these equations:

(a) $2n = 3$        (b) $2n = 7$        (c) $2n = -1$        (d) $2n = -5$

(e) $3n = 1$        (f) $4n = 6$        (g) $10n = -3$        (h) $2n = -9$

(i) $8n = 2$        (j) $5n = -4$        (k) $7n = -1$        (l) $9n = -2$

## Solving longer equations

(a) Solve $5n+2 = 17$                    OR            Solve $5n+2=17$

$\boxed{5n} + 2 = 17$

↑

This box $=15$ because $\boxed{15} + 2 = 17$

So $\boxed{5n} = 15$                                          Take off 2 from each pan

↓

$5n$ means $5 \times n$

So $5 \times n = 15$

So $n = 3$ because $5 \times \boxed{3} = 15$                Each $\boxed{n}$ must equal 3 because $5\boxed{n}$ boxes are equal to 15

So $n = 3$

**M12.4**

In Questions **1** to **6** , copy and fill the empty boxes.

**1** $\boxed{2n} +1 = 17$                    **2** $\boxed{4n} +3 = 23$                    **3** $\boxed{5n} + 7 = 17$

$\boxed{2n} = 16$                              $\boxed{4n} = 20$                              $\boxed{5n} = \boxed{\phantom{0}}$

$n = \boxed{\phantom{0}}$                        $n = \boxed{\phantom{0}}$                        $n = \boxed{\phantom{0}}$

322

**4** $\boxed{2n} - 4 = 20$

$\boxed{2n} = 24$

$n = \boxed{\phantom{0}}$

**5** $\boxed{3n} - 7 = 14$

$\boxed{3n} = 21$

$n = \boxed{\phantom{0}}$

**6** $\boxed{5n} - 4 = 26$

$\boxed{5n} = \boxed{\phantom{0}}$

$n = \boxed{\phantom{0}}$

Find the value of $n$ in Questions **7** to **10** :

**7** $\boxed{n}\boxed{n}\boxed{n}\boxed{4}$ $\boxed{10}$ ▲

**8** $\boxed{n}\boxed{n}\boxed{7}$ $\boxed{19}$ ▲

**9** $\boxed{n}\boxed{n}\boxed{n}\boxed{n}\boxed{n}\boxed{3}$ $\boxed{28}$ ▲

**10** $\boxed{n}\boxed{n}\boxed{n}\boxed{6}$ $\boxed{30}$ ▲

Solve these equations:

**11** $5n + 6 = 21$

**12** $5n + 7 = 17$

**13** $4n + 3 = 23$

**14** $4n + 7 = 19$

**15** $5n + 4 = 34$

**16** $3n - 6 = 9$

**17** $3n - 2 = 10$

**18** $6n - 1 = 29$

**19** $8n - 3 = 21$

**20** $7n + 6 = 34$

**21** $4n + 10 = 26$

**22** $5n - 5 = 45$

**23** $10n - 2 = 38$

**24** $4n - 9 = 23$

**25** $7n - 12 = 9$

**26** $9n - 5 = 22$

**27** $3n - 8 = 22$

**28** $6n + 8 = 26$

**29** $5n + 12 = 32$

**30** $10n + 13 = 73$

**31** $8n - 4 = 84$

## Equations with 'trickier' numbers

(a) Solve $3n + 1 = 2$
Subtract 1 from each
side of equation        $3n = 1$

divide each side of
equation by 3     $\dfrac{3n}{3} = \dfrac{1}{3}$

$n = \dfrac{1}{3}$

(b) Solve $5n + 13 = 3$
Subtract 13 from
each side of equation     $5n = -10$

divide each side of
equation by 5        $n = -2$

(d) Solve $18 = 20 + 3n$
Subtract 20 from each
side of equation        $-2 = 3n$

(c) Solve $2 - 3n = 14$
Subtract 2 from each
side of equation     $-3n = 12$

divide each side of
equation by -3     $n = -4$

divide each side of
equation by 2        $\dfrac{-2}{3} = \dfrac{3n}{3}$

$\dfrac{-2}{3} = n$

so $n = \dfrac{-2}{3}$

In Questions **1** to **6** , copy and fill the empty boxes.

**1** $\boxed{2n}$ + 1 = 4

$\boxed{2n}$ = 3

$n = \boxed{\phantom{x}}$

**2** $\boxed{10n}$ + 7 = 14

$\boxed{10n}$ = $\boxed{\phantom{x}}$

$n = \boxed{\phantom{x}}$

**3** $\boxed{4n}$ + 11 = 8

$\boxed{4n}$ = − 3

$n = \boxed{\phantom{x}}$

**4** 5 $\boxed{-2n}$ = 11

$\boxed{-2n}$ = 6

$n = \boxed{\phantom{x}}$

**5** − 4 $\boxed{-3n}$ = − 10

$\boxed{-3n}$ = − 6

$n = \boxed{\phantom{x}}$

**6** 30 = 40 $\boxed{+2n}$

$\boxed{\phantom{x}}$ = 2n

$\boxed{\phantom{x}}$ = n

Solve these equations:

**7** $3x + 4 = 6$

**8** $5x + 8 = 12$

**9** $2x + 9 = 8$

**10** $4x + 9 = 5$

**11** $3x + 8 = 7$

**12** $8x + 5 = 2$

**13** $6x + 10 = 5$

**14** $6x + 19 = 16$

**15** $4x + 3 = 17$

In questions **16** to **21** below, I am thinking of a number. Write down an equation then solve it to find the number.

> If we multiply the number by 3 and then add 1, the answer is 3.
>
> Let the number be $n$.       Equation is $3n + 1 = 3$
>
> Solve: $3n = 2$       so       $n = \dfrac{2}{3}$

**16** If we multiply the number by 4 and then add 2, the answer is 3.

**17** If we multiply the number by 7 and then add 5, the answer is 8.

**18** If we multiply the number by 5 and then add 11, the answer is 6.

**19** If we double the number and add 7, the answer is 1.

**20** If we multiply the number by 8 and subtract 4, the answer is −20.

**21** If we treble the number and add 8, the answer is −7.

Solve these equations:

**22** $7x + 8 = -6$

**23** $4x - 6 = -22$

**24** $6x - 2 = -20$

**25** $9x + 4 = -32$

**26** $14 = 20 + 2x$

**27** $31 = 39 + 4x$

**28** $8 = 33 + 5x$

**29** $9 - 2x = 17$

**30** $16 - 5x = 31$

**31** $13 - 7x = -22$

**32** $-6 = 9 + 3x$

**33** $20 = 48 - 7x$

**12B** **Multiply out brackets (see Unit 4)**

1. Jane says '3 $(2a + 1) = 6a + 1$'.

   Meg says '3 $(2a + 1) = 6a + 3$'.

   Who is correct?

Expand (multiply out)

2. $5(a + 2)$  
3. $2(3a + 2)$  
4. $6(2x - 1)$  
5. $4(5n + 3)$

6. $3(b + 2c)$  
7. $5(3a - 2b)$  
8. $9(2x - y)$  
9. $b(c - e)$

10. $x(x + 3)$  
11. $-4(x + 2)$  
12. $-6(y - 3)$  
13. $-3(3x - 2)$

## Equations with brackets

(a)  Solve          $3(n+2) = 12$

multiply out
brackets first          $3n + 6 = 12$

subtract 6 from each
side of equation          $3n = 6$

                              $n = 2$

(b)  Solve          $5(2n-1) = 45$

multiply out
brackets first          $10n - 5 = 45$

add 5 onto each
side of equation          $10n = 50$

                              $n = 5$

### M12.5

In Questions **1** to **3**, copy and fill the empty boxes.

**1**  $3(n + 1) = 12$

$3n + \boxed{\phantom{0}} = 12$

$3n = \boxed{\phantom{0}}$

$n = \boxed{\phantom{0}}$

**2**  $5(n - 2) = 30$

$\boxed{\phantom{0}} - 10 = 30$

$\boxed{\phantom{0}} = 40$

$n = \boxed{\phantom{0}}$

**3**  $4(2n + 3) = 28$

$8n + \boxed{\phantom{0}} = 28$

$8n = \boxed{\phantom{0}}$

$n = \boxed{\phantom{0}}$

Solve these equations:

**4** $4(n+2) = 20$      **5** $5(n+1) = 50$      **6** $8(n+3) = 40$

**7** $3(n-4) = 6$      **8** $3(2n+1) = 27$      **9** $2(4n-4) = 12$

**10** $5(2n+3) = 75$      **11** $9(2n+1) = 27$      **12** $3(5n-6) = 42$

**13** $2(2n-4) = 20$      **14** $5(4n+5) = 105$      **15** $3(3n-4) = 33$

**16** $4(2n+5) = 52$      **17** $2(5n-7) = 76$      **18** $6(n-9) = 12$

**19** $3(3n-7) = 24$      **20** $10(2n-6) = 40$      **21** $8(2n-3) = 8$

In Questions **22** to **25**, I am thinking of a number. Write down an equation then solve it to find the number.

---

Add double the number onto 4 then multiply the answer by 3. This gives 24.

Let the number be $n$.

Equation is          $(2n + 4) \times 3 = 24$

We write this as      $3(2n + 4) = 24$

Solve:            $6n + 12 = 24$

                       $6n = 12$

                       $n = 2$

---

**22** Add the number onto 5 then multiply the answer by 6. This gives 48.

**23** Add treble the number onto 2 then multiply the answer by 2. This gives 46.

**24** Take away 4 from double the number then multiply the answer by 5. This gives 30.

**25** Subtract 7 from treble the number then multiply the answer by 4. This gives 8.

### Equations with brackets and 'trickier' numbers

---

(a) Solve $2(n+3) = 5$

Multiply out brackets first      $2n + 6 = 5$

Subtract 6 from each side of equation      $2n = -1$

divide each side of equation by 2      $\dfrac{2n}{2} = \dfrac{-1}{2}$

                     $n = \dfrac{-1}{2}$

(b) Solve $36 = 4(1-2n)$

Multiply out brackets first      $36 = 4 - 8n$

Subtract 4 from each side of equation      $32 = -8n$

divide each side of equation by $-8$      $\dfrac{32}{-8} = \dfrac{-8n}{-8}$

                     $-4 = n$

                     so $n = -4$

---

In Questions **1** to **6** , copy and fill the empty boxes.

**1** $5(x + 3) = 10$

$\boxed{\phantom{x}} + 15 = 10$

$\boxed{\phantom{x}} = -5$

$x = \boxed{\phantom{x}}$

**2** $2(x + 9) = 14$

$2x + \boxed{\phantom{x}} = 14$

$2x = \boxed{\phantom{x}}$

$x = \boxed{\phantom{x}}$

**3** $3(2x + 5) = -3$

$6x + \boxed{\phantom{x}} = -3$

$6x = \boxed{\phantom{x}}$

$x = \boxed{\phantom{x}}$

**4** $3(x + 2) = 4$

$3x + \boxed{\phantom{x}} = 4$

$3x = \boxed{\phantom{x}}$

$x = \boxed{\phantom{x}}$

**5** $2(2x + 3) = 5$

$4x + \boxed{\phantom{x}} = 5$

$4x = \boxed{\phantom{x}}$

$x = \boxed{\phantom{x}}$

**6** $33 = 3(2 - 3x)$

$33 = 6 - \boxed{\phantom{x}}$

$27 = - \boxed{\phantom{x}}$

$\boxed{\phantom{x}} = x$

Solve these equations:

**7** $3(x + 2) = 6$

**8** $5(2x + 4) = 0$

**9** $4(x + 5) = 17$

**10** $5(x + 9) = 15$

**11** $2(4x + 10) = 4$

**12** $3(2x - 3) = -15$

**13** $4(2x - 3) = -20$

**14** $5(2x + 1) = 2$

**15** $5(4x + 3) = 8$

**16** $2(1 - 2x) = 14$

**17** $2(3 - 4x) = 30$

**18** $20 = 10(5 + x)$

**19** $85 = 5(5 - 2x)$

**20** $7 = 2(6 - 3x)$

**21** $25 = 8(4 + 5x)$

*Can you still?*

(12C) **Add, subtract and multiply decimals (see Unit 9)**

*Can you still?*

Work out

**1.** $16.2$
$+ \ 0.31$

**2.** $21.6$
$- \ 3.17$

**3.** $15.6 + 8 + 0.12$

**4.** $13.2 - 6$

**5.** $2.13 - 0.37$

**6.** $0.9 \times 0.02$

**7.** $0.7 \times 0.4$

**8.** $0.12 \times 7$

**9.** $0.5^2$

**10.** Copy and fill in the empty boxes

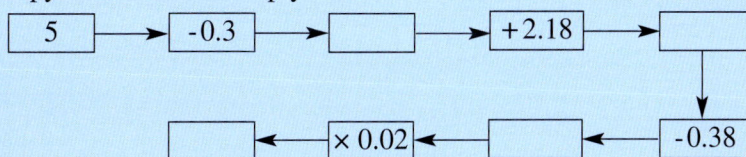

$\boxed{5} \rightarrow \boxed{-0.3} \rightarrow \boxed{\phantom{x}} \rightarrow \boxed{+2.18} \rightarrow \boxed{\phantom{x}}$

$\boxed{\phantom{x}} \leftarrow \boxed{\times 0.02} \leftarrow \boxed{\phantom{x}} \leftarrow \boxed{-0.38}$

## Equations with the unknown on both sides

(a)  Solve

$6n - 2 = 2n + 18$

Subtract $2n$ from each
side of equation                $4n - 2 = 18$

Add 2 onto each
side of equation                $4n = 20$

$n = 5$

(b)  Solve

$8n + 6 = 3n + 41$

Subtract $3n$ from each
side of equation                $5n + 6 = 41$

Subtract 6 from each
side of equation                $5n = 35$

$n = 7$

### M12.6

Find the value of $n$ in Questions **1** to **6** :

**1**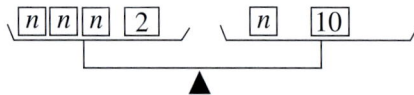

**2**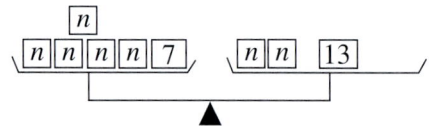

**3**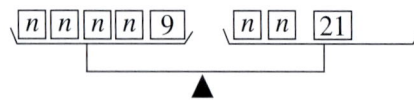

**4**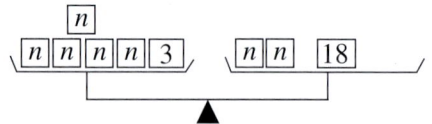

**5**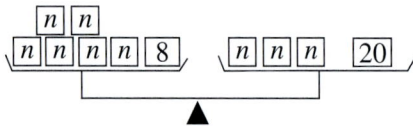

**6**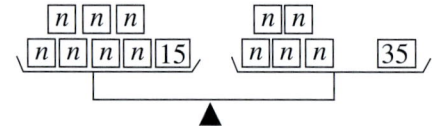

In Questions **7** to **9** , copy and fill the empty boxes.

**7**  $8n + 6 = 3n + 26$

$\boxed{5n} + 6 = 26$

$5n = \boxed{\phantom{0}}$

$n = \boxed{\phantom{0}}$

**8**  $9n - 4 = 5n + 20$

$\boxed{\phantom{0}} - 4 = 20$

$\boxed{\phantom{0}} = 24$

$n = \boxed{\phantom{0}}$

**9**  $6n - 1 = 4n + 11$

$2n - 1 = 11$

$2n = \boxed{\phantom{0}}$

$n = \boxed{\phantom{0}}$

Solve these equations:

**10** $7n + 3 = 3n + 27$

**11** $7n + 5 = 5n + 25$

**12** $10n + 2 = 7n + 14$

**13** $5n + 4 = 2n + 22$

**14** $6n + 8 = 2n + 36$

**15** $7n - 3 = 4n + 12$

Be careful!

**16** $5n - 2 = n + 10$

**17** $9n - 7 = 5n + 13$

**18** $11n - 9 = 5n + 27$

**19** $5n - 10 = 3n + 50$

**20** $8n - 3 = 2n + 39$

**21** $9n + 14 = 6n + 29$

**22** $10n + 17 = 3n + 52$

**23** $5n - 16 = n + 20$

**24** $8n - 22 = 2n + 8$

**25** $9n + 15 = 5n + 47$

## 'Trickier' equations with the unknown on both sides

(a)  Solve $7x - 2 = 3x - 10$

Subtract $3x$ from each
side of equation,    $4x - 2 = -10$
add 2 onto each side
of equation,                 $4x = -8$
                                      $x = -2$

(b)  Solve $8x + 4 = 34 - 2x$

Add $2x$ onto each
side of equation,      $10x + 4 = 34$
subtract 4 from each
side of equation,           $10x = 30$
                                         $x = 3$

(c)  Solve $5(2x + 3) = 2(3x + 8)$

multiply out brackets first,

subtract $6x$ from each side of equation,

subtract 15 from each side of equation,

divide each side of equation by 4,

$10x + 15 = 6x + 16$

$4x + 15 = 16$

$4x = 1$

$\dfrac{4x}{4} = \dfrac{1}{4}$

$x = \dfrac{1}{4}$

(d)  Solve $3(2x - 1) = 2(5 - x)$

multiply out brackets first,
add $2x$ onto each side of equation,
add 3 onto each side of equation,

divide each side of equation by 8,

$6x - 3 = 10 - 2x$

$8x - 3 = 10$

$8x = 13$

$\dfrac{8x}{8} = \dfrac{13}{8}$

$x = \dfrac{13}{8}$

we can write

$x = 1\dfrac{5}{8}$

In Questions **1** to **3** , copy and fill the empty boxes.

**1** $6x - 4 = 3x - 16$

$3x - 4 = -16$

$3x = \boxed{\phantom{00}}$

$x = \boxed{\phantom{00}}$

**2** $7x + 3 = 43 - x$

$\boxed{\phantom{00}} + 3 = 43$

$\boxed{\phantom{00}} = 40$

$x = \boxed{\phantom{00}}$

**3** $2(3x + 2) = 4(x + 3)$

$\boxed{\phantom{00}} + 4 = \boxed{\phantom{00}} + 12$

$\boxed{\phantom{00}} + 4 = 12$

$\boxed{\phantom{00}} = 8$

$x = \boxed{\phantom{00}}$

Solve these equations:

**4** $5x + 2 = 3 - 2x$

**5** $6x + 4 = 3 - 3x$

**6** $5x - 2 = x - 10$

**7** $9x + 4 = 3x - 1$

**8** $2x - 8 = 12 - 3x$

**9** $2 + 9x = 3 - x$

**10** $7x - 2 = 1 - 3x$

**11** $6x + 5 = 41 - 3x$

**12** $5x + 8 = 1 - 4x$

In Questions **13** to **16** below, I am thinking of a number. Write down an equation then solve it to find the number.

**13** If we multiply the number by 7 and add 4, the answer we get is the same as when we multiply the number by 3 and add 12.

**14** If we multiply the number by 8 and subtract 5, the answer we get is the same as when we multiply the number by 2 and add 19.

**15** If we treble the number and subtract from 9 we get the same answer as when we double the number and add 4.

**16** If we double the number, add 5 and then multiply the result by 3, the answer is 27.

Solve these equations:

**17** $3(2x + 3) = 2(x + 4)$

**18** $2(x + 2) = 5(x - 4)$

**19** $4(2x - 2) = 3(3x + 4)$

**20** $7(x - 1) = 2(2x + 4)$

**21** $8(x - 3) = 4(3 - x)$

**22** $6(x - 4) = 2(x - 1)$

**23** $3(x + 2) = 4(1 - x)$

**24** $3(2x + 1) = 4(7 - x)$

**25** $2(3x - 1) = 3(1 - 2x)$

**26** $5(2 - x) = 2(4 + 2x)$

**27** $2(3 - 2x) = 5(2 - x)$

**28** $4(x - 2) = 3(x + 3) - 4$

**29** $3(2x + 3) + 4(x - 2) = 8$

**30** $6(2x + 5) + 3(2 - 3x) = x$

(12D) **Dividing decimals** (see Unit 9)

Work out

1. $7\overline{)16.8}$

2. $9\overline{)41.4}$

3. $43.2 \div 6$

4. $3.44 \div 4$

5. $18 \div 0.5$

6. $4 \div 0.1$

7. 3 friends win £ 373.50 in a game. They share the money equally. How much does each friend get?

8. 4 people split a restaurant bill equally. If the bill is £ 78.40, how much does each person have to pay?

9. $3.8 \div 0.2$

10. $0.24 \div 0.3$

11. $17.2 \div 0.04$

12. A bottle of ginger beer holds 2 litres. How many glasses can be filled from this bottle if each glass holds 0.25 litres?

## Mixed equations

(a) The perimeter of this rectangle is 44 cm.

Find $x$ then write down the actual length and width of the rectangle.

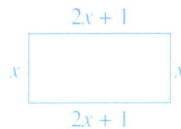

Perimeter $= x + 2x + 1 + x + 2x + 1 = 6x + 2$ (this is equal to 44 cm)

So $6x + 2 = 44$

$6x = 42$

$x = 7$

length $= 2x + 1 = 2 \times 7 + 1 = 15$ cm

width $= x = 7$ cm

(b) Solve $\dfrac{x}{3} + 4 = 6$

subtract 4 from each side of equation $\dfrac{x}{3} = 2$

$x = 6$

because $\dfrac{\boxed{6}}{3} = 2$

(c) Solve $\dfrac{x + 4}{3} = 6$

$x + 4 = 18$

because $\dfrac{18}{3} = 6$

so $x = 14$

Solve these equations:

**1**  $2x + 3 = 9$

**2**  $4x + 2 = 18$

**3**  $\dfrac{x}{2} + 5 = 10$

**4**  $\dfrac{x}{2} + 9 = 19$

**5**  $\dfrac{x}{3} + 4 = 9$

**6**  $\dfrac{x}{5} + 6 = 8$

**7**  $\dfrac{x}{3} + 12 = 19$

**8**  $3x - 2 = 16$

**9**  $6x - 1 = 23$

**10**  $5x - 3 = 32$

**11**  $\dfrac{x}{3} - 2 = 2$

**12**  $\dfrac{x}{4} - 3 = 2$

**13**  $\dfrac{x}{5} - 2 = 3$

**14**  $\dfrac{x}{6} - 3 = 2$

**15**  $\dfrac{x}{7} - 1 = 3$

**16**

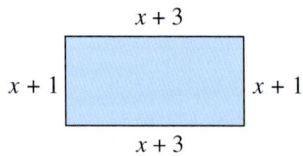

The perimeter of this rectangle is 28 cm.

(a) Write down an equation using the perimeter.

(b) Find $x$.

(c) Write down the actual length and width of the rectangle.

**17**

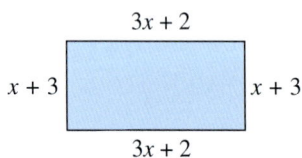

The perimeter of this rectangle is 58 cm.

(a) Write down an equation using the perimeter.

(b) Find $x$.

(c) Write down the actual length and width of the rectangle.

**18**  The perimeter of this rectangle is 34 cm.

(a) Write down an equation using the perimeter.

(b) Find $x$.

(c) Write down the actual length and width of the rectangle.

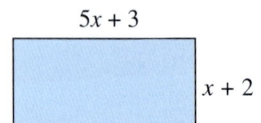

**19** The perimeter of this rectangle is 74 cm.

(a) Write down an equation using the perimeter.

(b) Find $x$.

(c) Write down the actual length and width of the rectangle.

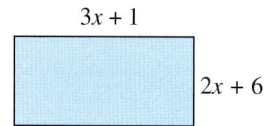

$3x + 1$

$2x + 6$

**20**

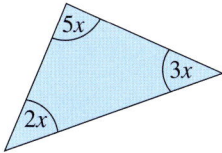

$5x$

$3x$

$2x$

(a) Write down an equation using the angles.

(b) Find $x$.

(c) Write down the actual value of each angle in this triangle.

**21**

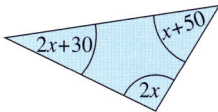

$2x+30$

$x+50$

$2x$

(a) Write down an equation using the angles.

(b) Find $x$.

(c) Write down the actual value of each angle in this triangle.

Solve these equations:

**22** $3x + 5 = 29$

**23** $\dfrac{x + 3}{2} = 4$

**24** $\dfrac{x + 5}{4} = 5$

**25** $\dfrac{x + 9}{3} = 7$

**26** $\dfrac{x}{3} + 2 = 7$

**27** $6x - 7 = 23$

**28** $\dfrac{x - 8}{2} = 5$

**29** $\dfrac{x - 3}{4} = 1$

**30** $\dfrac{x - 10}{3} = 2$

A rectangle has its length twice its width. If its perimeter is 42 cm, find the width of the rectangle.

Let $x$ = width    so length = $2x$

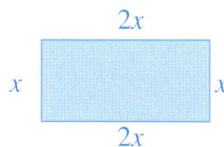

$2x$

$x$        $x$

$2x$

perimeter = $2x + x + 2x + x = 6x$

so $6x = 42$   (perimeter = 42)

$x = 7$

so width of rectangle = 7 cm.

Solve these equations:

**1**  $7x + 2 = 3x + 5$

**2**  $9x - 7 = 7x + 6$

**3**  $6x + 5 = 3x + 24$

**4**  $5x - 4 = x + 7$

**5**  $2(x + 9) = 5(x + 1)$

**6**  $6(x - 1) = 9(x - 3)$

**7**  $3(x - 1) = 2(x + 8)$

**8**  $5(2x - 3) = 2(3x + 3)$

**9**  $4(3x - 2) = 2(5x + 6)$

**10**  $3(2x - 1) = 4(x - 2)$

**11**  The area of this rectangle 20 cm².

**12**  The area of this rectangle is 46 cm².

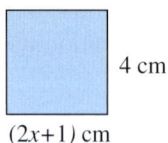

4 cm

2 cm

(2x+1) cm

(3x−1) cm

Find $x$ then write down the actual width of the rectangle.

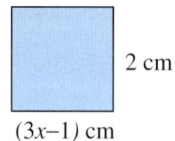

Find $x$ then write down the actual width of the rectangle.

**13**  A rectangle has its length 5 times its width. If the perimeter of the rectangle is 48 cm, find its length and width (remember: let width = $x$).

**14**  The length of a rectangle is 3 times its width. If the perimeter of the rectangle is 32 cm, find its length and width.

**15**

5x+30

2x+40

x+20

2x+30

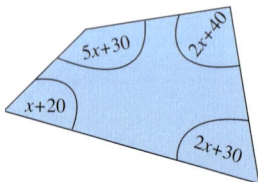

(a) Write down an equation using the angles.

(b) Find $x$.

(c) Write down the actual value of each angle in this quadrilateral.

**16**  A triangle has no angle 40° bigger than the smallest angle and the other angle 50° bigger than the smallest angle.

Find the size of each angle (hint : let $x$ = smallest angle).

**17**  A triangle has 2 angles which are each 4 times the size of the third angle. Find the size of each angle (hint : let $x$ = the third angle).

**18** There are 3 children in a family. Each is 3 years older than the next and the sum of the ages is 21. How old is each child? (hint : let $x$ = age of the youngest child)

**19** £190 is divided between Jack and Halle so that Jack receives £72 more than Halle. How much does each person get? (hint : let $x$ = Halle's money)

**20** A rectangular room is 2 m longer than it is wide. If its perimeter is 32 m, what is its area? (hint : let $x$ = width)

Solve these equations:

**21** $\dfrac{x - 5}{3} = 4$     **22** $\dfrac{x + 3}{2} = 7$     **23** $\dfrac{2x + 1}{4} = 5$     **24** $\dfrac{x + 6}{8} = -3$

**25** $\dfrac{3x - 2}{5} = 8$     **26** $\dfrac{7x - 3}{2} = 9$     **27** $\dfrac{9x - 5}{7} = 7$     **28** $\dfrac{5x + 29}{3} = 8$

**29** $\dfrac{20}{x} = 5$     **30** $8 = \dfrac{56}{x}$     **31** $\dfrac{36}{x} = 9$     **32** $7 = \dfrac{42}{x}$

*Can you still?*

*Can you still?*

**12E**    **Rounding off to decimal places/significant figures**

Round the numbers below to the accuracy shown in brackets:

1. 8.27 (1 decimal place)
2. 0.15 (1 decimal place)
3. 4.894 (2 decimal places)
4. 7.618 (3 significant figures)
5. 21.63 (2 significant figures)
6. 0.08236 (2 significant figures)
7. 8659 (3 significant figures)
8. 24.69 (1 decimal place)
9. 8.61847 (4 significant figures)
10. 481.93 (2 significant figures)

Use a calculator to work out the Questions below. Round each answer to 3 *significant figures*.

11. $6.2 \times 28.3$
12. $\sqrt{32}$
13. $418.6 \div 3.71$
14. $\dfrac{4.17 + 3.9}{8.67}$

## Trial and improvement

Sometimes it is not easy (or possible) to find the answer to a problem.

We can try out different numbers with a calculator until we get closer and closer to the answer.

$x$ cm

9 cm

The area of the rectangle is 65 cm².

Find $x$ to 1 decimal place.

Area $= 9 \times x$

so $9x = 65$

We will use trial and improvement to find $x$.

try $x = 8$        gives $9 \times 8 = 72$        too large

try $x = 7$        gives $9 \times 7 = 63$        too small

We want an answer of 65 so $x$ must be between 7 and 8.

try $x = 7.5$        gives $9 \times 7.5 = 67.5$        too large

try $x = 7.2$        gives $9 \times 7.2 = 64.8$        too small (by 0.2)

try $x = 7.3$        gives $9 \times 7.3 = 65.7$        too  large (by 0.7)

We want an answer of 65 so $x$ must be between 7.2 and 7.3. $x = 7.2$ gives an answer which is nearer than the answer given by $x = 7.3$.

$x = 7.2$ to 1 decimal place.

### M12.8

**1**

$x$ cm

6 cm

The area of this rectangle is 80 cm².

Copy and complete this table to find $x$ to one decimal place.

| trial | calculation | too large or too small? |
|---|---|---|
| $x = 13$ | $6 \times 13 = \ldots$ | too small |
| $x = 14$ | $6 \times 14 = \ldots$ | too large |
| $x = 13.5$ | $6 \times 13.5 = \ldots$ | too … |
| $x = 13.4$ | $6 \times 13.4 = \ldots$ | too … |
| $x = 13.3$ | $6 \times 13.3 = \ldots$ | too … |

so $x = \ldots$ to 1 decimal place.

**2**

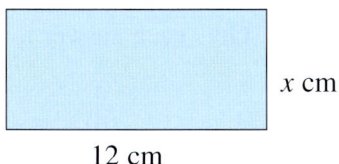

The area of this rectangle is 200 cm².

12 cm     $x$ cm

Copy and complete this table to find $x$ to one decimal place.

| trial | calculation | too large or too small? |
|---|---|---|
| $x = 17$ | $12 \times 17 = .....$ | too ...... |
| $x = 16.8$ | $12 \times 16.8 = .....$ | too ...... |
| $x = 16.6$ | $12 \times 16.6 = .....$ | too ...... |
| $x = 16.7$ | $12 \times 16.7 = .....$ | too ...... |

so $x = ...$ to 1 decimal place.

**3**

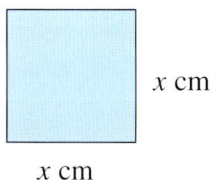

$x$ cm

$x$ cm

The area of this square is 130 cm².

Use trial and improvement to find $x$ to 1 decimal place.

**4** The volume of this cube is 100 cm³.

Volume $= x \times x \times x = x^3$

We want $x^3 = 100$

Copy and complete this table to find x to 1 decimal place.

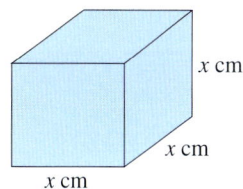

$x$ cm
$x$ cm
$x$ cm

| trial | calculation | too large or too small? |
|---|---|---|
| $x = 4$ | $4 \times 4 \times 4 = 64$ | too small |
| $x = 5$ | $5 \times 5 \times 5 =$ | too ... |
| $x = 4.5$ | $4.5 \times 4.5 \times 4.5 =$ | too ... |
| $x = 4.7$ | $4.7 \times 4.7 \times 4.7 =$ | too ... |
| $x = 4.6$ | $4.6 \times 4.6 \times 4.6 =$ | too ... |

so $x = ...$ to 1 decimal place.

**5**

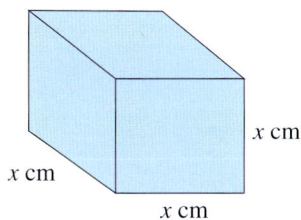

$x$ cm
$x$ cm
$x$ cm

The volume of this cube is 226 cm³.

Use trial and improvement to find $x$ to 1 decimal place.

337

**6** Solve these equations by trial and improvement. Give each answer to 1 decimal place.

(a) $x^2 = 60$        (b) $x^2 = 114$        (c) $x^3 = 71$        (d) $x^3 = 460$

**7**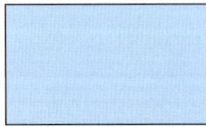

$x$ cm

$(x + 3)$ cm

The area of this rectangle is 250 cm².

area $= x \times (x + 3) = x(x + 3)$

we want $x(x + 3) = 250$

If we try $x = 15$, we get $15 \times 18 = 270$ which is too large.

Use trial and improvement to find $x$ to 1 decimal place.

### Greater accuracy

*Choosing the correct answer:*

Look at the earlier example.

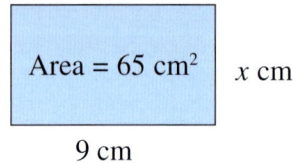

We found $x = 7.2$ gave an area of 64.8 cm²
and $x = 7.3$ gave an area of 65.7 cm²

To choose the correct value of $x$ to 1 decimal place, we should test the value *half way* between $x = 7.2$ and $x = 7.3$, ie. $x = 7.25$.

$x = 7.25$ gives area $= 9 \times 7.25 = 65.25$ cm².

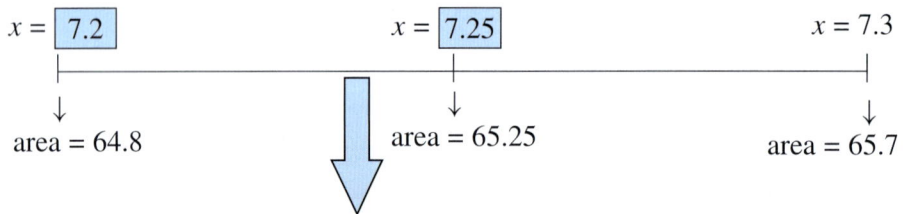

real area of 65 must be between these
2 values so is nearer to 7.2 than 7.3

so answer $= 7.2$ to 1 decimal place.

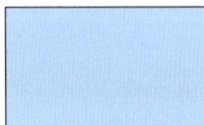

$x$ cm

$(x + 4)$ cm

The area of this rectangle is 325 cm².

Use trial and improvement to find $x$ to 2 *decimal places*.

area $= x(x + 4) = 325$.

| trial | calculation | too large or too small? |
|---|---|---|
| $x = 10$ | $10 \times 14 = 140$ | too small |
| $x = 20$ | $20 \times 24 = 480$ | too large |
| $x = 15$ | $15 \times 19 = 285$ | too small |
| $x = 17$ | $17 \times 21 = 357$ | too large |
| $x = 16$ | $16 \times 20 = 320$ | too small |
| **so $x$ is between 16 and 17.** | | |
| $x = 16.2$ | $16.2 \times 20.2 = 327.24$ | too large |
| $x = 16.1$ | $16.1 \times 20.1 = 323.61$ | too small |
| **so $x$ is between 16.1 and 16.2.** | | |
| $x = 16.15$ | $16.15 \times 20.15 = 325.4225$ | too large |
| $x = 16.14$ | $16.14 \times 20.14 = 325.0596$ | too large |
| $x = 16.13$ | $16.13 \times 20.13 = 324.4969$ | too small |
| **so $x$ is between 16.13 and 16.14.** | | |
| **Test the half way value to choose the correct answer.** | | |
| $x = 16.135$ | $16.135 \times 20.135 = 324.878225$ | too small |

So $x$ is between 16.135 and 16.14

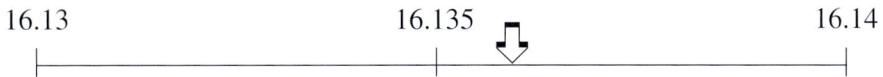

16.13        16.135        16.14

So $x$ is closer to 16.14

Answer: $x = 16.14$ to 2 decimal places.

## E12.8

**1**

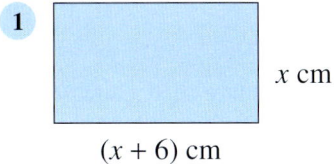

$x$ cm

$(x + 6)$ cm

The area of this rectangle is 270 cm$^2$.

area $= x(x + 6) = 270$

Use trial and improvement to find $x$ to 2 decimal places.

**2** The area of this rectangle is 500 cm$^2$

Use trial and improvement to find $x$ to 2 decimal places.

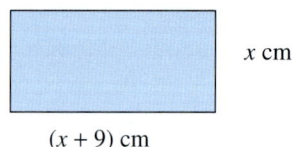

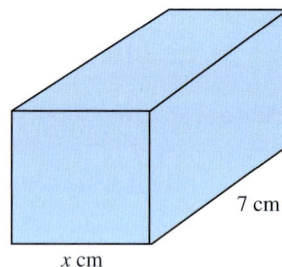

$x$ cm

$(x + 9)$ cm

**3** Solve these equations by trial and improvement. Give each answer to *1 decimal place*.

(a) $x^2+x = 24$     (b) $x^2-x = 62$     (c) $x^2+3x = 100$

(d) $x^3+x = 200$     (e) $x^3-x = 85$     (f) $x^3+2x = 170$

**4** $x$ cm

$x$ cm

$x$ cm

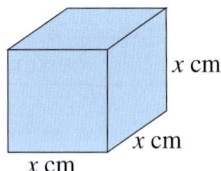

The volume of this cube is 650 cm$^3$.

Use trial and improvement to find $x$ to *2 decimal places*.

**5** Solve these equations by trial and improvement. Give each answer to *2 decimal places*.

(a) $x^3+x = 90$     (b) $x^3-2x = 120$     (c) $x^3+3x = 374$

**6** The volume of this cuboid is 300 cm$^3$

volume $= 7 \times x \times x = 7x^2$

so $7x^2 = 300$

Use trial and improvement to find $x$ to 2 decimal places.

(Remember: $7x^2 = x^2 \times 7$ not $(7x)^2$)

$x$ cm

$x$ cm

7 cm

**7** Solve these equations by trial and improvement. Give each answer to 2 decimal places.

(a) $9x^2 = 200$     (b) $4x^2 = 125$     (c) $5x^2 = 179$

**8** Solve $5^x = 62$ by trial and improvement. ($5^x$ is '5 to the power $x$'. On your calculator type | 5 | | y$^x$ | | your $x$ number | | = | )

Give your answer to 1 decimal place.

**9** Solve $8^x = 200$ by trial and improvement. Give your answer to 1 decimal place.

**10** $x$ cm

$x$ cm

6 cm

$x$ cm

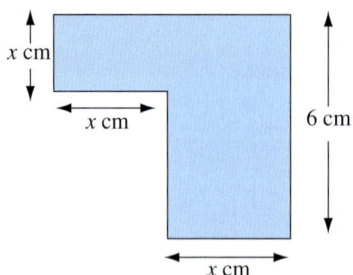

The total area of this shape is 74 cm$^2$

Use trial and improvement to find $x$. Give your answer to 2 decimal places.

If you do not have enough money to buy an item, you might buy *on credit*. There are different ways of doing this such as hire purchase, credit cards, store cards, bank overdrafts and personal loans.

**Make sure you know the true cost of buying on credit.**

This section deals with credit cards and store cards.

## Credit cards

- A credit card can be used to buy items now and pay for them at a later date. They can be used to get cash but this can be expensive to do.

- Credit cards are good if the person pays off the bill within a certain number of days. If the bill is not paid off, interest is charged which means the person will *owe even more money*.

- People usually have to be 18 or over to get a credit card (not everyone is able to get a credit card).

- Each person has a credit limit. If the person tries to spend more than this, the card will not work or the person will get a penalty charge.

## Monthly payment

If a person cannot pay off the bill in full, at least £5 or 5% of the total bill (whichever is the greater) has to be paid. The percentage may be different for some credit cards. If the person does not pay this, there will be a penalty charge and the person will *owe even more money*.

## APR (annual percentage rate)

Look at the APR to compare the cost of borrowing for different credit cards. The APR is given as a yearly percentage. It takes into account all the costs involved and the method of repayment.

In general, *the lower the APR, the better the deal.*

## Store cards

Credit cards can be an expensive way to borrow money over a long period of time. A store card often has a higher APR than a standard credit card so is even more expensive. The advantage of a store card is that you can spread out the cost of buying items and many stores give special offers with their cards at times.

### Richard's tale

Richard has a credit card with a credit limit of £3000. Each month the interest rate is 1.32%. During the first year of his credit card he spends up to his limit and at the end of January he owes £2998.

1  The credit card company want a payment of 5% of £2998. How much is this?

2  Richard cannot afford this payment so ignores it. The monthly interest of 1.32% of £2998 is added onto his debt. How much does he now owe? (give your answer to the nearest penny)

3  Richard did not make his monthly payment so has a penalty charge of £20. How much does he now owe?

4  The credit card company notice that Richard has gone over his credit limit and decide to increase his limit to £5000. How much money is Richard now allowed to spend before reaching this limit?

5  Over the next 4 months Richard spends happily and his credit card debt increases by another £1879. How much does he now owe?

6  The monthly payment is due. This is 5% of what Richard now owes. How much is the monthly payment? (give your answer to the nearest penny)

7  Richard can afford no more than £200. How much more would he need to make the monthly payment?

8  He fails to make this payment. The monthly interest of 1.32% of his debt is added onto his debt. How much does he now owe? (give your answer to the nearest penny)

9  Richard gets a penalty charge of £20 for not making his monthly payment. How much does he now owe?

10  Richard is now over his £5000 credit limit. He is getting more and more into debt. Maybe the credit card company will raise his credit limit again? What would be your advice to Richard? **Discuss with your teacher** the advantages and disadvantages of credit cards.

**1.** Finding numbers in sequences

For each sequence below, write down the *next 2 numbers*. What is the rule for each sequence?

(a) 5, 9, 13, 17...

(b) 3, 6, 12, 24...

(c) 25, 22, 19, 16...

(d) 1, 11, 21, 31...

(e)
    1    4    9    16    ...

(f) 160, 80, 40, 20...

(g)
    1    3    6    10    ...

(h) 3, 6, 11, 18...

**2.** Finding rules for sequences

(a) The first term of the sequence is 5 and the term-to-term rule is 'add 7'. Write down the first 5 terms of the sequence.

(b) Write down the term-to-term rule for the sequence:

    41, 33, 25, 17…

(c) Sequence 4, 7, 10, 13…

| n | 1 | 2 | 3 | 4 |
|---|---|---|---|---|
| term | 4 | 7 | 10 | 13 |
| 3n | 3 | 6 | 9 | 12 |

Use this table to find the $n^{th}$ term of the sequence.

(d) Make a table like the one above to find the $n^{th}$ term of the sequence 5, 7, 9, 11…

(e) Find the $n^{th}$ term of the sequence 3, 8, 13, 18…

(f) Here is a sequence of shapes made from sticks. Let $n$ = shape number and $s$ = number of sticks.

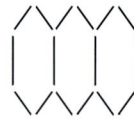

n = 1    n = 2    n = 3
s = 6    s = 11   s = 16

(i) Draw the next shape in the sequence.

(ii) Find a formula for the number of sticks (s) for the shape number $n$.

(iii) Use the formula to find out how many sticks are in shape number 100.

## 3. Solving equations

Solve these equations:

(a) $n + 4 = 11$  (b) $n - 3 = 12$  (c) $5n = 40$

(d) $\dfrac{n}{3} = 8$  (e) $6x = -18$  (f) $7x + 2 = 30$

(g) $4x - 9 = 23$  (h) $10n + 8 = 58$  (i) $9x - 7 = 38$

(j) Tom thinks of a number and then subtracts 8. If the answer is 19, what number did Tom think of?

## 4. Solving equations with brackets

Solve these equations:

(a) $3(n + 2) = 24$  (b) $5(n + 3) = 55$  (c) $2(2n - 5) = 30$

(d) $3(2n + 3) = 39$  (e) $4(n - 5) = 16$  (f) $2(3n + 4) = 56$

## 5. Solving equations with the unknown on both sides

Solve these equations:

(a) $9n + 3 = 7n + 13$  (b) $8n + 4 = 3n + 24$  (c) $7n - 4 = 3n + 24$

(d) $10x - 8 = 4x + 16$  (e) $6x + 2 = 4x + 3$  (f) $2x + 6 = 36 - 3x$

## 6. Setting up equations and solving them

(a) I think of a number. If I multiply the number by 5 and add 3, the answer is 38. What is my number?

(b)

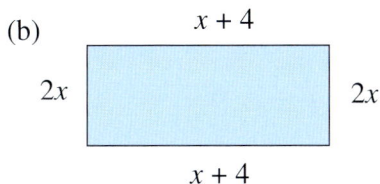

The perimeter of this rectangle is 50 cm.

(i) Write down an equation using the perimeter.

(ii) Find $x$.

(iii) Write down the actual length and width of the rectangle.

(c) One angle in a triangle is double the smallest angle and one angle is treble the smallest angle.

Find the size of each angle (hint : let $x$ = smallest angle).

## 7. Solving equations by trial and improvement

(a)

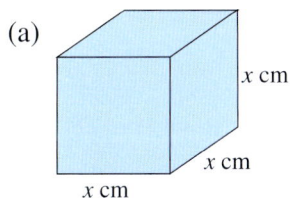

The volume of this cube is 280 cm³.

Use trial and improvement to find $x$ to 1 decimal place.

(b) Solve these equations by trial and improvement. Give each answer to 1 decimal place.

(i) $x^2 + x = 96$

(ii) $x^3 - 2x = 135$

(c) Solve $x^3 - x = 82$ by trial and improvement. Give the answer to *2 decimal places*.

## Mixed examination questions

**1** The first five terms of a sequence are given.

$$5, 3, 1, -1, -3\ldots$$

(i) What is the next term in the sequence?

(ii) Write down the $n^{th}$ term of the sequence.　　　　　　(AQA)

**2** Solve 　　(i) $5x - 7 = 23$ 　　(ii) $2(3x + 7) = 38$ 　　(CCEA)

**3** Solve these equations.

(a) $5x - 2 = 13$ 　　(b) $3(2x - 1) = 9$ 　　(WJEC)

**4** Use a trial and improvement method to find a solution to the equation

$$x^3 + x = 22.$$

Give your answer correct to one decimal place.

You must show all your trials. (AQA)

**5** (a) Here are the first five odd numbers: 1, 3, 5 , 7, 9

(i) Write down the tenth odd number

(ii) What is the twentieth odd number?

(b) Here are the first four terms of a sequence: 21, 20, 17, 12...
Write down the next two terms in the sequence. (CCEA)

**6** Solve these equations.

(i) $\dfrac{x}{3} = 10$      (ii) $5x - 3 = 7$      (iii) $2(3x + 2) = 7$      (OCR)

**7** Solve the following equations.

(a) $4x - 5 = 7$      (b) $\dfrac{x}{2} = -10$      (c) $3(z - 2) = 27$      (WJEC)

**8** Solve $2(5x + 3) = 23$ (OCR)

**9** Alistair is 3 years older than Simon. Simon is now $x$ years old.

(i) Write down Alistair's age in terms of $x$.
The total of their ages is 29 years.

(ii) Write down an equation in $x$.

(iii) Solve your equation to find $x$. (OCR)

**10** Use a trial and improvement method to find the value of $x$ correct to two decimal places when

$$x^3 + 4x = 9.$$

You must show all your trials. (OCR)

**In this unit you will learn how to:**

– find the mean, median, mode and range for sets of numbers

– use charts and graphs

– use stem and leaf diagrams

– use pie charts

– use two-way tables

– ( WATCH YOUR MONEY! ) – credit 3 –

personal loans.

## Averages and range

The shoe sizes of 6 people were:

$$6, 2, 8, 5, 8, 7$$

*add up all the numbers*

(a)  *mean* shoe size $= \dfrac{6 + 2 + 8 + 5 + 8 + 7}{6}$

*the total number of people*

$$= \dfrac{36}{6} = 6$$

(b)  arrange the shoe sizes in order:

$$2\ 5\ 6\ 7\ 8\ 8$$

$\uparrow$

the median is the $\frac{1}{2}$-way number

$$median = \dfrac{6 + 7}{2} = 6.5$$

(c)  *mode* = 8 because there are more 8s than any other number.

(d)  *range* = highest number – lowest number

$$= 8 - 2$$
$$= 6$$

# Key Facts

**mean** – add up the data then divide by the number of items

**median** – put numbers in order of size then choose middle item

**mode** – the item which occurs most often

**range** – largest value – smallest value

## M13. 1

1.  Copy and fill the empty boxes.
    The marks scored by 7 students in a test are:

    5    2    8    5    9    7    6

    (a) The *range* is the highest mark ☐ – the lowest mark ☐ = ☐

    (b) The *mode* is the most common value, which is ☐

    (c) The *median* is the middle value when the numbers are arranged in size order:

    ☐ ☐ ☐ ☐ ☐ ☐ ☐

    median = ☐

    (d) The *mean* is the total marks ☐ ÷ 7 = ☐

2.  Find the range of each set of numbers:

    (a) 12, 5, 17, 21, 3, 18, 14, 22, 16, 14

    (b) 17, 92, 36, 24, 35, 21, 53, 94, 68

    (c) 6, 7.5, 4.2, 6.8, 3.3, 7, 7.6, 5.7

3.  Find the mode of each set of numbers:

    (a) 7, 3, 4, 7, 6, 3, 7, 8, 1, 5, 6, 7, 6

    (b) 12, 13, 18, 13, 12, 19, 17, 13, 18, 12, 17, 13

    (c) 2.1, 0.8, 3.4, 0.4, 0.7, 2.6, 0.8, 0.7, 2.4, 0.8

**4** Find the median of each set of numbers:

(a) 3, 6, 2, 8, 5, 7, 9, 8, 6

(b) 12, 8, 7, 10

(c) 5.6, 2.1, 7.8, 6.3, 4.9

(d) 3, 7, 9, 4, 5, 3, 4, 7, 8, 5, 6, 1, 3, 7

**5** Find the mean average of each set of numbers:

(a) 8, 6, 9, 4, 8

(b) 3, 7, 5, 9, 5, 2, 9, 8

(c) 14, 16, 12, 15, 17, 16

(d) 5, 7, 4, 8, 7, 6, 5, 9, 4, 4

**6** The heights (in cm) of 8 people are:

162     183     171     169     153     171     168     170

Find the median height.

**7** The parents of 5 children were asked how much money they spent on each child last Christmas. The money is shown below:

£200        £300        £160        £280        £260

Find the mean average amount of money spent on each child last Christmas.

**8** The temperature was recorded at midnight in nine towns. The readings were:

2°, -3°, 0°, 1°, −1°, -2°, 0°, -4°, -2°

What was the range of the temperatures?

**9** On a school trip, the ages of the boys were 14, 14, 12, 15, 12, 11 and the ages of the girls were 13, 16, 15, 12.

(a) Find the mean age for the boys.

(b) Find the mean age for the girls.

(c) Find the mean age for all the children.

**10**

| 2 | 9 | 5 | 3 | 5 | 8 | 9 | 7 |

For the set of numbers above, find

(a) the mean

(b) the median

(c) the mode

(d) the range

**Mean, median or mode?**

When working out an average, how do I choose which one to use?

Look at the numbers 1, 1, 1, 1, 66

$$\text{mean} = \frac{70}{5} = 14 \qquad\qquad \text{median} = 1$$

Since each number is 1 except the last number, the median gives a more sensible idea of the average.

The mean average is distorted by the one high value 66.

# 🔑 Key Facts

If a set of numbers has extreme values, the mean average can be distorted so it is often better to use the median.

The median and mode are not calculated using all the numbers in the list but the mode is good for finding the most likely value and for data which are not numbers.

The mean average is better for numbers which are spread out in a balanced way.

## E13. 1

You may *use a calculator* for this exercise.

1   The shoe sizes of the students in a year 11 class were:

7,   8,   8,   5,   7,   7,   5,   7,   6,   7

5,   10,   7,   11,   9,   7,   7,   6,   8,   10

Find (a) the mode (b) the mean. Which average best describes these shoe sizes, the mode or the mean? Explain why.

2   For the set of numbers below, find (a) the mean and (b) the median.

| 0 | 1 | 1 | 1 | 2 | 2 | 70 |

(c) Which average best describes this set of numbers? Explain why.

3   The list below shows how many pupils are in each class in Marygate High School.

31   29   26   27   24   28   30   29   28

27   27   30   25   28   24   21   28   27

These numbers are spread out in a balanced way, so find the mean average number of pupils per class.

**4** The list below shows the yearly salaries of all the people who work at 'Easiprint'.

| £7000 | £6900 | £6900 | £138000 |
|-------|-------|-------|---------|
| £7500 | £5600 | £5900 | £7100 |
| £7000 | £7700 | £7900 | £7200 |

(a) Which kind of average would be the most sensible to use? Explain why.

(b) Work out this average.

**5** One year the first 12 rounds of golf for Tiger Woods were:

68   69   71   70   73   69   70   66   69   66   70   67

What was his mean average score?

**6** Write down 3 numbers with a mean of 7.

**7** Write down another 3 *different* numbers with a mean of 7.

**8** Write down 7 numbers with a median of 6.

**9** Jenny has 5 cards. The 5 cards have a mean of 9 and a range of 6.

| | 8 | 9 | 10 | |
|---|---|---|----|---|

What are the missing 2 numbers?

**10** The mean average pocket money received by 6 children is £5 each week.

(a) What is the total amount of pocket money received by the 6 children each week?

(b) Rowan joins the 6 children. Rowan gets £12 pocket money each week. What is the mean average pocket money for all 7 children?

**11** The mean height of 20 people is 160 cm.

(a) What is the total height of all 20 people?

(b) One person of height 179 cm leaves the group. Find the mean height of the remaining 19 people.

**12** A theatre needs a mean average of 220 people to attend each show if it is to make enough money to stay open.

The mean average for the first 23 shows is 216. How many people must attend the next show so that the mean average will become 220?

**13** In 3 cricket innings, Tariq has a median score of 42 and a mean score of 38. The range of the 3 scores is 14.

What are the three scores?

**14** The 6 months below have a mean of 9. What is the value of $x$?

| 12 | 3 | 8 | $x$ | 17 | 6 |

**15** In one football game, the mean age of the England team was equal to the mean age of the France team. 21 of the ages are shown below.

| England | 33 | 24 | 26 | 26 | 28 | 31 | 29 | 32 | 35 | 27 | 28 |
|---------|----|----|----|----|----|----|----|----|----|----|----|
| France  | 24 | 27 | $x$ | 27 | 34 | 29 | 33 | 22 | 33 | 29 | 30 |

Find the value of $x$.

*Can you still?*  *Can you still?*

**13A**  **Number Work (see Unit 1)**

Copy the crossnumber puzzle onto squared paper. Use the clues to complete the crossnumber puzzle.

| 1 | | 2 | | 3 |
|---|---|---|---|---|
| | | 4 | | |
| | | | | |
| 5 | | 6 | | |
| 7 | | 8 | | |

Clues across
**1.** 157 + 394
**4.** 831 - 236
**5.** 201 × 4
**7.** -3 + 17
**8.** -8 × -4

Clues down
**1.** 712 - 187
**2.** 130 × 12
**3.** 1575 ÷ 35
**5.** 504 ÷ 6
**6.** 602 ÷ 14

## Charts and graphs

**M13.2**

**1** The pictogram below shows how many year 10 students were absent from school during one week.

How many students were absent on:

(a) Friday?

(b) Wednesday?

(c) Thursday?

(d) How many *more* students were absent on Thursday than on Tuesday?

| Monday | ☺ ☺ |
| Tuesday | ☺ ☹ |
| Wednesday | ☺ ☺ ☹ |
| Thursday | ☺ ☺ ☺ ☹ |
| Friday | ☺ ☺ ☺ |

☺ means 10 students

**2** In Hart High School, students choose their year 10 options. 60 students choose History, 70 choose Geography, 30 choose Business Studies, 15 choose Spanish and 45 choose Art. Copy and complete the pictogram below:

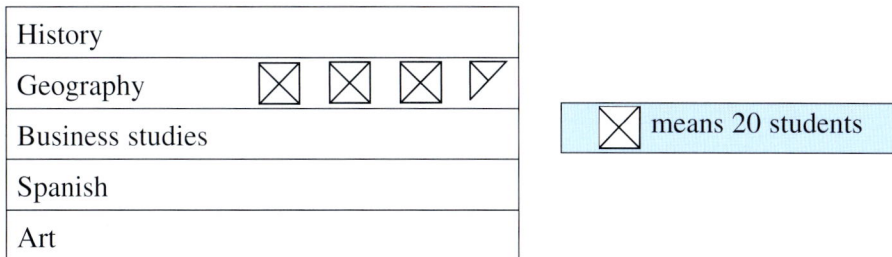

| History | |
|---|---|
| Geography | ⊠ ⊠ ⊠ ▷ |
| Business studies | |
| Spanish | |
| Art | |

⊠ means 20 students

**3** The chart below shows the amount of money spent on different items by the average household in Wales in 2002.

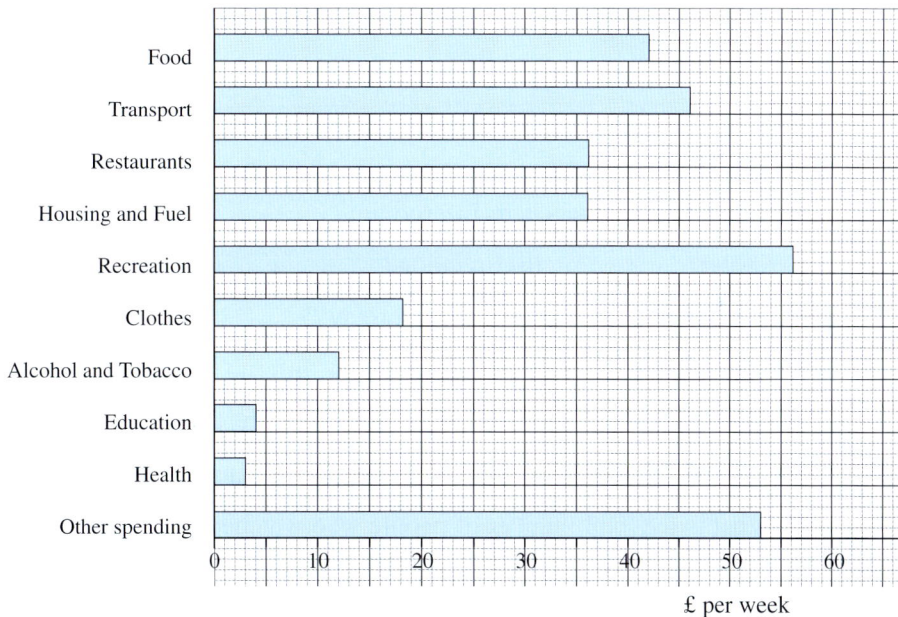

£ per week

How much money was spent on:

(a) transport          (b) education          (c) clothes

(d) How much *more* money was spent on recreation than on health?

(e) What was the total amount of money spent on food and restaurants?

(f) What was the total amount spent on everything each week?

**4** Two bands, 'Inferno' and 'Hotplay', tour part of the UK. The bar chart shows how many people watched each concert.

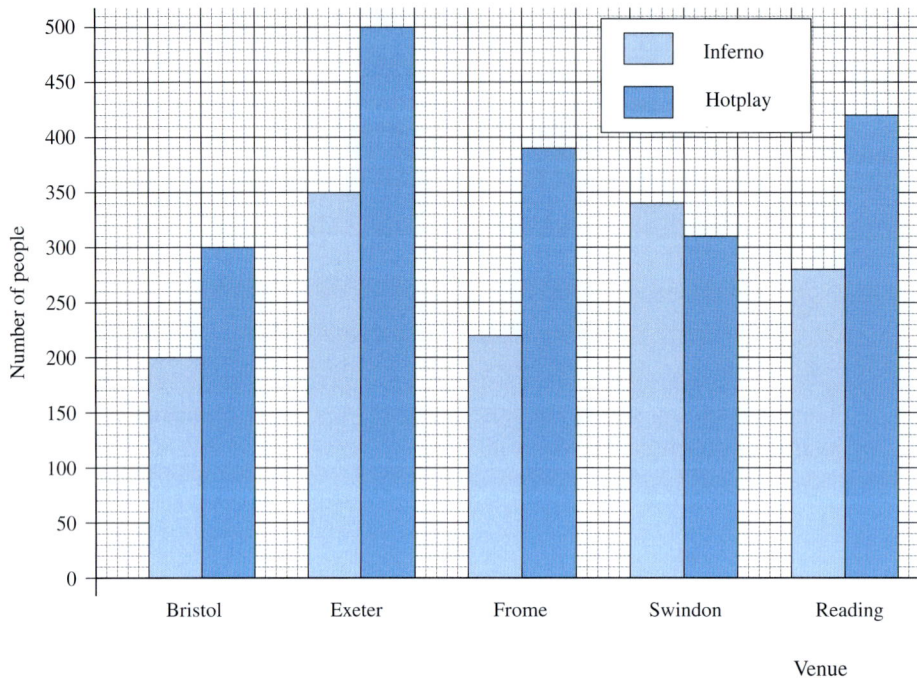

How many people watched 'Inferno' in:

(a) Exeter?          (b) Swindon?          (c) Reading?

(d) Where did 310 people watch 'Hotplay'?

(e) In which place did more people watch 'Inferno' than 'Hotplay'?

(f) How many *more* people watched 'Hotplay' than 'Inferno' in Bristol?

(g) How many *more* people watched 'Hotplay' than 'Inferno' in Reading?

(h) What is the total number of people who watched 'Hotplay' in all 5 venues?

**5** A supermarket is looking for new workers. The table shows how many people are interviewed each day during one week.

Draw a bar chart to show the information in the table.

| Day | Number of people |
|---|---|
| Monday | 6 |
| Tuesday | 8 |
| Wednesday | 4 |
| Thursday | 9 |
| Friday | 3 |
| Saturday | 5 |

**6** The graph shows the total number of pupils in Mount Henry High School from 1998 to 2005.

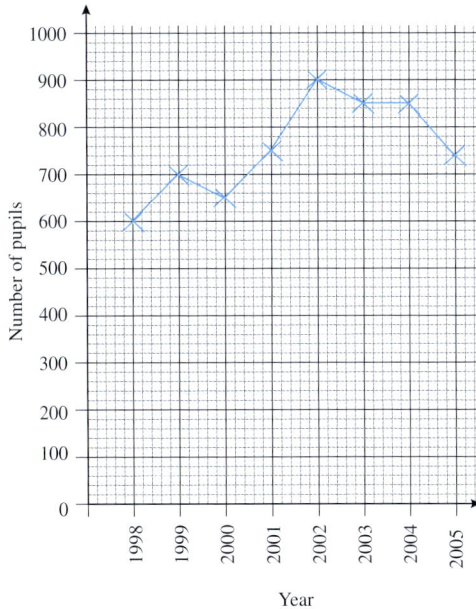

Year

How many pupils were at the school in:

(a) 2000

(b) 2001

(c) 2003

(d) 2005

(e) In which year were the highest number of pupils at the school?

(f) What is the *difference* between the number of pupils at the school in 2004 compared to 1999?

**7** The graph opposite shows the percentage of adults who smoked cigarettes in Great Britain.

What percentage of males smoked in:

(a) 1980

(b) 1986

(c) 1998

(d) What was the *drop* in the percentage of male smokers between 1974 and 2004?

(e) What was the *drop* in the percentage of female smokers between 1980 and 1998?

(f) What was the *difference* in the percentage of male smokers compared to female smokers in 1980?

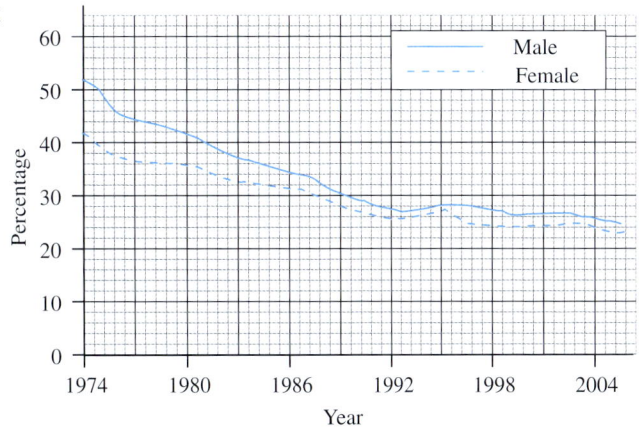

Year

**8** Some young people were asked how many computer games they have. The results are below:

| 8 | 3 | 13 | 7 | 15 | 5 | 11 | 18 | 23 | 2 | 0 | 1 | 16 | 8 |
|---|---|----|---|----|---|----|----|----|---|---|---|----|---|
| 26 | 9 | 8 | 24 | 12 | 0 | 28 | 13 | 9 | 15 | 13 | 21 | 19 | 4 |
| 12 | 8 | 11 | 21 | 17 | 7 | 16 | 22 | 18 | 6 | 0 | 14 | 22 | 12 |

(a) Copy and complete the tally chart below:

| Number of games | Tally | Total (Frequency) |
|---|---|---|
| 0–4 | JHT II | 7 |
| 5–9 | | |
| 10–14 | | |
| 15–19 | | |
| 20–24 | | |
| 25–29 | | |

(b) Copy and complete this frequency diagram:

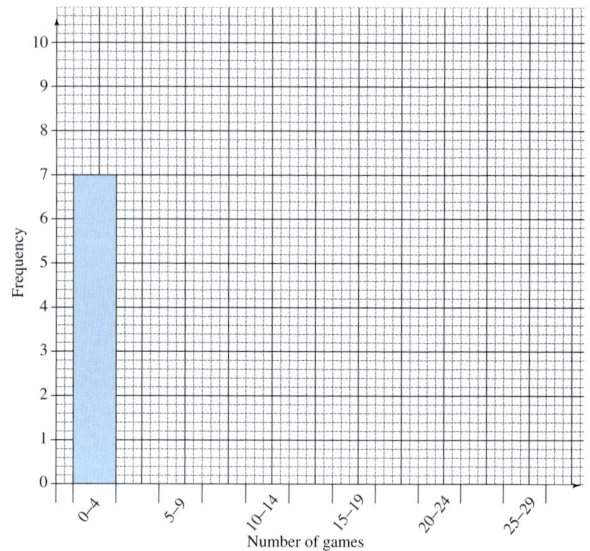

(c) How many people had 15 or more computer games?

9  The chart below shows the percentage of smokers for different age groups in 2003.

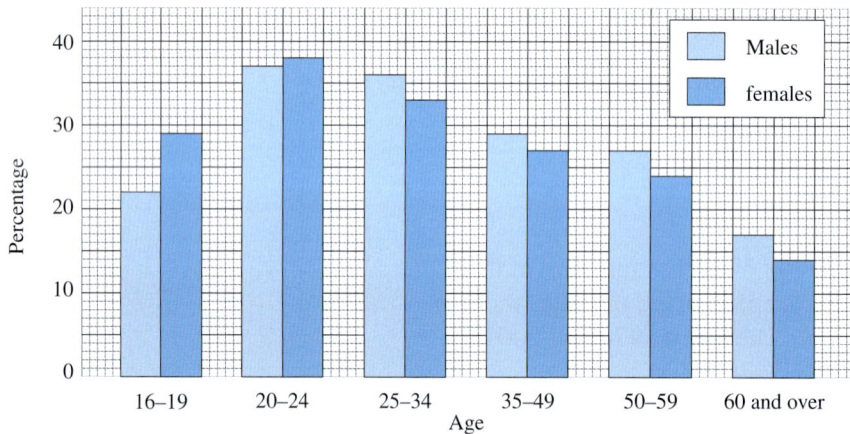

(a) In which age groups were the percentage of female smokers greater than the percentage of male smokers?

(b) What percentage of 25-34 year-old males are smokers?

(c) What percentage of 16-19 year-old females are smokers?

(d) What is the *difference* in the percentage of 16-19 year-old female smokers compared to 16-19 year-old male smokers?

(e) As people get older, what happens to the percentage of people who smoke?

## Stem and leaf diagrams

Data can be displayed in groups in a stem and leaf diagram.

Here are the marks of 20 girls in a science test.

| 47 | 53 | 71 | 55 | 28 | 40 | 45 | 62 | 57 | 64 |
|----|----|----|----|----|----|----|----|----|----|
| 33 | 48 | 59 | 61 | 73 | 37 | 75 | 26 | 68 | 39 |

We will put the marks into groups 20–29, 30–39..... 70–79.

We will choose the tens digit as the 'stem' and the units as the 'leaf'.

The first four marks are shown [47, 53, 71, 55]

| Stem (tens) | Leaf (units) |
|:-----------:|:-------------|
| 2 | |
| 3 | |
| 4 | 7 |
| 5 | 3 5 |
| 6 | |
| 7 | 1 |

The complete diagram is below …… and then with the leaves in numerical order:

| Stem | Leaf |
|:----:|:-----|
| 2 | 8 6 |
| 3 | 3 7 9 |
| 4 | 7 0 5 8 |
| 5 | 3 5 7 9 |
| 6 | 2 4 1 8 |
| 7 | 1 3 5 |

| Stem | Leaf |
|:----:|:-----|
| 2 | 6 8 |
| 3 | 3 7 9 |
| 4 | 0 5 7 8 |
| 5 | 3 5 7 9 |
| 6 | 1 2 4 8 |
| 7 | 1 3 5 |

We write a key next to the stem and leaf diagram to explain what the stem digit means and what the leaf digit means.

In this example    Key 4|7 = 47

The diagram shows the shape of the distribution. It is also easy to find the mode, the median and the range.

### E13.2

1  Draw a stem and leaf diagram for each set of data below:

| Stem | Leaf |
|:----:|:-----|
| 2 | |
| 3 | |
| 4 | |
| 5 | |
| 6 | |

(a)

| 32 | 29 | 41 | 38 | 52 | 53 | 41 | 28 | 36 | 52 |
|----|----|----|----|----|----|----|----|----|----|
| 44 | 26 | 47 | 43 | 38 | 27 | 36 | 63 | 62 | 28 |

(b)

| 29 | 42 | 41 | 35 | 23 | 46 | 23 | 36 |
|----|----|----|----|----|----|----|----|
| 42 | 53 | 27 | 51 | 29 | 36 | 27 | 43 |

**2** The heights of 26 pupils were recorded to the nearest cm.

162 153 155 146 149 161 155 163 146 155 153 162 148

157 146 148 162 153 151 164 147 149 152 158 149 157

(a) Show this data on a stem and leaf diagram.

(b) Write down the *range* of the data.

| Stem | Leaf |
|------|------|
| 14 | |
| 15 | |
| 16 | |

**3** The number of children in each class in Holland Bank School is recorded below:

| 28 | 31 | 27 | 28 | 30 | 24 | 23 | 32 | 29 |
|----|----|----|----|----|----|----|----|----|
| 29 | 29 | 30 | 26 | 27 | 31 | 27 | 26 | 31 |
| 25 | 27 | 30 | 28 | 27 | 29 | 30 | 28 | 27 |

(a) Draw a stem and leaf diagram to show this data.

(b) How many classes were there?

(c) What is the median number of children in a class?

(d) Find the range for the number of children in each class.

**4** A number of 16/17 year-olds were asked how much money they earned each week from part-time jobs.

The data is recorded below:

| 32 | 40 | 36 | 51 | 82 | 69 | 38 | 43 | 28 | 51 | 65 |
|----|----|----|----|----|----|----|----|----|----|----|
| 74 | 63 | 42 | 70 | 65 | 71 | 30 | 25 | 38 | 26 | 70 |
| 68 | 70 | 32 | 37 | 24 | 42 | 32 | 65 | 48 | 42 | 36 |

(a) Draw a stem and leaf diagram to show this data.

(b) How many people were asked?

(c) What is the median amount of money earned?

(d) Find the range for this data.

**5** Dan, Simon, Darryl and Julian try to play golf. The stem and leaf diagram shows the scores for each of their last 5 rounds of golf.

(a) What was their median score?

(b) Find the range of the scores.

| Stem | Leaf |
|------|------|
| 7 | 8 9 |
| 8 | 1 2 2 4 5 5 5 7 9 9 |
| 9 | 0 1 1 3 3 4 6 |
| 10 | 1 |

Key 8|2 = 82

**6**

| Stem | Leaf |
|------|------|
| 1 | 1 1 3 3 3 4 5 7 7 8 |
| 2 | 1 1 1 2 3 4 4 5 |

Key 2|3 = 2.3 litres

This stem and leaf diagram shows the engine sizes of some cars.

(a) What is the median engine size?

(b) What is the range of the engine sizes?

**7** The ages of the teachers in Holland Bank School and Grindley High School are shown in the back-to-back stem and leaf diagram.

| Holland Bank school | | Grindley High school |
|---|---|---|
| 9 6 6 4 | 2 | 2 3 3 5 7 7 7 8 |
| 9 8 5 5 4 2 | 3 | 0 0 1 3 4 4 6 |
| 9 8 8 6 6 6 5 5 0 | 4 | 1 2 2 5 7 7 8 8 8 |
| 7 7 7 5 5 5 3 2 2 | 5 | 0 6 6 7 |
| 3 2 2 1 | 6 | 0 |

Key 6|2 = 26          Key 4|5 = 45

(a) Find the median and range for Holland Bank School.

(b) Find the median and range for Grindley High School.

(c) Write a sentence to compare the ages of teachers in each school (use the median and range).

*Can you still?*

**13B**  **Add, subtract, multiply and divide fractions (see Unit 5)**

*Can you still?*

Work out

1. $\dfrac{1}{3}$ of 12

2. $\dfrac{3}{5}$ of 30

3. $\dfrac{1}{4} + \dfrac{1}{5}$

4. $\dfrac{2}{3} - \dfrac{3}{7}$

5. $\dfrac{3}{4} \times 24$

6. $\dfrac{3}{8} \times \dfrac{6}{9}$

7. $\dfrac{2}{9} \div \dfrac{7}{12}$

8. $\dfrac{8}{15} \div \dfrac{2}{3}$

9. $1\dfrac{1}{2} + 2\dfrac{1}{3}$

10. $3\dfrac{3}{4} - \dfrac{9}{10}$

11. $2\dfrac{3}{4} \times 1\dfrac{1}{5}$

12. $2\dfrac{1}{2} \div 3\dfrac{1}{3}$

## Drawing pie charts

Some people were asked what they had for breakfast. The data is recorded below:

| Breakfast | Frequency (number of people) |
|---|---|
| cereal | 18 |
| toast | 8 |
| egg | 4 |
| nothing | 15 |

To draw a pie chart:

(a) Add up the number of people.
   Total frequency = 18 + 8 + 4 + 15 = 45

(b) Whole angle in a pie chart = 360°
   This must be split between 45 people.
   Angle for each person = 360° ÷ 45 = 8°

(c) Angle for 'cereal'   = 18 × 8° = 144°
   Angle for 'toast'   = 8 × 8° = 64°
   Angle for 'egg'   = 4 × 8° = 32°
   Angle for 'nothing' = 15 × 8° = 120°

### Remember

Always find the total frequency then divide it into 360° to find out what angle is needed for each item in the pie chart.

## M13. 3

1   Some people were asked what their favourite kind of television programme was. The data is recorded below:

| Type of programme | Frequency (number of people) |
|---|---|
| soap | 25 |
| drama | 11 |
| news | 5 |
| comedy | 15 |
| other | 4 |

(a) Find the total frequency.

(b) Work out the angle for each person to help draw a pie chart (i.e. 360° ÷ 'total frequency').

(c) Work out the angle for each type of programme and draw a pie chart.

**2** Some people were asked where they were going to spend their Summer holiday. The table below shows the information.

| Country | Frequency |
|---------|-----------|
| France | 7 |
| Spain | 8 |
| USA | 4 |
| Greece | 6 |
| UK | 15 |

(a) Find the total frequency.

(b) Work out the angle for each person to help draw a pie chart.

(c) Work out the angle for each country and draw a pie chart.

In Questions **3**, **4** and **5**, work out the angle for each item and draw a pie chart.

**3** Favourite football team    **4** Most popular Briton    **5** Favourite snack

| Team | Frequency |
|------|-----------|
| Arsenal | 15 |
| Liverpool | 15 |
| Chelsea | 20 |
| Manchester Utd. | 25 |
| Everton | 6 |
| Aston Villa | 9 |

| Briton | Frequency |
|--------|-----------|
| Shakespeare | 15 |
| Churchill | 18 |
| Newton | 7 |
| Elizabeth 1 | 12 |
| Brunel | 8 |

| Snack | Frequency |
|-------|-----------|
| crisps | 60 |
| fruit | 35 |
| nuts | 10 |
| biscuits | 18 |
| chocolate | 34 |
| other | 23 |

**6** 120 children asked who their favourite 'Simpsons' character was. The information is shown below.

| Character | Frequency | Angle |
|-----------|-----------|-------|
| Homer | 52 | |
| Bart | 32 | |
| Mr. Burns | 17 | |
| Lisa | 12 | |
| Marge | 7 | |

Copy and complete the table then draw an accurate pie chart to show this information.

**7** Hal carries out a survey of 60 year 10 students. He asks them what their favourite cartoon is. He draws this accurate pie chart.

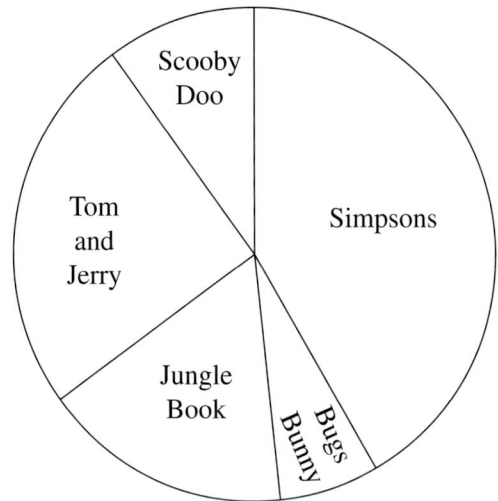

Measure the angles and complete the table.

| Cartoon | Frequency | Angle |
|---------|-----------|-------|
| Simpsons | 25 | |
| Bugs Bunny | | |
| Jungle Book | 10 | 60° |
| Tom and Jerry | | |
| Scooby Doo | | |
| Total | 60 | |

## Reading from pie charts

Marilyn has £120 to spend each week. The pie chart shows what she spends her money on. How much does she spend on rent?

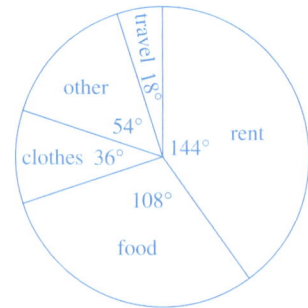

$$\text{fraction of pie chart} = \frac{144}{360} \quad \leftarrow \text{angle for 'rent'}$$
$$\leftarrow \text{total angle for pie chart}$$

$$= \frac{72}{180} = \frac{36}{90} = \frac{4}{10} = \frac{2}{5}$$

$$\text{money spent on rent} = \frac{2}{5} \text{ of £120}$$

$$= (120 \div 5) \times 2$$

$$= 24 \times 2$$

$$= £48$$

362

**1** The pie chart shows the 80 passengers travelling on a train. How many of the passengers were:

(a) men          (b) women

(c) girls          (d) boys

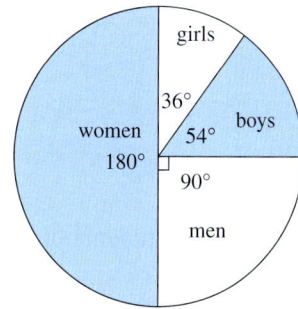

**2** Jack Jones runs a pub. He makes his money from 3 main things: food, drink and hiring out rooms. The pie chart shows what fraction of his money he gets from each of these things.

If Jack makes £ 900 one week, how much did he make from:

(a) food

(b) hiring out a room

(c) drink

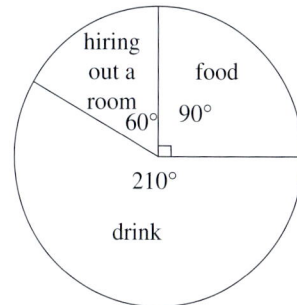

**3**

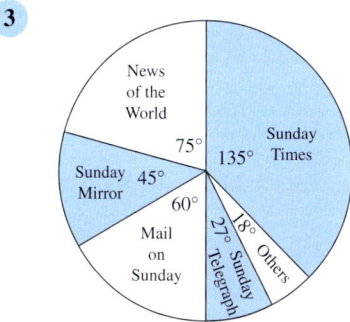

Penny delivers 240 newspapers each Sunday.

The pie chart shows the different newspapers which Penny delivers.

How many of the newspapers were:

(a) News of the World          (b) Sunday Mirror

(c) Sunday Telegraph          (d) Sunday Times

(e) Mail on Sunday          (f) Others

**4** Neil draws a pie chart to show what he does during a typical day (24 hours).

How many hours does he do the following?

(a) exercise          (b) school

(c) sleep          (d) eat

(e) watch TV          (f) other things

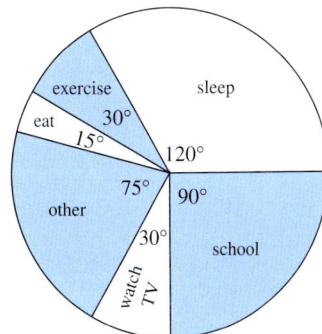

**5**

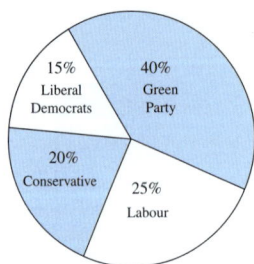

15% Liberal Democrats
40% Green Party
20% Conservative
25% Labour

Some young people were asked who they would vote for at the next general election. The information is shown on the pie chart.

Find the angle on the pie chart for:

(a) Labour            (b) the Green Party

(c) Conservative      (d) the Liberal Democrats

**6** The students of 2 different schools were asked to state their favourite children's film. Here are the results.

Holland Bank School

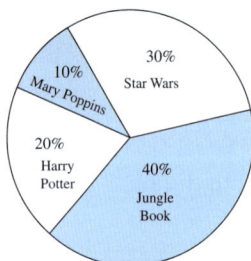

10% Mary Poppins
30% Star Wars
20% Harry Potter
40% Jungle Book

Hatton Green School

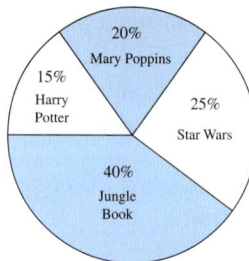

20% Mary Poppins
15% Harry Potter
25% Star Wars
40% Jungle Book

There were 800 students          There were 1000 students

(a) Carl says 'More students in Holland Bank School like Star Wars than the students in Hatton Green School.'
Use both charts to explain whether or not Carl is right.

(b) Yasmin says 'Less students in Holland Bank School like Harry Potter than the students in Hatton Green School,'

Use both charts to explain whether or not Yasmin is right.

**7** People in the North and the South of England were asked how many hours of Exercise they took each week. The information is shown in the pie charts below.

The North

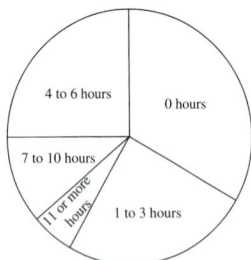

4 to 6 hours
0 hours
7 to 10 hours
11 or more hours
1 to 3 hours

The South

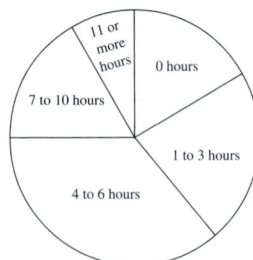

11 or more hours
0 hours
7 to 10 hours
1 to 3 hours
4 to 6 hours

Which of the statements below is correct?

(a) 'Less people in the North do some exercise than people in the South.'

(b) 'A smaller percentage of people in the North do some exercise than people in the South.'

(c) 'More people in the North do some exercise than people in the South.'
*Explain* why you chose your answer.

**8**

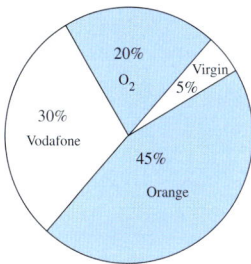

Over 2000 people were asked who their phone providers were. The results are shown in the pie chart.

Find the angle on the pie chart for:

(a) Vodafone     (b) $O_2$

(c) Virgin       (d) Orange

**9** The pie charts below show the ages in years of people in the UK and Kenya.

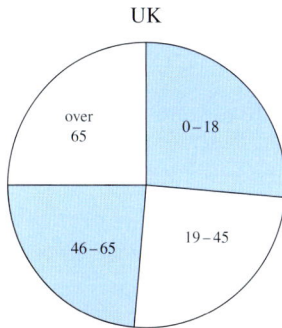

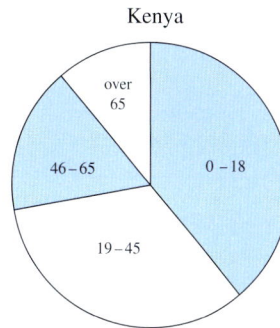

UK

Kenya

Which of the statements below are correct?

(a) 'There are more 0 to 18 year-olds in Kenya than in the UK.'

(b) 'There are less 0 to 18 year-olds in Kenya than in the UK.'

(c) A greater percentage of the people in Kenya are 0 to 18 year-olds than in the UK.'

*Explain* why you chose your answer.

*Can you still?*

**13C**  **Draw curves (see Unit 10)**

*Can you still?*

1. Draw an $x$-axis from –3 to 3 and a $y$-axis from 0 to 12
   Complete the table below then draw the curve $y = x^2 + 2$

| $x$ | –3 | –2 | –1 | 0 | 1 | 2 | 3 |
|---|---|---|---|---|---|---|---|
| $y$ | | 6 | | | 3 | | |

2. Draw an $x$-axis from the –3 to 3 and a $y$-axis from –2 to 12
   Complete the table below then draw the curve $y = x^2 - x$

| $x$ | –3 | –2 | –1 | 0 | 1 | 2 | 3 |
|---|---|---|---|---|---|---|---|
| $y$ | | | 2 | | | | |

70 students from years 10 and 11 were asked what sport they played in their last games lesson.

The information is shown in the table below.

| | Football | Rugby | Badminton | Total |
|---|---|---|---|---|
| Year 10 | 18 | 14 | B | 34 |
| Year 11 | 14 | E | 6 | C |
| Total | A | F | D | 70 |

↕ A column is vertica

↔ A row is horizontal

(a) The 'Football' column total is 18 + 14 = 32

(b) The year 10 row total is 34. Year 10 'Football' and 'Rugby' is 18 + 14 = 32 so the 'Badminton' must be 2 to make the total = 34.

(c) The 'Total' column adds up to 70 so the year 11 Total must be 36 so that 34 + 36 = 70.

(d) The 'Badminton' column total is B + 6 = 2 + 6 = 8.

(e) The year 11 row total is C = 36. Year 11 'Football' and 'Badminton' is 14 + 6 = 20 so the 'Rugby' must be 16 to make the total = 36.

(f) The 'Rugby' column total is 14 + E = 14 + 16 = 30.

| | Football | Rugby | Badminton | Total |
|---|---|---|---|---|
| Year 10 | 18 | 14 | 2 | 34 |
| Year 11 | 14 | 16 | 6 | 36 |
| Total | 32 | 30 | 8 | 70 |

We can *check* our answers by adding the totals along the bottom row to make sure they add up to 70 (32 + 30 + 8 = 70 ✓).

## M13.4

1  100 people were asked what their favourite kind of chocolate was. Copy and complete the two-way table below.

| | Plain chocolate | Milk chocolate | White chocolate | Total |
|---|---|---|---|---|
| Female | | | 5 | 43 |
| Male | 21 | | | |
| Total | | 46 | 14 | 100 |

**2** 80 children were asked if they went to the cinema, swimming or cycling one day in the Easter holidays. The information is shown in the two-way table below.

| | Cinema | Swimming | Cycling | Total |
|---|---|---|---|---|
| Boys | 18 | 17 | | 47 |
| Girls | 15 | | 8 | |
| Total | | | | 80 |

(a) Copy and complete the two-way table.

(b) How many children went swimming in total?

**3** 200 pupils were asked what their favourite school subjects were. The information is shown in the two-way table below.

| | Art | PE | Maths | Science | Total |
|---|---|---|---|---|---|
| Boys | | 53 | 28 | | 119 |
| Girls | | 28 | | 14 | |
| Total | 51 | | | 32 | 200 |

(a) Copy and complete the two-way table.

(b) One of these pupils is picked at random. Write down the *probability* that the pupil likes PE best.

**4** 400 students in years 10 and 11 were asked if they smoked or drank alcohol on a regular basis. The information is shown in the two-way table below.

| | Smoke | Drink alcohol | Neither | Smoke and drink alcohol | Total |
|---|---|---|---|---|---|
| Year 10 | 21 | 40 | | | |
| Year 11 | 23 | | | 38 | 227 |
| Total | | | 198 | 62 | 400 |

(a) Copy and complete the two-way table.

(b) One of these students is picked at random. Write down the *probability* that the student will not smoke or drink alcohol.

**5** 1000 people in Birmingham and Nottingham were asked how they travel to work. The information is shown in the two-way table below.

| | Car | Walk | Bike | Train | Total |
|---|---|---|---|---|---|
| Birmingham | 314 | 117 | | 69 | |
| Nottingham | | 175 | 41 | | |
| Total | 530 | | 72 | | 1000 |

(a) Copy and complete the two-way table.

(b) One of the people from Birmingham *only* is chosen. What is the *probability* that this person travels to work by bike?

**6** 500 football fans from Liverpool and Manchester were asked which football team they supported. The two-way table below shows the information.

| | Liverpool | Everton | Manchester United | Manchester City | Total |
|---|---|---|---|---|---|
| fans from Liverpool | | 83 | 15 | | 210 |
| fans from Manchester | 12 | 16 | | | |
| Total | 119 | | 156 | | 500 |

(a) Copy and complete the two-way table.

(b) *Use a calculator* to find what percentage of the fans supported Manchester City (reminder: 'number of Manchester City fans ÷ 500 then multiply by 100').

**7** 1800 people were asked if they had been in a car accident. The information is shown in the two-way table according to different age groups.

| | Car accident | No car accident | Total |
|---|---|---|---|
| 17 to 25 | 123 | 481 | |
| 26 to 60 | 65 | | 702 |
| over 60 | | | |
| Total | 286 | | 1800 |

(a) Copy and complete the two-way table.

(b) *Use a calculator* to find what percentage of the people had been in a car accident.

If you do not have enough money to buy an item, you might buy *on credit*. There are different ways of doing this such as hire purchase, credit cards, store cards, bank overdrafts and personal loans.

**Make sure you know the true cost of buying on credit.**

This section deals with personal loans.

**Personal loans**

- An amount of money borrowed from a bank or another organisation. The loan is paid back in fixed amounts, usually each month.

- The fixed amount must be paid each month. You cannot pay a little less one month then a little more the following month.

- The interest rate is usually a lot less than the interest rate on a credit card.

**Payment protection**

People are advised to take out insurance with their loan so that loan repayments will be made if people become ill, unemployed or have an accident. Payment protection increases the cost of a loan.

### WYM13

The table below shows the monthly repayments on loans from 1 year up to 5 years, with and without payment protection.

| Loan (£) | 12 months (£) | | 24 months (£) | | 36 months (£) | | 48 months (£) | | 60 months (£) | |
|---|---|---|---|---|---|---|---|---|---|---|
| | with protection | without protection | with protection | without protection | with protection | without protection | with protection | without protection | with protection | without protection |
| 1000 | 90.12 | 88.75 | 47.91 | 46.63 | 33.82 | 32.70 | 26.38 | 25.65 | 22.06 | 21.52 |
| 3000 | 269.09 | 265.31 | 142.38 | 139.65 | 100.83 | 98.12 | 79.18 | 77.36 | 66.32 | 64.91 |
| 5000 | 441.18 | 436.12 | 230.36 | 227.49 | 160.01 | 157.24 | 125.31 | 123.32 | 102.75 | 101.48 |
| 10000 | 879.83 | 873.51 | 458.31 | 453.62 | 318.09 | 314.21 | 248.03 | 245.72 | 204.89 | 202.27 |
| 15000 | 1316.42 | 1308.65 | 684.37 | 678.63 | 475.18 | 470.53 | 369.23 | 366.14 | 305.92 | 303.86 |
| 25000 | 2187.38 | 2177.28 | 1138.46 | 1130.36 | 788.41 | 782.08 | 611.74 | 607.83 | 506.99 | 504.69 |

**1** What is the monthly repayment on a £5000 loan over 36 months with protection?

**2** What is the monthly repayment on a £3000 loan over 24 months without protection?

**3** What is the monthly repayment on a £15000 loan over 60 months without protection?

**4** What is the monthly repayment on a £10000 loan over 12 months with protection?

**5** How much *more* will the monthly repayment on a £3000 loan with protection over 36 months cost than without protection?

**6** How much *more* will the monthly repayment on a £25000 loan with protection over 48 months cost than without protection?

**7** If Carl borrows £5000 over 60 months with protection for a holiday to Italy, how much money will he pay back *in total*? How much *interest* will he pay *in total*?

**8** If Sunita borrows £15000 for a new car over 36 months without protection, how much money will she pay back *in total*? How much *interest* will she pay *in total*?

**9** If you borrow £1000 over 24 months without protection, how much money will you pay back *in total*? How much *interest* will you pay *in total*?

**10** If you borrow £10000 over 60 months with protection, how much *more* will it cost you *in total* than borrowing the money without protection?

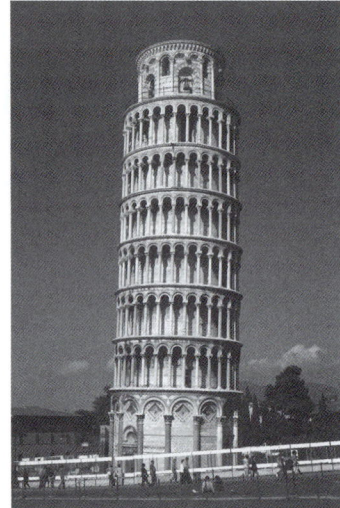

## TEST YOURSELF ON UNIT 13

**1. Finding the mean, median, mode and range for sets of numbers**

(a) 9, 7, 3, 7, 4, 8, 2, 7, 1, 6, 1

For the set of numbers above, find the (i) mode (ii) median (iii) mean (iv) range

(b) 8, 6, 5, 9, 8, 6

For the set of numbers above, which is larger – the mean or the median?

## 2. Using charts and graphs

The chart below shows the percentage of people in the USA who are obese (*very* overweight).

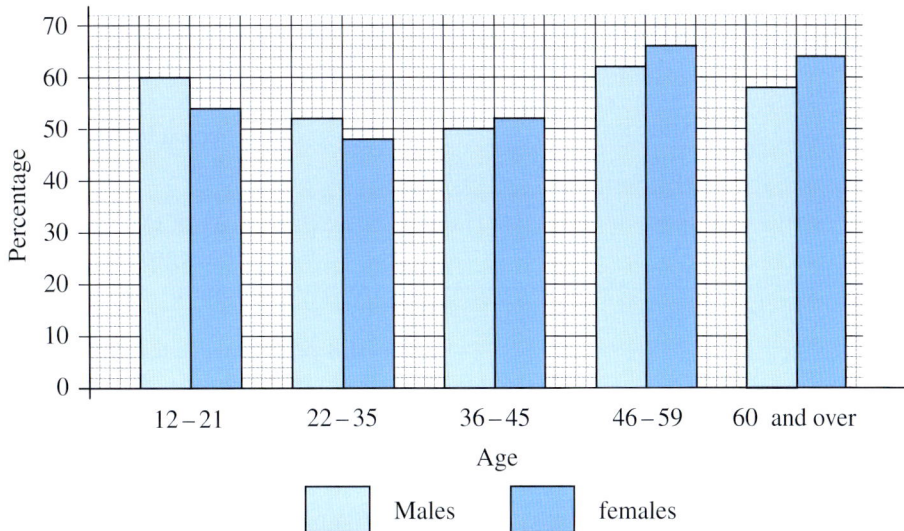

(a) In which age groups were the percentage of obese males greater than the percentage of obese females?

(b) What percentage of 46-59 year-old females are obese?

(c) What percentage of 22-35 year-old males are obese?

(d) What is the *difference* in the percentage of 46-59 year-old obese females compared to 46-59 year-old obese males?

## 3. Using stem and leaf diagrams

The ages of 25 people who work for a local newspaper are recorded below.

| | | | | |
|---|---|---|---|---|
| 31 | 42 | 27 | 50 | 21 |
| 26 | 19 | 19 | 62 | 35 |
| 32 | 23 | 53 | 27 | 46 |
| 48 | 43 | 28 | 53 | 58 |
| 37 | 51 | 36 | 47 | 20 |

(a) Draw a stem and leaf diagram to show this data.

(b) What is the median age?

(c) Find the range of the ages.

**4.** Using pie charts

(a) In a list of the richest people in a country, their backgrounds are listed below.

| Background | Number of people |
|---|---|
| inherited | 15 |
| business | 28 |
| music | 20 |
| sport | 17 |
| other | 10 |

(i) Find the total number of people.

(ii) Work out the angle for each person to help draw a pie chart.

(iii) Work out the angle for each background and draw a pie chart.

(b)

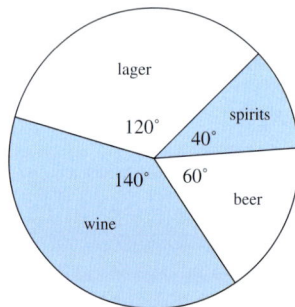

108 people were asked what their favourite drink is. The results are shown in the pie chart. How many people said:

(i) beer

(ii) lager

(iii) spirits

(iv) wine?

**5.** Using two-way tables

120 people were given the chance to go to Australia, India or the USA. The information showing their choices is in the two-way table.

|  | Australia | India | U.S.A | Total |
|---|---|---|---|---|
| Female |  | 32 |  | 71 |
| Male | 24 |  |  |  |
| Total | 47 |  | 33 | 120 |

(a) Copy and complete the two-way table.

(b) One of these people is picked at random. Write down the *probability* that the person has chosen India.

(c) *Use a calculator* to work out the *percentage* of the people who chose the USA.

1   Here is a pictogram.
It shows the number of people who had a meal in a café on each of four days.

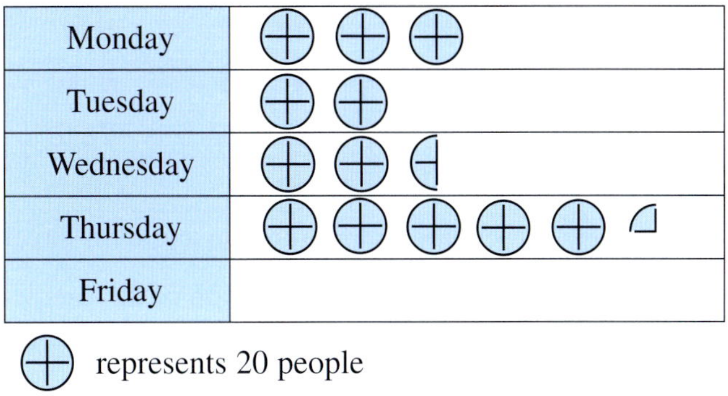

| Monday | ⊕ ⊕ ⊕ |
| Tuesday | ⊕ ⊕ |
| Wednesday | ⊕ ⊕ ◖ |
| Thursday | ⊕ ⊕ ⊕ ⊕ ⊕ ◪ |
| Friday | |

⊕ represents 20 people

(a) write down the number of people who had a meal in the café on

(i) Monday,

(ii) Wednesday,

(iii) Thursday.

On Friday, 55 people had a meal in the café.

(b) Show this information on the pictogram.                    (EDEXCEL)

2   John has a science test every week.
Here are John's scores in his last nine tests.

52, 59, 43, 49, 65, 68, 48, 53, 67

(a) Calculate his mean score.

(b) Find his median score.

(c) Find the range of his scores

3
```
2 | 3 7 8
3 | 0 2 3 6 6 9
4 | 1 4 5 6 7 8 8 9
5 | 0 0 0 0 3 6 7 7
6 | 1 2 2 4 5
```

Key: 2|7 represents 27 marks

The stem and leaf diagram shows the marks gained by 30 pupils in a test.

(a) Write down the highest mark.

(b) Find the median mark.

(c) Find the range of the marks.                    (OCR)

**4** Kim drew a pie chart to show the colours of the cars in the school car park.

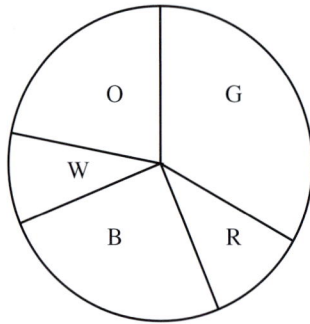

| Key | |
|---|---|
| G | Green |
| R | Red |
| B | Blue |
| W | White |
| O | Other |

(a) (i) Measure the angle for Green.

(ii) What fraction of the cars was Green?

(b) What percentage of the cars was Blue? (OCR)

**5** 60 British students each visited one foreign country last week.
The two-way table shows some information about these students.

| | France | Germany | Spain | Total |
|---|---|---|---|---|
| Female | | | 9 | 34 |
| Male | 15 | | | |
| Total | | 25 | 18 | 60 |

(a) Copy and complete the two-way table.

(b) One of these students is picked at random. Write down the probability that the student visited Germany last week. (EDEXCEL)

**6** Swimmers taking a survival test can achieve a gold, silver or bronze award.
Last month 240 swimmers took the test.
The results are shown in the table.

| Award | Number of Swimmers |
|---|---|
| Gold | 30 |
| Silver | 80 |
| Bronze | 120 |
| Failed | 10 |
| Total | 240 |

Draw a pie chart to illustrate this information. (AQA)

In this unit we will explore the data handling task which accounts for 10% of your final GCSE grade.

### What data will you look at?

Your teacher will probably set the task but you may be given some choice, for example: favourite music, memory tests or traffic issues in the area you live.

### The hypothesis

'A statement you believe to be true'.

Example: 'I believe that taller students weigh more than shorter students'.

### How is your work marked?

Three different 'strands' are being looked at:

Strand 1 – planning your project, deciding what data to collect, making it clear what you are going to do and stating any problems you expect to have.

Strand 2 – collecting and showing your data as well as looking at averages and spread.

Strand 3 – using the charts, graphs and any calculations to draw conclusion about your data. Does it show that your hypothesis is true or false?

Remember the *data handling cycle.*

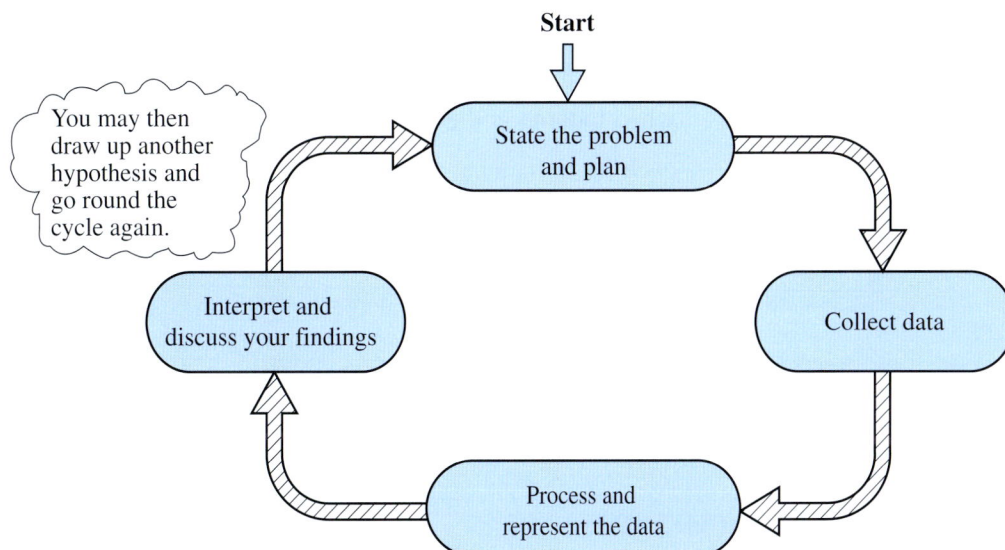

**Start**

State the problem and plan

Collect data

Process and represent the data

Interpret and discuss your findings

You may then draw up another hypothesis and go round the cycle again.

**Choosing the hypothesis**

Start with a *simple hypothesis*. This will involve *2 factors*.

Example: 'I believe boys are generally taller than girls in my school'.

This involves height and the sex (boy or girl).

When you have finished exploring this hypothesis, you *must* bring in another factor or you cannot work as high as a grade C.

Use age.

Example: 'I believe boys are generally taller than girls in year 11 but boys and girls are generally the same height in year 7'.

This involves *3 factors:* height, sex and age.

**The plan**

- is there a reason why you have chosen your hypothesis?
- where will you collect the data (it may have been provided or you may have to search for it)?
- will the data be reliable? How do you know?
- how will you take a sample from the data?
- how large will the sample size be?
- can you think of any problems at this stage?

You must write your plan down. Do not leave it until the end. Do it early on and show it to your teacher.

**The sample**

Sample size — use at least 30 sets of data or there will not be enough data to give reliable results.

Systematic sample – if you wanted 30 sets of data from 300 sets, you could take every $10^{th}$ set of data ($300 \div 10 = 30$). This might be suitable when looking at the simple hypothesis.

Random sample — each set of data has the same probability of being chosen.

(a) Write on identical pieces of card, mix up then choose how many you want.

(b) Use a computer or calculator. On some calculators SHIFT RAN # will give random three-digit numbers between, 0.001 and 0.999. Ignore the decimal point and use the number to select a piece of data.

**Use tables**

Put your data into clear tables.

**Process and represent the data**

- only do things which you are going to use to examine your hypothesis ( do not waste time drawing charts/graphs which you are not going to use).

- which charts/graphs will be useful?

- which averages can you work out from your data? Will they be of any use?

- can you measure how spread out the data is (range)? Would this be of any use?

- how will you check your calculations?

**Remember**

It is vital that you only produce charts, graphs and calculations if you are going to use them later.

The table below shows the typical things you might do for strand 2 to score the grades shown.

| grade G | bar charts, pictograms, mode, range |
|---------|--------------------------------------|

| | grade F | line graphs, frequency diagrams, mode of grouped data |
|--|---------|--------------------------------------------------------|

| | | grade E | stem and leaf diagrams, simple pie charts, mean and median |
|--|--|---------|-------------------------------------------------------------|

| | | | grade D | more difficult pie charts, simple histograms, scatter graphs and correlation |
|--|--|--|---------|-------------------------------------------------------------------------------|

| | | | | grade C | lines of best fit, frequency polygons, mean, median and modal class of grouped data |
|--|--|--|--|---------|--------------------------------------------------------------------------------------|

**Interpret and discuss your findings**

- You must compare any averages and ranges and *link it back to your hypothesis*.

  Example hypothesis: 'Boys are taller than girls in year 11'.

  If we had obtained:

| boys | girls |
|------|-------|
| mean = 170 cm<br>range = 41 cm | mean = 161 cm<br>range = 40 cm |

We could write: 'The boys have a greater mean average height than the girls and their heights are spread out in a similar way. This suggests that the boys are generally taller than the girls which supports my hypothesis'.

- You must examine all charts/graphs and write down any observations, *linking it back to your hypothesis*.

    Example hypothesis: 'I believe that taller students weigh more than shorter students'.

    We might have produced a scatter graph.

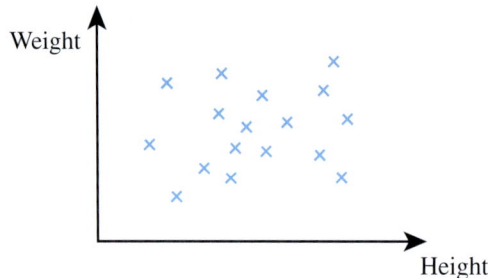

We could write: 'The scatter graph suggests no correlation between the heights and weights of the students. This suggests that my hypothesis was not correct'.

**Note**: It does not matter whether your hypothesis is true or false. The purpose of the coursework is how you go about showing whether your hypothesis is true or false.

- Can you suggest any real-life reasons why the results suggested your hypothesis was true or false?

- Can you write down any factors which might concern you about how reliable your findings are?

**The conclusion**

- write down your key findings, always linking them to your hypothesis.

- discuss any problems.

- how might you have improved what you did?

- what else might you have looked at if you had been given the time?

**Remember**

The highest coursework grade you can obtain by working once around the data handling cycle with a simple hypothesis is a D/E.

To push towards a grade C, you must work around the data handling cycle one more time. This must involve looking at another hypothesis with one more factor which is related in some way to your first simple hypothesis. Good luck!

# SHAPE 3

### In this unit you will learn how to:

– find perimeters of shapes

– find areas of triangles and rectangles

– find areas of trapeziums and parallelograms

– find circumferences of circles

– find areas of circles

– find surface areas and volumes of cuboids

– convert units of area and volume

– find volumes of prisms, particularly cylinders

– use similar triangles

– use dimensions to recognise a length, area or volume formula

– ⟨WATCH YOUR MONEY!⟩ – which is better value?

## Perimeter

The perimeter of a shape is the distance around its edges.

It is a length and is measured in units of length such as metres or centimetres.

8 cm

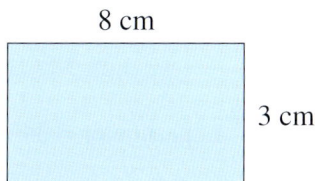

3 cm

Perimeter = 8 + 3 + 8 + 3 = 22 cm

distance around *all* its edges

**1** Find the perimeter of each rectangle. All lengths are in cm.

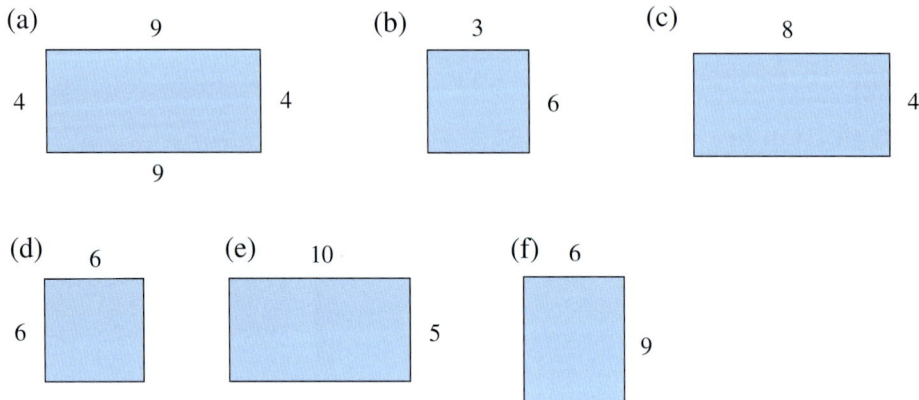

(a)

9

4        4

9

(b)

3

6

(c)

8

4

(d)

6

6

(e)

10

5

(f)

6

9

**2** Draw 3 different rectangles with a perimeter of 18 cm.

**3** Find the perimeter of a rectangle with a length of 12 cm and a width of 7 cm.

**4** Find the perimeter of each triangle. All lengths are in cm.

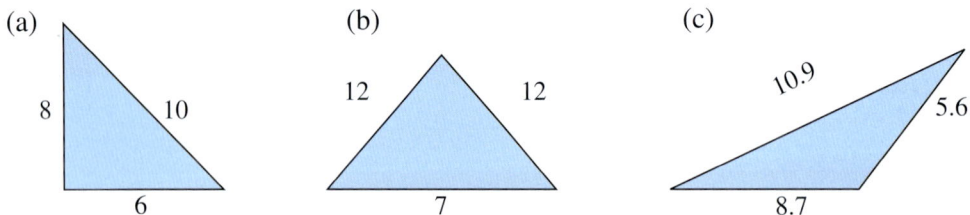

(a)

8        10

6

(b)

12        12

7

(c)

10.9

5.6

8.7

**5** For each triangle below you are given the perimeter. Find the missing value $x$. All lengths are in cm.

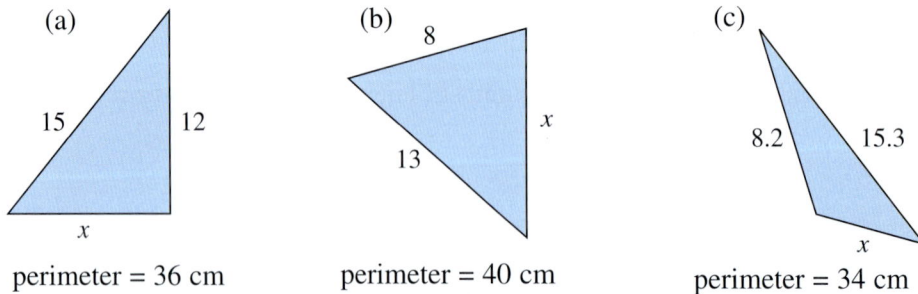

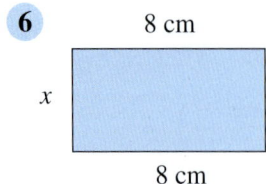

(a)

15        12

$x$

perimeter = 36 cm

(b)

8

$x$

13

perimeter = 40 cm

(c)

8.2        15.3

$x$

perimeter = 34 cm

**6**

8 cm

$x$

8 cm

The perimeter of this rectangle is 26 cm.

Find the missing value $x$.

380

**7** The perimeter of this rectangle is 44 cm.

Find the missing value $x$.

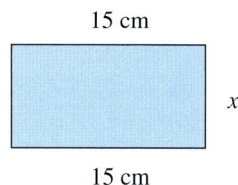

15 cm

15 cm

$x$

**8**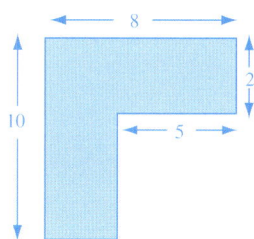

The perimeter of this square is 36 cm.

Find the missing value $x$.

**9** The perimeter of a square is 48 cm. How long is one of the sides of the square?

**10**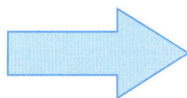

21 cm

$x$

The perimeter of this rectangle is 70 cm. Find the missing value $x$.

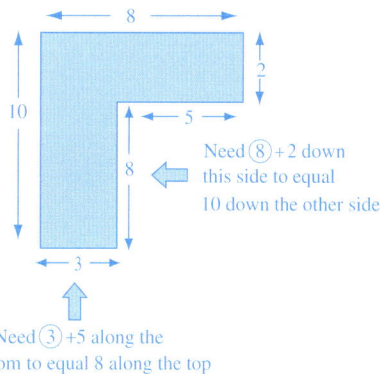

Find the perimeter of this shape.

Work out all missing lengths first.

Need ⑧+2 down this side to equal 10 down the other side

Need ③+5 along the bottom to equal 8 along the top

Perimeter = 8 + 2 + 5 + 8 + 3 + 10 = 36.
If the lengths are in cm, the perimeter = 36 cm.

**E15.1**

**1**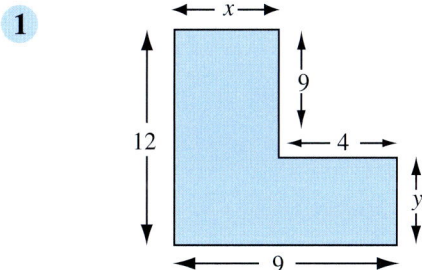

All lengths are in cm. Find the length of

(a) $x$

(b) $y$

(c) Find the perimeter of this shape.

381

In questions **2** to **7** , find the perimeter of each shape. All lengths are in cm.

**2**

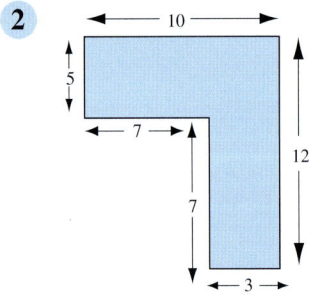

**3**

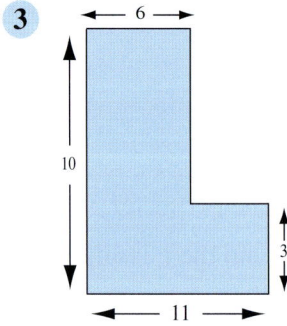

**4**

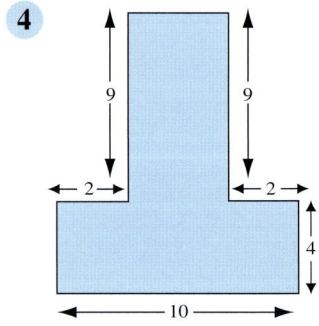

**5**

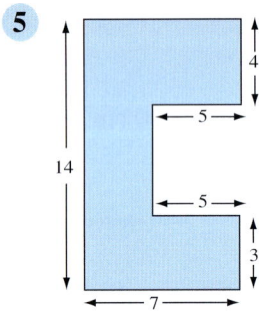

**6**

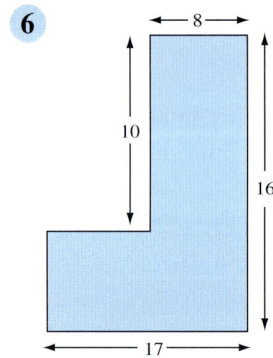

**7**

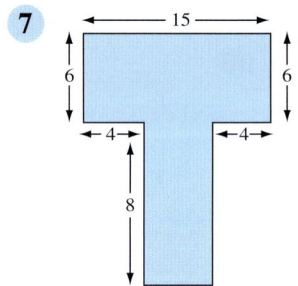

**8**

The perimeter of this shape is 60 cm.
Find the missing value $x$.

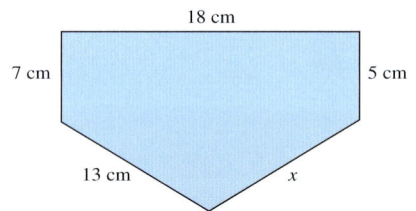

**9**

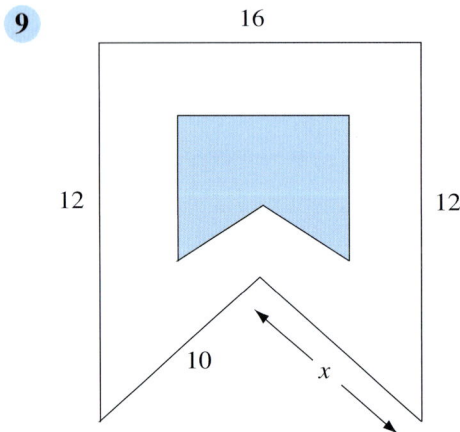

The perimeter of the large shape is twice the perimeter of the inside shape. All lengths are in cm.

The perimeter of the inside shape is 32 cm. Find the missing value $x$.

## Area of triangles and rectangles

The area of a shape is the amount of surface it covers.

It is measured in squares, usually square metres (m²) or square centimetres (cm²).

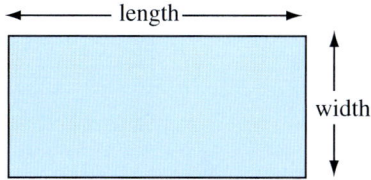

length / width

Area of rectangle = length × width

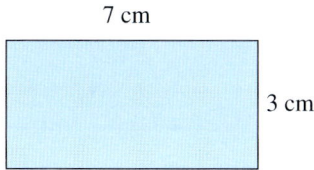

7 cm, 3 cm

Area = 7 × 3
     = 21 cm²

7 cm, 3 cm

height / base

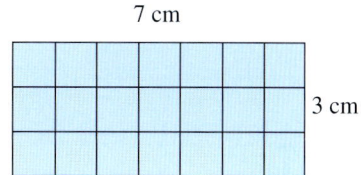

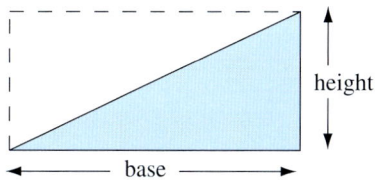

Area of triangle = $\frac{1}{2}$ area of rectangle

Area of triangle = $\frac{1}{2}$ (base × height)

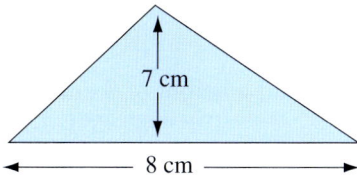

7 cm / 8 cm

Height = 7 cm    base = 8 cm

Area of triangle = $\frac{1}{2}$(base × height)

$= \frac{1}{2}(8 \times 7)$

$= \frac{1}{2}(56) = 28$ cm²

Find the area of this shape.

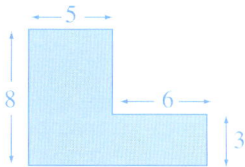

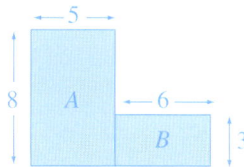

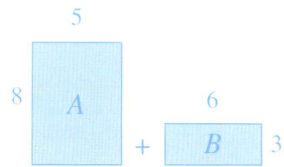

Area rectangle $A = 8 \times 5 = 40$

Area rectangle $B = 6 \times 3 = 18$

Total area       $= 40 + 18 = 58$

If each length is given in cm, the area of the shape is 58 cm².

Find the area of each shape below. All lengths are in cm.

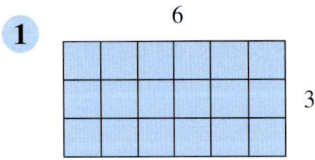

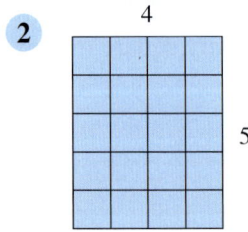

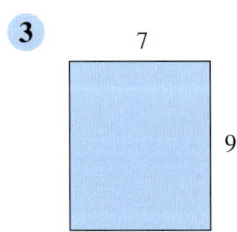

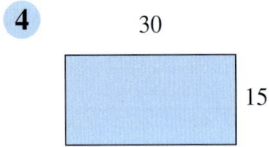

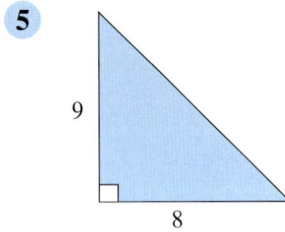

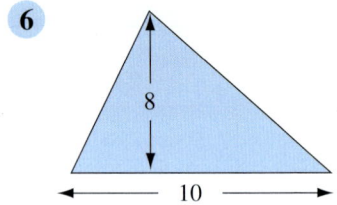

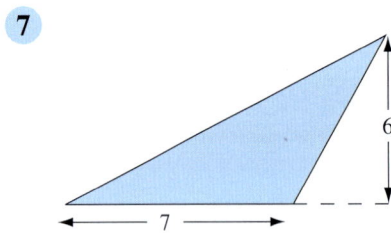

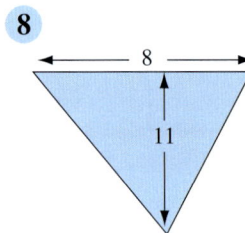

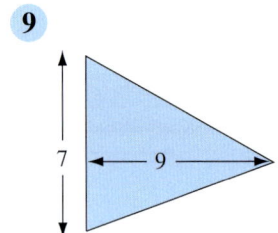

**1**

6

3

**2**

4

5

**3**

7

9

**4**

30

15

**5**

9

8

**6**

8

10

**7**

6

7

**8**

8

11

**9**

7

9

**10** Find the area of a triangle with a base of 20 cm and a height of 9 cm

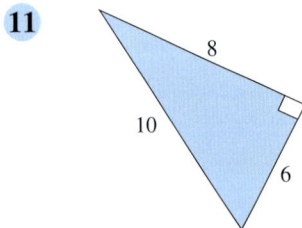

**11**

8

10

6

Find the area of this triangle.

**12** Find the area of this triangle.

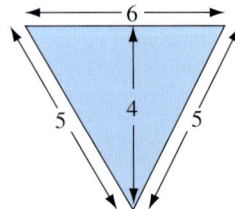

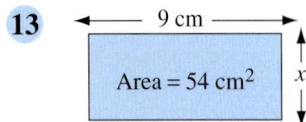

6

5

4

5

**13**

9 cm

Area = 54 cm²

x

Find the missing value x.

**14** Find the missing value $x$

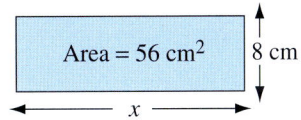

Area = 56 cm²    8 cm

Find the area of each shape in questions **15** to **20** by splitting them into rectangles.

**15**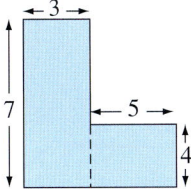

**16**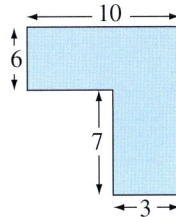

**17**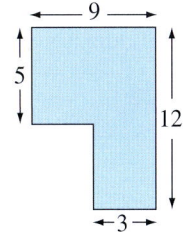

**18**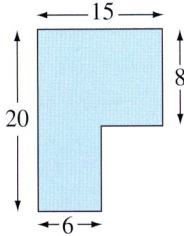

**19**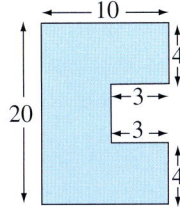

**20**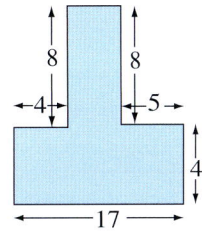

**21** Find the shaded area.

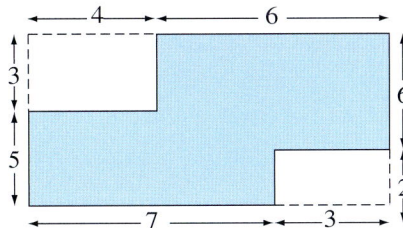

Find the area of each shape in questions **22** to **27** by splitting them into rectangles and triangles.

**22**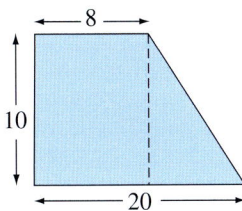

**23**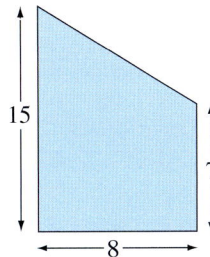

**24**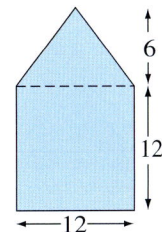

385

**25**

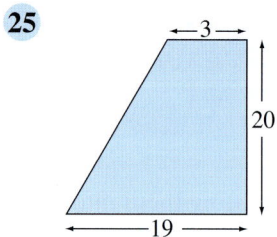

**26**

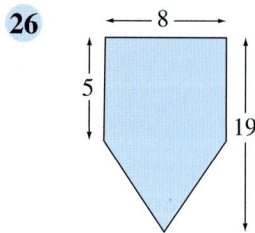

**27**

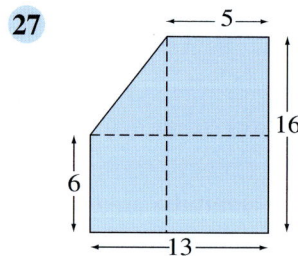

In questions **28** to **30** , find the shaded area.

**28**

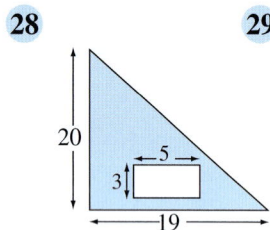

**29**

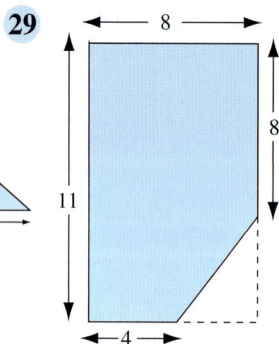

**30**

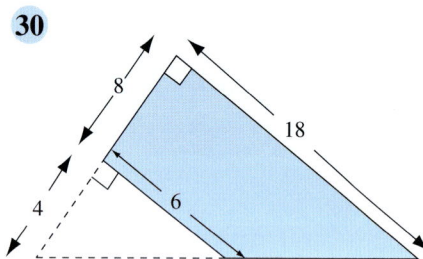

## Areas of trapeziums and parallelograms

**Parallelogram**

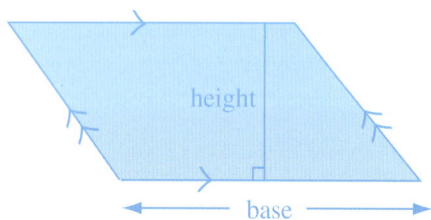

Area = base × height

Area = $b \times h$

**Trapezium** (2 parallel sides)

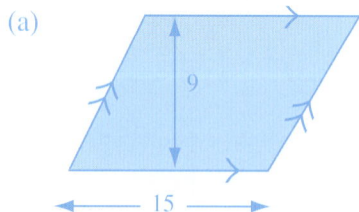

Area = $\frac{1}{2}(a + b) \times h$

(a)

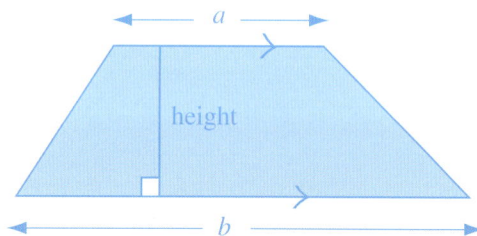

Area = base × height

= 15 × 9

= 135 cm²

(b)

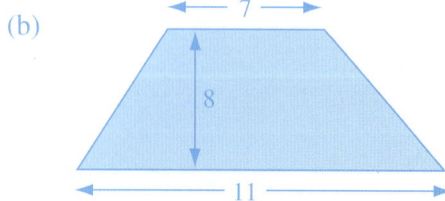

Area = $\frac{1}{2}(a + b) \times$ h

= $\frac{1}{2}(7 + 11) \times 8$

= $\frac{1}{2}(18) \times 8$

= 9 × 8 = 72 cm²

Find the area of each shape below. All lengths are in cm.

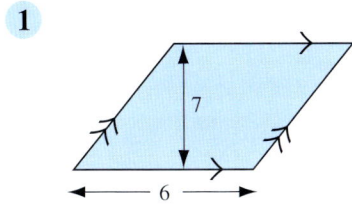

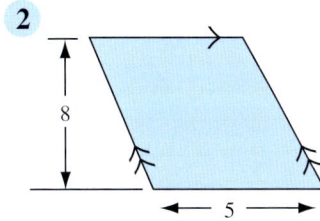

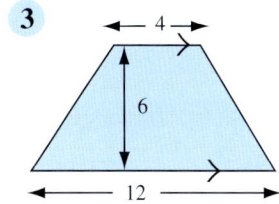

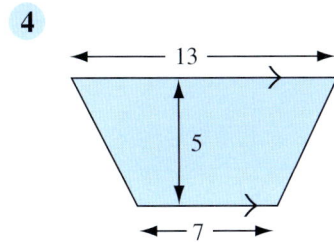

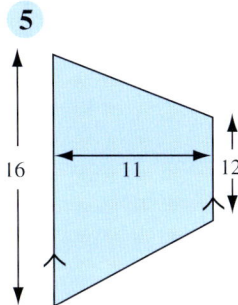

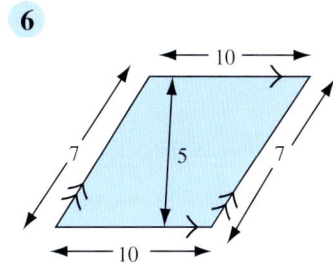

**1**

**2**

**3**

**4**

**5**

**6**

**7** Which of the 2 shapes below has the larger area?

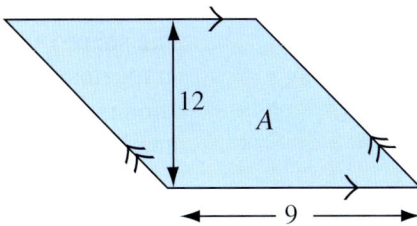

or

**8**

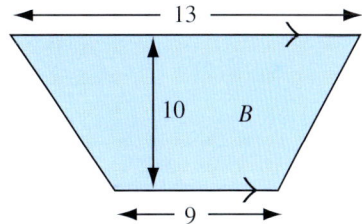

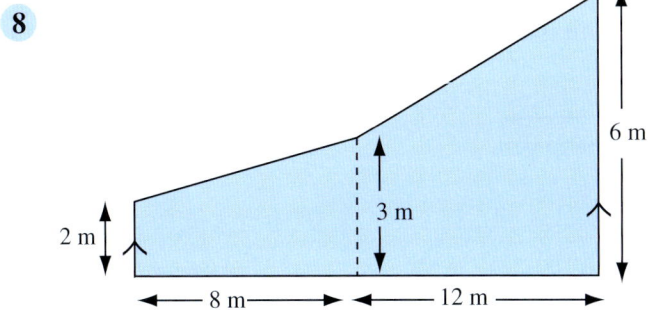

This is the plan of one end of a house. Find the area.

**9** Find the shaded area.

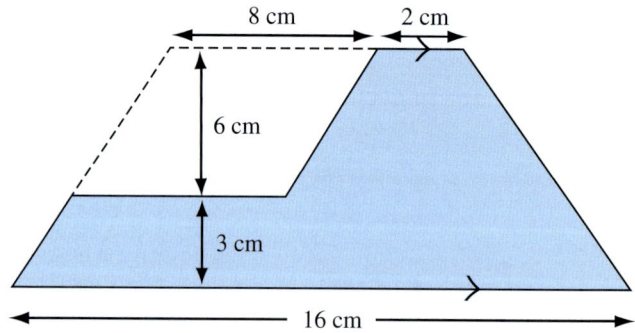

8 cm

2 cm

6 cm

3 cm

16 cm

**10** Find the area of the trapezium.

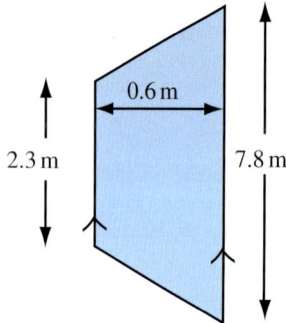

0.6 m

2.3 m

7.8 m

**11** Find the area of the parallelogram.

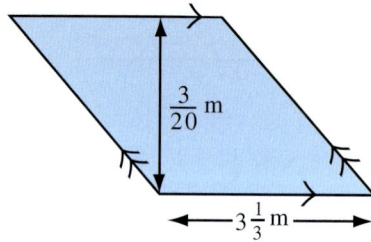

$\frac{3}{20}$ m

$3\frac{1}{3}$ m

**12**

24 m

20 m

20 m

16 m

30 m

34 m

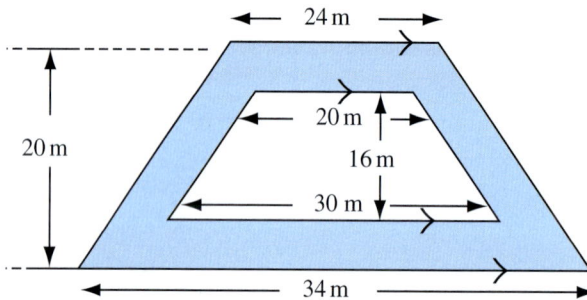

A garden is in the shape of a trapezium. It has a lawn also in the shape of a trapezium. The shaded area is a path around the lawn. Find the area of the path.

**13** The area of the trapezium is equal to the area of the parallelogram. Find the missing value $x$

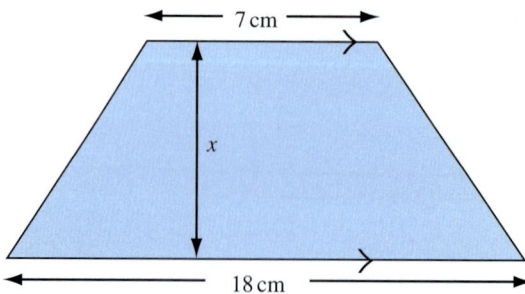

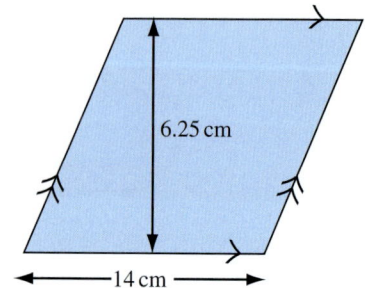

7 cm

$x$

18 cm

6.25 cm

14 cm

388

**14** Wayne wants to grass an area in his garden (the shaded area). If it costs him £13 to grass every 30 m², how much will it cost him to grass the shaded area? (Give your answer to the nearest pound)

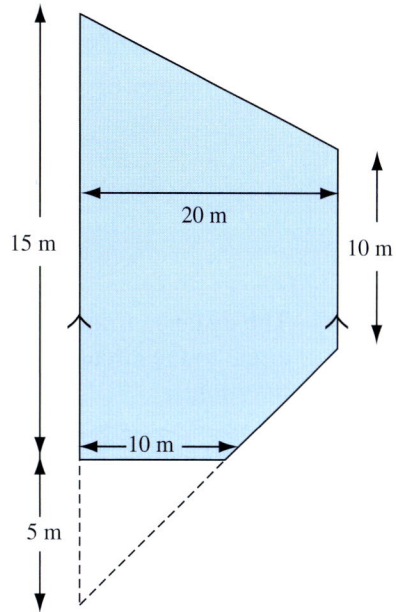

Can you still?

Can you still?

## (15A) Percentages (see Unit 6)

1. Which of the 3 questions below gives the largest answer?

   | 30% of £120 | or | 70% of £50 | or | 35% of £110 |

2. Sandeep gets a pay rise of 4%. If he used to earn £15000 each year, how much does he earn now?

3. Faye gets a 20% discount when she books a holiday to Spain. The holiday usually costs £650. How much does Faye pay for the holiday?

4. Beth scores 21 out of 35 in a science test. What percentage is this (to the nearest whole number)? *You may use a calculator.*

5. Kenny buys a digital radio for £190 + VAT. If VAT is 17.5%, how much will Kenny pay in total?

6. £6000 is invested in a bank at 4% per annum (year) compound interest. How much money will be in the bank after 2 years?

7. Sandra buys a caravan for £16000. Its value depreciates (goes down) each year by 5% of its value at the start of the year. How much is the caravan worth after 3 years?

The perimeter of a circle is called the *circumference*.

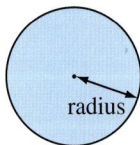

The distance from the centre of a circle to the circumference is called the *radius*.

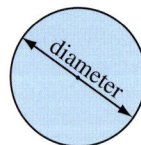

The distance across a circle through its centre is called the *diameter*.

The diameter is twice the radius

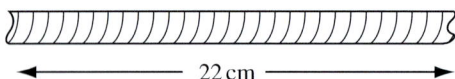

22 cm

A piece of string 22 cm long will make:

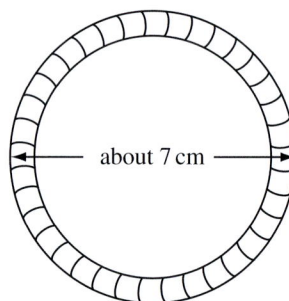

about 7 cm

A circle whose diameter is just over 7 cm.

If you divide the circumference of a circle by its diameter the number you obtain is always just over 3,

in fact                               3.14159265.....

This number has many digits so it is more convenient to give the number a name.

We call it 'pi'.

This is the Greek letter $\pi$.

$$\pi = 3.14159265.....$$

Most calculators have a $\boxed{\pi}$ button.

$$\frac{\text{circumference}}{\text{diameter}} = \pi \quad \text{for any circle}$$

so circumference = $\pi$ × diameter

$$C = \pi d \quad \text{*Learn* this formula.}$$

Find the circumference of each of the circles below (Give your answer correct to 1 decimal place).

(a)

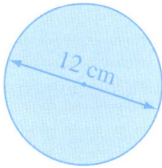

$C = \pi d$

$C = \pi \times 12 = 37.7$ cm.
(sometimes $\pi$ is not worked out and the answer is left as $12\pi$)

(b)

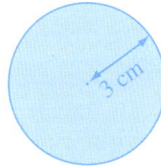

radius is 3 cm so diameter = 6 cm

$C = \pi d$

$C = \pi \times 6 = 18.8$ cm.

## M15.3

When necessary, give answers to 1 decimal place.

**1** *Use a calculator* to find the circumference of each circle below.

(a)

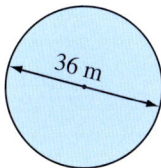
36 m

(b)

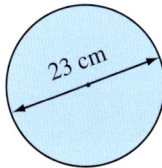
23 cm

(c)

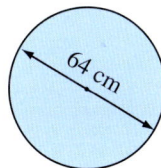
64 cm

(d)

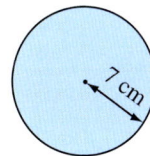
7 cm

(e)

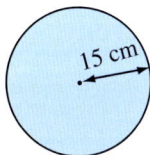
15 cm

(f)

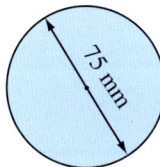
75 mm

(g)

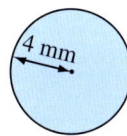
4 mm

(h)

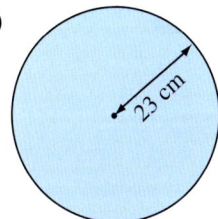
23 cm

**2** Which shape below has the larger perimeter – the square or the circle?

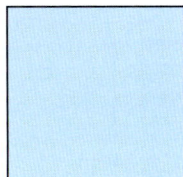
8 cm

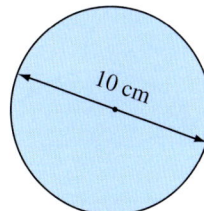
10 cm

**3** Kris walks around the edge of a circular lake of radius 250 m. If Kris walks once around the lake, how far does he walk? (Give your answer to the nearest metre)

(a) Find the perimeter of this shape (give the answer to 1 decimal place).

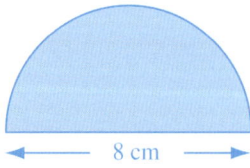

8 cm

The curved part is a semi-circle.

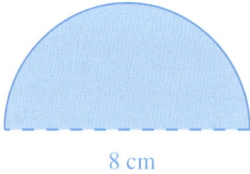

8 cm

$C = \pi d$ (whole circle)

$C = \pi \times 8 = 25.13$

We want half the circumference
= 25.13 ÷ 2 = 12.57

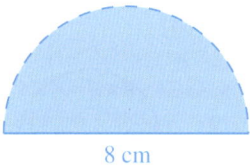

8 cm

Add on the straight line 8 cm

Perimeter of shape = 12.57 + 8 = 20.57

Perimeter = 20.6 cm (to 1 decimal place)

(b) A football of diameter 28 cm rolls in a straight line so that it makes 15 complete revolutions. How far does it roll? (Give your answer to the nearest cm).

$C = \pi d$

$C = \pi \times 28 = 87.96$

For one revolution (360° turn) the football rolls 87.96 cm (one circumference)

For 15 revolutions, the football rolls 15 × 87.96

= 1319.4 cm

= 1319 cm (to the nearest cm)

(ie. 13.19 m)

## E15.3

Calculate the perimeter of each shape. All arcs are either semi-circles or quarter circles. Give answers correct to 1 decimal place.

**1**

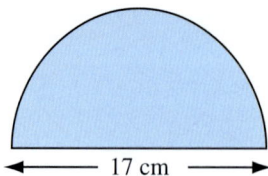

17 cm

**2**

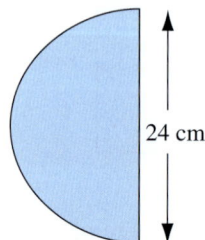

24 cm

**3**

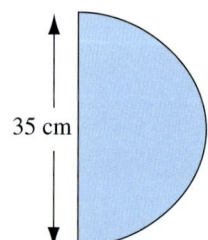

35 cm

**4**

7 cm
7 cm

**5**

100 m
60 m

**6**

8 cm
10 cm

**7**

9.4 cm
9.4 cm

**8**

18 cm
9 cm

**9**

45 cm
52 cm

**10**

10 cm
10 cm
15 cm

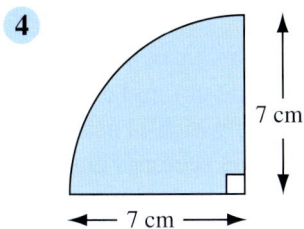

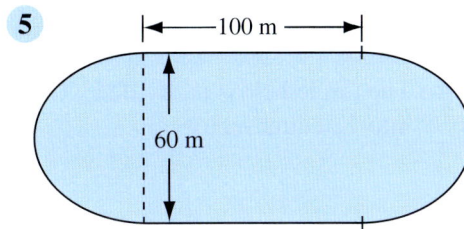

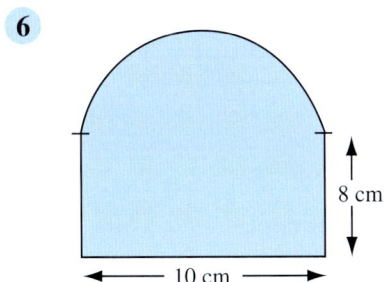

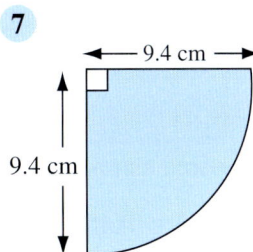

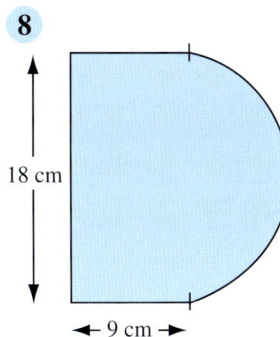

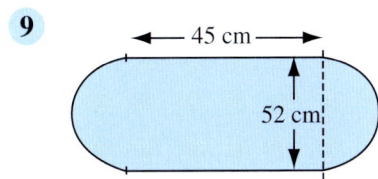

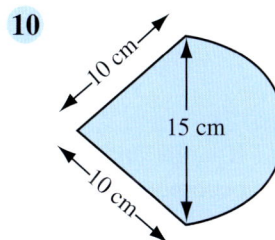

**11** The wheels on Inzaman's bike have a diameter of 65 cm. He travels so that the wheels go round completely 10 times. What distance does Inzaman travel? (Give your answer to the nearest cm).

**12** Dan kicks a football down the side of a steep hill and it rolls 80 metres. If the diameter of the football is 27 cm, how many *complete* revolutions did the football make before it stopped?

**13** A car tyre has a radius of 41 cm.

(a) How long is its circumference in cm?

(b) How many complete revolutions will the tyre make if the car travels 5 km?

**14** The circumference of a circular plate is 91 cm. Calculate the diameter of the plate to the nearest cm.

**15** A propeller rotates at 150 revolutions per minute. If the radius is 40 cm, how far does the end of the propeller travel in one hour? (Give your answer to the nearest kilometre).

## Area of a circle

(a) The circle below is divided into 12 equal sectors

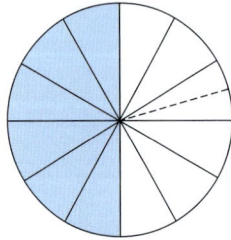

(b) The sectors are cut and arranged to make a shape which is nearly a rectangle. (one sector is cut in half).

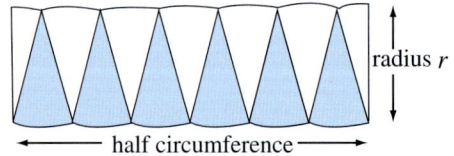

radius $r$

half circumference

(c) The approximate area can be found as follows:

length of rectangle $\approx$ half circumference of circle

$$\approx \frac{\pi \times 2r}{2} = \pi r^2$$

$$\approx \pi r^2$$

width of rectangle $\approx r$

$\therefore$ area of rectangle $\approx \pi r \times r$

$$\approx \pi r^2$$

If larger and larger numbers of sectors were used, this approximation would become more and more accurate.

This is a demonstration of an important result.

Area of a circle $= \pi r^2$    *Learn* this formula.

Note: $\pi r^2$ means '$r^2$ then multiply by $\pi$'

---

Find the area of each of the circles below (give your answer correct to 1 decimal place).

(a)

8 cm

radius = 8 cm

area   = $\pi r^2$

= $\pi \times 8^2$

= $\pi \times 64$

= 201.1 cm$^2$

(an 'exact' value of $64\pi$ could be given)

(b)

37 cm

diameter = 37 cm

so radius = 37 ÷ 2 = 18.5 cm

area    = $\pi r^2$

= $\pi \times 18.5^2$

= $\pi \times 342.25$

= 1075.2 cm$^2$

In questions **1** to **9**, calculate the area of each circle correct to 1 decimal place.

**1**
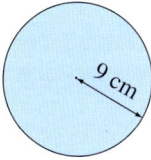
9 cm

**2**
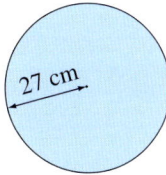
27 cm

**3**
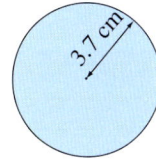
3.7 cm

**4**
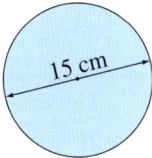
15 cm

**5**
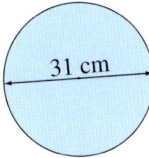
31 cm

**6**
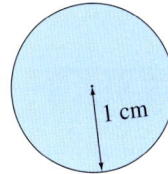
1 cm

**7**
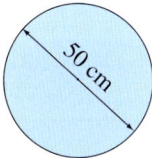
50 cm

**8**
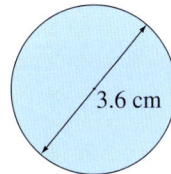
3.6 cm

**9**
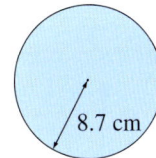
8.7 cm

**10** Tania creates a circular flower bed of radius 1.5 m. What is the area of this flower bed in m²?

**11** Which shape below has the larger area – the rectangle or the circle?

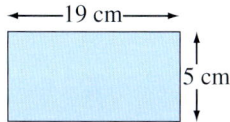
19 cm
5 cm

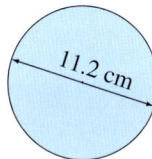
11.2 cm

**12** Do *not* use a calculator in this question. Find the area of each circle, leaving π in your answer (for example, 18π).

(a)
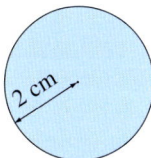
2 cm

(b)
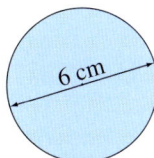
6 cm

(c)
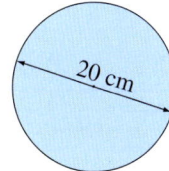
20 cm

Find the area of this shape (give the answer correct to 1 decimal place).

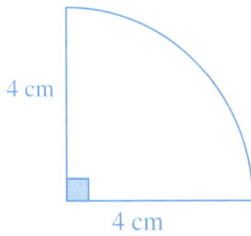

Area of circle $= \pi r^2$

$= \pi \times 4^2$

$= \pi \times 16 = 50.27$

Area of the quarter circle $= 50.27 \div 4$

$= 12.6 \text{ cm}^2$
(to 1 decimal place)

## E15.4

In questions **1** to **6** find the area of each shape. All arcs are either semi-circles or quarter circles and the units are cm. Give answers correct to 1 decimal place.

**1**

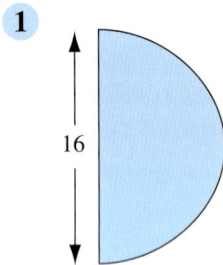

16

**2**

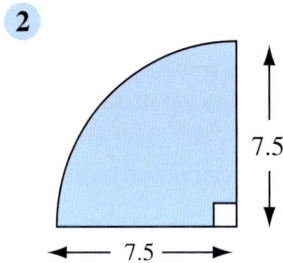

7.5

7.5

**3**

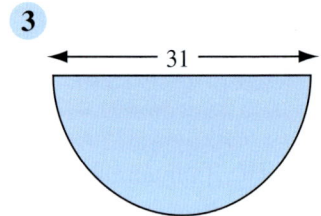

31

**4**

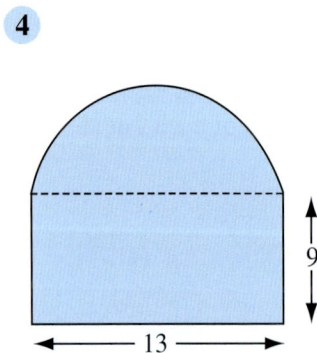

9

13

**5**

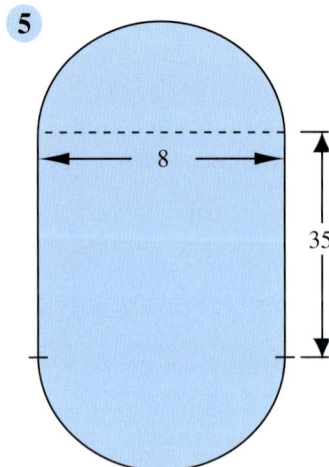

8

35

**6**

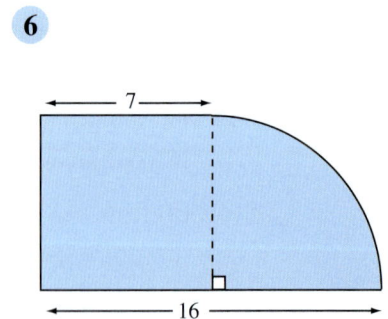

7

16

In questions **7** to **12** find the shaded area. Lengths are in cm. Give answers correct to 1 decimal place.

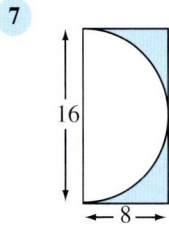

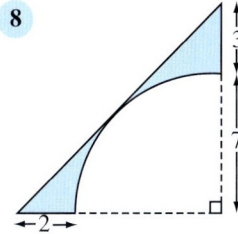

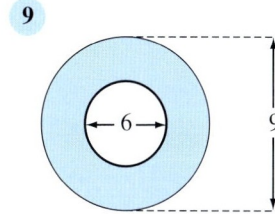

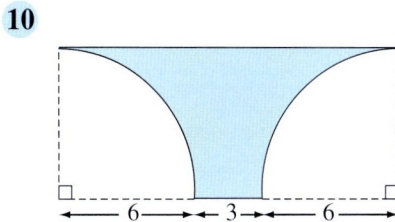

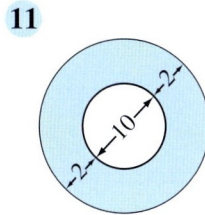

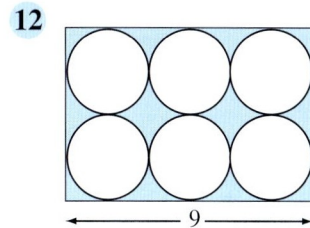

**7**

**8**

**9**

**10**

**11**

**12**

*Can you still?*

*Can you still?*

**15B**   **Probability (see Unit 11)**

**1.** Jake has 11 cards as shown below:

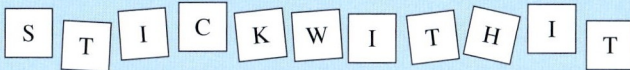

S   T   I   C   K   W   I   T   H   I   T

Jake picks a card at random. What is the probability that he picks the letter:

(a) K?   ( b) T?      (c) a letter in the first half of the alphabet?

**2.** Rena has 19 pencils. 9 are red, 3 are blue and the rest are black.

Rena takes out a pencil at random. What is the probability that she takes out:

(a) red?        (b) black?     (c) blue or black?

**3.** A dice is thrown 240 times. How many times would you expect to get:

(a) a 5?        (b) an odd number?        (c) a square number?

**4.** The probability that Pat will remember to bring his textbook to his next maths lesson is 0.8. How many times would you expect him to bring his textbook in the next 30 lessons?

## Key Facts

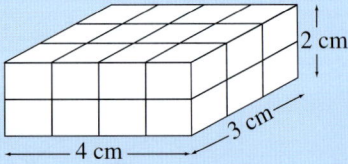

$$\text{Volume} = \text{length} \times \text{width} \times \text{height}$$

$$\begin{aligned}\text{Volume} &= 4 \times 3 \times 2 \\ &= 12 \times 2 \\ &= 24 \text{ cm}^3\end{aligned}$$

The cuboid has 6 faces.

| Face | | area (cm²) |
|------|------|------|
| Front | 4 × 2 = | 8 |
| Back | 4 × 2 = | 8 |
| Top | 4 × 3 = | 12 |
| Bottom | 4 × 3 = | 12 |
| Side 1 | 3 × 2 = | 6 |
| Side 2 | 3 × 2 = | 6 |
| | Total | 52 |

Total surface area = 52 cm²

### M15.5

1

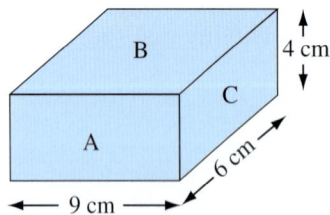

Write down the area of:

(a) the front face A

(b) the top face B

(c) the side face C

**2** Copy and complete the tables below to find the total surface area of each cuboid.

(a)

| Face | Area (cm²) |
|---|---|
| Front | |
| Back | |
| Top | |
| Bottom | |
| Side 1 | |
| Side 2 | |
| | Total = |

(b)

| Face | Area (cm²) |
|---|---|
| Front | |
| Back | |
| Top | |
| Bottom | |
| Side 1 | |
| Side 2 | |
| | Total = |

(c)

| Face | Area (cm²) |
|---|---|
| Front | |
| Back | |
| Top | |
| Bottom | |
| Side 1 | |
| Side 2 | |
| | Total = |

(d)

| Face | Area (cm²) |
|---|---|
| Front | |
| Back | |
| Top | |
| Bottom | |
| Side 1 | |
| Side 2 | |
| | Total = |

**3** Find the volume of each cuboid in question **2**. (The units for each answer will be cm³)

**4** Which of these 3 cuboids has the largest surface area?

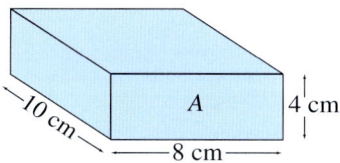

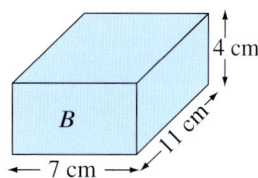

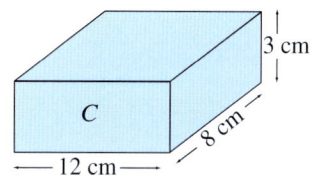

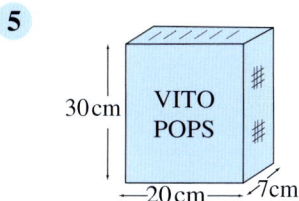

**5**

A breakfast cereal packet measures 30 cm × 20 cm × 7 cm.

The cereal packets are packed into large boxes which measure 1.2 m × 1 m × 0.42 m.

How many cereal packets can be packed into 1 large box?

**6** How many 2 cm × 2 cm × 2 cm cubes will fit into a box which measures 30 cm × 12 cm × 18 cm?

## Units of area and volume

*Length:* 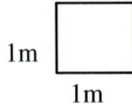   1 m = 100 cm

*Area:*  1 m × 1 m = 100 cm × 100 cm

1m ☐ 1m     $1 m^2 = 10000 cm^2$     ☐ 100 cm / 100 cm

*Volume:*  1 m × 1 m × 1 m = 100 cm × 100 cm × 100 cm

1m 1m 1m 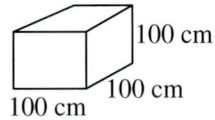   $1 m^3 = 1000000 cm^3$     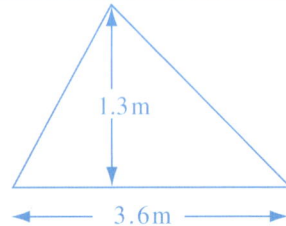 100 cm / 100 cm / 100 cm

*Capacity:*

1 litre = 1000 ml       1 ml is the same as 1cm$^3$

From above, 1 m$^3$ = 1000 000 cm$^3$  so 1 m$^3$ = 1000 000 ml

so   1 m$^3$ = 1000 litres

---

(a)  A rectangular tank measures 2 m by 1.2 m by 1.1 m. If the tank is completely full of water, how many litres of water does it contain?

Volume = 2 × 1.2 × 1.1

= 2.64 m$^3$

= 2.64 × 1000 litres

= 2640 litres.

(b)

1.3 m

3.6 m

Find the area *in cm²*.

**either**

Area = $\frac{1}{2}$ bh = $\frac{1}{2}$ × 3.6 × 1.3

= 2.34 m$^2$

= 2.34 × 10000 cm$^2$

= 23400 cm$^2$

**or change lengths first**

Area = $\frac{1}{2}$ bh = $\frac{1}{2}$ × 360 cm × 130 cm

= 23400 cm$^2$

**1** How many litres of water will each tank below contain when full.

(a)

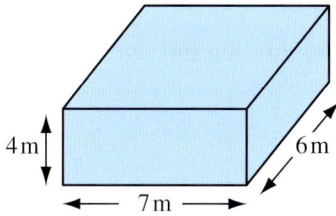

4 m    6 m    7 m

(b)

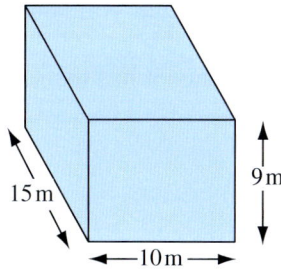

15 m    9 m    10 m

(c)

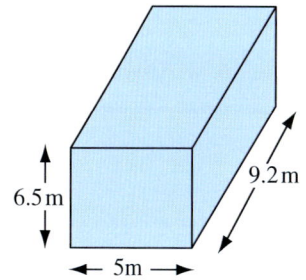

9.2 m    6.5 m    5 m

**2** Find the area of each shape below *in cm²*.

(a)

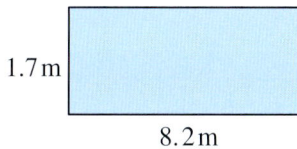

1.7 m    8.2 m

(b)

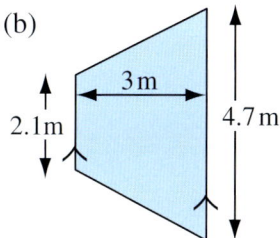

3 m    2.1 m    4.7 m

(c)

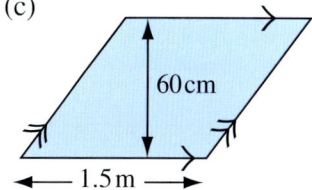

60 cm    1.5 m

**3** Copy and complete

(a) $1 \text{ m}^3 = \boxed{\phantom{xx}} \text{ cm}^3$

(b) $2 \text{ m}^3 = \boxed{\phantom{xx}} \text{ cm}^3$

(c) $4.7 \text{ m}^3 = \boxed{\phantom{xx}} \text{ cm}^3$

(d) $1 \text{ m}^2 = \boxed{\phantom{xx}} \text{ cm}^2$

(e) $3 \text{ m}^2 = \boxed{\phantom{xx}} \text{ cm}^2$

(f) $80000 \text{ cm}^2 = \boxed{\phantom{xx}} \text{ m}^2$

(g) $35000 \text{ cm}^2 = \boxed{\phantom{xx}} \text{ m}^2$

(h) $9.25 \text{ m}^2 = \boxed{\phantom{xx}} \text{ cm}^2$

(i) $1 \text{ m}^3 = \boxed{\phantom{xx}}$ litres

(j) $7 \text{ m}^3 = \boxed{\phantom{xx}}$ litres

(k) $5600$ litres $= \boxed{\phantom{xx}} \text{ m}^3$

(l) $3.9 \text{ m}^3 = \boxed{\phantom{xx}} \text{ cm}^3$

**4**

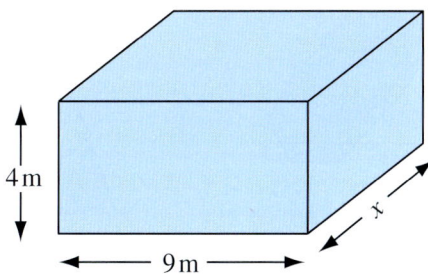

4 m    9 m    x

The capacity of this rectangular tank is 72000 litres.

Find the missing value $x$.

401

## Prisms

A prism has the same cross section throughout its length.

$$\text{Volume of prism} = (\text{Area of cross section}) \times (\text{length})$$

Any cuboid is a prism since it has the same cross section throughout its length.

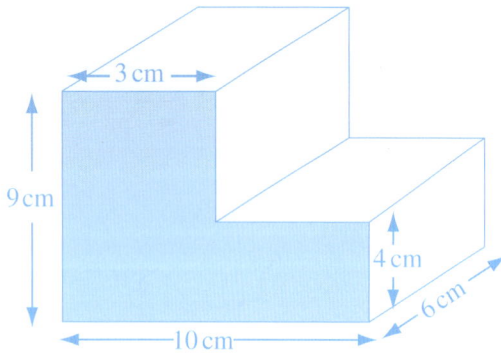

Find the volume of this prism.

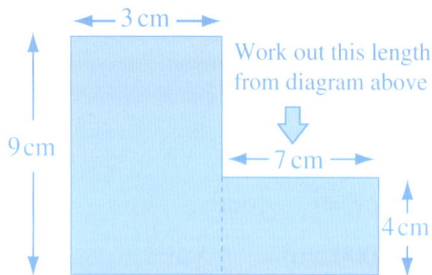

Work out this length from diagram above

Area of cross section = $(9 \times 3) + (7 \times 4)$

$= 27 + 28$

$= 55 \text{ cm}^2$

Volume of prism = Area of cross section $\times$ length

$= 55 \times 6$

$= 330 \text{ cm}^3$

### M15.6

**1** Which of the solids below are prisms?

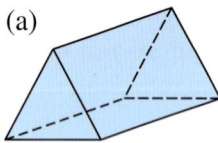

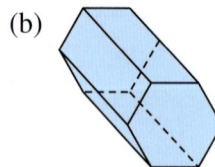

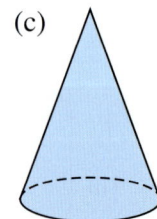

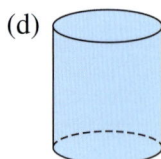

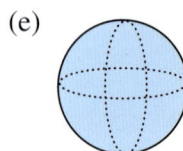

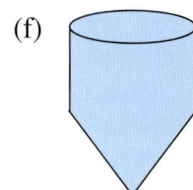

(a)

(b)

(c)

(d)

(e)

(f)

(g)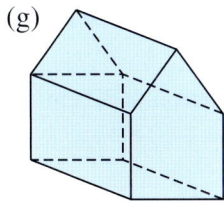

(h)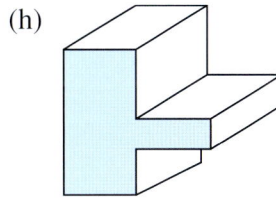

In questions **2** to **7** find the volume of each prism.

**2**

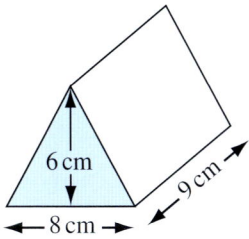
6 cm
8 cm
9 cm

**3**

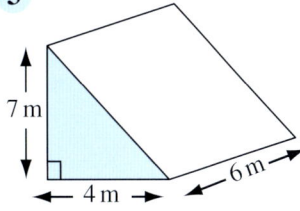
7 m
4 m
6 m

**4**

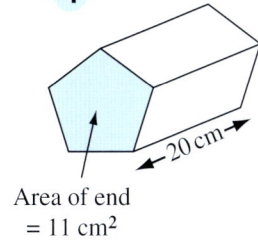
20 cm
Area of end
= 11 cm²

**5**

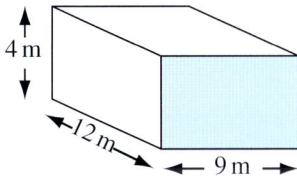
4 m
12 m
9 m

**6**

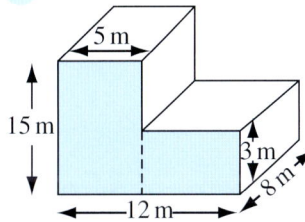
5 m
15 m
3 m
12 m
8 m

**7**

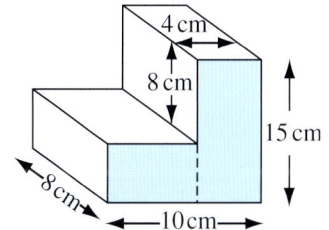
4 cm
8 cm
15 cm
8 cm
10 cm

**8** A garden shed is shown opposite.

Calculate the volume of this shed.

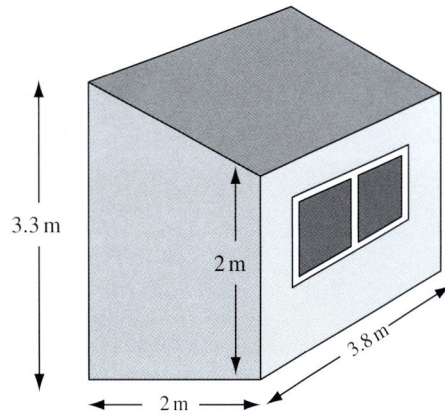
3.3 m
2 m
2 m
3.8 m

**9**

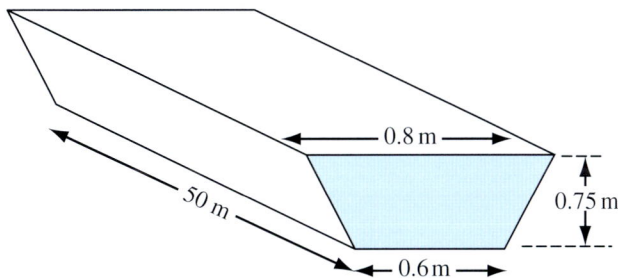
0.8 m
50 m
0.75 m
0.6 m

A trench is dug in a field. What volume of soil is removed?

**10**

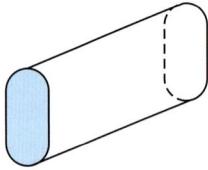

A piece of metal is in the shape of a prism. It has a volume of 6400 cm³.

If the area of the cross section is 32 cm², how long is the piece of metal?

In questions **11** and **12** find the *total surface area* of each prism.

**11**

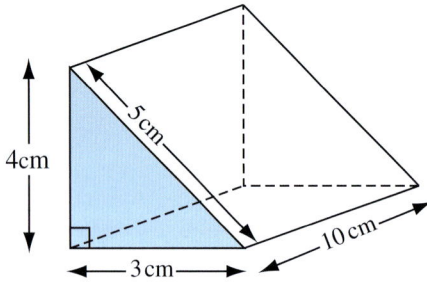

**12**

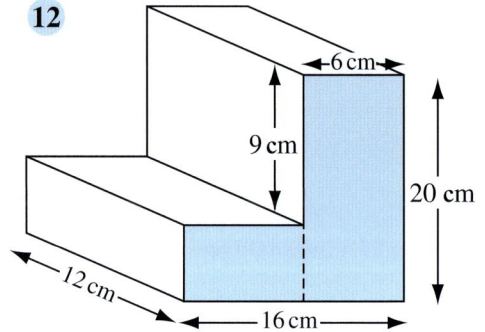

---

🔑 # Key Facts

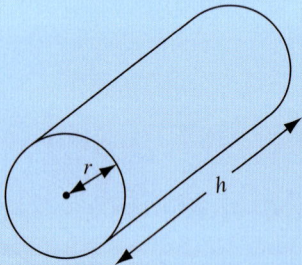

A cylinder is a prism because it has the same cross section throughout its length.

Volume = (area of cross section) × (length)

Volume = $\pi r^2 \times h$

$$V = \pi r^2 h$$

A cylinder has radius 5 cm and length 8 cm. Find the volume of the cylinder.

$V = \pi r^2 h$

$V = \pi \times 5^2 \times 8$

$V = 628.3$ cm³ (to 1 decimal place)

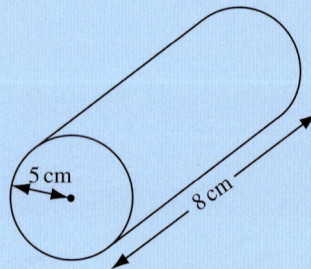

*Use a calculator* and give answers to 1 decimal place where necessary.

In questions **1** to **6** find the volume of each cylinder.

**1**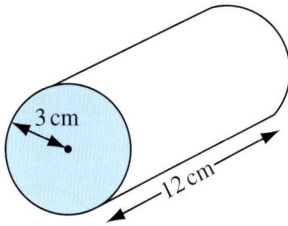

3 cm
12 cm

**2**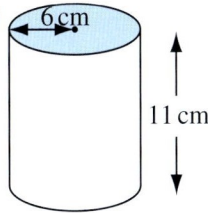

6 cm
11 cm

**3**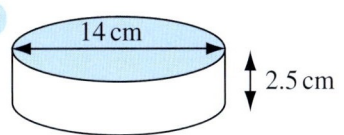

14 cm
2.5 cm

**4**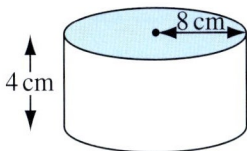

8 cm
4 cm

**5**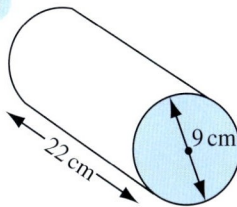

22 cm
9 cm

**6**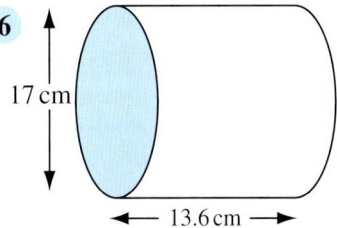

17 cm
13.6 cm

**7** Find the volume of a cylindrical container of radius 2 m and height 10 m. Leave π in your answer (for example, 24π).

**8** Find the volume in *litres* of a cylindrical tank of diameter 2.4 m and height 1.9 m.

**9** Which of the cylinders below has the larger volume?

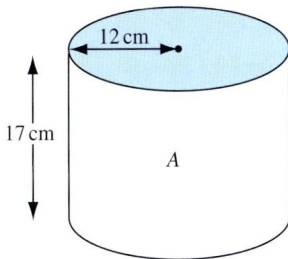

12 cm
17 cm
A

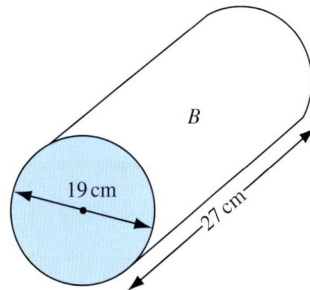

B
19 cm
27 cm

**10** A cylindrical can of dog meat has a radius of 3.5 cm and a height of 11 cm. If the can contains 400 cm³ of dog meat, how much empty space is there inside the can? (Give your answer correct to 1 decimal place).

**11** Cylinders are cut along the axis of symmetry. Find the volume of each object. (Give answers correct to 1 decimal place).

(a)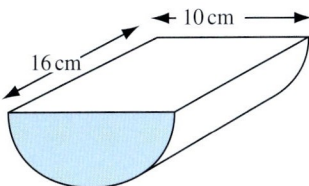

10 cm
16 cm

(b)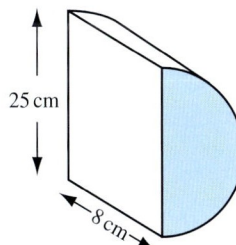

25 cm
8 cm

(c)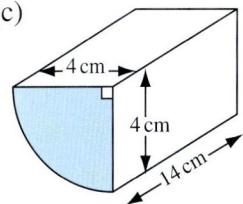

4 cm
4 cm
14 cm

**12**

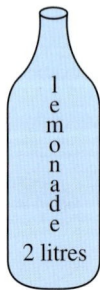

2 litres of lemonade is 2000 cm³.

How many glasses of radius 2.5 cm and height 10 cm can be completely filled from the bottle of lemonade?

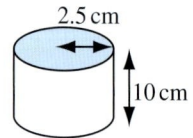

**13** A 300 m tunnel is dug. It forms a prism with the cross section shown.

(a) Calculate the area of the cross section.

(b) Calculate the volume of earth which is dug out for the tunnel.

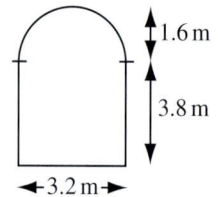

**14**

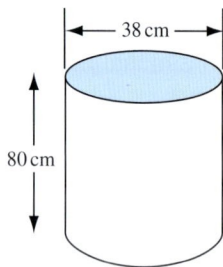

A cylindrical barrel is full of water. The water is poured into a trough as shown.

Will all the water go in without the trough overflowing?

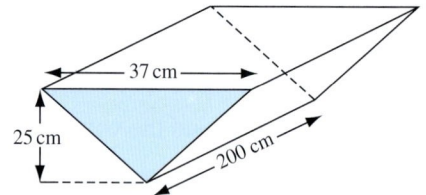

## Similar triangles

Two triangles are *similar* if they have the same angles.

Corresponding sides must be in the same proportion.

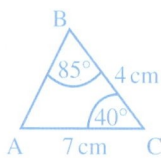

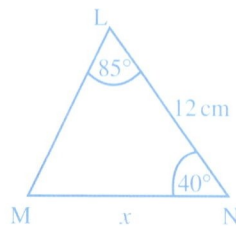

Find $x$

The triangles are similar because all 3 angles are the same.

Sides BC and LN correspond.

LN is $\frac{12}{4}$ times longer, ie. 3 times longer.

Each side in the larger triangle is 3 times longer than the corresponding side in the smaller triangle.

Sides MN and AC correspond so $x = 7 \times 3 = 21$ cm.

**1** For each part of the Question below, the shapes are similar. Find $x$.

(a)

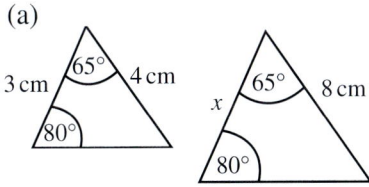

(b)

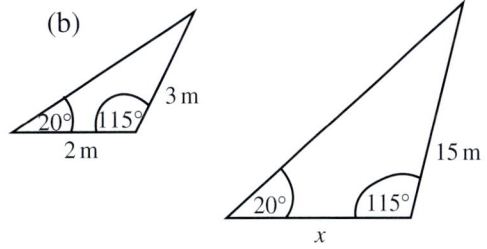

(c)

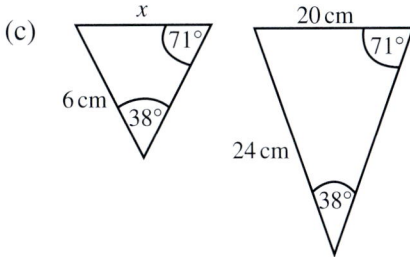

(d)

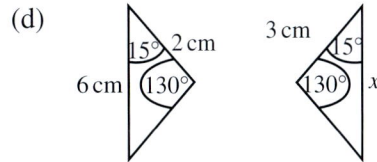

**2**

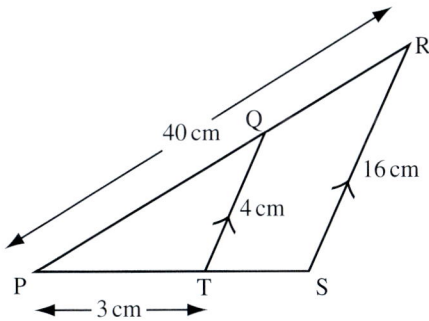

Triangles PQT and PRS are similar.

(a) Find PS

(b) Find PQ

**3**

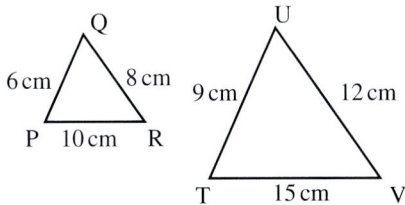

*Explain* why these triangles are similar.

**4** Use similar triangles to find $x$ in each diagram below.

(a)

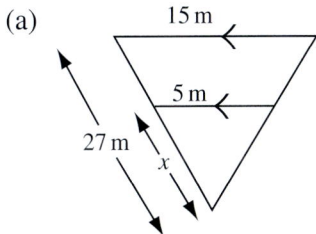

(b)

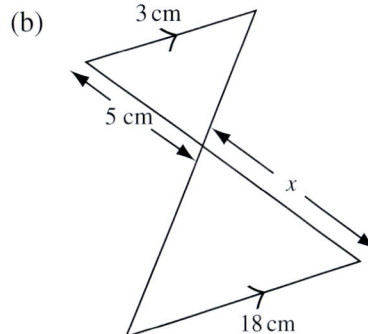

407

**5**

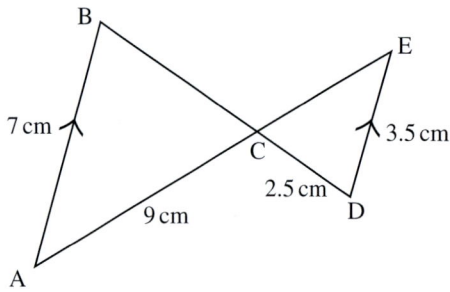

Triangles ABC and CDE are similar.

(a) Find BC

(b) Find CE

**6** Use similar triangles to find $x$.

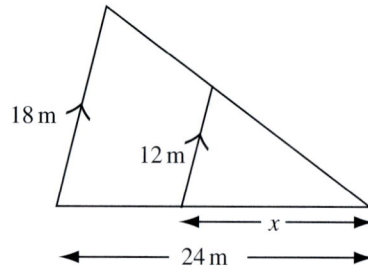

**7**

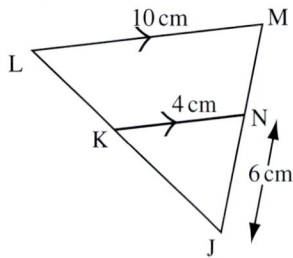

Use similar triangles to find the length of MN.

**8** Use similar triangles to find $x$ in each diagram below.

(a)

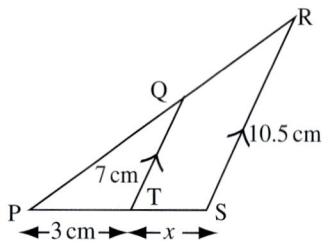

(b)

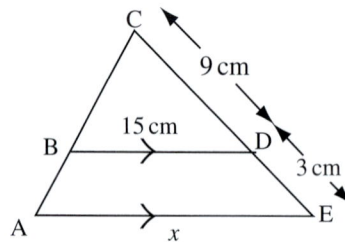

(c)

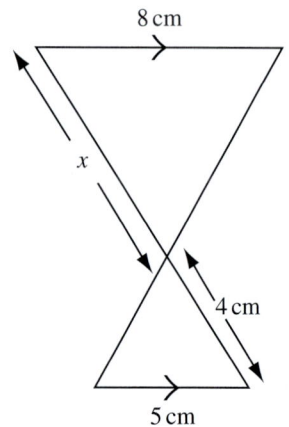

In this unit we have seen that a formula for an area involves multiplying 2 lengths together.

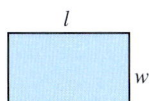

area = $l\, w$

length × length

area = $\pi\, r^2$

length × length

the number π written before the letter is not a length so has no dimension

A formula for a volume involves multiplying 3 lengths together.

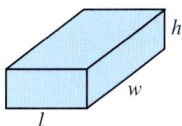

volume = $l\, w\, h$

length × length × length

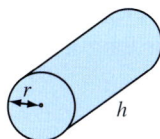

volume = $\pi\, r^2\, h$
= $\pi \times r \times r \times h$

the number π has no dimension

length × length × length

A formula with one length only represents a length.

Note: A number has no dimension unless it is defined as a length.

**E15.7**

**1** $x$ and $y$ are lengths.

P = $4xy$   Is this a formula for a length, area or volume?

**2** Each letter below is a length. For each expression write down if it represents a length, area or volume.

| | | | | |
|---|---|---|---|---|
| (a) $pq$ | (b) $5b$ | (c) $2xy$ | (d) $a^2$ | (e) $6y$ |
| (f) $abc$ | (g) $8b^2$ | (h) $5xyz$ | (i) $3xz$ | (j) $b^2c$ |
| (k) $4a^3$ | (l) $7x^2$ | (m) $9x$ | (n) $\pi y$ | (o) $a^2b$ |
| (p) $\pi y^2$ | (q) $4bc$ | (r) $\pi abc$ | (s) $5\pi a$ | (t) $8\pi ab$ |

**3** Here are 5 expressions:

| expression | length | area | volume | none of these |
|---|---|---|---|---|
| $\pi r^2$ | | | | |
| $4r^2 l^2$ | | | | |
| $\pi r l$ | | | | |
| $2\pi r$ | | | | |
| $\pi r^2 l$ | | | | |

$r$ and $l$ are lengths.

Copy the table and put a tick in the correct column to show whether the expression can be used for length, area, volume or none of these.

## WATCH YOUR MONEY! – Which is better value?

How do you spot the best value in a shop?

A pack of
2 kitchen rolls £1.20

A pack of
3 kitchen rolls £1.71

To compare the cost, find the cost of 1 kitchen roll (the *unit* cost) for each pack.

2 rolls for £1.20 gives 60 p per roll

3 rolls for £1.71 gives 57 p per roll

The pack of 3 rolls is the *best value* (obviously you would only buy the pack of 3 kitchen rolls if you do not mind having that many rolls or have enough money to buy that pack at that particular moment).

| Flakes £2.25 750 g | Which packet of flakes is the best value? | Flakes £1.60 500 g |
|---|---|---|

750 g costs 225 p, so 1g costs $\dfrac{225}{750}$ = 0.3 p

500 g costs 160 p, so 1g costs $\dfrac{160}{500}$ = 0.32 p

so the 750 g box is the best value.

*OR*

500 g costs 160 p so 250 g costs 80 p

At this price, 3 × 250 g = 750 g costs 3 × 80 p = £2.40

This is more expensive than the 750 g box.

## WYM15

For each of questions **1** to **4** , decide which is the better value.

| A pack of 2 light bulbs 92 p | or | A pack of 5 light bulbs £2.40 |
|---|---|---|
| *A* | | *B* |

**2**

| 1 can of cola 45 p | or | A pack of 6 cans of cola £2.34 |
|---|---|---|
| *A* | | *B* |

| 150 g tin of baked beans 33 p | or | 400 g tin of baked beans 56 p |
|---|---|---|
| *A* | | *B* |

**4**

| 500 g punnet of strawberries £1.89 BUY ONE AND GET ONE FREE | or | 1 kg punnet of strawberries £3.82 |
|---|---|---|
| *A* | | *B* |

**5**  Carl is buying paper plates and plastic cups for a party. Paper plates cost 80 p for a pack of 20 or £1.50 for a pack of 50.

Plastic cups cost 78 p for a pack of 12 or £1.80 for a pack of 30.

Carl needs 60 plates and 75 cups. What is the cheapest way of buying them?

411

**6** Jordan buys some tomato ketchup from the local supermarket. There are 3 different sized bottles.

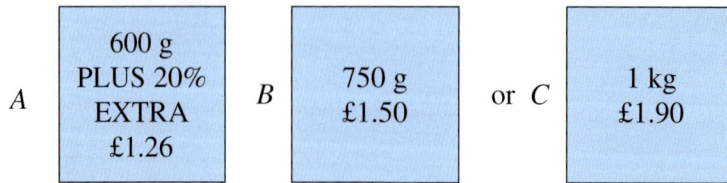

A | 600 g PLUS 20% EXTRA £1.26    B | 750 g £1.50    or  C | 1 kg £1.90

Which bottle gives the best value for money?

**7** Which box of washing powder below is the best value?

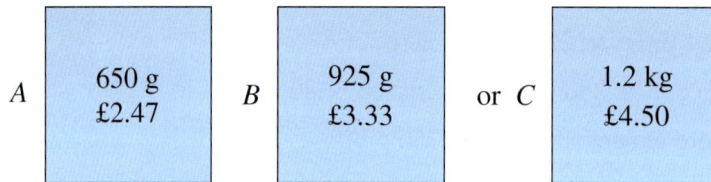

A | 650 g £2.47    B | 925 g £3.33    or  C | 1.2 kg £4.50

## TEST YOURSELF ON UNIT 15

**1.** Finding perimeters of shapes

Find the perimeter of each shape below. All lengths are in cm.

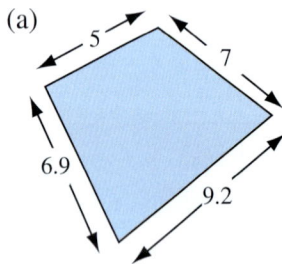

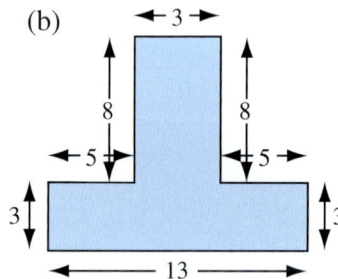

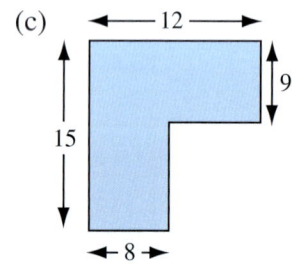

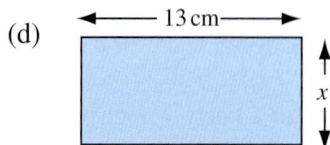

(a)

5, 7, 6.9, 9.2

(b)

3, 8, 8, 5, 5, 3, 13

(c)

12, 9, 15, 8

(d)

13 cm, x

The perimeter of this rectangle is 64 cm.
Find the missing value x.

## 2. Finding areas of triangles and rectangles

Find the area of each shape below. All lengths are in cm.

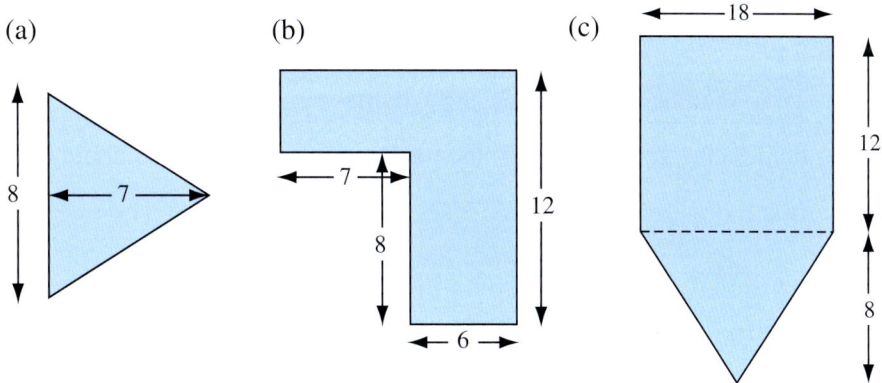

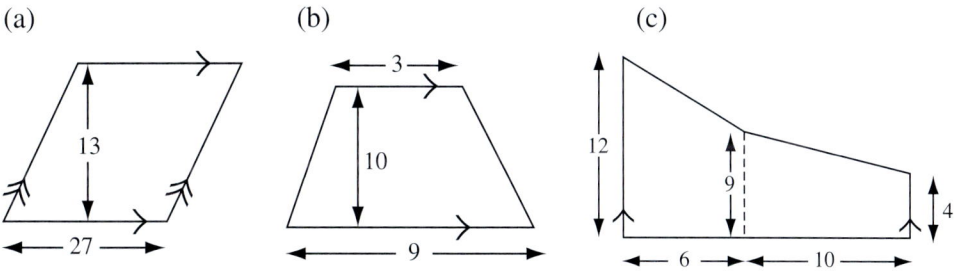

(a)

(b)

(c)

## 3. Finding areas of trapeziums and parallelograms

Find the area of each shape below. All lengths are in cm.

(a)

(b)

(c)

## 4. Finding circumferences of circles

*Use a calculator* to find the circumference or perimeter of each shape below. When necessary, give answers to 1 decimal place.

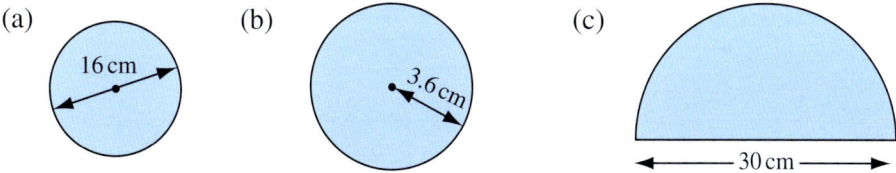

(a)

(b)

(c)

## 5. Finding areas of circles

*Use a calculator* to find the area of each shape below. When necessary, give answers to 1 decimal place.

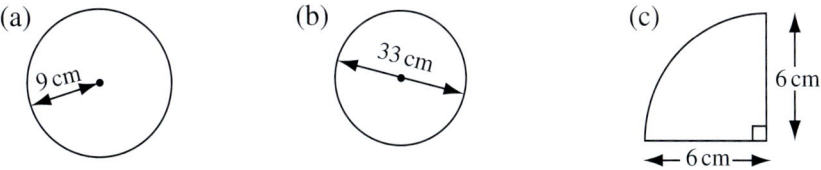

(a)

(b)

(c)

(d) Find the shaded area.

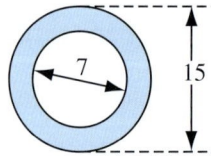

**6.** Finding surface areas and volumes of cuboids

Find (i) the volume and (ii) the total surface area of each cuboid below.

(a)

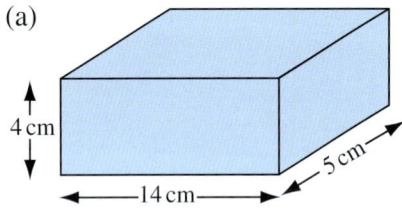

(b)

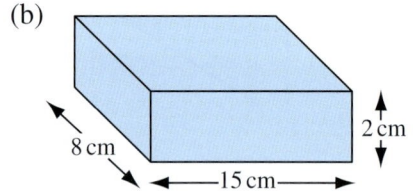

(c) A cuboid has a length of 20 cm and a width of 5 cm. What is the height of the cuboid if the volume is 320 cm³?

**7.** Converting units of area and volume

Copy and complete

(a) $1 m^2 = \boxed{\phantom{x}}$ cm² 

(b) $5 m^3 = \boxed{\phantom{x}}$ cm³ 

(c) $9.4 m^3 = \boxed{\phantom{x}}$ cm³

(d) $5.6 m^2 = \boxed{\phantom{x}}$ cm² 

(e) $2 m^3 = \boxed{\phantom{x}}$ litres 

(f) $3.72 m^3 = \boxed{\phantom{x}}$ litres

(g) How many litres of water will this tank contain when full?

(h) Find the area of the shape below in cm².

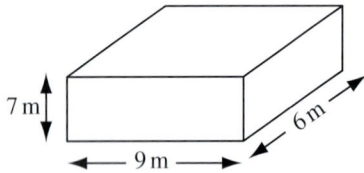

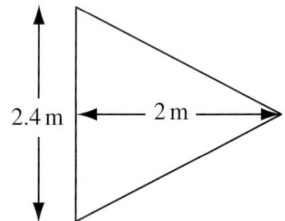

**8.** Finding volumes of prisms, particularly cylinders

Find the volume of each prism below. When necessary, give answers to 1 decimal place.

(a)

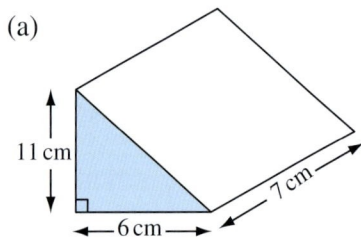

(b)

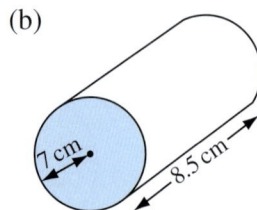

(c)

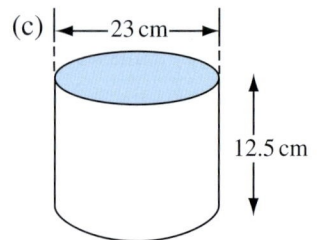

414

**9.** Using similar triangles

(a)

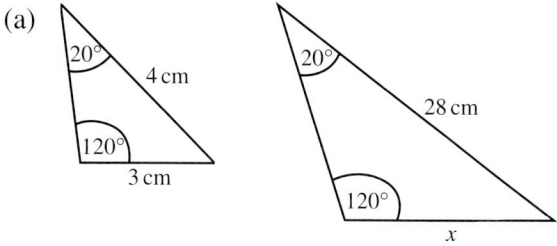

These 2 triangles are similar.

Find $x$.

(b)

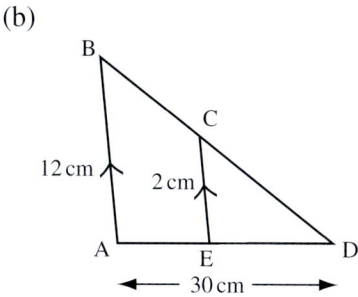

Find the length of DE.

(c)

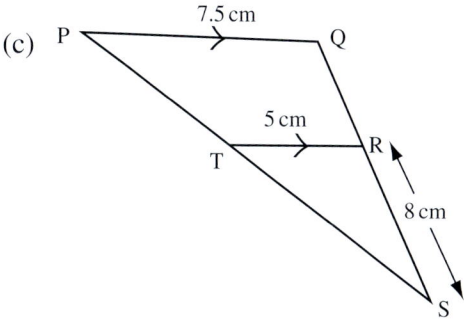

Find the length of QR.

**10.** Using dimensions to recognise a length, area or volume formula

Each letter below is a length. For each expression write down if it represents a length, area, volume or if it is none of these.

(a) $5ab$  (b) $6r$  (c) $\pi a^3$  (d) $ab^2$  (e) $\pi l$

(f) $2\pi x$  (g) $abcd$  (h) $3\pi ab$  (i) $4\pi a$  (j) $9r^2h$

## Mixed examination questions

1

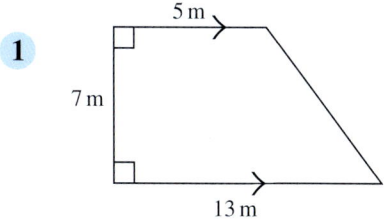

Work out the area of the shape.  (CCEA)

2  A circular pond has radius 8.2 metres.

(a) Calculate the circumference of the pond.

(b) Calculate the area of the pond.

(OCR)

415

**3** A photo frame is a square of side 20 cm.

It has a circular glass section and the rest is brass.

Work out the area of the brass part of the photo frame. Take the value of $\pi$ to be 3.142.

Give your answer to an appropriate degree of accuracy. (OCR)

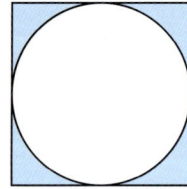

**4** Change 8 m³ to cm³.

**5** The diagram shows a bale of straw.

The bale is a cylinder with radius 70 cm and height 50 cm.

(a) Calculate the circumference of the bale.

   Give your answer to an appropriate degree of accuracy.

(b) Calculate the volume of the bale.

   State your units. (AQA)

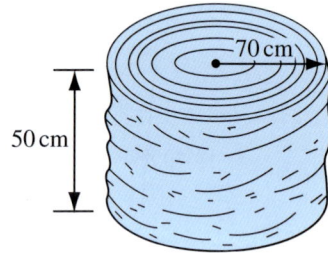

**6** The diagram shows a right-angled triangle $ABC$ and a circle. $A$, $B$ and $C$ are points on the circumference of the circle. $AC$ is a diameter of the circle. The radius of the circle is 10 cm. $AB = 16$ cm and $BC = 12$ cm. Work out the area of the shaded part of the circle. Give your answer correct to the nearest cm². 

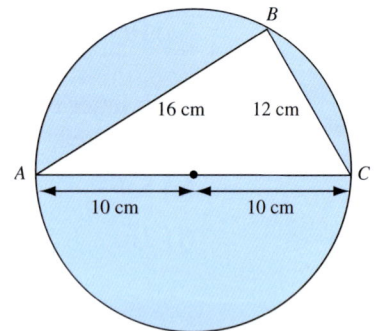

(EDEXCEL)

**7** The area of a trapezium is 7430 mm².

Change 7430 mm² to cm².

**8** The roof of a barn is a triangular prism as shown in the diagram. The dimensions, in metres, are given on the diagram.

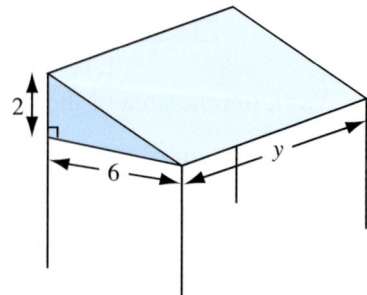

The volume of the roof space is 48 m³. Work out the length of the roof, $y$ metres. (OCR)

**In this unit you will learn how to**:

– draw scatter diagrams and describe correlation

– draw a line of best fit and use it to estimate values

– find the median and mode from tables of information

– find mean averages from tables of information (including grouped data)

– compare sets of data

– WATCH YOUR MONEY! – car insurance

## Scatter graphs

Sometimes it is important to find out if there is a connection between 2 sets of data.

**Examples**

- Do tall people weigh more?

- Do people who smoke die younger?

- Do people drink more when the weather is hot?

If there is a relationship, it will be easy to spot if the data is plotted on a scatter diagram – that is a graph in which one set of data is plotted on the horizontal axis and the other on the vertical axis.

- Here is a scatter diagram showing the number of hours without sleep for a group of people and their reaction time.

- We can see a connection. The longer people went without sleep, the greater their reaction time (ie. people reacted more slowly as they went without sleep).

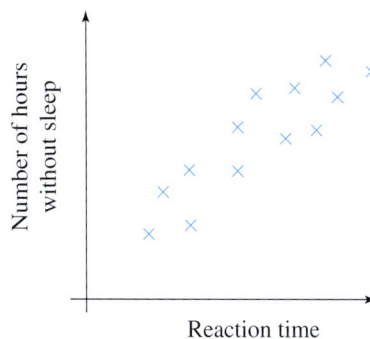

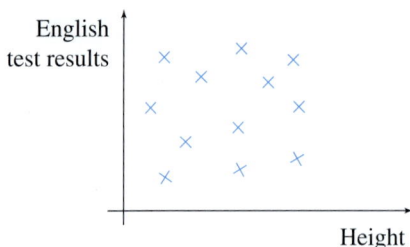

• This scatter graph shows the English test results for a group of students and their heights. We can see there is *no connection* between these 2 sets of data.

## Correlation

The word 'correlation' describes how things *co-relate*. There is 'correlation' between 2 sets of data if there is a connection or relationship.

The correlation between 2 sets of data can be positive or negative and it can be strong or weak.

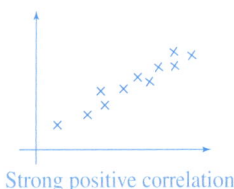

Strong positive correlation

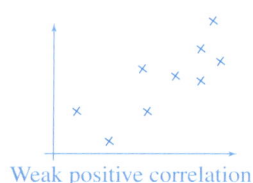

Weak positive correlation

When the points are around a line which slopes *upwards* to the right, the *correlation* is *positive* (as the values for one set of data increases, the values for the other set of data also increases).

*Strong* correlation – the points are bunched close to a line through their midst.

*Weak* correlation – the points are more scattered.

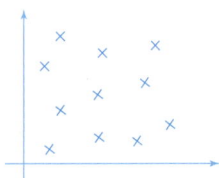

*No correlation*

Points are completely spread out.

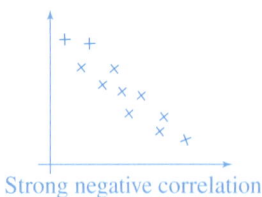

Strong negative correlation

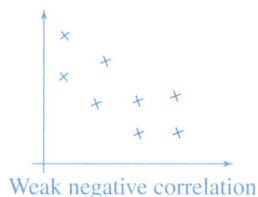

Weak negative correlation

When the points are around a line which slopes *downwards* to the right, the *correlation* is *negative* (as the values for one set of data increases, the values for the other set of data decreases).

**1** The table below shows the number of days absence for 15 year 10 pupils and their maths test results.

| Number of days absent | 5 | 9 | 0 | 1 | 10 | 7 | 0 | 5 | 2 | 9 | 10 | 2 | 6 | 8 | 4 |
|---|---|---|---|---|---|---|---|---|---|---|---|---|---|---|---|
| Test score | 7 | 3 | 10 | 9 | 2 | 5 | 9 | 6 | 8 | 4 | 3 | 9 | 6 | 4 | 7 |

(a) Copy and complete this scatter graph to show the data in the table (the first point (5, 7) is done for you).

(b) Describe the correlation in this scatter graph.

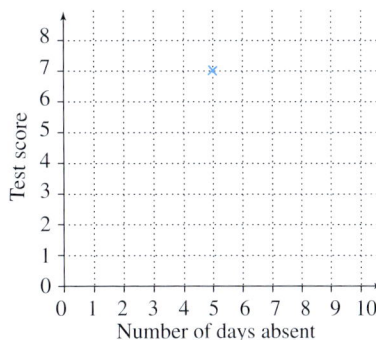

**2** The table below shows the heights and weights of 12 people.

| Weight (kg) | 72 | 60 | 66 | 55 | 80 | 63 | 70 | 79 | 57 | 60 | 77 | 65 |
|---|---|---|---|---|---|---|---|---|---|---|---|---|
| Height (cm) | 175 | 167 | 177 | 168 | 184 | 173 | 180 | 188 | 171 | 173 | 178 | 170 |

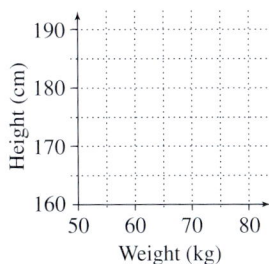

(a) Copy and complete this scatter graph to show the data in the table.

(b) Describe the correlation in this scatter graph.

**3** Describe the correlation, if any, in these scatter graphs.

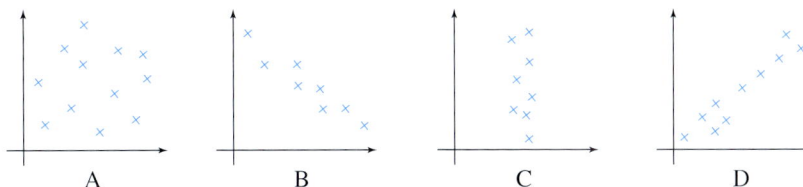

**4** The table below shows the age and value of 12 used cars.

| Age (years)      | 4 | 8 | 1 | 7 | 2 | 6 | 5 | 7 | 1 | 4 | 7 | 5 |
|------------------|---|---|---|---|---|---|---|---|---|---|---|---|
| Value (£1000's)  | 7 | 2 | 8 | 3 | 7 | 2 | 6 | 5 | 9 | 5 | 4 | 4 |

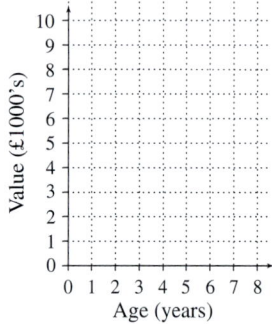

(a) Copy and complete this scatter diagram to show the data in the table.

(b) Describe the correlation in this scatter graph.

**5** **Whole class activity**

(a) *If your teacher allows*, each person in your class must do as many step-ups onto a chair as possible in one minute. When a person finishes, that person must find his/her pulse rate by counting how many beats in one minute.

Also each person needs to find out his/her height (to the nearest cm) and record his/her shoe size.

Enter all the data in a table, either on the board or on a sheet of paper.

| height | shoe size | number of step-ups | pulse rate |
|--------|-----------|--------------------|------------|
|        |           |                    |            |

(b) Draw the scatter graphs shown below

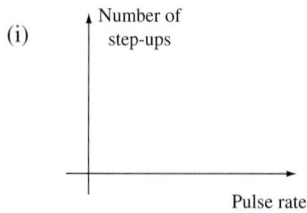

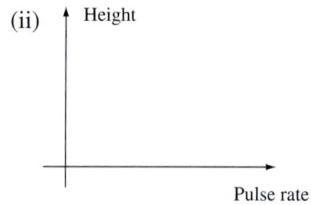

(i)

(ii)

(c) Describe the correlation, if any, in the scatter graphs you drew in part (b).

(d) (i) Draw a scattergram of 2 sets of data where you think there might be positive correlation.

   (ii) Was there indeed a positive correlation?

## (16A) Add, subtract, multiply and divide decimals
### (see Unit 9)

Do not use a calculator

1. Gary buys a magazine for £2.10 and spends £2.35 on the bus. How much change will he have left from £20?

2. Which calculation below gives the biggest answer?

   | 0.07 × 32 | or | 3.1 × 0.8 | or | 310 × 0.006 |

3. 5 friends go to a Premiership football game. The total cost is £167.50. How much does each friend pay if they split the cost equally?

4. Which sum below gives the larger answer?

   | 2.7 + 9 + 1.36 | or | 1.95 + 2.2 + 8 |

5. Imran has £28.30 and spends £19.45. Terry has £41.65 and spends £32.90. Who has more money left?

6. A piece of wood 3.04 m long is cut into 8 equal pieces. How long will each short piece of wood be?

7. Copy the questions below and fill in the empty boxes.

   (a) $1.26 \div 0.3 = \boxed{\phantom{x}} \div 3 = \boxed{\phantom{x}}$    (b) $2.76 \div 0.06 = \boxed{\phantom{x}} \div 6 = \boxed{\phantom{x}}$

8. Copy and complete this number chain.

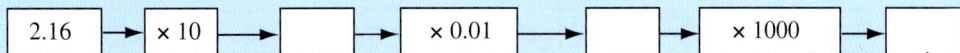

   $2.16 \rightarrow \times 10 \rightarrow \boxed{\phantom{x}} \rightarrow \times 0.01 \rightarrow \boxed{\phantom{x}} \rightarrow \times 1000 \rightarrow \boxed{\phantom{x}}$

### Line of best fit

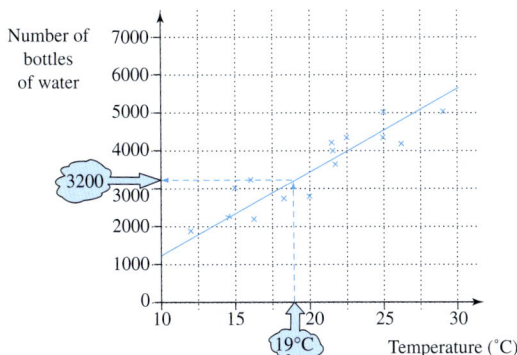

This scatter diagram shows the number of bottles of water sold by a supermarket each week and the average weekly temperature.

(a) A line of best fit is drawn (try to get the same number of points above the line as below).

(b) How many bottles of water are likely to be sold if the average weekly temperature is 19°C?

Draw a line up from the temperature axis to the line of best fit and then across to the vertical axis (as shown). We can estimate that 3200 bottles of water will be sold if the average weekly temperature is 19°C.

421

1 The table below shows the marks of 10 students in a Maths exam and a Science exam.

| Maths | 74 | 60 | 40 | 80 | 52 | 66 | 50 | 84 | 58 | 70 |
|---|---|---|---|---|---|---|---|---|---|---|
| Science | 70 | 62 | 44 | 76 | 54 | 56 | 46 | 70 | 56 | 64 |

(a) Copy and complete the scatter graph to show the data in the table.

(b) Draw the line of best fit.

(c) A student scored 72% in the Maths test but missed the Science test. Use your line of best fit to find out the Science mark that the student would have been most likely to get.

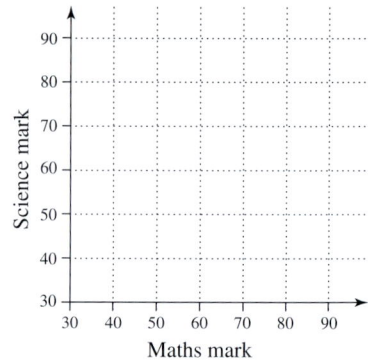

2 15 people were given a short term memory test where they could achieve a maximum score of 20. The table below shows their ages and marks.

| Age | 55 | 65 | 75 | 50 | 45 | 64 | 70 | 59 | 67 | 50 | 72 | 48 | 80 | 57 | 60 |
|---|---|---|---|---|---|---|---|---|---|---|---|---|---|---|---|
| Score | 17 | 12 | 10 | 16 | 18 | 13 | 15 | 15 | 15 | 17 | 12 | 19 | 10 | 15 | 12 |

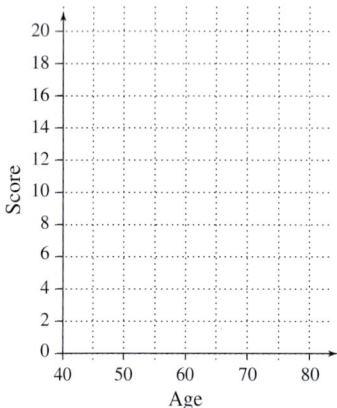

(a) Copy and complete the scatter diagram to show the data in the table.

(b) Draw the line of best fit.

(c) What score would you expect a 63 year-old to get?

**3** In a certain area, 15 people are asked what their yearly household salary is and how much their house is worth. The information is shown in the table below.

| Salary (£1000's) | 47 | 70 | 23 | 40 | 32 | 55 | 15 | 49 |
|---|---|---|---|---|---|---|---|---|
| Value of house (£1000's) | 275 | 340 | 180 | 240 | 205 | 310 | 125 | 250 |

| Salary (£1000's) | 35 | 25 | 60 | 15 | 62 | 52 | 28 |
|---|---|---|---|---|---|---|---|
| Value of house (£1000's) | 250 | 210 | 130 | 300 | 290 | 275 | 190 |

(a) Draw a scatter diagram to show this data. Use the x-axis for salaries from 10 to 70. Use the y-axis for the values of the houses from 100 to 350.

(b) Draw the line of best fit.

(c) What would you expect the salary to be for the people living in a house worth £230,000?

(d) 2 points on the scatter diagram seem 'odd'. Give reasons why these points might have occurred.

**4** A golfer records his weekly average score and how many hours be practises each week (in golf a score of 70 is *better* than a score of 80!). The information is shown in the table below.

| Weekly average score | 79 | 75 | 87 | 81 | 84 | 73 | 77 | 88 | 72 | 78 | 84 | 76 |
|---|---|---|---|---|---|---|---|---|---|---|---|---|
| Weekly hours practising | 22 | 24 | 19 | 21 | 22 | 23 | 24 | 17 | 26 | 22 | 19 | 21 |

(a) Draw a scatter graph to show this data. Use the x-axis for the weekly average score from 70 to 90. Use the y-axis for the weekly hours practising from 0 to 30.

(b) Describe the correlation in this scatter graph.

(c) Draw the line of best fit.

(d) If the golfer practised for 25 hours one week, what average score would you expect the golfer to get that week?

**5** Information was recorded about 12 smokers. The table shows how many cigarettes they smoked each day and their age when they died.

| Age | 65 | 51 | 58 | 80 | 46 | 72 | 61 | 80 | 75 | 48 | 52 | 68 |
|---|---|---|---|---|---|---|---|---|---|---|---|---|
| Number of cigarettes per day | 37 | 42 | 40 | 10 | 44 | 23 | 35 | 20 | 26 | 49 | 44 | 32 |

(a) Draw a scatter graph to show this data. Use the $x$-axis for ages from 40 to 90. Use the $y$-axis for the number of cigarettes per day from 0 to 50.

(b) Describe the correlation in this scatter graph.

(c) Draw the line of best fit.

(d) If a person smoked 38 cigarettes each day, what age would you expect that person to live to?

**6** 15 teenagers with part-time jobs were asked how much they earn each week and how much they spend on clothes/shoes on average each week. The information is shown in the table below.

| Weekly earnings (£) | 43 | 58 | 35 | 48 | 53 | 28 | 38 | 59 | 34 | 55 | 22 | 45 | 30 | 40 | 50 |
|---|---|---|---|---|---|---|---|---|---|---|---|---|---|---|---|
| Weekly amount spent on clothes/ shoes (£) | 23 | 32 | 20 | 30 | 32 | 13 | 27 | 40 | 17 | 36 | 10 | 29 | 18 | 19 | 34 |

(a) Draw a scatter diagram to show this data. Use the $x$-axis for weekly earnings from 20 to 60. Use the $y$-axis for the weekly amount spent on clothes/shoes from 0 to 50.

(b) Describe the correlation in this scatter diagram.

(c) Draw the line of best fit.

(d) If a teenager earned £37 each week, how much would you expect the teenager to spend on clothes/shoes on average each week?

( **16B** ) **Sequences (see Unit 12)**

1. For each sequence below, write down the *next 2 numbers*. What is the term-to-term rule for each sequence?

   (a) 29, 24, 19, 14,..

   (b) 48, 24, 12, 6,..

   (c) 2, 6, 12, 20,..

   (d) 64, 49, 36, 25,..

2. Sequence 8, 13, 18, 23,..

| $n$ | 1 | 2 | 3 | 4 |
|-----|---|---|---|---|
| term | 8 | 13 | 18 | 23 |
| $5n$ | 5 | 10 | 15 | 20 |

   Use this table to find the $n^{th}$ term of the sequence.

3. Make a table like the one above to find the $n^{th}$ term of the sequence 6, 13, 20, 27,...

4. Here is a sequence of shapes made from sticks. Let $n$ = shape number and $s$ = number of sticks.

   $n = 1$
   $s = 6$

   $n = 2$
   $s = 10$

   $n = 3$
   $s = 14$

   (a) Draw the next shape in the sequence.

   (b) Find a formula for the number of sticks ($s$) for the shape number $n$.

   (c) Use the formula to find out how many sticks are in shape number 50.

## Median and mode from tables of information

The table below shows the ages of some children.

| Age | 7 | 8 | 9 | 10 |
|-----|---|---|---|----|
| Frequency | 4 | 2 | 1 | 2 |

Find  (a) the modal age                 (b) The median age

Answers

(a) 'frequency' is 'how many'. There are 4 ages of 7.
   7 occurs the most, so the mode = 7 ( modal age)

(b) The table shows

| 7 7 7 7 | 8 8 | 9 | 10 10 |
|---------|-----|---|-------|
| 4 lots | 2 lots | 1 lot | 2 lots |

The numbers are in order of size. The middle number is the median which is 8.

We do not want to have to write out all the numbers.
To find out the median directly from the table, add up the frequency row
$(4 + 2 + 1 + 2 = 9)$.

> If you have $n$ numbers, the middle number is always at position $\dfrac{n + 1}{2}$

## M16.2

1  The table below shows the shoe sizes of some people.

| Shoe size | 6 | 7 | 8 | 9 |
|-----------|----|----|----|----|
| Frequency | 11 | 7 | 15 | 24 |

Find   (a) the modal shoe size and (b) the median shoe size

2  The table below shows the heights of some children in year 11.

| Height (cm) | 171 | 172 | 173 | 174 | 175 |
|-------------|-----|-----|-----|-----|-----|
| Frequency | 9 | 27 | 15 | 21 | 17 |

Find   (a) the modal height and (b) the median height

3  Some people were asked how many holidays abroad they had taken in the last 2 years. The information is shown in the table below.

| Number of holidays | 0 | 1 | 2 | 3 | 4 |
|--------------------|----|----|----|----|---|
| Frequency | 28 | 37 | 21 | 12 | 6 |

Find

(a) the modal number of holidays

(b) the median number of holidays

4  The 2 tables below show the number of visits made to the doctor during last year.

| Number of visits | 0 | 1 | 2 | 3 | 4 |
|------------------|----|----|----|---|---|
| Frequency | 32 | 29 | 15 | 9 | 3 |

14 to 21 year-olds

| Number of visits | 0 | 1 | 2 | 3 | 4 |
|------------------|---|----|----|----|----|
| Frequency | 8 | 19 | 42 | 35 | 31 |

Over 65 year-olds

(a) Find the median number of visits for *each* age group.

(b) Which age group has the higher median number of visits?

**1** The table below shows how many days absence from school for some Year 10 pupils during the last term.

| Number of days | 0 to 2 | 3 to 5 | 6 to 8 | over 8 |
|---|---|---|---|---|
| Frequency | 103 | 44 | 16 | 6 |

Find (a) the modal interval

(b) the interval which contains the median

**2** The table below shows the weights of some newborn babies at the local hospital.

| Weight (in pounds) | 4 to 6 | 6 to 7 | 8 to 9 | 10 or more |
|---|---|---|---|---|
| Frequency | 26 | 27 | 31 | 4 |

Find (a) the modal interval

(b) the interval which contains the median

**3** The tables below show the salaries earned by workers in 2 firms,

| EASITECH | |
|---|---|
| Salary (£1000's) | Frequency |
| 4 to 6 | 7 |
| 7 to 10 | 15 |
| 11 to 15 | 29 |
| 16 to 25 | 36 |
| 26 or more | 12 |

| COMPFIX PLC | |
|---|---|
| Salary (£1000's) | Frequency |
| 4 to 6 | 29 |
| 7 to 10 | 43 |
| 11 to 15 | 19 |
| 16 to 25 | 16 |
| 26 or more | 13 |

(a) For each firm, find the interval which contains the median.

(b) For which firm do you think people generally earn more money?
Explain why you think this.

**4** This table shows how many goals were scored by the football teams in the Premiership one season.

| Number of goals | Frequency |
|---|---|
| 20 to 29 | 1 |
| 30 to 39 | 2 |
| 40 to 49 | 8 |
| 50 to 59 | 4 |
| 60 to 69 | 3 |
| 69 to 70 | 2 |

Find (a) the modal interval

(b) the interval which contains the median

## Mean averages from tables of information

Some students are asked how many pairs of shoes they have. The table shows the information.

Find the mean average.

$$\text{mean average} = \frac{\text{total number of pairs of shoes}}{\text{total number of people}}$$

total number of pairs of shoes
$= (5 \times 1) + (3 \times 2) + (3 \times 3) + (4 \times 5) + (4 \times 5)$

$= 5 + 6 + 9 + 20 + 20 = 60$

| Number of pairs of shoes | Frequency |
|---|---|
| 1 | 5 |
| 2 | 3 |
| 3 | 3 |
| 4 | 5 |
| 5 | 4 |

total number of people = total frequency = $5 + 3 + 3 + 5 + 4 = 20$

so mean average $= \dfrac{60}{20} = 3$ pairs of shoes.

### M16.3

*Use a calculator if you need to.*

1. This table shows the number of cars owned by people who live in Beech Grove.

   (a) Find the total number of cars.

   (b) Find the mean average.

| Number of cars | Frequency |
|---|---|
| 0 | 1 |
| 1 | 4 |
| 2 | 4 |
| 3 | 6 |

2. Some teenagers were asked how often they had been to the cinema in the last month. The information is shown in the table below.

| Cinema trips | 0 | 1 | 2 | 3 | 4 | 5 |
|---|---|---|---|---|---|---|
| Frequency | 98 | 42 | 34 | 15 | 8 | 3 |

   (a) Find the total number of cinema trips.

   (b) Find the mean average.

**3**

| Number of children | Frequency |
|---|---|
| 0 | 12 |
| 1 | 38 |
| 2 | 30 |
| 3 | 14 |
| 4 | 6 |

100 families are asked how many children they have. The information is recorded in this table.

(a) Find the total number of children.

(b) Find the mean average.

**4** Some people were asked how many portions of fruit and vegetables they ate each day. The information is shown in the table below.

| Number of portions | 0 | 1 | 2 | 3 | 4 | 5 | 6 | 7 |
|---|---|---|---|---|---|---|---|---|
| Frequency | 17 | 20 | 16 | 28 | 11 | 4 | 3 | 1 |

(a) Find the total number of portions eaten.      (b) Find the mean average.

**5** 3 different hotels are rated by guests using a points score out of 20. The scores are shown in the table below.

| HOTEL PARADISE | | HOTEL DE VERE | | TROPIC HOTEL | |
|---|---|---|---|---|---|
| Score | Frequency | Score | Frequency | Score | Frequency |
| 14 | 21 | 14 | 31 | 14 | 86 |
| 15 | 38 | 15 | 21 | 15 | 91 |
| 16 | 33 | 16 | 49 | 16 | 33 |
| 17 | 49 | 17 | 42 | 17 | 75 |
| 18 | 17 | 18 | 21 | 18 | 61 |
| 19 | 24 | 19 | 17 | 19 | 47 |
| 20 | 6 | 20 | 9 | 20 | 18 |

(a) Work out the mean average for each hotel, giving your answers to 2 decimal places.

(b) Which hotel had the highest points score?

**6** A group of young people visited Alton towers theme park. The number of major rides they had is shown in the table below.

| Number of rides | 2 | 3 | 4 | 5 | 6 | 7 |
|---|---|---|---|---|---|---|
| Frequency | 9 | 24 | 31 | 16 | 8 | 3 |

(a) Find the total number of rides.

(b) Find the mean average (give your answer to the nearest whole number).

## Mean averages for grouped data

Some year 11 students are asked how many CDs they have. The table shows the information.

Estimate the mean average.

We need to find the total number of CDs. The problem is we do not know *exactly* how many CDs each person has.

| Number of CDs | Frequency |
|---|---|
| 0–9 | 28 |
| 10–19 | 18 |
| 20–29 | 33 |
| 30–39 | 21 |

We will get a reasonable answer if we take the mid-value of each interval and assume that is how many CDs each person has.

To find the mid-value of an interval, add the first and last values then halve the answer.

For the 10–19 interval,

$$\text{mid-value} = \frac{10 + 19}{2} = 14.5$$

| Number of CDs | Frequency | Mid-value |
|---|---|---|
| 0–9 | 28 | 4.5 |
| 10–19 | 18 | 14.5 |
| 20–29 | 33 | 24.5 |
| 30–39 | 21 | 34.5 |

We now use the mid-value and the frequency to find the total number of CDs.

Total number of CDs $= (28 \times 4.5) + (18 \times 14.5) + (33 \times 24.5) + (21 \times 34.5)$

$$= 1920$$

Total number of people = total frequency = 28 + 18 + 33 + 21 = 100

$$\text{Mean average} = \frac{\text{total number of CDs}}{\text{total number of people}} = \frac{1920}{100} = 19.2 \text{ CDs.}$$

This is an *estimate* because we used the mid-values not the exact number of CDs.

### Note

Sometimes the interval 10–19 might be written as $10 \leq n \leq 19$ where $n$ is the number of CDs. ($n \leq 19$ means $n$ is less than or equal to 19. See Unit 18 for more detail on inequalities.)

### Examples

$20 \leq n \leq 29$ means $n$ lies between 20 and 29 and can also equal 20 and 29.

$20 \leq n < 29$ means $n$ lies between 20 and 29. It can equal 20 but it *cannot* equal 29.

| Number of trips abroad | Frequency | Mid-value |
|---|---|---|
| 0–2 | 6 | |
| 3–5 | 8 | |
| 6–10 | 5 | 8 |
| 11–15 | 1 | |

Some teenagers were asked how often they had been abroad in their lifetime. The information is shown in the table.

(a) Copy and complete the table.

(b) Estimate the total number of trips abroad.

(c) Estimate the mean average.

**2**  100 people were asked how many cups of tea they drank each week. The information is shown in the table.

(a) Copy and complete the table.

(b) Estimate the total number of cups of tea.

(c) Estimate the mean average.

| Number of cups of tea ($n$) | Frequency | Mid-value |
|---|---|---|
| $0 \leq n < 10$ | 23 | |
| $10 \leq n < 20$ | 29 | 15 |
| $20 \leq n < 30$ | 38 | |
| $30 \leq n < 40$ | 7 | |
| $40 \leq n < 50$ | 3 | 45 |

**3**  The table below shows how many days off work were taken by staff at a hospital during the last year.

| Number of days off work | 0 to 9 | 10 to 19 | 20 to 29 | 30 to 39 | 40 to 59 |
|---|---|---|---|---|---|
| Frequency | 88 | 57 | 31 | 18 | 6 |
| Mid-value | | | | | |

(a) Copy and complete the table.

(b) Estimate the total number of days off work.

(c) Estimate the mean average.

**4**  The table below shows how many DVD's were owned by 250 families.

| Number of DVD's ($n$) | $0 \leq n < 10$ | $10 \leq n < 20$ | $20 \leq n < 30$ | $30 \leq n < 40$ | $40 \leq n < 50$ | $50 \leq n < 60$ |
|---|---|---|---|---|---|---|
| Frequency | 21 | 23 | 91 | 74 | 32 | 9 |
| Mid-value | | | | | | |

(a) Estimate the total number of DVD's.    (b) Estimate the mean average.

**5** 1000 people were asked how many hours of exercise they do during an average week. The information is shown in the table.

(a) Estimate the total number of hours of exercise.

(b) Estimate the mean average.

| Number of hours of exercise ($n$) | Frequency |
|---|---|
| $0 \leq n < 1$ | 225 |
| $1 \leq n < 3$ | 301 |
| $3 \leq n < 5$ | 260 |
| $5 \leq n < 7$ | 134 |
| $7 \leq n < 9$ | 56 |
| $9 \leq n < 12$ | 24 |

**6** The tables below show the salaries earned by people in 3 different firms.

| JETBUILD | |
|---|---|
| Salary($s$) (£1000's) | Frequency |
| $4 \leq s < 6$ | 6 |
| $6 \leq s < 10$ | 15 |
| $10 \leq s < 15$ | 18 |
| $15 \leq s < 25$ | 8 |
| $25 \leq s < 70$ | 3 |

| KABINSEAL | |
|---|---|
| Salary($s$) (£1000's) | Frequency |
| $4 \leq s < 6$ | 8 |
| $6 \leq s < 10$ | 21 |
| $10 \leq s < 15$ | 24 |
| $15 \leq s < 25$ | 17 |
| $25 \leq s < 70$ | 5 |

(a) Which firm offers the higher mean average salary?

(b) Write down an estimate of this mean average salary.

**7** The table below shows how many hours of TV were watched by 500 people last week.

| Hours of TV ($h$) | $0 \leq h < 10$ | $10 \leq h < 20$ | $20 \leq h < 35$ | $35 \leq h < 50$ | $50 \leq h < 60$ | $60 \leq h < 80$ |
|---|---|---|---|---|---|---|
| Frequency | 83 | 112 | 155 | 102 | 36 | 12 |

Estimate the mean average number of hours of TV watched.

**8**

| Number of lengths swum ($n$) | Frequency |
|---|---|
| 0 to 20 | 25 |
| 21 to 30 | 65 |
| 31 to 40 | 32 |
| 41 to 60 | 46 |
| 61 to 80 | 24 |
| 81 to 100 | 8 |

200 people took part in a sponsored swim. The table shows how many lengths they swam.

Estimate the mean number of lengths swum.

## 🔑 Key Facts

To compare 2 sets of data, always write at least 2 things:

1. Compare an *average* (i.e. mean, median or mode).

2. Compare the *range* of each set of data ( this shows how spread out the data is).

---

6 members of the Harris family weigh 40 kg, 53 kg, 71 kg, 75 kg, 79 kg and 90 kg.

5 members of the Collins family weigh 61 kg, 62 kg, 84 kg, 86 kg and 87 kg.

Harris family: median  = 73 kg (half way between 71 kg and 75 kg)
$\qquad$ range  = 90 – 40  = 50 kg

Collins family: median = 84 kg
$\qquad$ range  = 87 – 61 = 26 kg.

Compare the weights of the Harris family and the Collins family.

**Answer**

The *median* for the Harris family is less than the median for the Collins family but the *range* for the Harris family is greater than the range for the Collins family (i.e. the weights are more spread out).

---

### M16.4

**1** 7 members of the Truman family weigh 46 kg, 51 kg, 52 kg, 67 kg, 74 kg, 79 kg and 82 kg.

4 members of the Jenkins family weigh 42 kg, 68 kg, 70 kg and 86 kg.

Copy and complete the statements below to compare the weights of the Truman family and the Jenkins family.

Truman family:  median = ____kg   range = ____kg

Jenkins family:  median = ____ kg   range = ____ kg

'The median for the Truman family is (*greater/smaller*) than the median for the Jenkins family and the range for the Truman family is (*greater/smaller*) than the range for the Jenkins family (i.e. weights for the Truman family are (*more/less*) spread out).'

**2** Some 16 year-olds and 17 year-olds are asked how much they earn per hour in their part-time jobs. The information is shown below.

| 16 year-olds: | £5 | £4.50 | £4.30 | £4.80 | £5.20 |
| | £5.75 | £6.10 | £5.15 | £4.70 | £4.60 |

| 17 year-olds: | £4.90 | £5.30 | £5 | £5.25 | £4.95 | £6.20 | £5.06 | £5.50 |

Copy and complete the statements below to compare the hourly rate of pay for these 16 year-olds and 17 year-olds.

16 year-olds: mean = £ _____    range = £ _____

17 year-olds: mean = £ _____    range = £ _____

'The mean for the 16 year-olds is (*greater/smaller*) than the mean for the 17 year-olds and the range for the 16 year-olds is (*greater/smaller*) than the range for the 17 year-olds (i.e. the hourly rate of pay for the 16 year-olds is (*more/less*) spread out).'

**3** The Wolves and the Sentinels are 2 basketball teams. The ages (in years) of the players in each team are listed below:

| The Wolves: | 23 | 18 | 19 | 25 | 20 | 27 | 23 | 22 | 20 | 26 |
| The Sentinels: | 22 | 28 | 19 | 27 | 21 | 21 | 29 | 21 | 25 | 22 |

Copy and complete the statements below to compare the ages of the players for the Wolves and the Sentinels.

The Wolves:    median = _____    range = _____

The Sentinels:  median = _____    range = _____

'The median for the Wolves is (*greater/smaller*) than the median for the Sentinels and the range for the Wolves is (*greater/smaller*) than the range for the Sentinels (i.e. the ages for the Wolves are (*more/less*) spread out).'

## E16.4

**1** The marks obtained by 2 classes in a maths test are shown in the back-to-back stem and leaf diagram.

| Class 10A | | Class 10B |
|---:|:---:|:---|
| 9 6 | 4 | 3 3 7 8 |
| 7 7 7 3 2 | 5 | 0 1 4 6 6 6 8 |
| 9 9 8 8 4 1 | 6 | 2 5 5 8 9 |
| 6 6 5 2 | 7 | 4 5 7 7 9 9 |
| 8 7 4 0 | 8 | 1 3 6 |
| 1 1 | | 2 4 |

Key 4|6 = 64                Key 6|5 = 65

(a) Find the median and range for each class.

(b) Write a sentence to compare the test marks for the two classes.

2   Ten students from year 10 and ten students from year 11 were asked how often they had their hair cut each year. The information is shown below:

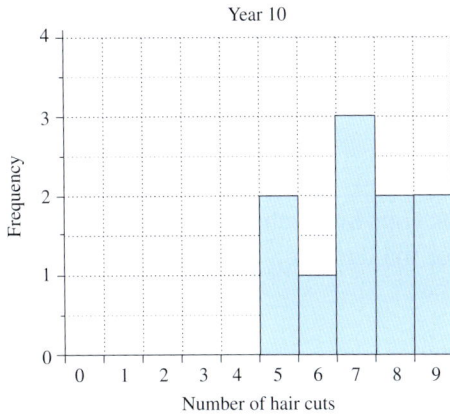

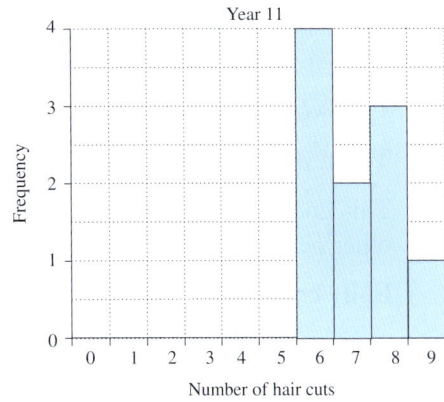

Year 10

Frequency

Number of hair cuts

Year 11

Frequency

Number of hair cuts

(a) Work out the mean and range for Year 10.

(b) Work out the mean and range for Year 11.

(c) Write a sentence to compare the number of hair cuts for the students in Year 10 and Year 11.

3   The tables below show how many televisions are owned by families living in 2 streets.

| Ash Lane | |
| --- | --- |
| Number of TV's | Frequency |
| 0 | 3 |
| 1 | 5 |
| 2 | 7 |
| 3 | 4 |
| 4 | 1 |

| Tibbs Drive | |
| --- | --- |
| Number of TV's | Frequency |
| 0 | 1 |
| 1 | 2 |
| 2 | 4 |
| 3 | 1 |
| 4 | 2 |

(a) Work out the mean and range for Ash Lane.

(b) Work out the mean and range for Tibbs Drive.

(c) Write a sentence to compare the number of televisions owned by families in Ash Lane and Tibbs Drive.

The law says you must have car insurance if you drive on public roads.

The car insurance will pay out money if you injure or kill somebody or damage another person's property.

The two main types of car insurance are:

### Third party, fire and theft

This does not provide much cover for your own vehicle but will deal with the other person if you are responsible for the damage.

### Fully comprehensive

This provides full cover for your own vehicle and any other vehicle involved.

### Cost

The amount you pay for car insurance depends on several factors:

- the value of your car
- where your live
- your age
- if you have made a claim on the car insurance in recent years

### No claims bonus

The amount you pay is reduced by 10% each year you do not claim on your car insurance. The biggest discount you can usually have is 60% which is a considerable saving. This percentage reduction is called the 'no claims bonus'.

The bonus is lost if you make a claim on your car insurance then you build up the bonus again over the next few years. Some people pay extra to protect their 'no claims bonus'.

### Payments

Some people pay the annual (yearly) cost of their car insurance in one payment but many people spread the cost over 12 equal monthly instalments.

---

This year Karen's fully comprehensive car insurance quote is £700. She gets a 60% no claims bonus and wants to pay 12 equal monthly instalments. How much is each monthly payment (to the nearest penny)?

No claims bonus = 60% of £700 = £420

Amount to pay = £700 – £420 = £280

Monthly payment = £ 280 ÷ 12 = £23.33 (to the nearest penny)

**1** Warren is given a quote of £620 this year for third party, fire and theft insurance on his Nissan Micra. He gets a 60% no claims bonus and wants to pay 12 equal monthly instalments. How much is each monthly payment (to the nearest penny)?

**2** Helen's fully comprehensive car insurance quote this year for her Astra is £1154. She has a 40% no claims bonus. If she pays 12 equal monthly instalments, how much is each payment (to the nearest penny)?

Copy and complete the table below to work out the monthly insurance payments for each car.

| | Car | annual car insurance (£) | no claims bonus | annual insurance to pay (£) | monthly payment (£) |
|---|---|---|---|---|---|
| **3** | Corsa | 950 | 60% | 380 | |
| **4** | Lexus | 1260 | 60% | | |
| **5** | Shogun | 1530 | 30% | | |
| **6** | Ford Escort | 1125 | 50% | | |
| **7** | Saab 900S | 935 | 20% | | |
| **8** | Ford Fiesta | 870 | 60% | | |
| **9** | VW Golf | 1060 | 20% | | |

**10** Sally bumps her car and has to claim on her car insurance. Her annual insurance is £1280. Before her claim she had a 60% no claims bonus. After the claim, her no claims bonus is reduced by 20% (ie. she has a 40% no claims bonus).

(a) What was her monthly payment before the claim?

(b) What is her monthly payment after the claim?

(c) How much more does she have to pay each month?

**11** David is involved in a car accident and puts in a claim on his car insurance. His annual insurance is £1370. Before the accident he had a 50% no claims bonus. After the claim, his no claims bonus is reduced *to* 20%. How much more will he have to pay each month for his car insurance?

**12** There are many other insurances that people are advised to take out, for example: life insurance, medical insurance, buildings insurance, contents insurance, critical illness insurance and income protection insurance.

(a) Find out what these insurances cover you for.

(b) **Discuss with your teacher** the advantages and disadvantages of taking out these types of insurance.

**1.** Drawing scatter diagrams and describing correlation

Describe the correlation, if any, in these scatter graphs.

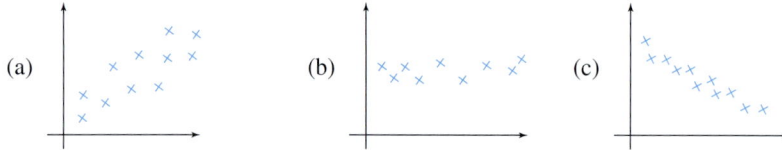

(a)    (b)    (c)

**2.** Drawing a line of best fit and using it to estimate values

The table below shows the engine sizes of 12 cars and how many miles per gallon they operate at.

| Engine size (litres) | 1.8 | 1.1 | 2 | 1.6 | 1 | 1.8 | 1.5 | 2.8 | 1.2 | 2 | 1.6 | 1.4 | 2.4 | 2.1 |
|---|---|---|---|---|---|---|---|---|---|---|---|---|---|---|
| Miles per gallon | 35 | 53 | 24 | 33 | 47 | 31 | 33 | 16 | 46 | 30 | 40 | 42 | 20 | 22 |

(a) Copy and complete the scatter diagram to show the data in the table.

(b) Draw the line of best fit.

(c) Use the line of best fit to estimate how many miles per gallon a 1.3 litre car would do.

(d) Roughly with what engine size would you expect the car to do 23 miles per gallon?

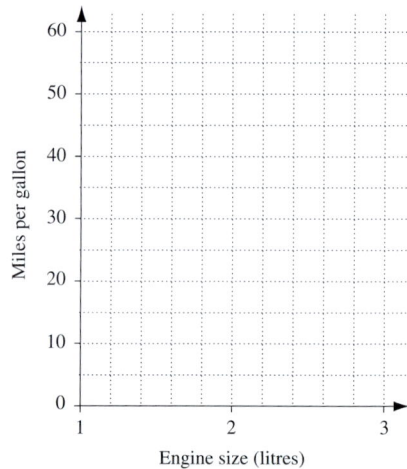

**3.** Finding the median and mode from tables of information

Some 16 year-olds were asked how many dental fillings they had been given during their lifetimes. The table shows the information.

| Number of fillings | 0 | 1 | 2 | 3 | 4 | 5 |
|---|---|---|---|---|---|---|
| Frequency | 12 | 17 | 24 | 18 | 7 | 3 |

Find (a) the modal number of fillings

(b) the median number of fillings

(a) This table shows the number of bicycles owned by families who live in Camden Terrace.

    (i) Find the total number of bicycles.

    (ii) Find the mean average.

| Number of bicycles | Frequency |
|:---:|:---:|
| 0 | 8 |
| 1 | 4 |
| 2 | 17 |
| 3 | 24 |
| 4 | 16 |
| 5 | 6 |

(b) The table below shows how many hours were spent using a computer by 200 people last week.

| Hours using a computer(h) | $0 \leq h < 5$ | $5 \leq h < 10$ | $10 \leq h < 20$ | $20 \leq h < 30$ | $30 \leq h < 40$ | $40 \leq h < 60$ |
|:---:|:---:|:---:|:---:|:---:|:---:|:---:|
| Frequency | 49 | 68 | 36 | 23 | 17 | 7 |

Estimate the mean number of hours spent using a computer.

(a) 30 young people were asked how many cards they received on their last birthday (10 nine year-olds and 20 nineteen year-olds). The information is shown below:

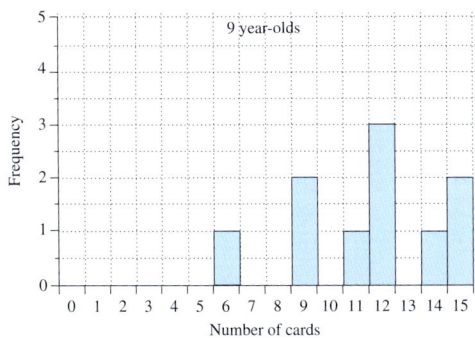

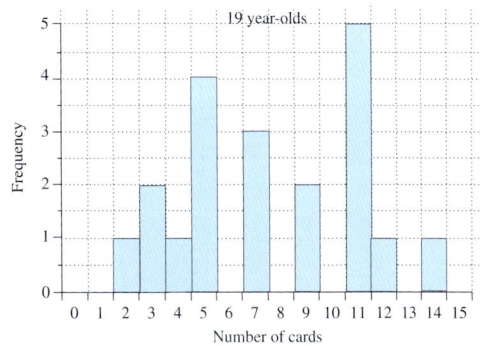

    (i) Work out the mean and range for the 9 year-olds.

    (ii) Work out the mean and range for the 19 year-olds.

    (iii) Use the means and ranges to *compare* the number of birthday cards received by 9 year-olds and 19 year-olds.

(b) The heights of 6 members of the Kallis family are 151 cm, 153 cm, 164 cm, 170 cm, 184 cm, and 186 cm.

The heights of 5 members of the Moore family are 162 cm, 169 cm, 175 cm, 177 cm and 180 cm.

(i) Find the median height and the range of the heights for each family.

(ii) Use the medians and ranges to *compare* the heights of the Kallis family and the Moore family.

## Mixed examination questions

1 The table below shows the heights of a group of Year 7 pupils together with the height of each of their fathers. All measurements are in centimetres.

| Pupil | A | B | C | D | E | F | G | H | I |
|---|---|---|---|---|---|---|---|---|---|
| Height of pupil | 138 | 141 | 145 | 148 | 149 | 154 | 155 | 161 | 162 |
| Height of father | 151 | 155 | 153 | 170 | 161 | 176 | 185 | 186 | 192 |

(a) Draw a scatter graph to show this information.

The first three points are plotted for you.

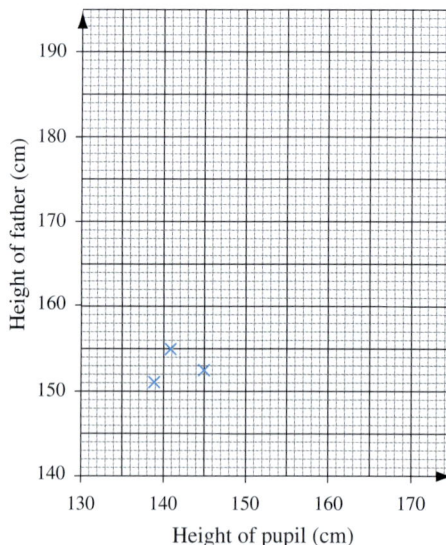

(b) Describe the correlation between the two sets of heights.

(c) Draw a line of best fit on the scatter diagram.

(d) A new pupil joins the group. His height is 151 cm. Use your line of best fit to estimate the height of his father.

(OCR)

**2** Rosie had 10 boxes of drawing pins.

She counted the number of drawing pins in each box.

The table gives information about her results.

| Number of drawing pins | Frequency | |
|---|---|---|
| 29 | 2 | |
| 30 | 5 | |
| 31 | 2 | |
| 32 | 1 | |

(a) Write down the modal number of drawing pins in a box.

(b) Work out the range of the number of drawing pins in a box.

(c) Work out the mean number of drawing pins in a box.          (EDEXCEL)

**3** One hundred batteries were tested to see how long they lasted.

The results are shown in the table below.

| Time ($t$ hours) | Frequency |
|---|---|
| $0 \leq t < 4$ | 12 |
| $4 \leq t < 8$ | 20 |
| $8 \leq t < 12$ | 34 |
| $12 \leq t < 16$ | 25 |
| $16 \leq t < 20$ | 9 |

Use the mid-points of the intervals to calculate an estimate of the mean time that a battery lasted.          (OCR)

**4** The maximum load for a lift is 1200 kg.

The table shows the distribution of the weights of 22 people waiting for the lift.

| Weight ($w$ kg) | Frequency |
|---|---|
| $30 \leq w < 50$ | 8 |
| $50 \leq w < 70$ | 10 |
| $70 \leq w < 90$ | 4 |

Will the lift be overloaded if all of these people get in?

You must show working to support your answer.          (AQA)

# SHAPE 4

**In this unit you will learn how to:**

– read scales

– use and convert metric units

– deal with 'time' problems

– use and convert imperial units

– convert between metric and imperial units

– find upper and lower bounds

– calculate with speed, density and other compound measures

– WATCH YOUR MONEY! – income tax

## Reading scales

### M17.1

For each of the scales work out:

    (a) the measurement indicated by each of the arrows.

    (b) the difference between the two arrows.

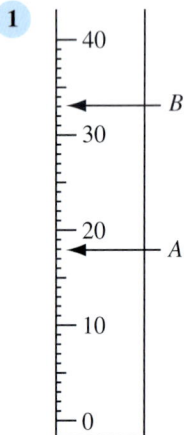 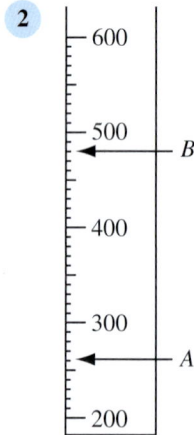 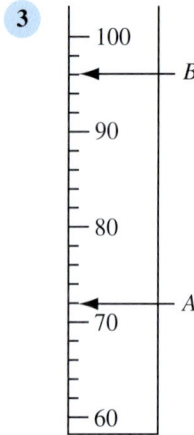 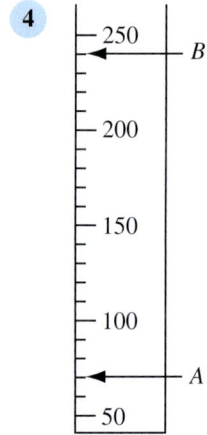

**5**  cm  40  50  60  70  80  A  B

**6**  kg  0  20  40  60  80  100  A  B

**7**  g  20  30  40  A  B

**8**  cm  50  60  70  80  A  B

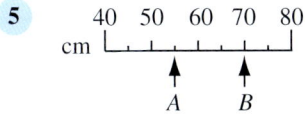

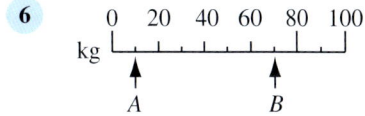

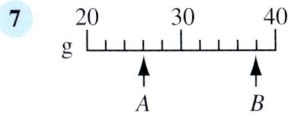

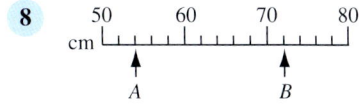

Write down the measurement shown by the arrow on each dial below.

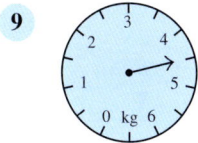

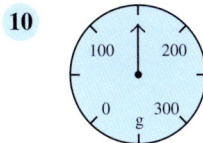

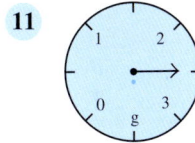

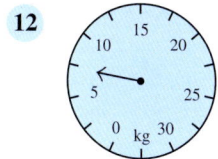

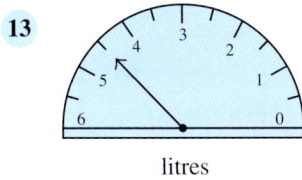

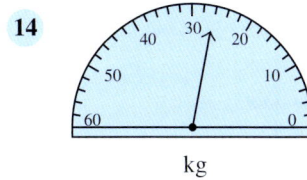

**9**  3  2  4  1  5  0  kg  6

**10**  100  200  0  g  300

**11**  1  2  0  g  3

**12**  15  10  20  5  25  0  kg  30

**13**  4  3  2  5  1  6  0  litres

**14**  40  30  20  50  10  60  0  kg

Write down the time shown by each clock below:

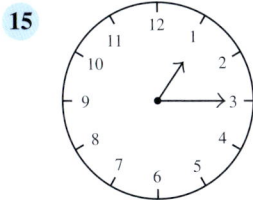

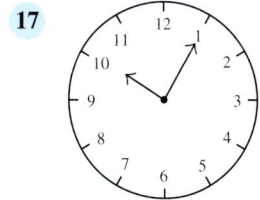

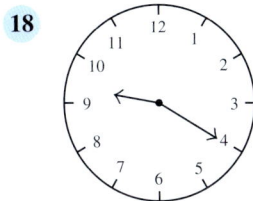

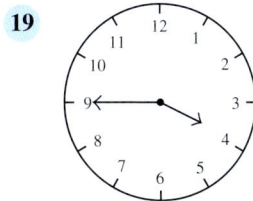

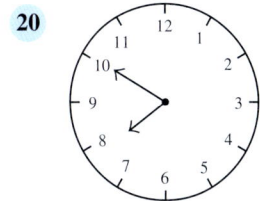

**15**  12 11 10 9 8 7 6 5 4 3 2 1

**16**  12 11 10 9 8 7 6 5 4 3 2 1

**17**  12 11 10 9 8 7 6 5 4 3 2 1

**18**  12 11 10 9 8 7 6 5 4 3 2 1

**19**  12 11 10 9 8 7 6 5 4 3 2 1

**20**  12 11 10 9 8 7 6 5 4 3 2 1

A  2  3  4

What number does A point to?

5 divisions cover 1 unit

so 1 division means $1 \div 5 = 0.2$

so A points to 3.6

For each of the scales work out:

    (a) the measurement indicated by each of the arrows.

    (b) the difference between the two arrows.

**1**

kg scale, arrows A and B, marks 7, 8, 9

**2**

cm scale, arrows A and B, marks 4, 5, 6

**3**

litres scale, arrows A and B, marks 2, 4, 6

**4**

m scale, arrows A and B, marks 16, 17, 18

**5** litres scale: 0.6, 0.5, 0.4, 0.3; B near top, A lower

**6** ml scale: 27, 26, 25, 24; B and A

**7** ml scale: 47, 45, 43, 41; B and A

**8** kg scale: 0.06, 0.05, 0.04, 0.03; B and A

**9**

kg scale, arrows A and B, marks 6, 7, 8, 9

**10**

cm scale, arrows A and B, marks 25, 26, 27, 28

**11**

kg scale, arrows A and B, marks 0.3, 0.4, 0.5, 0.6

**12**

ml scale, arrows A and B, marks 600, 850, 1100, 1350

**13**

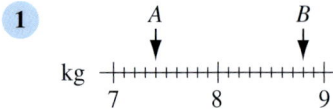

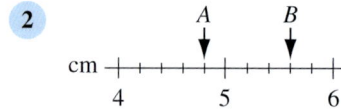

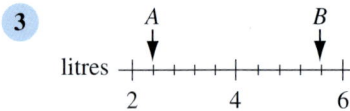

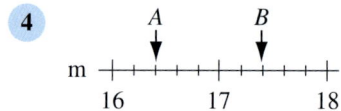

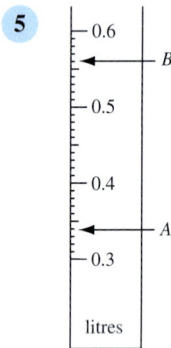

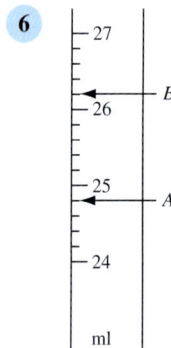

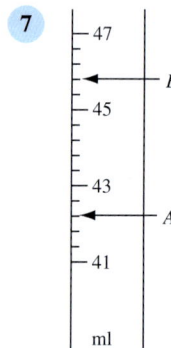

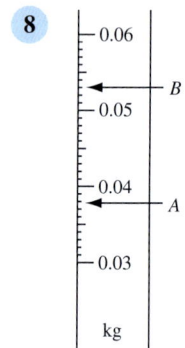

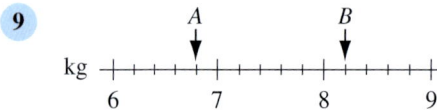

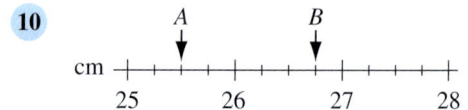

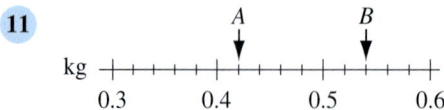

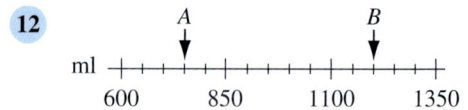

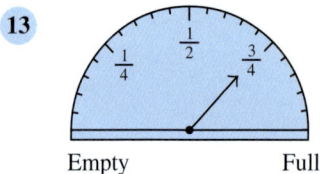

This is a fuel gauge on a car.
It is full with 50 litres of petrol.
How much petrol is there in the car now?

Empty — Full ; marks $\frac{1}{4}$, $\frac{1}{2}$, $\frac{3}{4}$

**14** Here is another fuel gauge.
This is full with 60 litres of petrol.
How much petrol is there in the car now?

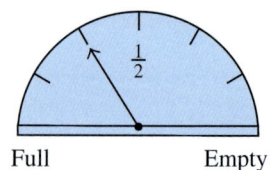

Full — Empty ; mark $\frac{1}{2}$

Write down the measurement shown by the arrow on each dial below.

**15**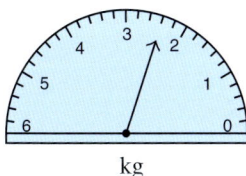
kg

**16**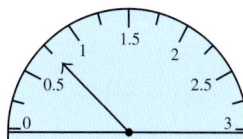
litres

**17**
kg

**18**
litres

**19**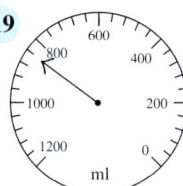
ml

**20**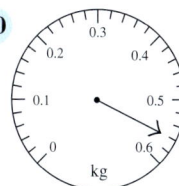
kg

*Can you still?*

*Can you still?*

**17A**  **Draw graphs and find gradients (see Unit 10)**

**1.**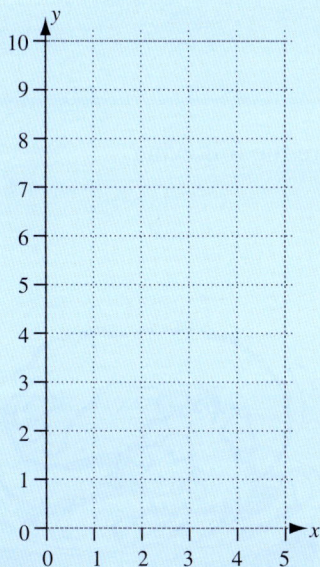

Draw these axes.

(a) Complete the table below then draw $y = 3x + 2$.

| $x$ | 0 | 1 | 2 |
|-----|---|---|---|
| $y$ |   |   |   |

(b) Find the gradient of the line $y = 3x + 2$.

(c) Complete the table below then draw $y = 5 - x$ on the same axes.

| $x$ | 0 | 1 | 2 |
|-----|---|---|---|
| $y$ |   |   |   |

(d) Find the gradient of the line $y = 5 - x$.

**2.** Draw these axes.

Complete the table below then draw the curve $y = x^2 - 5$.

| $x$ | −3 | −2 | −1 | 0 | 1 | 2 | 3 |
|-----|----|----|----|---|---|---|---|
| $y$ |    |    |    |   |   |   |   |

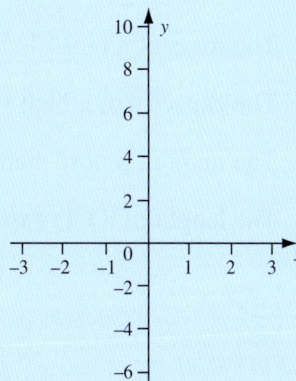

445

## 🔑 Key Facts

| length | mass | volume |
|---|---|---|
| 10 mm = 1 cm | 1000 g = 1 kg | 1000 ml = 1 litre or 1 l |
| 100 cm = 1 m | 1000 kg = 1 tonne | 1 ml = 1 cm$^3$ |
| 1000 m = 1 km | | |

**Examples**

Convert the following metric units.

(a) 7000 g into kg ⇨ $\boxed{\div 1000}$ ⇨ 7 kg

(b) 2.5 m into cm ⇨ $\boxed{\times 100}$ ⇨ 250 cm

(c) 4.32 tonnes into kg ⇨ $\boxed{\times 1000}$ ⇨ 4320 kg

(d) 400 ml into litres ⇨ $\boxed{\div 1000}$ ⇨ 0.4 l

### M17.2

Write down which metric unit you would use to measure the following.

**1** The distance from Bristol to London (m or km?)

**2** The length of a pen (cm or mm?)

**3** The mass of a dog (kg or tonnes?)

**4** The length of a garden (cm or m?)

**5** The contents of a full wine glass (litres or ml?)

**6** The length of a submarine.

**7** The mass of a tank.

**8** The capacity of a bath full of water.

**9** The mass of a nose stud.

**10** The length of a CD case.

**11** Write each length in cm.

(a) 7 m      (b) 4.5 m      (c) 1.62 m      (d) 50 mm      (e) 0.3 m

**12** Write each mass in g.

(a) 5 kg      (b) 3.6 kg      (c) 9.2 kg      (d) 0.632 kg      (e) 6.42 kg

**13** Write each volume in ml.

(a) 3 l      (b) 24 cm$^3$      (c) 143 cm$^3$      (d) 9.6 l      (e) 3.125 l

**14** Write each length in m.

(a) 8 km      (b) 300 cm      (c) 940 cm      (d) 6.3 km      (e) 8.092 km

**15** Copy each sentence below and choose the most sensible estimate.

(a) A baby weighs (*400 g / 4 kg*).

(b) A bottle of wine contains (*7 ml / 0.7 l*).

(c) A woman weighs (*6 kg / 60 kg*).

(d) The height of the door is (*100 cm / 2 m*).

(e) The length of a toothbrush is (*16 mm / 16 cm*).

(f) A can of lemonade contains (*330 ml / 33 l*).

**16** Write each mass in kg.

(a) 6000 g      (b) 5 tonnes      (c) 8.24 tonnes      (d) 9500 g      (e) 350 g

**17** Write each length in km.

(a) 3000 m      (b) 9500 m      (c) 2471 m      (d) 4650 m      (e) 23000 m

**18** Write each volume in litres.

(a) 2000 ml      (b) 60000 ml      (c) 8400 ml      (d) 670 ml      (e) 4 ml

**19** Roy buys 1 kg of potatoes. 700 g are eaten. What is the weight of the potatoes that are left?

**20** Gemma has a 2 litre bottle of cola. She pours out 4 glasses of cola each of 200 ml. What volume of cola is left in the bottle?

**21** Nazim cuts 27 cm off a 2 m metal rod. What is the length of the metal rod now?

**22** Lola runs one 1500 m race and one 800 m race. How many kilometres has she run in total?

**23** A lorry and its load weigh 3.1 tonnes. If the load weighs 600 kg, how much does the lorry weigh?

Copy and complete the following:

1   6.35 m = ☐ cm        2   1.57 m = ☐ cm        3   8.1 m = ☐ cm

4   28 cm = ☐ m          5   1 cm = ☐ m           6   320 cm = ☐ m

7   9 cm = ☐ m           8   60 mm = ☐ cm         9   200 mm = ☐ cm

10  8 mm = ☐ cm          11  2500 m = ☐ km        12  350 m = ☐ km

13  9000 m = ☐ km        14  3 kg = ☐ g           15  9.5 kg = ☐ g

16  0.375 kg = ☐ g       17  575 g = ☐ kg         18  1849 g = ☐ kg

19  6 tonnes = ☐ kg      20  530 ml = ☐ l         21  1832 ml = ☐ l

22  5500 ml = ☐ l        23  4.5 litres = ☐ ml    24  65 ml = ☐ l

25  85 l = ☐ ml          26  2.18 l = ☐ ml        27  3.84 tonnes = ☐ kg

28  248 cm = ☐ m

29  A bag contains 2 kg of flour. 1350 g is used. What is the weight of the flour left in the bag?

30  One tin of baked beans weighs 270 g. How many *kilograms* do 9 tins weigh?

31  There are 48 tiles in a stack. Each tile is 7 mm thick. How high is the stack in centimetres?

32  How many 400 ml plastic beakers can be filled from an 88 litre barrel of beer?

33  Al has a 5.4 m piece of wood. He cuts it into small lengths of 45 cm. How many small pieces of wood will he have?

34  14 people have the following weights:

| 78 kg | 69 kg | 81 kg | 83 kg | 81 kg | 77 kg | 60 kg |
|-------|-------|-------|-------|-------|-------|-------|
| 52 kg | 63 kg | 50 kg | 71 kg | 51 kg | 86 kg | 81 kg |

They get into a lift. The lift is *not* safe if the total weight of the people is more than 1 tonne. Will these 14 people be safe in this lift?

35  Write down the larger amount from each pair below.

(a) 19 m or 0.19 km            (b) 6 cm or 71 mm

(c) 2.3 tonnes or 285 kg       (d) 9200 ml or 9.4 l

(e) 5.7 m or 569 cm            (f) 38 g or 0.04 kg

(g) 620 mm or 70 cm            (h) 9.6 kg or 9700 g

(i) 380 ml or 0.35 l           (j) 3.2 km or 318000 cm.

**17B**   **Solve equations by trial and improvement (see Unit 12)**

**1.**

$x$ cm

$(x + 5)$ cm

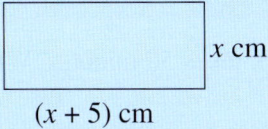

The area of this rectangle is 73 cm².

area $= x (x + 5) = 73$.

Copy the table below then carry it on to find $x$ to *1 decimal place* by trial and improvement.

| Trial | Calculation | Too large or too small? |
|---|---|---|
| $x = 5$ | $5 \times 10 = 50$ | too small |
| $x = 8$ | $8 \times 13 = 104$ | too large |
| $x = 6$ | $6 \times 11 = 66$ | too small |
| $x = 7$ | $7 \times 12 = 84$ | too large |
| $x = 6.5$ | $\cdots$ | $\cdots$ |

**2.** Solve this equation by trial and improvement. Give the answer to *1 decimal place*.

$$x^3 - x = 100$$

Try $x = 4$ and $x = 5$ first.

**3.** Solve $x^2 + 4x = 150$ by trial and improvement. Give the answer to *2 decimal places*.

## Time

1 year = 12 months = 365 days = 52 weeks

3:20 a.m. (before midday) = 03:20 p.m. (after midday) = 15:20

**M17.3**

**1** Change these times into 24-hour clock time.

    (a) 11:15 a.m.     (b) 2:45 p.m.     (c) 5:30 p.m.     (d) 9:40 a.m.

    (e) 6:50 p.m.     (f) 9:32 p.m.     (g) 8:24 a.m.     (h) 3:56 p.m.

**2** Change these times into 12-hour clock time.

    (a) 10:40           (b) 16:20           (c) 19:35           (d) 21:10

    (e) 02:05           (f) 08:05           (g) 17:26           (h) 23:47

**3** Calli gets on a bus at 08:20. The bus journey is 45 minutes. What time does Calli get off the bus?

**4** Ravi leaves for work at 7:50 a.m. His journey to work takes 50 minutes. What time does he arrive at work?

**5** Karen spends a day shopping in London. She leaves home at 08:10 and arrives home at 17:00. How many hours and minutes is she out shopping?

**6** A meeting at work begins at 2:30 p.m. and ends at 4:15 p.m. How long did the meeting last for?

**7** Copy and complete the following:

    (a) 1 year = ☐ weeks        (b) 5 years = ☐ weeks

    (c) 2 years = ☐ months     (d) 10 years = ☐ months

    (e) 2 years = ☐ days       (f) 3 years = ☐ days

**8** Dom borrows some money from a bank. He must pay some money back each month for 3 years. For how many months must he pay back money?

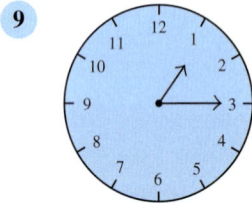

**9**

Coach leaves           Coach arrives

How long was the coach journey?

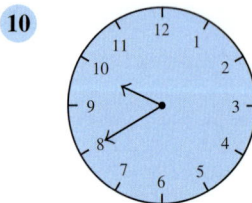

**10**

Train leaves           Train arrives

How long was the train journey?

**11** Copy and complete the table below.

| Old time | Add on | New time |
|---|---|---|
| 16:30 | 25 minutes | 16:55 |
| 13:50 | 30 minutes | |
| 15:25 | 1 hour 40 minutes | |
| 07:45 | 3 hours 30 minutes | |
| 09:05 | 4 hours 50 minutes | |
| 16:24 | 1 hour 45 minutes | |
| 11:38 | 2 hours 50 minutes | |

**12**

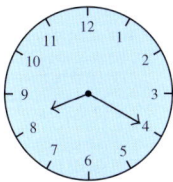

Film starts

A film lasts for 2 hours 40 minutes. At what time does the film end?

**13**

Plane leaves

A plane journey lasts for 3 hours 45 minutes. At what time does the plane journey end?

**14** Simone arrives at the Gym at 16:25 and works out for 1 hour 40 minutes. At what time does she leave the Gym?

**15** Phil drives from Reading up to Bromsgrove. He leaves at 08:45 and the journey takes 2 hours 45 minutes. When does he arrive at Bromsgrove?

**16** Carol goes out to a party at 19:50. She arrives home 3 hours 35 minutes later. At what time does she arrive home?

**17** Copy and complete this train timetable. Each train takes the same time between stations.

| | Train 1 | Train 2 | Train 3 | Train 4 | Train 5 | Train 6 |
|---|---|---|---|---|---|---|
| Henton | 09:00 | 09:57 | 10:30 | 11:23 | 12:15 | 13:12 |
| Oldhill | 09:08 | | | | | |
| Eastham | 09:23 | | | 11:46 | | |
| Colston | 09:40 | | | | | |
| Todwick | 09:55 | | 11:25 | | | |

## 🔑 Key Facts

Many people still 'think' using the old imperial units.

'Jack is 6 feet tall', 'Wendy weighs 10 stone'.

We have

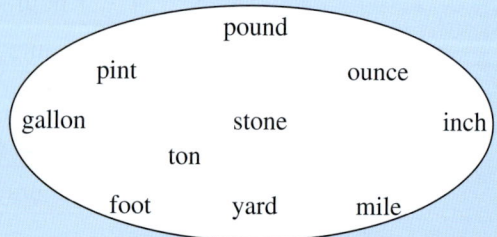

| length mass | volume | |
|---|---|---|
| 12 inches = 1 foot | 8 pints = 1 gallon | 16 ounces = 1 pound |
| 3 feet = 1 yard | | 14 pounds = 1 stone |
| 1760 yards = 1 mile | | 2240 pounds = 1 ton |

**Examples**

Convert the following imperial units.

(a) 5 feet into inches ⇨ | × 12 | ⇨ 60 inches

(b) 6 stone 5 pounds into pounds.
   6 stone into pounds ⇨ | × 14 | ⇨ 84 pounds.
   so 6 stone 5 pounds = 84 + 5 = 89 pounds.

(c) 28 pints into gallons ⇨ | ÷ 8 | ⇨ 3.5 gallons.

---

### E17.3

Write down which imperial unit you would use to measure the following.

**(The key facts before the next Exercise may help you).**

1  The length of a calculator (inches or yards?)

2  The mass of a cat (ounces or stone?)

3  The distance from London to York (yards or miles?)

4  The volume of a supermarket milk carton (pints or gallons?)

5  The length of a football pitch (yards or miles?)

6  The mass of a feather.

**7** The length of a biro.

**8** The capacity of a car petrol tank.

**9** The capacity of a wine bottle.

**10** The mass of a caravan.

**11** Write each length in inches.

(a) 2 feet      (b) 6 feet      (c) 5 feet 2 inches      (d) 6 feet 5 inches

**12** Write each mass in pounds.

(a) 3 stone      (b) 32 ounces      (c) 2 stone 4 pounds      (d) 5 stone 8 pounds

**13** Write each volume in pints.

(a) 2 gallons      (b) 9 gallons      (c) 4½ gallons      (d) 7¼ gallons

**14** Write each length in feet.

(a) 5 yards      (b) 7 yards 2 feet      (c) 48 inches      (d) 3 yards 1 foot

**15** Copy each sentence below and choose the most sensible estimate.

(a) A bag of sugar weighs (*2 pounds / 2 ounces*).

(b) A teapot contains (*2 pints / 5 gallons*).

(c) A baby weighs (*7 stone / 7 pounds*).

(d) The length of a cricket pitch is (*22 inches / 22 yards*).

**16** Copy and complete the following:

(a) 4 pounds = ☐ ounces          (b) 4 feet 10 inches = ☐ inches

(c) 2 miles = ☐ yards            (d) 9.5 gallons = ☐ pints

(e) 3 tons = ☐ pounds            (f) 2 stone 6 pounds = ☐ pounds

(g) 70 pounds = ☐ stone          (h) 7040 yards = ☐ miles

(i) 3 pounds 6 ounces = ☐ ounces  (j) 2½ tons = ☐ pounds

(k) 68 pints = ☐ gallons         (l) 3 stone 12 pounds = ☐ pounds

**17** Henry weighs 15 stone 3 pounds. He goes on a diet and loses 1 stone 9 pounds. How much does Henry weigh now?

**18** Ignes is 5 feet 4 inches tall. Nigel is 9 inches taller. How tall is Nigel?

**19** During her lifetime Jackie gives 54 pints of blood. How many gallons is this?

**20** Copy and complete the clues that go across. What word is shown going down the shaded boxes?

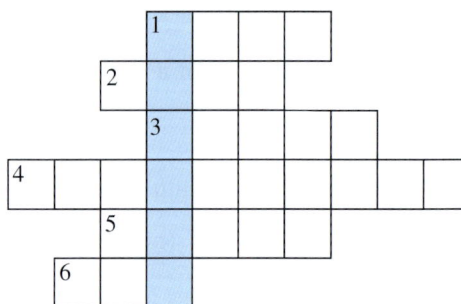

### Clues

**1.** One thousand of these make a kilogram.

**2.** 3 feet.

**3.** 1000 millilitres.

**4.** Ten of these make a centimetre.

**5.** 16 ounces.

**6.** 2240 pounds.

---

*Can you still?*

**17C** **Find the mean, median, mode and range for sets of numbers (see Unit 13)**

*Can you still?*

**1.** For each set of numbers below find the

   (i) mode        (ii) median        (iii) mean        (iv) range

   (a) 9, 7, 1, 3, 8, 3, 4

   (b) 4, 4, 4, 8, 8, 8, 8, 4, 8

   (c) 0.9, 0.3, 0.7, 0.4, 0.7, 0.6

**2.** Write down 4 numbers with a mean of 5.

**3.** Write down 5 numbers which have a mean of 7 *and* a median of 10.

**4.** The mean weight of 50 people is 61 kg.

   (a) What is the total weight of all 50 people?

   (b) Another 30 people have a mean weight of 69 kg. What is the mean weight of all 80 people?

## Converting between metric and imperial units

### Key Facts

(The '≈' sign means 'is approximately equal to'.)

We have

| length | mass | capacity |
|---|---|---|
| 1 inch ≈ 2.5 cm | 1 ounce ≈ 30 g | 1 litre ≈ 1.8 pints |
| 1 foot ≈ 30 cm | 1 kg ≈ 2.2 pounds | 1 gallon ≈ 4.5 litres |
| 1 yard ≈ 90 cm | | |
| 1 mile ≈ 1.6 km | | |

To *change units*, use the values above and *multiply* or *divide*.

**Examples**

Convert the units shown.

(a) 2 yards into cm ⇨ $\boxed{\times 90}$ ⇨ 180 cm

(b) 3 gallons into litres ⇨ $\boxed{\times 4.5}$ ⇨ 13.5 litres

(c) 33 pounds into kg ⇨ $\boxed{\div 2.2}$ ⇨ 15 kg.

### M17.4

*You may use a calculator.*

**1**  Write each length in cm.

(a) 4 inches　　(b) 3 feet　　(c) 5 yards　　(d) 2.5 yards　　(e) 1.5 feet

**2**  Write each mass in pounds.

(a) 3 kg　　(b) 5 kg　　(c) 3.5 kg　　(d) 8.5 kg　　(e) 6.2 kg

**3**  Write each capacity in litres.

(a) 2 gallons　(b) 9 gallons　(c) 20 gallons　(d) 5.5 gallons　(e) 4.6 gallons

**4**  On a journey, Tom's car used 6 gallons of petrol and Sarah's car used 26 litres of petrol. Which car used more petrol?

**5** On a hiking holiday, Maggie walked 32 miles and Ed walked 53 km. Who walked further?

Copy and complete:

**6** 10 ounces ≈ ☐ g

**7** 5 litres ≈ ☐ pints

**8** 5 miles ≈ ☐ km

**9** 32 km ≈ ☐ miles

**10** 27 pints ≈ ☐ litres

**11** 4 kg ≈ ☐ pounds

**12** 66 pounds ≈ ☐ kg

**13** 31.5 litres ≈ ☐ gallons

**14** 19.2 km ≈ ☐ miles

**15** 7 yards ≈ ☐ cm

**16** 60 kg ≈ ☐ pounds

**17** 150 g ≈ ☐ ounces

**18** 6 feet ≈ ☐ cm

**19** 14 miles ≈ ☐ km

**20** 72 litres ≈ ☐ gallons

**21** Which weighs more, A or B?

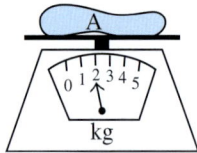

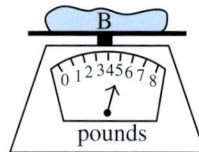

**22** Which weighs more, C or D?

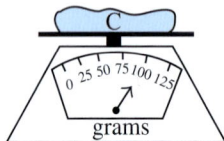

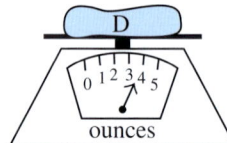

In questions **23** to **30**, which amount is the larger

**23** 5 kg or 12 pounds?

**24** 12 inches or 28 cm?

**25** 4 km or 3 miles?

**26** 35 pints or 21 litres?

**27** 250 g or 8 ounces?

**28** 8.5 feet or 250 cm?

**29** 2.5 gallons or 12 litres?

**30** 12 miles or 20 km?

**31** Sandra fills up her car with 8 gallons of petrol.

How much will it cost if petrol costs 90 p per litre?

**32** The distance from Leeds to York is about 24 miles.
How many km is this?

**33** Jamie needs 6 ounces of bacon to put in a stew. He buys 170 g of bacon. Will he have enough?

**34** Which is larger – a yard or a metre?

**35** An exercise machine is only strong enough to take weights up to 16 stone. Arnie weighs 100 kg. Should he use the exercise machine?

(remember: 1 stone = 14 pounds).

**36** On a building site, 50 kg of soil is moved every minute. How many tonnes of soil will be moved in 1 hour?

## Measuring – upper and lower bounds

When you measure something, the measurement is never exact.

If you measure the diameter of a 5 pence coin with a ruler, you might read 1.7 cm. If you use a more accurate device for measuring you might read the diameter as 1.71 cm. An even more accurate device might give the diameter as 1.712 cm. None of these figures is precise.

They are all approximations to the actual diameter.

This means that there is always an error in making any kind of measurement such as length, weight, time, temperature and so on. This kind of error cannot be avoided.

Suppose the width of a book is measured at 16 cm to the nearest cm.

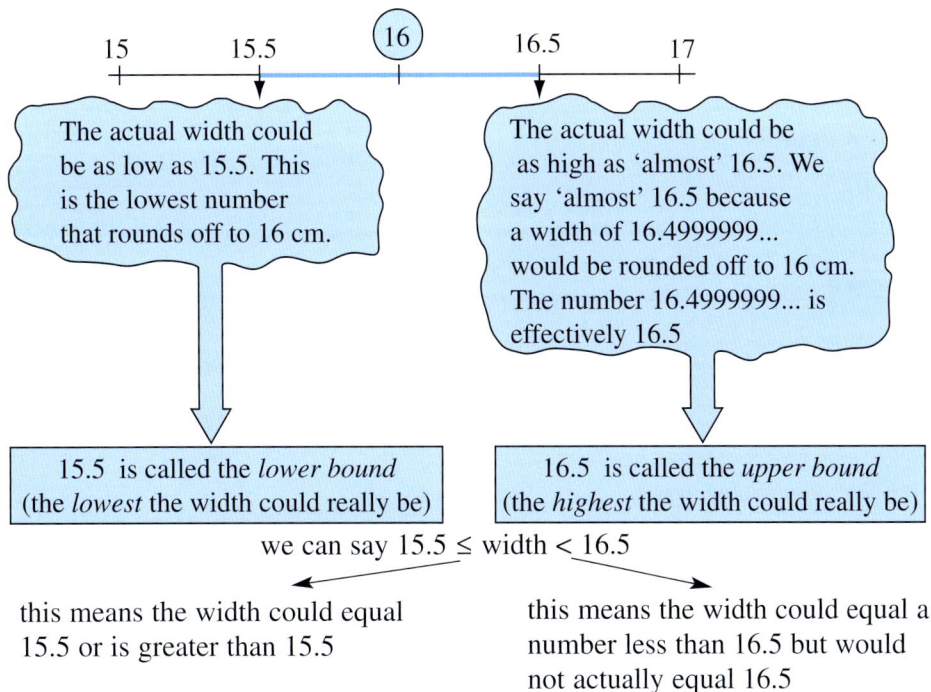

```
  15      15.5      16      16.5      17
  +---------+---------+---------+---------+
```

The actual width could be as low as 15.5. This is the lowest number that rounds off to 16 cm.

The actual width could be as high as 'almost' 16.5. We say 'almost' 16.5 because a width of 16.4999999... would be rounded off to 16 cm. The number 16.4999999... is effectively 16.5

15.5 is called the *lower bound*
(the *lowest* the width could really be)

16.5 is called the *upper bound*
(the *highest* the width could really be)

we can say $15.5 \leq$ width $< 16.5$

this means the width could equal 15.5 or is greater than 15.5

this means the width could equal a number less than 16.5 but would not actually equal 16.5

The length of a nail is measured at 3.4 cm to the nearest *0.1 cm*.

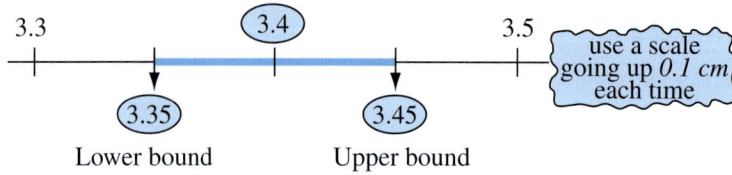

```
3.3              3.4              3.5
 +       +        +        +       +
       3.35            3.45
    Lower bound     Upper bound
```

use a scale going up *0.1 cm* each time

we can say 3.35 ≤ length < 3.45

The length of a park is measured at 3800 m to the nearest *100 m*.

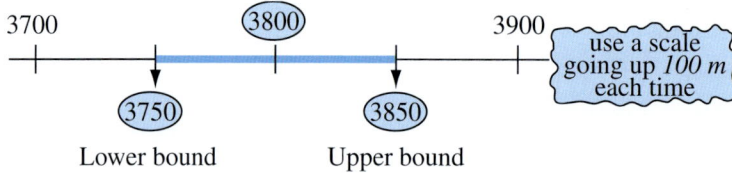

```
3700            3800            3900
 +      +        +        +       +
      3750            3850
   Lower bound     Upper bound
```

use a scale going up *100 m* each time

we can say 3750 ≤ length < 3850

---

(a) temperature of a room is 23.5°C to one decimal place.

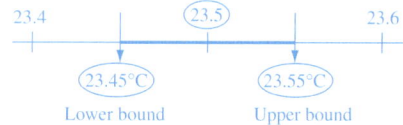

```
23.4        23.5        23.6
 +    +       +    +       +
   23.45°C      23.55°C
  Lower bound  Upper bound
```

(b) length of a table is 1430 mm to the nearest 10 mm.

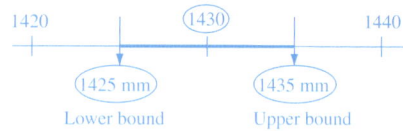

```
1420        1430        1440
 +    +       +    +       +
   1425 mm      1435 mm
  Lower bound  Upper bound
```

(c) weight of a lorry is 21000 kg to 2 significant figures.

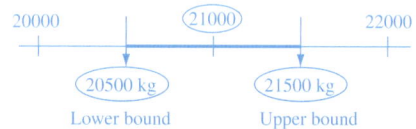

```
20000       21000       22000
 +    +       +    +       +
  20500 kg     21500 kg
  Lower bound  Upper bound
```

## E17.4

1   The length of a pen is measured at 14 cm to the nearest cm.

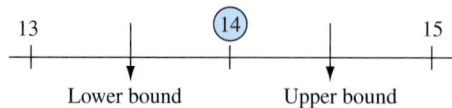

```
13           14           15
 +    +        +    +       +
   Lower bound   Upper bound
```

Write down   (a) the lower bound   (b) the upper bound

2   The height of a church tower is 42 m, measured to the nearest metre.

Write down   (a) the lower bound   (b) the upper bound

**3** A man weighs 83 kg, measured to the nearest kg.

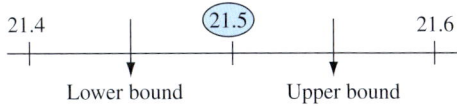

Write down  (a) the lower bound   (b)  the upper bound

**4** The diameter of a one pound coin is 21.5 mm,

measured to the nearest 0.1 mm.

```
        21.4              (21.5)              21.6
        +-----+-------------+-------------+-----+
              |             |             |
              v             v             v
          Lower bound         Upper bound
```

Write down   (a) the lower bound   (b)  the upper bound

**5** A baby weighs 3.6 kg, measured to the nearest 0.1 kg. Write down
(a) the lower bound  (b) the upper bound

**6** Copy and complete the table.

|     |                                         | Lower bound | Upper bound |
| --- | --------------------------------------- | ----------- | ----------- |
| (a) | length = 79 cm, to nearest cm           |             |             |
| (b) | mass = 32 kg, to nearest kg             |             |             |
| (c) | length = 6.3 m, to nearest 0.1 m        |             |             |
| (d) | volume = 15.7 m³, to nearest 0.1 m³     |             |             |
| (e) | width = 9.1 cm, to nearest 0.1 cm       |             |             |

**7** A coin weighs 10.3 g, correct to one decimal place. What is the least possible weight of the coin?

**8** A famous rock singer has a fortune of £24,712,000, correct to the nearest £1000. What is the least amount of money the rock singer might have?

**9** The width of a field is 530 m, correct to the nearest 10 m. What is the least possible width of the field?

**10** In a 100 m race a sprinter is timed at 10.12 seconds to the nearest 0.01 seconds. Write down the least possible time.

**11** Copy and complete each statement. Part (a) is done as an example.

(a) A mass $m$ is 48 g, to the nearest g, so $47.5 \leq m < 48.5$.

(b) A length $l$ is 92.6 mm, to the nearest 0.1 mm, so $92.55 \leq l <$ ☐.

(c) A diameter $d$ is 16.2 cm, to the nearest 0.1 cm, so ☐ $\leq d <$ ☐.

(d) A capacity $C$ is 1200 l, to the nearest 100 l, so ☐ $\leq C < 1250$.

(e) A height $h$ is 3.86 m, to the nearest 0.01 m, so ☐ $\leq h <$ ☐.

**12**

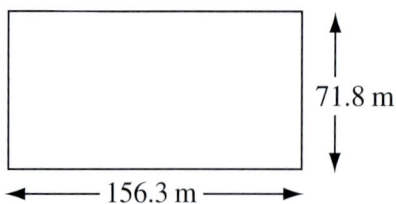

The length and width of a field are measured to the nearest 0.1 m.

71.8 m

156.3 m

(a) Write down the lower bound for the length of the field.

(b) Write down the upper bound for the width of the field.

(c) The area of the field is length × width. Use a calculator to find the *lowest* possible value of the area of the field.

**13**

8.4 cm

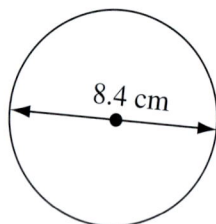

The diameter of the circle is measured to the nearest 0.1 cm.

Circumference $= \pi \times$ diameter

Use a calculator to find the *greatest* possible value of the circumference of the circle. (Give the answer to 1 decimal place).

*Can you still?*

*Can you still?*

**17D**   **Find averages from tables of information (see Unit 16)**

**1.** 89 people were asked how many cars they had owned during their lifetimes. The table below shows the information.

| Number of cars | 0 | 1 | 2 | 3 | 4 | 5 | 6 | 7 |
|---|---|---|---|---|---|---|---|---|
| Frequency | 11 | 8 | 12 | 21 | 22 | 8 | 5 | 2 |

Find  (a) the modal number of cars.          (b) the median number of cars.

(c) the total number of cars.          (d) the mean average number of cars.

**2.** 500 people were asked how much their houses were worth. The table below shows the information.

| Value of house (£1000's)($v$) | $50 \leq v < 100$ | $100 \leq v < 200$ | $200 \leq v < 300$ | $300 \leq v < 400$ | $400 \leq v < 500$ | $500 \leq v < 700$ |
|---|---|---|---|---|---|---|
| Frequency | 75 | 184 | 112 | 72 | 41 | 16 |

Find  (a) the modal interval.

(b) the interval which contains the median.

(c) estimate the mean average value of a house.

# Speed

When Carl walks at a constant speed of 5 km per hour, it means he moves 5 km in 1 hour. In 2 hours he walks 10 km. In 3 hours he moves 15 km and so on. We see that the distance moved is equal to the speed multiplied by the time taken.

$$\text{Distance} = \text{speed} \times \text{time}$$

Speed can be measured in km per hour

$$\text{Speed} = \frac{\text{Distance}}{\text{Time}}$$

we also have

$$\text{Time} = \frac{\text{Distance}}{\text{Speed}}$$

These three important formulas can be remembered using a triangle as shown.

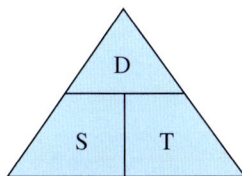

To find S: cover S and you have $\dfrac{D}{T}$

To find T: cover T and you have $\dfrac{D}{S}$

To find D: Cover D and you have $S \times T$

These formulas can only be used for objects moving at a *constant* speed.

*Be careful!*

- If the speed is in miles per hour, the distance must be in miles and the time must be in hours.

- If the speed is in metres per second, the distance must be in metres and the time must be in seconds.

---

(a) A car travels 100 miles in 2 hours 30 minutes.
Find the speed in mph

Time must be in hours only: 2 hours 30 minutes = 2.5 hours.

$$S = \frac{D}{T} = \frac{100}{2.5} = 40 \text{ mph.}$$

(b) Hazel runs at a steady speed of 8 m/s.

How far does she travel in 4.3 s?

$$D = S \times T = 8 \times 4.3 = 34.4 \text{ m.}$$

**1** Find the speed of a car for each distance and time shown below.

(a) distance = 90 miles, time = 2 hours

(b) distance = 200 miles, time = 4 hours

(c) distance = 165 miles, time = 3 hours

(d) distance = 60 miles, time = 1.5 hours

**2** Find how far a person runs for each speed and time below.

(a) speed = 7 m/s, time = 8 s        (b) speed = 5 m/s, time = 9 s

(c) speed = 6.5 m/s, time = 3 s       (d) speed = 4.9 m/s, time = 10 s

**3** Find how long it takes a train to travel for each distance and speed below.

(a) distance = 160 km, speed = 80 km/hr

(b) distance = 210 km, speed = 70 km/hr

(c) distance = 250 km, speed = 100 km/hr

(d) distance = 100 km, speed = 80 km/hr

**4** A plane flies 480 km at 320 km/hr. How long does the journey take?

**5** A person cycles for 3 hours at a speed of 12 mph. How far does he travel?

**6** Eurostar travels 420 km from London to Paris in 3 hours. Find the average speed of the train.

**7** Charlie drives from Wells to Bristol at 40 mph in 30 minutes. How far is it from Wells to Bristol?

**8** A hiker walks 28.5 miles at 3 mph. How long does the hiker walk for?

**9** Find the speed in mph for each of the following.

| Distance | Time | Speed (mph) |
|---|---|---|
| 30 miles | 30 minutes | |
| 9 miles | 15 minutes | |
| 15 miles | 20 minutes | |
| 6 miles | 5 minutes | |
| 30 miles | 45 minutes | |

**10** Terry cycles at 16 mph for 30 minutes then slows down to 12 mph for 15 minutes. How far does he travel in total?

**11** Janine walks at 6 km/hr for 1 hour 30 minutes then 4 km/hr for 2 hours 15 minutes. How far does she walk in total?

**12** A lorry leaves Cardiff at 09:30 and arrives in London at 12:00. The journey is 130 miles. What was the average speed of the lorry?

**13** A magpie flies 2 miles in 10 minutes. What is its speed in mph?

**14** Sima drives 50 miles from Leeds to Manchester at an average speed of 40 mph. If she left Leeds at 10:20, when did she arrive at Manchester?

**15** The speed of light is 300,000,000 m/s. How long will it take light to travel 6,000,000 km? (Be careful with the units)

## Density and other compound measures

If the density of a substance is 30 g/cm$^3$, it means that 1 cm$^3$ of the substance has a mass of 30 g.

$$\text{Density} = \text{Mass per unit Volume} \quad \text{so} \quad \text{Density} = \frac{\text{Mass}}{\text{Volume}}$$

We can use a triangle again to remember the formulas.

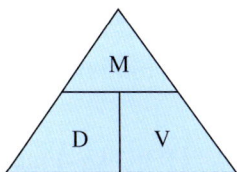

To find M: cover M and you have D × V

To find D: cover D and you have $\dfrac{M}{V}$

To find V: cover V and you have $\dfrac{M}{D}$

*Note*

There is a difference between 'mass' and 'weight' but in this book you may assume they have the same meaning.

(a) The density of silk is 1.3 g/cm$^3$. What is the mass of 8 cm$^3$ of silk?

    M = D × V = 1.3 × 8 = 10.4 g.

(b) The density of copper is 8.9 g/cm$^3$. The mass of a copper bar is 106.8 g. Find the volume of the copper bar.

    $V = \dfrac{M}{D} = \dfrac{106.8}{8.9} = 12$ cm$^3$.

*Note*

Speed and density are known as *compound measures*. Below is an example of different compound measures.

(c) A van can be hired at £45 per day. How much will it cost to hire the van for a fortnight (14 days)?

cost = 45 × 14 = £630

1 Copy and complete the table below:

| Density (g/cm³) | Mass (g) | Volume (cm³) |
|---|---|---|
| | 200 | 50 |
| | 80 | 5 |
| 13 | | 8 |
| 24 | | 36 |
| 10 | 150 | |
| 60 | | 0.5 |
| | 36 | 9 |
| 16 | 320 | |
| 0.1 | 19 | |
| | 42 | 10 |

2 The density of brass is 8.2 g/cm³. The volume of a brass ring is 20 cm³. Find the mass of the brass ring.

3 A gold bar has a volume of 80 cm³ and a mass of 1544 g. Find the density of the gold.

4 A piece of cotton has a volume of 250 cm³ and a mass of 385 kg. Find the density of the cotton.

5 A liquid weighs 500 g and has a density of 2.5 g/cm³. Find the volume of the liquid.

6 Which has a greater mass – 30 cm³ of cast iron with density 7.4 g/cm³ or 25 cm³ of pure nickel with density 8.9 g/cm³? Write down by how much.

7 Find the volume of some lead weighing 3 kg. The density of lead is 11.4 g/cm³ (note: you must change 3 kg into grams first). Give your answer to the nearest whole number.

8 High alloy steel has a density of 8.3 g/cm³. Find the weight of some steel with a volume of 50 cm³.

9 Brass has a density of 8.2 g/cm³. Find the volume of a brass fitting which weighs 0.574 kg.

10 Find the volume of a piece of zinc alloy weighing 2 kg. The density of zinc alloy is 6 g/cm³. Give your answer to the nearest whole number.

11 50 m [ ] 100 m
A farmer grows strawberries in this field. If the farmer makes £1.20 per m², how much money will the farmer make in total?

12 40 m² of carpet costs £878. What is the cost per m² of the carpet?

13 A supermarket chain makes £900,000 profit per day. How much profit do they make in one year? Assume 365 days in one year.

# WATCH YOUR MONEY! – Income tax

Tim starts a job earning £200 each week. When he gets his first pay packet, he finds £18.42 has been taken off his money already. This is *income tax*.

This does not make Tim happy but this money is used by the government to pay for things like hospitals, schools and defence.

Most people have income tax deducted from their pay *before* they receive it, by their employer, who then pays the tax to the government. This method of paying income tax is called *PAYE* (*Pay As You Earn*).

## Tax allowance

An amount of money a person may earn before paying income tax (at the time of writing) is £4745 each year for a single person.

## Taxable income

Taxable income = income – tax allowance
   (per year)

Income tax is worked out as a percentage of the taxable income.

## Percentage rate of income tax

10% on first £1960 of taxable income.

22% on the next £28540 of taxable income.

40% on any other taxable income.

---

If Tim earns £200 each week, that will be £10,000 in one year (assuming 50 working weeks in one year).

Tax allowance = £ 4745

Taxable income = income – tax allowance

$$= 10000 - 4745$$

$$= £5255$$

Tim pays 10% of £1960 on first £1960 of taxable income.
This leaves 5255 – 1960 = £3295 of taxable income.
Tim must then pay 22% of £3295

Income tax = 10% of 1960  = £196

   and 22% of 3295  = £724.90

Total income tax for the year = £920.90  (this is £18.42 for each week if divided by 50 weeks)

465

**1** Sophie earns £15000 each year. She has a tax allowance of £4745. Copy and complete the statements below to find out how much income tax Sophie must pay.

Taxable income = income − tax allowance

$$= 15000 - \boxed{\phantom{xxx}}$$

$$= £ \boxed{10255}$$

Income tax = 10% of 1960 = £ $\boxed{\phantom{xxx}}$

and 22% of $\boxed{\text{'taxable income'} - 1960}$

$$= 22\% \text{ of } \boxed{\phantom{xx}} = £ \boxed{\phantom{xx}}$$

Total income tax = £ $\boxed{\phantom{x}}$ + £ $\boxed{\phantom{x}}$ = £ $\boxed{\phantom{x}}$

**2** Callum earns £13400 each year. He has a tax allowance of £4745. Copy and complete the statements below to find out how much income tax Callum must pay.

Taxable income = income − tax allowance

$$= \boxed{\phantom{xx}} - \boxed{\phantom{xx}}$$

$$= £ \boxed{\phantom{xx}}$$

Income tax = 10% of 1960 = £ $\boxed{\phantom{xx}}$

and 22% of $\boxed{\text{'taxable income'} - 1960}$

$$= 22\% \text{ of } \boxed{\phantom{xx}} = £ \boxed{\phantom{xx}}$$

Total income tax = £ $\boxed{\phantom{x}}$ + £ $\boxed{\phantom{x}}$ = £ $\boxed{\phantom{x}}$

**3** Wendy earns £28500 each year. She has a tax allowance of £4745.

(a) What is Wendy's taxable income?

(b) How much income tax will Wendy have to pay?

**4** Alex earns £1450 each month. He has a tax allowance of £4745.

(a) What is his annual (yearly) taxable income?

(b) How much income tax will he pay for one year?

(c) How much income tax will he pay each month?

**5** Angus earns £6000 each year. How much income tax will he pay? (He has a tax allowance of £4745)

**6** Dom earns £90 each week. His tax allowance is £4745. Assuming 52 weeks in one year, how much income tax will Dom pay each week?

**7** Millie earns £320 each week. She has a tax allowance of £4745.

(a) Find her annual salary (assuming 52 weeks in one year).

(b) What is her taxable income?

(c) How much income tax will she pay for one year?

(d) How much income tax will she pay each week?

**8** Emma earns £896 each month from her work in a shop. She also works in a pub, earning £30 each week. Her tax allowance is £4745. Assuming 52 weeks in one year, how much income tax will Emma pay each week?

## TEST YOURSELF ON UNIT 17

### 1. Reading scales

For each of the scales below, write down the measurement indicated by the arrow.

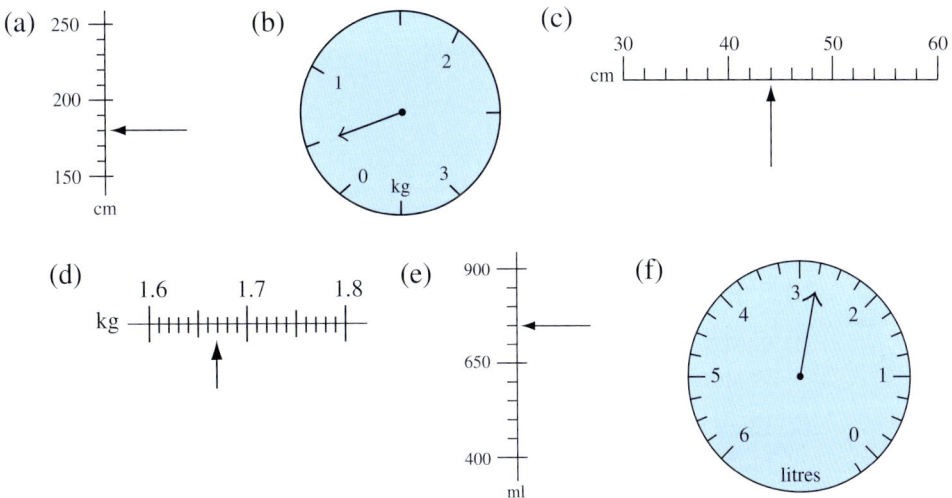

### 2. Using and converting metric units

Copy and complete the following:

(a) 9.5 m = ☐ cm      (b) 7.5 kg = ☐ g      (c) 6.12 kg = ☐ g

(d) 2000 ml = ☐ l      (e) 3200 g = ☐ kg      (f) 2.6 km = ☐ m

(g) 850 m = ☐ km      (h) 5.9 l = ☐ ml      (i) 46 ml = ☐ l

(j) 4 tonnes = ☐ kg      (k) 6 g = ☐ kg      (l) 85 mm = ☐ cm

(m) Chas has 1.4 kg of flour and uses 638 g. How much flour does he have left?

(n) Sarah knocks over a 2 litre bottle of water and spills 735 ml. How much water is left in the bottle?

### 3. Dealing with 'time' problems

(a) Shanta catches a train at 14:45. Is this in the morning or the afternoon?

(b)

Plane leaves                      Plane arrives

How long was the plane journey?

(c) Ravi and Bella start watching a DVD at 7:40 p.m. The DVD lasts for 2 hours 25 minutes. At what time do they stop watching the DVD?

(d) A game of football starts at 12:30. The game finishes 1 hour 40 minutes later. At what time does the game finish?

(e) Joey gets up at 07:45 and goes to bed at 23:30. How long is he up for?

### 4. Using and converting imperial units

Copy and complete the following:

(a) 5 stone = ☐ pounds

(b) 7 yards = ☐ feet

(c) 3 gallons = ☐ pints

(d) 24 inches = ☐ feet

(e) 48 ounces = ☐ pounds

(f) 12 feet = ☐ yards

(g) 3.5 gallons = ☐ pints

(h) 2 stone 3 pounds = ☐ pounds

(i) 5 feet 9 inches = ☐ inches

(j) Carl weighs 11 stone 10 pounds. He has a wonderful holiday and puts on a ½ stone. How much does Carl now weigh?

(k) Lucy is 4 feet 11 inches tall when she is 11 years old. She grows another 7 inches by the time she is 16 years old. How tall is Lucy when she is 16 years old?

### 5. Converting between metric and imperial units

Copy and complete the following:

(a) 10 inches ≈ ☐ cm

(b) 100 cm ≈ ☐ inches

(c) 10 miles ≈ ☐ km

(d) 25 miles ≈ ☐ km

(e) 32 km ≈ ☐ miles

(f) 4 gallons ≈ ☐ litres

(g) 5 kg ≈ ☐ pounds

(h) 88 pounds ≈ ☐ kg

(i) 90 litres ≈ ☐ gallons

(j) Which is further – 6 miles or 10 km?

(k) A barrel contains 30 litres of beer. How many whole pints of beer would this provide?

**6.** Finding upper and lower bounds

(a) The diameter of a 10 pence coin is 2.4 cm, measured to the nearest 0.1 cm.

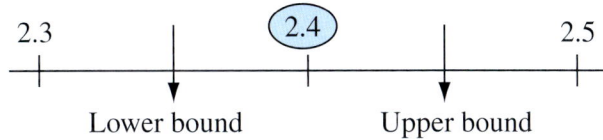

```
        2.3              2.4              2.5
         +       +        |       +        +
                 ▼                 ▼
             Lower bound       Upper bound
```

Write down    (i) the lower bound    (ii) the upper bound

(b) The length of a road is 364 m, measured to the nearest metre.
Write down    (i) the lower bound    (ii) the upper bound

(c) A woman weighs 65 kg, measured to the nearest kg.
Write down    (i) the lower bound    (ii) the upper bound

(d) The width of a book is 18.8 cm, measured to the nearest 0.1 cm.
Write down    (i) the lower bound    (ii) the upper bound

**7.** Calculating with speed, density and other compound measures

(a) Sharon walks for 3 hours at a speed of 5 km/hr. How far
does Sharon walk?

(b) Greg cycles 63 km at a speed of 14 km/hr. How long
does the journey take him?

(c) 12 cm$^3$ of gold weighs 231.6 g. Find the density of gold.

(d) A steel bar has a volume of 600 cm$^3$. If the density of
steel is 8.3 g/cm$^3$, find the mass of the steel bar.

(e) A car costs £39 per day to hire. How much will it cost to
hire the car for 12 days?

(f) A lorry travels at 51 mph for 20 minutes. How far does the lorry travel?

## Mixed examination questions

**1** (a) How many grams are there in 1½ kilograms?

(b) How many centimetres are there in 2 metres?

(c) How many millilitres are there in 3 litres?

(d) Which **metric** unit would be the most useful to measure

(i) the area of a football pitch

(ii) the capacity of a car's petrol tank?                    (OCR)

**2** What is the reading on each of these scales?

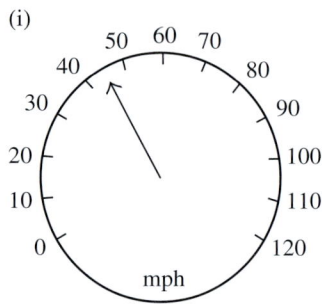

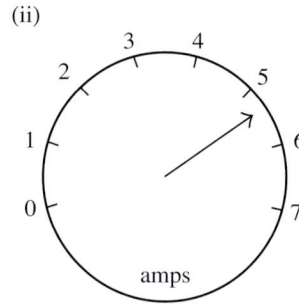

(i)

mph

(ii)

amps

(EDEXCEL)

**3** Two villages are 40 km apart.

(a) Change 40 km into metres.

(b) How many miles are the same as 40 km?

(AQA)

**4** Here is part of a train timetable from Crewe to London.

(a) At what time should the train leave Coventry?

The train should arrive in London at 10:45

(b) How long should the train take to travel from Crewe to London?

Verity arrived at Milton Keynes station at 09:53

| Station | Time of Leaving |
|---------|-----------------|
| Crewe | 08:00 |
| Wolverhampton | 08:40 |
| Birmingham | 09:00 |
| Coventry | 09:30 |
| Rugby | 09:40 |
| Milton Keynes | 10:10 |

(c) How many minutes should she have to wait before the 10:10 train leaves?

(EDEXCEL)

**5** The speed limit in London is 30 miles per hour.
In Paris the speed limit is 50 kilometres per hour.

Which of these two speeds is slower?
Show clear working to support your answer.

(OCR)

**6** The mass of 5 $m^3$ of copper is 44 800 kg.

(a) Work out the density of copper.

The density of zinc is 7130 kg/$m^3$.

(b) Work out the mass of 5 $m^3$ of zinc.

(EDEXCEL)

**7** Each side of a regular pentagon has a length of 101 mm, correct to the nearest millimetre.

(i) Write down the **least** possible length of each side.

(ii) Write down the **greatest** possible length of each side.

(EDEXCEL)

# ALGEBRA 4

**In this unit you will learn how to:**

– change the subject of a formula

– deal with inequalities

– use the laws of indices

– write numbers in standard form

– use numbers written in standard form

– 〈WATCH YOUR MONEY!〉 – buying a house.

## Changing the subject of a formula

(a) $a = 3b$

Make $b$ the subject of the formula.

$a = 3 \times b$

$\dfrac{a}{3} = \dfrac{3 \times b}{3}$

$\dfrac{a}{3} = b$    we say that $b = \dfrac{a}{3}$

(b) $p = 5q + 8$ Make q the subject of the formula.

$\boxed{p} = \boxed{5q}\ \boxed{+8}$

$\boxed{p} - 8 = \boxed{5q}\ \boxed{+8} - 8$

$p - 8 = 5q$

$\dfrac{p - 8}{5} = \dfrac{5q}{5}$

$\dfrac{p - 8}{5} = q$    we say that $q = \dfrac{p - 8}{5}$

### M18.1

Copy and complete each statement below:

**1** If $x = y + 5$ then $x\ \square\ 5 = y$

**2** If $x = y + 8$ then $x\ \square\ 8 = y$

**3** If $a = b - 3$ then $a\ \square\ 3 = b$

**4** If $a = b + 9$ then $a\ \square\ 9 = b$

**5** If $a = 6b$ then $\dfrac{a}{\square} = b$

**6** If $x = y - 2$ then $x\ \square\ 2 = y$

**7** $p = 3q$ Make $q$ the subject of the formula.

**8** $a = 7b$ Make $b$ the subject of the formula.

**9** $x = \dfrac{y}{9}$ Make $y$ the subject of the formula.

**10** Make $x$ the subject of each formula given below:

(a) $y = x - 9$      (b) $y = \dfrac{x}{12}$      (c) $y = x + 6$      (d) $y = x + 20$

(e) $y = 8x$      (f) $y = 10x$      (g) $y = x - 4$      (h) $y = x - 25$

(i) $y = \dfrac{x}{3}$      (j) $y = \dfrac{x}{15}$      (k) $y = x + 100$      (l) $y = 18x$

**11** Match up pairs of formulas which are the same. There will be one odd formula left over.

A   $a = b + 5$

B   $a = 5b$

C   $a = b - 5$

P   $b = \dfrac{a}{5}$

Q   $b = a - 5$

R   $b = 5a$

S   $b = a + 5$

**12** Copy and fill each box below:

(a) $x = 3y + 2$

     $x - \square = 3y + 2 - \square$

     $x - \square = 3y$

     $\dfrac{x - \square}{\square} = y$

(b) $x = 4y - 9$

     $x + \square = 4y - 9 + \square$

     $x + \square = 4y$

     $\dfrac{x + \square}{\square} = y$

**13** $a = 2b - 5$ Make $b$ the subject of the formula.

**14** $p = 9q + 7$ Make $q$ the subject of the formula.

**15** $a = 7b + 1$ Make $b$ the subject of the formula.

**16** $x = 3y - 10$ Make $y$ the subject of the formula.

**17** Make $x$ the subject of each formula given below:

(a) $y = 2x + 8$      (b) $y = 6x - 5$      (c) $y = 8x - 10$

(d) $y = \dfrac{x}{3} + 2$      (e) $y = \dfrac{x}{5} - 6$      (f) $y = \dfrac{x}{2} - 4$

$c(x - d) = y$   Make $x$ the subject of the formula

$c(x - d) = y$   *multiply out the bracket first*

$\boxed{cx}\;\boxed{-cd} = \boxed{y}$   add $cd$ onto *both* sides of the equation

$\boxed{cx}\;\boxed{-cd} + cd = \boxed{y} + cd$

$cx = y + cd$   divide *both* sides of the equation by $c$

$$\frac{\cancel{c}x}{\cancel{c}} = \frac{y + cd}{c} \quad \text{the } c \text{ cancels down}$$

$$x = \frac{y + cd}{c}$$

## E18.1

**1**   Copy and fill each box below:

(a)   $y = ax - b$

$y + \square = ax - b + \square$

$y + \square = ax$

$\dfrac{y + \square}{\square} = x$

(b)   $v = at + u$

$v - \square = at + u - \square$

$v - \square = at$

$\dfrac{v - \square}{\square} = t$

**2**   Make $x$ the subject of each formula given below:

(a)   $y = px + q$     (b)   $y = cx - h$     (c)   $y = rx - 2p$

(d)   $q = cx + 3s$     (e)   $bx + 5c = 2f$     (f)   $y = ax + b - c$

**3**   Copy and fill each box below:

(a)   $y = \dfrac{fx - g}{h}$

$\square = fx - g$

$\square + g = fx - g + g$

$\square + g = fx$

$\dfrac{\square + g}{\square} = x$

(b)   $\dfrac{px + 2h}{c} = y$

$px + 2h = \square$

$px + 2h - 2h = \square - \square$

$px = \square - \square$

$x = \dfrac{\square - \square}{\square}$

473

**4** Make $x$ the subject of each formula given below:

(a) $c(x + d) = y$      (b) $m(x - n) = q$      (c) $r(x + 5) = y$

(d) $a(x + 7) = 3b$      (e) $y = f(x - g)$      (f) $4b = s(x - t)$

**5** Make $x$ the subject of each formula given below:

(a) $\dfrac{ax + d}{4} = e$      (b) $\dfrac{bx + 3c}{y} = p$      (c) $\dfrac{ax - r}{5} = q$

(d) $y = \dfrac{cx - 2d}{7}$      (e) $y = \dfrac{ax - 3c}{b}$      (f) $\dfrac{px + qr}{8} = y$

**6** $h = 3g + m$ Make $g$ the subject of the formula.

**7** $v = u + fy$ Make $y$ the subject of the formula.

*Can you still?*

**18A** **Find the circumference and area of circles (see Unit 15)**

*Can you still?*

1. *Use a calculator* to find (i) the perimeter (ii) the area of each shape below. When necessary, give answers to 1 decimal place.

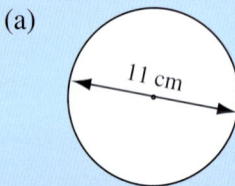

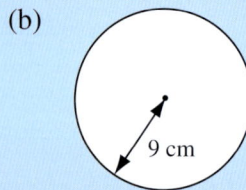

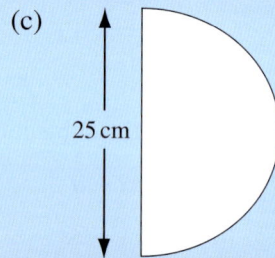

(a)

11 cm

(b)

9 cm

(c)

25 cm

2. Find the total distance once around this running track.

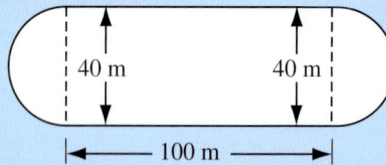

40 m      40 m

100 m

3. Find the *area* of this shape.

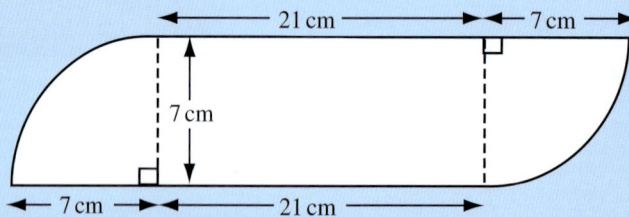

21 cm    7 cm

7 cm

7 cm    21 cm

## Inequalities

Show on a number line the range of values of $x$ for the inequalities shown.

(a)        $x > 2$

↑

| | | ⊕ | | |
0    1    2    3    4

The circle at the left hand end of the range is open. This means $x$ *cannot* equal 2.

'$x$ is greater than 2'

(b)        $x \leq -1$

↑

−4    −3    −2    −1    0

The circle at −1 is filled in. This means $x$ *can* equal −1.

'$x$ is less than or equal to −1'

(c)    $-2 \leq x < 1$

−3    −2    −1    0    1    2

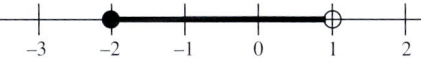

$x$ is greater than −2 and *can equal −2*.

$x$ is also less than 1 but *cannot equal 1*.

## M18.2

**1**   Write down the inequalities shown below:

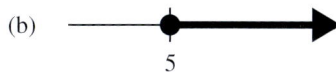

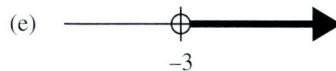

(a)   1

(b)   5

(c)   −2

(d)   −4

(e)   −3

(f)   2    5

(g)   −6    −1

(h)   0    8

(i)   $\frac{1}{2}$

(j)   −5    −1

(k)   −4    7

(l)   −1    2.5

**2**   Draw a number line to show the following inequalities.

(a) $x \geq 3$        (b) $x < 6$        (c) $x \leq -3$

(d) $3 < x < 8$        (e) $-6 < x \leq 2$        (f) $n > -1$

(g) $-7 \leq n < -3$        (h) $2 \leq t \leq 4$        (i) $-2 < p \leq 0$

**3** If ☐ < 120, write a possible number for ☐

**4** If ☐ > 50, write a possible number for ☐

**5** Write a possible number for ☐ in each of the following:

    (a) ☐ > 820      (b) ☐ < 175      (c) 300 < ☐

    (d) 1100 < ☐      (e) 185 < ☐      (f) ☐ < 362

**6** Write a possible number for ☐ in each of the following:

    (a) 150 < ☐ < 250    (b) 730 < ☐ < 750    (c) 1241 < ☐ < 1243

    (d) 428 < ☐ < 430    (e) −6 < ☐ < 0    (f) − 8 < ☐ < − 4

**7** Copy and fill each box below with < or >

    (a) 17 ☐ 13    (b) 228 ☐ 241    (c) 7.5 ☐ 7.05    (d) − 6 ☐ − 5

**8** Answer true or false:

    (a) − 4 > 3    (b) 3.6 < 3.17    (c) 5.23 > 5.1    (d) $6\frac{1}{4} < 6.5$

---

Solve the inequalities:

(a)  $x + 6 > 14$    (b) $x - 3 \leq 6$    (c)  $4x < 320$    (d) $\dfrac{x}{7} \geq -3$

      $x > 8$         $x \leq 9$         $x < \dfrac{320}{4}$      $x \geq -3 \times 7$

                                               $x < 80$       $x \geq - 21$

---

## E18.2

**1** Copy and fill in the boxes below:

    (a) $x - 5 > 3$      (b) $\dfrac{x}{4} \leq 9$      (c) $2x + 4 < 10$

        $x > 3 + $ ☐        $x \leq 9 \times$ ☐        $2x < 10 - $ ☐

        $x > $ ☐            $x \leq$ ☐             $2x < $ ☐

                                               $x < $ ☐

Solve the inequalities in Questions **2** to **13**.

**2** $x + 8 < 15$      **3** $x - 2 \geq 9$      **4** $n - 8 < 1$

**5** $n + 6 \geq -2$      **6** $a - 7 > -2$      **7** $b - 6 \geq -4$

**8** $5 + x \leq 17$      **9** $4n \leq 20$      **10** $6y > 42$

**11** $\dfrac{b}{3} \geq 8$      **12** $\dfrac{x}{5} < -9$      **13** $3x \geq -12$

Find the range of values of $x$ which satisfy each inequality in Questions **14** to **19** and show each answer on a number line.

**14** $5x \leq 30$

**15** $9x > -27$

**16** $2 + x \geq 6$

**17** $\dfrac{x}{2} \geq 1$

**18** $x + 3 < 0$

**19** $\dfrac{x}{4} \leq -2$

In Questions **20** to **25** write down all the *integer* values (*whole numbers*) of $x$ which satisfy the given inequalities.

**20** $0 < x < 4$

**21** $2 \leq x \leq 4$

**22** $1 \leq x < 7$

**23** $-2 \leq x \leq 2$

**24** $-4 < x \leq 0$

**25** $-5 \leq x < 4$

**26** Write down the smallest integer $x$ for which $2x > 5$.

**27** Write down the largest integer $x$ for which $10x < 56$.

Solve the inequalities in Questions **28** to **39**.

**28** $2x + 7 > 19$

**29** $3x - 1 \leq 14$

**30** $6n - 5 \geq 43$

**31** $4b + 12 \leq 28$

**32** $3 + 7x > -4$

**33** $4n - 8 < 0$

**34** $3(a - 2) < 15$

**35** $4(x + 3) \leq 20$

**36** $\dfrac{a}{6} - 4 \geq 2$

**37** $5x + 3 \geq 2x + 21$

**38** $8n - 2 > 3n + 33$

**39** $6x + 8 < 38 - 4x$

*Can you still?*

*Can you still?*

**18B**    **Find surface areas and volumes of cuboids (see Unit 15)**

**1.** Which of these 3 cuboids has the *smallest* surface area?

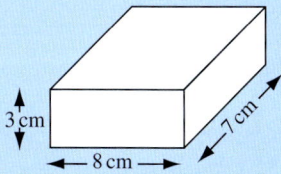

A

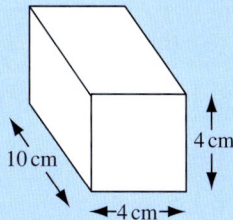

B

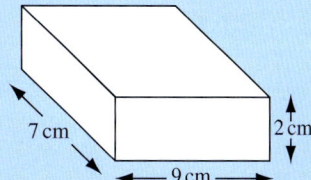

C

**2.** Which of the 3 cuboids in Question ② has the *largest volume*?

**3.** The *volume* of this cuboid is 420 cm³.

What is the length $l$ of the cuboid?

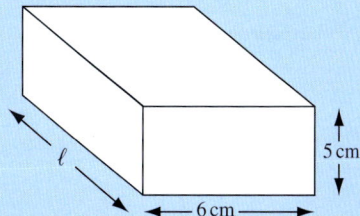

## Key Facts

$3^4 \Leftarrow$ the 'power' 4 is also called the 'index' ('indices' for more than one index)

$\Uparrow$

this number is called the 'base'

To *multiply* numbers with indices, *add the indices*. The base numbers must be the same.

$$a^m \times a^n = a^{m+n}$$

To *divide* numbers with indices, *subtract the indices*. The base numbers must be the same.

$$a^m \div a^n = a^{m-n}$$

### M18.3

**1** Copy and complete. Write the answer as a number in index form.

(a) $3^3 \times 3^4 =$      (b) $5^2 \times 5^4 =$      (c) $8^3 \times 8^3 =$

(d) $7^2 \times 7^3 =$      (e) $4^6 \times 4 =$      (f) $6^5 \times 6^2 =$

**2** Copy and complete. Write the answer as a number in index form.

(a) $7^6 \div 7^2$      (b) $4^7 \div 4^4$      (c) $3^9 \div 3$

(d) $5^8 \div 5^5$      (e) $6^{10} \div 6^7$      (f) $4^6 \div 4^5$

**3** Work out and write each answer as a number in index form.

(a) $8^6 \times 8^2$      (b) $4^7 \times 4^3$      (c) $9^8 \div 9^5$

(d) $6^4 \times 6^4$      (e) $8^7 \div 8$      (f) $5^5 \div 5^2$

(g) $3^3 \times 3^2 \times 3^4$      (h) $2^6 \times 2 \times 2^3$      (i) $(4^3)^2$

**4**

$\longleftarrow 2^6\,\text{cm} \longrightarrow$

$2^3\text{cm}$

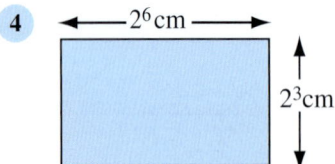

Write down the area of this rectangle in index form.

**5** Copy and complete

(a) $3^4 \times 3^2 = \square$

(b) $\square \times 6^4 = 6^6$

(c) $\square \times 9^4 = 9^7$

(d) $4^6 \times \square = 4^8$

(e) $9^3 \times \square = 9^4$

(f) $4^8 \div 4^2 = \square$

(g) $3^8 \div \square = 3^2$

(h) $8^{10} \div \square = 8^5$

(i) $\square \div 4^5 = 4^7$

**6** Write down the area of this square in index form.

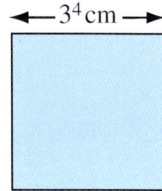

$\longleftarrow 3^4\,\text{cm} \longrightarrow$

**7** Work out and write each answer as a number in index form.

(a) $5^3 \times 5^9 \times 5^2$

(b) $8^7 \times 8^2 \times 8^4$

(c) $\dfrac{4^8 \times 4^3}{4^7}$

(d) $\dfrac{7^6 \times 7^8}{7^4}$

(e) $\dfrac{8^9}{8^2 \times 8^3}$

(f) $\dfrac{6^8}{6^3 \times 6^3}$

**8** Which statements below are true?

(a) $4^3 \times 4^2 = 4^5$

(b) $7^9 \div 7^3 = 7^6$

(c) $2^8 \times 2 = 2^9$

(d) $3^6 \times 3 = 3^6$

(e) $5^6 \div 5^3 = 5^2$

(f) $8^7 \div 8 = 8^6$

# Key Facts

To raise an index number to another power, multiply the indices.

$(a^m)^n = a^{mn}$

(a) $\dfrac{a^2 \times a^7}{(a^2)^2} = \dfrac{a^9}{a^4} = a^5$

(b) $\dfrac{n^4 \times n^6}{(n^4)^2} = \dfrac{n^{10}}{n^8} = n^2$

$4^2 \div 4^2 = 4^{2-2} = 4^0$

$4^2 \div 4^2 = 16 \div 16 = 1$

so $4^0 = 1$

*LEARN!*    $a^0 = 1$    for any number $a$ (apart from $a = 0$)

**1** Copy and complete. Write the number in index form.

(a) $(3^2)^4$     (b) $(5^3)^2$     (c) $(6^3)^4$     (d) $(7^4)^2$

(e) $(5^6)^3$     (f) $(8^2)^5$     (g) $(3^5)^3$     (h) $(6^3)^5$

**2** Which is larger? $\boxed{10^0}$ or $\boxed{3^0}$

**3** Copy and complete. Write the number in index form.

(a) $(3^4)^2 \times 3^3$     (b) $(2^3)^4 \times 2^6$     (c) $6^5 \times (6^2)^2$

(d) $\dfrac{7^3}{7^0}$     (e) $\dfrac{(5^2)^4}{(5^3)^2}$     (f) $\dfrac{9 \times (9^3)^3}{9^7}$

(g) $\dfrac{8^2 \times 8^6}{(8^2)^3}$     (h) $\dfrac{4^3 \times (4^5)^2}{4^7}$     (i) $\dfrac{(2^3)^2 \times (2^3)^2}{2^4 \times 2^3}$

**4** What is the value of $(4^0)^6$?

**5** Simplify the expressions below.

(a) $a^4 \times a^3$     (b) $x^7 \times x^4$     (c) $x^9 \div x^4$

(d) $(n^3)^2$     (e) $a^{10} \div a^6$     (f) $(x^3)^3$

(g) $n^0$     (h) $p^8 \times p$     (i) $m^{14} \div m^8$

(j) $(x^2)^0$     (k) $(a^2)^4 \times a^5$     (l) $x^p \div x^p$

**6**

Write down the area of this picture in index form.

**7** Simplify the expressions below.

(a) $5x^3 \times x^6$     (b) $4x^2 \times 4x^2$     (c) $5p^3 \times 2p^2$

(d) $8a^2 \times 3a^4$     (e) $\dfrac{8a^5}{a^2}$     (f) $\dfrac{10x^6}{2x^4}$

**8** Which is larger? $\boxed{\dfrac{(3^3)^2 \times 3^2}{3^3 \times (3^2)^2}}$   or   $\boxed{\dfrac{(3^2)^3 \times 3^3}{3^5 \times 3^2}}$

                A                       B

**9** Simplify the expressions below.

(a) $\dfrac{x^5 \times x^3}{x^6}$

(b) $\dfrac{a^2 \times a^6}{(a^2)^2}$

(c) $\dfrac{(m^3)^2 \times m^4}{(m^3)^3}$

(d) $\dfrac{a^8}{a^3 \times a}$

(e) $\dfrac{n^9 \times (n^2)^4}{(n^3)^5}$

(f) $\dfrac{x^8 \times x^4}{(x^3)^2 \times x^2}$

(g) $\dfrac{(x^3)^6}{x^2 \times (x^2)^5}$

(h) $\dfrac{a^{20}}{(a^3)^4 \times (a^2)^2}$

(i) $\dfrac{n^2 \times (n^4)^2}{(n^2)^3 \times n}$

**10** Multiply out the brackets below, leaving each answer in index form.

(a) $x^3 (x^3 + x^2)$

(b) $n^4 (n^5 - n)$

(c) $x^7 (x^2 + x^5)$

*Can you still?*

**18C**  **Find volumes of prisms (see Unit 15)**

*Can you still?*

Find the volume of each prism below. When necessary, give answers to 1 decimal place.

**1.**

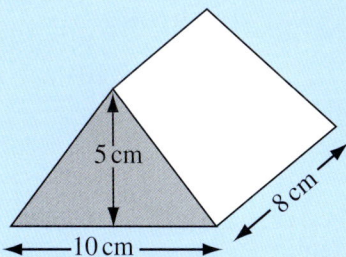

**2.**

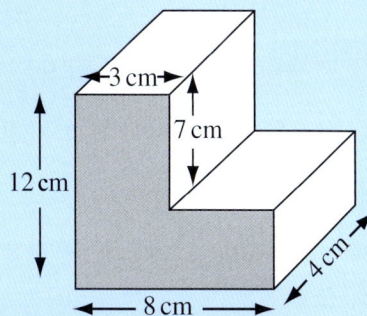

**3.**

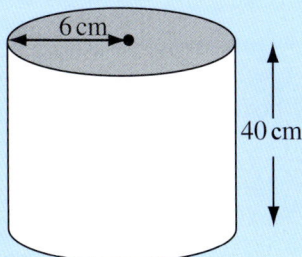

**4.**

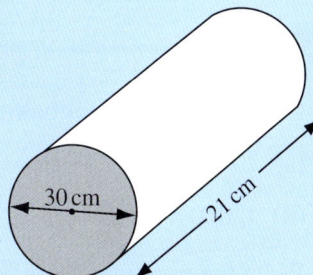

---

🔑 # Key Facts

---

A number written in standard form will have the form

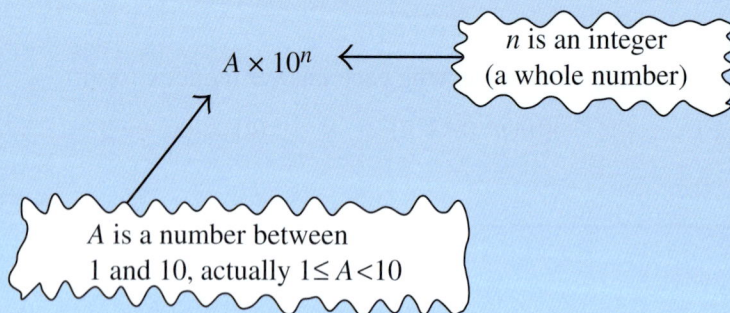

$$A \times 10^n$$ ← *n* is an integer (a whole number)

*A* is a number between 1 and 10, actually $1 \leq A < 10$

Very large numbers and very small numbers are usually written in standard form.

**Changing ordinary numbers into standard form**

| 6000 | $= 6 \times 1000$ | $= 6 \times 10 \times 10 \times 10$ | $= 6 \times 10^3$ |
|---|---|---|---|
| 1980 | $= 1.98 \times 1000$ | $= 1.98 \times 10 \times 10 \times 10$ | $= 1.98 \times 10^3$ |
| 5300000 | $= 5.3 \times 1000000$ | $= 5.3 \times 10 \times 10 \times 10 \times 10 \times 10 \times 10$ | $= 5.3 \times 10^6$ |

**Numbers between 0 and 1**

$0.0082 = 8.2 \times 10^{-3}$ ← the decimal point moves to the right
↑  ↑            3 places from *A* to *B*.
*A*  *B*

---

### M18.4

**1** Copy each statement below and fill in the empty boxes.

(a) $7000 = 7 \times 10^{\square}$    (b) $400000 = 4 \times 10^{\square}$  (c) $360 = 3.6 \times 10^{\square}$

(d) $42000 = 4.2 \times 10^{\square}$    (e) $82000 = \square \times 10^{\square}$  (f) $6400 = \square \times 10^3$

**2** Write the numbers below in standard form.

(a) 60000  (b) 900  (c) 5800  (d) 690000

(e) 850  (f) 74000000  (g) 47000  (h) 4 million

(i) 72 million  (j) 382  (k) 42 thousand  (l) 213 million

**3** Copy each statement below and fill in the empty boxes.

(a) $0.08 = 8 \times 10^{\square}$  (b) $0.009 = 9 \times 10^{\square}$  (c) $0.052 = 5.2 \times 10^{\square}$

(d) $0.000067 = 6.7 \times 10^{\square}$  (e) $0.4 = \square \times 10^{-1}$  (f) $0.00082 = \square \times 10^{-4}$

**4** Write the numbers below in standard form.

(a) 0.0008  (b) 0.003  (c) 0.00000007  (d) 0.95

(e) 0.0061  (f) 0.2  (g) 0.0000000039  (h) 0.000062

(i) 0.00000057  (j) 0.0625  (k) 0.00437  (l) 0.812

**5** Write each number below as an ordinary number.

(a) $5 \times 10^2$  (b) $6.8 \times 10^3$  (c) $8.1 \times 10^5$  (d) $7 \times 10^{-2}$

(e) $9.8 \times 10^{-4}$  (f) $6.12 \times 10^4$  (g) $3.7 \times 10^{-3}$  (h) $8.41 \times 10^{-2}$

(i) $2.5 \times 10^6$  (j) $4.6 \times 10^{-1}$  (k) $1.72 \times 10^{-4}$  (l) $5.36 \times 10^5$

**6** Write down which numbers below are *not* written in standard form.

(a) $7.1 \times 10^{-2}$  (b) $0.32 \times 10^8$  (c) $48 \times 10^3$

(d) $59 \times 10^{-3}$  (e) $5.6 \times 10^{-3}$  (f) $0.02 \times 10^7$

**7** The population of the UK is about 60 million. Write this in standard form.

**8** The annual budget for the Bayford High School is £4126000. Write this in standard form.

**9** A rock star has sold a total of 127 million albums. Write this in standard form.

**10** Write the numbers below in standard form.

(a) 0.02  (b) 0.0006  (c) 209  (d) 31600

(e) 5800000  (f) 316.8  (g) 32.71  (h) 0.000624

(i) 0.39  (j) 0.0065  (k) 80.64  (l) 590000

(m) 63700000  (n) 627.91  (o) 0.073  (p) 0.0000416

**Standard form calculations**

**Using a calculator**

A number like 720 000 000 000 000 is too large to type into a calculator. Write it in standard form as $7.2 \times 10^{14}$.

Use the $\boxed{\text{EXP}}$ button to enter numbers in standard form.

$7.2 \times 10^{14}$ is typed in as $\boxed{7}$ $\boxed{\cdot}$ $\boxed{2}$ $\boxed{\text{EXP}}$ $\boxed{1}$ $\boxed{4}$

**Note.** you do **not** press the $\boxed{\text{X}}$ button after the $\boxed{\text{EXP}}$ button!

The calculator display may be $\boxed{7.2^{14}}$ or $\boxed{7.2\ 14}$ but more and more calculators now show $\boxed{7.2 \times 10^{14}}$

'*On paper*' the standard form number must be written properly as $7.2 \times 10^{14}$

---

**Without a calculator**

**Multiplication**

**Multiply the numbers and add the powers.**

$(2 \times 10^3) \times (3 \times 10^2) = 2000 \times 300 = 600000 = 6 \times 10^5$

**Division**

**Divide the numbers and subtract the powers.**

$(6 \times 10^5) \div (2 \times 10^2) = 600000 \div 200 = 3000 = 3 \times 10^3$

---

**E18.4**

1   Use a calculator to work out the following and write each answer in standard form.

(a) $(5 \times 10^9) \times (9 \times 10^6)$

(b) $(4 \times 10^{11}) \times (3 \times 10^{24})$

(c) $(7 \times 10^{19}) \times (9 \times 10^{12})$

(d) $(3 \times 10^6) \times (2.1 \times 10^7)$

(e) $(3 \times 10^{16}) \times (5 \times 10^{-9})$

(f) $(1.8 \times 10^6) \times (2.3 \times 10^{14})$

(g) $(7.2 \times 10^{-6}) \times (4 \times 10^{-12})$

(h) $(6.3 \times 10^{-8}) \times (2 \times 10^{26})$

(i) $(8 \times 10^{-14}) \times (3.6 \times 10^{-17})$

(j) $(9 \times 10^{21}) \div (3 \times 10^6)$

(k) $(7.2 \times 10^{34}) \div (3 \times 10^{-16})$

(l) $(4.8 \times 10^{16}) \div (4 \times 10^{-6})$

(m) $(4.2 \times 10^{16}) \div (7 \times 10^{-12})$

(n) $(5.1 \times 10^{-8}) \div (1.7 \times 10^{-19})$

(o) $(8.1 \times 10^{-14}) \div (3 \times 10^{-8})$

**2** The distance of the Earth from the Sun is about $1.496 \times 10^{11}$ m. The distance of Pluto from the Sun is about $5.91 \times 10^{12}$ m. How many times further from the Sun is Pluto compared to the Earth? (give your answer to the nearest whole number)

**3** The mass of a substance is $9 \times 10^{-8}$ kg. Its volume is $5 \times 10^{-9}$ m³. What is its density in kg/m³?

**4**

The radius of this circle is $4.7 \times 10^{-8}$ m. Calculate the area of the circle (give your answer to 3 significant figures).

**5** $m = 7.1 \times 10^{19}$ and $n = 3.6 \times 10^{33}$

Work out the following, leaving each answer in standard form correct to 3 significant figures.

(a) $m \times n$      (b) $m \div n$      (c) $m^2$      (d) $m^2 \div n^2$

**6** The mass of an electron is $9.1 \times 10^{-28}$ grams. What is the total mass of $5 \times 10^{12}$ electrons?

**7** Work out the following, leaving each answer in standard form correct to 3 significant figures.

(a) $\dfrac{(2.1 \times 10^{9}) \times (4.6 \times 10^{16})}{4 \times 10^{7}}$

(b) $\dfrac{(3.8 \times 10^{21}) \times (6.1 \times 10^{32})}{4.6 \times 10^{19}}$

(c) $\dfrac{(2.7 \times 10^{31}) \times (8.6 \times 10^{-14})}{5.6 \times 10^{-12}}$

(d) $\dfrac{(5.6 \times 10^{37}) \times (3.1 \times 10^{8})}{6.2 \times 10^{-12}}$

(e) $\dfrac{(4.3 \times 10^{9}) \times (2.6 \times 10^{24})}{(6.6 \times 10^{5})^2}$

(f) $\dfrac{(3.7 \times 10^{-9}) \times (2.6 \times 10^{-18})}{(5.3 \times 10^{17}) \times (1.8 \times 10^{-4})}$

**8** **Do not use a calculator**. Work out the following, leaving each answer in standard form.

(a) $(4 \times 10^{3}) \times (2 \times 10^{5})$      (b) $(3.5 \times 10^{7}) \times (2 \times 10^{9})$

(c) $(2 \times 10^{-8}) \times (3 \times 10^{20})$      (d) $(3 \times 10^{9}) \times (1.8 \times 10^{12})$

(e) $(3 \times 10^{4})^2$      (f) $(8 \times 10^{6}) \times (2 \times 10^{5})$

(g) $(9 \times 10^{7}) \times (4 \times 10^{6})$      (h) $(5 \times 10^{14}) \times (3 \times 10^{-4})$

(i) $(2 \times 10^{7})^3$

Now *check* your answers *with a calculator*.

**9** **Do not use a calculator**. Work out the following, leaving each answer in standard form.

(a) $(8 \times 10^{14}) \div (2 \times 10^6)$

(b) $(3 \times 10^{26}) \div (2 \times 10^{13})$

(c) $(9 \times 10^{17}) \div (3 \times 10^4)$

(d) $\dfrac{6 \times 10^{21}}{2 \times 10^8}$

(e) $\dfrac{8.1 \times 10^{42}}{3 \times 10^{17}}$

(f) $\dfrac{2 \times 10^{27}}{4 \times 10^9}$

Now *check* your answers *with a calculator*.

**10** **Do not use a calculator**. Work out the following by changing the numbers into ordinary numbers first. Write your *final answer* in *standard form*.

(a) $(6 \times 10^3) + (3 \times 10^4)$

(b) $(5 \times 10^3) - (4 \times 10^2)$

(c) $(2 \times 10^5) - (6 \times 10^4)$

(d) $(3.5 \times 10^3) - (2.1 \times 10^2)$

(e) $(6.7 \times 10^4) + (3.1 \times 10^5)$

(f) $(8.3 \times 10^6) + (1.6 \times 10^4)$

Now *check* your answers *with a calculator*.

## WATCH YOUR MONEY! – Buying a house

Although house prices may seem very expensive at the moment, you may one day in the future wish to buy a house.

### Mortgages

Most people need to take out a mortgage which they usually pay back over 25 years. Interest has to be paid on the mortgage so it is important to shop around for the best deal.

### Repayment mortgage

An amount is paid each month to pay the interest and some of the borrowed money. The monthly amount is worked out so that all the money is paid back after 25 years.

### Interest – only mortgage

This costs less than a repayment mortgage because only the interest is paid back each month. This means that after 25 years you will still owe the same amount of money as you borrowed at the start.

You would have to save money to pay back the mortgage at the end or have another plan. If not, you would have to sell your home to pay back the mortgage at the end.

## Deposit

If you save some money towards your new home before you buy it, your mortgage payments will be smaller. Often if you have at least a 5% deposit you will get a better deal on the mortgage interest rate.

## Hidden costs

### Stamp Duty

Money paid to the government when a property is bought.

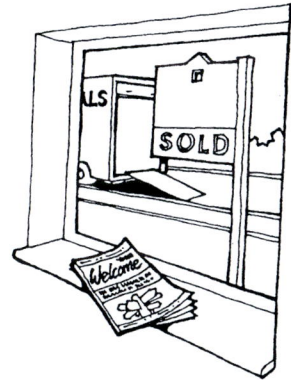

If you buy a flat for £90000, you have to pay stamp duty of 1% of £90000 to the government. That is £900.

| At the time of writing, | stamp duty |
|---|---|
| property worth up to £60000 | – no stamp duty |
| £60001 to £250000 | – 1% of the cost of the property |
| £250001 to £500000 | – 3% of the cost of the property |
| more than £500000 | – 4% of the cost of the property |

## Solicitor

You have to pay a solicitor to make sure there are no legal problems with your new property.

## Surveyor

You need a surveyor to check that your new property is safe and will not cost you expensive repairs in the future.

### WYM18

1   Dan wants to buy a house for £140,000. He earns £35,000 each year. A building society will give him a mortgage of 3.5 times his annual (yearly) salary.

(a) How much mortgage can Dan get?

(b) How much more money does he need to buy the house?

(c) Stamp duty is 1% of £140,000. The solicitor and surveyor bills amount to £2000. How much money will he really need to have saved to buy this house if he takes the full mortgage?

**2** Jim and Hannah have saved £40,000. They earn £30,000 between them each year. A bank will give them a mortgage of 4 times their joint annual salary.

(a) How much mortgage can they get?

(b) They want to buy a house for £155,000. Stamp duty is 1%. The solicitor and surveyor bills amount to £2800. Can they afford this house?
How much money will be left over if they take out the full mortgage?

**3** Donna sells her flat and makes £73,000 profit. She earns £27000 each year. A bank will give her a mortgage of 3.5 times her annual salary.

(a) What is the most money she will have available to buy a new property?

(b) If she bought a house for this amount of money, how much stamp duty would be payable at 1%?

**4** 4 friends want to buy a house together. They can jointly raise a mortgage of £240,000 and have a total deposit of £41,000.

They buy a house costing £268,000. Stamp duty is 3%. The solicitor and surveyor bills amount to £3420.

How much money will they have left over if they take out the full mortgage?

**5** Laura earns £26,000 each year and Bruce earns £19,000. They can both get a mortgage of 3.5 times their salary.

(a) How much mortgage can Laura get?

(b) How much mortgage can Bruce get?

(c) They have a joint deposit of £33,000. They buy a property costing £182,000. Stamp duty is 1%. The solicitor and surveyor bills amount to £2950. What is the *lowest* joint mortgage they would need to take out?

**6** Peter and Sonia can *rent* a flat for £560 each month. They could *buy* a similar flat and the monthly mortgage payments would be £560. *Discuss with your teacher* the advantages and disadvantages of buying the flat compared to renting the flat.

**1.** Changing the subject of a formula

Make $x$ the subject of each formula given below:

(a) $y = x + 3$       (b) $y = 4x$       (c) $y = x - 9$       (d) $y = 2x + 1$

(e) $y = 5x - 2$      (f) $y = ax - b$      (g) $a(x + b) = y$      (h) $\dfrac{x}{a} - b = y$

**2.** Dealing with inequalities

Write down the inequalities shown below:

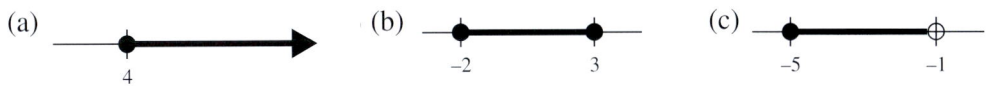

(a)

4

(b)

-2      3

(c)

-5      -1

Draw a number line to show the following inequalities:

(d) $x < -2$       (e) $4 < x < 7$       (f) $-6 \leq x < 1$

Solve the inequalities below:

(g) $x + 3 \geq 7$       (h) $x - 4 > 8$       (i) $5x \leq 35$

(j) $\dfrac{x}{9} \geq 6$       (k) $3x + 5 < 29$       (l) $2(x - 3) > 14$

(m) Write down all the integer values (whole numbers) of $x$ which satisfy the inequality

$$-4 \leq x < 2$$

**3.** Using the laws of indices

Work out and write each answer as a number in index form.

(a) $5^3 \times 5^4$       (b) $6^7 \div 6^5$       (c) $8^9 \div 8^4$

(d) $\dfrac{3^7 \times 3^4}{3^6}$       (e) $4^0$       (f) $(3^2)^3$

(g) $\dfrac{4^2 \times 4^6}{(4^3)^2}$       (h) $\dfrac{(2^4)^3 \times 2^3}{2^9}$       (i) $\dfrac{5^7 \times 5^0}{(5^2)^3}$

Simplify the expressions below.

(j) $a^8 \div a^2$       (k) $(x^4)^5$       (l) $y^6 \times y^3 \times y^4$

(m) $m^3 \times m$       (n) $\dfrac{x^4 \times x^5}{x^7}$       (o) $\dfrac{x^3 \times (x^2)^4}{(x^3)^3}$

### 4. Writing numbers in standard form

Write the numbers below in standard form.

(a) 70000      (b) 3800      (c) 513.4      (d) 0.05

(e) 0.0081      (f) 9700000      (g) 0.75      (h) 5168.3

Write down each number below as an ordinary number.

(i) $6 \times 10^5$      (j) $4 \times 10^{-3}$      (k) $3.6 \times 10^{-2}$      (l) $2.94 \times 10^7$

### 5. Using numbers written in standard form

**Do not use a calculator**. Work out the following, leaving each answer in standard form.

(a) $(2 \times 10^{17}) \times (4.5 \times 10^8)$      (b) $(1.8 \times 10^7) \times (3 \times 10^{12})$

(c) $(3.7 \times 10^{19}) \times (2 \times 10^{-4})$      (d) $(8 \times 10^{21}) \div (4 \times 10^6)$

(e) $(3.9 \times 10^8) \div (3 \times 10^{-8})$      (f) $(7 \times 10^8) \times (6 \times 10^9)$

**Use a calculator.** Work out the following, leaving each answer in standard form correct to 3 significant figures where appropriate.

(g) $(8.6 \times 10^9) \times (2.4 \times 10^{23})$      (h) $(2.9 \times 10^{-7}) \times (4.6 \times 10^{-16})$

(i) $(7.8 \times 10^6) \div (2.9 \times 10^{31})$      (j) $(5.3 \times 10^{14}) - (3.4 \times 10^{13})$

(k) $\dfrac{(5.1 \times 10^{19}) \times (6.2 \times 10^{13})}{(1.8 \times 10^{11})^2}$      (l) $\dfrac{(7.1 \times 10^{23}) + (4.9 \times 10^{22})}{(3.3 \times 10^9) - (8.4 \times 10^8)}$

(m) In a country, 23 million adults work. The total money they earn in one year is £$5.175 \times 10^{11}$. How much does one person earn on average?

## Mixed examination questions

**1**   Evaluate $7^6 \div 7^4$                                        (CCEA)

**2**   Write each of these expressions as a single power of $y$.

(i) $y^2 \times y^3$      (ii) $\dfrac{y^8}{y^2}$      (iii) $(y^4)^2$      (OCR)

**3**   Make $t$ the subject of the formula

$v = u + 8t$

**4** Rearrange the following formula to make L the subject.

$P = 2L + 2W$ (OCR)

**5** Multiply out $n^2 (n - n^4)$

**6** Simplify $\dfrac{5^4 \times 5^6}{5^3}$ Give your answer as a single power of 5 (OCR)

**7** Solve the inequality $3 + 4x > 9$ (AQA)

**8** (i) Write down the integer values of $n$ for which $1 < 3n \leq 12$

(ii) Solve the inequality $5x - 2 \geq 1$ (OCR)

**9** Simplify $2a^5 \times 3a^2$ (AQA)

**10** 420 000 carrot seeds weigh 1 gram.

Each carrot seed weighs the same.

(a) Write the number 420 000 in standard form.

(b) Calculate the weight, in grams, of one carrot seed.
Give your answer in standard form, correct to 2 significant
figures. (EDEXCEL)

**11** List the values of $x$, where $x$ is an integer, such that $-1 < x - 2 \leq 1$ (AQA)

**12** Rearrange the formula $y = r + 3x$ to make $x$ the subject. (EDEXCEL)

**13** On a Saturday 1.5 million copies of a newspaper are printed.

(a) Write 1.5 million in standard form.

(b) Each copy of the newspaper has 80 pages.

Calculate the total number of pages printed on a Saturday.

Give your answer in standard form.

(c) The total weight of the newspapers is $3 \times 10^5$ kg.

Calculate the weight of one newspaper.

Give your answer in grams. (AQA)

# 19

# SHAPE 5

**In this unit you will learn how to**:

– measure lengths and angles

– construct triangles

– construct perpendicular bisectors, angle bisectors and angles without using a protractor

– make scale drawings

– use map scales

– draw loci

– ⟨WATCH YOUR MONEY!⟩ – council tax

## Measuring lengths and angles

### M19.1

1  Read the measurements shown on the ruler.

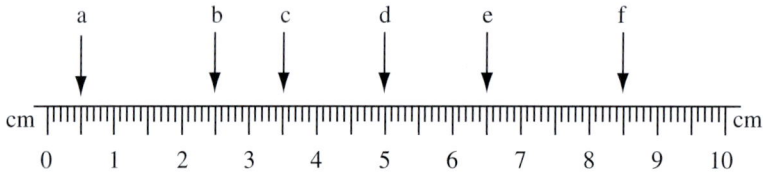

Measure these lines to the nearest tenth of centimetre.

2 _____

3 _____   4 _____

5 _____   6 _____

7

8

**9** Measure the perimeter of each shape below to the nearest tenth of a centimetre.

(a)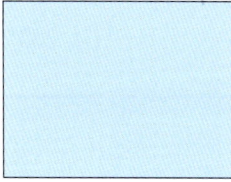

(b)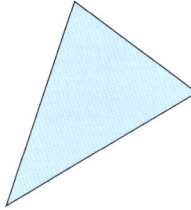

(c)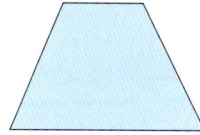

Using a protractor, measure the following angles.

**1**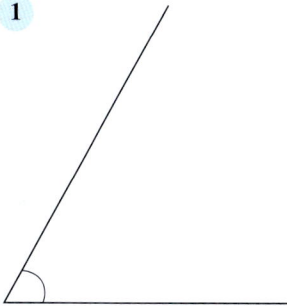

**2**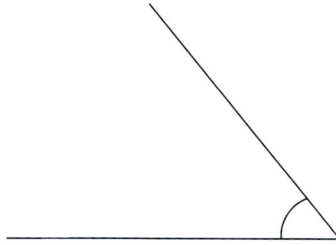

**3**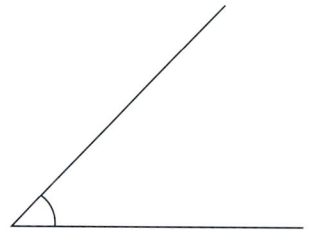

**4**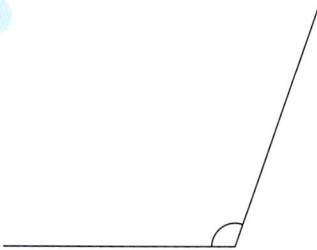

**5**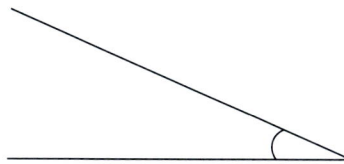

**6**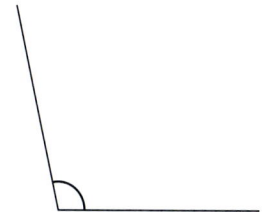

**7**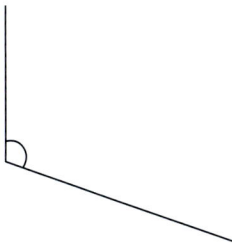

**8**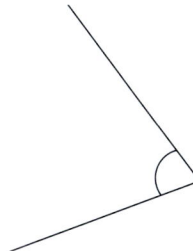

**9**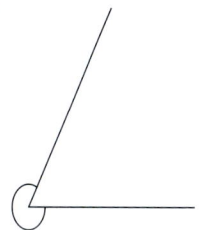

**10** Use a protractor to draw the following angles. Label each angle acute, obtuse or reflex.

| | | | |
|---|---|---|---|
| (a) 70° | (b) 25° | (c) 54° | (d) 31° |
| (e) 165° | (f) 108° | (g) 172° | (h) 15° |
| (i) 310° | (j) 230° | (k) 126° | (l) 283° |

*Can you still?*

*Can you still?*

**19A** Use fractions (see Unit 5)

1. Which fraction is larger – $\frac{2}{5}$ or $\frac{2}{3}$?

2. How many quarters make $5\frac{3}{4}$?

3. Work out (a) $\frac{5}{9} - \frac{1}{9}$      (b) $\frac{5}{8} + \frac{2}{9}$

4. 
> Buy 36 eggs then get $\frac{1}{3}$ extra FREE

If you buy 36 eggs, how many eggs will you get in total?

5. Work out $\frac{2}{5}$ of £40.

6. Marie has £40. She spends $\frac{3}{5}$ of her money on Saturday. How much money does she have left?

7. Work out (a) $\frac{3}{7} \times \frac{2}{9}$      (b) $2\frac{2}{3} \times 1\frac{1}{5}$

8. What fraction of these animals are rabbits?

9. $4\frac{1}{2}$ bars of chocolate are shared equally between 5 children. What fraction of a bar of chocolate does each child get?

10. Work out (a) $\frac{2}{9} \div \frac{5}{6}$      (b) $3\frac{3}{4} \div \frac{5}{12}$

**M19.2**

This Exercise deals with triangles where 2 sides and an angle are known or 2 angles and a side are known.

Use a ruler and protractor to draw:

**1**

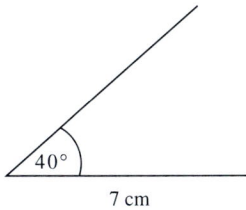

40°
7 cm

**2**

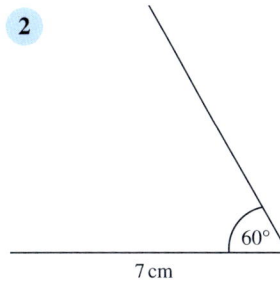

60°
7 cm

Now draw both of these on the same diagram like below:

**3**

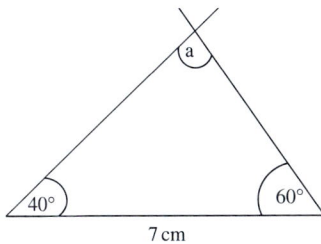

a

40°          60°
7 cm

Measure angle *a*. It should be 80°.

**4** Use a ruler and protractor to draw:

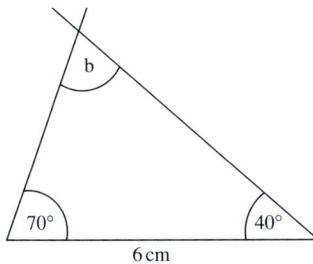

b

70°          40°
6 cm

Measure and write down angle *b*.

**5** Draw accurately:

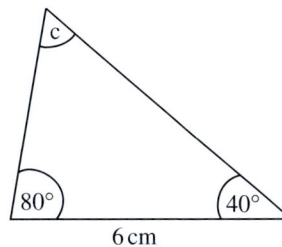

c

80°          40°
6 cm

Measure and write down angle *c*.

**6** Use a ruler and protractor to draw:

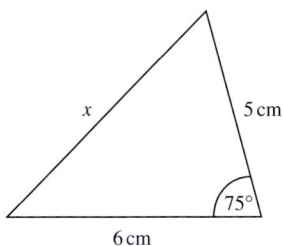

*x*          5 cm

75°

6 cm

Measure the length of the side marked *x*.

In questions **7** to **12**, construct the triangles and measure the lengths of the sides marked $x$.

**7**

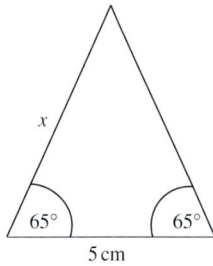

$x$

$65°$   $65°$

5 cm

**8**

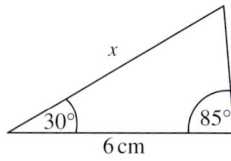

$x$

$30°$   $85°$

6 cm

**9**

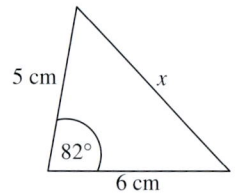

5 cm   $x$

$82°$

6 cm

**10**

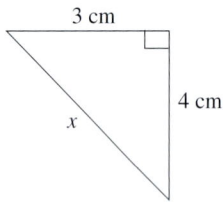

3 cm

4 cm

$x$

**11**

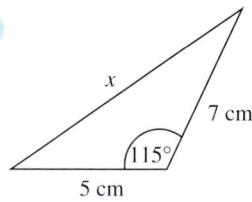

$x$

7 cm

$115°$

5 cm

**12**

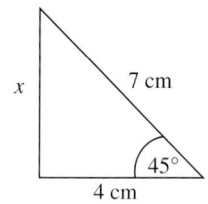

$x$   7 cm

$45°$

4 cm

---

If we know all 3 sides, a triangle can be drawn with a ruler and a pair of compasses only.

Draw accurately

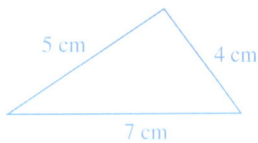

5 cm   4 cm

7 cm

(a) Draw one side with a ruler

(b) Set your pair of compasses to 5 cm. Put the point of the pair of compasses on one end of the line and draw an arc of radius 5 cm.

(c) Set your pair of compasses to 4 cm. Put the point of the pair of compasses on the other end of the line and draw an arc of radius 4 cm.

Join the point where the 2 arcs cross to each end of the 7 cm line to make a *perfect* triangle.

7 cm

arc radius 5 cm

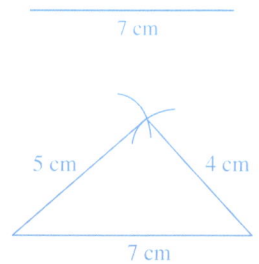

7 cm

5 cm   4 cm

7 cm

**E19.2**

In questions **1** to **6**, use a ruler and compasses only to draw each triangle. Use a protractor to measure each angle $x$.

**1**

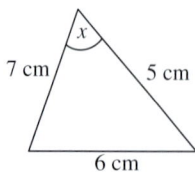

$x$

7 cm   5 cm

6 cm

**2**

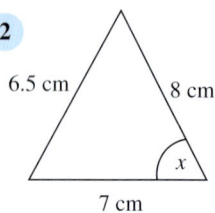

6.5 cm   8 cm

$x$

7 cm

**3**

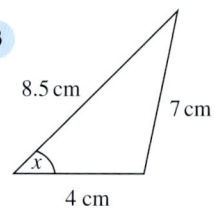

8.5 cm   7 cm

$x$

4 cm

**4**

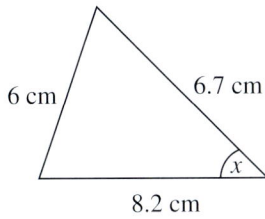

**5**

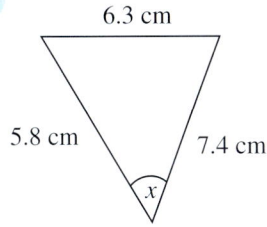

**6**

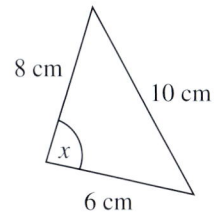

**7** Construct an equilateral triangle with each side equal to 6 cm. Measure the angles to check that each one is 60°.

**8** Draw a right-angled triangle with shorter sides equal to 4.5 cm and 6 cm. Measure the longest side of the triangle.

**9**

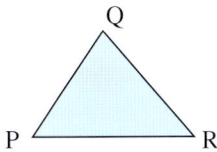

Draw a triangle PQR, where PR = 7.5 cm, QP̂R = 55° and PQ = 5 cm.

Measure the length of QR.

**10** Draw a triangle XYZ, where XY = 4.8 cm, YZ = 6.1 cm and XZ = 7 cm. Measure XŶZ, YẐX and ZX̂Y.

Draw accurately the diagrams in questions **11** to **14** .

**11**

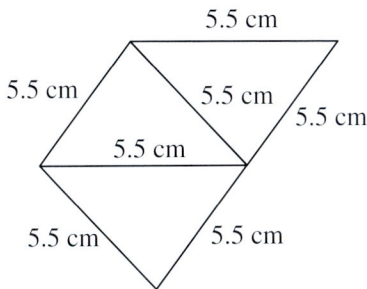

**12**

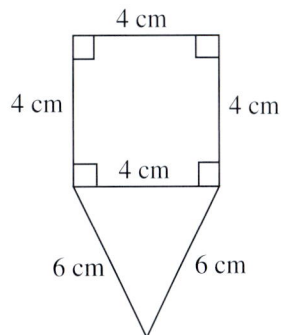

**13**

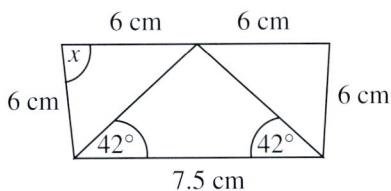

Measure *x*.

**14**

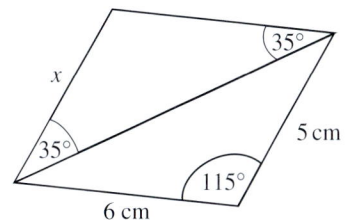

Measure *x*.

497

### Perpendicular bisector

Draw a line AB 8 cm long.

Set the pair of compasses to more than 4 cm (half the line AB). Put the compass point on A and draw an arc as shown.

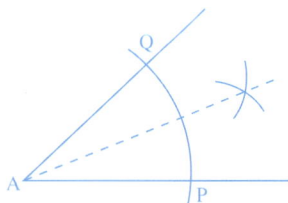

Put the compass point on B (**Do not let the compasses slip**). Draw another arc as shown.

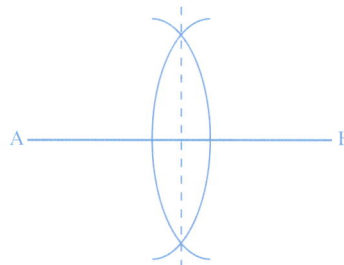

This broken line cuts line AB in half (*bisects*) and is at right angles to line AB (*perpendicular*).

The broken line is called the *perpendicular* bisector of line AB.

### Bisector of an angle

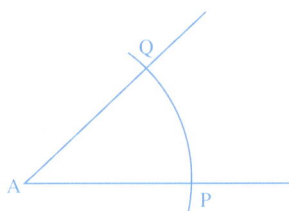

Put the compass point on A and draw an arc as shown.

Put the compass point on P and draw an arc as shown.

Put the compass point on Q and draw an arc as shown.

This broken line cuts the angle in half (*bisects*).

This broken line is called the *angle bisector*.

### M19.3

1. Draw a horizontal line AB of length 9 cm. Construct the perpendicular bisector of AB. Check that each half of the line measures 4.5 cm exactly.

2. Draw a horizontal line CD of length 6 cm. Construct the perpendicular bisector of CD. Check that each half of the line measures 3 cm exactly.

3. Draw a *vertical* line EF of length 10 cm. Construct the perpendicular bisector of EF.

4. Draw an angle of 80°. Construct the bisector of the angle. Use a protractor to check that each half of the angle now measures 40°.

**5** Draw an angle of 110°. Construct the bisector of the angle.

**6** (a) Use a pencil, ruler and a pair of compasses *only* to *construct* the triangle ABC shown opposite.

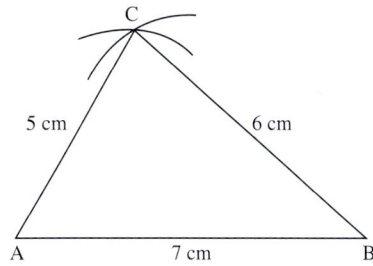

(b) Construct the perpendicular bisector of line AB.

(c) Construct the perpendicular bisector of line BC.

(d) Construct the perpendicular bisector of line AC. The 3 perpendicular bisectors should cross at the same point.

**7** Draw any triangle XYZ and construct:

(a) the perpendicular bisector of XY.

(b) the perpendicular bisector of XZ.

Mark the point of intersection M.

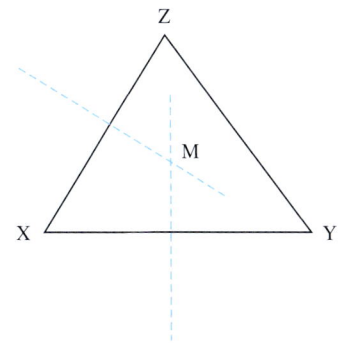

(c) Take a pair of compasses and, with centre at M and radius MX, draw a circle through the points X, Y and Z. This is the *circumcircle of triangle XYZ*.

(d) Repeat this construction for another triangle with different sides.

**8** Draw any triangle ABC and then construct the bisectors of angles A, B and C. If done accurately the three bisectors should all pass through one point.

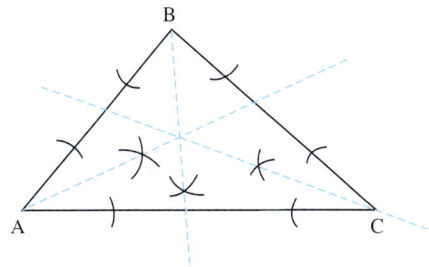

**9** Draw any triangle XYZ and construct the bisectors of angles X and Y to meet at point M.

With centre at M draw a circle which just touches the sides of the triangle. This is the *inscribed circle of the triangle*.

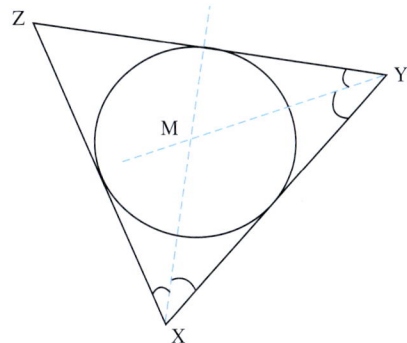

Repeat the construction for a different triangle.

**Constructing a 60° angle**

Draw a line 6 cm long.

A ———————— 6 cm ———————— B

Set the pair of compasses to less than 6 cm. Put the compass point on A and draw an arc as shown.

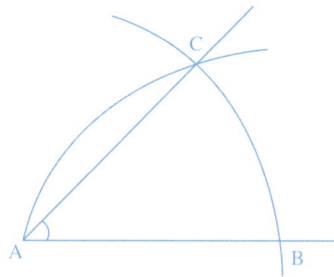

Put the compass point on B (**Do not let the compasses slip**). Draw another arc as shown.

Join C to the end of the line. The two lines make an angle of 60°. BÂC = 60°

**Constructing a 90° angle at a point on a line**

Draw any line and mark a point on that line.

Set the pair of compasses to around 3 cm. Put the compass point on A and draw 2 small arcs which cross the line on each side of A. (If necessary, make the line longer)

Put the compass point on B and set the compasses longer than BA. Draw an arc above the line.

Put the compass point on C (**Do not let the compasses slip**). Draw another arc as shown.

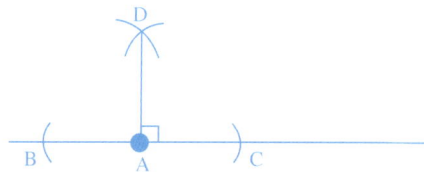

Join D and A with a straight line.

The two lines make an angle of 90°. CÂD = 90°

---

**E19.3**

**1** (a) Draw a line 9 cm long and mark the point A on the line as shown.

4 cm    A    5 cm

(b) Construct an angle of 90° at A.

**2** Construct an angle of 60°.

**3** (a) Draw a line 7 cm long and mark the point B on the line as shown.

4 cm      B      3 cm

(b) Construct and an angle of 45° at B.

**4** Construct an angle of 30°.

**5** Construct an equilateral triangle with each side equal to 5 cm.

**6** Construct these triangles (only use a protractor to *check* at the end).

(a)

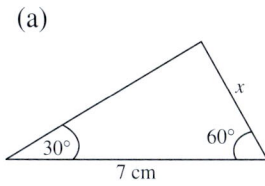

Measure *x*.

(b)

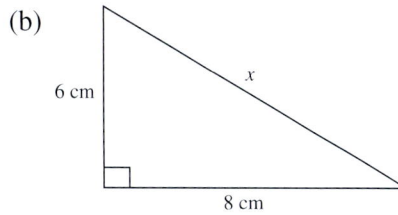

Measure *x*.

**7** Construct each shape below and measure *x*.

(a)

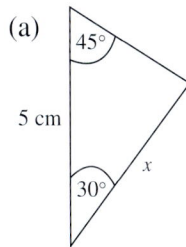

(b)

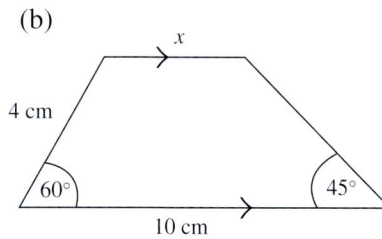

(c)

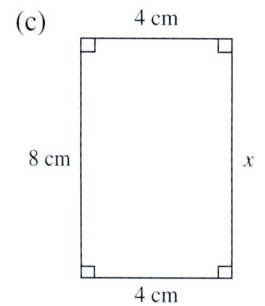

**8** (a) Draw any line and any point as shown opposite.

A •

_____

(b) Put the compass point on A and set the compasses so that an arc can be drawn as shown.

(c) Now draw the perpendicular bisector of the line BC.

The line AD is described as the *perpendicular from the point A to the line*.

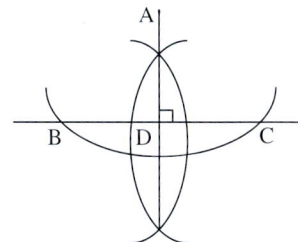

**9** Construct an angle of 15°.

**10** Construct a right-angled triangle ABC, where AB = 7 cm, $A\hat{B}C = 90°$ and $B\hat{A}C = 45°$. Measure the length of BC.

**11** Construct an angle of 22.5°.

**12** Draw any vertical line and any point as shown opposite.

*Construct* the perpendicular from the point to the line.

Can you still?

Can you still?

**(19B)** **Round off to decimal places and significant figures (see Unit 9)**

**1.** Which numbers below round to 6.8 (to 1 decimal place)?

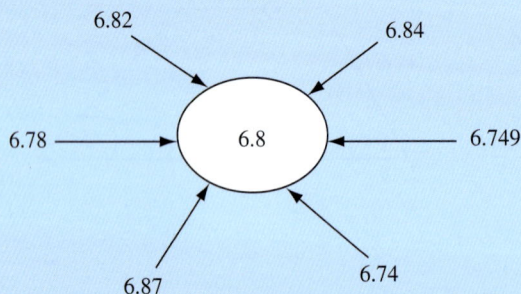

**2.** Round these numbers to 2 decimal places.

(a) 4.138        (b) 8.216        (c) 9.462

**3.** Round these numbers to 3 significant figures.

(a) 4.176        (b) 2381        (c) 51635

**4.** 0.06028 = 0.0603 to 3 significant figures. Is this true or false?

**5.** Round off 52.516 to 2 significant figures.

**6.** Use a calculator to work out each question below giving each answer to 3 significant figures.

(a) $5.86 \times 2.7$        (b) $9.86^2$        (c) $17 \div 0.18$

(d) $281 - 2.1983$        (e) $\sqrt{(28.5 - 9.1)}$        (f) $\dfrac{5.12 \times 3.9}{6.75}$

## M19.4

Draw an accurate scale drawing of each shape below using the scale shown.

**1**

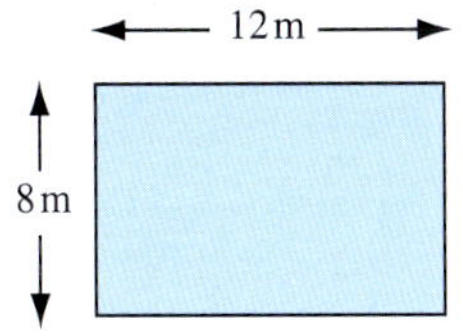
12m
8m

Scale: 1 cm for every 4 m

**2**

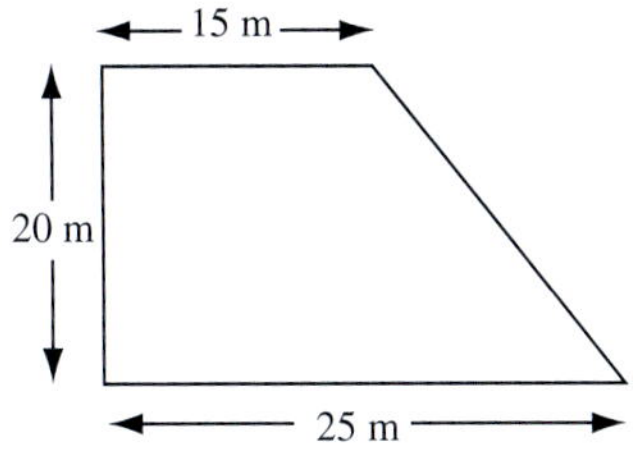
15 m
20 m
25 m

Scale: 1 cm for every 5 m.

**3**

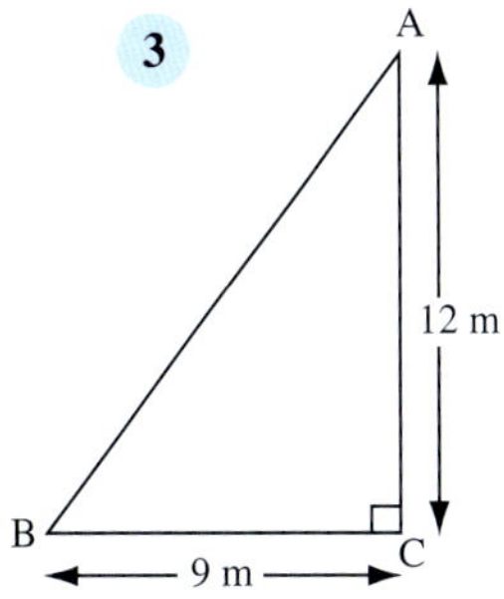
A
12 m
B
C
9 m

Scale: 1 cm for every 3 m. Measure (in cm) then write down the actual length of AB (in m).

**4**

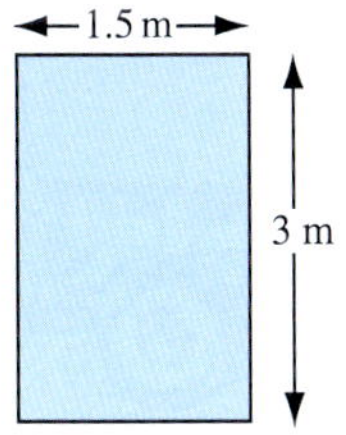
1.5 m
3 m

Scale: 2 cm for every 1 m.

**5**

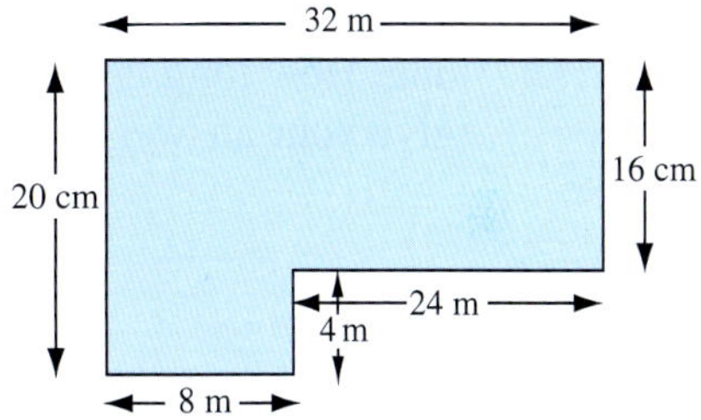
32 m
20 cm
16 cm
24 m
4 m
8 m

Scale: 1 cm for every 8 m.

**6**

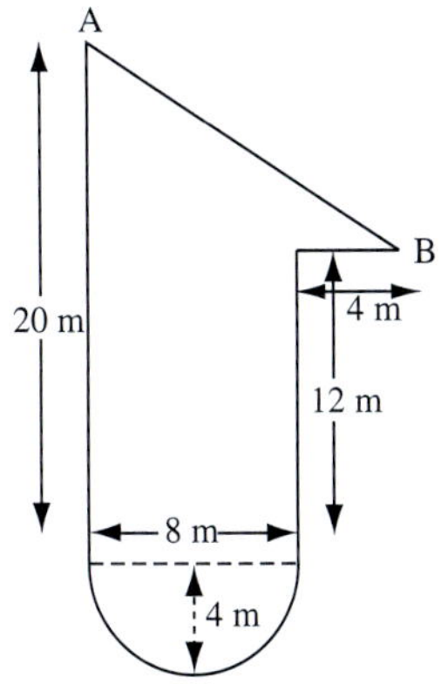
A
B
4 m
20 m
12 m
8 m
4 m

Scale: 1 cm for every 4 m. Measure in cm the length of AB.

On a map of scale 1:3000 000, Leeds and Manchester are 2 cm apart. What is the actual distance between the cities?

1 cm on map     = 3000 000 cm for real

2 cm on map     = 2 × 3000 000 cm for real

             = 6000 000 cm     (÷ 100 to change cm into m)

             = 60000 m     (÷ 1000 to change m into km)

             = 60 km

The actual distance between Leeds and Manchester is 60 km.

### E19.4

You may use a calculator.

1  A model of a dustcart is made using a scale of 1:50. The model is 16 cm long. How long is the real dustcart? (give your answer in metres)

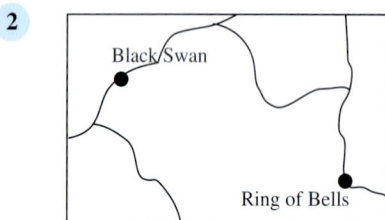

2

Black Swan

Ring of Bells

Scale is 1:50000

Measure the shortest distance between the Black Swan and the Ring of Bells (give your answer in km).

3  Two towns are 3 cm apart on a map whose scale is 1:5000 000. Find the actual distance (in km) between the two towns.

**4** A lake is 5 cm long on a map whose scale is 1:50000. Find the actual length (in km) of the lake.

**5** Copy and complete the table below.

| Map length | Scale | Real length |
|---|---|---|
| 6 cm | 1:80 | m |
| 4 cm | 1:5000 | m |
| 9 cm | 1:200 000 | km |
| cm | 1:2000 | 160 m |
| cm | 1:3000 000 | 120 km |
| cm | 1:1000 000 | 35 km |

**6** The length of part of a railway track is 18 km. How long will it be on a map of scale 1:200 000?

**7**

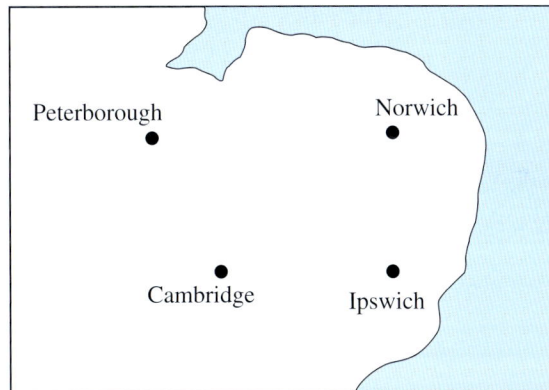

Scale is 1:3000000

Measure then write down the actual distances (in km) between:

(a) Norwich and Ipswich

(b) Peterborough and Norwich

(c) Cambridge and Ipswich

**8** The distance between two cities is 110 km. How far apart will they be on a map of scale 1:2000 000?

**9** The length of a house is 8.4 m. A plan of the house is drawn using a scale of 1:70. How long will the house be on the plan?

Can you still?

Can you still?

**19C**   **Using ratios (see Unit 6)**

1.  Write down the ratio of black squares to white squares.

2. In Hatton High School there are 120 girls and 150 boys in year 11. Find the ratio of girls to boys, giving your answer in its *simplest form*.

3. Divide £240 in the ratio 5:7.

4. A shandy is made by mixing beer and lemonade in the ratio 2:7. If 100 ml of beer is used, how much shandy is made in total?

5. A small firm makes £40000 profit which is to be shared between 3 people (Tom, Gus and Mel) in the ratio 8:11:6. How much money does Mel get?

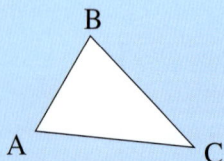

6.  The sides AB and BC in a triangle are in the ratio 2:3. If AB = 12 cm, how long is BC?

7. 8 magazines cost £24. How much do 7 magazines cost?

8. 14 packets of crisps cost £3.78. How much will 9 packets of crisps cost?

9. 4 new car tyres cost £168. How much will 3 new car tyres cost?

## Locus

Sarah walks so that she is always 2 km from a point A.

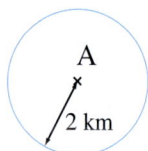

She ends up walking in a circle. She walks in a circle because she is following the rule that she is always 2 km from point A. The circle is called a '*locus*'.

A *locus* is the *set of points* which fit a given rule.

The plural of locus is '*loci*'.

For Sarah walking above, the circle is the *locus* of points 2 km from point A.

(a) Draw the locus of all points which are 2 cm from the line AB.

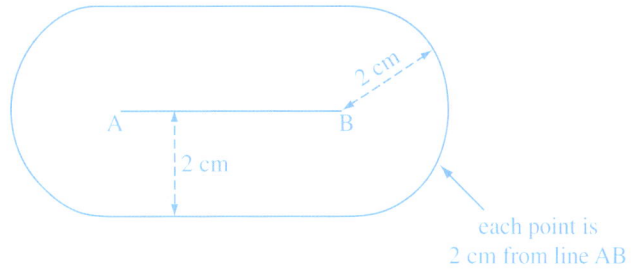

2 cm

A — B

2 cm

each point is 2 cm from line AB

(b) A garden has a tree at the corner B. A lawn is made so that it is greater than or equal to 1 m from the edge of the garden and *at least* 2 m from the tree. Draw the lawn in the garden.

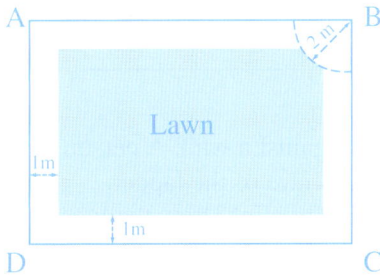

12 m

A — B

8 m

D — C

A — B

2 m

Lawn

1m

1m

D — C

The lawn is a 'locus' even though the word 'locus' was *not* used in the question.

## M19.5

You will need a ruler and a pair of compasses.

**1** Draw the locus of all points which are 4 cm from a point A.

**2** Draw the locus of all points which are 3 cm from the line AB.

A —— 6 cm —— B

**3** A goat is tied by a 5 m rope to a peg in the middle of a large field. Using a scale of 1 cm for 1 m, shade the area that the goat can graze in.

**4** Draw the locus of all points which are less than or equal to 1.5 cm from the line PQ.

P —— 5 cm —— Q

**5** A wild headteacher is placed in a cage. The pupils are not allowed to be within one metre of the cage. Using a scale of 1 cm for 1 m, sketch the cage and show the locus of points where the pupils are *not* allowed.

3 m

4 m

**6**

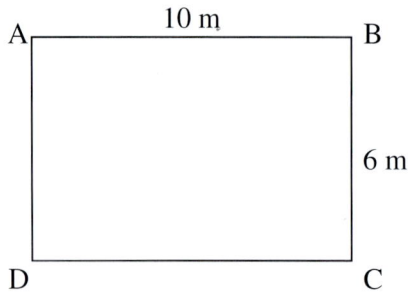

A garden has a tree at the corners C and D. The whole garden is made into a lawn except for anywhere less than or equal to 4 m from any tree. Using a scale of 1 cm for 2 m, draw the garden and shade in the lawn.

**7** Another garden has a tree at the corner A. A lawn is made so that it is greater than or equal to 2 m from the edge of the garden and *at least* 5 m from the tree.

Using a scale of 1 cm for 2 m, draw the garden and shade in the lawn.

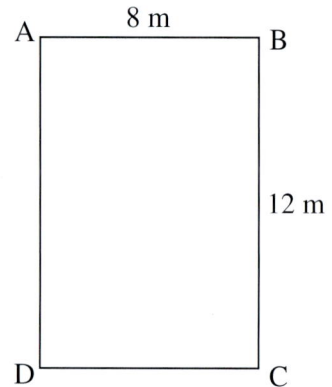

**8**

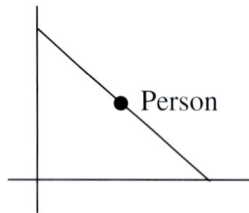

A ladder leans against a wall. A person is standing at the centre of the ladder. The ladder starts to slip! Draw the locus of the person as the ladder falls (make sure in your drawing, the ladder stays the same length!).

**9**

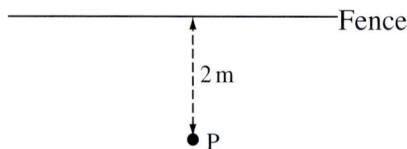

A goat is tied by a 3 m rope to a peg P as shown. Using a scale of 1 cm for 1 m, copy the diagram then shade the area that the goat can graze in.

**10**

The goat is moved so that it is tied by a 3 m rope to a peg P as shown. Using a scale of 1 cm for 1 m, copy the diagram then shade the area that the goat can graze in.

You will need a ruler and a pair of compasses.

**1** Draw the locus of points which are the same distance from P and Q below.

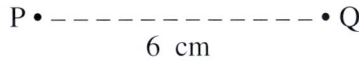

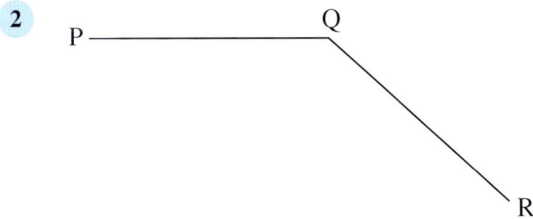

P •− − − − − − − − − − − − − •Q

6 cm

**2**

P —————— Q
          \
           \
            \
             \ R

Draw the locus of points which are the same distance from the lines PQ and QR.

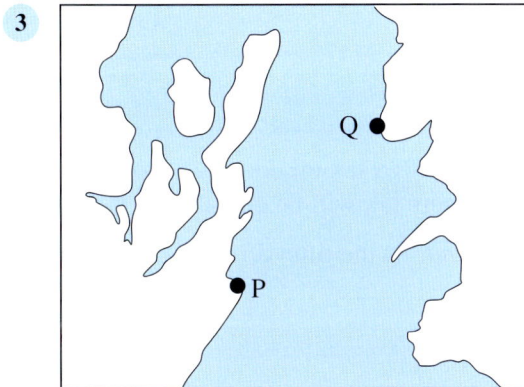

**3**

A ship sails so that it is *equidistant* from ports P and Q. Using a scale of 1 cm for 1 km, draw a rough copy of this diagram with P and Q 4 km apart.

Construct the path taken by the ship.

**4** Draw this square.

Show the locus of points inside the square which are nearer to A than to C *and* are more than 3 cm from B.

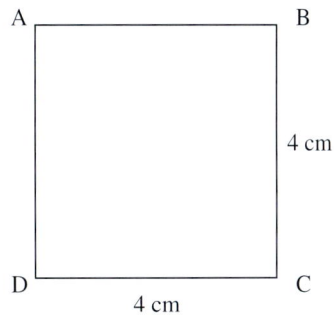

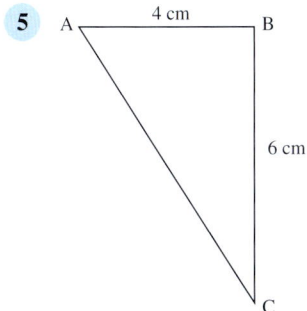

A ——————— B
|         |
|         | 4 cm
|         |
D ——————— C
    4 cm

**5**

A — 4 cm — B
|        |
|        | 6 cm
|        |
         C

Draw one copy of triangle ABC and show on it:

(a) the locus of points equidistant from A and B

(b) the locus of points equidistant from lines AB and AC

(c) the locus of points nearer to AC than to AB

509

**6** A transmitter at Redford has a range of 80 km and another transmitter at Hatton has a range of 60 km. The 2 transmitters are 120 km apart.

Using a scale of 1 cm for 20 km, draw the 2 transmitters then shade the area where a signal can be received from both transmitters.

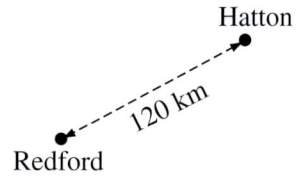

**7** A child's block is rolled along the floor by rotating about its corners.

Draw the locus of B.

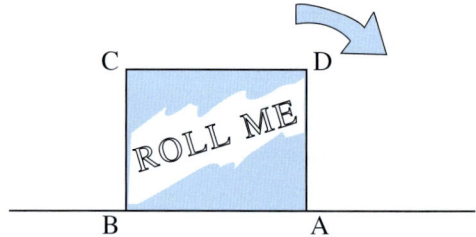

## WATCH YOUR MONEY! – Council tax

This is tax collected by local authorities. It is a tax on domestic property. In general, the bigger the property is, the more tax will be charged.

Each property is put into a *valuation band*. At the time of writing the bands are as listed below.

| Valuation band | Range of values |
|----------------|-----------------|
| A | up to £40000 |
| B | over £40000 and up to £52000 |
| C | over £52000 and up to £68000 |
| D | over £68000 and up to £88000 |
| E | over £88000 and up to £120000 |
| F | over £120000 and up to £160000 |
| G | over £160000 and up to £320000 |
| H | over £320000 |

The council tax is used to pay for local services such as rubbish collection, schools and the fire service.

Council tax is not paid on some properties, for example any property that only students live in or a property where all the people who live in it are aged under 18.

If only one person lives in a property they will get a 25% discount on the council tax bill.

Jack lives on his own in a flat worth £75000. This year's council tax rates in his area are shown in the table below:

| Band | A | B | C | D | E | F | G | H |
|---|---|---|---|---|---|---|---|---|
| Annual council tax (£) | 650 | 800 | 1000 | 1200 | 1350 | 1550 | 1900 | 2300 |

(a) How much council tax will Jack have to pay this year?

(b) If he spreads the council tax payment over 10 months, how much will he pay each month?

(a) Using the table at the start of this section, Jack's flat is in band D. The other table shows he must pay £1200 this year.

Jack lives on his own so gets a 25% discount.

25% of £1200 = £300

Jack pays £1200 – £300 = £900

(b) If the payment is spread over 10 months, each month Jack pays £900 ÷ 10 = £90.

## WYM19

For this exercise use the council tax rates shown in the table below.

| Band | A | B | C | D | E | F | G | H |
|---|---|---|---|---|---|---|---|---|
| Annual council tax (£) | 661 | 798 | 1109 | 1252 | 1420 | 1675 | 1910 | 2405 |

Use the table at the start of this section to find out which band each property belongs to in the following Questions.

1   Harry and Erica Smith live in a house worth £105000. How much council tax will they have to pay?

2   Simon and Shanice live in a house worth £132000.

(a) How much council tax will they have to pay?

(b) If the council tax payment is spread over 10 months, how much will the monthly payments be?

3   Molly lives on her own in a bedsit valued at £50000. How much council tax will Molly have to pay this year?

4   The Jackson family live in a house valued at £210 000. If they spread their council tax payment over 10 months, what will the monthly payments be?

5 Jenny, David and Matt are all students. They live in a house valued at £90000. How much council tax will they have to pay this year?

6 Mr. and Mrs. Pickford live in a flat valued at £102,000. They are allowed to pay their council tax in 4 equal (quarterly) payments. How much will each quarterly payment be?

7 Rhys lives on his own in a bungalow valued at £110 000. If he spreads his council tax payment over 10 months, what will his monthly payments be?

8 Find out what the council tax bill for a band D property in *your area* is this year. Do you think council tax is a fair way of collecting money for local services or not? Give reasons. Discuss with your teacher.

## TEST YOURSELF ON UNIT 19

**1.** Measuring lengths and angles

(a) Measure AB to the nearest tenth of a centimetre.

A ——————————————— B

(b) Measure the perimeter of this trapezium to the nearest tenth of a centimetre.

(c) Using a protractor, measure each angle stated below:

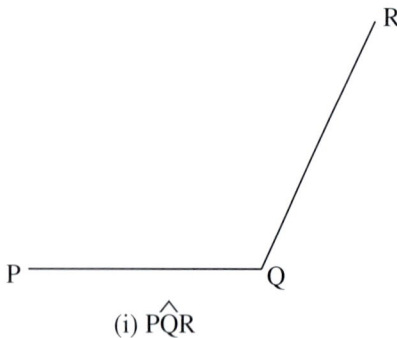

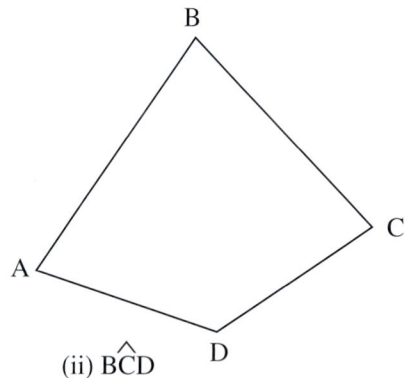

(i) $P\hat{Q}R$

(ii) $B\hat{C}D$

**2.** Constructing triangles

(a) Use a ruler and protractor to draw:

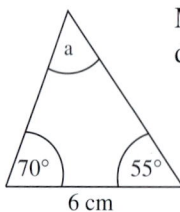

Measure and write down angle *a*.

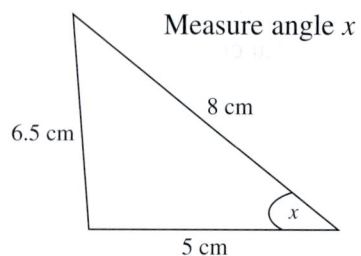

70° 55°

6 cm

(b) Use a ruler and compasses only to construct:

Measure angle *x*

8 cm

6.5 cm

5 cm

### 3. Constructing perpendicular bisectors, angle bisectors and angles

(a) Draw a *vertical* line PQ of length 8 cm.

Construct the perpendicular bisector of PQ.

(b) Draw an angle of 70°. Construct the bisector of the angle.

(c) Construct this triangle.

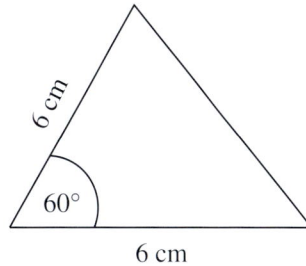

(d) Construct an angle of 30°.

### 4. Making scale drawings

Draw an accurate scale drawing of each shape below using the scale shown.

(a)

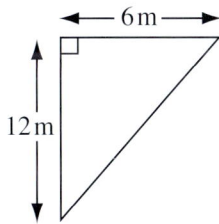

Scale: 1 cm for every 3 m

(b)

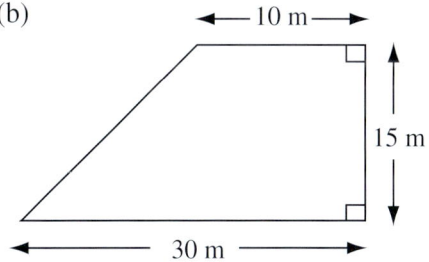

Scale: 1 cm for every 5 m

### 5. Using map scales

(a) A model of a building is made using a scale of 1:200. The model length of the building is 15 cm. How long is the real building (give your answer in metres)?

(b) Cara is making a scale drawing of her garden using a scale of 1:50. If her pond has a diameter of 3 m, what is the diameter of the pond on the scale drawing (give the answer in cm)?

(c) The distance between two villages is 7.5 km. How far apart will they be (in cm) on a map of scale 1:300 000?

## 6. Drawing loci

(a) Draw the locus of all points which are 3.5 cm from the line PQ.

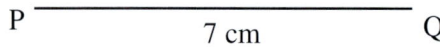

P ——————————————— Q
7 cm

(b) The diagram shows a rectangular room ABCD. Draw *three* diagrams using a scale at 1 cm for every 1 m. Use a separate diagram to show each locus below:

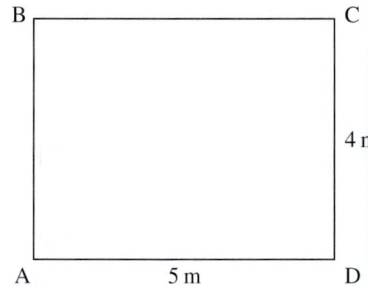

(i) Points in the room less than or equal to 3 m from B.

(ii) Points in the room which are an equal distance from both B and C. (*'equidistant'* from B and C).

(iii) Points in the room which are greater than or equal to 2 m from D.

## Mixed examination questions

**1**

55°     38°
12 cm

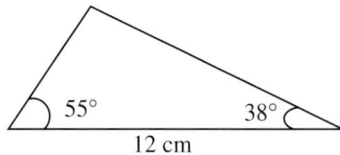

Use your ruler, compasses and protractor to make an accurate construction of this triangle. (WJEC)

**2** Copy the line AB. Draw the locus of all points which are 3 cm away from the line AB.

A

B

(EDEXCEL)

**3** Make an accurate drawing of a triangle with sides 5 cm, 7 cm and 8 cm long.

**4** The diagram represents a triangular garden *ABC*. The scale of the diagram is 1 cm represents 1 m. A tree is to be planted in the garden so that it is nearer to *AB* than to *AC*, within 5 m of point *A*.

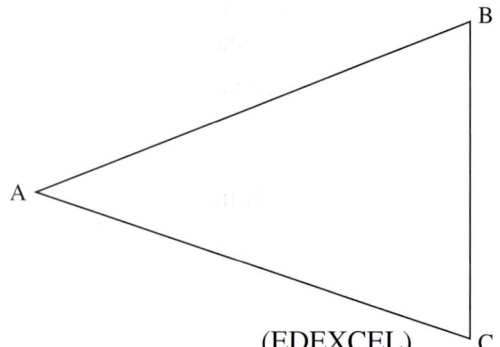

Copy the diagram and shade the region where the tree may be planted. (EDEXCEL)

**5**

O ——————— A

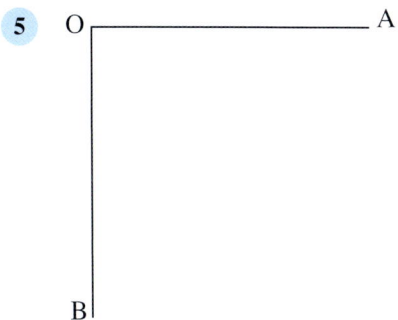

(a) Copy the diagram opposite. Draw the locus of points which are the same distance from the line OA and the line OB.

B

Some points are the same distance from the line OA and the line OB and are also 4 cm from the point B.

(b) Mark the positions of these points with crosses.     (EDEXCEL)

**6**  Copy the diagram below.

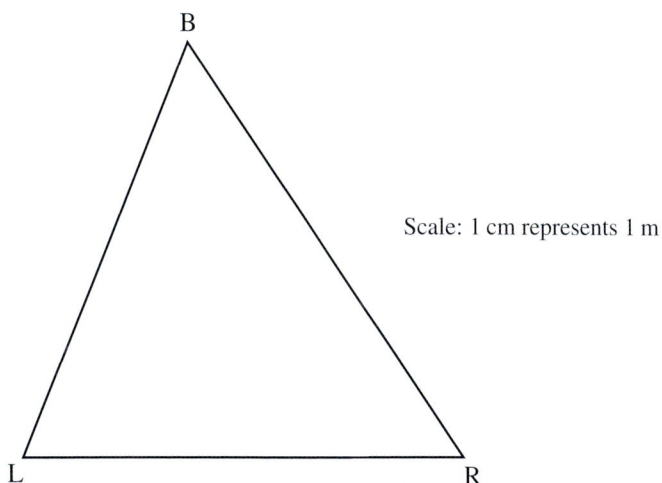

B

Scale: 1 cm represents 1 m

L                                    R

Triangle LRB is the plan of a garden drawn to a scale of 1 cm to 1 m.

A lime tree (*L*), a rowan tree (*R*) and a beech tree (*B*) are at the corners of the garden.

(a) Construct the perpendicular bisector of *LR*. Show your construction lines clearly.

(b) Diana wants to put a bird table in the garden.

The bird table must be nearer the rowan tree than the lime tree.

It must also be within 4 metres of the beech tree.

Shade the region on the plan where the bird table may be placed.     (OCR)

**In this unit you will learn how to:**

- draw nets

- draw 3-D objects

- draw and use plans and elevations

- use bearings

- use Pythagoras' theorem

- solve problems with shapes and lines using co-ordinates

- use 3 co-ordinates for a point in 3-D space

- WATCH YOUR MONEY! – old age pensions.

## Nets

### Key Facts

A shape which folds up to make a solid is called a *net*.

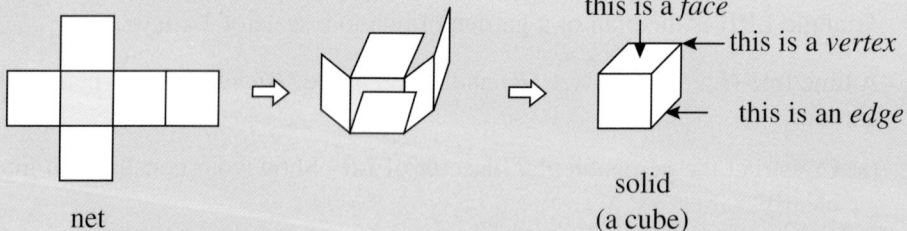

this is a *face*

this is a *vertex*

this is an *edge*

net

solid
(a cube)

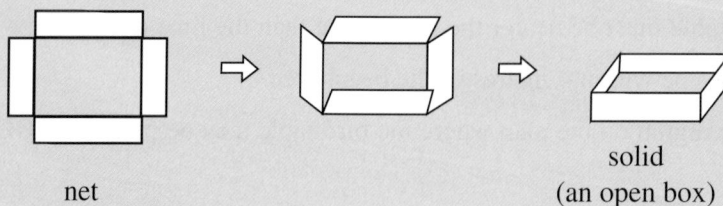

net

solid
(an open box)

**1** 

A    B    C    D    E

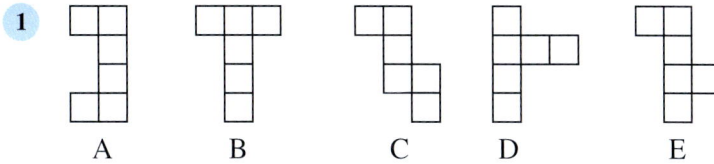

Which of these nets will fold to make a cube?
*If your teacher wants you to*, draw the nets on squared paper, cut them out and fold them to see which ones do make cubes.

**2** Draw an accurate *net* for this cube.

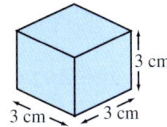

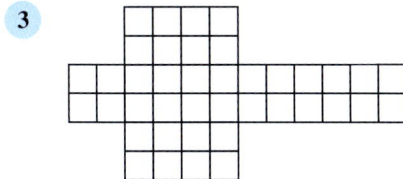

3 cm
3 cm    3 cm

**3** 

This net makes a cuboid.
Each small square is 1 cm long.

(a) How long will the cuboid be?

(b) How wide will it be?

(c) How high will it be?

(d) What is the volume of the cuboid?

**4** Draw an accurate net for this cuboid.

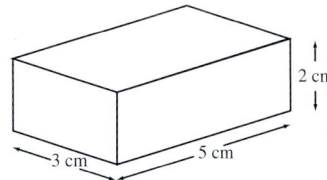

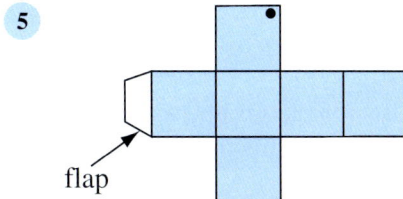

2 cm
3 cm    5 cm

**5** 

flap

(a) Sketch this net.

(b) Which edge will the flap be stuck to? Put a ✓ on this edge.

(c) Two other corners will meet the corner with a •
Put a • in each corner that meets the corner with a •

**6** Draw a net for this *open* box.
*If your teacher want you to*, cut out the net and fold it to check it is right.

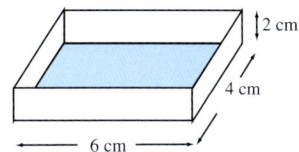

2 cm
4 cm
6 cm

**7** 

The dots on opposite faces of a die add up to seven. There must be 4 dots on the bottom face of this die.

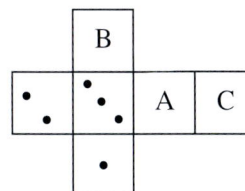

B
A  C

This is a net of a die. How many dots are on faces A, B and C?

517

**8** Which of the nets below will make a closed box?

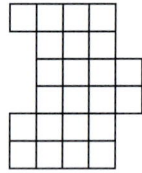

A

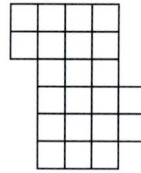

B

**1** This diagram shows the net of a solid.

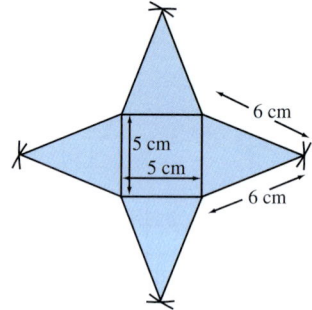

(a) Use *compasses* and a *ruler* to draw the net accurately on paper or card.

(b) Draw on some flaps.

(c) Cut out the net, fold and glue it to make the solid.

(d) What is the name of the solid?

**2** The diagram shows a triangular prism.

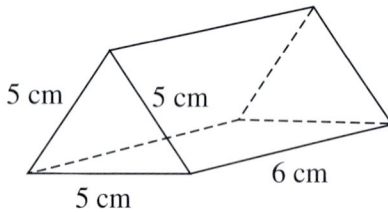

(a) Use *compasses* and a *ruler* to construct the net for this prism on paper or card.

(b) Draw on some flaps.

(c) Cut out the net, fold and glue it to make the solid.

**3** Here is another triangular prism (a wedge).

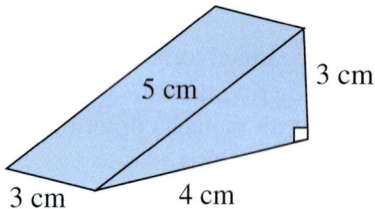

(a) Use *compasses* and a *ruler* to construct the net for this prism on paper or card.

(b) Draw on some flaps.

(c) Cut out the net, fold and glue it to make the solid.

**4** Draw an *accurate net* for this square-based pyramid.

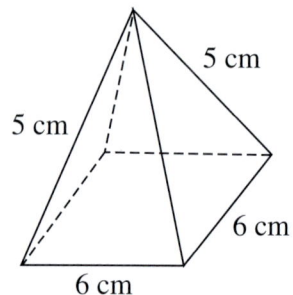

518

(20A)  **Use metric units (see Unit 17)**

1. Which of the amounts below are the same as 30 cm?

   (3 m)    (300 mm)    (0.3 m)    (30 m)

2. Which of the amounts below are the same as 40 kg?

   (4000 g)    (40000 g)    (400 g)    (4 tonnes)

3. Copy and complete the following:

   (a) 7.5 kg = ☐ g          (b) 8 l = ☐ ml          (c) 300 ml = ☐ l

   (d) 0.6 m = ☐ cm          (e) 4200 g = ☐ kg          (f) 2.8 km = ☐ m

4. Mary has a 1.5 litre bottle of ginger beer. She and a friend drink 860 ml. How much ginger beer is left in the bottle?

5. Sandra runs in a 40 km race. She has to stop 2700 m *before* the end of the race. How many km has Sandra run?

## 3-D objects

### M20.2

You will need isometric dot paper.

**1**

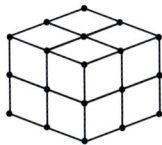

Here is a cube made from eight 1 cm cubes.

Draw a cuboid with a volume of 18 cm$^3$.

**2**  Draw a cuboid with a volume of 20 cm$^3$.

**3**  Make a copy of each object below. For each drawing state the number of 'multilink' cubes needed to make the object.

(a)

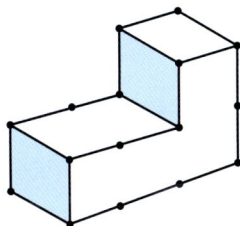

(b)

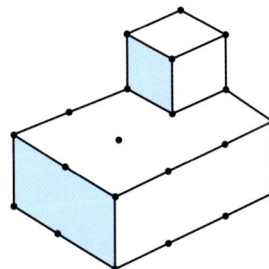

**4** Using four cubes, you can make several different shapes. A and B are different shapes but C is the same as A.

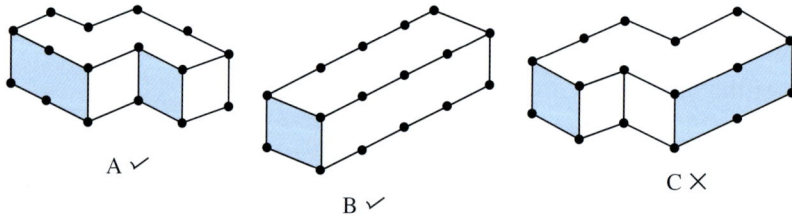

A ✓

B ✓

C ✗

Make as many *different* shapes as possible, using four cubes, and draw them all (including shapes A and B above) on isometric paper.

**5**

This shape falls over onto the shaded face.

Draw the shape after it has fallen over.

---

🔑 # Key Facts

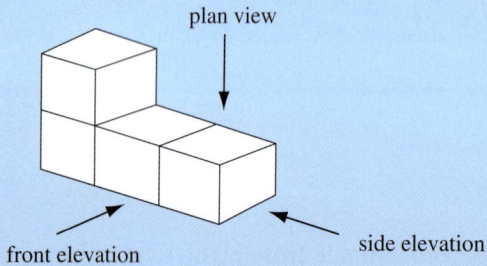

plan view

front elevation

side elevation

Here is a 3-D object made from centimetre cubes.

A plan view is when the object is looked at from above.

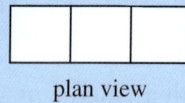

plan view

A front elevation is when the object is viewed from the front.

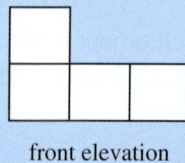

front elevation

A side elevation is when the object is viewed from the side.

side elevation

520

**E20.2**

In Questions **1** to **6** draw (a) the plan view, (b) the front view and (c) the side view of the object.

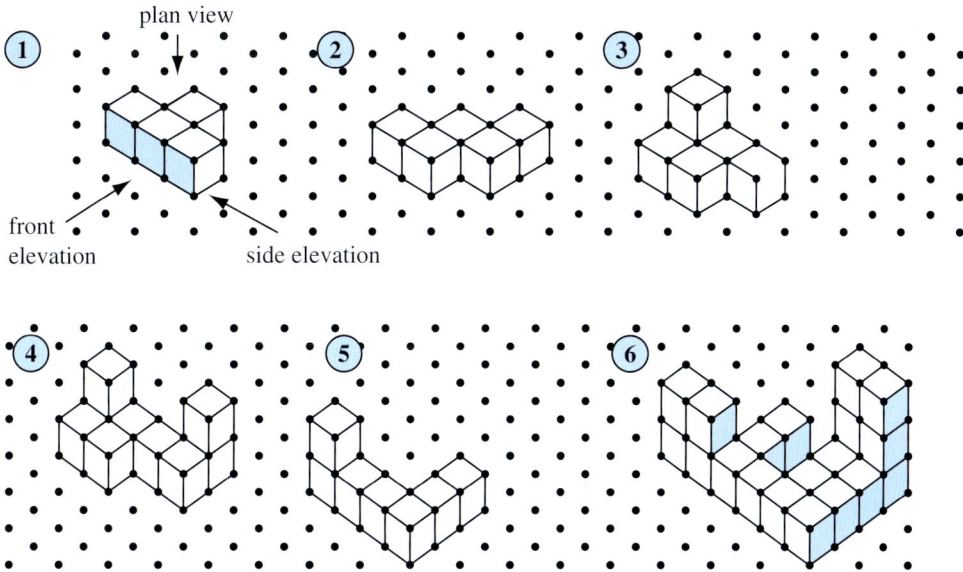

In Questions **7** to **10** you are given the plan and two elevations of an object. Use the information to make the shape using centimetre cubes. Draw the object on isometric paper if you can.

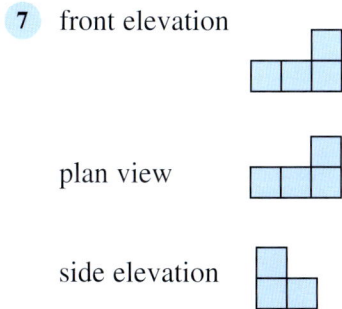

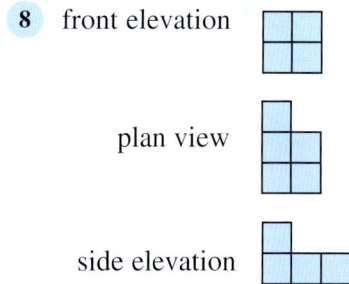

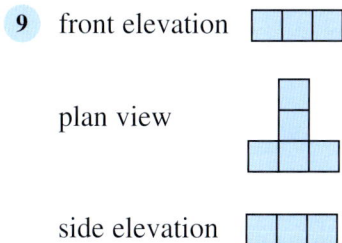

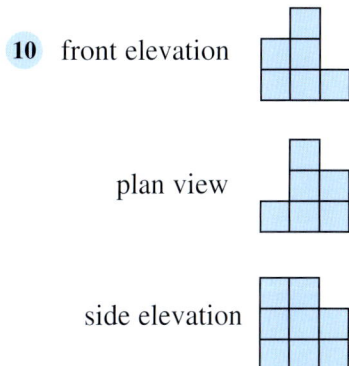

**7** front elevation

plan view

side elevation

**8** front elevation

plan view

side elevation

**9** front elevation

plan view

side elevation

**10** front elevation

plan view

side elevation

## 🔑 Key Facts

Bearings are used by navigators on ships and aircraft and by people travelling in open country.

> Bearings are measured from the *North* line in a *clockwise* direction.
> A bearing is always given as a *three-figure number*.

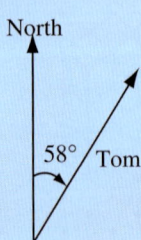

North

58° Tom

Tom is walking on
a bearing of 058°.

↑
3-figures used

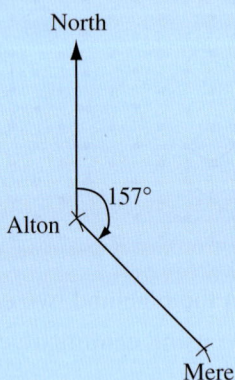

North

Alton ✕ 157°

✕ Mere

Mere is on a bearing
of 157° *from Alton*.

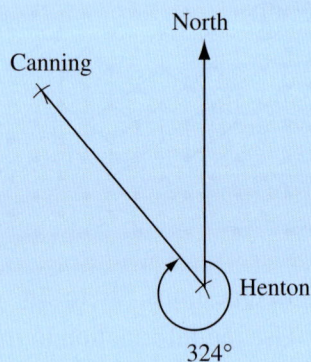

Canning
✕

North

✕ Henton

324°

Canning is on a bearing
of 324° *from Henton*.

### M20.3

**1**

North

North-west          North-east

45° 45°
45°        45°
West ←                    → East
45°        45°
45° 45°

South-west          South-east

South

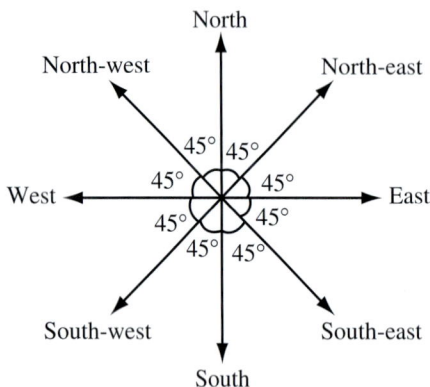

Write down the bearing for each compass direction below:

(a) East

(b) South-east

(c) West

(d) North-east

(e) South-west

(f) North-west

(g) South

(h) North

**2** Peter hits 6 golf balls, aiming north, with his usual precision. The golf balls travel in the directions shown. On what bearing does each golf ball fly?

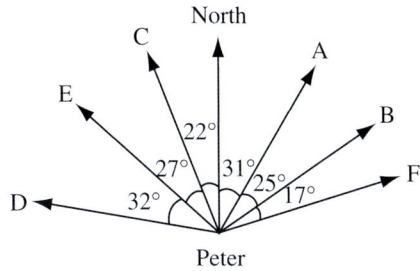

**3**

Write down the bearing of:

(a) Henly *from Dinder*

(b) Dinder *from Weare*

(c) Weare *from Dinder*

(d) Weare *from Henly*

(e) Dinder *from Henly*

(f) Henly *from Weare*

**4** Seven travellers head off from camp on their search for the 'meaning of life'. They begin walking in the directions shown. On what bearing is each traveller walking?

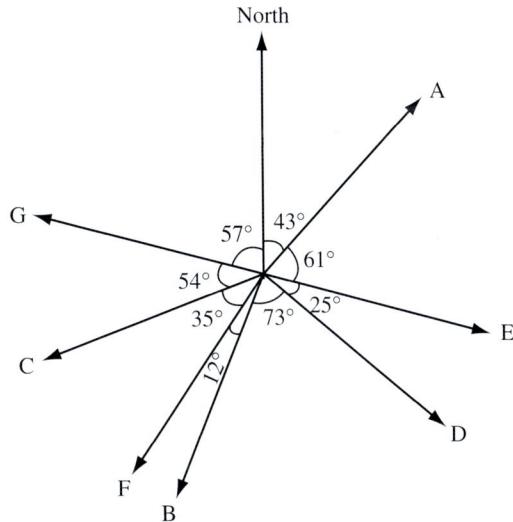

## E20.3

**1**

Find the bearing of:

(a) Cowling *from Colton*

(b) Colton *from Cowling*

**2**

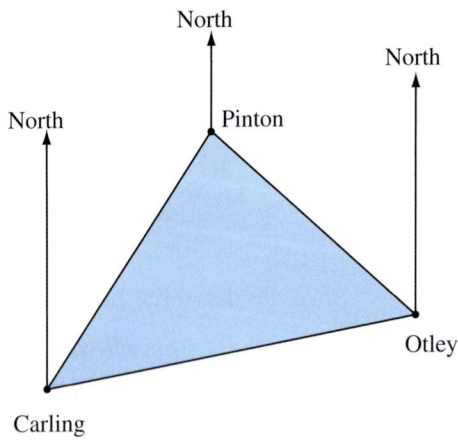

Use a protractor to measure the bearing of:

(a) Carling *from Pinton*

(b) Otley *from Carling*

(c) Pinton *from Otley*

(d) Carling *from Otley*

**3**

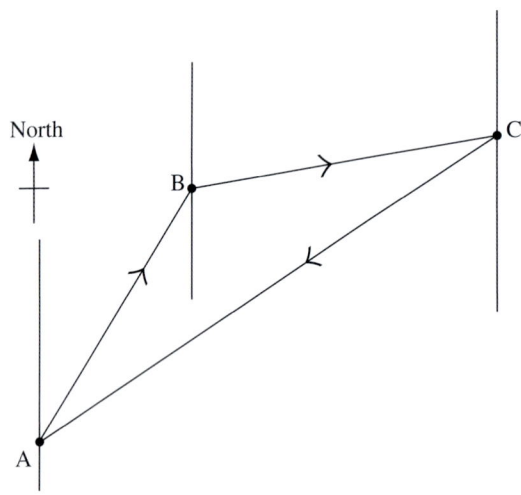

A hiker walks from A to B then B to C and finally from C to A.

Use a protractor to measure the bearing of the walk from

(a) *A to B*

(b) *B to C*

(c) *C to A*

**4** Yasmin goes on a sponsored walk. Her route is shown opposite.

Work out the bearing of the journey from:

(a) Start to Jam Hill

(b) Jam Hill to Pilling Mount

(c) Pilling Mount to the White Swan

(d) The White Swan back to the Finish

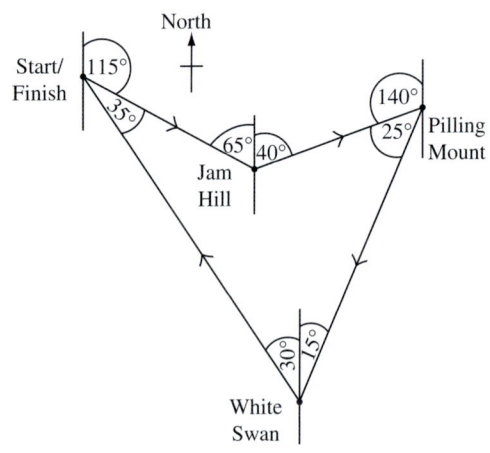

524

**5** A ship sails 6 km due north and then a further 8 km on a bearing of 070°.

Use a scale of 1 cm for every 1 km to show the ship's journey. How far is the ship now from its starting point?

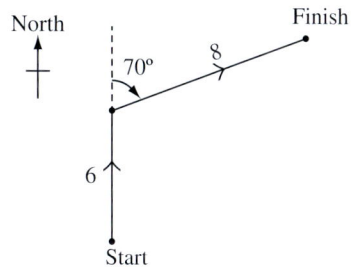

**6** A ship sails 7 km due south and then a further 5 km on a bearing of 120°. Use a scale of 1 cm for every 1 km to show the ship's journey. How far is the ship from its starting point?

**7** A ship sails 6 km on a bearing of 065° and then a further 7 km on a bearing of 165°. Use a scale of 1 cm for every 1 km to show the ships journey. Find the distance of the ship from its starting point?

*Can you still?*

**20B** **Use percentages (see Unit 6)**

*Can you still?*

1. Which 2 numbers below are equal to each other?

$\frac{7}{25}$  2.8  28%  $\frac{1}{28}$

2. At a local garage, 8 out of 40 cars fail their MOT. What *percentage* of the cars fail their MOT?

3. 9 out of 36 children say that their favourite film is 'Star Wars'. What *percentage* of children say that their favourite film is *not* 'Star Wars'?

4. Which 2 answers below are the same?

20% of £80    15% of £60    5% of £180

5. A computer costs £780 + VAT. If VAT is 17.5%, work out how much the computer costs altogether.

6. In June, Rebecca earns £160 each week. After a pay rise she earns £168 each week. What is the *percentage increase* in her pay?

7. £3000 is invested at 5% per annum (year) compound interest. How much money will there be after 2 years?

8. There are 5000 fish in a lake. Each year, the lake loses 4% of its fish at the start of the year. How many fish are in the lake after 2 years?

## Pythagoras' theorem

Here is a dissection which demonstrates a result called Pythagoras' theorem. Pythagoras was a famous Greek mathematician who proved the result in about 550 B.C. The dissection works only for isosceles right angled triangles.

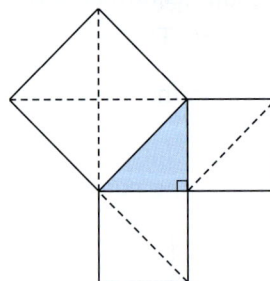

---

## 🔑 Key Facts

**Pythagoras' theorem**

> In a *right angled* triangle, the square on the hypotenuse is equal to the sum of the squares on the other two sides.

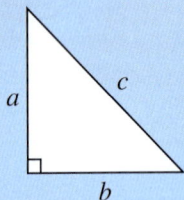

$$a^2 + b^2 = c^2$$

The 'hypotenuse' is the *longest* side in a right angled triangle.

To find the *hypotenuse*, square the known sides, *add* then square root. To find one of the *shorter sides*, square the known sides, *subtract* then square root.

---

(a) Find the length $x$.

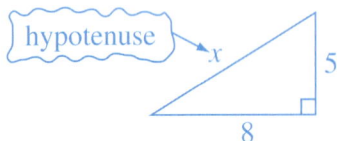

hypotenuse

$x^2 = 5^2 + 8^2$

$x^2 = 25 + 64$

$x^2 = 89$

$x = \sqrt{89}$

$x = 9.43$ (to 2 decimal places)

(b) Find the length $y$.

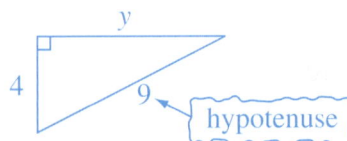

hypotenuse

$y^2 + 4^2 = 9^2$

$y^2 + 16 = 81$

$y^2 = 81 - 16$

$y^2 = 65$

$y = \sqrt{65}$

$y = 8.06$ (to 2 decimal places)

You will need a calculator. Give your answers correct to 2 decimal places where necessary. The units are cm.

**1** Find the length $x$. $x$ is the hypotenuse.

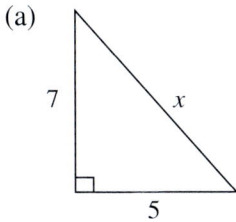

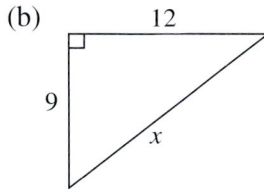

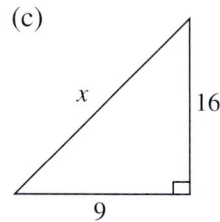

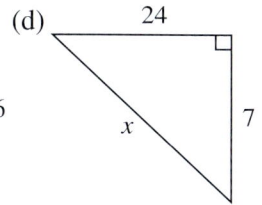

(a)
7
5
$x$

(b)
12
9
$x$

(c)
$x$
16
9

(d)
24
$x$
7

**2** Find the length $x$. $x$ is one of the shorter sides.

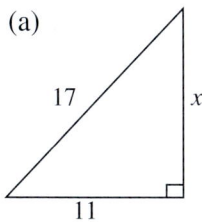

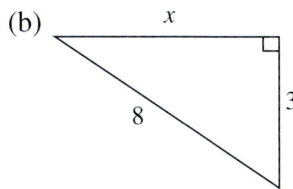

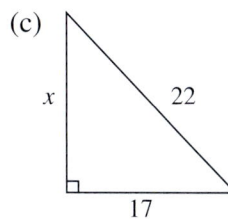

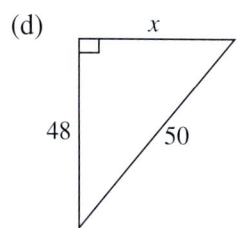

(a)
17
$x$
11

(b)
$x$
8
3

(c)
$x$
22
17

(d)
$x$
48
50

**3** Find the length $x$.

Be careful! Check whether $x$ is the hypotenuse or one of the shorter sides.

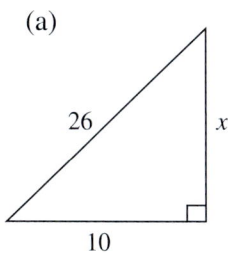

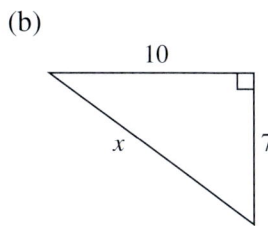

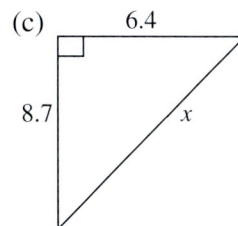

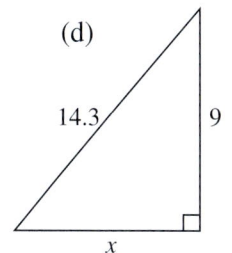

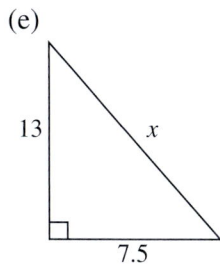

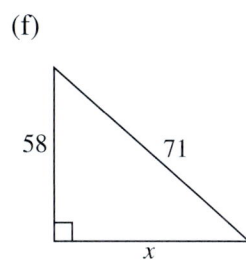

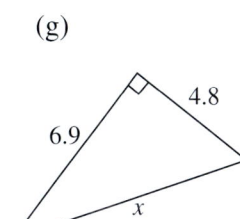

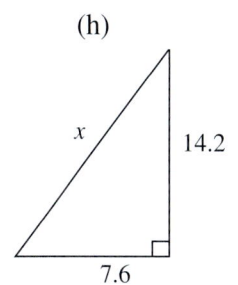

(a)
26
$x$
10

(b)
10
$x$
7

(c)
6.4
8.7
$x$

(d)
14.3
9
$x$

(e)
13
$x$
7.5

(f)
58
71
$x$

(g)
4.8
6.9
$x$

(h)
$x$
14.2
7.6

527

**4** Find the length AB.

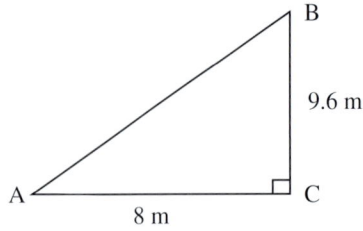

**5** Find the length PQ.

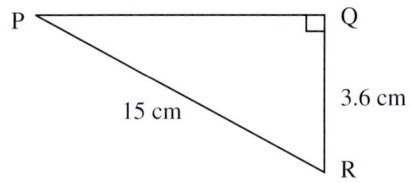

**6** Find the length MN.

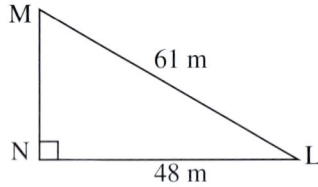

**7** Find the length YZ.

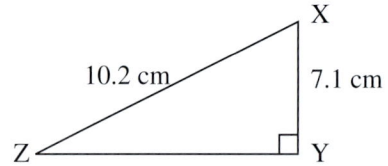

A ladder of length 6 m reaches 4.8 m up a vertical wall. How far is the foot of the ladder from the wall?

$x$ is one of the shorter sides in a right angled triangle.
Use Pythagoras' theorem.

$x^2 + 4.8^2 = 6^2$

$x^2 + 23.04 = 36$

$x^2 = 12.96$

$x = \sqrt{12.96}$

$x = 3.6$ m

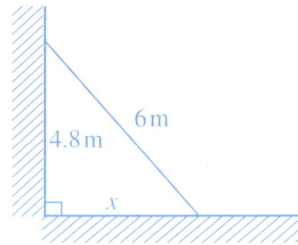

### E20.4

You will need a calculator (give answers to 2 decimal places)

**1** A ladder of length 6 m rests against a vertical wall, with its foot 2.4 m from the wall. How far up the wall does the ladder reach?

**2**

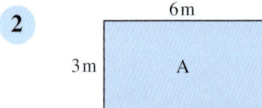

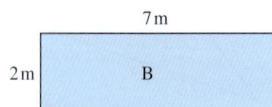

Which rectangle has the longer diagonal and by how much?

**3** A ladder of length 7 m reaches 5 m up a vertical wall. How far is the foot of the ladder from the wall?

528

**4**

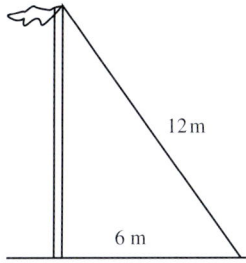

A rope attached to a flagpole is 12 m long. The rope is fixed to the ground 6 m from the foot of the flagpole. How tall is the flagpole?

**5** Towley is 8 km due east of Hapton. Castleton is 12 km due south of Hapton. How far is Towley from Castleton?

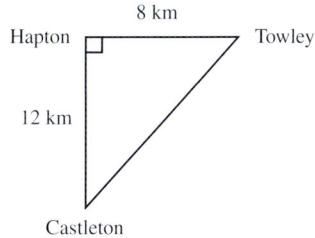

**6** Redford is 9 km due north of Hagshed. Peltsham is 7 km due west of Hagshed. How far is Redford from Peltsham?

**7** A ship sails 50 km due north and then a further 62 km due east. How far is the ship from its starting point?

**8**

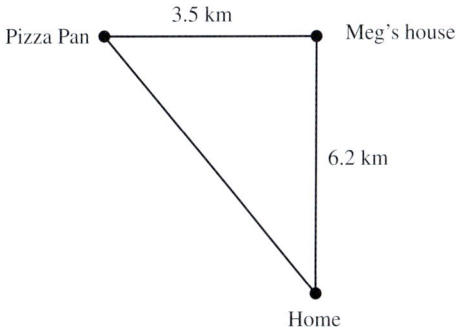

Kat and Holly are sisters. They are meeting friends at Pizza Pan. Kat drives *directly* to Pizza Pan. Holly has to pick up Meg on the way to Pizza Pan. How much further does Holly drive than Kat?

**9** A clothes line is attached to 2 vertical walls as shown. How long is the clothes line?

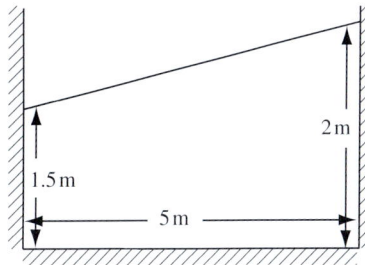

**10**

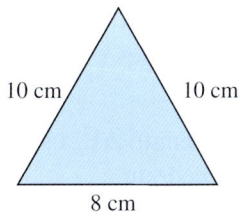

An *isosceles* triangle has a line of symmetry which divides the triangle into two right-angled triangles as shown.

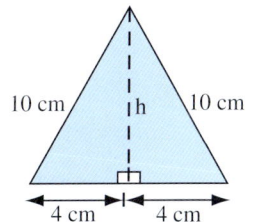

Use Pythagoras' theorem to find the height *h* of the triangle.

**11** Find the height of each isosceles triangle below.

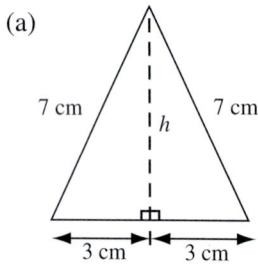

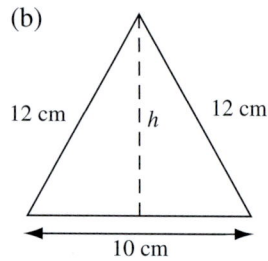

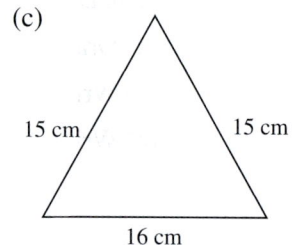

(a)

7 cm    7 cm
      $h$
3 cm   3 cm

(b)

12 cm    12 cm
      $h$
10 cm

(c)

15 cm    15 cm
16 cm

**12** Area of triangle $= \frac{1}{2}bh$
Find the area of this isosceles triangle.

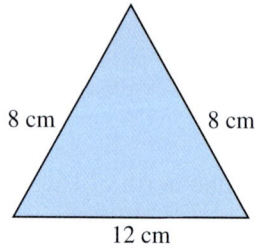

8 cm    8 cm
12 cm

**13** Calculate the vertical height and hence the area of an equilateral triangle of side 16 cm.

**14** Find the length $x$. The units are cm.

(a)

6
10
9
$x$

(b)

13
12
10
$x$

(c)

3
3
5
$x$
3

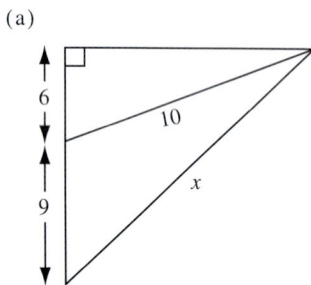

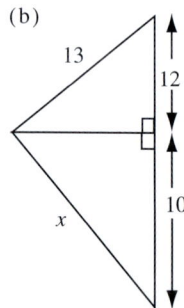

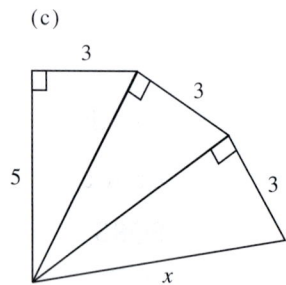

## Shapes and lines using co-ordinates

### M20.5

You may use a calculator.

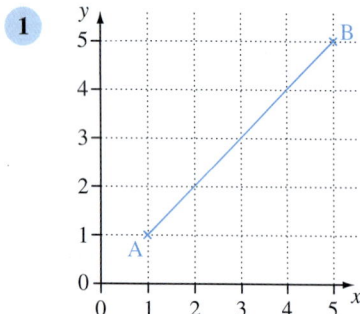

**1**

(a) Find the co-ordinates of the midpoint of line AB.

(b) Calculate the length AB, using Pythagoras' theorem.

**2** Draw an *x*-axis from –5 to 5 and a *y*-axis from –5 to 5.

ABCD is a square. A is (– 3, 2), B is (– 3, – 4), C is (3, – 4).

(a) Draw the square.

(b) Write down the co-ordinates of D.

(c) Write down the co-ordinates of the centre of the square.

(d) Calculate the length of the diagonal AC.

**3**

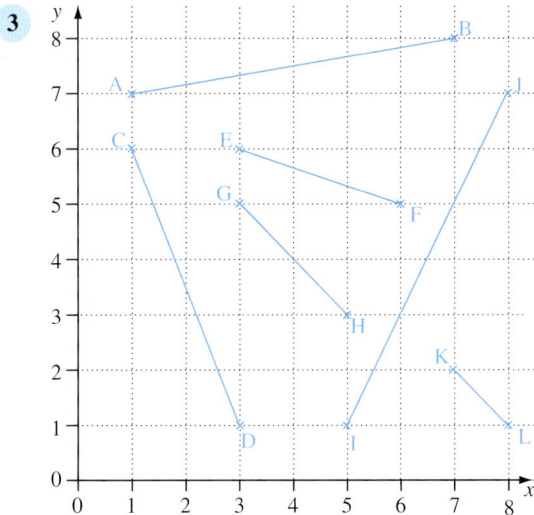

Calculate the length of each line *and* write down the co-ordinates of the midpoint of each line.

**4** Calculate the length of the line joining (2, 1) to (8, 9).

**5** Draw an *x*-axis from 0 to 7 and a *y*-axis from – 3 to 3.

PQRS is a parallelogram. P is (4, 1), Q is (2, – 2), R is (6, – 2).

(a) Draw the parallelogram.

(b) Write down the co-ordinates of S.

(c) Write down the co-ordinates of the midpoint of diagonal QS.

(d) Calculate the length of the diagonal QS.

**6** Draw an *x*-axis from –5 to 5 and a *y*-axis from –5 to 5.

ABCD is a rhombus. A is (– 4, 2), B is (1, 2), C is (4, – 2).

(a) Draw the rhombus.

(b) Write down the co-ordinates of D.

(c) Write down the co-ordinates of the midpoint of diagonal BD.

(d) Calculate the length of the diagonal AC.

531

A point in 3-D space has co-ordinates $(x, y, z)$ using 3 axes.

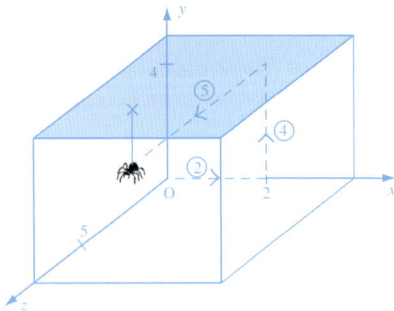

Start at the origin O. This has co-ordinates $(0, 0, 0)$. To get to the spider, move 2 units parallel to the $x$-axis then 4 units parallel to the $y$-axis then 5 units parallel to the $z$-axis. The spider is at $(2, 4, 5)$.

**E20.5**

**1**

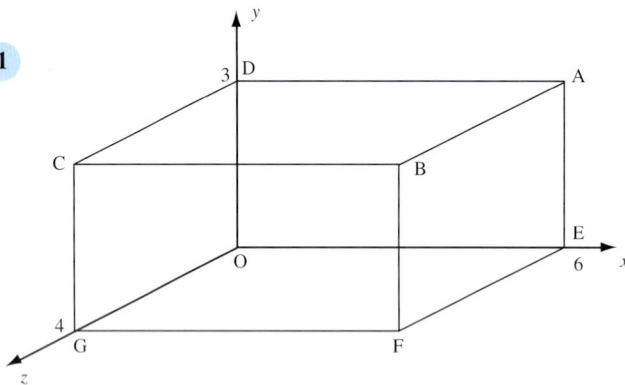

A has co-ordinates $(6, 3, 0)$. B has co-ordinates $(6, 3, 4)$. Write down the co-ordinates of C, D, E, F and G.

**2** (a) Write down the co-ordinates of the vertices L, M, N, O, P, Q, R and S.

(b) Write down the co-ordinates of the midpoint of edge PL.

(c) Calculate the length of QS.

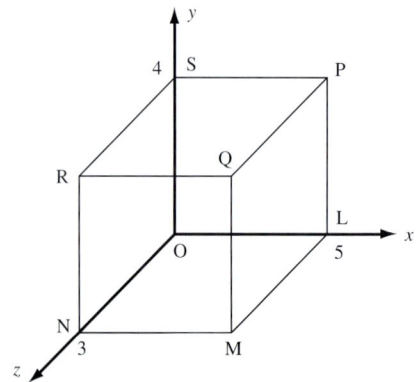

The co-ordinates of G are $(6, 4, 10)$.

(a) Write down the co-ordinates of the vertices O, A, B, C, D, E and F.

(b) Calculate the length AG.

(c) Write down the co-ordinates of the midpoint of edge FG.

(d) Write down the co-ordinates of the midpoint of edge BC.

**3**

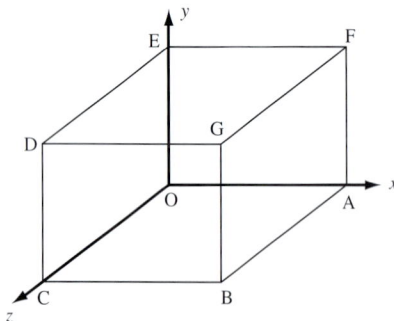

Hopefully you will have a long and happy life. How will you pay for things when you get a lot older? What kind of life will you be able to have?

By 2050 there will be 14 million people over 65 in the UK.

If you do not save some money during your working years you will rely on the government for your money. How much might that be?

**The state pension**

The state pension at the time of writing is £3150 per annum for a single person. That is £60.58 each week. The government might give a person allowances to make sure the amount is at least £90 a week.

How would you manage?

### WYM20

1  Billy receives £90 a week pension and allowances. He has no other savings. He owns his own house. He has to spend the following *each week*:

|  |  |
|---|---|
| food | £40 |
| electricity | £11 |
| gas | £7 |
| water rates | £7 |
| council tax | £16 |
| phone | £6 |

(a) How much money does Billy have left for each week?

(b) Billy needs to buy clothes, see friends and family. He wants to have the occasional drink and he would still like to run a car. He is 67 years old. What is your advice to Billy?

2  Mike started paying a *small amount* of money into a *personal pension* plan each month when he was 26 years old. He carried on paying a small amount each month throughout his working life. Mike is now 65 years old and has a pension of £14000 per annum. When he adds his state pension of £3150, he has £329.81 each week. *Compare* the life he could now lead compared to Billy in Question 1.

3  Throughout your working life a small amount of money could be saved each month towards a pension.

(a) Write down (*or discuss with your teacher*) reasons for saving.

(b) Write down (*or discuss with your teacher*) reasons for *not* saving like this.

**1.** Drawing nets

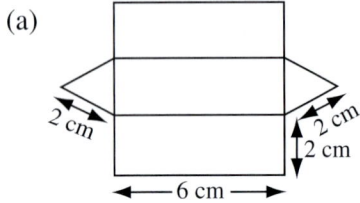

(a)

This diagram shows the net of a solid.

Name the solid.

2 cm 2 cm 2 cm 6 cm

(b)

7 cm 4 cm 3 cm

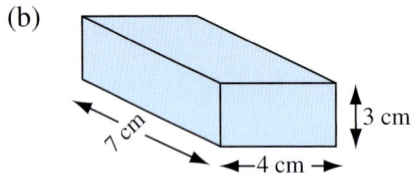

Draw an accurate net for this cuboid.

**2.** Drawing 3-D objects

(a) On isometric dot paper, draw any solid with a volume of 10 cm³.

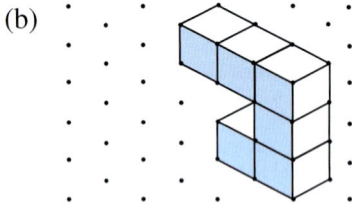

(b)

This shape falls over onto the shaded face.

Draw the shape after it has fallen over.

(c) Draw a hexagonal prism.

**3.** Drawing and using plans and elevations

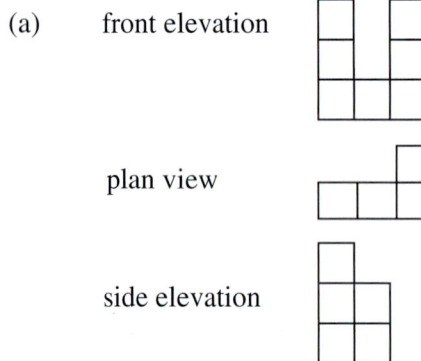

(a)  front elevation

Draw this object on isometric paper.

plan view

side elevation

(b) Draw and label the plan and a side elevation for this solid (called a frustum).

(c)

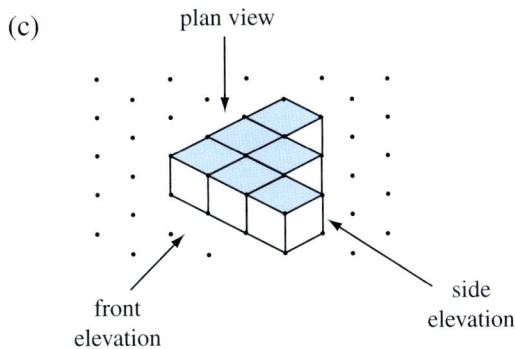

plan view

front elevation

side elevation

Draw the plan view, the front view and the side view of this object.

### 4. Using bearings

(a)

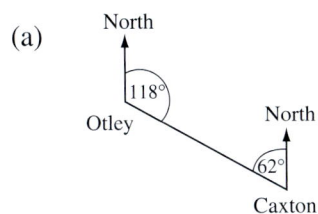

North

118°

Otley

North

62°

Caxton

(i) Write down the bearing of Caxton from Otley.

(ii) Write down the bearing of Otley from Caxton.

(b) *Use a protractor* to measure the bearing of:

  (i) Ambleford from Cayton

 (ii) Berwick from Cayton

(iii) Berwick from Ambleford

(iv) Cayton from Ambleford

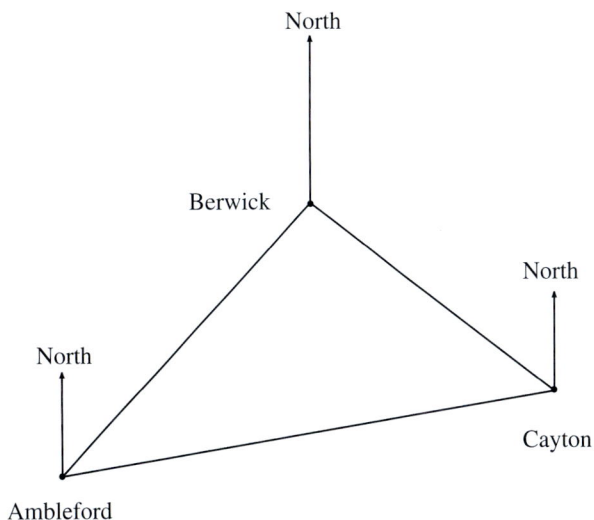

North

Berwick

North

North

Cayton

Ambleford

### 5. Using Pythagoras' theorem

(a)

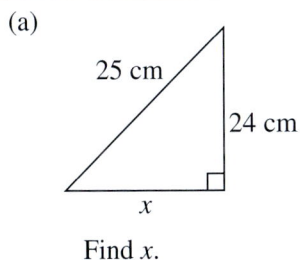

25 cm

24 cm

$x$

Find $x$.

(b)

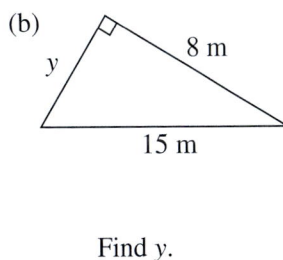

$y$

8 m

15 m

Find $y$.

(c)

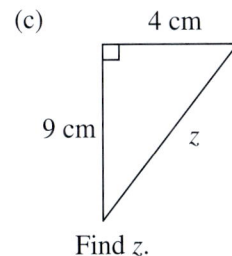

4 cm

9 cm

$z$

Find $z$.

535

## 6. Solving problems with shapes and lines using co-ordinates

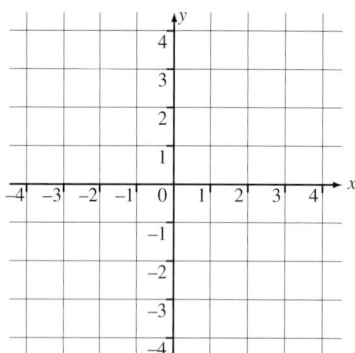

(a) Copy this grid.

(b) ABCD is a rectangle. A is (−3, 2), B is (3, 2), C is (3, −3).

Draw the rectangle.

(c) Write down the co-ordinates of D.

(d) Write down the co-ordinates of the midpoint of diagonal BD.

(e) Calculate the length of the diagonal BD.

(f) Calculate the length of the line joining (3, 1) to (7, 6).

## 7. Using 3 co-ordinates for a point in 3-D space

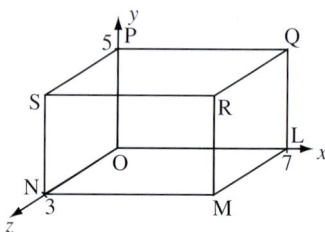

(a) Write down the co-ordinates of the vertices L, M, N, O, P, Q, R and S.

(b) Write down the co-ordinates of the midpoint of edge NS.

(c) Calculate the length of LN.

## Mixed examination questions

1   Write down which of the following are nets of a cube.

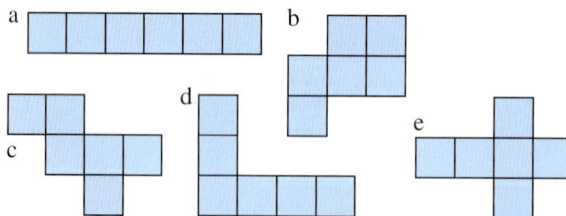

(WJEC)

2

XYZ is a right-angled triangle.
XY = 3.2 cm.
XZ = 1.7 cm.

Calculate the length of YZ.

Give your answer correct to 3 significant figures.

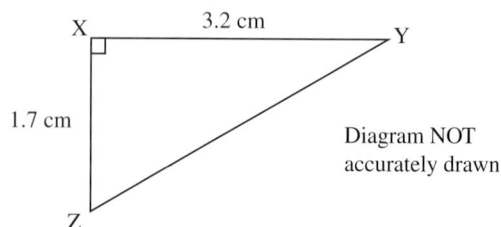

Diagram NOT accurately drawn

(EDEXCEL)

**3** These drawings show two views of the same solid made with centimetre cubes. The base of the solid is horizontal.

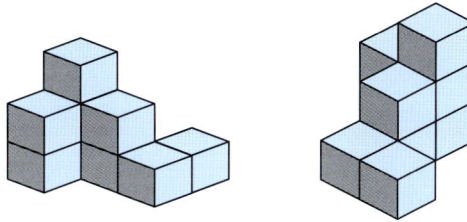

(a) How many centimetre cubes are there in the solid?

(b) Draw an accurate full-sized plan view of the solid on a centimetre grid. (OCR)

**4** The diagram shows three villages. Abshelf (A), Grasston (G) and Haswell (H). The North line through Grasston is shown.

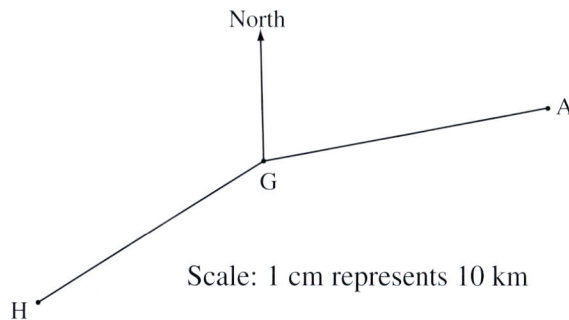

Scale: 1 cm represents 10 km

(a) What is the distance, in kilometres, between Abshelf and Grasston?

(b) Measure and write down the bearing of Abshelf from Grasston.

(c) Measure and write down the bearing of Haswell from Grasston. (OCR)

**5** A lift at the seaside takes people from sea level to the top of a cliff, as shown.

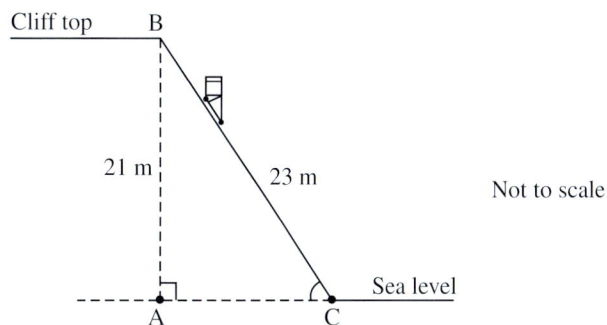

From sea level to the top of the cliff, the lift travels 23 m and rises a height of 21 m.

Calculate the distance AC. (AQA)

## Page 1    M1.1

6. (a) 600    (b) 4    (c) 8    (d) 3000    (e) 6
   (f) 700    (g) 80    (h) 5000    (i) 10    (j) 600
   (k) 6    (l) 5000    (m) 100    (n) 700    (o) 5

7. (a) 863    (b) 368    **8.** (a) 741    (b) 147

## Page 3    E1.1

1. (a) $\frac{2}{100}$   (b) $\frac{9}{10}$   (c) $\frac{5}{10}$   (d) $\frac{7}{1000}$   (e) $\frac{9}{10}$
  (f) $\frac{7}{1000}$   (g) $\frac{8}{1000}$   (h) $\frac{2}{100}$   (i) 7 units   (j) $\frac{2}{10}$
  (k) 8 units   (l) 10   (m) $\frac{8}{10}$   (n) $\frac{8}{1000}$   (o) 30
  (p) $\frac{2}{100}$   (q) $\frac{7}{100}$   (r) 70   (s) $\frac{1}{1000}$   (t) $\frac{0}{10}$

2. 0.1    **3.** 0.7    **4.** 0.5

5. (a) 87.643   (b) 34.678   (c) 98.654   (d) 14.568

## Page 4    M1.2

| | | | | |
|---|---|---|---|---|
| **1.** 60 | **2.** 50 | **3.** 40 | **4.** 80 | **5.** 20 |
| **6.** 20 | **7.** 70 | **8.** 40 | **9.** 10 | **10.** 40 |
| **11.** 80 | **12.** 100 | **13.** 310 | **14.** 290 | **15.** 460 |
| **16.** 240 | **17.** 420 | **18.** 820 | **19.** 1320 | **20.** 6150 |
| **21.** 200 | **22.** 400 | **23.** 500 | **24.** 600 | **25.** 700 |
| **26.** 800 | **27.** 700 | **28.** 300 | **29.** 900 | **30.** 700 |
| **31.** 700 | **32.** 900 | **33.** 700 | **34.** 700 | **35.** 1400 |
| **36.** 2700 | **37.** 4600 | **38.** 1600 | **39.** 2200 | **40.** 5400 |
| **41.** £17000 | **42.** 3000 | **43.** 17000 | **44.** 1000 | **45.** £39000 |
| **46.** 482000 | **47.** 8 | **48.** 3 | **49.** 3 | **50.** 12 |
| **51.** 8 | **52.** £3 | **53.** £3 | **54.** £7 | **55.** £13 |
| **56.** £25 | **57.** 7 kg | **58.** 4 kg | **59.** 14 kg | **60.** 9 kg |

61. 23 kg

## Page 6    E1.2

1. (a) 2320   (b) 2300   (c) 2000
2. (a) 4630   (b) 4600   (c) 5000
3. (a) 6280   (b) 6300   (c) 6000
4. (a) 4190   (b) 4200   (c) 4000
5. (a) 1000   (b) 1000   (c) 1000
6. (a) 3280   (b) 3300   (c) 3000
7. (a) 8170   (b) 8200   (c) 8000
8. (a) 17450   (b) 17500   (c) 17000
9. 550, 610, 619, 583
10. China 1100, India 900, USA 300, Brazil 200, Pakistan 100, Japan 100, Mexico 100 (All Millions)
11. 50,351: 49,681: 50,018: 49,899
12. (a) 102   (b) 40   (c) 296   (d) 12   (e) 15   (f) 17
    (g) 53   (h) 13   (i) 26   (j) 210   (k) 184   (l) 5

## Page 7    M1.3

| | | | | |
|---|---|---|---|---|
| **1.** 162 | **2.** 287 | **3.** 592 | **4.** 5766 | **5.** 8902 |
| **6.** 39 | **7.** 44 | **8.** 55 | **9.** 415 | **10.** 2461 |
| **11.** 1177 | **12.** 819 | **13.** 248 | **14.** 366 | **15.** 3131 |
| **16.** 508 | **17.** 11390 | **18.** 843 | **19.** 3669 | **20.** 117831 |

21.

| 9 | 2 | 4 | | 2 |
|---|---|---|---|---|
| 5 | | 2 | 4 | 3 |
| 8 | 8 | 4 | | 2 |
| | 3 | | 5 | 8 |
| 6 | 4 | 2 | 5 | 9 |

## Page 8    E1.3

1. 505    **2.** 1170    **3.** 79    **4.** 161    **5.** 368    **6.** 355    **7.** 160

8. 465    **9.** 308    **10.** 123    **11.** 388    **12.** 342    **13.** 861    **14.** 147

15.

| + | 38 | 87 | 245 | 66 |
|---|---|---|---|---|
| 109 | 147 | 196 | 254 | 175 |
| 326 | 364 | 413 | 571 | 392 |
| 163 | 201 | 250 | 408 | 229 |
| 446 | 484 | 533 | 691 | 512 |

16.

| + | 443 | 148 | 516 | 244 |
|---|---|---|---|---|
| 384 | 827 | 532 | 900 | 628 |
| 252 | 695 | 400 | 768 | 496 |
| 87 | 530 | 235 | 603 | 331 |
| 226 | 669 | 374 | 742 | 670 |

17. £377      **18.** £261

19. (a) £1262   (b) £263   (c) £138   (d) £39

20. (a) 57   (b) 61   (c) 4   (d) 16     **21.** 32350     **22.** 15792

## Page 10    M1.4

| | | | |
|---|---|---|---|
| **1.** 7690 | **2.** 31000 | **3.** 268000 | **4.** 41600 |
| **5.** 2400 | **6.** 38610 | **7.** 630 | **8.** 8170 |
| **9.** 39700 | **10.** 418 | **11.** 5270 | **12.** 48 |
| **13.** 516 | **14.** 316000 | **15.** 53000 | **16.** 4170 |
| **17.** 684 | **18.** 5370000 | **19.** £5200 | **20.** £1300 |
| **21.** 110 | **22.** 893 | **23.** 460 | **24.** 21800 |
| **25.** 49000 | **26.** 84100 | **27.** 93 | **28.** 100 |
| **29.** 1000 | **30.** 100 | **31.** 382000 | **32.** 92400 |

33. 10     **34.** 3160 → 316000 → 31600 → 316

35. 8640 → 8640 → 864

## Page 11    E1.4

| | | | | |
|---|---|---|---|---|
| **1.** 180 | **2.** 400 | **3.** 280 | **4.** 270 | |
| **5.** 360 | **6.** 2100 | **7.** 4000 | **8.** 3600 | |
| **9.** 12000 | **10.** 48000 | **11.** 14000 | **12.** 160000 | |
| **13.** 27000 | **14.** 560000 | **15.** 240000 | **16.** £8000 | |
| **17.** 6000 | **18.** 4 | **19.** 9 | **20.** 9 | |
| **21.** 2 | **22.** 8 | **23.** 8 | **24.** 8 | **25.** 7 |
| **26.** 8 | **27.** 3 | **28.** 6 | **29.** 60 | **30.** 90 |
| **31.** 30 | **32.** 40 | **33.** £5000 | **34.** 90 | **35.** 5 |
| **36.** 30 | **37.** 20 | **38.** 70 | **39.** 50 | **40.** 1500 |

41. 35000    **42.** 50    **43.** 30    **44.** 800, 24000, 40, 2

45. 30, 1500, 45000, 500

## Page 12    Can you still?    1A

| | | | | |
|---|---|---|---|---|
| **1.** 800 | **2.** 900 | **3.** 1700 | **4.** 2200 | **5.** 20 |
| **6.** 70 | **7.** 450 | **8.** 250 | **9.** 9 | **10.** 7 |
| **11.** 3 | **12.** 7 | **13.** 8000 | **14.** 8000 | **15.** 28000 |
| **16.** 54000 | **17.** 17 | **18.** 56 | **19.** 66 | **20.** 560 |

## Page 13  M1.5

1. (a)

| × | 7 | 2 | 12 | 8 | 6 | 3 | 11 | 9 | 4 | 5 |
|---|---|---|----|---|---|---|----|---|---|---|
| 7 | 49 | 14 | 84 | 56 | 42 | 21 | 77 | 63 | 28 | 35 |
| 2 | 14 | 4 | 24 | 16 | 12 | 6 | 22 | 18 | 8 | 10 |
| 12 | 84 | 24 | 144 | 96 | 72 | 36 | 132 | 108 | 48 | 60 |
| 8 | 56 | 16 | 96 | 64 | 48 | 24 | 88 | 72 | 32 | 40 |
| 6 | 42 | 12 | 72 | 48 | 36 | 18 | 66 | 54 | 24 | 30 |
| 3 | 21 | 6 | 36 | 24 | 18 | 9 | 33 | 27 | 12 | 15 |
| 11 | 77 | 22 | 132 | 88 | 66 | 33 | 121 | 99 | 44 | 55 |
| 9 | 63 | 18 | 108 | 72 | 54 | 27 | 99 | 81 | 36 | 45 |
| 4 | 28 | 8 | 48 | 32 | 24 | 12 | 44 | 36 | 16 | 20 |
| 5 | 35 | 10 | 60 | 40 | 30 | 15 | 55 | 45 | 20 | 25 |

(b)

| × | 2 | 9 | 6 | 3 | 5 | 11 | 12 | 8 | 7 | 4 |
|---|---|---|---|---|---|----|----|---|---|---|
| 2 | 4 | 18 | 12 | 6 | 10 | 22 | 24 | 16 | 14 | 8 |
| 9 | 18 | 81 | 54 | 27 | 45 | 99 | 108 | 72 | 63 | 36 |
| 6 | 12 | 54 | 36 | 18 | 30 | 66 | 72 | 48 | 42 | 24 |
| 3 | 6 | 27 | 18 | 9 | 15 | 33 | 36 | 24 | 21 | 12 |
| 5 | 10 | 45 | 30 | 15 | 25 | 55 | 60 | 40 | 35 | 20 |
| 11 | 22 | 99 | 66 | 33 | 55 | 121 | 132 | 88 | 77 | 44 |
| 12 | 24 | 108 | 72 | 36 | 60 | 132 | 144 | 96 | 84 | 48 |
| 8 | 16 | 72 | 48 | 24 | 40 | 88 | 96 | 64 | 56 | 32 |
| 7 | 14 | 63 | 42 | 21 | 35 | 77 | 84 | 56 | 49 | 28 |
| 4 | 8 | 36 | 24 | 12 | 20 | 44 | 48 | 32 | 28 | 16 |

2. 93  3. 136  4. 244  5. 195  6. 623
7. 208  8. 1664  9. 1625  10. 1539  11. 1715
12. 1296  13. 548  14. 3488  15. 2163  16. 924
17. 1968  18. 1040  19. 2214  20. 18912  21. 44688
22. £511  23. 288  24. £2508  25. £1304

## Page 14  E1.5

1. 368  2. 560  3. 2511  4. 3128
5. 3952  6. 2006  7. 1792  8. 31692
9. 23482  10. 27812  11. 41741  12. 2274
13. 9464  14. 57996  15. 395304  16. £46336
17. 780  18. 9000 kg  19. £13578  20. £22060

## Page 15  M1.6

**Part One**
1. 2  2. 2  3. 6  4. 8  5. 8  6. 5
7. 7  8. 10  9. 4  10. 9  11. 10  12. 8
13. 4  14. 2  15. 9  16. 10  17. 7  18. 5
19. 0  20. 1

**Part Two**
1. 33  2. 21  3. 12  4. 12  5. 13
6. 12  7. 121  8. 62  9. 16  10. 81
11. 339  12. 562  13. 243  14. 145  15. 257

16. 232  17. 216  18. 49  19. 729  20. 466
21. 257  22. 205  23. 1296  24. 726  25. 305
26. 1387  27. 5457  28. 1754  29. 5231  30. 698
31. 3214  32. 2234

## Page 16  E1.6

1. 86r12  2. 178r3  3. 149r1  4. 54r2  5. 64r2
6. 41r6  7. 528r2  8. 3570r1  9. 582r5  10. 426r2
11. 501r5  12. 39r1  13. 65r7  14. 832r7  15. 14285r4
16. 536r2  17. 286r5  18. 1110r8  19. 612  20. 12080r3
21. 6  22. 14  23. 118  24. 17  25. 13

## Page 17  M1.7

1. 36  2. 27  3. 25  4. 23  5. 43
6. 24  7. 32  8. 25  9. 38  10. 29
11. 26  12. 23  13. 18  14. 36  15. 18
16. Charlie 29  Ron 82  Tessa 43  Teresa 15  17. 35

## Page 18  E1.7

1.

| 3 | 8 |   | 5 | 2 | 8 |
|---|---|---|---|---|---|
| 1 |   | 4 | 7 |   | 6 |
| 6 | 8 |   | 2 | 4 | 3 |
|   | 1 | 8 |   | 2 |   |
| 4 | 9 |   | 3 | 7 | 2 |
| 3 |   | 7 | 3 |   | 4 |
| 6 | 2 | 6 |   | 8 | 3 |

2. 12 Classes, 8 over  3. 42  4. 74  5. 423

## Page 18  Can you still?  1B

1. 637  2. 1355  3. 523  4. 153  5. 4803
6. 6376  7. 7845  8. 5318  9. 4457  10. 147
11. 218  12. 430  13. 286  14. 552  15. 571

## Page 19  M1.8

1. $-1°, -5°, -1°, -9°, 3°, -3°, 8°, -7°, -5°, -4°$
   (in order vertically)

2. $-3, -2, -1, 0, 7, 9$

3. $-10, -8, -4, 4, 1$

4. $-6, -5, -3, 0, 2, 6$

5. (a) 2°  (b) 4°  (c) 5°  (d) 3°  (e) 7°  (f) 12°

6. $-1°$  7. 4°  8. London  9. Belfast

10. 5°  11. 3°  12. 7° C  13. Liverpool

14. (a) $-3$  (b) $-6$  (c) $-4$  (d) 0

   (e) $-3$  (f) $-6$  (g) $-8$  (h) $-9$

   (i) $-2$  (j) $-4$  (k) $-9$  (l) $-1$

**15.**

| Old Temp.°C | Change °C | New Temp.°C |
|---|---|---|
| −2 | Rises 7 | 5 |
| −1 | Rises 3 | 2 |
| 2 | Falls 6 | −4 |
| −8 | Falls 2 | −10 |
| −7 | Rises 7 | 0 |
| −6 | Rises 4 | −2 |
| −12 | Rises 8 | −4 |
| −4 | Rises 3 | −1 |
| −2 | Falls 5 | −7 |
| −10 | Falls 4 | −14 |

## Page 22　E1.8

**1.** (a) 2　(b) 3　(c) −6　(d) −5

(e) 5　(f) 6　(g) −7　(h) −1

(i) −3　(j) −2　(k) −9　(l) −4

(m) 8　(n) 9　(o) −7　(p) −7

**2.** £30　**3.** (a) £40　(b) £10　(c) £80

**4.** £114　**5.** yes

**6.** (a) −1　(b) −10　(c) 11　(d) −6

(e) 2　(f) −11　(g) −6　(h) −4

(i) −14　(j) −4　(k) 6　(l) −11

(m) −7　(n) −8　(o) 1　(p) −7

(q) 1　(r) −10　(s) −5　(t) −8

## Page 23　M1.9

**1.** (a) −15　(b) −18　(c) 24　(d) 21

**2.** (a) 32　(b) −42　(c) 12　(d) −36

**3.** (a) −30　(b) −3　(c) 45　(d) 16

**4.** (a) −2　(b) −7　(c) 5　(d) −5

**5.** (a) 6　(b) −6　(c) −3　(d) 6

**6.** (a) −6　(b) 6　(c) 5　(d) −7

**7.**

| × | −3 | −6 | 8 | −2 |
|---|---|---|---|---|
| 7 | −21 | −42 | 56 | −14 |
| −3 | 15 | 30 | −40 | 10 |
| −4 | 12 | 24 | −32 | 8 |
| 9 | −27 | −54 | 72 | −18 |

**8.**

| × | −7 | 4 | −3 | −8 |
|---|---|---|---|---|
| 4 | −28 | 16 | −12 | −32 |
| −6 | 42 | −24 | 18 | 48 |
| −5 | 35 | −20 | 15 | 40 |
| −7 | 49 | −28 | 21 | −56 |

**9.** (a) −5　(b) 12　(c) 9　(d) −9

**10.** (a) −132　(b) 384　(c) −238　(d) 782

**11.** (a) 4　(b) −8　(c) 16　**12.** (a) −27　(b) 32　(c) −60

## Page 24　E1.9

**1.**

| 20 | ÷ | −4 | → | −5 |
|---|---|---|---|---|
| ÷ | | × | | |
| −10 | × | −3 | → | 30 |
| ↓ | | ↓ | | |
| −2 | × | 12 | → | −24 |

**2.**

| −30 | × | −2 | → | 60 |
|---|---|---|---|---|
| ÷ | | × | | |
| −5 | × | 4 | → | −20 |
| ↓ | | ↓ | | |
| 6 | × | −8 | → | −48 |

**3.**

| −8 | ÷ | −2 | → | 4 |
|---|---|---|---|---|
| × | | × | | |
| 3 | × | −6 | → | −18 |
| ↓ | | ↓ | | |
| −24 | ÷ | 12 | → | −2 |

**4.**

| −8 | + | −4 | → | −12 |
|---|---|---|---|---|
| − | | + | | |
| 2 | − | 12 | → | −10 |
| ↓ | | ↓ | | |
| −10 | + | 8 | → | −2 |

**5.**

| −11 | − | −1 | → | −10 |
|---|---|---|---|---|
| + | | + | | |
| 6 | − | 8 | → | −2 |
| ↓ | | ↓ | | |
| −5 | − | 7 | → | −12 |

**6.**

| −10 | − | −2 | → | −8 |
|---|---|---|---|---|
| − | | − | | |
| −4 | + | 7 | → | 3 |
| ↓ | | ↓ | | |
| −6 | − | −9 | → | 3 |

**7.**

| −10 | ÷ | 5 | → | −2 |
|---|---|---|---|---|
| × | | − | | |
| −2 | × | 9 | → | −18 |
| ↓ | | ↓ | | |
| 20 | ÷ | −4 | → | −5 |

**8.**

| 30 | ÷ | −5 | → | −6 |
|---|---|---|---|---|
| − | | − | | |
| 40 | ÷ | −8 | → | −5 |
| ↓ | | ↓ | | |
| −10 | × | 3 | → | −30 |

**9.**

| −16 | + | 4 | → | −12 |
|---|---|---|---|---|
| ÷ | | × | | |
| −8 | − | −6 | → | −2 |
| ↓ | | ↓ | | |
| 2 | × | −24 | → | −48 |

## Page 25　M1.10

| | | | | | |
|---|---|---|---|---|---|
| **1.** 11 | **2.** 23 | **3.** 10 | **4.** 10 | **5.** 24 | **6.** 40 |
| **7.** 6 | **8.** 5 | **9.** 14 | **10.** 9 | **11.** 56 | **12.** 34 |
| **13.** 4 | **14.** 33 | **15.** 55 | **16.** 17 | **17.** 56 | **18.** 35 |
| **19.** 8 | **20.** 13 | **21.** 5 | **22.** 20 | **23.** 19 | **24.** 5 |
| **25.** 11 | **26.** 18 | **27.** 38 | **28.** 10 | **29.** 14 | **30.** 33 |
| **31.** 19 | **32.** 2 | **33.** 16 | **34.** 10 | **35.** 13 | **36.** 5 |
| **37.** 16 | **38.** 4 | **39.** 1 | **40.** 0 | | |

## Page 26  E1.10

1.  16      2.  6      3.  20      4.  4      5.  20
6.  7      7.  55      8.  17      9.  4      10.  34
11.  56      12.  16      13.  14      14.  10      15.  8
16.  26      17.  78      18.  100      19.  11      20.  2
21.  57      22.  $(3 + 2) \times 5 = 25$      23.  $(7 + 4) \times 4 = 44$
24.  $5 \times (2 + 3) = 25$      25.  $8 + (3 \times 6) = 26$
26.  $5 \times (9 - 4) = 25$      27.  $6 \times (15 - 6) = 54$
28.  $(40 - 25) \times 3 = 45$      29.  $(63 - 7) \div 8 = 7$
30.  $42 \div (6 + 1) = 6$      31.  $(18 - 12) \div (12 \div 4) = 2$
32.  $(16 + 14) \div 2 = 15$      33.  $(7 + 25) \div 4 = 8$
34.  $(7 + 3) \times (8 - 5) = 30$      35.  $(13 + 2) \times 4 = 60$
36.  $(3 + 8 + 19) \div 3 = 10$      37.  $(5 + 6) \times (10 - 4) = 66$

## Page 27  WYM 1

1.  £40      2.  £35      3.  £54      4.  £48      5.  £40
6.  £32.80      7.  £39      8.  £63      9.  £32.90      10.  £63
11.  £61.60      12.  £85      13.  £85.50      14.  £151.50      15.  £121.25

## Page 28    TEST YOURSELF ON UNIT 1

1.  (a) 400    (b) 20    (c) $\frac{9}{100}$    (d) $\frac{6}{10}$    (e) $\frac{7}{1000}$
2.  (a) (i)  3290      (ii)  3300      (iii)  3000
    (b) (i)  5610      (ii)  5600      (iii)  6000
    (c) (i)  12320      (ii)  12300      (iii)  12000
    (d) (i)  22830      (ii)  22800      (iii)  23000
    (e) 4      (f) 8
3.  (a) 92    (b) 315    (c) 6011    (d) 37    (e) 117    (f) 1315
4.  (a) 56    (b) 5600    (c) 972    (d) 2304    (e) 1242
    (f) 3042    (g) 11313    (h) 19186
5.  (a) 171    (b) 328    (c) 326    (d) 54    (e) 67    (f) 53
    (g) 7
6.  (a) $46°$    (b) $-3°C$    (c) $-3$    (d) $-4$    (e) $-4$    (f) 4
    (g) 1    (h) $-12$    (i) $-2$    (j) $-7$
7.  (a) $-24$    (b) 20    (c) $-28$    (d) $-2$    (e) 8    (f) $-72$
    (g) $-8$    (h) 7
8.  (a) 13    (b) 9    (c) 4    (d) 2    (e) 16    (f) 45
    (g) $7 \times (4 + 5)$    (h) $(10 - 7) \times (8 + 2)$

## Page 30    Mixed examination questions

1.  (a) (5, 33) (2, 12) (7, 47)    (b) 4
2.  (a) Ben Nevis, Snowdon, Scafell Pike, Clisham, Sawell, Yes Tor
    (b) $799\,\text{m} < \text{height} < 979\,\text{m}$
3.  (a) 46602    (b) 47000
4.  (a) 43914    (b) 30.5 or 30 remainder 13
5.  (a) $124°C$    (b) (i) $T > -62°\,C$    (ii) $-273° < T < -62$
6.  14

7.  (a) (i)  52602    (ii)  53000
    (b) (i)  in twenty thousand three hundred and eighty seven
        (ii)  20400
8.  (a) Glasgow    (b) $6°C$    (c) Cardiff    (d) Hull    9.  £15244
10.  (a) 7    (b) £2.40    11.  20250

# UNIT 2

## Page 33    M2.1

1.  1, 4, 9, 16, 25, 36, 49, 64, 81, 100, 121, 144
2.  (a) 16    (b) 64    (c) 81    (d) 100    (e) 400
3.  149    4.  39    5.  28    6.  65    7.  34
8.  16    9.  84    10.  81    11.  30
12.  (a) 3    (b) 7    (c) 10    13.  8
14.  (a) 1    (b) 5    (c) 9    (d) 2    (e) 4
15.  (a) 2    (b) 16    (c) 6    (d) 8
16.  (a) 289    (b) 784    (c) 12996    (d) 0.16    (e) 14.44    (f) 0.01
17.  (a) 17    (b) 24    (c) 50    (d) 41    (e) 2.9    (f) 0.3
18.  (a) 0.4    (b) 0.5    (c) 0.6    (d) 0.7    (e) 0.8    (f) 0.9
19.  (a) 49, 16 or 1, 64    (b) 9,1    (c) 25,4    (d) 64,9    (e) 25,36
20.  (a) 8    (b) 5    (c) 60

## Page 35    E2.1

1.  1, 8, 27, 64, 125, 216, 343, 512, 729, 1000
2.  Yes    3.  No    4.  3
5.  (a) 3    (b) 2    (c) 5    (d) 4    (e) 6
6.  (a) 2744    (b) 9261    (c) 3.375    (d) 0.001    (e) 0.008
7.  (a) 15    (b) 24    (c) 40    (d) 0.3    (e) 0.4
8.  (a) 3    (b) 4    (c) 6    9.  (a) 6    (b) 8    (c) 125
10.  (a) 6    (b) 90    (c) 15

## Page 37    M2.2

1.  $8 \times 8 \times 8 \times 8$                2.  $6 \times 6 \times 6 \times 6 \times 6$
3.  $10 \times 10 \times 10 \times 10$            4.  $12 \times 12$
5.  $7 \times 7 \times 7 \times 7 \times 7$        6.  $3 \times 3 \times 3 \times 3 \times 3 \times 3 \times 3$
7.  $8 \times 8 \times 8 \times 8 \times 8 \times 8$    8.  $2 \times 2 \times 2 \times 2 \times 2 \times 2 \times 2 \times 2$
9.  $4^5$    10.  $2^6$    11.  $5^3$    12.  $3^8$    13.  $10^5$    14.  $6^4$
15.  $3^3$    16.  same    17.  45    18.  24    19.  48    20.  72
21.  100    22.  54    23.  64    24.  128

## Page 37    E2.2

1.  (b) $2^5, 32$            (c) $7 \times 7 \times 7, 343$    (d) $8^4, 4096$
    (e) $7 \times 7 \times 7 \times 7 \times 7$    (f) $4^6, 4096$        (g) $5^4, 625$
    (h) 16384                (i) $9^5, 59049$        (j) $10^6, 1000000$
2.  (a) 9 times        (b) $2^{10}$
3.  (a) 625        (b) 3125        (c) 1953125        (d) 244,140,625

## Page 38    Can you still?    2A

**1.** $-7°$ C    **2.** $31°$ C

**3.** (a) $-7$  (b) $2$  (c) $-5$  (d) $-3$  (e) $6$  (f) $-2$

(g) $-2$  (h) $-5$  (i) $-7$  (j) $-1$  (k) $1$  (l) $-7$

**4.** (a) $-2$  (b) $-2$  (c) $5$

## Page 38    M2.3 _____

**1.** 1, 2, 4, 8    **2.** 1, 2, 4, 8, 16        **3.** 1, 11

**4.** 1, 3, 5, 15  **5.** 1, 2, 3, 4, 6, 8, 12, 24  **6.** 1, 19

**7.** 1, 5, 7, 35  **8.** 1, 2, 4, 7, 14, 28      **9.** 1, 2, 4, 5, 8, 10, 20, 40

**10.** 1, 23    **11.** 1, 2, 3, 5, 15, 30  **12.** 1, 2, 3, 6, 7, 14, 21, 42

**13.** 1, 17    **14.** 1, 2, 13, 26      **15.** 1, 2, 5, 10, 25, 50

**16.** 11, 15, 17, 19, 23, 35    **17.** 8, 16, 24, 26, 28, 30, 40, 42, 50

**18.** 11, 17, 19, 23    **19.** 20    **20.** 22    **21.** No  **22.** 21, 28

**23.** 51, 53, 55, 57    **24.** 77

## Page 40    E2.3 _____

**1.** 20, 24, 28, 32, 36, 40    **2.** 21, 28, 35, 42, 49, 56, 63, 70

**3.** 8, 16, 24, 32, 40, 48, 56, 64, 72, 80

**4.** 30, 60, 90, 120, 150, 180, 210, 240, 270, 300

**5.** 16, 32, 48, 64, 80, 96, 112, 128, 144, 160

**6.** 11, 54  **7.** 22, 38, 91  **8.** 23  **9.** 30

**10.** 12, 16, 20; 12, 18, 24, 30 LCM 12

**11.** (a) 30    (b) 21    (c) 45    (d) 70

(e) 6    (f) 40    (g) 60    (h) 60

**12.** 15, 30

## Page 41    M2.4 _____

**1.** (a) 1, 2, 3, ④ ⑥ ⑫    (b) 1, 2, 3, ⑥ ⑨ ⑱    (c) 6

**2.** (a) 1, 2, ④ ⑤ ⑩ ⑳    (b) 1, 2, ③ ⑤ ⑥ ⑩ ⑮ ㉚
(c) 10

**3.** (a) 1, 2, 4, 8, 16, 32    (b) 1, 2, 4, 5, 8, 10, 20, 40    (c) 8

**4.** (a) 1, 2, 3, 4, 6, 8, 12, 24    (b) 1, 2, 3, 4, 6, 9, 12, 18, 36    (c) 12

**5.** (a) 2    (b) 10    (c) 5    (d) 5

(e) 4    (f) 8    (g) 1    (h) 16

**6.** (a) 2    (b) 5    (c) 12

## Page 43    E2.4 _____

**1.** (a) 20 (b) 30 (c) 45 (d) 42 (e) 165 (f) 100

**2.** (a) $70 = \boxed{2} \times \boxed{5} \times \boxed{7}$    (b) $72 = \boxed{3} \times \boxed{3} \times \boxed{2} \times \boxed{2} \times \boxed{2}$

**3.** (a) $24 = \boxed{2} \times \boxed{2} \times \boxed{2} \times \boxed{3}$    (b) $84 = \boxed{2} \times \boxed{2} \times \boxed{3} \times \boxed{7}$

**4.** (a) $2 \times 3 \times 3$      (b) $2 \times 2 \times 7$

(c) $2 \times 11$      (d) $2 \times 2 \times 2 \times 2 \times 2$

(e) $2 \times 2 \times 2 \times 2 \times 3$  (f) $2 \times 5 \times 5$

(g) $3 \times 3 \times 3 \times 3$    (h) $2 \times 2 \times 2 \times 2 \times 2 \times 3$

(i) $2 \times 2 \times 2 \times 5 \times 5$  (j) $2 \times 2 \times 2 \times 3 \times 5$

(k) $2 \times 2 \times 7 \times 7$    (l) $2 \times 2 \times 2 \times 7 \times 7$

**5.** (a) 60  (b) 120  (c) 70

## Page 44    Can you still?    2B

**1.** (a) $-6$  (b) $-20$  (c) $12$  (d) $-30$

(e) $-4$  (f) $-5$  (g) $8$  (h) $6$

(i) $-3$  (j) $-80$  (k) $5$  (l) $-4$

**2.** (a) $-4$  (b) $-9$  (c) $5$

(d) $-2$  (e) $-36$  (f) $-8$

**3.** (a) $9$  (b) $25$  (c) $81$  (d) $-1$  (e) $-16$

## Page 44    M2.5 _____

**1.** $\frac{1}{3}, \frac{2}{6}$  **2.** $\frac{1}{4}, \frac{2}{8}$  **3.** $\frac{6}{12}, \frac{3}{6}$  **4.** $\frac{2}{3}, \frac{4}{6}$  **5.** $\frac{12}{32}, \frac{6}{16}$

**6.** $\frac{4}{6}, \frac{2}{3}$  **7.** $\frac{3}{4}, \frac{9}{12}$  **8.** $\frac{2}{6}, \frac{4}{12}$  **9.** $\frac{1}{4}, \frac{25}{100}$  **10.** $\frac{2}{12}$

**11.** $\frac{14}{16}$  **12.** $\frac{4}{8}$  **13.** $\frac{12}{20}$  **14.** $\frac{16}{20}$  **15.** $\frac{10}{12}$

**16.** $\frac{15}{24}$  **17.** $\frac{12}{21}$  **18.** $\frac{15}{20}$  **19.** $\frac{40}{45}$  **20.** $\frac{18}{60}$

**21.** $\frac{8}{20}$  **22.** $\frac{12}{27}$  **23.** $\frac{9}{18}$  **24.** $\frac{15}{40}$  **25.** $\frac{56}{80}$

**26.** $\frac{24}{160}$  **27.** $\frac{30}{42}$  **28.** $\frac{42}{54}$  **29.** $\frac{24}{66}$  **30.** $\frac{20}{90}$

**31.** $\frac{36}{42}$  **32.** $\frac{27}{300}$  **33.** $\frac{32}{200}$

## Page 45    E2.5 _____

**1.** $\frac{3}{4}$  **2.** $\frac{1}{5}$  **3.** $\frac{1}{3}$  **4.** $\frac{3}{4}$

**5.** $\frac{3}{5}$  **6.** $\frac{3}{5}$  **7.** $\frac{3}{8}$  **8.** $\frac{1}{2}$

**9.** $\frac{5}{6}$  **10.** $\frac{1}{8}$  **11.** $\frac{4}{5}$  **12.** $\frac{2}{3}$

**13.** $\frac{1}{3}$  **14.** $\frac{1}{3}$  **15.** $\frac{1}{2}$  **16.** $\frac{3}{4}$

**17.** (a) $\frac{2}{5}$  (b) $\frac{2}{5}$  (c) $\frac{1}{3}$  (d) $\frac{2}{9}$  (e) $\frac{1}{3}$

(f) $\frac{2}{3}$  (g) $\frac{2}{3}$  (h) $\frac{5}{6}$  (i) $\frac{8}{9}$  (j) $\frac{2}{5}$

(k) $\frac{1}{3}$  (l) $\frac{3}{5}$  (m) $\frac{3}{5}$  (n) $\frac{7}{9}$  (o) $\frac{1}{2}$

(p) $\frac{2}{3}$  (q) $\frac{2}{5}$  (r) $\frac{1}{4}$  (s) $\frac{3}{4}$  (t) $\frac{2}{3}$

**18.** (c) and (f)    **19.** (a) (c) and (d)

**20.** (b) CHINA  (c) PEAR  (d) ENGLISH  (e) HOCKEY

## Page 47    Can you still?    2C

**1.** 19    **2.** 4    **3.** 40    **4.** 18

**5.** 18    **6.** 10    **7.** 27    **8.** 4

**9.** 13    **10.** 26    **11.** 17    **12.** 3

**13.** 15    **14.** 15    **15.** 2    **16.** 14

**17.** $(7 + 4) \times 3 = 33$    **18.** $(25 - 20) \times 4 = 20$

**19.** $(9 + 21) \div 6 = 5$    **20.** $(7 - 2) \times (5 + 1) = 30$

## Page 48    M2.6 _____

**1.** (a) 1/2  (b) 2/5    **2.** 1/2 = 3/6, 1/3 = 2/6, 1/2

**3.** 3/4 = 6/8, 7/8

**4.** (a) 1/3 (b) 1/5 (c) 3/4 (d) 3/4 (e) 2/5 (f) 3/5

**5.** (a) $\frac{1}{6}, \frac{1}{3}, \frac{1}{2}$    (b) $\frac{3}{8}, \frac{1}{2}, \frac{3}{4}$    (c) $\frac{1}{6}, \frac{7}{12}, \frac{2}{3}$

(d) $\frac{3}{10}, \frac{2}{5}, \frac{1}{2}$  (e) $\frac{13}{20}, \frac{7}{10}, \frac{4}{5}$  (f) $\frac{5}{8}, \frac{11}{16}, \frac{3}{4}$

Answers 6

## Page 48    E2.6

1. (a) $\frac{11}{20}$   (b) $\frac{13}{20}$   (c) $\frac{3}{4}$   (d) $\frac{8}{9}$   (e) $\frac{4}{7}$   (f) $\frac{7}{40}$

2. (a) 3/5, 1/2, 9/20   (b) 3/4, 9/16, 3/8
   (c) 5/6, 5/12, 1/4   (d) 2/3, 11/18, 5/9
   (e) 1/2, 1/3, 1/4, 1/6   (f) 3/5, 11/20, 3/10, 1/4

3. 1/2 = 6/12, 1/3 = 4/12, 5/12

4. 1/5 = 4/20, 3/4 = 15/20, Any from 5/20 → 14/20 inc.

5. (a) Any from 4/12 → 7/12 inc.
   (b) 3/10 or 4/10
   (c) Any from 5/12 → 8/12 inc.
   (d) Any from 17/40 → 24/40 inc.
   (e) Any from 9/16 → 13/16 inc.
   (f) Any from 25/56 → 34/56 inc.

## Page 49    Can you still?    2D

1. 9   2. 64   3. 6   4. 9   5. 100   6. 20   7. (b)   8. 1, 8, 27
9. 2   10. 1   11. 27   12. 64   13. 8
14. 72   15. 12   16. 36   17. 3   18. 16 + 25

## Page 51    M2.7

1. T   2. T   3. F   4. T   5. F   6. T
7. T   8. T   9. T   10. F   11. T   12. T
13. $\frac{11}{100}$   14. $\frac{1}{25}$   15. $\frac{9}{10}$   16. $\frac{3}{5}$
17. $\frac{1}{500}$   18. $\frac{37}{100}$   19. $\frac{3}{250}$   20. $\frac{4}{5}$
21. $\frac{7}{20}$   22. $\frac{3}{200}$   23. $\frac{2}{25}$   24. $\frac{9}{20}$
25. $\frac{1}{125}$   26. $\frac{9}{25}$   27. $\frac{1}{8}$   28. $\frac{3}{8}$
29. 0.43   30. 0.7   31. $\frac{8}{10}$ = 0.8   32. $\frac{15}{100}$ = 0.15
33. $\frac{28}{100}$ = 0.28   34. $\frac{34}{100}$ = 0.34
35. $\frac{36}{100}$ = 0.36   36. $\frac{55}{1000}$ = 0.055
37. 0.05   38. 0.45   39. 0.4   40. 0.04
41. 0.12   42. 0.84   43. 0.29   44. 0.015
45. 0.25   46. 0.105   47. 0.125   48. 0.365
49. 0.875   50. 0.75   51. 0.119   52. 0.85
53. $0.\dot{6}$   54. $0.4\dot{5}$   55. $0.\dot{2}$   56. $0.\dot{7}$
57. $0.1\dot{6}$   58. $0.8\dot{3}$

## Page 53    E2.7

1. F   2. T   3. T   4. T   5. F   6. T
7. T   8. T   9. F   10. F   11. <   12. <
13. <   14. =   15. <   16. >   17. <   18. <
19. 30000 → 0.0003
20. 0.008, 0.08, 0.8       21. 0.042, 0.4, 0.41
22. 0.702, 0.72, 0.73      23. 0.83, 0.832, 0.85
24. 0.06, 0.063, 0.61      25. 0.053, 0.503, 0.51, 0.52
26. 0.014, 0.017, 0.1, 0.107   27. 0.03, 0.034, 0.303, 0.31, 0.32
28. 0.087, 0.806, 0.81, 0.812, 0.82   29. 0.06, 0.061, 0.064, 0.603, 0.61

30. 0.015, 0.107, 0.11, 0.121, 0.13
31. 3.04, 3.16, 3.18, 3.2, 3.6
32. 8.019, 8.021, 8.1, 8.13, 8.14
33. 0.51, 0.53, 5.02, 5.1, 5.17
34. 0.19, 1.03, 1.07, 1.16, 1.72
35. EAT MY SHORTS
36. HOW YOU DOING
37. SHARPEN

## Page 55    WYM 2

1. £215   2. £285   3. £396
4. (a) £216   (b) £264   (c) £255   (d) £330 (e) £312
5. £123.75   6. £218.40   7. £254.40   8. £303.40
9. (a) £265.20   (b) £235   (c) £229.60   (d) £303.60   (e) £374
10. £442   11. £446.25   12. Jenny by £1.00

## Page 57    TEST YOURSELF ON UNIT 2

1. (a) 49 (b) 25 (c) 4 (d) 3 (e) 7 (f) 1, 36, 81
2. (a) 8 (b) 64 (c) 4 (d) 2 (e) 125 (f) 1, 8, 27
3. (a) $3 \times 3 \times 3 \times 3$ (b) $2 \times 2 \times 2 \times 2 \times 2$ (c) $6^3$
   (d) $5^4$ (e) $3^6$ (f) 64
4. (a) 1, 2, 3, 6, 9, 18 (b) 1, 2, 4, 8, 16, 32 (c) 3, 5, 7, 17
5. (a) 6, 12, 18, 24, 30 (b) 42, 49 (c) 24, 28 (d) 15 (e) 24 (f) 24
6. (a) 1, 3, 5, 15 (b) 1, 2, 4, 5, 10, 20 (c) 5 (d) 8 (e) 7 (f) 4
7. (a) $2^2 \times 3$ (b) $2^2 \times 3^2$ (c) $2 \times 3^3$ (d) $2^2 \times 5^2$ (e) $2^4 \times 3^2$
8. (a) $\boxed{21}$ /24 (b) $\boxed{20}$ /36 (c) 10/ $\boxed{35}$ (d) $\boxed{18}$ /27
   (e) $\boxed{4}$ /5 (f) 3/ $\boxed{10}$
9. (a) 3/5 (b) 3/8 (c) 3/8 (d) 3/7 (e) 3/4 (f) 1/3
10. (a) 1/4 (b) 2/3 (c) 5/7 (d) 1/4, 3/8, 2/5
    (e) 7/12, 2/3, 3/4, 5/6
11. (a) 37/100 (b) 2/25 (c) 4/5 (d) 7/250 (e) 21/50
12. (a) 0.3   (b) 0.17
    (c) 0.07, 0.071, 0.7   (d) 0.062, 0.064, 0.6, 0.63
    (e) 0.034, 0.318, 0.32, 0.331
    (f) 2.047, 2.14, 2.183, 2.318, 2.714, 2.83

## Page 60    Mixed examination questions

1. $\frac{2}{3}$   2. $\frac{1}{2}, \frac{3}{5}, \frac{5}{8}$
3. (i) 6, 12   (ii) 4, 16   (iii) 3, 4, 6, 12
4. (a) (i) 1000   (ii) 2   (b) (i) 27   (ii) 23 or 29
5. (a) $\frac{7}{20}$   (b) 0.375
6. (a) 1, 2, 5, 10   (b) 23, 29   (c) 216
7. (i) $3^2 \times 5$   (ii) 225
8. $\frac{1}{6}, \frac{3}{8}, \frac{1}{2}, \frac{2}{3}, \frac{3}{4}$     9. (i) $p = 2, q = 3$   (ii) $2 \times 3^2$   (iii) 72

# UNIT 3

## Page 63   M3.1

**1.** b, d   **2.** b, d   **3.** b, d

**4.** (a) Obtuse   (b) Acute   (c) Acute   (d) Reflex   (e) Reflex
(f) Obtuse   (g) Reflex   (h) Acute   (i) Obtuse   (j) Obtuse

**5.** (a) Acute   (b) Obtuse   (c) Acute   (d) Obtuse   (e) Obtuse
(f) Reflex   **6.** (c) No

## Page 64   E3.1

**1.** $P\hat{Q}R$   **2.** $S\hat{T}U$   **3.** $C\hat{A}B$   **4.** $E\hat{F}G$

**5.** $S\hat{P}Q$   **6.** $P\hat{S}R$   **7.** Obtuse

**8.** (a) $I\hat{A}B, B\hat{C}D, C\hat{D}E, D\hat{E}F, F\hat{G}H$, (Any 3)
(b) $A\hat{B}C, E\hat{F}G, G\hat{H}I, H\hat{I}A$ (Any 3)   (c) Obtuse   (d) Acute

**9.** (a) 70°  (b) 60°   **10.** (a) 150°  (b) 30°   **11.** (a) 110°  (b) 60°

## Page 65   M3.2

**1.** $a$ 40°   **2.** $b$ 110°   **3.** $c$ 30°   **4.** $d$ 160°

**5.** $e$ 60°   **6.** $f$ 75°   **7.** $g$ 45°   **8.** $h$ 95°

**9.** $i$ 50°   **10.** $j$ 80°   **11.** $k$ 160°   **12.** $l$ 100°

**13.** $m$ 155°   **14.** $n$ 90°   **15.** $o$ 85°   **16.** $p$ 70°

**17.** $q$ 328°   **18.** $r$ 70°   **19.** $s$ 61°   **20.** $t$ 67°

**21.** $u$ 55°   **22.** $v$ 148°   **23.** $w$ 145°   **24.** $x$ 39°

## Page 67   E3.2

**1.** $a$ 100°   **2.** $b$ 120°   **3.** $c$ 115°

**4.** $d$ 40°, $e$ 140°   **5.** $f$ 90°   **6.** $g$ 60°

**7.** $h$ 65°   **8.** $i$ 50°   **9.** $j$ 80°

**10.** $k$ 30°   **11.** $l$ 30°   **12.** $m$ 85°

**13.** $n$ 25°   **14.** $o$ 75°   **15.** $p$ 42°

**16.** $q$ 63°, $r$ 117°   **17.** $s$ 80°, $t$ 100°   **18.** $u$ 75°, $v$ 105°

**19.** $w$ 59°, $x$ 121°   **20.** $y$ 50°, $z$ 50°   **21.** $a$ 60°, $b$ 60°

**22.** $c$ 58°, $d$ 58°   **23.** $e$ 46°, $f$ 62°   **24.** $g$ 67°, $h$ 42°

**25.** $EF, IJ$

## Page 67   Can you still?   3A

**1.** (a) 15, 105   (b) 18, 72, 936, 3744, 29952
(c) 72, 1656, 19872, 139104

**2.** (a) 4 (b) 9 (c) 32   **3.** (a) 48 (b) 63 (c) 39 (d) 28

## Page 69   M3.3

**1.** $a$ 50°   **2.** $b$ 65°

**3.** $c$ 80°, $d$ 20°   **4.** $e$ 40°, $f$ 100°

**5.** $g$ 35°, $h$ 110°   **6.** $i$ 75°, $j$ 30°

**7.** $k$ 70°, $l$ 70°   **8.** $m$ 80°, $n$ 80°

**9.** $o, p, q$ all 60°   **10.** $r$ 50°, $s$ 50°

**11.** $t$ 65°, $u$ 65°   **12.** $v$ 70°, $w$ 110°

**13.** $a$ 28°, $b$ 152°   **14.** $c$ 25°, $d$ 130°, $e$ 155°

**15.** $f$ 33°, $g$ 114°, $h$ 114°   **16.** $i$ 85°, $j$ 85°, $k$ 85°

**17.** $l$ 42°, $m$ 96°, $n$ 96°   **18.** $o$ 60°, $p$ 120°

**19.** $q$ 45°, $r$ 45°, $s$ 135°   **20.** $t$ 60°, $u$ 60°

## Page 71   E3.3

**1.** $a$ 80°   **2.** $b$ 115°

**3.** $c$ 125°   **4.** $d$ 35°

**5.** $e$ 56°   **6.** $f$ 128°

**7.** $g$ 50°, $h$ 130°   **8.** $i$ 75°, $j$ 105°

**9.** $k$ 60°, $l$ 120°   **10.** $m$ 40°, $n$ 140°

**11.** $o$ 155°, $p$ 25°   **12.** $q$ 63°, $r$ 117°

**13.** $s$ 42°, $t$ 138°   **14.** $u$ 107°, $v$ 73°, $w$ 73°

**15.** $x$ 37°, $y$ 37°, $z$ 143°   **16.** $a$ 71°, $b$ 71°, $c$ 80°, $d$ 100°

**17.** $e$ 48°, $f$ 48°, $g$ 27°, $h$ 27°   **18.** $i$ 67°, $j$ 113°, $k$ 56°, $l$ 124°

**19.** $m$ 90°, $n$ 117°, $o$ 117°   **20.** $p$ 77°, $q$ 103°, $r$ 126°, $s$ 126°, $t$ 54°

**21.** $u$ 30°, $v$ 80°, $w$ 70°   **22.** $x$ 40°, $y$ 65°, $z$ 75°

**23.** $a$ 85°, $b$ 60°, $c$ 35°   **24.** $d$ 100°, $e$ 100°, $f$ 38°, $g$ 142°

## Page 72   Can you still?   3B

**1.** (a) 1, 2, 5, 10   (b) 1, 5, 25   (c) 1, 2, 3, 4, 6, 8, 12, 24

**2.** 15, 22   **3.** 12, 30, 42

**4.** (a) 7, 14, 21, 28, 35, 42 (b) 5, 10, 15, 20, 25, 30, 35, 40 (c) 35

**5.** (a) 28   (b) 18   (c) 24

## Page 73   M3.4

**1.** $a, c, d, f$   **2.** $a, c, f$

## Page 75   E3.4

**1.** 3   **2.** 1   **3.** 2   **4.** 1   **5.** 4   **6.** 2   **7.** 4   **8.** 2

**9.** 5   **10.** 8   **11.** 5   **12.** 1   **13.** 6   **14.** 6   **15.** 4   **16.** 4

## Page 76   M3.5

**2.** (a) 8   (b) 2   (c) 2

## Page 77   Can you still?   3C

**1.** (a) $2 \times 2 \times 3 \times 5$   (b) $2 \times 2 \times 2 \times 2 \times 5$

**2.** (a) $2 \times 3 \times 5$   (b) $2 \times 2 \times 3 \times 3$   (c) $2 \times 5 \times 5$
(d) $2 \times 2 \times 2 \times 2 \times 3 \times 3$

**3.** (a) 1, 2, 4, 7, 14, 28   (b) 1, 3, 7, 21   (c) 7

**4.** (a) 12   (b) 15   (c) 27

## Page 77   M3.6

**1.** $A, B, D, F$   **2.** (a) Equal/90°   (b) equal   **4.** (b) 4

**5.** (a) yes   (b) 4   (c) 4   **6.** (a) equal   (b) equal

**8.** (a) 2   **9.** (a) yes   (b) 2   **10.** $B, E, F$   **12.** (b) 2

**13.** (a) yes   (b) 2   (c) 2

**15.** (a) 0   (c) 0   **16.** (a) yes   (b) 2   (c) 2   **17.** $A, C, D$

**21.** (a) 1   (c) 1   **22.** (a) No   (b) 0   (c) 0

**26.** 90°   **27.** (a) $a, c, f$   (b) $a, b$   (c) $a, b, c, f$

## Page 81   E3.6

**1.** $a$ 60°   **2.** $b$ 100°   **3.** $c$ 120°   **4.** $d$ 140°

**5.** $e$ 35°   **6.** $f$ 125°   **7.** $g$ 96°, $h$ 84°   **8.** $i$ 42°, $j$ 138°

**9.** $k$ 57°, $l$ 115°

**10.** $m$ 45°, $n$ 135°

**11.** $o$ 50°

**12.** $p$ 55°

**13.** $q$ 73°

**14.** $r$ 91°, $s$ 91°

**15.** $t$ 90°

**16.** $u$ 107°, $v$ 107°

**17.** $w$ 100°, $x$ 100°

**18.** $y$ 115°, $z$ 115°, $a$ 40°

**19.** $b$ 115°

**20.** $c$ 120°

**21.** $d$ 72°, $e$ 72°, $f$ 45°

**22.** $g$ 28°

**23.** $h$ 100°, $i$ 80°, $j$ 80°, $k$ 20°

**24.** $l$ 126°, $m$ 54°, $n$ 54°, $o$ 72°

## Page 82    Can you still?    3D

**1.** $\frac{4}{12}$    **2.** $\frac{12}{30}$    **3.** $\frac{12}{40}$    **4.** $\frac{10}{15}$    **5.** $\frac{15}{27}$

**6.** $\frac{20}{35}$    **7.** $\frac{4}{5}$    **8.** $\frac{5}{7}$    **9.** $\frac{1}{4}$    **10.** $\frac{1}{3}$

**11.** $\frac{1}{4}$    **12.** $\frac{3}{5}$    **13.** $\frac{2}{3}$    **14.** $\frac{3}{5}$    **15.** $\frac{4}{9}$

**16.** $\frac{5}{7}$    **17.** $\frac{3}{8}$    **18.** $\frac{9}{11}$    **19.** b, c, e    **20.** a, b, d

## Page 83    M3.7

**1.** $a$ 70°

**2.** $b$ 74°, $c$ 68°

**3.** $d$ 74°, $e$ 24°

**4.** $f$ 70°, $g$ 70°

**5.** $h$ 40°, $i$ 100°

**6.** $j$ 112°

**7.** $k$ 108°, $l$ 72°

**8.** $m$ 22°

**9.** $n$ 76°, $o$ 95°, $p$ 85°

**10.** $q$ 170°

**11.** $r$ 61°, $s$ 119°

**12.** $t$ 120°

**13.** $u$ 118°, $v$ 118°, $w$ 62°

**14.** $x$ 37° , $y$ 37°, $z$ 106°

**15.** $a$ 150°, $b$ 30°

**16.** $c$ 35°, $d$ 35°

**17.** $e$ 51°, $f$ 85°, $g$ 95°

**18.** $h$ 50°

**19.** $i$ 45°, $j$ 135°

**20.** $k$ 74°, $l$ 106°, $m$ 84°, $n$ 96°

**21.** $o$ 40°

**22.** $p$ 50°, $q$ 130°, $r$ 25°

**23.** $s$ 65°, $t$ 75°, $u$ 75°

**24.** $v$ 28°, $w$ 76°, $x$ 76°

## Page 83    Can you still?    3E

**1.** 4    **2.** 8    **3.** 1    **4.** 6

**5.** (a) 6420    (b) 6400    (c) 6000

**6.** (a) 8910    (b) 8900    (c) 9000

**7.** (a) 13150    (b) 13100    (c) 13000

**8.** (a) 36880    (b) 36900    (c) 37000    **9.** 47

**10.** 242    **11.** 7    **12.** 40    **13.** 28    **14.** 7    **15.** 1

**16.** 15    **17.** 32

## Page 87    E3.8

**1.** $a$ 108°,    $b$ 90°,    $c$ 120°,    $d$ 144°

**2.** $a$ 76°,    $b$ 141°,    $c$ 122°,    $d$ 67°,    $e$ 51°,    $f$ 128°,    $g$ 113°,    $h$ 122°,    $i$ 85°,    $j$ 92°,    $k$ 88°

**3.** $a$ 30°,    $b$ 150°    **4.** $a$ 40°,    $b$ 140°

**5.** $a$ 24°,    $b$ 18°,    $c$ 6°,    $d$ 4°

**6.** $a$ 156°,    $b$ 162°,    $c$ 174°,    $d$ 176°

**7.** 45    **8.** 18    **9.** 30    **10.** 165°

## Page 89    WYM 3

**1.** £684    **2.** £642    **3.** £1652    **4.** £834

**5.** £2810    **6.** £840    **7.** £5580    **8.** £2284

## Page 90    TEST YOURSELF ON UNIT 3

**1.** (a) Obtuse    (b) Acute (c) Obtuse (d) Rt. angle (e) Reflex (f) Rt. angle (g) Acute (h) Obtuse

**2.** (a) $P\hat{Q}R$ (b) $F\hat{G}H$ (c) $A\hat{B}D$ (d) $P\hat{R}Q$

**3.** $a$ 35°, $b$ 109°, $c$ 110°

**4.** $a$ 67°, $b$ 39°,    $c$ 41°, $d$ 41°

**5.** $a$ 80°, $b$ 80°,    $c$, 64°, $d$ 52°, $e$ 52°, $f$ 60°, $g$ 120°

**6.** $a$ 74°, $b$ 123°, $c$ 79°, $d$ 79°, $e$ 75°, $f$ 105°

**7.** (a) (i) 2 (ii) 2    (b) (i) 4 (ii) 4    (c) (i) 1 (ii) 1

**8.** (a) trapezium (i) 0 (ii) 0    (b) rhombus    (i) 2    (ii) 2    (c) Kite (i) 1 (ii) 0    (d) parallelogram    (i) 0    (ii) 2

**9.** $a$ 70°, $b$ 80°, $c$ 80°, $d$ 120°, $e$ 60°

## Page 92    Mixed examination questions

**1.** (i) Acute angle    (ii) 180°

**2.** (a) 54°    (b) (i) 72°

**3.** (a) 4    (b) 2    (c) 1

**4.** $x = 11°$, $y = 53°$, $z = 42°$

**5.** 64°    **7.** 142°

# UNIT 4

## Page 95    M4.1

| | | | | |
|---|---|---|---|---|
| **1.** 24 | **2.** 12 | **3.** 10 | **4.** 4 | **5.** 8 |
| **6.** 7 | **7.** 12 | **8.** 22 | **9.** 16 | **10.** 36 |
| **11.** 40 | **12.** 24 | **13.** 6 | **14.** 20 | **15.** 1 |
| **16.** 12 | **17.** 36 | **18.** 16 | **19.** 3 | **20.** 4 |
| **21.** 18 | **22.** 16 | **23.** 1 | **24.** 35 | **25.** 31 |
| **26.** 11 | **27.** 11 | **28.** 2 | **29.** 30 | **30.** 9 |
| **31.** 9 | **32.** 9 | **33.** 0 | **34.** 0 | **35.** 0 |
| **36.** 73 | **37.** 42 | **38.** 24 | **39.** 292 | **40.** 2 |
| **41.** 14 | **42.** 23 | **43.** 19 | **44.** 40 | **45.** 12 |
| **46.** 19 | **47.** 16 | **48.** 9 | **49.** 18 | |

## Page 96    E4.1

| | | | | |
|---|---|---|---|---|
| **1.** 65 | **2.** 25 | **3.** 100 | **4.** 400 | **5.** 64 |
| **6.** 98 | **7.** 48 | **8.** 140 | **9.** 82 | **10.** 23 |
| **11.** 90 | **12.** 34 | **13.** 44 | **14.** 196 | **15.** 3 |
| **16.** 54 | **17.** 104 | **18.** 50 | **19.** 186 | **20.** 10 |
| **21.** 46 | **22.** 18 | **23.** 3 | **24.** 0 | **25.** 16 |
| **26.** −6 | **27.** 14 | **28.** −9 | **29.** −20 | **30.** 6 |
| **31.** 14 | **32.** −11 | **33.** −20 | **34.** 4 | **35.** 20 |
| **36.** 18 | **37.** −30 | **38.** −2 | **39.** 24 | **40.** −27 |
| **41.** 36 | **42.** 48 | **43.** 27 | **44.** −5 | **45.** 11 |

## Page 97  M4.2

| | | | | |
|---|---|---|---|---|
| **1.** 17 | **2.** 15 | **3.** 10 | **4.** 3 | **5.** 33 |
| **6.** 22 | **7.** 26 | **8.** 34 | **9.** 44 | **10.** 6 |
| **11.** 16 | **12.** 12 | **13.** 56 | **14.** 752 | **15.** 943 |
| **16.** 14.76 | **17.** 85 | **18.** 761 | **19.** 34.1 | **20.** 25.89 |
| **21.** 60 | **22.** 30.38 | **23.** 14 | **24.** 41 | **25.** 5 |

## Page 99  E4.2

**1.** (a) 29 (b) 9 (c) 52          **2.** (a) 112 (b) 300 (c) 101

**3.** (a) 43 (b) 32 (c) 38          **4.** (a) $720°$ (b) $18000°$

**5.** (a) 29 (b) $-6$ (c) 2          **6.** (a) 39 (b) $-33$ (c) $-27$

**7.** (a) 75 (b) 300 (c) 12 (d) 192          **8.** (a) 600 (b) 300

**9.** (a) 2 (b) 15 (c) 21 (d) 9          **10.** (a) 13 (b) 125 (c) $-1$

**11.** 52          **12.** (a) 3 (b) $-5$

**13.** (a) 3 (b) 1          **14.** (a) $-2$ (b) 2

**15.** (a) 5 (b) 9 (c) 5          **16.** (a) 7 (b) 13 (c) 17

**17.** (a) 6 (b) 2 (c) $-9$          **18.** (a) 53 (b) 58 (c) 2000

**19.** (a) 2 (b) 6 (c) 4

## Page 102  M4.3

| | | | |
|---|---|---|---|
| **1.** $5a + 4b$ | **2.** $12a$ | **3.** $7a + 4b$ | **4.** $7p + 8q$ |
| **5.** $11p + 5q$ | **6.** $7p + 9q$ | **7.** $13p + 8q$ | **8.** $4x + 5y$ |
| **9.** $3y$ | **10.** $5x + 3y$ | **11.** $9a$ | **12.** $15x + 4y$ |
| **13.** $9x$ | **14.** $4x + 2y$ | **15.** $11a + 1$ | **16.** $7x - 3$ |
| **17.** $5p + 8q$ | **18.** $14c - 2$ | **19.** $18a + 4$ | **20.** $4x + 9y$ |
| **21.** $3c + 9$ | **22.** $16c + 15$ | **23.** $6a + 12b + 14$ | |
| **24.** $15a + 14$ | **25.** $15x + 8y + 18$ | **26.** $5m + 2n$ | |
| **27.** $5a + 8b$ | **28.** $3b$ | **29.** $17x + 7y$ | |
| **30.** $8a + 10$ | **31.** $11x + 4$ | **32.** $2p + q$ | |
| **33.** $8a + 7$ | **34.** $5a + 3b - 2$ | **35.** $5x + y$ | |

## Page 103  E4.3

| | | | |
|---|---|---|---|
| **1.** $9a$ | **2.** $2c$ | **3.** $-6a$ | **4.** $5b$ |
| **5.** 0 | **6.** $10a + 3b$ | **7.** $7p + 7q$ | **8.** $10m - 2n$ |
| **9.** $-2a + b$ | **10.** $b$ | **11.** $2a - 2b$ | **12.** $-3x$ |
| **13.** $4p + 6$ | **14.** $-4p - 2$ | **15.** $4a - 2$ | **16.** $5x - y$ |
| **17.** $9a - 2$ | **18.** $2c - 7$ | **19.** $-3p + 2q$ | **20.** $5a - 9$ |

**21.** $3x - 5$   **22.** (a) $13a + 6b - 6$ (b) $5a + 6b - 7$ (c) $8a + 6b - 8$

**23.** $9c + 11d + 4$   **24.** $8x + x^2$          **25.** $12x^2$

**26.** $7x^2 + 8x$   **27.** $12a^2 + 9a$          **28.** $5ab + a$

**29.** $8ab + 5a$   **30.** $3xy$          **31.** $3xy - 5$

**32.** $17ab + 6$   **33.** $6xy$          **34.** $10ab - 2a + 4b$

**35.** $3xy - 3x$   **36.** $5a^2 + 7$          **37.** $12a^2 - 5a$

**38.** $7ab + 7a^2$   **39.** $9x^2 + y^2 + 2x - y$   **40.** $2a^2 + 4ab + 6a$

**41.** $-2pq + 5p$

## Page 104  Can you still?  4A

| | | | |
|---|---|---|---|
| **1.** 0.07 | **2.** 0.19 | **3.** 0.75 | **4.** 0.2 |
| **5.** 0.15 | **6.** 0.36 | **7.** $\frac{3}{10}$ | **8.** $\frac{67}{100}$ |

**9.** $\frac{25}{100} = \frac{1}{4}$   **10.** $\frac{4}{10} = \frac{2}{5}$   **11.** $\frac{8}{100} = \frac{2}{25}$   **12.** $\frac{32}{100} = \frac{8}{25}$

**13.** $\frac{4}{5}$          **14.** 0.28          **15.** $\frac{7}{20}$

## Page 105  M4.4

| | | | | |
|---|---|---|---|---|
| **1.** $8x$ | **2.** $15x$ | **3.** $16x$ | **4.** $8y$ | **5.** $20y$ |
| **6.** $42a$ | **7.** $80x$ | **8.** $36a$ | **9.** $18d$ | **10.** $24c$ |
| **11.** $36p$ | **12.** $45x$ | **13.** $14c$ | **14.** $27d$ | **15.** $48x$ |
| **16.** $2x$ | **17.** $6x$ | **18.** $2p$ | **19.** $5x$ | **20.** $7A$ |
| **21.** $3Q$ | **22.** $7n$ | **23.** $3A$ | **24.** $9N$ | **25.** $4r$ |
| **26.** $10t$ | **27.** $12T$ | **28.** $7a$ | **29.** $8R$ | **30.** $4b$ |
| **31.** $a^2$ | **32.** $c^2$ | **33.** $Q^2$ | **34.** $3c^2$ | **35.** $4p^2$ |
| **36.** $5d^2$ | **37.** $2r^2$ | **38.** $B^2$ | **39.** $5c^2$ | **40.** $6a^2$ |
| **41.** $8ab$ | **42.** $18y^2$ | **43.** $14a^2$ | **44.** $25t^2$ | |

## Page 105  E4.4

| | | | |
|---|---|---|---|
| **1.** $6ab$ | **2.** $18xy$ | **3.** $10pq$ | **4.** $21e^2$ |
| **5.** $24mn$ | **6.** $54c^2$ | **7.** $24x^2$ | **8.** $16B^2$ |
| **9.** $45PQ$ | **10.** $36uv$ | **11.** $4c$ | **12.** $5A$ |
| **13.** $8p$ | **14.** $8x$ | **15.** $abc$ | **16.** $12abc$ |
| **17.** $60xyz$ | **18.** $72abcd$ | **19.** $T$ | **20.** $T$ |
| **21.** $F$ | **22.** $T$ | **23.** $F$ | **24.** $T$ |
| **25.** $T$ | **26.** $T$ | **27.** $T$ | **28.** $F$ |
| **29.** $F$ | **30.** $F$ | **31.** $T$ | **32.** $F$ |
| **33.** $T$ | **34.** $-m^2$ | **35.** $-6ab$ | **36.** $-20cd$ |
| **37.** $8xy$ | **38.** $-3y$ | **39.** $3a$ | **40.** $-2p$ |
| **41.** $18cd$ | **42.** $-40xy$ | **43.** $-7q$ | **44.** $-54y$ |
| **45.** $-21a^2$ | **46.** $7x$ | **47.** $-54ab$ | **48.** $54P^2$ |

## Page 106  Can you still?  4B

| | | | | |
|---|---|---|---|---|
| **1.** $-2$ | **2.** $-10$ | **3.** 1 | **4.** $-6$ | **5.** $-8$ |
| **6.** $-4$ | **7.** $-13$ | **8.** $-5$ | **9.** $-13$ | **10.** 0 |
| **11.** $-24$ | **12.** 24 | **13.** 30 | **14.** $-18$ | **15.** $-16$ |
| **16.** $-4$ | **17.** 8 | **18.** $-4$ | **19.** $-6$ | **20.** 7 |

## Page 107  M4.5

| | | |
|---|---|---|
| **1.** $2a + 6$ | **2.** $16y - 8$ | **3.** $24x - 12$ |
| **4.** $15x + 20$ | **5.** $21x - 35$ | **6.** $28y + 8$ |
| **7.** $5a - 5b$ | **8.** $4a + 2b$ | **9.** $21x + 7y$ |
| **10.** $3x + 6y$ | **11.** $18x + 12$ | **12.** $4p + 4q$ |
| **13.** $4p + 8q$ | **14.** $18a - 30b$ | **15.** $36c + 72d$ |
| **16.** $x^2 + xy$ | **17.** $2x^2 + xy$ | **18.** $ab - ac$ |
| **19.** $ab + a^2$ | **20.** $p^2 - pq$ | **21.** $2c^2 + cd$ |
| **22.** $p^2 + 3p$ | **23.** $a^2 - 7a$ | **24.** $3a^2 + 3a$ |
| **25.** $5xy + 10x$ | **26.** $3bc + 6bd$ | **27.** $4a^2 + 8ab$ |
| **28.** $6m^2 - 15mn$ | **29.** $24ab - 48ac$ | **30.** $6x^2 + 9xy$ |

## Page 108   E4.5

1. $-2x - 12$
2. $-5y + 15$
3. $-3a + 6$
4. $-2x - 8$
5. $-5c - 50$
6. $-6x + 2y$
7. $-12p + 20$
8. $-10a - 5$
9. $-32b + 8$
10. $-6c - 12$
11. $-15a - 6$
12. $-18x + 18$
13. $-20a + 24$
14. $9b - 21$
15. $7 - 14x$
16. $-ab - ac$
17. $-ef + eg$
18. $-x^2 + xy$
19. $-2p^2 - pq$
20. $-3y^2 - yz$
21. $-2x^2 + xy$
22. $-a^2 - ab$
23. $-m^2 + mn$
24. $-3x + y$
25. $-2p - 5q$
26. $-3a^2 - 3ab$
27. $6ab - 4b^2$
28. $15x^2 - 10xy$

## Page 108   M4.6

1. $2x + 11$
2. $10x + 8$
3. $14x + 8$
4. $22x + 20$
5. $18x + 13$
6. $4a + 12$
7. $16a + 18$
8. $27y + 12$
9. $9a + 12$
10. $9x + 24$
11. $12x + 18$
12. $14a + 7$
13. $14a + 18$
14. $26x + 25$
15. $26d + 32$
16. $18x + 15$
17. $11a + 4$
18. $28x + 5$
19. $22a + 20$
20. $19x + 3$

## Page 109   E4.6

1. $10a + 10$
2. $6x + 11$
3. $4x + 10$
4. $9a + 7$
5. $13$
6. $4y - 13$
7. $5x + 17$
8. $14a - 5$
9. $3x + 18$
10. $2c + 26$
11. $11a + 22$
12. $2c + 54$
13. $6c + 10$
14. $4x + 26$
15. $a + 5$
16. $21a + 48$
17. $21m + 3n$
18. $7a + 2b$
19. $7x + 42$
20. $8x + 22$

## Page 110   M4.7

1. (a) $x^2 + 7x + 12$ (b) $x^2 + 7x + 6$ (c) $x^2 + 13x + 36$
2. $x^2 + 8x + 12$
3. $p^2 + 6p + 5$
4. $a^2 + 10a + 21$
5. $m^2 + 10m + 16$
6. $y^2 + 9y + 18$
7. $n^2 + 2n + 1$
8. $x^2 + 10x + 21$
9. $y^2 + 9y + 20$
10. $p^2 + 13p + 30$
11. $a^2 + 16a + 63$
12. $f^2 + 12f + 32$
13. $y^2 + 14y + 48$
14. $a^2 + 5a + 6$
15. $x^2 + 14x + 40$
16. $x^2 + 6x + 9$
17. $x^2 + 6x + 9$
18. $x^2 + 10x + 25$
19. $x^2 + 16x + 64$
20. $x^2 + 4x + 4$
21. $x^2 + 18x + 81$

## Page 111   E4.7

1. (a) $x^2 - 4x - 12$ (b) $a^2 - 2a - 15$ (c) $m^2 - 14m + 49$
2. $m^2 + 2m - 3$
3. $n^2 - 3n - 10$
4. $b^2 - 5b - 24$
5. $x^2 + 2x - 48$
6. $c^2 - 11c + 24$
7. $q^2 - 9q + 14$
8. $f^2 - 12f + 20$
9. $a^2 + 5a - 36$
10. $y^2 - 13y + 36$
11. $x^2 - 8x + 16$
12. $x^2 - 8x + 16$
13. $x^2 - 12x + 36$
14. $m^2 - 2m + 1$
15. $y^2 - 20y + 100$
16. $a^2 - 16a + 64$
17. $n^2 + 5n + 6$
18. $x^2 + 11x + 30$
19. $12 - y - y^2$
20. $2x^2 + 8x + 10$
21. $2n^2 + 4n + 20$

## Page 112   Can you still?   4C

1. 0.04, 0.35, 0.4
2. 0.089, 0.09, 0.1
3. 0.04, 0.14, 0.2, 0.53
4. 0.12, 0.21, 1.12, 1.2
5. 0.09, 0.85, 2.04, 2.4
6. 0.137, 0.37, 0.4, 0.703, 0.73
7. 0.091, 0.109, 0.19, 0.901, 0.91
8. 0.608, 0.628, 0.68, 0.806, 0.816, 0.86

## Page 113   M4.8

1. $3(2a + 5)$
2. $3(3c + 2)$
3. $5(x - 3)$
4. $6(2a + 3)$
5. $5(3m + 4)$
6. $7(n - 5)$
7. $8(x + 4)$
8. $9(x + 4)$
9. $7(2a - 5)$
10. $8(2n - 3)$
11. $9(5x + 4)$
12. $8(6a - 5)$
13. $2(4a + 5)$
14. $3(2x + 9)$
15. $5(x - 4)$
16. $6(m + 7)$
17. $5(5a - 7)$
18. $4(4x - 1)$
19. $9(3p - 2)$
20. $6(3a + 4b)$
21. $8(2x + 5y)$
22. $7(2a - 3b)$
23. $4(6m - 5n)$
24. $7(3x + 4y)$
25. $8(7a + 4b)$
26. $10(2x - y)$
27. $9(4x - 3y)$
28. $8(9c + 5d)$
29. $5(2a + 3b + 5c)$
30. $3(2p + 3q + r)$
31. $7(x + 2y - z)$
32. $3(3a - 3b - 7c)$
33. $4(6m + 3n + 4p)$
34. $7(6a + 5b - 2)$
35. $9(2a - 3b + 4c)$
36. $4(7x - 9y + 4)$

## Page 114   E4.8

1. $x(y + z)$
2. $a(b - c)$
3. $x(x + 6)$
4. $a(5 + a)$
5. $3b(b - 4)$
6. $c(d + c)$
7. $3x(y + 5z)$
8. $8b(a - 3c)$
9. $4x(3x - 2)$
10. $m(6m - 1)$
11. $f(e + g)$
12. $p(p + 3)$
13. $a(7 - a)$
14. $x(x - 8)$
15. $a(a + 5)$
16. $2p(q + 2r)$
17. $4b(2a - 3c)$
18. $3y(2x - 3z)$
19. $5x(x - 3)$
20. $5s(t + 7)$
21. $8p(r - 5q)$
22. $2b(3a + 2)$
23. $a(3a + 8)$
24. $4x(3 - 4x)$
25. $x(x + y)$
26. $3x(x + 7y)$
27. $10b(2a - 5)$
28. $a^2(b - c)$
29. $a(a + bc)$
30. $x(5x - 6y)$
31. $10p(2p - 3q)$
32. $4b(9ac - 4b)$
33. $7x(7x + 6y)$
34. $7a(9a - 5b)$

## Page 115   WYM 4

1. 290 E
2. 6944 Pesos
3. 358.50 Aus$
4. 10782 Rand
5. £165
6. £600
7. £68
8. 3105.36 riyals
9. £700
10. £15.00
11. Japan
12. Australia
13. Shabina
14. £76.80
15. £38.80

## Page 116   TEST YOURSELF ON UNIT 4

1. (a) 15 (b) 17 (c) 81 (d) 22
   (e) 65 (f) −9 (g) 12

2. (a) 17 (b) 11 (c) 124.62 (d) 45 (e) 7

**3.** (a) $6x + 7y$    (b) $5a + 6b$    (c) $7p + 2$
   (d) $6m + 4n$    (e) $5x + 3$    (f) $x$
   (g) $3p + q$    (h) $3x^2$    (i) $4a + 5ab$

**4.** (a) $15a$    (b) $14c$    (c) $A^2$    (d) $6b^2$
   (e) $3p$    (f) $9b$    (g) $24mn$    (h) $4F$

**5.** (a) $3x + 21$    (b) $12a - 6b$    (c) $5x + 25y$
   (d) $pq + 6p$    (e) $2a^2 - 5a$    (f) $2b^2 + 3bc$
   (g) $3xy - 6x^2$    (h) $-8a + 4b$    (i) $x^2 + 10x + 21$
   (j) $y^2 - 4y - 12$    (k) $p^2 - 4p + 4$

**6.** (a) $5a + 13$    (b) $7x + 20$    (c) $8x + 36$
   (d) $23m + 17$    (e) $14a + 19$    (f) $x + 6$

**7.** (a) $5(x + 3)$    (b) $8(a - 3)$    (c) $7(5p - 3)$
   (d) $2(2a + 5b - 4c)$    (e) $c(d + e)$    (f) $x(x - 4y)$
   (g) $2q(3p - 5r)$    (h) $5a(a + 6b)$

## Page 118    Mixed examination questions

**1.** 35    **2.** (a) (i) $4c$ (ii) $4r - p$   (b) (i) 27 (ii) 16

**3.** (a) $2a$   (b) 14    **4.** $2x - y + 4z$    **5.** (a) $x + 1$   (b) 3

**6.** (a) (i) 21 (ii) $-2$   (b) $14x + 21y$

**7.** (a) $3x$   (b) $3a + 2b$ (c) $3a + 6$ (d) $8x + 1$

**8.** (a) (i) $5p - q$ (ii) $12xy$   (b) (i) $15h - 10$ (ii) $-3r + 4$

**9.** (a) $F = 2c + 30$   (b) (i) 138 (ii) 12    **10.** $14x + 7$

**11.** (i) $5(2x + 3)$ (ii) $x(x - 3)$    **12.** $a(a + 3)$

**13.** (a) $x + 2$   (b) $4x + 14$

# UNIT 5

## Page 120   M5.1

**1.** a, d

**2.** (a) $\frac{5}{8}$   (b) $\frac{1}{6}$   (c) $\frac{1}{4}$   (d) $\frac{3}{8}$   (e) $\frac{5}{6}$   (f) $\frac{7}{9}$   (g) $\frac{5}{16}$   (h) $\frac{7}{12}$

**3.** (a) $\frac{18}{33}$   (b) $\frac{15}{33}$    **4.** $\frac{3}{5}$    **5.** $\frac{1}{6}$    **6.** $\frac{5}{14}$    **7.** $\frac{1}{3}$

**8.** (a) $\frac{1}{10}$   (b) $\frac{1}{4}$   (c) $\frac{2}{5}$   (d) $\frac{3}{100}$   (e) $\frac{13}{20}$   (f) $\frac{12}{25}$

**9.** $\frac{19}{100}$    **10.** (a) 3   (b) 7   (c) 13   (d) 25

**11.** (a) 5   (b) 9   (c) 8   (d) 20

**12.** (a) 3   (b) 8   (c) 12   (d) 20

**13.** £7    **14.** £7    **15.** $6g$    **16.** 8    **17.** 12    **18.** 24

**19.** 12    **20.** 35    **21.** 8    **22.** $36\,l$    **23.** $63\,\text{kg}$    **24.** 18

**25.** £48    **26.** £84    **27.** $850\,\text{m}$    **28.** 162    **29.** £96    **30.** £1866

**31.** $1\frac{1}{2}\,l$    **32.** 16    **33.** $70\,\text{cm}$    **34.** $125\,\text{kg}$    **35.** £7.50

## Page 122   E5.1

**1.** 33    **2.** 27    **3.** 15    **4.** 100    **5.** £48    **6.** 72 g

**7.** £200    **8.** $84\,\text{cm}$    **9.** £7    **10.** PERFECT    **11.** £12

## Page 123    Can you still?    5A

**1.** $a\ 140°$    **2.** $b\ 85°$    **3.** $c\ 80°$   **4.** $d\ 49°$

**5.** $e\ 65°,\ f\ 115°$    **6.** $g\ 61°,\ h\ 69°$

**7.** $i\ 93°$    **8.** $j\ 42°,\ k\ 42°$

## Page 124   M5.2

**1.** $3\frac{1}{2}$    **2.** $2\frac{1}{6}$    **3.** $3\frac{3}{4}$    **4.** $3\frac{2}{3}$    **5.** $2\frac{1}{4}$

**6.** $2\frac{1}{7}$    **7.** $3\frac{1}{8}$    **8.** $1\frac{3}{4}$    **9.** $2\frac{6}{7}$    **10.** $2\frac{1}{9}$

**11.** $2\frac{1}{2}$    **12.** $5\frac{5}{6}$    **13.** $7\frac{2}{3}$    **14.** $8\frac{1}{2}$    **15.** $5\frac{1}{8}$

**16.** $5\frac{4}{5}$    **17.** $2\frac{5}{6}$    **18.** $3\frac{2}{9}$    **19.** $8\frac{4}{5}$    **20.** $6\frac{3}{4}$

## Page 124   E5.2

**1.** $\frac{7}{3}$    **2.** $\frac{7}{2}$    **3.** $\frac{19}{4}$    **4.** $\frac{17}{3}$    **5.** $\frac{9}{2}$    **6.** $\frac{23}{4}$

**7.** $\frac{19}{3}$    **8.** $\frac{31}{8}$    **9.** $\frac{14}{3}$    **10.** $\frac{28}{5}$    **11.** $\frac{29}{9}$    **12.** $\frac{31}{7}$

**13.** $\frac{35}{4}$    **14.** $\frac{67}{9}$    **15.** $\frac{68}{7}$    **16.** $\frac{32}{5}$    **17.** $\frac{62}{7}$    **18.** $\frac{43}{8}$

## Page 125    Can you still?    5B

**1.** $a\ 55°$      **2.** $b\ 80°$

**3.** $c\ 75°\ d\ 30°$    **4.** $e\ 38°\ f\ 142°$

**5.** $g\ 60°\ h\ 60°$    **6.** $i\ 54°\ j\ 54°\ k\ 72°$

**7.** $l\ 72°\ m\ 72°$    **8.** $q\ 60°\ r\ 120°$

## Page 126   M5.3

**1.** $\frac{3}{5}$   **2.** $\frac{5}{7}$   **3.** $\frac{6}{7}$   **4.** $\frac{7}{9}$   **5.** $\frac{6}{8}\left(\frac{3}{4}\right)$   **6.** $\frac{5}{10}\left(\frac{1}{2}\right)$   **7.** $\frac{2}{7}$

**8.** $\frac{4}{11}$   **9.** $\frac{8}{20}\left(\frac{2}{5}\right)$   **10.** $\frac{7}{10}$   **11.** $\frac{3}{9}\left(\frac{1}{3}\right)$   **12.** $\frac{2}{8}\left(\frac{1}{4}\right)$

**13.** (a) $\frac{3}{11}$   (b) $\frac{5}{11}$   (c) $\frac{8}{11}$   (d) $\frac{9}{11}$   (e) $\frac{10}{11}$

**14.** (a) $\frac{5}{9}$   (b) $\frac{2}{9}$   (c) $\frac{6}{9}\left(\frac{2}{3}\right)$   (d) $\frac{1}{9}$   (e) $\frac{3}{9}\left(\frac{1}{3}\right)$

**15.** c      **16.** b      **17.** b

**18.** $\frac{3}{15} + \frac{10}{15} = \frac{13}{15}$    **19.** $\frac{21}{28} - \frac{8}{28} = \frac{13}{28}$    **20.** $\frac{15}{40} + \frac{12}{40} = \frac{27}{40}$

**21.** $\frac{7}{15}$   **22.** $\frac{3}{8}$   **23.** $\frac{9}{10}$   **24.** $\frac{5}{6}$   **25.** $\frac{7}{10}$   **26.** $\frac{1}{8}$

**27.** $\frac{1}{20}$   **28.** $\frac{3}{8}$   **29.** $\frac{1}{12}$   **30.** $\frac{5}{6}$   **31.** $\frac{11}{12}$   **32.** $\frac{5}{12}$

**33.** $1\frac{3}{4}$   **34.** $2\frac{11}{12}$   **35.** $3\frac{19}{20}$   **36.** $2\frac{23}{24}$   **37.** $2\frac{17}{24}$   **38.** $6\frac{1}{10}$

**39.** $3\frac{5}{6}$    **40.** $A \rightarrow R, B \rightarrow P, C \rightarrow Q$

**41.** (a) $1\frac{1}{8}$   (b) $1\frac{1}{2}$   (c) $1\frac{13}{20}$   (d) $1\frac{3}{4}$    **42.** $4\frac{7}{12}$ km

**43.** (a) $2\frac{7}{20}$   (b) $2\frac{3}{20}$   (c) $2\frac{1}{10}$

## Page 129   E5.3

**1.** (a) $\frac{1}{8}$   (b) $\frac{1}{9}$   (c) $\frac{1}{12}$   (d) $\frac{1}{12}$

**3.** (a) $\frac{1}{30}$   (b) $\frac{1}{15}$   (c) $\frac{1}{24}$   (d) $\frac{1}{20}$

**4.** (a) $\frac{3}{8}$   (b) $\frac{1}{2}$   (c) $\frac{1}{6}$   (d) $\frac{1}{5}$

**5.** (a) $\frac{8}{35}$   (b) $\frac{1}{6}$   (c) $\frac{1}{4}$   (d) $\frac{2}{5}$    **6.** $\frac{2}{21}$    **7.** $\frac{1}{90}$    **8.** $\frac{3}{20}$

9. $\frac{2}{3}$  10. $\frac{1}{24}$  11. $\frac{1}{12}$  12. $\frac{1}{2}$  13. $\frac{1}{12}$  14. $\frac{1}{36}$

15. $\frac{1}{12}$  16. $\frac{1}{3}$  17. $\frac{1}{6}$  18. 28  19. (a) 6 (b) 4

20. 8  21. 15  22. $\frac{3}{4}$  23. $1\frac{1}{20}$  24. $8\frac{1}{3}$  25. $\frac{3}{4}$

26. $1\frac{1}{3}$  27. $\frac{3}{4}$  28. 3  29. $3\frac{2}{3}$  30. $7\frac{1}{5}$  31. 12

32. $\frac{8}{15}$  33. 6  34. $A \rightarrow R, B \rightarrow P, C \rightarrow Q$

35. $\frac{3}{4}$  36. $\frac{18}{35}$  37. $\frac{7}{40}$  38. 27  39. 4

40. 32  41. 30  42. 10  43. 48  44. 6

45. 63  46. $A \rightarrow R, B \rightarrow P, C \rightarrow Q$

47. 4  48. $6\frac{3}{7}$  49. $\frac{21}{32}$  50. $2\frac{3}{20}$  51. $5\frac{1}{4}$

52. $1\frac{61}{100}$  53. $\frac{4}{7}$  54. $\frac{49}{106}$  55. $11\frac{1}{5}$  56. $2\frac{2}{17}$

57. $1\frac{3}{5}$  58. $2\frac{13}{14}$  59. 9  60. 15

## Page 132  WYM 5 _____

5. 300  6. £12  7. Tariff P  8. Tariff Q

9. (b) 200  (c) Tariff Z  (d) Tariff Y

## TEST YOURSELF ON UNIT 5

1. (a) $\frac{17}{29}$ (b) $\frac{6}{11}$ (c) $\frac{5}{9}$ (d) $\frac{2}{7}$

2. (a) £6 (b) £3 (c) £14 (d) 35 kg (e) £300 (f) £390

3. (a) $5\frac{3}{4}$ (b) $4\frac{1}{2}$ (c) $3\frac{2}{5}$ (d) $6\frac{2}{5}$ (e) $\frac{9}{4}$ (f) $\frac{17}{3}$ (g) $\frac{23}{7}$ (h) $\frac{35}{8}$

4. (a) $\frac{5}{7}$ (b) $\frac{13}{35}$ (c) $\frac{7}{12}$ (d) $\frac{29}{35}$ (e) $3\frac{1}{10}$ (f) $1\frac{1}{8}$ (g) $3\frac{1}{12}$ (h) $4\frac{1}{12}$

5. (a) $\frac{1}{24}$ (b) $\frac{2}{15}$ (c) $\frac{3}{14}$ (d) $\frac{3}{10}$ (e) $\frac{2}{3}$ (f) $6\frac{3}{5}$ (g) $10\frac{2}{3}$  $15\frac{1}{5}$

6. (a) $\frac{8}{9}$ (b) $\frac{18}{35}$ (c) $\frac{1}{16}$ (d) $\frac{11}{6}$ (e) $2\frac{5}{8}$ (f) $1\frac{9}{25}$ (g) $1\frac{13}{21}$

## Page 136  Mixed examination questions

1. (b) (i) $\frac{5}{6}$ (ii) $\frac{1}{6}$  2. (a) $\frac{1}{10}$ (b) $\frac{3}{20}$  3. (i) $\frac{5}{12}$ (ii) $\frac{1}{16}$

4. $1\frac{1}{2}$ inches  5. $\frac{3}{8}$  6. $3\frac{7}{8}$

# UNIT 6

## Page 138  M6.1 _____

1. (a) 37/100  (b) 37%  2. 5%  3. 30%  4. 65%

5. 57%  6. 33%  7. (a) 25%  (b) 55%

8. 12%  9. 11%  10. 60%

## Page 139  E6.1 _____

1. (a) 1/10  (b) 3/100  (c) 11/100  (d) 2/5

   (e) 3/4  (f) 3/20  (g) 4/5  (h) 11/50

   (i) 8/25  (j) 19/20  (k) 12/25  (l) 1/20

2. 3/10  3. 11/20  4. 16/25

5. (a) 25%  (b) 7%  (c) 80%  (d) 35%  (e) 75%

   (f) 12%  (g) 36%  (h) 9%  (i) 40%  (j) 70%

   (k) 56%  (l) 90%  (m) 85%  (n) 42%

6. 78%  7. 52%  8. 55%

9. (a) 71%  (b) 28%  (c) 31%  (d) 28%  (e) 81%  (f) 29%

   (g) 16%  (h) 74%  (i) 79%  (j) 28%  (k) 96%  (l) 62%

10. 59%

## Page 141  M6.2 _____

1. (a) 24%  (b) 18%  (c) 40%  (d) 20%

2. (a) 35%  (b) 45%  (c) 20%  3. 52%

4. (a) 65%  (b) 36%  (c) MATHS  5. 70%

6. (a) 59%  (b) 41%  7. (a) 58%  (b) 42%

8. (a) 30%  (b) 20%  (c) 10%  (d) 5%  (e) 25%  (f) 10%

9. 70%

10. English 85% Maths 56% Science 46% Arts 65% Geog. 70% Meg.

## Page 142  E6.2 _____

1. (a) 33%  (b) 86%  (c) 31%  (d) 75%  (e) 71%  (f) 77%

2. 29%  3. 69%  4. 9%  5. 42%  6. 19%

7. (a) 8%  (b) 36%  8. (a) 9%  (b) 16%  (c) 21%

9. Juice 15%, Wine 13%, Cola 23%, Lemonade 15%, Beer 25%, Cider 9%  10. (a) 15%  (b) 60%  (c) 25%

## Page 144  Can you still?  6A

1. (a) 3/10  (b) 1/5  (c) 29/100  (d) 9/25  (e) 18/25

2. (a) 0.31  (b) 0.9  (c) 0.35  (d) 0.25  (e) 0.64

3. $A \rightarrow U$,  $B \rightarrow Q$,  $C \rightarrow T$,  $D \rightarrow V$,  $E \rightarrow S$,  $F \rightarrow P$

## Page 145  M6.3 _____

1. (a) 40  (b) 21  (c) 14  (d) 60  (e) 4.5  (f) 12.5

2. (a) 20  (b) 7  (c) 12  (d) 25  (c) 50  (f) 7.5

3. (a) 15  (b) 24  (c) 60  (d) 9  (e) 300  (f) 39

4. 210  5. (a) 4  (b) 10  (c) 20  (d) 6

6. (a) 10  (b) 14  (c) 30  (d) 40  (e) 200  (f) 48

7. (a) 8  (b) 9  (c) 2  (d) 20  (e) 5  (f) 60

8. (a) 24  (b) 27  (c) 6  (d) 60  (e) 15  (f) 180

9. (a) 28  (b) 7  (c) 56  (d) 28  (e) 210  (f) 98

10. (a) 4  (b) 1  (c) 3  (d) 7  (e) 1.5  (f) 4.5

11. (a) 12  (b) 9  (c) 18  (d) 30  (e) 7.5  (f) 4.5

12. (a) 15 g  13. (a) 10%  (b) 15 g  14. (b)  15. (b)

16. 100  17. 8  18. 252

20.

| 60 | 38 | 3 | | 63 | 90 | 38 | 11 | | 66 | 15 |
|---|---|---|---|---|---|---|---|---|---|---|
| Y | O | U | | K | N | O | W | | I | T |

| 40 | 12 | 63 | 50 | 9 | | 9 | 50 | 90 | 9 | 50 |
|---|---|---|---|---|---|---|---|---|---|---|
| M | A | K | E | S | | S | E | N | S | E |

## Page 147  E6.3 _____

1. (a) 6  (b) 4  (c) 3.5  (d) 8.5  (e) 0.65  (f) 0.09

2. (a) 18  (b) 12  (c) 10.5  (d) 25.5  (e) 1.95  (f) 0.27

3. (a) 18  (b) 63  (c) 27  (d) 58.5  (e) 28.8  (f) 0.72

4. (a) 120  (b) 192  (c) 108  (d) 57.6  (e) 16.32  (f) 0.72

5. (a) 243 (b) 324 (c) 121.5 (d) 607.5 (e) 39.69 (f) 5.67
6. (a) 35 (b) 21 (c) 66.5 (d) 119.875 (e) 12.6 (f) 0.7
7. £40.50 8. £30.80 9. £86.95 10. £38.50 11. £510 12. £28
13. 29,760 14. 689 15. (b) 16. $A \to R, B \to P, C \to Q,$
17. (a) £2.11 (b) £23.66 (c) £1.19 (d) £1.99 (e) £7.55
(f) £5.14 (g) £11.31 (h) 85$p$ (i) £4.77
18. 67.5 g 19. £316.20 20. (a)

## Page 149 Can you still? 6B

1. 6 2. 2 3. 5 4. 19 5. 25 6. 10
7. 18 8. 26 9. 14 10. 36 11. 8 12. 26
13. 10 14. 3 15. 20 16. 48 17. 31 18. 2

## Page 150 M6.4

1. (a) £66 (b) £117 (c) £48 (d) £30 (e) £225 (f) £856
(g) £20 (h) £192 (i) £57 (d) £26 2. £270
3. £5600 4. £882 5. 825 g 6. (a) £120 (b) £480
7. (a) £9 (b) £81 8. (a) £22.50 (b) £67.50
9. (a) £60 (b) £20 10. (a) £46 (b) £46 11. £126 (b) £294
12. (a) £30 (b) £60 13. (a) £140 (b) £210
14. (a) £48 (b) £16 15. £55
16. £164,800 17. 63 kg 18. £22,880 19. £470 20. £658

## Page 151 E6.4

1. (a) £94.50 (b) £278.10 (c) £69.75 (d) £60.48 (e) £292.80
(f) £6.63 (g) £8.21 (h) £175.94 (i) £19.68 (j) £9.53
2. £42.75 3. £7.72 4. 11270 5. £945.14 6. £484.10
7.

| ITEM | PRICE(£) | VAT(17.5%) | PRICE + VAT |
|---|---|---|---|
| TV | 325 | 56.88 | 381.88 |
| Fridge | 217 | 37.98 | 254.98 |
| Mobile Phone | 185 | 32.38 | 217.38 |
| CD Player | 133 | 23.28 | 156.28 |
| Sofa | 899 | 157.33 | 1056.33 |
| Camera | 326 | 57.05 | 383.05 |
| Car | 12121 | 2121.18 | 14242.18 |
| Bed | 582 | 101.85 | 683.85 |
| Computer Game | 47 | 8.23 | 55.23 |
| Guitar | 332 | 58.10 | 390.10 |

8. £2883 9. £2276.85 10. £72.80 11. £410.28
12.

| Money put into Bank (£) | Interest each year | Extra Money(£) | Total money after 1 year (£) |
|---|---|---|---|
| 80 | 3% | 2.40 | 82.40 |
| 500 | 5.5% | 27.50 | 527.50 |
| 360 | 2.9% | 10.44 | 370.44 |
| 25 | 5% | 1.25 | 26.25 |
| 2100 | 4.7% | 98.70 | 2198.70 |
| 5350 | 3.85% | 205.96 | 5555.96 |
| 473 | 5.05% | 23.89 | 496.89 |
| 204 | 4.79% | 9.77 | 213.77 |
| 8 | 5.8% | 0.46 | 8.46 |
| 791 | 6.7% | 53 | 844 |

13. (a) £2726 (b) £1990 14. (a) £323.13 (b) £274.66
15. (a) £646.25 (b) £529.93

## Page 153 Can you still? 6C

1. $5a$ 2. $4a$ 3. $7a + 3b$
4. $14x + 4y$ 5. $3x + 4y$ 6. $5p + 5q$
7. $7m + n$ 8. $9a + 4$ 9. $9m + 2n + 3$
10. $7a + 5b + 30$ 11. $6m + 12n + 14$

## Page 154 M6.5

1. (a) 0.69 (b) 0.31 (c) 0.93 (d) 0.21 (e) 0.15 (f) 0.6
2. (a) 29% (b) 84% (c) 14% (d) 67% (e) 90% (f) 2%
3. (a) 0.53 (b) 0.28 (c) 0.18 (d) 0.4 (e) 0.03 (f) 0.92
4. (a) 8% (b) 80% (c) 90% (d) 9% (e) 5% (f) 50%
5. (a) (d) (f) (h) are true
6. $A \to T, B \to R, C \to U, D \to Q, E \to P$
7. (a) 0.035 (b) 0.067 (c) 1 (d) 1.2 (e) 2.48 (f) 1.92
8. $21\% = 0.21 = \frac{21}{100}, \quad 7\% = 0.07 = \frac{7}{100}, \quad 19\% = 0.19 = \frac{19}{100},$
$25\% = 0.25 = \frac{1}{4}, \quad 30\% = 0.3 = \frac{3}{10}, \quad 70\% = 0.7 = \frac{7}{10}$
9. $0.32 = 32\% = \frac{8}{25}, 0.43 = 43\% = \frac{43}{100}, 0.06 = 6 = \frac{3}{50},$
$0.14 = 14\% = \frac{7}{50}, 0.8 = 80\% = \frac{4}{5}, \quad 0.15 = 15\% = \frac{3}{20}$

## Page 156 E6.5

1. 8% 2. 15% 3. 5% 4. 20%, 8%, 5%, 15%, 45%, 35%
5. $33\frac{1}{3}\%$ 6. 3% 7. 22.5% 8. 10.2%
9. 25%, 30%, 23%, 21%, 68%, 56.25% 10. 12% 11. 20% 12. 4%
13. Lager 125%, Crisps 140%, Bitter 117%, Nuts 178%, 14. 73%

## Page 159 M6.6

1. £6050 2. £6615
3. (a) £10,714.14 (b) £4764.06 (c) £2809 (d) £674.16
4. (a) £392 (b) £274.40 5. (a) 9500 (b) 9025
6. (a) £53.05 (b) 54.64 7. £14,124.88 8. 7,077.888
9. 6912 10. (a) Geena (b) £2.42

## Page 160 E6.6

1. (a) £1064.80 (b) £1288.41 (c) £2074.99
2. (a) £457.96 (b) £490.02 (c) £561.02
3. (a) £1377.28 4. (a) £0.85 (b) £5129.23 5. £85.43
6. 630, 694.58, 756.77, 977.34
7. 11863.80, 7217.94, 5629.99, 1625.48
8. 21.6, 23.22, 25.19, 27.21
9. 2670000, 2376300, 2114907, 1882267 10. £37,178.76

## Page 161 Can you still? 6D

1. $3a + 9$ 2. $5x - 15$ 3. $8x + 24$ 4. $35m - 10$
5. $28a + 14b$ 6. $18y - 9z$ 7. $14x - 63y$ 8. $ab + ac$
9. $m^2 - 6m$ 10. $-3a - 12$ 11. $-5x + 25$ 12. $-4b + 12$

## Page 162 M6.7

1. $4 : 3$ 2. $3 : 4$ 4. $4 : 1$
8. (a) $1 : 5$ (b) $2 : 1$ (c) $1 : 5$ 9. $2 : 5$ 10. $8 : 5$
11. (a) $3 : 1$ (b) $1 : 6$ (c) $1 : 3$ (d) $9 : 4$

**12.** (a) 8 (b) 9 (c) 6 (d) 12 (e) 6 white 9 red

**13.** 5 : 1 **14.** 3 : 2

**15.** (a) 3 : 2 (b) 2 : 3 (c) 3 : 5 (d) 5 : 11
(e) 3 : 2 (f) 6 : 7 (g) 3 : 4 (h) 7 : 4
(i) 3 : 4 (j) 3 : 5 (k) 8 : 5 (l) 2 : 5
(m) 4 : 2 : 1 (n) 2 : 3 : 4 (o) 8 : 3 : 5 (p) 4 : 9 : 7

**16.** 6 : 1 **17.** 4 : 5

**18.** (a) 1 : 2 (b) 5 : 1 (c) 10 : 1 (d) 6 : 1
(e) 1 : 8 (f) 1 : 4 (g) 25 : 2 (h) 1 : 40
(i) 1 : 4 (j) 1 : 10 (k) 1 : 40 (e) 1 : 10

## Page 164   E6.7

**1.** 45p **2.** 60p **3.** 90p **4.** 40p
**5.** £9 **6.** £35 **7.** 55p **8.** £48
**9.** 108 g **10.** £1350 **11.** 64 km **12.** £3.50
**13.** £5.10 **14.** 61.10 kg
**15.** 35 p, £2.45, £3.50, £17.50 **16.** 96 p, £4.80, £14.40, £16.80
**17.** 1.90, 15.20, 61.75, 142.50 **18.** 1.65, 8.25, 24.75, 206.25, 104.61
**19.** 1125 g **20.** £18.62 **21.** £82.20
**22.** 450 g cheese, 900 g flour, 750 g Margarine, 3 onions, 9 eggs, 90 g butter, 9 Table spoons water
**23.** 330 g butter, 330 g sugar, 3 Table spoons water, 6 eggs, 330 g flour, 3 Table spoons cocoa
**24.** 180 g flour, 420 ml milk, 3 eggs
**25.** 450 g cheese, 324 g flour, 270 ml water, 45 g peperoni

## Page 167   M6.8

**1.** (a) £40 : £120 (b) £50 : £40 (c) £140 : £100
(d) 32 g : 48 g (e) 90 g : 210 g (f) 350 g : 100 g
(g) 45 m : 15 m (h) £500 : £100 : £200
(i) £80 : £120 : £160 (j) 2000 g : 1250 g : 1750 g
**2.** 16 boys, 12 girls **3.** Cath £500, Ben £300 **4.** Colin 14, Lily 21
**5.** 6 cm, 21 cm **6.** (a) 260 (b) 325 (c) 390
**7.** Omar £120, Molly £40, Sachin £160
**8.** BMW 48 $l$, Mini 27 $l$ **9.** 16 $l$ blue, 40 $l$ yellow
**10.** 420 g Copper, 180 g tin, 300 g nickel
**11.** $x = 100°$, $y = 20°$ $z = 60°$
**12.** $p = 108°$, $q = 36°$, $r = 72°$, $s = 144°$

## Page 168   E6.8

**1.** (a) 54 ml (b) 10 ml **2.** £165 **3.** (a) 18 (b) 20
**4.** 10 **5.** 20 years old
**6.** (a) 24 $l$ (b) 24 $l$ (c) 32 $l$ Red, 48 $l$ Yellow
**7.** (a) 29 g (b) 10.5 kg
**8.** (a) 12 (b) 14 **9.** (a) 16 (b) 165 **10.** £336 **11.** 94
**12.** 540 g Flour, 180 g Sugar **13.** 49 $l$
**14.** (a) 51 kg (b) 15 kg (c) 27 kg
**15.** Dopey £120, Doc £135, Happy £60, Bashful £45, Grumpy £150, Sneezy £105, Sleepy £180 Total £795

## Page 171   WYM 6

**1.** £40.19 **2.** £47.25 **3.** £116.52
**4.** (a) 17-26-19 (b) 32718425 (c) www.sb.co.uk (d) 417327
(e) the amount in figures and words do not agree **5.** £37.14

## Page 172   TEST YOURSELF ON UNIT 6

**1.** (a) 29/100 (b) 1/5 (c) 1/25 (d) 71/100
(e) 17/20 (f) 3/25 (g) 3% (h) 50%
(i) 51% (j) 30% (k) 28% (l) 55%
**2.** (a) 40% (b) Faye by 8% (c) 8% (d) 19%
**3.** (a) £9 (b) £12 (c) £9 (d) £27
(e) £2 (f) £6 (g) £19.50 (h) £21.16
(i) £53.04
**4.** (a) £44 (b) £56 (c) £570 (d) £40
(e) £392 (f) £737.90 (g) £634.40 (h) £338.80
**5.** (a) 0.29 (b) 0.79 (c) 0.34 (d) 0.25
(e) 0.7 (f) 0.22 (g) 61% (h) 80%
(i) 8% (j) 64% (k) 30% (l) 127%
**6.** (a) 19% (b) 25% (c) 6% (d) 20%
**7.** (a) £4410 (b) £45592 (c) £14745.60
**8.** (a) 1.12 (b) £1233.64 (c) 0.79 (d) £51.85
**9.** (a) 2 : 5 (b) 17 : 12 (c) 1 : 3 (d) 3 : 8 (e) 4 : 1
(f) 1 : 4 (g) 1 : 12
**10.** (a) 42 p (b) £25 (c) 2355 g
**11.** (a) 20 boys, 16 girls (b) Ally £1650, Jane £600, Rob £750
(c) 9 ml (d) 18 litres

## Page 175   Mixed examination questions

**1.** (a) £97.50 (b) £20.68 **2.** £20709
**3.** (a) (i) $\frac{1}{4}$ (ii) $\frac{1}{5}$ (iii) 30%
(b) 0.2, 25%, $\frac{3}{10}$ (c) (i) $\frac{9}{100}$ (ii) 0.09
**4.** £8.10 **5.** 250 g
**6.** 200 g pl. flour, 150 g almonds, 225 g sugar, 150 g butter, 10 pears
**7.** A. £320, B. £256, C. £192
**8.** (a) 656 (b) No (c) 360 (d) 22%
**9.** (a) 128 (b) 1 hour (c) 4% (d) £3200 **11.** £144
**12.** (a) £650 (b) £465.66

# UNIT 8

## Page 186   M8.1

**1.** B, C, E **2.** Q, T, R **3.** R, T **4.** B, D
**5.** A, H, M; B, E, N; C, O, Q; D, I, L; F, P, R; G, J, S; K, T, U

## Page 188   E8.1

No answers

## Page 189  M8.2

**1.** I LOVE BLING

**2.** (5, 2)(2, 2)(6, 3)(5, 1)(0, 1)(5, 2)(2, 2)(6, 3)(4, 4)(5, 5)

**3.** WHAT LIES AT THE BOTTOM OF THE SEA AND SHIVERS?
A NERVOUS WRECK

**5.** (a) (2, 4) (b) (5, 2) (c) (2, 1) (d) bird (e) shirt (f) tap

## Page 191  E8.2

**1.** THIS IS EASY

**2.** (a) (3, −2)    (b) (−3, 2)    (c) (2, 5)    (d) (−2, 3)

(e) (−4, −2)    (f) (0, −2)    (g) worm    (h) crab

(i) swimmer    (j) fly    (k) duck    (l) wasp

**3.** (a) (−3, −1)    (b) (−1, 2)    (c) (2, 1)

(d) (1, −3)    (e) bottle    (f) bone

(g) clock    (h) mirror    (i) worm

## Page 193  M8.3

**1.** (a) (1R, 3D)    (b) (3R, 1D)    (c) (1L, 3D)    (d) (3R, 4D)

(e) (4R, 0D)    (f) (2R, 2U)    (g) (1L, 2U)    (h) (2R, 1D)

(i) (0R, 3U)    (j) (1R, 1U)

**2.** (a) (2R, 2D)    (b) (0R, 4D)    (c) (5R, 5D)    (d) (3L, 4D)

(e) (2L, 4U)    (f) (2L, 2D)    (g) (5L, 0D)    (h) (1L, 4U)

(i) (5L, 1U)    (j) (2L, 1D)    (k) (6R, 6U)    (l) (3L, 6U)

## Page 195  E8.3

**1.**
(a) $\begin{pmatrix} -3 \\ -1 \end{pmatrix}$   (b) $\begin{pmatrix} 1 \\ -4 \end{pmatrix}$   (c) $\begin{pmatrix} -2 \\ -2 \end{pmatrix}$   (d) $\begin{pmatrix} 3 \\ -2 \end{pmatrix}$

(e) $\begin{pmatrix} -3 \\ 2 \end{pmatrix}$   (f) $\begin{pmatrix} 1 \\ 2 \end{pmatrix}$   (g) $\begin{pmatrix} -4 \\ 0 \end{pmatrix}$   (h) $\begin{pmatrix} 4 \\ -3 \end{pmatrix}$

**2.**
(a) $\begin{pmatrix} 1 \\ -3 \end{pmatrix}$   (b) $\begin{pmatrix} 3 \\ -7 \end{pmatrix}$   (c) $\begin{pmatrix} -4 \\ -9 \end{pmatrix}$

(d) $\begin{pmatrix} 1 \\ -10 \end{pmatrix}$   (e) $\begin{pmatrix} 0 \\ -6 \end{pmatrix}$   (f) $\begin{pmatrix} 2 \\ -8 \end{pmatrix}$

(g) $\begin{pmatrix} 5 \\ 0 \end{pmatrix}$   (h) $\begin{pmatrix} 4 \\ 3 \end{pmatrix}$   (i) $\begin{pmatrix} -2 \\ -4 \end{pmatrix}$

(j) $\begin{pmatrix} -7 \\ 2 \end{pmatrix}$   (k) $\begin{pmatrix} -5 \\ -6 \end{pmatrix}$   (l) $\begin{pmatrix} 9 \\ 0 \end{pmatrix}$

(m) $\begin{pmatrix} 7 \\ 4 \end{pmatrix}$   (n) $\begin{pmatrix} -3 \\ 4 \end{pmatrix}$   (o) $\begin{pmatrix} -2 \\ -3 \end{pmatrix}$

(p) $\begin{pmatrix} 5 \\ 6 \end{pmatrix}$   (q) $\begin{pmatrix} 5 \\ 6 \end{pmatrix}$   (r) $\begin{pmatrix} -5 \\ 7 \end{pmatrix}$

**3.**
(f) $\begin{pmatrix} 4 \\ 4 \end{pmatrix}$   (g) $\begin{pmatrix} -2 \\ -8 \end{pmatrix}$   (h) $\begin{pmatrix} 0 \\ 8 \end{pmatrix}$

## Page 199  E8.4

**3.** (d) reflect in $x$-axis    **4.** (d) reflect in $y$-axis

**6.** (a) $x = 3$ (b) $y$-axis (c) $y = -1$ (d) $x$-axis

## Page 201    Can you still?    8A

**1.** 6    **2.** 18    **3.** 5    **4.** 25    **5.** 21    **6.** 6

**7.** 20    **8.** 63    **9.** £576    **10.** £12    **11.** 440 g    **12.** 88%

## Page 203  M8.5

**17.** (a) (7, 5)    (b) (5, 5)    (c) (5, 4)    (d) (3, 7)

## Page 205  E8.5

**1.** (a) rotate 90° clockwise about (1.5, 2.5)

(b) rotate 180° about (0, 2)

(c) rotate 90° anticlockwise about (−1, 1)

**5.** (f) rotate 90° clockwise about (−3, −5)

**6.** (g) rotate 90° clockwise about (−2, −2)

## Page 207  M8.6

**10.** S.F.2    **11.** Not an enlargement    **12.** S.F.2

## Page 210  E8.6

**1.** S.F.2 centre (1, 0)    **2.** S.F. centre (2, 4)

**3.** S.F.4 centre (−6, 5)    **4.** S.F.2 centre (4, 3)

**5.** S.F.2 centre (−5, 5)

**12.** (a) $3u^2$ (b) $27u^2$ (c) 9 times larger = (scale factor)$^2$

**13.** (b) $3u^2$ (c) $12u^2$ (d) 4 times larger = (scale factor)$^2$

## Page 212    Can you still?    8B

**1.** $\frac{1}{20}$    **2.** $\frac{4}{7}$    **3.** $\frac{1}{20}$    **4.** $\frac{5}{12}$

**5.** $\frac{2}{9}$    **6.** $\frac{8}{11}$    **7.** 21    **8.** 6

**9.** $\frac{5}{9}$    **10.** $\frac{5}{12}$    **11.** $\frac{5}{4}$    **12.** $\frac{14}{15}$

**13.** $\frac{6}{7}$    **14.** $\frac{5}{27}$    **15.** $\frac{3}{10}$    **16.** $\frac{5}{22}$

## Page 213  M8.7

**4.** (a) 90° clockwise about (6, 2)  (b) $\begin{pmatrix} -3 \\ 2 \end{pmatrix}$

**7.** (a) 180° about (3, 4) (b) 90° clockwise about (3, 1) (c) $\begin{pmatrix} 3 \\ 2 \end{pmatrix}$

## Page 214    Can you still?    8C

**1.** $3x + 12$    **2.** $10x - 15$    **3.** $12x + 26$

**4.** $8x + 11$    **5.** $5x + 12$    **6.** $18x + 25$

**7.** $20x + 1$    **8.** $4x + 16$    **9.** $11x + 10$

## Page 215  E8.7

**2.** (a) reflection in $x$-axis    (b) $\begin{pmatrix} -4 \\ 1 \end{pmatrix}$ translation

(c) rotation 180° about (−1, 0)    (d) $\begin{pmatrix} 2 \\ 1 \end{pmatrix}$ translation

**4.** (a) translation $\begin{pmatrix} 9 \\ 5 \end{pmatrix}$ (b) enlargement S.F. $\frac{1}{2}$ centre (0, 0)

(c) reflection in $y = 1$ (rotation 180°, centre $(2\frac{1}{2}, 1)$)

(d) rotation 180°, centre (4, 3)    (e) rotation 180°, centre (0, 0)

**5.** (f) translation $\begin{pmatrix} 6 \\ 0 \end{pmatrix}$    **6.** (f) reflection in $y = \frac{1}{2}$

## Page 218  WYM 8

**1.** £353.15    **2.** £1044.98    **3.** £1016.34    **4.** £125.60

**5.** £785.29  **6.** £65  **7.** £807.03  **8.** £785.08  **9.** £785.08

**10.** money taken to pay bills

**11.** money taken out from a cash machine

**12.** amount overdrawn (owed to bank)

## TEST YOURSELF ON UNIT 8

**1.** B  **2.** (1, 2)(3, 1)(2, 0)(0, 3)

**3.** (b) (i) $\begin{pmatrix} -5 \\ -4 \end{pmatrix}$ (ii) $\begin{pmatrix} -1 \\ -5 \end{pmatrix}$ (iii) $\begin{pmatrix} -4 \\ 4 \end{pmatrix}$ (iv) $\begin{pmatrix} 5 \\ 1 \end{pmatrix}$

**5.** (b) (i) 90° anticlockwise about $(1, -1)$

(ii) 90° clockwise about $(0, 0)$

**6.** (c) S.F.2 centre $(3, 9)$

## Page 221    Mixed examination questions

**1.** $a$ and $d$    **2.** C $(1, 2)$, D $(-2, 3)$

**3.** (a) Rotation 180°, centre $(0, 0)$ (b) Reflection in $y = x$

**4.** Rotation 180°, centre $(0, 4)$

**5.** (c) 2 (d) Rotation 90° Anticlockwise, centre $(0, 0)$

# UNIT 9

## Page 224   M9.1

**1.** (a) 35.9  (b) 394.5  (c) 15.74  (d) 32  (e) 38.55

(f) 13.39  (g) 11.3  (h) 5.56  (i) 11.4

**2.** $0.71 + 0.29$,  $0.54 + 0.46$,  $0.96 + 0.04$,

$0.37 + 0.63$,  $0.22 + 0.78$,  $0.8 + 0.2$,

$0.41 + 0.59$,  $0.61 + 0.39$

**3.** (a) 73.68  (b) 4323.5  (c) 2312.11

(d) 41.85  (e) 152.36  (f) 620.5

**4.** (a) 4.97  (b) 10.15  (c) 3.152  (d) 6.31  (e) 12.47

(f) 52.44  (g) 25.5  (h) 34.9  (i) 22.4  (j) 2.6

(k) 5.7  (l) 2.31

## Page 225   E9.1

**1.** $0.281 + 0.019$,  $0.049 + 0.251$,  $0.213 + 0.087$,

$0.12 + 0.18$,  $0.17 + 0.13$,  $0.28 + 0.02$,

$0.06 + 0.24$,  $0.202 + 0.098$

**2.** (a) 909.3  (b) 1060.8  (c) 221.86

(d) 47.97  (e) 39.06  (f) 0.794

**3.** 19.13

**4.** (a) £16.28  (b) £5.47  (c) £8.94

(d) £13.15  (e) £15.52  (f) £16.01

(g) £11.37  (h) £2.43

**5.** £28.10  **6.** £10.63  **7.** Yes £24.31

**8.** (a)  **9.** (b)  **10.** (a)  **11.** 'B'

**12.** (a) $8.56 - 4.83 = 3.73$  (b) $4.07 + 4.96 = 9.03$

(c) $3.176 - 2.428 = 0.748$

## Page 227    Can you still?    9A

**1.** $2\frac{1}{4}$  **2.** $2\frac{3}{5}$  **3.** $2\frac{7}{10}$  **4.** $2\frac{5}{6}$  **5.** $5\frac{3}{7}$

**6.** $\frac{11}{3}$  **7.** $\frac{11}{2}$  **8.** $\frac{37}{5}$  **9.** $\frac{27}{7}$  **10.** $\frac{35}{4}$

## Page 227   M9.2

**1.** 61.2  **2.** 39.7  **3.** 61.8  **4.** 581  **5.** 0.93

**6.** 0.81  **7.** 3226  **8.** 13600  **9.** 736  **10.** 61.2

**11.** 573  **12.** 32.98  **13.** 380  **14.** 6100  **15.** 30

**16.** 500  **17.** 1  **18.** 790  **19.** 21.4  **20.** 82.4

**21.** 0.4  **22.** 0.02  **23.** 0.18  **24.** 0.074  **25.** 0.9

**26.** 0.08  **27.** 0.02  **28.** 1.5  **29.** 1.9  **30.** 0.036

**31.** 0.64  **32.** 0.5  **33.** 2.5  **34.** 0.01  **35.** 0.87

**36.** 0.04

**37.** (a) 3.9 $\boxed{\times 10}$ 39 $\boxed{\times 10}$ 390 $\boxed{\times 0.01}$ 3.9 $\boxed{\times 0.1}$ 0.39

(b) 670 $\boxed{\times 0.1}$ 67 $\boxed{\times 0.1}$ 6.7 $\boxed{\times 100}$ 670 $\boxed{\times 0.01}$ 6.7

(c) 83.2 $\boxed{\times 100}$ 8320 $\boxed{\times 0.1}$ 832 $\boxed{\times 0.01}$ 8.32 $\boxed{\times 0.1}$ 0.832

(d) 0.24 $\boxed{\times 100}$ 24 $\boxed{\times 0.1}$ 2.4 $\boxed{\times 100}$ 240 $\boxed{\times 0.001}$ 0.24

## Page 228   E9.2

**1.** (a) 2.66  (b) 0.234  (c) 51.6  (d) 0.0493  (e) 2.914

(f) 9.184  (g) 2.2284  (h) 5.13  (i) 0.0835  (j) 8.672

**2.** (a) 0.36  (b) 0.16  (c) 0.021  (d) 0.016

(e) 0.018  (f) 0.0035  (g) 0.012  (h) 0.56

(i) 0.00012  (j) 0.64  (k) 0.09  (l) 0.81

**3.** (a) 2.16  (b) 27.6  (c) 61.5

(d) 87.6  (e) 92.4  (f) 0.216

**4.** £14.22  **5.** £9.45  **6.** £16.53  **7.** £21.16

**8.** £165.96  **9.** £8.82

**10.** (a) 4.56  (b) 10.64  (c) 12.16  (d) 30.4

**11.** (a) 0.54  (b) 0.70  (c) 0.54  (d) 0.025  (e) 0.88

(f) 0.64  (g) 2.05  (h) 0.789  (i) 2.04  (j) 0.343

(k) 0.0076  (l) 0.0066  (m) 0.4354  (n) 14.72  (o) 12.27

**12.** (a) 1.2  (b) 6  (c) 0.3  (d) 0.7  (e) 0.06  (f) 0.09

## Page 230   M9.3

**1.** 6.2  **2.** 9.12  **3.** 3.41  **4.** 2.56  **5.** 4.9  **6.** 4.35

**7.** (a) 3.3  (b) 4.735  (c) 3.25  (d) 6.75

**8.** (a) 2.64  (b) 0.45  (c) 2.125  (d) 3.875

**9.** 4.63  **10.** 2.47  **11.** 34.2  **12.** 3.155

**13.** 0.217  **14.** 3.81  **15.** 0.49  **16.** 10.04

**17.** 1.74  **18.** 0.0725  **19.** 0.00392  **20.** 0.0532

**21.** £43.25  **22.** £5.75  **23.** £6.47  **24.** £12.45

**25.** £1.99  **26.** 48.25 kg  **27.** 4 p  **28.** 47 cm

## Page 231   E9.3

1. (a) $\boxed{46} \div 2 = \boxed{23}$    (b) $\boxed{320} \div 4 = \boxed{80}$
   (c) $\boxed{16.5} \div 5 = 3.5$    (d) $\boxed{2640} \div 2 = \boxed{1320}$
2. (a) 7    (b) 8    (c) 13    (d) 16
3. (a) 20    (b) 8    (c) 12    (d) 0.6
4. (a) 4    (b) 9    (c) 30    (d) 0.6
5. 18   6. 19   7. 2.3   8. 21.4   9. 2.8
10. 6.2   11. 7.4   12. 65   13. 38   14. 25
15. 3.6   16. 32.5   17. 5   18. 16   19. b
20. a   21. a
23. (a) 561540   (b) 5615400   (c) 561.54   (d) 5615.4
24. (a) 2316   (b) 23.16   (c) 23.16   (d) 64848

## Page 233   Can you still?   9B

1. $a = 61°$                    2. $b = 80°, c = 100°$
3. $d = 105°$                   4. $e = 77°, f = 26°$
5. $g = h = i = 51.5°$          6. $j = 123°, k = 57°$
7. $l = 71°$, m $= 102°$        8. $n = 114°, o = 66°$

## Page 233   M9.4

1. $65 - 74$ inclusive
2. $135 - 144$ inclusive
3. 350, 351, 375, 399, 400, 401, 408, 420, 437, 440, 445, 449
4. (a) 700   (b) 400   (c) 800   (d) 800   (e) 500
   (f) 800   (g) 1600   (h) 2100   (i) 6400   (j) 3400
5. 2500, 2506, 2700, 2900, 3000, 3100, 3300, 3400, 3450, 3499
6. Oban 1000, Perth 2000, Dundee 6000, Edinburgh 44000, Ayr 4000, Peebles 1000
7. (a) 5    (b) 9    (c) 3    (d) 3    (e) 9
   (f) 1    (g) 12   (h) 26   (i) 41   (j) 69
   (k) 250  (l) 175  (m) 3    (n) 8    (o) 8
8. (a), (b), (d), (g), (h)   9. 815   10. 2749   11. 41500   12. 12449

## Page 235   E9.4

1. (a) £4   (b) £8   (c) £1   (d) £5   (e) £9
2. (a) 7m   (b) 3m   (c) 11m   (d) 8m   (e) 1m
3. (a) 7    (b) 3    (c) 9    (d) 5    (e) 4
   (f) 13   (g) 18   (h) 11   (i) 34   (j) 1
4. (a) 17   (b) 47   (c) 367   (d) 2323   (e) 23   (f) 98
   (g) 494  (h) 5    (i) 41   (j) 2204   (k) 7    (l) 18
5. (a) 420  (b) 1830  (c) 2950  (d) 210  (e) 170
   (f) 2990  (g) 630  (h) 3520  (i) 5250

## Page 236   M9.5

1. 3.4
2. (a) 6.3   (b) 5.8   (c) 8.4   (d) 6.8
   (e) 0.4   (f) 9.8   (g) 12.6   (h) 15.7
3. 7.319, 7.31, 7.341, and 7.33
4. (a) 2.35   (b) 7.05   (c) 13.33   (d) 2.07
   (e) 0.24   (f) 23.68   (g) 0.94   (h) 7.09

5. 8.164, 8.1623, 8.1649
6. (a) 2.168   (b) 5.641   (c) 8.326   (d) 4.232
   (e) 7.252   (f) 13.711   (g) 17.330   (h) 41.614
7. (a) 1.39   (b) 0.31   (c) 6.60   (d) 7.66   (e) 0.33   (f) 1.14
   (g) 2.02   (h) 0.76   (i) 0.01   (j) 2.76   (k) 4.12   (l) 0.16
8. (a) A 3.0, 3.7, 4.5;  B 3.0, 3.2, 2.8   (b) 11.2, 9

## Page 238   E9.5

1. B   2. A   3. A   4. C   5. A   6. B
7. C   8. B   9. B   10. A   11. C   12. B
13. (a) £14, £19,    (b) £14.95, £20.29 both smaller
14. A → Q , B → S, C → P, D → T, E → R
15. £5000   16. 12000 KCals   17. $210\text{cm}^3$
18. A → T, B → P, C → R, D → Q, E → S

## Page 240   Can you still?   9C

$7\%, \frac{7}{100}, 0.07 : \frac{3}{50}, 0.06, 6\% : 0.35, \frac{7}{20}, 35\% : \frac{7}{10}, 70\%, 0.7 : \frac{1}{4},$
$25\%, 0.25 : 0.6, 60\%, \frac{3}{5} : 0.04, 4\%, \frac{1}{25}.$

## Page 241   M9.6

1. (a) 15   (b) 9   (c) 51   (d) 8   (e) 8   (f) 2   (g) 38
   (h) 1   (i) 18   (j) 58   (k) 30   (l) 20   (m) 2   (n) 13
2. A → Q , B → S , C → P , D → T, E → R
3. Across Answers
   1. 6.92   3. 11.9   5. 40.12   7. 735
   9. 49   10. 34.8   11. 81   12. 245
   Down Answers
   1. 6.8   2. 250.848   3. 11.27   4. 94.65
   6. 91.68   8. 31.45   10. 34

## Page 243   E9.6

1. (a) 196   (b) 53.29   (c) 17.64   (d) 79.21
   (e) 529   (f) 15   (g) 19   (h) 3.2
   (i) 5.3   (j) 0.7   (k) 225   (l) 484
   (m) 12   (n) 24   (o) 56.45   (p) 261.68
2. A → R , B → P , C → S , D → U , E → Q , F → T
3. (a) $\frac{2}{7}$   (b) $\frac{5}{9}$   (c) $3\frac{2}{5}$   (d) $6\frac{4}{9}$   (e) $\frac{8}{11}$   (f) $7\frac{2}{7}$
4. (a) $\frac{29}{35}$   (b) $1\frac{3}{8}$   (c) $\frac{26}{99}$   (d) $4\frac{3}{8}$
   (e) $14\frac{2}{5}$   (f) $13\frac{3}{4}$   (g) 56   (h) $17.64 = 17\frac{16}{25}$

5.

| + | $\frac{3}{8}$ | $\frac{7}{20}$ | $2\frac{1}{2}$ | $1\frac{2}{3}$ |
|---|---|---|---|---|
| $\frac{1}{4}$ | $\frac{5}{8}$ | $\frac{3}{5}$ | $2\frac{3}{4}$ | $1\frac{11}{12}$ |
| $\frac{3}{5}$ | $\frac{39}{40}$ | $\frac{19}{20}$ | $3\frac{1}{10}$ | $2\frac{4}{15}$ |
| $2\frac{1}{3}$ | $2\frac{17}{24}$ | $2\frac{41}{60}$ | $4\frac{5}{6}$ | 4 |
| $1\frac{3}{10}$ | $1\frac{27}{40}$ | $2\frac{13}{20}$ | $1\frac{13}{20}$ | $2\frac{29}{40}$ |

7.

| H | | L | E | G | I | B | L | E |
|---|---|---|---|---|---|---|---|---|
| E | | | | E | | | O | |
| D | | O | I | L | | G | O | B |
| G | | | | | H | I | S | |
| E | | | B | | | B | E | D |
| H | | B | O | G | | | | I |
| O | | | O | | | S | | G |
| G | O | | Z | | H | | | |
| | | B | E | S | I | E | G | E |

**6.** (a) 136.68   (b) 0.63   (c) 12.27   (d) 3.84   (e) 5.15
(f) 5.15   (g) 0.38   (h) 0.31   (i) 3.47   (j) 47.82

## Page 246   Can you still?   9D

**1.** £84   **2.** £49   **3.** £15600   **4.** £51
**5.** £70.50   **6.** £79.46   **7.** £1056.33

## Page 247   M9.7

**1.** (a) T   (b) T   (c) F   (d) T   (e) T
(f) F   (g) T   (h) F   (i) T   (j) F

**2.** 3.9639, 3.9641, 3.9568

**3.** (a) 2.19   (b) 32.9   (c) 0.855   (d) 183
(e) 18.4   (f) 0.0876   (g) 48900   (h) 0.656
(i) 3280   (j) 6280   (k) 0.0214   (l) 376000

**4.** (a) 14   (b) 8   (c) 6.4
(d) 0.836   (e) 1740   (f) 51.4
(g) 32000   (h) 0.055   (i) 30000

**5.** Across Answers
  **1.** 17.97   **3.** 11   **6.** 830
  **8.** 14.52   **9.** 224   **11.** 12
  **12.** 8.8   **13.** 31.8   **14.** 3.3
  Down Answers
  **1.** 1.98   **2.** 900   **4.** 138.268   **5.** 0.041
  **7.** 3.02   **9.** 2.23   **10.** 418   **12.** 83

## Page 249   E9.7

**1.** (a) 1850, $1850 \div 20 = 92.5$   (b) 4952, $4952 \div 328 = 14$
(c) 50.4, $50.4 + 12.6 = 63$   (d) 31.6, $31.6 \times 7 = 221.2$
(e) 42.3, $42.3 \times 9.1 = 384.93$   (f) $39.51 - 25.8 = 13.71$
(g) 21.2, $21.2 \times 4.5 = 95.4$   (h) 42.4, both ways
(i) 6.2449..., check by squaring   (j) 29.63, both ways

**2.** $A \to T$, $B \to P$, $C \to S$, $D \to R$, $E \to Q$

**3.** (a) 28   (b) 36   (c) 101.16

**4.** £1000   **5.** 6 times

**6.** (a) 5   (b) 100   (c) £3000
(d) 1   (i) 0.2 kg   (f) 2
(g) 100   (h) £2000   (i) 400

## Page 251   WYM 9

**1.** (a) £963.50   (b) 528.75   (c) £740.25
**2.** 'Electrics'   **3.** £213.85   **4.** £3231.25   **5.** £108.10 total
**6.** No   **7.** Yes   **8.** £502.90 total

## Page 252   TEST YOURSELF ON UNIT 9

**1.** (a) 27.2   (b) 3.31   (c) 10.6   (d) 6.7
(e) 13.77   (f) 17.82   (g) 11.6   (h) £13.73

**2.** (a) 49.8   (b) 34.2   (c) 6.7   (d) 0.03
(e) 0.018   (f) 0.48   (g) 0.49   (h) 6.36

**3.** (a) 3.32   (b) 2.25   (c) 1.407   (d) 3.75
(e) 0.128   (f) 0.72   (g) £15.75

**4.** (a) $7.8 \div 0.2 = \boxed{78} \div 2 = 39$
(b) $1.71 \div 0.3 = \boxed{17.1} \div 3 = 5.7$
(c) 23   (d) 104   (e) 0.36   (f) 15.6

**5.** (a) (i) 20   (ii) 50   (iii) 80   (iv) 140   (v) 460
(b) (i) 400   (ii) 800   (iii) 1200   (iv) 8400   (v) 1700
(c) (i) 3000   (ii) 9000   (iii) 17000   (iv) 22000   (v) 24000
(d) (i) 7   (ii) 9   (iii) 3   (iv) 19   (v) 27

**6.** (a) (i) 8.2   (ii) 6.4   (iii) 4.2   (iv) 14.3   (v) 8.2
(b) (i) 3.39   (ii) 2.19   (iii) 15.38   (iv) 0.90   (v) 28.18
(c) (i) 8.193   (ii) 0.724   (iii) 7.486   (iv) 27.209   (v) 14.813

**7.** (a) C   (b) B   (c) B   (d) C   (e) A   (f) B   (g) A   (h) B

**8.** (a) 68.89   (b) $\frac{7}{20}$   (c) 0.36   (d) 49
(e) $5\frac{32}{35}$   (f) 3.8   (g) 19.683   (h) 24
(i) 20   (j) 38.5   (k) 4624   (l) 64

**9.** (a) 17.8   (b) 24   (c) 31.7
(d) 213000   (e) 380   (f) 0.611
(g) 0.021   (h) 400000   (i) 2400

**10.** (a) Yes   (b) Yes   (c) Yes   (d) Yes   (e) Yes
(f) Yes   (g) 3   (h) 200   (i) 9   (j) 10

## Page 255   Mixed examination questions

**1.** (i) £5.21   (ii) £4.79   (iii) 6
**2.** £40.72   **3.** 855.4 kg   **4.** £3.85
**5.** (a) 30   (b) 6.5   **6.** 1, 7   **7.** $250 (\approx 10^2 \div 0.4)$

# UNIT 10

## Page 257   M10.1

**1.** A, $x = 1$;   B, $x = 4\frac{1}{2}$;   C, $x = -3$
**2.** P, $y = 1$;   Q, $y = 3\frac{1}{2}$;   R, $y = -3$;   S, $y = -1\frac{1}{2}$
**3.** (c) (i) A, C   (ii) $x = -3$   (iii) $y = 3$
**4.** (a) A   (b) L   (c) B D   (d) E J G K   (e) 2   (f) J
**5.** $y = 1, y = 5, y = 9, x = 1, x = 3, x = 7, x = 9$

## Page 258   Can you still?   10A

**1.** 10%   **2.** 2.5%   **3.** 25%   **4.** 25%   **5.** 6.25%

## Page 259   E10.1

**1.** $(0, 4)(1, 5)(2, 6)(3, 7)$   **2.** $(0, 6)(1, 7)(2, 8)(3, 9)$
**3.** $(0, 0)(1, 2)(2, 4)(3, 6)$   **4.** $(0, 2)(1, 4)(2, 6)(3, 8)$
**5.** $(0, 1)(1, 4)(2, 7)(3, 10)$   **6.** $(0, 0)(1, 3)(2, 6)(3, 9)$
**7.** $(0, 6)(1, 5)(2, 4)(3, 3)$   **8.** $(0, 8)(1, 7)(2, 6)(3, 5)$
**10.** (b) $(2, 2)$   **11.** (a) 1   (b) $-6$   (c) $-4$   (d) $-4$   (e) $-1$
**12.** (a) $-2$   (b) $-6$   (c) $-6$   (d) $-9$   (e) $-11$

13. $(-2, -4)\ (-1, -3)\ (0, -2)\ (1, -1)\ (2, 0)$
14. $(-2, 0)\ (-1, 2)\ (0, 4)\ (1, 6)\ (2, 8)$
15. $(-2, -5)\ (-1, -4)\ (0, -3)\ (1, -2)\ (2, -1)$
16. $(-2, -5)\ (-1, -3)\ (0, -1)\ (1, 1)\ (2, 3)$
17. $(-2, 4)\ (-1, 2)\ (0, 0)\ (1, -2)\ (2, -4)$
18. $(-3, -10)\ (-2, -7)\ (-1, -4)\ (0, -1)\ (1, 2)\ (2, 5)$
19. $(-2, -8)\ (-1, -5)\ (0, -2)\ (1, 1)\ (2, 4)$
20. $(-2, 6)\ (-1, 3)\ (0, 0)\ (1, -3)\ (2, -6)$

## Page 262 Can you still? 10B
1. £4410  2. £13310  3. £6489.60  4. £8960

## Page 263 M10.2
1. (a) 9 (b) 10 (c) 6 (d) 12 (e) 15
2. (a) 16 (b) −12 (c) 18 (d) 10 (e) 12
3. (a) −2 (b) 1 (c) 4 (d) 2 (e) −1
4. $(-3, 9)\ (-2, 4)\ (-1, 1)\ (0, 0)\ (1, 1)\ (2, 4)\ (3, 9)$
5. $(-3, 10)\ (-2, 5)\ (-1, 2)\ (0, 1)\ (1, 2)\ (2, 5)\ (3, 10)$
6. $(-3, 6)\ (-2, 1)\ (-1, -2)\ (0, -3)\ (1, -2)\ (2, 1)\ (3, 6)$
7. $(-3, 7)\ (-2, 2)\ (-1, -1)\ (0, -2)\ (1, -1)\ (2, 2)\ (3, 7)$
8. $(-3, 14)\ (-2, 9)\ (-1, 6)\ (0, 5)\ (1, 6)\ (2, 9)\ (3, 14)$
9. $(-3, 18)\ (-2, 8)\ (-1, 2)\ (0, 0)\ (1, 2)\ (2, 8)\ (3, 18)$
10. $(-3, 27)\ (-2, 12)\ (-1, 3)\ (0, 0)\ (1, 3)\ (2, 12)\ (3, 27)$
11. $(-3, 19)\ (-2, 9)\ (-1, 3)\ (0, 1)\ (1, 3)\ (2, 9)\ (3, 19)$
12. $(1, 6)\ (2, 3)\ (3, 2)\ (4, 15)\ (5, 1.2)\ (6, 1)$
13. $(1, 12)\ (2, 6)\ (3, 4)\ (4, 3)\ (5, 2.4)\ (6, 2)$

## Page 265 E10.2
1. (a) $(-4, 14)(-3, 8)(-2, 4)(-1, 2)(0, 2)(1, 4)(2, 8)$
2. (a) $(-3, 6)\ (-2, 2)\ (-1, 0)\ (0, 0)\ (1, 2)\ (2, 6)\ (3, 12)$
3. (a) $(-3, 3)\ (-2, 0)\ (-1, -1)\ (0, 0)\ (1, 3)\ (2, 8)\ (3, 15)$
4. (a) $(-3, 15)\ (-2, 8)\ (-1, 3)\ (0, 0)\ (1, -1)\ (2, 0)\ (3, 3)$ (b) −0.75
5. (a) $(-3, 14)\ (-2, 8)\ (-1, 4)\ (0, 2)\ (1, 2)\ (2, 4)\ (3, 8)$ (b) 1.75
6. $(-4, 2)\ (-3, -2)\ (-2, -4)\ (-1, -4)\ (0, -2)\ (1, 2)\ (2, 8)$
7. $(-3, -27)\ (-2, -8)\ (-1, -1)\ (0, 0)\ (1, 1)\ (2, 8)\ (3, 27)$

## Page 267 M10.3
1. (b) 2 (c) 4   2. $x = 0, y = 3; y = 0, x = 1$

## Page 269 E10.3
1. $x = 2, y = 5$
2. (a) $x = 3, y = 2$ (b) $x = 0, y = 5$ (c) $x = 1, y = 6$
3. (d) $x = 4, y = 3$   4. $x = 1\frac{1}{2}, y = 4\frac{1}{2}$
5. $x = 1\frac{1}{2}, y = 3\frac{1}{2}$   6. $x = 5, y = 3$
7. (a) $x = 10, y = 1$ (b) $x = 3, y = 8$ (c) $x = 1, y = 4$

## Page 272 M10.4
1. 1  2. $\frac{1}{2}$  3. 3  4. 1  5. $\frac{1}{3}$  6. $\frac{3}{4}$
7. (A) 4, (B) $1\frac{1}{2}$, (C) $\frac{1}{4}$  8. (a) 3 (b) $\frac{1}{4}$ (c) $-\frac{2}{3}$

## Page 273 E10.4
1. −3  2. $-\frac{1}{2}$  3. −1
4. (A) −2, (B) −5, (C) $-\frac{1}{3}$, (D) $\frac{3}{2}$, (E) $\frac{5}{2}$
5. all gradients = 2
6. (a) $y = 3x + 1, y = 3x - 2, y = 7 + 3x$
   (b) $y = 3 + 4x$ and $y = 4x - 2$
7. (a) 7 (b) 9 (c) 2 (d) $\frac{1}{2}$ (e) −2

## Page 274 Can you still? 10C
1. £50 : £250  2. 126g : 294g  3. £500 : £1250 : £750
4. 180 ml  5. 63°, 81°

## Page 275 M10.5
1. (a) 100 cm (b) (i) 2 days (ii) 6 days (c) 30 cm (d) 140 cm
2. (a) 40 (b) 30 (c) 10 (d) 55 (e) 11 am–12 noon, 20 cars
3. (a) (b) 40 (c) 24 (d) 72 (e) 8 (f) 40 (g) 35
   (h) 10 (i) 20
4. (a) 28 (b) 112 (c) 70 (d) 40 (e) 60 (f) 100 (g) 110
5. (a) 160 (b) 120 (c) 6.30 pm (d) 8.30 pm (e) $1\frac{1}{2}$ hrs.
   (f) the first

## Page 277 E10.5
1. (a) 3 km (b) 11 km (c) 16 km (d) 4 km (e) 14 km (f) 17 km
2. (a) 100 m (b) 150 m (c) 400 m (d) 20 secs (e) 35 secs
   (f) 45 secs (g) kris
3. (a) 80 km (b) 54 km (c) 75 km (d) 100 km
4. (a) 40 km/h (b) 60 km/h (c) 20 km/h
5. (a) 13.00 (b) 15 mins. (c) 10.15 (d) 75 mins.
   (e) 25 km/h (f) 70 km/h (g) 60 km/h
8. A 3, B 1, C 2, D 4   9. A 2, B 3, C 1   10. A3, B1, C2
11. A 5, B 1, C 6, D 3, E 2, F 4

## Page 283 WYM 10
1. £193.53 + 5%(£9.68) = £203.21
2. (a) £119.13 (b) £131.91 (c) £61.37 (d) £109.16
   (e) £94.54 (f) £110.72 (g) £15951

# TEST YOURSELF ON UNIT 10
1. (a) $(0, 1)\ (1, 5)\ (2, 9)$
   (b) $(0, 7)\ (1, 6)\ (2, 5)\ (3, 4)\ (4, 3)$
   (c) $(2, 0)\ (3, 1)\ (4, 2)\ (5, 3)$ (d) $y = x - 2$
2. (a) $(-3, 11)\ (-2, 6)\ (-1, 3)\ (0, 2)\ (1, 3)\ (2, 6)\ (3, 11)$
   (b) $(-3, 5)\ (-2, 0)\ (-1, -3)\ (0, -4)\ (1, -3)\ (2, 0)\ (3, 5)$
3. $x = 0, y = 2;\quad y = 0, x = 6$
4. $x = 2, y = 3$   5. (c) $\frac{1}{3}$ (d) $-\frac{2}{3}$ (e) −4 (f) $\frac{5}{2}$
7. (a) 61.5 kg (b) 65 kg (c) 64 kg (d) July (e) 62 kg
   (f) August (g) 2 kg (h) 1 kg

## Page 286 Mixed examination questions
2. (a) boat slowed (b) 70 minutes (c) 8 mph   4. (b) $(2\frac{1}{2}, 4)$

# Unit 11

## Page 289   M11.1

**1.** unlikely  **2.** unlikely  **3.** certain  **4.** even chance  **5.** likely

**6.** unlikely  **7.** certain  **8.** unlikely  **9.** impossible  **10.** unlikely

## Page 290   Can you still? 11A

**1.** 11, 3, 13, 2, 7 prime numbers     **2.** parrot

## Page 291   E11.1

**1.** (a) 50     (b) 0.71     (c) No, pupils' explanations

**2.** (a) 50     (b) 0.18     (c) Yes, pupils' explanations

**3.** (a) 0.39     (b) 122     (c) 0.61

**4.** (a) 50     (b) 1, 0.088;   2, 0.096;   3, 0.102;   4, 0.1;

                5, 0.094;   6, 0.104;   7, 0.08;   8, 0.164;

                9, 0.09;   10, 0.082

   (c) No, pupils' explanations.     **5.** (a) 0.2     (b) 0.3

   (c) Cottage pie 270, Chicken kurma 180, Spaghetti bolognese 450.

## Page 292   Can you still? 11B

**1.** (c) translation $\begin{pmatrix} 3 \\ -4 \end{pmatrix}$     (d) B and C

## Page 293   M11.2

**1.** $\frac{2}{5}$     **2.** (a) $\frac{1}{6}$     (b) $\frac{1}{6}$     (c) $\frac{1}{6}$     (d) $\frac{2}{6}$

**3.** (a) $\frac{1}{9}$  (b) $\frac{2}{9}$  (c) $\frac{3}{9}$     **4.** (a) $\frac{4}{11}$     (b) $\frac{5}{11}$     (c) $\frac{6}{11}$

**5.** (a) $\frac{1}{5}$  (b) $\frac{2}{5}$  (c) $\frac{3}{5}$     **6.** (a) $\frac{5}{10}$     (b) $\frac{3}{10}$     (c) $\frac{5}{10}$

**7.** (a) $\frac{5}{15}\left(\frac{1}{3}\right)$  (b) $\frac{3}{15}\left(\frac{1}{5}\right)$  (c) $\frac{10}{15}\left(\frac{2}{3}\right)$  (d) 0

**8.** (a) $\frac{1}{10}$     (b) $\frac{4}{10}$     (c) $\frac{5}{10}$

**9.** (a) $\frac{1}{52}$     (b) $\frac{26}{52}\left(\frac{1}{2}\right)$     (c) $\frac{13}{52}\left(\frac{1}{4}\right)$

**10.** (a) $\frac{5}{12}$     (b) $\frac{7}{12}$

## Page 295   E11.2

**1.** 60     **2.** (a) 30     (b) 30     (c) 90     (d) 60     **3.** 30     **4.** 5

**5.** 15     **6.** 24     **7.** 4     **8.** (a) 28     (b) 20     (c) 32

**9.** 48     **10.** 180     **11.** 12     **12.** (a) 1     (c) black

**13.** 25     **14.** (a) $\frac{1}{4}$     (b) 1     (c) 6     **15.** bag B

## Page 298   M11.3

**1.** Cereal + Juice, Cereal + tea, toast + juice, toast + tea

**2.** H1, H2, H3, H4, H5, H6, T1, T2, T3, T4, T5, T6

**3.** (a) (2, 1) (2, 4) (2, 9) (2, 16) (3, 1) (3, 4) (3, 9) (3, 16) (5, 1) (5, 4) (5, 9) (5, 16) (7, 1) (7, 4) (7, 9) (7, 16)   (b) 16

**4.** CC, CV, CR, VV, VR, RR

**5.** MLC, MTC, MPC, SLC, STC, SPC, MLA, MTA, MPA, SLA, STA, SPA, MLR, MTR, MPR, SLR, STR, SPR

**6.** Tom Sasha : Tom Becky : Tom Ronnie : Sasha Becky
    Sasha Ronnie : Becky Ronnie

**7.** HHH, HHT, HTH, HTT, THH, THT, TTH, TTT.

**8.** Coke Fanta; Coke sprite, Coke Diet coke, Fanta sprite,
    Fanta Diet coke, Sprite Diet Coke

**9.** (a)

| + | 1 | 3 | 5 |
|---|---|---|---|
| 2 | 3 | ⑤ | ⑦ |
| 4 | ⑤ | 7 | ⑨ |
| 6 | ⑦ | ⑨ | ⑪ |

Answers ringed

(b) $\frac{3}{9}$     **10.** (b) $\frac{5}{36}$   (c) $\frac{1}{2}$   (d) $\frac{1}{6}$

## Page 300   E11.3

**1.** b, c, f     **2.** (a) 0.8   (b) 0.2     **3.** (a) 0.9   (b) 0.1

**4.** 0.2     **5.** (a) 0.3   (b) 0.85     **6.** (a) 0.4   (b) 0.2   (c) 12

**7.** (a) 0.2   (b) 0.2   (c) 15     **8.** $\frac{12}{13}$     **9.** (a) 0.6   (b) 0.15   (c) 15

**10.** (a) $\frac{3}{8}$   (b) $\frac{15}{16}$   (c) $\frac{9}{16}$   (d) 2     **11.** $\frac{2}{3}$     **12.** $\frac{1}{4}$

## Page 304   WYM11

**1.** (a) £42     (b) £504     (c) £546     (d) £126

**2.** (a) £84     (b) £558     (c) £642     (d) £82

**3.** (a) total credit price £820 Extra cost £85     (b) £440, £50

   (c) £13752, £1352     (d) £250, £20     (e) £594.64, £129.64

**4.** £988.     **5.** £980

## Page 305   Test yourself on Unit 11

**2.** (a) 0.32     (b) 0.42     (c) 0.26     (d) 84

**3.** (a) (i) $\frac{1}{8}$     (ii) $\frac{3}{8}$     (iii) $\frac{2}{8}\left(\frac{1}{4}\right)$     (iv) $\frac{3}{8}$

   (b) (i) $\frac{4}{12}$     (ii) $\frac{2}{12}\left(\frac{1}{2}\right)$     (iii) $\frac{7}{12}$

   (c) (i) 5     (ii) 25     (iii) 25

**4.** (a) (1, 1) (1, 2) (1, 3) (1, 4) (2, 1) (2, 2) (2, 3) (2, 4) (3, 1) (3, 2)
    (3, 3) (3, 4) (4, 1) (4, 2) (4, 3) (4, 4) (5, 1) (5, 2) (5, 3) (5, 4)
    (6, 1) (6, 2) (6, 3) (6, 4)

   (b) French History Art; French History dt; French Geography Art;
       French Geography dt; German History Art; German
       History dt; German Geography Art; German Geography dt;
       Spanish History Art; Spanish History dt; Spanish Geography
       Art; Spanish Geography dt.     (c) 12

**5.** (a) 0.99     (b) (i) $\frac{5}{6}$     (ii) $\frac{1}{6}$     (c) (i) 0.2   (ii) 0.3   (iii) 25

## Page 307   Mixed examination questions

**1.** (a) GBC, GCB, BCG, BGC, CBG, CGB     (b) (i) $\frac{17}{20}$     (ii) 0.6

**2.** (b) 200     **3.** (a) $\frac{7}{9}$     (b) $\frac{16}{45}$     (c) 0.24

**4.** (a) $\frac{3}{5}$     (b) 0.4     **5.** 0.25     **6.** 90

# Unit 12

## Page 311   M12.1

**1.** (a) 14  (b) 7  (c) 24  (d) 13     **2.** 18, 22, (+ 4)     **3.** 15, 17, (+ 2)

**4.** 39, 47, (+ 8)  **5.** 4, 1, (− 3)     **6.** 7, 3, (− 4)

**7.** 41, 50, (+ 9)  **8.** 28, 34, (+ 6)     **9.** 46, 55, (+ 9)

**10.** 19, 25, (+ 1 to previous difference)

**11.** 11, 16, (+ 1 to previous difference)

**12.** 8, 3, (subtract 1 more each time)

**13.** 30, 5, (substact 5 more each time)    **14.** −3, −5, (− 2)

**15.** −6, −8, (−2)  **16.** 15, 23    **17.** 14, 20    **18.** 11, 1

**19.** 14, 8    **20.** 19, 33    **21.** −6, −2    **22.** −3, −9

**23.** 49, 45    **24.** 4, −4    **25.** 14, 19    **26.** 15, 21

**27.** (a) 16    (b) 25    **28.** (a) 13    (b) 17

**29.** (a) 21    (b) 26    **30.** (a) 13    (b) 16

## Page 312    E12.1

**1.** 16, 32, (× 2)    **2.** 81, 243, (× 3)    **3.** 80, 160, (× 2)

**4.** 50, 25, (÷ 2)    **5.** $2\frac{1}{2}$, 3, (+ $\frac{1}{2}$)    **6.** 162, 486, (× 3)

**7.** 625, 3125, (× 5)  **8.** 3, 1, (÷ 3)    **9.** 20,000, 200,000, (× 10)

**10.** 50, 0, (subtract 10 more each time)    **11.** 2.9, 3.3, (+ 0.4)

**12.** 0.03, 0.003, (÷ 10)    **13.** (a) 48    (b) 96    **14.** 36, 49

**15.** 31, 42    **16.** 19, 25    **17.** 63, 90    **18.** 46, 64

**19.** 50, 71    **20.** 37, 53    **21.** 121, 169    **22.** 79, 109

**23.** 32, 43    **24.** 21, 34, (Add previous 2 numbers)

**25.** 24, 44    **26.** (a) 1, 7, 21, 35, 35, 21, 7, 1

          (b) 1, 2, 4, 8…, doubles each time

## Page 314    M12.2

**1.** 6, 11, 16, 21, 26        **2.** Subtract 7

**3.** (a) 4, 11, 18, 25, 32    (b) 26, 23, 20, 17, 14    (c) 3, 6, 12, 24, 48

  (d) 8000, 800, 80, 8, 0.8

**4.** (a) − 6        (b) ÷ 2        (c) + 1.5        (d) × 3

**5.** (a) 283        (b) 2        **6.** (a) 17        (b) 4

**7.** $5n − 2$

**8.** (a) $2n + 6$        (b) $4n − 1$        (c) 4, 8, 12, 16, $4n + 1$

  (d) 3, 6, 9, 12, $3n − 1$

**9.** (a) $6n − 3$        (b) $7n − 3$        (c) $10n + 3$        (d) $5n + 3$

  (e) $8n − 7$        (f) $9n − 2$

**10.** (a) $14 − 2n$        (b) $21 − 4n$        (c) $0.5n + 2$        (d) $49 − 9n$

## Page 317    E12.2

**1.** (b) 23    (c) $w = 5n + 3$    (d) 103

**2.** (a) 6, 10, 14, etc    (b) 18        (c) $w = 4n + 2$        (d) 82

**3.** (c) $s = 6n − 2$    (d) 298    **4.** (c) $s = 2n + 1$    (d) 101

**5.** (c) $s = 8n − 4$    (d) 396    **6.** (c) $s = 4n + 1$    (d) 201

**7.** (c) $s = 9n + 1$    (d) 451    **8.** (b) $p = 3n + 2$    (c) 62

**9.** (c) $w = 2n + 6$    (d) 106

## Page 319    Can you still? 12A

**1.** $9a$        **2.** $6a$        **3.** $4a$        **4.** $9x + 2y$

**5.** $2a + 2b$    **6.** $6x + 7y$    **7.** $5p + 4q$    **8.** $4x + 2$

**9.** $4a + 5b + 5$    **10.** $£(2a + z)$    **11.** $(5m + 5n + 2)$ cm

**12.** $(8x + 4)$ cm

## Page 320    M12.3

**1.** (a) 4    (b) 3    (c) 3    (d) 5    (e) 11    (f) 27    (g) 17

  (h) 22    (i) 10    (j) 7    (k) 3    (l) 16

**2.** (a) 23    (b) 29    (c) 12    (d) 14    (e) 21    (f) 32    (g) 44

  (h) 57

**3.** (a) 7    (b) 6    (c) 4    (d) 16    (e) 6    (f) 7    (g) 6

  (h) 9    (i) 7    (j) 8    (k) 4    (l) 5

**4.** (a) 6    (b) 12    (c) 20    (d) 10    (e) 30    (f) 32    (g) 70

  (h) 36

**5.** 8        **6.** 17        **7.** 27        **8.** 9        **9.** 4

**10.** (a) 12    (b) 14    (c) 5    (d) 7    (e) 18    (f) 39    (g) 28

  (h) 53    (i) 35    (j) 5    (k) 22    (l) 36

## Page 321    E12.3

**1.** (a) −1    (b) −5    (c) −5    (d) −5    (e) 1    (f) −5    (g) −4

  (h) −5    (i) 3    (j) −7    (k) −8    (l) −8

**2.** (a) −5    (b) −3    (c) −7    (d) −2    (e) −6    (f) −6    (g) −3

  (h) −8    (i) 4    (j) 7    (k) −6    (l) 6

**3.** (a) −18    (b) −16    (c) −6    (d) −15    (e) −8    (f) −21    (g) −6

  (h) 6    (i) −20    (j) −18    (k) 4    (l) −14

**4.** (a) $\frac{3}{2}$    (b) $\frac{7}{2}$    (c) $\frac{-1}{2}$    (d) $\frac{-5}{2}$    (e) $\frac{1}{3}$    (f) $\frac{3}{2}$    (g) $\frac{-3}{10}$

  (h) $\frac{-9}{2}$    (i) $\frac{1}{4}$    (j) $\frac{-4}{5}$    (k) $\frac{-1}{7}$    (l) $\frac{-2}{9}$

## Page 322    M12.4

**1.** $n = 8$  **2.** $n = 5$    **3.** $5n = 10$, $n = 2$    **4.** $n = 12$  **5.** $n = 7$

**6.** $5n = 30$, $n = 6$    **7.** 2    **8.** 6    **9.** 5    **10.** 8

**11.** 3    **12.** 2    **13.** 5    **14.** 3    **15.** 6    **16.** 5

**17.** 4    **18.** 5    **19.** 3    **20.** 4    **21.** 4    **22.** 10

**23.** 4    **24.** 8    **25.** 3    **26.** 3    **27.** 10    **28.** 3

**29.** 4    **30.** 6    **31.** 11

## Page 324    E12.4

**1.** $1\frac{1}{2}$    **2.** $10n = 7$, $n = \frac{7}{10}$    **3.** $\frac{-3}{4}$    **4.** −3    **5.** 2

**6.** $−10 = 2n$, $n = −5$    **7.** $\frac{2}{3}$    **8.** $\frac{4}{5}$    **9.** $−\frac{1}{2}$    **10.** −1

**11.** $\frac{-1}{3}$    **12.** $\frac{-3}{8}$    **13.** $\frac{-5}{6}$    **14.** $\frac{-1}{2}$    **15.** $\frac{7}{2}$

**16.** $4n + 2 = 3$, $n = \frac{1}{4}$        **17.** $7n + 5 = 8$, $n = \frac{3}{7}$

**18.** $5n + 11 = 6$, $n = −1$        **19.** $2n + 7 = 1$, $n = −3$

**20.** $8n − 4 = −20$, $n = −2$        **21.** $3n + 8 = −7$, $n = −5$

**22.** −2    **23.** −4    **24.** −3    **25.** −4    **26.** −3    **27.** −2

**28.** −5    **29.** −4    **30.** −3    **31.** 5    **32.** −5    **33.** 4

## Page 325    Can you still? 12B

**1.** Meg        **2.** $5a + 10$    **3.** $6a + 4$    **4.** $12x − 6$

**5.** $20n + 12$    **6.** $3b + 6c$    **7.** $15a − 10b$    **8.** $18x − 9y$

**9.** $bc − be$    **10.** $x^2 + 3x$    **11.** $−4x − 8$    **12.** $−6y + 18$

**13.** $−9x + 6$

## Page 325   M12.5

**1.** $n = 3$ **2.** $n = 8$ **3.** $n = 2$ **4.** 3 **5.** 9 **6.** 2 **7.** 6
**8.** 4 **9.** $\frac{5}{2}$ **10.** 6 **11.** 1 **12.** 4 **13.** 7 **14.** 4
**15.** 5 **16.** 4 **17.** 9 **18.** 11 **19.** 5 **20.** 5 **21.** 2
**22.** $6(n + 5) = 48$, $n = 3$   **23.** $2(3n + 2) = 46$, $n = 7$
**24.** $5(2n - 4) = 30$, $n = 5$   **25.** $4(3n - 7) = 8$, $n = 3$

## Page 327   E12.5

**1.** $-1$ **2.** $-2$ **3.** $-3$ **4.** $-\frac{2}{3}$ **5.** $-\frac{1}{4}$ **6.** $-3$ **7.** 0
**8.** $-2$ **9.** $\frac{-3}{4}$ **10.** $-6$ **11.** $-2$ **12.** $-1$ **13.** $-1$ **14.** $\frac{-3}{10}$
**15.** $\frac{-7}{20}$ **16.** $-3$ **17.** $-3$ **18.** $-3$ **19.** $-6$ **20.** $\frac{5}{6}$ **21.** $\frac{-7}{40}$

## Page 327   Can you still? 12C

**1.** 16.51 **2.** 18.43 **3.** 23.72 **4.** 7.2 **5.** 1.76 **6.** 0.018
**7.** 0.28 **8.** 0.84 **9.** 0.25 **10.** $4.7 \to 6.88 \to 6.5 \to 0.13$

## Page 328   M12.6

**1.** 4 **2.** 2 **3.** 6 **4.** 5 **5.** 4 **6.** 10
**7.** $5n = \boxed{20}$, $n = \boxed{4}$ **8.** $\boxed{4n} - 4 = 20$, $\boxed{4n} = 24$, $n = \boxed{6}$
**9.** $2n = \boxed{12}$, $n = \boxed{6}$ **10.** 6 **11.** 10 **12.** 4 **13.** 6
**14.** 7 **15.** 5 **16.** 3 **17.** 5 **18.** 6 **19.** 30
**20.** 7 **21.** 5 **22.** 5 **23.** 9 **24.** 5 **25.** 8

## Page 330   E12.6

**1.** $-4$ **2.** 5 **3.** 4 **4.** $\frac{1}{7}$ **5.** $\frac{-1}{9}$ **6.** $-2$
**7.** $-\frac{5}{6}$ **8.** 4 **9.** $\frac{1}{10}$ **10.** $\frac{3}{10}$ **11.** 4 **12.** $\frac{-7}{9}$
**13.** $7x + 4 = 3x + 12$, $x = 2$ **14.** $8x - 5 = 2x + 19$, $x = 4$
**15.** $9 - 3x = 2x + 4$, $x = 1$ **16.** $3(2x + 5) = 27$, $x = 2$
**17.** $\frac{-1}{4}$ **18.** 8 **19.** $-20$ **20.** 5 **21.** 3 **22.** $\frac{11}{2}$
**23.** $\frac{-2}{7}$ **24.** $2\frac{1}{2}$ **25.** $\frac{5}{12}$ **26.** $\frac{2}{9}$ **27.** 4 **28.** 13
**29.** $\frac{7}{10}$ **30.** $-18$

## Page 331   Can you still? 12D

**1.** 2.4 **2.** 4.6 **3.** 7.2 **4.** 0.86 **5.** 36 **6.** 40
**7.** £124.50 **8.** £19.60 **9.** 19 **10.** 0.8 **11.** 430 **12.** 8

## Page 332   M12.7

**1.** 3 **2.** 4 **3.** 10 **4.** 20 **5.** 15 **6.** 10 **7.** 21
**8.** 6 **9.** 4 **10.** 7 **11.** 12 **12.** 20 **13.** 25 **14.** 30
**15.** 28 **16.** (a) $4x + 8 = 28$, (b) $x = 5$ (c) length 8 cm, width 6 cm
**17.** (a) $8x + 10 = 58$ (b) $x = 6$ (c) length 20 cm, width 9 cm
**18.** (a) $12x + 10 = 34$ (b) $x = 2$ (c) length 13 cm, width 4 cm
**19.** (a) $10x + 14 = 74$ (b) $x = 6$ (c) length 19 cm width 18
**20.** (a) $10x = 180°$ (b) $x = 18°$ (c) $90°, 54°, 36°$
**21.** (a) $5x + 80° = 180°$ (b) $x = 20°$ (c) $70°, 70°, 40°$
**22.** 8 **23.** 5 **24.** 15 **25.** 12 **26.** 15 **27.** 5 **28.** 18
**29.** 7 **30.** 16

## Page 334   E12.7

**1.** $\frac{3}{4}$ **2.** $6\frac{1}{2}$ **3.** $\frac{19}{3}$ **4.** $\frac{11}{4}$ **5.** $\frac{13}{3}$ **6.** 7
**7.** 19 **8.** $\frac{21}{4}$ **9.** 10 **10.** $\frac{-5}{2}$ **11.** $x = 2$, width 5 cm
**12.** $x = 8$, width 23 cm   **13.** width 4 cm, length 20 cm
**14.** width 4 cm. length 12 cm   **15.** (a) $10x + 120 = 360$,
 (b) $x = 24°$   (c) $44°, 88°, 150°, 78°$
**16.** $30°, 70°, 80°$   **17.** $20°, 80°, 80°$   **18.** 4 yrs, 7 yrs, 10 yrs
**19.** £59 for Halle, £131 for Jade   **20.** 63 m² **21.** 17 **22.** 11
**23.** $\frac{19}{2}$ **24.** $-30$ **25.** 14 **26.** 3 **27.** 6 **28.** $-1$
**29.** 4 **30.** 7 **31.** 4 **32.** 6

## Page 335   Can you still? 12E

**1.** 8.3 **2.** 0.2 **3.** 4.89 **4.** 7.62 **5.** 22 **6.** 0.082
**7.** 8660 **8.** 24.7 **9.** 8.618 **10.** 480 **11.** 175 **12.** 5.66
**13.** 113 **14.** 0.931

## Page 336   M12.8

**1.** 13.3 **2.** 16.7 **3.** 11.4 **4.** 4.6 **5.** 6.1
**6.** (a) 7.7 (b) 10.7 (c) 4.1 (d) 7.7 **7.** 14.4

## Page 339   E12.8

**1.** 13.70 **2.** 18.31
**3.** (a) 4.4 (b) 8.4 (c) 8.6 (d) 5.8 (e) 4.5 (f) 5.4
**4.** 8.66
**5.** (a) 4.41 (b) 5.07 (c) 7.04 **6.** 6.55
**7.** (a) 4.71 (b) 5.59 (c) 5.98
**8.** 2.6 **9.** 2.5 **10.** 6.1

## Page 342   WYM12

**1.** £149.90 **2.** £3037.57 **3.** £3057.57 **4.** £1942.43 **5.** £4936.57
**6.** £246.83 **7.** £46.83 **8.** £5001.73 **9.** £5021.73

## Page 343   Test yourself on Unit 12

**1.** (a) 21, 25 (+ 4) (b) 48, 96 (× 2) (c) 13, 10 (− 3)
 (d) 41, 51 (+10) (e) 25, 36 (f) 10, 5 (÷ 2)
 (g) 15, 21 (h) 27, 38 (+3, +5, +7…)
**2.** (a) 5, 12, 19, 26, 33 (b) substract 8 (c) $3n+1$
 (d) $2n + 3$ (e) $5n - 2$ (f) (ii) $s = 5n + 1$ (iii) 501
**3.** (a) 7 (b) 15 (c) 8 (d) 24 (e) −3 (f) 4 (g) 8 (h) 5
 (i) 5 (j) 27
**4.** (a) 6 (b) 8 (c) 10 (d) 5 (e) 9 (f) 8
**5.** (a) 5 (b) 4 (c) 7 (d) 4 (e) $\frac{1}{2}$ (f) 6
**6.** (a) 7 (b) 7 (c) $30°, 60°, 90°$
**7.** (a) 6.5 (b) (i) 9.3 (ii) 5.3 (c) 4.42

## Page 345   Mixed examination questions

**1.** (i) −5 (ii) $7 - 2n$
**2.** (i) $x = 6$ (ii) $x = 4$

**3.** (a) $x = 3$    (b) $x = 2$        **4.**  2.7

**5.** (a) (i) 19    (ii) 39        (b) 5, −4

**6.** (i) $x = 30$    (ii) $x = 2$    (iii) $x = \frac{1}{2}$

**7.** (a) $x = 3$    (b) $x = -20$    (c) $z = 11$        **8.** $x = 1.7$

**9.** (i) $x + 3$    (ii) $2x + 3 = 29$    (iii) $x = 13$        **10.** 1.46

# Unit 13

## Page 348    M13.1 ─────────────

**1.** (a) 7    (b) 5    (c) 6    (d) 6    **2.** (a) 19    (b) 77

   (c) 4.3    **3.** (a) 7    (b) 13    (c) 0.8    **4.** (a) 6    (b) 9

   (c) 5.6    (d) 5    **5.** (a) 7    (b) 6    (c) 15    (d) 5.9

**6.** (a) 169.5 cm        **7.** £240    **8.** 6°

**9.** (a) $11\frac{1}{3}$    (b) 14    (c) 12.4    **10.** (a) 6    (b) 6    (c) 5    (d) 7

## Page 350    E13.1 ─────────────

 **1.** (a) 7    (b) 7.35 Mode is better – most common size

 **2.** (a) 11    (b) 1    (c) Median because 70 distorts the data

 **3.** 27.2    **4.** (a) Median    (b) £7050        **5.** 69

 **9.** 6, 12    **10.** (a) £30  (b) £6    **11.** (a) 3200 cm    (b) 159 cm

**12.** 312    **13.** 29, 42, 43    **14.** 8    **15.** 31

## Page 352    Can you still? 13A

Across: **1.** 551    **4.** 595    **5.** 804    **7.** 14    **8.** 32

Down: **1.** 525    **2.** 1560    **3.** 45    **5.** 84    **6.** 43

## Page 352    M13.2 ─────────────

 **1.** (a) 30    (b) 25    (c) 35    (d) 20        **3.** (a) £46

   (b) £4    (c) £18    (d) £53    (e) £78    (f) £306

 **4.** (a) 350    (b) 340    (c) 420    (d) Swindon  (e) Swindon

   (f) 100    (g) 140    (h) 2200

 **6.** (a) 650    (b) 750    (c) 850    (d) 740    (e) 2002    (f) 150

 **7.** (a) 42%    (b) 34%    (c) 37→38%    (d) 26%    (e) 12%    (f) 6%

 **8.** (a) frequencies: 7, 10, 9, 8, 6, 2    (c) 16

 **9.** (a) 16 – 19, 20 – 24    (b) 36%    (c) 29%    (d) 7%

   (e) gets lower

## Page 357    E13.2 ─────────────

 **2.** (b) 18    **3.** (b) 27    (c) 28    (d) 9    **4.** (b) 33    (c) £42

   (d) £58  **5.** (a) 88    (b) 23    **6.** (a) 1.75 litres

   (b) 1.4 litres        **7.** (a) 47, 39    (b) 36, 38

   (c) The age range is similar for both schools but the median age is
   lower at Grindley H.S.

## Page 359    Can you still? 13B

**1.** 4    **2.** 18    **3.** $\frac{9}{20}$    **4.** $\frac{5}{21}$    **5.** 18    **6.** $\frac{1}{4}$

**7.** $\frac{8}{21}$    **8.** $\frac{4}{5}$    **9.** $4\frac{5}{6}$    **10.** $2\frac{17}{20}$  **11.** $3\frac{3}{10}$  **12.** $\frac{3}{4}$

## Page 360    M13.3 ─────────────

**1.** (a) 60    (b) 6°    (c) 150°, 66°, 30°, 90°, 24°

**2.** (a) 40    (b) 9°    (c) 63°, 72°, 36°, 54°, 135°

**3.** 60°, 60°, 80°, 100°, 24°, 36°        **4.** 90°, 108°, 42°, 72°, 48°

**5.** 120°, 70°, 20° 36°, 68°, 46°        **6.** 156°, 96°, 51°, 36°, 21°

**7.** frequencies 25, 4, 10, 15, 6; angles 150°, 24°, 60°, 90°, 36°

## Page 363    E13.3 ─────────────

**1.** (a) 20  (b) 40  (c) 8  (d) 12    **2.** (a) £225  (b) £150  (c) £525

**3.** (a) 50    (b) 30    (c) 18    (d) 90    (e) 40    (f) 12

**4.** (a) $2h$    (b) $6h$    (c) $8h$    (d) $1h$    (e) $2h$    (f) $5h$

**5.** (a) 90°    (b) 144°    (c) 72°    (d) 54°

**6.** (a) wrong. 10 more at Hatton Green

   (b) wrong. 10 more at Holland Bank    **7.** (a) wrong    (b) true

   (c) wrong    **8.** (a) 108°    (b) 72°    (c) 18°    (d) 162°

**9.** (a) depends on population    (b) depends on population    (c) true

## Page 365    Can you still? 13C

**1.** $y$ values 11, 6, 3, 2, 3, 6, 11        **2.** 12, 6, 2, 0, 0, 2, 6

## Page 366    M13.4 ─────────────

**1.**

| 19 | 19 | 5 | 43 |
|----|----|----|-----|
| 21 | 27 | 9 | 57 |
| 40 | 46 | 14 | 100 |

**2.**

| 18 | 17 | 12 | 47 |
|----|----|----|-----|
| 15 | 10 | 8 | 33 |
| 33 | 27 | 20 | 80 |

(b) 27

**3.** (a)

| 20 | 53 | 28 | 18 | 119 |
|----|----|----|----|-----|
| 31 | 28 | 8 | 14 | 81 |
| 51 | 81 | 36 | 32 | 200 |

**4.** (a)

| 21 | 40 | 88 | 24 | 173 |
|----|----|----|----|-----|
| 23 | 56 | 110 | 38 | 227 |
| 44 | 96 | 198 | 62 | 400 |

(b) $\frac{81}{200}$

(b) $\frac{198}{400}$

**5.** (a)

| 314 | 117 | 31 | 69 | 531 |
|-----|-----|----|----|-----|
| 216 | 175 | 41 | 37 | 469 |
| 530 | 292 | 72 | 106 | 1000 |

**6.** (a)

| 107 | 83 | 15 | 5 | 210 |
|-----|----|----|----|-----|
| 12 | 16 | 141 | 121 | 290 |
| 119 | 99 | 156 | 126 | 500 |

(b) $\frac{31}{531}$

(b) 25.2%

**7.** (a)

| 123 | 481 | 604 |
|-----|-----|-----|
| 65 | 637 | 702 |
| 98 | 396 | 494 |
| 286 | 1514 | 1800 |

(b) 15.9%

## Page 369    WYM13 ─────────────

**1.** £160.01    **2.** £139.65    **3.** £303.86    **4.** £879.83

**5.** £2.71    **6.** £3.91    **7.** £6165, £1165

**8.** £16939.08, £1939.08    **9.** £1119.12, £119.12    **10.** £157.20

## Page 370    Test yourself on Unit 13

**1.** (a) (i) 7    (ii) 6    (iii) 5    (iv) 8    (b) both the same (7)

**2.** (a) 12 – 21, 22 – 35    (b) 66%    (c) 52%    (d) 4%

**3.** (b) 36    (c) 43

**4.** (a) (i) 90    (ii) 4°    (iii) 60°, 112°, 80°, 68°, 40°

   (b) (i) 18    (ii) 36    (iii) 12    (iv) 42

**5.** (a)

| 23 | 32 | 16 | 71 |
|----|----|----|----|
| 24 | 8 | 17 | 49 |
| 47 | 40 | 33 | 120 |

(b) $\frac{1}{3}$    (c) 27.5%

## Page 373    Mixed examination questions

**1.** (a) (i) 60    (ii) 50    (iii) 105    **2.** (a) 56    (b) 53    (c) 25

**3.** (a) 65    (b) 48    (c) 42    **4.** (a) (i) 120°    (ii) $\frac{1}{3}$    (b) 25%

**5.** (a)

| 2 | 23 | 9 | 34 |
|----|----|----|----|
| 15 | 2 | 9 | 26 |
| 17 | 25 | 18 | 60 |

(b) $\frac{25}{60} = \frac{5}{12}$    **6.** angles: 45°, 120°, 180°, 15°

# Unit 15

## Page 380    M15.1

**1.** (a) 26    (b) 18    (c) 24    (d) 24    (e) 30    (f) 30
**3.** 38 cm    **4.** (a) 24 cm    (b) 31 cm    (c) 25.2 cm
**5.** (a) 9 cm    (b) 19 cm    (c) 10.5 cm    **6.** 5 cm
**7.** 7 cm    **8.** 9 cm    **9.** 12 cm    **10.** 14 cm

## Page 381    E15.1

**1.** (a) 5 cm    (b) 3 cm    (c) 42 cm    **2.** 44    **3.** 42
**4.** 46    **5.** 45    **6.** 66    **7.** 58    **8.** 17 cm    **9.** 14 cm

## Page 384    M15.2

**1.** 18 cm²    **2.** 20 cm²    **3.** 63 cm²    **4.** 450 cm²
**5.** 36 cm²    **6.** 40 cm²    **7.** 21 cm²    **8.** 44 cm²
**9.** 31.5 cm²    **10.** 90 cm²    **11.** 24 cm²    **12.** 12 cm²
**13.** 6 cm    **14.** 7 cm    **15.** 41 cm²    **16.** 81 cm²
**17.** 66 cm²    **18.** 192 cm²    **19.** 164 cm²    **20.** 132 cm²
**21.** 62 cm²    **22.** 140 cm²    **23.** 88 cm²    **24.** 180 cm²
**25.** 220 cm²    **26.** 96 cm²    **27.** 168 cm²    **28.** 175 cm²
**29.** 82 cm²    **30.** 96 cm²

## Page 387    E15.2

**1.** 42 cm²    **2.** 40 cm²    **3.** 48 cm²    **4.** 50 cm²
**5.** 154 cm²    **6.** 50 cm²    **7.** B (by 2 cm²)    **8.** 74 m²
**9.** 69 cm²    **10.** 3.03 m²    **11.** $\frac{1}{2}$ m²    **12.** 340 m²
**13.** 7 cm    **14.** £206

## Page 389    Can you still? 15A

**1.** (c)    **2.** £15600    **3.** £520    **4.** 60%
**5.** £223.25    **6.** £6489.60    **7.** £13718

## Page 391    M15.3

**1.** (a) 113.1 cm    (b) 72.3 cm    (c) 201.1 cm    (d) 44 cm
(e) 94.2 cm    (f) 235.6 cm    (g) 25.1 cm    (h) 1445.1 cm
**2.** square    **3.** 1571 m

## Page 392    E15.3

**1.** 43.7 cm    **2.** 61.7 cm    **3.** 90 cm    **4.** 25 cm
**5.** 388.5 m    **6.** 41.7 cm    **7.** 33.6 cm    **8.** 64.3 cm
**9.** 253.4 cm    **10.** 43.6 cm    **11.** 2042 cm    **12.** 94
**13.** (a) 257.6 cm    (b) 1940    **14.** 29 cm    **15.** 23 km

## Page 395    M15.4

**1.** 254.5 cm²    **2.** 2290.2 cm²    **3.** 43 cm²    **4.** 176.7 cm²
**5.** 754.8 cm²    **6.** 3.1 cm²    **7.** 1963.5 cm²    **8.** 10.2 cm²
**9.** 237.8 cm²    **10.** 7.1 m²    **11.** Circle (by 3.52 cm²)
**12.** (a) 4π    (b) 9π    (c) 100π

## Page 396    E15.4

**1.** 201.1 cm²    **2.** 176.7 cm²    **3.** 754.8 cm²
**4.** 249.7 cm²    **5.** 330.3 cm²    **6.** 126.6 cm²
**7.** 27.5 cm²    **8.** 6.5 cm²    **9.** 35.3 cm²
**10.** 33.5 cm²    **11.** 75.4 cm²    **12.** 11.6 cm²

## Page 397    Can you still? 15B

**1.** (a) $\frac{1}{11}$    (b) $\frac{3}{11}$    (c) $\frac{6}{11}$    **2.** (a) $\frac{9}{19}$    (b) $\frac{7}{19}$    (c) $\frac{10}{19}$
**3.** (a) 40    (b) 120    (c) 80    **4.** 24

## Page 398    M15.5

**1.** (a) 36 cm²    (b) 54 cm²    (c) 24 cm²    **2.** (a) 166 cm²
(b) 216 cm²    (c) 342 cm²    (d) 812 cm²    **3.** (a) 140 cm³
(b) 180 cm³    (c) 324 cm³    (d) 1320 cm³    **4.** c
**5.** 120    **6.** 810

## Page 401    E15.5

**1.** (a) 168000    (b) 1350000    (c) 299000
**2.** (a) 139400 cm²    (b) 102000 cm²    (c) 9000 cm²
**3.** (a) 1000000 cm³    (b) 2000000 cm³    (c) 4700000 cm³
(d) 10000 cm²    (e) 30000 cm²    (f) 8 m²
(g) 3.5 m²    (h) 92500 cm²    (i) 1000 litres
(j) 7000 litres    (k) 5.6 m³    (l) 3900000 cm³
**4.** 2 m

## Page 401    Can you still? – Probability 15C

**1.** 0.5    **2.** 0.15    **3.** (a) 0.35    (b) 0.25    (c) 3

## Page 402    M15.6

**1.** a, b, d, g, h    **2.** 216 cm³    **3.** 84 cm³    **4.** 220 cm³
**5.** 432 m³    **6.** 768 m³    **7.** 816 cm³    **8.** 20.14 m³
**9.** 26.25 m³    **10.** 200 cm    **11.** 132 cm²    **12.** 1324 cm²

## Page 405    E15.6

**1.** 339.3 cm³    **2.** 1244.1 cm³    **3.** 384.8 cm³    **4.** 804.2 cm³
**5.** 1399.6 cm³    **6.** 3086.9 cm³    **7.** 40π    **8.** 8595.4 litres
**9.** A larger    **10.** 23.3 cm³

**11.** (a) 628.3   (b) 1963.5   (c) 175.9

**12.** 10   **13.** (a) 16.2 m$^2$   (b) 4854.4 m$^3$   **14.** YES

## Page 407   M15.7

**1.** (a) 6 cm   (b) 10 m   (c) 5 cm   (d) 9 cm

**2.** (a) 12 cm   (b) 10 cm

**3.** corresponding sides are in the same ratio

**4.** (a) 9 m   (b) 30 cm   **5.** (a) 5 cm   (b) 4.5   **6.** 16 m

**7.** 15 cm   **8.** (a) 1.5 cm   (b) 20 cm   (c) 6.4 cm

## Page 409   E15.7

**1.** area.

**2.** (a) A   (b) L   (c) A   (d) A   (e) L   (f) V   (g) A
(h) V   (i) A   (j) V   (k) V   (l) A   (m) L   (n) L
(o) V   (p) A   (q) A   (r) V   (s) L   (t) A

**3.** area, none of these, area, length, volume

## Page 411   WYM15

**1.** A   **2.** B   **3.** B   **4.** A

**5.** Plates : 1 pack of 50 + 1 pack of 20 – cups : 2 packs of 30 + 2 packs of 12

**6.** A   **7.** B

## Page 412   Test yourself on Unit 15

**1.** (a) 28.1 cm   (b) 48 cm   (c) 54 cm   (d) 19 cm

**2.** (a) 28 cm$^2$   (b) 100 cm$^2$   (c) 288 cm$^2$

**3.** (a) 351 cm$^2$   (b) 60 cm$^2$   (c) 128 cm$^2$

**4.** (a) 50.3 cm   (b) 22.6 cm   (c) 77.1 cm

**5.** (a) 254.5 cm$^2$   (b) 855.3 cm$^2$   (c) 28.3 cm$^2$   (d) 138.2 cm$^2$

**6.** (a) (i) 280 cm$^3$   (ii) 292 cm$^2$   (b) (i) 240 cm$^3$   (ii) 332 cm$^2$
(c) 3.2 cm

**7.** (a) 10000 cm$^2$   (b) 5000000 cm$^3$   (c) 9400000 cm$^3$
(d) 56000 cm$^2$   (e) 2000 litres   (f) 3720 litres
(g) 378000 litres   (h) 24000 cm$^2$

**8.** (a) 231 cm$^3$   (b) 1308.5 cm$^3$   (c) 5193.4 cm$^3$

**9.** (a) 21 cm   (b) 5 cm   (c) 4

**10.** (a) A   (b) L   (c) V   (d) V   (e) L   (f) L   (g) N
(h) A   (i) L   (j) V

## Page 415   Mixed examination questions

**1.** 63 m$^3$   **2.** (a) 51.5 m   (b) 211.2 m$^2$   **3.** 85.8 cm$^2$

**4.** 8000000 cm$^3$   **5.** (a) 440 cm   (b) 0.77 m$^3$   **6.** 218 cm$^2$

**7.** 74.3 cm$^2$   **8.** 8 m

# Unit 16

## Page 419   M16.1

**1.** (b) strong negative

**2.** (b) positive

**3.** A no correlation,   B strong negative,   C no correlation,
D strong positive

**4.** (b) weak negative

## Page 421   Can you still?  16A

**1.** £15.55   **2.** 3.1 × 0.8   **3.** £33.50   **4.** 2.7 + 9 + 1.36

**5.** Imran (by 10 p)   **6.** 38 cm   **7.** (a) 4.2   (b) 46 (final answers)

**8.** 21.6, 0.216, 216

## Page 422   E16.1

**1.** (b) about 66   **2.** (c) 13→14   **3.** (c) about £37000
(d) 2nd home, inheritance?   **4.** (d) about 72–73

**5.** (b) negative correlation   (d) about 59

**6.** (a) positive correlation   (d) about £21

## Page 425   Can you still?  16B

**1.** (a) 9, 4   (b) 3, 1$\frac{1}{2}$   (c) 30, 42   (d) 16, 9

**2.** 5n + 3   **3.** 7n – 1   **4.** (b) s = 4n + 2   (c) 202

## Page 426   M16.2

**1.** (a) 9   (b) 8   **2.** (a) 172 cm   (b) 173 cm   **3.** (a) 1   (b) 1

**4.** (a) 14 – 21, 1 visit : 65+, 2 visits   (b) over 65

## Page 427   E16.2

**1.** (a) 0–2 days   (b) 0–2 days   **2.** (a) 8–9 lbs   (b) 6.7 lbs

**3.** (a) Easitech 11–15, compfix 7–10   (b) Easitech, higher median

**4.** (a) 40–49   (b) 40–49

## Page 428   M16.3

**1.** (a) 30   (b) 2   **2.** (a) 202   (b) 1.01

**3.** (a) 164   (b) 1.64   **4.** (a) 225   (b) 2.25

## Page 431   E16.3

**1.** (a) 30   (b) 2   **2.** (a) 202   (b) 1.01   **3.** (a) 164   (b) 1.64

**4.** (a) 225   (b) 2.25

**5.** (a) Paradise 16.53, Devere 16.46, Tropic 16.36   (b) Paradise

**6.** (a) 363   (b) 4

## Page 431   E16.3

**1.** (b) 91   (c) about 4.55   **2.** (b) 1880   (c) about 18.8

**3.** (b) 2900   (c) 14.5   **4.** (b) 7250   (c) 29

**5.** (a) 3258.2   (b) about 3.26   **6.** (a) Kabinseal   (b) about £14500

**7.** about 27 hours   **8.** 38.9

## Page 433   M16.4

**1.** Truman ; median 67 kg, range 36 kg; Jenkins; median 69 kg, range 44 kg. Truman median *smaller*. Truman range smaller. Truman weights *less* spread out.

**2.** 16 yr olds mean £5.01, range £1.80.

17 yr olds mean £5.27, range £1.30

16 yr olds mean is smaller, range greater. So 16 yr old hourly rate is more spread out

**3.** Wolves median 22.5, range 9

Sentinels median 22, range 10

Wolves median is greater and the range is smaller. So the ages for the Wolves are less spread out

## Page 434   E16.4

**1.** (a) 10 A median 69, range 45:10 B median 65, range 51

**2.** (a) yr.10 mean 7.1 haircuts, range = 4

(b) yr.11 mean 7.1 haircuts, range = 3

**3.** (a) Ash Lane mean 1.75, range = 4

(b) Tibbs Drive mean 2.1, range = 4

## Page 437   WYM16

| | | |
|---|---|---|
| **1.** £20.67 | **2.** £57.70 | **3.** £31.67 |
| **4.** £504, £42 | **5.** £1071, £89.25 | **6.** £562.50, £46.88 |
| **7.** £748, £62.33 | **8.** £348, £29 | **9.** £848  £70.67 |
| **10.** £42.67  (b) £64  (c) £21.33 | | **11.** £34.25 |

## Page 438   Test yourself on Unit 16

**1.** (a) positive correlation        (b) no correlation

(c) strong negative correlation

**2.** (c) about 44 mpg        (d) 2.2→2.3 litres        **3.** (a) 2        (b) 2

**4.** (a) (i) 204        (ii) 2.72        (b) 13.5 hours

**5.** (a) (i) mean 11, range 9        (ii) mean 7.6, range 12

(b) (i)  Kallis median 167 cm, range 35 cm; Moore median 175 cm, range 18 cm

(ii) The Moore family are taller than the Kallis family and their heights are less spread out.

## Page 440   Mixed examination questions

**1.** (b) strong positive correlation        (d) about 170 cm

**2.** (a) 30        (b) 3        (c) 30.2

**3.** 9.96 hours

**4.** Load is 1260 g if all weights are at the centre of each weight range. So the lift could be overloaded but it is not certain to be.

# Unit 17

## Page 442   M17.1

**1.** (a) A 18, B 33        (b) 15        **2.** (a) A 260, B 480        (b) 220

**3.** (a) A 72, B 96        (b) 24        **4.** (a) A 70, B 240        (b) 170

**5.** (a) A 55 cm, B 70 cm  (b) 15 cm        **6.** (a) A 10 kg, B 70 kg

(b) 60 kg        **7.** (a) A 26 g, B 38 g        (b) 12 g

**8.** (a) A 54 cm, B 72 cm        (b) 18 cm        **9.** 4.5 kg        **10.** 150 g

**11.** 2.5 g        **12.** 7.5 kg        **13.** 4.5 l        **14.** 26 kg        **15.** 1.15

**16.** 8.30        **17.** 10.05        **18.** 9.20        **19.** 3.45        **20.** 7.50

## Page 444   E17.1

**1.** (a) A 7.4, B 8.8        (b) 1.4        **2.** (a) A 4.8, B 5.6        (b) 0.8

**3.** (a) A 2.4 l, B 5.6 l  (b) 3.2 l        **4.** (a) A 16.4 m, B 17.4 m  (b) 1 m

**5.** (a) A 0.34 l, B 0.56 l        (b) 0.22 l

**6.** (a) A 24.8 ml, B 26.2 ml        (b) 1.4 ml

**7.** (a) A 42.2 ml, B 45.8 ml        (b) 3.6 ml

**8.** (a) A 0.038 kg, B 0.053 kg        (b) 0.015 kg

**9.** (a) A 6.8 kg, B 8.2 kg        (b) 1.4 kg

**10.** (a) A 25.5 cm, B 26.75 cm        (b) 1.25 cm

**11.** (a) A 0.42 kg, B 0.54 kg        (b) 0.12 kg

**12.** (a) A 750 ml, B 1200 ml        (b) 450 ml

**13.** 12.5 l        **14.** 20 l        **15.** 2.4 kg        **16.** 0.75 l

**17.** 9.6 kg        **18.** 3.25 l        **19.** 840 ml        **20.** 0.56 kg

## Page 445   Can you still?  17A

**1.** (a) y-values: 2, 5, 8        (b) 3        (c) y-values: 5, 4, 3        d) –1

**2.** y-values: 4, –1, –4, –5, –4, –1, 4

## Page 446   M17.2

| | | | | |
|---|---|---|---|---|
| **1.** km | **2.** cm | **3.** kg | **4.** m | **5.** ml |
| **6.** m | **7.** tonnes | **8.** litres | **9.** g | **10.** cm |

**11.** (a) 700 cm  (b) 450 cm  (c) 162 cm  (d) 5 cm  (e) 30 cm

**12.** (a) 5000 g  (b) 3600 g  (c) 9200 g  (d) 632 g  (e) 6420 g

**13.** (a) 3000 ml  (b) 24 ml  (c) 143 ml  (d) 9600 ml  (e) 3125 ml

**14.** (a) 8000 m  (b) 3 m  (c) 9.4 m  (d) 6300 m  (e) 8092 m

**15.** (a) 4 kg  (b) 0.7 l  (c) 60 kg  (d) 2 m  (e) 16 cm  (f) 330 ml

**16.** (a) 6 kg  (b) 5000 kg  (c) 8240 kg  (d) 9.5 kg  (e) 0.35 kg

**17.** (a) 3 km  (b) 9.5 km  (c) 2.471 km  (d) 4.65 km  (e) 23 km

**18.** (a) 2 l  (b) 60 l  (c) 8.4 l  (d) 0.67 l  (e) 0.004 l

**19.** 300 g        **20.** 1200 ml        **21.** 173 cm        **22.** 2.3 km

**23.** 2.5 tonnes

## Page 448   E17.2

**1.** 635 cm        **2.** 157 cm        **3.** 810 cm        **4.** 0.28 m        **5.** 0.01 m

**6.** 3.2 m        **7.** 0.09 m        **8.** 6 cm        **9.** 20 cm        **10.** 0.08 cm

**11.** 2.5 km        **12.** 0.35 km        **13.** 9 km        **14.** 3000 m        **15.** 9500 g

**16.** 375 g        **17.** 0.575 kg        **18.** 1.849 kg        **19.** 6000 kg        **20.** 0.53 l

**21.** 1.832 l        **22.** 5.5 l        **23.** 4500 ml        **24.** 0.065 l

**25.** 85000 ml  **26.** 2180 ml        **27.** 3840 kg        **28.** 2.48 m        **29.** 650 g

**30.** 2.43 kg        **31.** 33.6 cm        **32.** 220        **33.** 12        **34.** yes

**35.** (a) 0.19 km    (b) 71 mm        (c) 2.3 tonnes    (d) 9.4 l        (e) 5.7 m

(f) 0.04 kg        (g) 70 cm        (h) 9700 g        (i) 380 ml    (j) 3.2 km

## Page 449   Can you still?  17B

**1.** x = 6.4        **2.** 4.7        **3.** x = 10.41

## Page 449   M17.3

**1.** (a) 11:15        (b) 14:45        (c) 17:30        (d) 09:40

(e) 18:50        (f) 21:32        (g) 08:24        (h) 15:56

**2.** (a) 10.40 am        (b) 4.20 pm        (c) 7.35 pm        (d) 9.10 pm

(e) 2.05 am        (f) 8.05 am        (g) 5.26 pm        (h) 11.47 pm

**3.** 9.05 am (09:05)        **4.** 8.40 am (08:40)        **5.** 8 hrs 50 minutes

**6.** 1hr 45 mins    **7.** (a) 52 wks    (b) 260 wks    (c) 24 months

(d) 120 months    (e) 730 days    (f) 1095 days

**8.** 36 months    **9.** 2 hrs 50 mins    **10.** 2 hrs 35 mins

**11.** 16:30 → 16:55 (given); 13:50 → 14:20; 15:25 → 17:05;

07:45 → 11:15; 09:05 → 13:55; 16:24 → 18:09; 11:38 → 14:28

**12.** 11o'clock    **13.** 8.20    **14.** 18:05    **15.** 11:30    **16.** 23.25

**17.**

|          | Train 1 | Train 2 | Train 3 | Train 4 | Train 5 | Train 6 |
|----------|---------|---------|---------|---------|---------|---------|
| Henton   | 09:00   | 09:57   | 10:30   | 11:23   | 12:15   | 13:12   |
| Oldhill  | 09:08   | 10:05   | 10:38   | 11:31   | 12:23   | 13:20   |
| Eastham  | 09:23   | 10:20   | 10:53   | 11:46   | 12:38   | 13:35   |
| Colston  | 09:40   | 10:37   | 11:10   | 12:03   | 12:55   | 13:52   |
| Todwick  | 09:55   | 10:52   | 11:25   | 12:18   | 13:10   | 14:07   |

## Page 452    E17.3

**1.** inches    **2.** stones    **3.** miles    **4.** pints    **5.** yards

**6.** ounces    **7.** inches    **8.** gallons    **9.** pints    **10.** tons

**11.** (a) 24    (b) 72    (c) 62    (d) 77

**12.** (a) 42    (b) 2    (c) 32    (d) 78

**13.** (a) 16    (b) 72    (c) 36    (d) 58

**14.** (a) 15    (b) 23    (c) 4    (d) 10

**15.** (a) 2 pounds    (b) 2 pints    (c) 7 pounds    (d) 22 yards

**16.** (a) 64 ounces    (b) 58 inches    (c) 3520 yards    (d) 76 pints

(e) 6720 pounds    (f) 34 pounds    (g) 5 stones    (h) 4 miles

(i) 54 ounces    (j) 5600 pounds    (k) $8\frac{1}{2}$ gallons    (l) 56 pounds

**17.** 13 stone 8 pounds    **18.** 6 ft 1 inch    **19.** $6\frac{3}{4}$ pints    **20.** GALLON

## Page 454    Can you still?  17C

**1.** (a) (i) 3    (ii) 4    (iii) 5    (iv) 8

(b) (i) 8    (ii) 6    (iii) 6    (iv) 4

(c) (i) 0.7    (ii) 0.65    (iii) 0.6    (iv) 0.6

**2.** Any 4 numbers with a sum of 20    **3.** 1, 1, 10, 11, 12, (for example)

**4.** (a) 3050 kg    (b) 64 kg

## Page 455    M17.4

**1.** (a) 10 cm    (b) 90 cm    (c) 450 cm    (d) 225 cm    (e) 45 cm

**2.** (a) 6.6 pounds    (b) 11 pounds    (c) 7.7 pounds

(d) 18.7 pounds    (e) 13.64 pounds

**3.** (a) 9 l    (b) 40.5 l    (c) 90 l    (d) 24.75 l    (e) 20.7 l

**4.** Tom's    **5.** Ed    **6.** 300 g    **7.** 9 pints    **8.** 8 km

**9.** 20 miles    **10.** 15 litres    **11.** 8.8 pounds    **12.** 30 kg

**13.** 7 gallons    **14.** 12 miles    **15.** 630 cm    **16.** 132 pounds

**17.** 5 ounces    **18.** 180 cm    **19.** 22.4 km    **20.** 16 gallons

**21.** B    **22.** D    **23.** 12 pounds    **24.** 12 inches

**25.** 3 miles    **26.** 21 litres    **27.** 250 g    **28.** 8.5 feet

**29.** 12 litres    **30.** 20 km    **31.** £32.40    **32.** 38.4 km

**33.** No    **34.** a metre    **35.** yes    **36.** 3

## Page 458    E17.4

**1.** (a) 13.5 cm    (b) 14.5 cm    **2.** (a) 41.5 m    (b) 42.5 m

**3.** (a) 82.5 kg    (b) 83.5 kg    **4.** (a) 21.45 mm    (b) 21.55 mm

**5.** (a) 3.55 kg    (b) 3.65 kg

**6.** (a) lower bound 78.5 cm  upper bound 79.5 cm

(b) lower bound 31.5 kg  upper bound 32.5 kg

(c) lower bound 6.25 m  upper bound 6.35 m

(d) lower bound 15.65 m³  upper bound 15.75 m³

(e) lower bound 9.05 cm  upper bound 9.15 cm

**7.** 10.25 g    **8.** £24,711,500    **9.** 525 m    **10.** 10.115 sec

**11.** (b) 92.55 mm ≤ l < 92.65 mm    (c) 16.15 cm ≤ d < 16.25 cm

(d) 1150 l ≤ c < 1250 l    (e) 3.855 m ≤ h < 3.865 m

**12.** (a) 156.25 m    (b) 71.85 m    (c) 11210.9375 m²    **13.** 26.5 cm

## Page 460    Can you still?  17D

**1.** (a) 4    (b) 3    (c) 267    (d) 3

**2.** (a) £100,000–£200,000    (b) £100,000–£200,000    (c) £228,950

## Page 462    M17.5

**1.** (a) 45 m.p.h    (b) 50 m.p.h    (c) 55 m.p.h    (d) 40 m.p.h

**2.** (a) 56 m    (b) 45 m    (c) 19.5 m    (d) 49 m

**3.** (a) 2 hrs    (b) 3 hrs    (c) 2.5 hrs    (d) $1\frac{1}{4}$ hrs

**4.** $1\frac{1}{2}$ hrs    **5.** 36 miles    **6.** 140 km/hr    **7.** 20 miles    **8.** 9.5 hrs

**9.** 60 m.p.h, 36 m.p.h, 45 m.p.h, 72 m.p.h, 40 m.p.h    **10.** 52 m.p.h

**11.** 11 miles    **12.** 18 km    **13.** 12 m.p.h    **14.** 11.35    **15.** 20 sec

## Page 464    E17.5

**1.**

| Density (g/cm³) | Mass (g) | Volume (cm³) |
|-----------------|----------|--------------|
| (4)             | 200      | 50           |
| (16)            | 80       | 5            |
| 13              | (104)    | 8            |
| 24              | (864)    | 36           |
| 10              | 150      | (15)         |
| 60              | (30)     | 0.5          |
| (4)             | 36       | 9            |
| 16              | 320      | (20)         |
| 0.1             | 19       | (190)        |
| (4.2)           | 42       | 10           |

**2.** 164 g    **3.** 19.3 g/cm³    **4.** 1.54 g/cm³    **5.** 200 cm³

**6.** Nickel by 0.5 g    **7.** 263 cm³    **8.** 415 g    **9.** 70 g

**10.** 333 cm³    **11.** £6000    **12.** £21.95

**13.** £328,500,000

## Page 466    WYM17

**1.** 15000 – 4745 = 10255, 10% of 1960 = £196,

22% of £8295 = £1824.90

Total income tax = £196 + £1824.90 = £2020.90

**2.** $13400 - 4745 = 8655$, 10% of 1960 = £196,

22% of £6695 = £1472.90

Total income tax = 196 + 1472.90 = £1668.90

**3.** (a) £23755     (b) £4990.90

**4.** (a) £17400     (b) £3592.80     (c) £299.40     **5.** £125.50

**6.** (a) £16640     (b) £11895     (c) £2381.70     (d) £45.80

**7.** None     **8.** £27.49

## Page 467    Test yourself on Unit 17

**1.** (a) 180 cm     (b) 0.5 kg     (c) 44 cm     (d) 1.67 kg     (e) 750 ml

(f) 2.75 l

**2.** (a) 950 cm     (b) 7500 g     (c) 6120 g     (d) 2 l     (e) 3.2 kg

(f) 2600 m     (g) 0.85 km     (h) 5900 ml     (i) 0.046 l     (j) 4000 kg

(k) 0.006 kg     (l) 8.5 cm     (m) 762 g     (n) 1265 ml

**3.** (a) Afternoon     (b) 4 hrs 55 mins     (c) 22:05 or 10:05 pm

(d) 14:10     (e) 15 hrs 45 mins

**4.** (a) 70     (b) 21     (c) 24     (d) 2     (e) 3     (f) 4     (g) 28

(h) 31     (i) 69     (j) 12 stone 3 pounds     (k) 5 feet 6 inches

**5.** (a) 25     (b) 40     (c) 16     (d) 40     (e) 20     (f) 18     (g) 11

(h) 40     (i) 20     (j) 10 km  (k) 54

**6.** (a) (i) 2.35 cm     (ii) 2.45 cm     (b) (i) 363.5 m     (ii) 364.5 m

(c) (i) 64.5 kg     (ii) 65.5 kg     (d) (i) 18.75 cm     (ii) 18.85 cm

**7.** (a) 15 km     (b) 4.5 hrs     (c) 19.3 g/cm$^3$     (d) 4980 g

(e) £468     (f) 17 miles

## Page 469    Mixed examination questions

**1.** (a) 1500     (b) 200     (c) 3000     (d) (i) Hectares     (ii) litres

**2.** (i) 45 m.p.h     (ii) 5.3 amps

**3.** (a) 40,000     (b) 25

**4.** (a) 09.30     (b) 2 hrs 45 mins   (c) 17

**5.** 30 m.p.h

**6.** (a) 8960 kg/m$^3$     (b) 35650 kg

**7.** (i) 100.5 mm     (ii) 101.5 mm

# Unit 18

## Page 471    M18.1

**1.** $x - 5 = y$     **2.** $x - 8 = y$     **3.** $a + 3 = b$     **4.** $a - 9 = b$

**5.** $\dfrac{a}{6} = b$     **6.** $x + 2 = y$     **7.** $q = \dfrac{p}{3}$     **8.** $b = \dfrac{a}{7}$     **9.** $y = 9x$

**10.** (a) $x = y + 9$     (b) $x = 12y$     (c) $x = y - 6$     (d) $x = y - 20$

(e) $x = \dfrac{y}{8}$     (f) $x = \dfrac{y}{10}$     (g) $x = y + 4$     (h) $x = y + 25$

(i) $x = 3y$     (j) $x = 15y$     (k) $x = y - 100$     (l) $x = \dfrac{y}{18}$

**11.** A→Q,  B→P,  C→S     **12.** (a) $y = \dfrac{x - 2}{3}$     (b) $y = \dfrac{x + 9}{4}$

**13.** $b = \dfrac{a + 5}{2}$     **14.** $q = \dfrac{p - 7}{9}$     **15.** $b = \dfrac{a - 1}{7}$     **16.** $y = \dfrac{x + 10}{3}$

**17.** (a) $\dfrac{y - 8}{2}$     (b) $\dfrac{y + 5}{6}$     (c) $\dfrac{y + 10}{8}$     (d) $3(y - 2)$

(e) $5(y+6)$     (f) $2(y+4)$

## Page 473    E18.1

**1.** (a) $\dfrac{y + b}{a} = x$     (b) $\dfrac{v - u}{a} = t$     **2.** (a) $\dfrac{y - q}{p}$     (b) $\dfrac{y + h}{c}$

(c) $\dfrac{y + 2p}{r}$     (d) $\dfrac{q - 3s}{c}$     (e) $\dfrac{2f - 5c}{b}$     (f) $\dfrac{y - b + c}{a}$

**3.** (a) $x = \dfrac{yh + g}{f}$     (b) $x = \dfrac{cy - 2h}{p}$

**4.** (a) $\dfrac{y - cd}{c}$     (b) $\dfrac{q + mn}{m}$     (c) $\dfrac{y - 5r}{r}$     (d) $\dfrac{3b - 7a}{a}$

(e) $\dfrac{y + fg}{f}$     (f) $\dfrac{4b + st}{s}$

**5.** (a) $\dfrac{4e - d}{a}$     (b) $\dfrac{py - 3c}{b}$     (c) $\dfrac{5q + r}{a}$     (d) $\dfrac{7y + 2d}{c}$

(e) $\dfrac{yb + 3c}{a}$     (f) $\dfrac{8y - qr}{p}$     **6.** $g = \dfrac{h - m}{3}$     **7.** $y = \dfrac{v - u}{f}$

## Page 474    Can you still?  18A

**1.** (a) P = 34.6 cm,  A = 95.0 cm$^2$     (b) P = 56.5 cm,  A = 254.5 cm$^2$

(c) P = 64.3 cm,  A = 245.4 cm$^2$     **2.** 325.7 m     **3.** 224.0 cm$^2$

## Page 475    M18.2

**1.** (a) $x < 1$     (b) $x \geq 5$     (c) $x < -2$     (d) $x \geq -4$

(e) $x > -3$     (f) $2 \leq x \leq 5$     (g) $-6 < x < -1$     (h) $0 < x \leq 8$

(i) $x > \dfrac{1}{2}$     (j) $-5 \leq x < 1$     (k) $-4 \leq x \leq 7$     (l) $-1 < x \leq 2.5$

**2.** (a) ——●——→ 3     (b) ←——○—— 6     (c) ←——●—— −3

(d) ○——————○ 3  8     (e) ○——————● −6  2     (f) ○——————→ −1

(g) ●——————○ −7  −3     (h) ●——————○ 2  4     (i) ○——————● −2  0

Questions 3–6 – Pupils' answers to fit given inequality

**7.** (a) >     (b) <     (c) >     (d) <

**8.** (a) F     (b) F     (c) T     (d) T

## Page 476    E18.2

**1.** (a) $x > 8$  (b) $x \leq 36$     (c) $x < 3$     **2.** $x < 7$     **3.** $x \geq 11$

**4.** $n < 9$     **5.** $n \geq -8$     **6.** $a > 5$     **7.** $b \geq 2$     **8.** $x \leq 12$

**9.** $x \leq 5$     **10.** $y > 7$     **11.** $b \geq 24$     **12.** $x < -45$     **13.** $x \geq -4$

**14.** $x \leq 6$     **15.** $x > -3$     **16.** $x \geq 4$     **17.** $x \geq 2$     **18.** $x < -3$

**19.** $x \leq -8$     **20.** 1, 2, 3     **21.** 2, 3, 4     **22.** 1, 2, 3, 4, 5, 6

**23.** −2, −1, 0, 1, 2     **24.** −3, −2, −1, 0     **25.** −5, −4, −3, −2, −1, 0, 1, 2, 3

**26.** 3     **27.** 5     **28.** $x > 6$     **29.** $x \leq 5$     **30.** $n \geq 8$

**31.** $b \leq 4$     **32.** $x > -1$     **33.** $n < 2$     **34.** $a < 7$     **35.** $x \leq 2$

**36.** $a \geq 36$     **37.** $x \geq 6$     **38.** $n > 7$     **39.** $x < 3$

# Answers 29

## Page 477 Can you still? 18B

**1.** C  **2.** A  **3.** 14 cm

## Page 478 M18.3

**1.** (a) $3^7$ (b) $5^6$ (c) $8^6$ (d) $7^5$ (e) $4^7$ (f) $6^7$

**2.** (a) $7^4$ (b) $4^3$ (c) $3^8$ (d) $5^3$ (e) $6^3$ (f) $4$

**3.** (a) $8^8$ (b) $4^{10}$ (c) $9^3$ (d) $6^8$ (e) $8^6$ (f) $5^3$

(g) $3^9$ (h) $2^{10}$ (i) $4^6$  **4.** $2^9$

**5.** (a) $3^6$ (b) $6^2$ (c) $9^3$ (d) $4^2$ (e) $9$ (f) $4^6$

(g) $3^6$ (h) $8^5$ (i) $4^{12}$  **6.** $3^8$

**7.** (a) $5^{14}$ (b) $8^{13}$ (c) $4^4$ (d) $7^{10}$ (e) $8^4$ (f) $6^2$

**8.** (a) T (b) T (c) T (d) F (e) F (f) T

## Page 480 E18.3

**1.** (a) $3^8$ (b) $5^6$ (c) $6^{12}$ (d) $7^8$ (e) $5^{18}$ (f) $8^{10}$ (g) $3^{15}$ (h) $6^{15}$

**2.** same  **3.** (a) $3^{11}$ (b) $2^{18}$ (c) $6^9$ (d) $7^3$ (e) $5^2$

(f) $9^3$ (g) $8^2$ (h) $4^6$ (i) $2^5$  **4.** $1$

**5.** (a) $a^7$ (b) $x^{11}$ (c) $x^5$ (d) $n^6$ (e) $a^4$ (f) $x^9$

(g) $1$ (h) $p^9$ (i) $m^6$ (j) $1$ (k) $a^{13}$ (l) $1$

**6.** $3x^5$  **7.** (a) $5x^9$ (b) $16x^4$ (c) $10p^5$ (d) $24a^6$ (e) $8a^3$ (f) $5x^2$

**8.** B  **9.** (a) $x^2$ (b) $a^4$ (c) $m$ (d) $a^4$ (e) $n^2$

(f) $x^4$ (g) $x^6$ (h) $a^4$ (i) $n^3$

**10.** (a) $x^6 + x^5$ (b) $n^9 - n^5$ (c) $x^9 + x^{12}$

## Page 481 Can you still? 18C

**1.** 200 cm³  **2.** 244 cm³  **3.** 4523.6 cm³  **4.** 14844.0 cm³

## Page 482 M18.4

**1.** (a) $7 \times 10^3$ (b) $4 \times 10^5$ (c) $3.6 \times 10^2$ (d) $4.2 \times 10^4$

(e) $8.2 \times 10^4$ (f) $6.4 \times 10^3$

**2.** (a) $6 \times 10^4$ (b) $9 \times 10^2$ (c) $5.8 \times 10^3$ (d) $6.9 \times 10^5$

(e) $8.5 \times 10^2$ (f) $7.4 \times 10^7$ (g) $4.7 \times 10^4$ (h) $4 \times 10^6$

(i) $7.2 \times 10^7$ (j) $3.82 \times 10^2$ (k) $4.2 \times 10^4$ (l) $2.13 \times 10^8$

**3.** (a) $8 \times 10^{-2}$ (b) $9 \times 10^{-3}$ (c) $5.2 \times 10^{-2}$ (d) $6.7 \times 10^{-5}$

(e) $4 \times 10^{-1}$ (f) $8.2 \times 10^{-4}$

**4.** (a) $8 \times 10^{-4}$ (b) $3 \times 10^{-3}$ (c) $7 \times 10^{-8}$ (d) $9.5 \times 10^{-1}$

(e) $6.1 \times 10^{-3}$ (f) $2 \times 10^{-1}$ (g) $3.9 \times 10^{-9}$ (h) $6.2 \times 10^{-5}$

(i) $5.7 \times 10^{-7}$ (j) $6.25 \times 10^{-2}$ (k) $4.37 \times 10^{-3}$ (l) $8.12 \times 10^{-1}$

**5.** (a) 500 (b) 6800 (c) 810000 (d) 0.07

(e) 0.00098 (f) 61200 (g) 0.0037 (h) 0.0841

(i) 2500000 (j) 0.46 (k) 0.000172 (l) 536000

**6.** b, c, d, f  **7.** $6 \times 10^7$  **8.** $4.126 \times 10^6$  **9.** $1.27 \times 10^8$

**10.** (a) $2 \times 10^{-2}$ (b) $6 \times 10^{-4}$ (c) $2.09 \times 10^2$ (d) $3.16 \times 10^4$

(e) $5.8 \times 10^6$ (f) $3.168 \times 10^2$ (g) $3.271 \times 10$ (h) $6.24 \times 10^{-4}$

(i) $3.9 \times 10^{-1}$ (j) $6.5 \times 10^{-3}$ (k) $8.064 \times 10$ (l) $5.9 \times 10^5$

(m) $6.37 \times 10^7$ (n) $6.2791 \times 10^2$ (o) $7.3 \times 10^{-2}$ (p) $4.16 \times 10^{-5}$

## Page 484 E18.4

**1.** (a) $4.5 \times 10^{16}$ (b) $1.2 \times 10^{36}$ (c) $6.3 \times 10^{32}$

(d) $6.3 \times 10^{13}$ (e) $1.5 \times 10^8$ (f) $4.14 \times 10^{20}$

(g) $2.88 \times 10^{-17}$ (h) $1.26 \times 10^{19}$ (i) $2.88 \times 10^{-30}$

(j) $3 \times 10^{15}$ (k) $2.4 \times 10^{50}$ (l) $1.2 \times 10^{22}$

(m) $6 \times 10^{27}$ (n) $3 \times 10^{11}\,kg/m^3$ (o) $2.7 \times 10^{-6}$

**2.** 40  **3.** $1.8 \times 10$  **4.** $6.94 \times 10^{-15}$

**5.** (a) $2.56 \times 10^{53}$ (b) $1.97 \times 10^{-14}$ (c) $5.04 \times 10^{39}$

(d) $3.89 \times 10^{-28}$

**6.** $4.55 \times 10^{-15}$ grams

**7.** (a) $2.42 \times 10^{18}$ (b) $5.04 \times 10^{34}$ (c) $4.15 \times 10^{29}$

(d) $2.8 \times 10^{57}$ (e) $2.57 \times 10^{22}$ (f) $1.01 \times 10^{-40}$

**8.** (a) $8 \times 10^8$ (b) $7 \times 10^{16}$ (c) $6 \times 10^{12}$

(d) $5.4 \times 10^{21}$ (e) $9 \times 10^8$ (f) $1.6 \times 10^{12}$

(g) $3.6 \times 10^{14}$ (h) $1.5 \times 10^{11}$ (i) $8 \times 10^{21}$

**9.** (a) $4 \times 10^8$ (b) $1.5 \times 10^{13}$ (c) $3 \times 10^{13}$

(d) $3 \times 10^{13}$ (e) $2.7 \times 10^{25}$ (f) $5 \times 10^{17}$

**10.** (a) $3.6 \times 10^4$ (b) $4.6 \times 10^3$ (c) $1.4 \times 10^5$

(d) $3.29 \times 10^3$ (e) $3.77 \times 10^5$ (f) $8.316 \times 10^6$

## Page 487 WYM18

**1.** (a) £122500 (b) £17500 (c) £20900

**2.** (a) £120000 (b) Yes, £650

**3.** (a) £167500 (b) £1675  **4.** £1540

**5.** (a) £91000 (b) 66500 (c) £153770

## Page 489 Text yourself on Unit 18

**1.** (a) $y - 3$ (b) $\frac{y}{4}$ (c) $y + 9$ (d) $\frac{y-1}{z}$

(e) $\frac{y+z}{5}$ (f) $\frac{y+b}{a}$ (g) $\frac{y-ab}{a}$ (h) $a(y+b)$

**2.** (a) $x \geq 4$ (b) $2 \leq x \leq 3$ (c) $-5 \leq x < -1$

(d), (e), (f) [number line diagrams: $-2$, $4$, $7$, $-6$, $1$]

(g) $x \geq 4$ (h) $x > 12$ (i) $x \leq 7$ (j) $x \geq 54$

(k) $x < 8$ (l) $x > 10$ (m) $-4, -3, -2, -1, 0, 1$

**3.** (a) $5^7$ (b) $6^2$ (c) $8^5$ (d) $3^5$ (e) $1$ (f) $3^6$

(g) $4^2$ (h) $2^6$ (i) $5$ (j) $a^6$ (k) $x^{20}$ (l) $y^{13}$

(m) $m^4$ (n) $x^2$ (o) $x^2$

**4.** (a) $7 \times 10^4$   (b) $3.8 \times 10^3$   (c) $5.134 \times 10^2$   (d) $5 \times 10^{-2}$

(e) $8.1 \times 10^{-3}$   (f) $9.7 \times 10^6$   (g) $7.5 \times 10^{-1}$   (h) $5.1683 \times 10^3$

(i) 60000   (j) 0.004   (k) 0.036   (l) 29400000

**5.** (a) $9 \times 10^{25}$   (b) $5.4 \times 10^{19}$   (c) $7.4 \times 10^{15}$   (d) $2 \times 10^{15}$

(e) $1.3 \times 10^{16}$   (f) $4.2 \times 10^{18}$   (g) $2.06 \times 10^{33}$

(h) $1.33 \times 10^{-22}$   (i) $2.69 \times 10^{-25}$   (j) $4.96 \times 10^{14}$

(k) $9.76 \times 10^{10}$   (l) $3.09 \times 10^{14}$

### Page 490   Mixed examination questions

**1.** 49   **2.** (i) $y^5$   (ii) $y^6$   (iii) $y^8$   **3.** $t = \dfrac{v-u}{8}$

**4.** $L = \dfrac{p-2w}{2}$   **5.** $n^3 - n^6$   **6.** $5^7$   **7.** $x > 1\frac{1}{2}$

**8.** (i) 2, 3, 4   (iii) $x \geq \dfrac{3}{5}$   **9.** $6a^7$

**10.** (a) $4.2 \times 10^5$   (b) $2.4 \times 10^{-6}$   **11.** 2, 3   **12** $x = \dfrac{y-r}{3}$

**13.** (a) $1.5 \times 10^6$   (b) $1.2 \times 10^8$   (c) 200 g

# Unit 19

### Page 492   M19.1

**1.** (a) 0.5   (b) 2.5   (c) 3.5   (d) 5   (e) 6.5   (f) 8.5
**2.** 5.3   **3.** 3.9   **4.** 2.9   **5.** 2.1   **6.** 4.0   **7.** 6.8, 4.0
**8.** 7.1, 1.7, 4.0   **9.** (a) 10.6 cm   (b) 7.7 cm   (c) 7.3 cm

### Page 493   E19.1

**1.** 60°   **2.** 50°   **3.** 45°   **4.** 110°   **5.** 23°   **6.** 102°
**7.** 107°   **8.** 72°   **9.** 294°

### Page 494   Can you still?  19A

**1.** $\frac{2}{3}$   **2.** 23   **3.** (a) $\frac{4}{9}$   (b) $\frac{61}{72}$   **4.** 48   **5.** £16
**6.** £16   **7.** (a) $\frac{2}{21}$   (b) $3\frac{1}{5}$   **8.** $\frac{4}{7}$   **9.** $\frac{9}{10}$
**10.** (a) $\frac{4}{15}$   (b) 9

### Page 495   M19.2

**4.** 70°   **5.** 60°   **6.** 6.7 cm (accept 6.6 – 6.8)   **7.** 5.9 cm
**8.** 6.6 cm   **9.** 7.25 cm   **10.** 5 cm   **11.** 10.2 cm   **12.** 5 cm

### Page 496   E19.2

**1.** 57°   **2.** 51°   **3.** 55°   **4.** 46°   **5.** 55°   **6.** 90°
**8.** 7.5 cm   **9.** 6.2 cm   **10.** XŶZ = 79°, YẐX = 31°, ZX̂Y = 70°
**13.** 50°   **14.** 5.7 cm

### Page 500   E19.3

**6.** (a) 3.5 cm   (b) 10 cm
**7.** (a) 3.7 cm   (b) 4.5 → 4.6 cm   (c) 8 cm

### Page 502   Can you still?  19B

**1.** 6.82, 6.84, 6.78
**2.** (a) 4.14   (b) 8.22   (c) 9.46
**3.** (a) 4.18   (b) 2380   (c) 51600
**4.** True   **5.** 53
**6.** (a) 15.8   (b) 97.2   (c) 94.4   (d) 279   (e) 4.40   (f) 2.96

### Page 503   M19.4

**3.** 15 m   **6.** 3.6 cm

### Page 504   E19.4

**1.** 8 m   **2.** 1.65 km   **3.** 150 km   **4.** 2.5 km
**5.** (missing numbers) 4.8, 200, 18, 8, 4, 3.5
**6.** 9 cm   **7.** (a) 54 km   (b) 96 km   (c) 66 km
**8.** 5.5 cm   **9.** 12 cm

### Page 506   Can you still?  19C

**1.** 3:8   **2.** 4:5   **3.** £100, £140   **4.** 450 ml
**5.** £9600   **6.** 18 cm   **7.** £21   **8.** £2.43
**9.** £126

### Page 511   WYM19

**1.** £1420   **2.** (a) £1675   (b) £167.50   **3.** £598.50
**4.** £191   **5.** 0   **6.** £355   **7.** £106.50

### Page 512   Test yourself on Unit 19

**1.** (a) 5.3 → 5.4 cm   (b) 9.2 cm   (c) 115°   (d) 80°
**2.** (a) 55°   (b) 54°
**5.** (a) 30 m   (b) 6 cm   (d) 2.5 cm

# Unit 20

### Page 517   M20.1

**1.** B, C, E   **3.** (a) 4 units   (b) 2 units   (c) 2 units   (d) 16 u³
**5.**

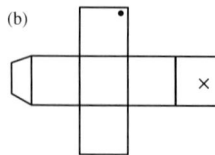

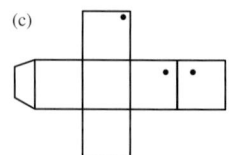

(b)

(c)

**7.** A5, B6, C4   **8.** B

### Page 519   Can you still?  20A

**1.** 300 mm, 0.3 m   **2.** 40000 g   **3.** (a) 7500 g   (b) 8000 ml
(c) 0.3 litres   (d) 60 cm   (e) 4.2 kg   (f) 2800 m
**4.** 640 ml   **5.** 37.3 km

## Page 521    E20.2

**1.** (a) (b) (c)

**2.** (a) (b) (c)

**3.** (a) (b) (c)

**4.** (a) (b) (c)

**5.** (a) (b) (c)

**6.** (a) (b) (c)

## Page 522    M20.3

**1.** (a) 090° (b) 135° (c) 270° (d) 045° (e) 225° (f) 315°
(g) 180° (h) 000°

**2.** A 031°, B 056°, C 338°, D 279°, E 311°, F 073°

**3.** (a) 135° (b) 025° (c) 205° (d) 255° (e) 315° (f) 075°

**4.** A 043°, B 202°, C 249°, D 129°, E 104°, F 214°, G 303°

## Page 523    E20.3

**1.** (a) 125° (b) 305° **2.** (a) 213° (b) 078° (c) 310° (d) 258°

**3.** (a) 032° (b) 081° (c) 238°

**4.** (a) 115° (b) 040° (c) 195° (d) 330°

**5.** 11.5 km **6.** 10.4 km **7.** 8.4 km

## Page 525    Can you still?  20B

**1.** $\frac{7}{25}$ = 28% **2.** 20% **3.** 75% **4.** 15% of £60 = 5% of £180

**5.** £916.50 **6.** 5% **7.** £3307.50 **8.** 4608

## Page 527    M20.4

**1.** (a) 8.60 (b) 15 (c) 18.36 (d) 25

**2.** (a) 12.96 (b) 7.42 (c) 13.96 (d) 14

**3.** (a) 24 (b) 12.21 (c) 10.80 (d) 11.11

(e) 15.01 (f) 40.95 (g) 8.41 (h) 16.11

**4.** 12.50 m **5.** 14.56 cm **6.** 37.64 m **7.** 7.32 cm

## Page 528    E20.4

**1.** 5.50 m **2.** B by 0.57 m **3.** 4.90 m **4.** 10.39 m

**5.** 14.42 km **6.** 11.40 km **7.** 79.65 km **8.** 2.58 km

**9.** 5.02 m **10.** 9.17 cm **11.** (a) 6.32 (b) 10.91 (c) 12.69

**12.** 31.75 cm$^2$ **13.** 110.85 cm$^2$ **14.** (a) 17 (b) 11.18 (c) 7.21

## Page 530    M20.5

**1.** (a) (3, 3) (b) 5.66 **2.** (b) (3, 2) (c) (0, –1) (d) 8.49

**3.** AB$\left(4, 7\frac{1}{2}\right)$, 6.08; CD$\left(2, 3\frac{1}{2}\right)$, 5.39, EF$\left(4\frac{1}{2}, 5\frac{1}{2}\right)$, 3.16

GH(4, 4), 2.83, IJ$\left(6\frac{1}{2}, 4\right)$, 6.71, KL$\left(7\frac{1}{2}, 1\frac{1}{2}\right)$, 1.41

**4.** 10 **5.** (b) (8, 1) (c) $\left(5, -\frac{1}{2}\right)$ (d) 6.71

**6.** (b) (–1, –2) (c) (0, 0) (d) 8.94

## Page 532    E20.5

**1.** C(0, 3, 4), D (0, 3, 0), E (6, 0, 0), F (6, 0, 4), G (0, 0, 4)

**2.** (a) L (5, 0, 0), M (5, 0, 3), N (0, 0, 3), O (0, 0, 0)
P (5, 4, 0), Q (5, 4, 3), R (0, 4, 3), S (0, 4, 0)
(b) (5, 2, 0) (c) 5.83 units

**3.** (a) O(0, 0, 0), A(6, 0, 0), B(6, 0, 10), C(0, 0, 10)
D(0, 4, 10), E(0, 4, 0), F(6, 4, 0)
(b) 10.77 units (c) (6, 4, 5) (d) (3, 0, 10)

## Page 534    Test yourself on Unit 20

**1.** (a) prism (triangular based)

**3.** (b) (c)

**4.** (a) (i) 118° (ii) 298°
(b) (i) 260° (ii) 307° (iii) 043° (iv) 080°

**5.** (a) 7 cm (b) 12.69 m (c) 9.85 cm

**6.** (c) D (–3, –3) (d) $\left(0, -\frac{1}{2}\right)$ (e) 7.81

**7.** (a) L(7, 0, 0), M(7, 0, 3), N(0, 0, 3), O(0, 0, 0)
P(0, 5, 0), Q(7, 5, 0), R(7, 5, 3), S(0, 5, 3)
(b) $\left(0, 2\frac{1}{2}, 4\right)$ (c) 7.62

## Page 536    Mixed examination questions

**1.** c, e **2.** 3.62 cm

**3.** (a) 9 (b)

**4.** (a) 39 km (b) 080° (c) 240°

**5.** 9.4 m

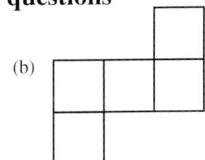

# Index